# Victimology and Victim Assistance

# Victimology and Victim Assistance

## Advocacy, Intervention, and Restoration

Yoshiko Takahashi

*California State University, Fresno, USA*

Chadley James

*California State University, Fresno, USA*

Los Angeles | London | New Delhi
Singapore | Washington DC | Melbourne

FOR INFORMATION:

SAGE Publications, Inc.
2455 Teller Road
Thousand Oaks, California 91320
E-mail: order@sagepub.com

SAGE Publications Ltd.
1 Oliver's Yard
55 City Road
London EC1Y 1SP
United Kingdom

SAGE Publications India Pvt. Ltd.
B 1/I 1 Mohan Cooperative Industrial Area
Mathura Road, New Delhi 110 044
India

SAGE Publications Asia-Pacific Pte Ltd
18 Cross Street #10-10/11/12
China Square Central
Singapore 048423

Acquisitions Editor:   Jessica Miller
Editorial Assistant:   Rebecca Lee
Production Editor:   Kimaya Khashnobish
Copy Editor:   Michelle Ponce
Typesetter:   C&M Digitals (P) Ltd.
Proofreader:   Alison Syring
Indexer:   Sylvia Coates
Cover Designer:   Gail Buschman
Marketing Manager:   Jillian Ragusa

Printed in the United States of America

*Library of Congress Cataloging-in-Publication Data*

Names: Takahashi, Yoshiko, author. | James, Chadley, author.

Title: Victimology and victim assistance : advocacy, intervention, and restoration / Yoshiko Takahashi, California State University, Fresno, USA, Chadley James, California State University, Fresno, USA.

Description: Thousand Oaks : SAGE Publications, [2018] | Includes bibliographical references and index.

Identifiers: LCCN 2018028867 | ISBN 9781506359557 (pbk. : alk. paper)

Subjects: LCSH: Victims of crimes—United States. | Justice, Administration of—United States. | Victims of crimes. | Justice, Administration of.

Classification: LCC HV6250.3.U5 T35 2018 | DDC 362.880973—dc23
LC record available at https://lccn.loc.gov/2018028867

This book is printed on acid-free paper.

18 19 20 21 22 10 9 8 7 6 5 4 3 2 1

# Brief Contents

# Detailed Contents

## CHAPTER 3   THE NATURE AND EXTENT OF VICTIMIZATION     35

# Preface

••••••••••••••••••••••••••••••••••••••••••••••••••••••••••••••••••••••••••••••••

This book is designed as a primary resource for victimology, victim services, and victim advocacy courses. There is growing interest in studying victim assistance by criminal justice and criminology students who intend to pursue careers as service providers in the criminal justice system or community-based agencies. Also, students in other disciplines such as social work and child development would benefit from this text to build on their knowledge of the criminal justice system and victim assistance.

The value and distinctiveness of the text is that it will discuss the criminal justice system and how victims' rights have been recognized in the system. To achieve this, the authors have divided the material into four sections, starting with a general discussion and overview of victimology and victim assistance and moving to more specific areas. The four sections are: Foundations, Understanding the Criminal Justice System and Victim Assistance, Impact of Crime on Victims, and New Directions in Victim Assistance.

The Foundations section is designed to provide students with an overview of victim assistance and assessing the impact on victimization through victimological theories, available data, and the trauma and recovery process. The second section addresses how victim services have been integrated into the main areas of the criminal justice system—law enforcement, the courts, corrections, and the juvenile justice system. Restorative justice is also discussed. The third section discusses effective responses to specific crime victims, including victims of family violence, sexual assault, and cyber-crime. The fourth section discusses challenges for victim assistance, which includes discussions on professionalism in victim services, compassion fatigue, and barriers to services. The final section also covers multicultural competency issues using some examples of the LGBTQ, Asian Pacific Islander, and Native American communities.

The authors build on the growing interest in victimology and victim assistance and provide a context within which to understand the major challenges and possible ethical dilemmas that victim advocates could face, along with discussing the future direction of victim assistance.

## Key Features

••••••••••••••••••••••••••••••••••••••••••••••••••••••••••••••••••••••••••••••••

- Victim assistance programs are highlighted in boxes within the chapters to orient students toward programs that are actively working to support victims.

- Case studies are used throughout the book to provide realistic and factual depictions of victims, humanizing the topics covered and facilitating discussion.

- Coverage of crucial topics like human trafficking, cyber-crime, and trauma-informed care offer students contemporary insights into the field of victim assistance.

# Digital Resources

study.sagepub.com/takahashi

The password-protected **Instructor Resource Site** includes the following:

**Test banks** provide a diverse range of prewritten options as well as the opportunity to edit any question and/or insert personalized questions to effectively assess students' progress and understanding

Editable, chapter-specific **PowerPoint® slides** offer complete flexibility for creating a multimedia presentation for the course

**Lecture notes** summarize key concepts by chapter to ease preparation for lectures and class discussions

**Sample course syllabi** for semester and quarter courses provide suggested models for structuring one's course

# Acknowledgments

M any individuals have supported us putting our ideas into a book. We would like to thank the editorial and production staff at SAGE for their professional work and support. Especially, our acquisitions editor, Jessica Miller, has been great to work with, and your professional advice, encouragement, and flexibility have been so meaningful to us. Also, we would like to thank and greatly miss Jerry Westby, who visited our campus and initiated the idea of a victim assistance book.

Special thanks goes to Suleman Masood, who is our former student in victimology. Suleman, your journey to success made us re-realize the importance of education for crime victims, and education is a healing process for many survivors.

We would like to thank John P. Dussich, Paul C. Friday, and Gerd Fredinand Kirchhoff for your guidance and mentorship.

We thank our spouses, Michael D. Evans and Natasha James, for their patience and support.

The authors and SAGE gratefully acknowledge the insightful comments and contributions of the following reviewers:

Ronicka Schottel, PLADC, MSCJ, MPA
Assistant Professor
Peru State College

Geri Barber
The University of Scranton

Ellen G. Cohn, PhD
Associate Professor
Department of Criminal Justice
Florida International University

Molly R. Wolf, LMSW, PhD
Edinboro University of Pennsylvania

Kevin M. Beaver
Florida State University

Elvira White-Lewis, JD/PhD
Associate Professor
Texas A&M University—Commerce

Joy D. Patton, PhD, LMSW, MA
Assistant Professor of Human Services
University of North Texas at Dallas

Keith J. Bell, PhD
West Liberty University

Caron Jacobson
Senior Lecturer
Governors State University

Allyson S. Maida, LCSW
Associate Adjunct
St. John's University

Karen L. Bune
Adjunct Professor
Marymount University

Dr. Mary M. Breaux
College of Criminal Justice and
    Criminology
Sam Houston State University

Rachael Gossett
Lindenwood University

Michelle L. Foster
Kent State University

Cheryl A. S. McFarland, PhD
Florida State University

# About the Authors

Yoshiko Takahashi, **PhD**, is an associate professor in the Department of Criminology at California State University, Fresno. While teaching undergraduate victimology courses, she coordinates the Victimology Option program and oversees the Victim Services Certificate program at the same institution. Her current research focuses on domestic violence and gender inequality issues among Asian communities in the United States and Southeast Asian student success in higher education. Dr. Takahashi is serving on the Board of Directors of the Central California Asian Pacific Women (CCAPW). She is also an elected executive committee member of the World Society of Victimology (WSV).

Chadley James, **PhD** is an assistant professor in the Department of Criminology at California State University, Fresno. Dr. James has published in international journals and textbooks and has presented papers at international conferences, courses, and seminars in Africa, Asia, Europe, the Middle East, and the United States. He is the organizing codirector of the longest running two-week graduate course in Victimology, Victim Assistance, and Criminal Justice held every year in Dubrovnik, Croatia, at the Inter-University Center. In 2015, the World Society of Victimology (WSV) awarded Dr. James the Beniamin Mendelsohn Young Victimologist Award, and he is also an elected executive committee member of the WSV.

# Foundations

# Historical Perspectives of Victimology and Victim Assistance

The old saying of victims being the forgotten actors in the criminal justice system is slowly beginning to no longer apply. This is because much has been done to bring attention to and assist those who have been harmed by crime (Spalek, 2006). The plight of crime **victims** in the United States to be recognized and have access to services following victimization emanates from enormous efforts made by social movements during the mid-to-late 1900s, along with the political will that has recognized the advantage of reintegrating victims into the criminal justice system. Today, there exists an expanding body of victim legislation that affords rights to victims during criminal proceedings, has created and expanded state compensation programs, and provides funding for victim assistance programs (Office for Victims of Crime [OVC], 2016). These developments have significantly influenced the recovery of individuals who have suffered the emotional and psychological trauma, physical injuries, and financial losses of crime.

**Victims:**
"persons who individually or collectively have suffered harm, including physical or mental injury, emotional suffering, economic loss or substantial impairment of their fundamental rights, through acts or omissions that are in violation of criminal laws operative within Member States, including those laws proscribing criminal abuse of power" (United Nations General Assembly, 1985)

The framework for the acknowledgment and advancement in services offered to victims has developed from the study of victimology. Victimology, as a scientific discipline, has drawn its knowledge from research from a variety of backgrounds, such as law, social work, nursing, psychology, and medicine (Mawby & Walklate, 1994; Kirchhoff, 2005, 2010; Fattah, 2010). Arguably, however, the most significant influence in the development of victimology has come from criminology. Criminologists have concentrated a large portion of their work on analyzing criminal victimization and ways to prevent it (Spalek, 2006; Moriarty, 2008). This has led some to argue that victimology is a subfield of criminology and not a discipline on its own. Irrespective of this debate, criminology and victimology are complementary areas of study (Fisher, Reyns, & Sloan, 2016). While criminologists focus on studying criminal behavior, which includes the process of making laws, breaking laws, and reacting toward those breaking of laws (Sutherland, Cressey, & Luckenbill, 1992), the focus for victimologists is the opposite. Victimologists are interested in understanding the impact of the victimization on victims and how best they can be restored to their previctimization state; victimologists, too, analyze how the criminal justice system accommodates and assists victims and how society, along with the media and the Internet, react to criminal victimization and victims (Kirchhoff, 2005; Karmen, 2013; Daigle & Muftic, 2016). Victimology, then, is "the scientific study of victims, victimizations, and the social reaction to both of these" (Kirchhoff, 2010, p. 96).

## History of Victimology

Victimization is not a new concept; it is in fact as old as humanity itself. However, it was not until after the Second World War that a more scientific approach to studying crime victims emerged (Fattah, 2000, p. 18) and when the term *victimology* was first coined. Attribution of the term is given to Beniamin Mendelsohn, who first used it in a set of papers presented in Bucharest, Romania, in 1947. Frederick Wertham, however, is argued to be the first to have published the term *victimology*, in his book *The Show of Violence* (1949) (Van Dijk, 1997; Kirchhoff, 2010). Irrespective of when the term *victimology* first appeared, the concepts of victimization and victims have been issues of consideration dating back to ancient cultures and civilizations (Fisher et al., 2016).

History reveals that before written laws existed, when a person or property was harmed, the victim and his or her family were responsible for obtaining justice. Victims typically obtained justice through retaliation. This system of justice was referred to as **lex talions**, which is the principle of an-eye-for-an-eye. Here criminals would be dealt punishment equal to that of the harm caused. This notion of punishment is like that of retribution. This was a period where crime was viewed as harm against the victim, and not the state, as it is in today's criminal justice system (Daigle & Muftic, 2016). However, to avoid certain forms of retaliation, offenders could return the stolen property or make some form of payment to the injured party, which is referred to as restitution. The principles of retribution and restitution were both acceptable means of obtaining justice for victims.

**lex talions:** the principle of an-eye-for-an-eye. Here criminals would be dealt punishment equal to that of the harm caused

These principles were included into the earliest written law, Code of *Ur-Nammu* (c. 2100 BCE—2050 BCE), and later, the *Code of Hammurabi* (c. 1792 BCE—1750 BCE). Along with the death penalty and imprisonment, special considerations were made to protect vulnerable groups from the powerful, and restoration of equity between the offender and the victim was emphasized (Kirchhoff, 2010; Daigle & Muftic, 2016). To state that the oldest codes focused solely on the needs of the victims is wrong, but it does reflect a period in history referred to as "The Golden Age of the Victim" (Schafer, 1968, p. 7), where victims played a more central role in legal proceedings.

Writings on the way victimizations were interpreted and the impact it had on people and communities can also be found in religious texts. References about persons intentionally injured or killed (either as a religious sacrifice or for a wrong doing for personal benefit) are found in many of the world's religions, and remain today, significant influences on cultures' and societies' normative guidelines throughout the world (Kirchhoff, 2010; Dussich, 2015, p. 2).

The move away from viewing crime against the victim to crime against the state began in the Middle Ages and was fully in place by the industrial revolution. Once the state began to assume control over criminal matters and public interest, the interests of the victims became secondary, excluding them from formal proceedings of the justice system (Peacock, 2013; Daigle & Muftic, 2016). This did not mean that the struggle for recognition of the oppressed and injured ended. During the Era of Enlightenment, Cesare Beccaria's (1738-1794) and Jeremy Bentham's (1748-1832) work focused on eliminating the tyrannical nature of criminal law—where they advocated on the side of the victim (the powerless)—, from the indifference and ignorance of the rich and powerful (Kirchhoff, 2010). The classical school emphasized the concepts of rationality and free will, where it was assumed that crime victims only wanted revenge. Being unable to pursue revenge, victims needed the state to act on their behalf, highlighting their secondary position in the system while the state pursued justice (Beirne, 1994). The move away from this theoretical approach (classical school) to criminal law began with a new direction in the philosophy of science, and which today is still important for science generally, called *positivism*. The proponents of this new way of approaching science, Cesare Lombroso (1835-1909), and later, Rafaele Garrafalo (1851-1934), and Enrico Ferri (1856-1929) argued that using the scientific method to study human behavior provides a "real understanding of things, far better than the theory that a man is a criminal because he wants to be" (Ferri, 1908, p.75). Positivistic research is broadly reflected in the criminological literature and in policy recommendations for reducing crime (Conklin, 2012). However, just as much as positivists believe that everyone who commits crime is responsible to the state, victims, too, must be indemnified (compensated) by the state because it has not prevented their victimization (Ferri, 1908; Kirchhoff, 2010).

The period following World War II was arguably the most salient for victimology. Compensation provided for the wounded and killed in the Holocaust and by atomic bombs signaled a clear engagement and reemergence of victims. In 1948, Hans von Hentig produced one of the first English-language texts on crime victims in *The Criminal and His Victim*, where he showed that crime was a social process, an interaction between an offender and a victim (Kirchhoff, 2010), where both in some way influenced the criminal act. This led to the first victimological theory of victim precipitation. Beniamin Mendelsohn expanded the parameters of victimology to focus not only on crime victims but also victims of various other factors and circumstances, which he termed *general victimology* (Hoffman, 1992) (the early contributors to victimology and theories will be discussed more in Chapter 2).

Greater awareness for the plight of the victim and the need for governmental schemes to provide compensation and restitution began in the United Kingdom in 1957; however, it was New Zealand that introduced the first compensation legislation in 1963. In the United States, California was the first state to establish a compensation program in 1965; today, they exist in every state (Mawby & Walklate, 1994; Daigle & Muftic, 2016). During this same period in the United States, victimology was being driven forward, by what remains today the most influential social movements affecting the plight of crime victims. In particular, the civil rights movement and the women's movement in the 1960s and 1970s were instrumental in advocating for greater awareness of the needs of minorities, women, and children and how the criminal justice system reacts to them (Fisher et al., 2016).

It was then in 1973, in Israel, in mutual cooperation and concern for victims that the first international symposium on victimology was held. Six years later, in Germany, at the third international symposium on victimology, the World Society of Victimology (WSV) was founded. The WSV brings together a network of victimologists that encourages the advancement of research and cooperation between "international, national, regional, and local agencies and other groups who are concerned with the problems of victims" (World Society of Victimology, 2016). The WSV continues to host triennially its symposia around the world, along with postgraduate courses on victimology in Croatia, India, and South Africa annually. Further recognition of the victim internationally was established when the United Nations adopted the *Declaration of Basic Principles of Justice for Victims of Crime and Abuse of Power in 1985*. The aim of the declaration has been to improve victims' access to justice, fair treatment, restitution, compensation, and support, as well as taking steps to prevent victimization linked to the abuse of power (Kirchhoff, 2010; Groenhuijsen, 2013; Peacock, 2013). Many of the principles in the declaration have been implemented into legislation around the world, particularly in the United States, where laws supporting victims' rights continue to expand.

The development and growth of victimology has been meteoric; today there are dedicated journals and textbooks related to the study of victimology, published in many different languages and taught in universities all over the world. Victimology continues to grow and recognize the many "needs of an expanding range of victims in a complex world" (Dussich, 2015, p. 19).

# History of Victim Assistance

Victimology's development and recognition of the needs of crime victims was significantly influenced by a rising social consciousness during the 1960s and 1970s. During this period, different social movements were occurring simultaneously. These movements were led and inspired by persons who had personally suffered the effects of victimization and supported by others who showed empathy and provided insight into advancing the plight of these victims (Young & Stein, 2004). The civil rights movement, the women's movement, the children's movement, and the concern about increasing crime all contributed to what is referred to today as the crime victims' movement.

## The Civil Rights Movement

The civil rights movement during the 1950s and 1960s was the first in modern American history to use civil disobedience to challenge the discrimination that was taking place in society (Underwood, 2003). The movement concerned itself with ending the lack of political and economic power for African Americans and other American minorities. It took on the issues of inequality in education, housing, employment, and the criminal justice system. The movement's influence on the criminal justice system was of particular significance. During this time, African Americans' relationships with law enforcement officers, who were predominately White and male, were very strained. Because of the tension between the two communities, many crime victims would not report their victimizations to the police, limiting their access to needed assistance and justice (Fisher et al., 2016). For those who did report their victimizations and enter the criminal justice system, the treatment given was notably different to that provided to White people. This led the movement to challenge law enforcement and the criminal justice system to adopt a more compassionate and humane approach to the problems of those fighting for equality (Alexander, 2012). According to Underwood (2003), the movement paved the way for the powerless in society to show that with social action social change is possible.

## The Women's Movement

Arguably, the most influential of the movements during the 1960s and 1970s was the women's movement. It was in this period where many brave women who had personally suffered the effects of sexual abuse and domestic violence, along with feminist groups, advocated against the poor treatment they received in society. It was argued that the inequality women experienced in education and in the workplace was the result of a patriarchal society. Poor recognition and treatment of women was also seen in the criminal justice system. This led early female victim advocates to set up shelters and counselling centers to assist these victims (Young & Stein, 2004; Fisher et al., 2016). The first three victim assistance programs in the United States all began in 1972, of which, two were rape crisis centers in Washington, DC, and in the San Francisco Bay area (Young & Stein, 2004). The women's movement, in addition to advocating and providing direct assistance to female victims of crime, fought to change the social norms in society that led to their unfair treatment. Their advocating, while achieving much more than can be stated here, led to the repeal of marital exemption laws, which meant wives could pursue rape charges against their husbands. Additionally, the women's movement fought for changes in the way the criminal justice system responded to domestic violence. Often law enforcement officers would be hesitant to intervene in domestic disputes, as it was believed that such issues should be resolved in the home behind closed doors, leaving the female victim powerless and in danger (Gosselin, 2014). Today, significant government intervention has taken place in the way law enforcement responds to domestic violence, in large part due to the concerns that the women's movement raised about the problem. The movement's contribution to the development of victimology and the continued recognition and growth of assistance offered to female victims of crime was pivotal and helped to make the home a safer place for women and children (Underwood, 2003).

## The Children's Movement

Dovetailing off the women's movement was the children's movement. Like women, children were often ignored in society, despite crimes such as abuse and neglect occurring throughout history (Fisher et al., 2016). Just before the turn of the 20th century, the first high-profile case, of Mary Ellen Wilson, brought attention to the problem of child abuse and that there were no laws to protect children from abuse and cruelty by parents and guardians. Following the case of Miss Wilson, the New York Society for the Prevention of Cruelty to Children (NYSPCC) was created. This society was dedicated entirely to the protection of children. By 1922, there were 300 nongovernmental child protection agencies throughout the United States. These agencies, however, were mainly in the big cities, meaning that often children in rural areas had little to no formal child protective services. In accordance with the spread of these nongovernmental agencies, the first juvenile court was established in Chicago, Illinois, in 1899, eventually spreading across the country. Despite juvenile courts focusing on troublesome youth, they had the jurisdiction to intervene in cases of abuse and neglect. Juvenile courts today remain an important component in the child protection system (Myers, 2008). However, it was not until the 1960s that child abuse was recognized as a social problem. The strength of the women's movement and the recognition of violence within the household helped to expose the fact that children are victimized and in need of assistance, too. It was found that when mothers leave the abusive relationship, children often accompanied the mothers to the shelters (Katz, 2006). Then, in 1962, Dr. Henry Kempe, published his seminal work on "The Battered-Child Syndrome," which highlighted the problem of child abuse. His work additionally pointed out that the medical community is in a position to recognize and report instances of child abuse. Kempe's work, too, provided the evidence for the early victim advocates to push for better legal protection and assistance for children of abuse and neglect (Daigle & Muftic, 2016; Fisher et al., 2016). The strength and dedication of those who fought to change societies' norms by starting these social movements have been prolific for victims in American society.

## Early Programs for Crime Victims

As mentioned earlier in this chapter, one of the first methods designed and used to compensate victims for their losses was crime victims' compensations programs. The activism for compensation programs began in the 1950s in the United Kingdom. Margery Fry was an instrumental figure in the development of these programs. She argued that there were many inadequacies in how the state secured and/or made available compensation for victims of crime (Floyd, 1970). Despite Miss Fry's early proposals to the British Parliament for the development of these programs being denied in 1961, the idea of victim compensation was developing around the world. The first compensation program to be introduced to the United States was in 1965 in California. New York followed in 1966, Hawaii in 1967, and Massachusetts in 1968 (Floyd, 1970; Young & Stein, 2004). It was in 1984 when the Federal Government enacted the Victims of Crime Act (VOCA), and the federal crime victims' fund was established. The VOCA authorizes compensation when federal crimes are committed and provides monetary assistance to state compensation programs. Today, there are compensation programs in every state in the country, with nearly $500 million paid annually to more than 200,000 people suffering criminal injury, including victims of spousal and child abuse, rape, assault, and drunk driving, as well as families of murder victims (National Association of Crime Victim Compensation Boards, 2016).

Then, victimology was growing in the 1970s and bringing greater attention to the victim being the neglected party in the criminal justice system. The system, too, began to notice that the biggest reason for prosecution failure was the loss of cooperative witnesses—victims—and a system that was indifferent to their most basic needs (Young & Stein, 2004). To counter the problem of prosecution failure, the Federal Law Enforcement Assistance Administration (LEAA) funded and piloted three victim/witness programs in district attorneys' Offices. These programs were designed to provide better notification to victims about dates and processes relating to their cases, along with separate waiting areas in the courts, and to encourage victim participation in the criminal justice system (Young & Stein, 2004). As they succeeded, more victim/witness programs started and began to expand on the services provided to victims. These services included prosecutor-based staff training in crisis intervention (as court appearances can be crisis inducing for victims), social services referrals, assistance with compensation programs, and notifications beyond court dates, that is, bail determinations, continuances, plea bargains, dismissals, sentences, restitution, protective measures, and parole hearings (Young & Stein, 2004; Daigle & Muftic, 2016). These programs continue today offering the same services to crime victims.

## Development of Victim Assistance Organizations

The energy and growth the victims' movement ignited into victim assistance during the 1970s was immense. It brought to the surface the criminal violence that was taking place against women and children. These brave victims of rape and domestic violence began to fight back and founded programs and shelters to assist similar victims. However, as these victims were taking back their lives, other victims, too, began to realize they were often neglected and found that services were not readily available to them. The families and loved ones of homicide victims were an isolated group, as people did not know how to act or how to help them (Young & Stein, 2004; Daigle & Muftic, 2016). Recognizing the needs of this over-looked group of victims, Families and Friends of Missing Persons was established in 1974 to support loved ones of murdered or missing persons. This was followed by the establishment of Parents of Murdered Children in 1978 and Mothers Against Drunk Driving (MADD) in 1980. These organizations sought to provide the necessary assistance to these victims following the loss of their loved ones. They also advocated for changes in laws and policy to bring greater awareness to and hopefully remedy the problem (Young & Stein, 2004; Daigle & Muftic, 2016). It was from the outgrowth of these movements and organizations that the first two national conferences on victim assistance were held in 1975 and 1976, and the National Organization for Victim Assistance (NOVA) was founded (Dussich, 2015). NOVA today promotes the networking between victim assistance organizations, holds national conferences that provide training opportunities to those working with victims, and continues to draft and ensure the passage of various laws to assist crime victims (Young & Stein, 2004; Spalek, 2006). The development of victim assistance organizations and their advocacy opened the door for legislative and policy changes, which began the push for victims' rights.

## Legislative and Policy Development of Victims' Rights

Discussed at the beginning of the chapter was that victimization is not a new concept, but it was not until after the Second World War that greater attention was given to victims (Fattah, 2000). Following the Holocaust and various other atrocities that took place at that time, the United Nations was established in 1945 to confront issues that challenged the peace and security of people around world. The need to protect vulnerable groups and address the plight of crime victims began with the development of international instruments and legislation, eventually leading to the establishment of victims' rights.

**United Nations Universal Declaration of Human Rights:** the declaration is a document drafted by representatives with different legal and cultural backgrounds from around the world. Its aim is to set a common standard of achievements of all peoples and all nations to protect their fundamental human rights (United Nations, 2004)

## United Nations Universal Declaration of Human Rights

The United Nations (UN) was established in 1945 as an intergovernmental organization committed to promoting peace, security, and strengthening of friendship between nations. The UN began with 50 countries, known as member states, which signed the Charter of the UN detailing the organization's purposes and principles, which include helping solve economic, social, and humanitarian problems (United Nations, 2004). The UN Charter divides the organization into six principal bodies, which are the General Assembly, the Security Council, the International Court of Justice, the Economic and Social Council (ECOSOC), the Trusteeship Council, and the Secretariat. Each body has specific and complementary responsibilities and powers, which help to achieve the goals of the organization. Today there are 193 member states. It was the principal body of ECOSOC that convened the UN Commission on Human Rights in 1946 (replaced in 2006 by the UN Human Rights Council), headed by Eleanor Roosevelt, that developed the **Universal Declaration of Human Rights**. The declaration is a document drafted by representatives with different legal and cultural backgrounds from around the world. Its aim is to set a common standard of achievements of all peoples and all nations to protect their fundamental human rights (United Nations, 2004). Eleanor Roosevelt wrote,

> Every man, woman, and child seeks equal justice, equal opportunity, equal dignity without discrimination. (Sears, 2008, p. 4)

The document consists of 30 fundamental rights, which include the right that all humans are born free and (should be) treated equal (with) dignity and rights; have freedom of speech; and have the right to life, liberty, and security of person. The declaration was formally adopted by the United Nations on December 10, 1948. It is arguably the most historic human rights document and forms the basis for a democratic society (Morsink, 1999). The UN has played an important role in preventing the abuse of power and violations of human rights around the world by developing international guidelines that have positioned the victim within the framework of criminal law and procedure (United Nations Office for Drug Control and Crime Prevention [UNODCCP], 1999).

## United Nations Declaration of Basic Principles of Justice for Victims of Crime and Abuse of Power 1985

One of the most significant international documents the UN prompted was the Declaration of the Basic Principles of Justice for Victims of Crime and Abuse of Power. The declaration resulted from the reemergence of the victim and the recognition that the criminal justice system needed to evolve and adapt to the increasing need for safety and the well-being of victims. Globally, it was the work of many individuals, organizations, governments, and international bodies that fought to restore the plight of victims into the legal system and improve the quantity and quality of assistance available to victims (UNODCCP, 1999). The idea for the declaration was to create national and international standards for how victims of crime needed to be treated in the criminal justice system. It provides an internationally recognizable definition of "victims," which is

> Persons who individually or collectively have suffered harm, including physical or mental injury, emotional suffering, economic loss or substantial impairment of their fundamental rights, through acts or omissions that are in violation of criminal laws operative within Member States, including those laws proscribing criminal abuse of power. (United Nations General Assembly, 1985)

The declaration also provides recommendations on measures to be taken on behalf of victims to improve access to justice, fair treatment, restitution, compensation, and assistance. It also outlines steps to assist prevention of victimization linked to abuse of power and to provide remedies for the victims (UNODCCP, 1999). After 31 years, the declaration is still a fundamental document and recognized as the "Magna Carta of victims' rights" (Groenhuijsen, 2009, p. 7). The principles the document contains form the basis of all local and international protocols on victims' rights (Groenhuijsen, 2009).

## U.S. Legislation and Policy

During the same time that the plight of crime victims in the United States was gaining attention through the social justice movements, so was the law and order movement developing in response to rising social unrest and an increasing crime rate. The increase in the public fear of crime heightened by media attention enabled politicians to implement a particular philosophy of crime control. This philosophy emphasized harsher punishment and greater efficiency in seeking justice and the criminal justice process (Fisher et al., 2016). However, the greater focus on punishment revealed that the victim was the neglected party in the criminal justice system. Therefore, coupled with this recognition and the victims' movement, an emphasis was placed on trying to address this issue. In 1965, the President's Commission on Law Enforcement and the Administration of Justice was created. The commission, after surveying the whole criminal justice process, released a report in 1967 making recommendations for addressing the crime problem. The report indicated that the education and training of police officers needed improving and more should be done to compensate victims of crime. This marked a shift toward incorporating victims' rights into criminal justice processes (Fisher et al., 2016).

Further based on the recommendation of the Presidents Commission, Congress created the Law Enforcement Assistance Administration (LEAA). The LEAA's task was to improve the criminal justice system in the United States, and it did this by financing programs with federal funds to improve police, corrections, and courts (Rogovin & Velde, 1969). In particular, it funded the first three victim/witness programs in district attorneys' Offices and funded many other training and education programs for criminal justice professionals dealing with victims of crime (Young & Stein, 2004; Dussich, 2015; Fisher et al., 2016). The funding for the LEAA ended in 1982, which sadly led to the closure of many programs. Despite its ending, the victims' movement was well underway, with public officials encouraged to continue to pursue recognition of victims and improving their treatment within the criminal justice system. This led to Wisconsin becoming the first state to enact a "Victims' Bill of Rights" in 1980. Then, in 1982, in response to an executive order by President Ronald Reagan, the President's Task Force on Victims of Crime was formed. The objective of the task force was to conduct a nationwide study and assess the poor treatment of crime victims in the criminal justice system. The study gathered information from both victims and experts in the field of victim assistance and criminal justice. The findings from the report highlighted that the needs of victims were indeed great and in need of assistance (Hook & Seymour, 2004; Young & Stein, 2004). The report, in light of this information, made 68 recommendations to the federal government on how victims could be treated better, which was a watershed movement for victims' rights. "The final report of the task force provided and continues to provide a workable framework for the development of policy, programs, and protocols to define and protect victims' rights in the 21st century" (Hook & Seymour, 2004, np.).

One of the first federal legislations to be enacted from the task force, was the **Victims' of Crime Act (VOCA)** in 1984. The act established the Crime Victims Fund, which was made up of federal criminal fines, penalties, forfeitures, and special assessments, for state compensation programs and local victim assistance programs. Subsequent revisions to the act expanded victim eligibility to include victims of domestic violence, drunk driving

**Victims' of Crime Act (VOCA):** the act established the Crime Victims Fund, which was made up of federal criminal fines, penalties, forfeitures, and special assessments, for state compensation programs and local victim assistance programs. Subsequent revisions to the act expanded victim eligibility to include victims of domestic violence, drunk driving accidents, nonresident commuters and visitors, and saw the establishment of the Office for Victims of Crime (Hook & Seymour, 2004; Young & Stein, 2004)

accidents, and nonresident commuters and visitors, and saw the establishment of the Office for Victims of Crime (Hook & Seymour, 2004; Young & Stein, 2004). The VOCA funds help to support victims throughout the country in their recovery efforts after victimization through victim assistance and compensation training and technical assistance for victim support (Fisher et al., 2016).

Another significant piece of legislation is the **Violence Against Women Act (VAWA) of 1994**. The VAWA was enacted as part of the Violent Crime Control and Law Enforcement Act of 1994, acknowledging domestic violence and sexual assault as crimes, along with providing federal resources to encourage community-coordinated responses to combating violence against women. It focused on legal assistance programs for victims and expanded the definition of crime to include dating violence and stalking. The VAWA has been reauthorized and expanded upon three times, in 2000, 2005, and 2013 (National Network to End Domestic Violence [NNEDV], 2016). Some of the expansions to the act include housing protections for victims of domestic violence in federally subsidized housing programs, protection for dating violence on college campuses, better protection for victims of stalking over the Internet, and protections for LGBT victims from discrimination in receiving services. The purpose of many of the changes to the VAWA has been to eliminate discrimination and ensure equal provisions regardless of gender, race, or sexual orientation of the victim (NNEDV, 2016). The VOCA and the VAWA, along with other key federal legislation (see Table 1) have demonstrated the government's recognition of the importance of developing and protecting crime victims' rights.

**Violence Against Women Act (VAWA) of 1994:** enacted as part of the Violent Crime Control and Law Enforcement Act of 1994, it acknowledges domestic violence and sexual assault as crimes, along with providing federal resources to encourage community-coordinated responses to combating violence against women

## Common State Victims' Rights

The President's Task Force on Victims of Crime report made 68 recommendations for the better treatment of victims by providing a workable framework for the development of policy, programs, and protocols to define and protect victims' rights. The 68th recommendation was for an amendment to be made to the constitution for the provision and expansion of victims' rights at the federal level (Beloof, 1999). Victims' rights constitutional amendments have been introduced to Congress on several occasions but have yet to be adopted. The latest attempt for such an amendment was in 2012 (National Victims' Constitutional Amendment Passage [NVCAP], 2016). Irrespective of a constitutional amendment to victims' rights not being made at the federal level, all states do provide some legal rights to crime victims as part of their state code. However, 32 states have made amendments to their constitutions to include rights for crime victims (National Center for Victims of Crime, 2012). The purposes of the amendments are as follows:

- Crime victims' rights are protected in the same way that defendants' rights are protected.

- Crime victims' rights are a permanent part of the criminal justice system.

- Courts would have the power to enforce crime victims' rights if they are violated.

(National Center for Victims of Crime, 2012)

# Table 1.1
## KEY VICTIMS' RIGHTS LEGISLATION

2014 Sean and David Goldman International Abduction Prevention and Return Act

**2014**

2013 Kilah Davenport Child Protection Act

2011 Ike Skelton National Defense Authorization Act

2010 Tribal Law and Order Act

2006 Adam Walsh Child Protection and Safety Act

2004 Justice for All Act

**2004**

2003 Prison Rape Elimination Act

2003 Fair and Accurate Credit Transaction Act

2003 PROTECT Act ("Amber Alert" law)

2001 Air Transportation Safety and System Stabilization Act

2000 Trafficking Victims Protection Act

1998 Crime Victims with Disabilities Awareness Act

1998 Identity Theft and Deterrence Act

1997 Victims' Rights Clarification Act

1996 Community Notification Act ("Megan's Law")

1996 Mandatory Victims' Restitution Act

1996 Antiterrorism and Effective Death Penalty Act

1994 Violence Against Women Act

**1994**

1994 Violent Crime Control and Law Enforcement Act

1993 Child Sexual Abuse Registry Act

1992 Battered Women's Testimony Act

1990 Victims of Child Abuse Act

1990 Hate Crimes Statistics Act

1990 Student Right-To-Know and Campus Security Act

1990 Victims' Rights and Restitution Act

1990 National Child Search Assistance Act

1988 Drunk Driving Prevention Act

1985 Children's Justice Act

1984 Missing Children's Assistance Act

**1984**

1984 Family Violence Prevention and Services Act

1984 Victims of Crime Act

1982 Missing Children's Act

1982 Victim and Witness Protection Act

1980 Parental Kidnapping Prevention Act

**1974**

1974 Child Abuse Prevention and Treatment Act

*Source:* Office for Victims of Crime (2014).

Not all states provide all victims' rights. Common victims' rights provided in all states are the right to notification of rights, notification of court appearances, victim participation at various stages of the criminal justice process, and compensation (Beloof & Pugach, 2014). Then, depending on the state, other common rights may include the right to consult with court officials before plea bargains are entered and or offenders are released from custody, the right to restitution, to protection, and a speedy trial (National Center for Victims of Crime, 2012; Beloof & Pugach, 2014). The criminal justice process can be lengthy and time consuming; therefore, some states offer the right to protection of employment while the victim participates in the criminal justice system (National Center for Victims of Crime, 2012).

Despite the adoption of legislation and amendments to state constitutions for crime victims' rights, there have been problematic issues identified with victims' rights. Arguments have been made that victims' rights create administrative issues (Miers, 1992), and by trying to facilitate these rights it may result in "delays in trials, and add expenses to an already overburdened system" (Johnson & Morgan, 2008 p. 120). Another issue raised is that by providing victims certain rights, it may tip the balance between the rights of the offender and the victim (Johnson & Morgan, 2008). This has been argued with the right the victim has to participate in various stages of the CJS, particularly delivering a victim impact statement at the sentencing phase of a criminal trial. Then, questions have been raised around the enforcement of these rights, that is, what happens when victims' rights are not protected? In many instances there is no protection for victims when a right is violated. It is specifically noted in many states constitutions that if victims' rights are violated, victims cannot sue civilly a government agency or official (Daigle & Muftic, 2016). Irrespective of the issues raised with these rights, the political will and effort to develop and refine victims' rights instruments have been significant in improving the needs and developing services for those who suffer the consequences of crime.

# Types of Victim Services

The progression of victims' rights and legislative policy has prompted an increase in services offered to victims. Following a crime, victims may be in need of assistance to help them and their families recover from the traumatic experiences (Petersen, 2003). Victims are able to access assistance from victim advocates from a variety of different sources. **Victim advocates** are persons trained to support victims of crime. They assist victims by providing information, emotional support and resources; filling out paperwork; and accompanying victims to court. Many advocates are paid staff, but there are volunteer advocates, too. Assistance from advocates can be found in different areas of society (National Center for Victims of Crime, 2012). Within the criminal justice system, advocates can be found in police stations, prosecutors' Offices, courts, probation or parole departments, or correctional institutions. Many advocates also work for nonprofit organizations, such as domestic violence shelters and sexual assault crisis centers (Edmunds & Underwood, 2003; National Center for Victims of Crime, 2012). The following text will provide a brief description of the different types of victim services.

> **Victim advocates:** trained professionals who offer victims information, support, and help finding resources and assisting victims with paperwork

## Victim Services in the Criminal Justice System

Following a victimization, law enforcement is the first contact crime victims have with the criminal justice system. The initial impression the victim has with the system is argued to be long lasting and to influence his or her further participation within it. Significant improvements have been made to police training that have bettered officers' understanding of victimization and how they interact with victims, along with the direct assistance offered to victims (Underwood, 2003). Today, many police departments offer victim assistance programs through which police may refer the victims to victim services or provide the victims with information about where they can receive additional services. Then, depending on whether an offender is apprehended, the victim may move forward with criminal justice system processes and interact with prosecutors and judges. In order to make these interactions and the court process less intimidating, many prosecutors' Offices have victim/witness assistance programs. These programs offer court orientation, accompaniment to court, information on the progress of the case, and assistance with participation at various stages of the criminal justice process (i.e., creating and delivering victim impact statements) (Underwood, 2003; OVC, 2016).

## Victim Services in Human Services

Much of the assistance offered to crime victims is provided through services away from the CJS and in the community. These services offered to victims are provided through nonprofit organizations and community services agencies. They range from domestic violence shelters, sexual assault crisis centers, group homes and halfway houses, community mental health centers, and youth services agencies, along with programs designed to help people with alcoholism, drug abuse, family violence, and aging (Martin, 2007). Professionals in these services include but are not limited to the following:

- Case Worker
- Family Support Worker
- Youth Worker
- Social Worker
- Alcohol Counselor
- Adult Day Care Worker
- Drug Abuse Counselor

- Life Skills Instructor
- Probation Officer
- Parole Officer
- Child Advocate
- Gerontology Worker
- Juvenile Court Liaison

Victim services in human services have arisen from the desire and recognition that people are sometimes in need of assistance. The assistance crime victims may receive may not always come from social service agencies accustomed to helping victims but also from many different resources in the community (National Organization for Human Services (NOHS), 2016).

## Victim Services in the Health Care System

In many instances following victimization, a victim may not report the crime but seek assistance for injuries from doctors, clinics, and or hospitals. The health care system offers services to people impacted by crime to assist them in their recovery with support and information. Many professionals within this system are trained to provide crisis counseling, emotional support, and education and referral information to victims (Palmer & Edmunds, 2003). Additionally, many clinics and hospitals provide forensic examinations for victims of sexual assault, rape, or child abuse. The examinations are performed by Sexual Assault Nurse Examiner's (SANE). The SANE program was developed in the 1970s to train nurses on how to better collect and preserve the evidence from sexual assault victims and, also, to deal with the sensitive nature of the victimization (Campbell et al., 2014). In addition to SANEs, Sexual Assault Response Teams (SARTs) have been initiated to work alongside law enforcement agencies, prosecutors' Offices, and victim assistance organizations. The SARTs, when notified about a sexual assault case, assist victims in receiving medical care, including a forensic medical exam (by a SANE), provide additional information regarding other services, and help to ensure that the victim is treated with dignity and respect by the those working in the CJS (Greeson & Campbell, 2013; OVC, 2016).

The trauma experienced from victimization may, too, require victims to seek mental health care. The counseling services offered by victim assistance organizations may not be enough to assist victims, in which case, they are referred to psychologists and psychiatrists to better assist in the recovery of the victim's mental health.

## Victim Services in Religious Organizations

In times of crisis, it is not uncommon for people to call upon religious institutions and their leaders (imams, pastors, priests, and rabbis, etc.) for spiritual guidance, support, and information. Faith-based assistance programs have typically been found in prisons; however, religious institutions have begun to develop programs specifically to serve crime victims and their families (OVC, 2016). Some faith communities have benefited from funding from the Victims of Crime Act to develop their own programs, while other have collaborated with secular victim service programs to develop and train providers and members of the faith community to meet the needs of victims. Faith-based victim service programs have included in the assistance they offer victims transitional housing or housing assistance, financial assistance (rental or utilities payment assistance), transportation, childcare services, counseling, and employment counseling (DeHart, 2010; OVC, 2016).

## Other Types of Victim Services

Criminal victimization affects each victim differently. However, the advancement in understanding of the impact of victimization has led to improved treatment programs for victims. For victims of federal crimes, services were introduced in the mid-1980s with the passing of the Victims' Rights and Restitution Act (VRRA) in 1990. The VRRA provides guidelines for how and when victims of federal crimes will be assisted by U.S. Attorneys' Offices (Underwood, 2003). The guidelines detail how in federal cases victims' safety must be assured, along with providing the necessary crisis intervention and counseling support. Providing information about case status and financial relief through compensation or restitution is equally important in assisting victims of federal crimes. The U.S. Attorneys' Offices' victim-witness personnel are trained to provide support to particularly vulnerable victims (e.g., children, victims of human trafficking, sexual assault) and will assist in making appropriate service referrals (United States Department of Justice, 2014).

High rates of crime, poverty, and chronic lack of services for crime victims in many American Indian/Alaskan Native communities is compounded by complex jurisdictional issues and cultural diversity amongst tribes (OVC, 2016). To address the needs of criminal victimization on tribal lands, the U.S. Department of Justice has supported justice initiatives for tribal organizations. With funding from the OVC, innovative partnerships have developed and expanded assistance programs that offer services to victims in tribal communities. These services focus on culturally specific training and understanding, bilingual counseling services, and court assistance (Underwood, 2003). In the U.S. Attorneys' Offices, there are 42 victim specialist positions dedicated to American Indian communities, 12 victim specialist positions at the Bureau of Indian Affairs, and the Department of the Interior that provide services to victims in tribes in the West and Southwest of the country (OVC, 2016).

The military justice system is designed to ensure order and discipline within the military, along with protecting the lives and property of members of its community

(Department of Defense, 2016). The U.S. military has its own justice system to deal with offenses involving military personnel. To address the needs of victims, the Department of Defense has established a victim and witness assistance council. The purpose of the council is to facilitate the distribution of information and resources in support of providing assistance to victims and witnesses of crimes on military installations (Department of Defense, 2016). Additionally, the military has a family advocacy program designed to intervene and prevent family violence.

The rich history of victimology and growth of victim assistance has broadened our understanding of victims and the impact support has on their lives. This text will provide an overview of the causes and consequences of victimization, along with discussing the trauma and recovery process for victims. The different types of victim services and the responses to victims at various stages of the criminal justice system will be outlined. Additionally, the text addresses the barriers to services, ethical dilemmas victim advocates may face, and the challenges for victim advocacy.

## SUMMARY

Victimization is not a new concept; in fact it is as old as humanity itself. However, the growth of victimology did not begin until the mid-to-late 1900s, where, following World War II, greater awareness for the plight of the victim and the need for governmental schemes were developed. Social movements in the 1960s and 1970s drove victimology and victims' assistance forward. These movements included the civil rights movement, the women's movement, and the children's movement, which is referred to today as the crime victims' movement. The first victim services agencies were developed in the early 1970s. Brave victims of rape and domestic violence, and survivors of homicide established multiple advocacy groups such as Family and Friends of Missing Persons, Parents of Murdered Children, and Mothers Against Drunk Driving. Important international instruments following World War II, along with the victims' movement, lead the way for legislation to be enacted that has changed the way victims are treated in the criminal justice system and the support offered to them. This, too, has led to state constitutional amendments to incorporate victims' rights. The progression of victims' rights and legislative policy has increased the types of services offered to victims. Today, many victims are able to access assistance from victim advocates from a variety of different sources. Services to victims are offered in the criminal justice system (at both the state and federal level), within the community, the health care system, tribal communities, and the military.

## KEY WORDS

*lex talions*   3
United nations
   universal declaration of
   human rights   8

Victim advocate   13
Victims   2
Victims' of crime act
  (VOCA)   10

Violence against women act
  (VAWA)   11

# INTERNET RESOURCES

**The American Society of Victimology (http://www.american-society-victimology.us)**

This organization advances the discipline of victimology by promoting evidence-based practices and providing leadership in research and education. The website contains information about victimology and victimologists. This organization looks at advancements in victimology through research, practice, and teaching.

**The World Society of Victimology (http://www.worldsocietyofvictimology.org)**

This is a not-for-profit, nongovernmental organization with Special Category consultative status with the ECOSOC of the United Nations and the Council of Europe. The purpose of the WSV is to advance victimological research and practices around the world; to encourage interdisciplinary and comparative work and research in this field; and to advance cooperation between international, national, regional, and local agencies and other groups who are concerned with the problems of victims.

**The National Organization for Victim Assistance (http://www.trynova.org)**

NOVA is a private, nonprofit, 501(c)(3) charitable organization. Its mission is to champion dignity and compassion for those harmed by crime and crisis. It is the oldest national victim assistance organization of its type in the United States and is the recognized leader in this noble cause. This website contains information about victim assistance.

**The Office for Victims of Crime (http://www.ovc.gov/help/index.html)**

The OVC is committed to enhancing the nation's capacity to assist crime victims and to providing leadership in changing attitudes, policies, and practices to promote justice and healing for all victims of crime. The OVC website offers a list of helplines of national organizations that provide services to crime victims, including the National Domestic Violence Hotline and Disaster Distress Helpline.

# CRITICAL THINKING QUESTIONS

1. Explain how the concept of victimization is not new and how World War II and the social movements of the 1960s and 1970s reignited the attention given to victims and victimization.

2. Why is the women's movement arguably one of the most influential in the victims' movement?

3. List two international instruments developed after World War II that have changed the way victims are treated in the criminal justice system.

4. List three victim assistance organizations started in the 1970s, and describe their influence on the growth and development of victim assistance organizations.

5. Compare and contrast the different types of services offered to victims in the criminal justice system and human services.

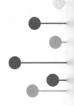

# CHAPTER 2

# Theories of Victimization

For centuries, people have been attempting to explain why crime happens and also why some people become victims. In this respect, we have organized our concepts and understanding of crime and victims through scientific knowledge, religious beliefs, and the social structures of the time in which they originate (Burgess, Regehr, & Roberts, 2013). Despite the enormous amount of research studies that have been carried out to better our understanding of victimization, we do not have one set of consolidated arguments to explain the complexity of victims and victimization (Rock, 2007). Instead, we have different theoretical positions in which different notions of, and emphasis upon, sociostructural processes and human action influence the ways in which victimization is understood and analyzed and impacts the lives of individuals (Spalek, 2006). **Theories** are the ideas that provide a framework for investigating the cause-and-effect relationship of events. Research is driven by theory. In the social sciences, it is argued that social interactions are not random acts; for example, victimization does not just happen, it is caused. Why it happens and what are its consequences are the questions (Gosselin, 2014). Tracing the development of theories for understanding victimization, it is important to examine the pioneering victimologists whose work focused on expanding the criminological perspective to pay attention not only to the perpetrators of crime but also to the victims, too. Moving forward, the present-day constructions of routine activities and lifestyle-exposure theory, the opportunity model, the differential risk model of criminal victimization, social learning theory, extended low self-control theory, and extended control balance theory will be examined to illustrate how a focus on theory has enhanced our understanding of victimization.

**Theories:** the ideas that provide a framework for investigating the cause-and-effect relationship of events

## Pioneers in Victimology

For most of criminology's history, the focus has been on the causes and consequences of crime. It wasn't until the 1940s that early victimologists began to view criminal activity as an interactive event between the offender and the victim (Kirchhoff, 2005, 2010; Fisher, Reyns, & Sloan, 2016). These early scholars expanded the criminological perspective by exploring the role victims play in their own victimization. This was done by examining victims' actions and reactions that might have provoked, unintentionally triggered, or facilitated their own victimization. Explaining victimization in this way assumes that each party has some responsibility for the crime, which lead to the development of the concept of victim precipitation. This concept became the characteristic feature of the pioneering victimologists' work and theories (Fisher et al., 2016). Victim *precipitation* is

*Precipitation:* the extent to which the victims contributed to the criminal event that harmed them, and it can take two forms, victim facilitation and victim provocation

# CASE STUDY
## "Sneaking Out"

Michael recently moved to the United States to live with his aunt and uncle and to complete his senior year of high school, and he was taking some time to adjust to his new academic schedule. Michael was a very talented soccer player and was hoping to attain a scholarship to play soccer at a Division 1 university. Since moving to the United States, Michael's uncle, Paul, had to remind him that while soccer was important to him, he needed to concentrate more on his studies and improving his grades. After practices and matches, Michael would always go and hang out with his friends, often neglecting his homework and other responsibilities. One day, the school contacted Paul, notifying him that Michael was a promising student, but his grades were not where they should be and that they were going to suggest that he not be eligible to play soccer until his grades improved. Paul knew that this would upset Michael but thought this was the motivation he needed to improve his school work. That afternoon, Michael came home very upset at his recent suspension from playing soccer. Paul tried to encourage Michael by saying that it was only until his grades improved and it was all up to him. Michael did not see it that way

and asked if he could use the car to go and see his friends. Paul said no and that he should instead use his time effectively to catch up with his school work. Michael went to his room but later that night snuck out and walked to his friend's house. On the way home, he was attacked by two strangers who roughed him up and took his cell phone and wallet. Stunned and very frightened, he ran the rest of the way home. Once home, he was very shaken up and tried to explain to his aunt and uncle what had happened. They were very upset that he had disobeyed them but were happy that he at least made it home safely.

## Questions:

1. What theory would you apply to this case study, and why?

2. Although it may be easy to blame Michael for his victimization, why is it wrong to think this way?

3. Can we compare his victimization to other victims to see how similar he is to them?

defined as the extent to which the victims contributed to the criminal event that harmed them, and it can take two forms, victim facilitation and victim provocation. Fisher et al. (2016) describes that in cases of victim *facilitation*, the victims, often unknowingly, make it easier for offenders to target them or set in motion the events that lead to the victimization. A professor who leaves his laptop in the classroom while he goes to his office to get something and then has it stolen would be a victim who facilitated his own victimization. The professor is not blameworthy, as the offender should not take the professor's property. However, leaving the laptop unattended made him a likely target and the laptop easily available to steal.

**Facilitation:** when the victim, often unknowingly, makes it easier for offenders to target him or her or set in motion the events that lead to the victimization

Victim **provocation** occurs when the victim overtly acts to incite another person to commit an illegal act resulting in his or her victimization. For example, if Paul were to attack Mark, and Mark defends himself, and Paul gets more seriously hurt, then Paul in this case is ultimately the victim. However, if Paul did not attack Mark, he would not have been hurt. Daigle and Muftic (2016) argue that the distinctions between these concepts—victim precipitation, victim facilitation, and victim provocation—are not always clear-cut and can be problematic when used to blame the victims without considering the offenders' roles. The contributions of the pioneering victimologists, including Hans von Hentig, Benjamin Mendelsohn, Stephen Schafer, and Marvin Wolfgang, are discussed below.

## Hans von Hentig

Shortly after World War II began, Hans von Hentig immigrated to the United States where he resumed his work as a scholar investigating the causes of criminality. Through his research, von Hentig argued that too much attention was being given to the perpetrators of crime, and not enough attention was being paid to the victims (Spalek, 2006). He wrote that only examining the outcome of a criminal event can blur the lines of who the real victim is and who the real offender is, and it is therefore necessary to examine the dynamics that surround the event to determine whether or not the victim in any way contributed to his or her own victimization (von Hentig, 1940). By viewing the criminal event as a social interaction (Kirchhoff, 2010), von Hentig in his seminal publication, *The Criminal and His Victim* (1948), dedicated a whole chapter to victims, identifying characteristics which he considered to contribute to the likelihood of being victimized. He proposed an extensive list of 13 victim types based on their propensity for victimization and acting as an agent provocateur (Daigle & Muftic, 2016). These victim types included (1) the young; (2) females; (3) the old; (4) mentally defective and deranged; (5) immigrants; (6) minorities; (7) the dull normal; (8) the depressed; (9) the acquisitive; (10) the wanton; (11) the lonesome and heartbroken; (12) the tormentor; and (13) the blocked, exempted, or fighting. Von Hentig (1948) argued that these victim types, because of their characteristics, contribute to the cause of crime. For example, he reasoned that the young, females, and the elderly are likely to lack the physical strength to resist offenders. Because of cultural differences or lack of familiarity, immigrants and minorities may lead themselves into situations in which they are more easily targeted by offenders. The mentally defective victims and those victims who are depressed may not understand what is occurring around them or may not be able to resist criminal advances. The wanton, acquisitive, and the tormentor are those victims who are directly involved in the criminal act or place themselves in situations where there is a high risk of victimization due to promiscuous, greedy, or abusive behavior. In considering von Hentig's victim types, it is important to be mindful of the fact that they are based on anecdotal observations rather than empirical evidence. Nonetheless, his work highlighted that not only do offenders affect victims, but victims influence offenders, too (Fisher et al., 2016).

## Benjamin Mendelsohn

Benjamin Mendelsohn is credited as being the "Father of Victimology" for the enormous amount of energy he expended into the field through his writings and the promotion of his ideas. Mendelsohn, in his later years, advocated for victimology to be broadened and studied in colleges and universities, for victimological textbooks and journals to be established, and for international conferences to be held, where the focus would be not only on crime victims but also on all forms of victims, including those of disasters, accidents, wars, and discrimination. He called this broader perspective "general victimology" (Hoffman, 1992; Kirchhoff, 2005). However, it is his earlier work for which he is most remembered. Mendelsohn, like von Hentig, became interested in how the victim may have in some way contributed to his or her own victimization. While working as a defense attorney, he conducted an extensive study with his clients before going to trial (Hoffman, 1992). He would ask them to answer a questionnaire from which he established that often there was a strong interpersonal relationship between victims and offenders. He also found in his study that victims precipitated their own victimization to some degree. Mendelsohn, therefore, became interested in establishing to what degree victims were responsible for their victimization (Fattah, 1991) and from this created six categories of victims. Viewing criminal interactions in this way, Mendelsohn reinforced the idea that responsibility assigned to either the offender or the victim is blurred due to the various circumstances surrounding the incident (Fisher et al., 2016). The categories he developed included (1) the completely innocent victim; (2) the victim with minor guilt; (3) the victim as guilty as the offender; (4) the victim that is more guilty than the offender; (5) the most guilty victim; and (6) the imaginary victim. The first category of victim, *the completely innocent victim*, are persons who bear no responsibility for their victimization. He placed children and the unconscious in this category. His second category, *the victim with minor guilt*, are those who are partially responsible. He argued that their actions may be accidental or inadvertent or due to ignorance the danger or harm could have been avoided by planning or awareness. The third category of victim, *the victim as guilty as the offender*, shares equal responsibility with the offender for the victimization. These victims can include people who voluntarily engage in behaviors that knowingly increase their risk of victimization, for example, fighting. *The victim who is more guilty than the offender* is the fourth category of victim. These are people who have provoked the offender to act and in so doing caused their victimization. For example, in an abusive intimate partner relationship, a wife retaliates and injures her abusive husband who in this case is the victim but is more guilty than his wife (the offender and the victim of intimate partner violence). Mendelsohn's fifth category of victim, *the most guilty victim*, includes people responsible for initiating the victimization in the perpetration of a crime. For example, in the commission of a robbery, the offender is killed or injured by the victim acting in self-defense. The final category of victim is *the imaginary victim*. These are people who are not actually victimized but instead fabricate their victimization. Mendelsohn argues that these persons may have mental health problems that cause them to create false events (Schafer, 1977). While both Mendelsohn and von Hentig provided categorizations of victims, their ideas contrasted each other's. Von Hentig focused on identifying the risk factors for victimization, whereas Mendelsohn assigned degrees of blame to victims. It is important to take into consideration that while Mendelsohn's categorizations were an important early set for better understanding criminal victimization, if they are applied broadly, simplistically, and without careful investigation into the facts, the concepts could be misused. Ferguson and Turvey (2009) argue that before these descriptors can be applied to a specific case, attention must be paid to the details. For example, not every bar fight involves a more guilty or most guilty victim, and not everyone who fails to exhibit provocative behavior prior to an attack is completely innocent. Theoretically, Mendelsohn's categories are interesting, however, when applying them to specific cases, especially they can be problematic, especially when contextual information is not taken into consideration (Ferguson & Turvey, 2009).

## Stephan Schafer

Stephen Schafer was the first to author an English book on restitution, titled *Restitution to Victims of Crime,* in 1960 (Dussich, 2015), and he also furthered the interest in understanding the role victims play in criminal victimizations in his book titled *The Victim and His Criminal* (1968). In this play on words on von Hentig's seminal work, Schafer focused on what is called "functional responsibility" (Schafer, 1968, p. 61). **Functional responsibility** refers to the role victims play in not provoking others into victimizing or harming them and indicates that victims should also do everything possible to prevent a victimization from occurring. Similar to von Hentig, Schafer developed seven categories of victims where he emphasized the concepts of precipitation and functional responsibility. These categories are (1) unrelated victims, (2) provocative victims, (3) precipitative victims, (4) biologically weak victims, (5) socially weak victims, (6) self-victimizing victims, (7) and political victims. Schafer's categories of victims differed from von Hentig's in that he was interested in the culpability of the victim, whereas von Hentig placed an emphasis on risk factors. The *unrelated victim* refers to a victim who bears no responsibility and is the unfortunate target of the perpetrator. The *provocative victim* is a person who shares responsibility with the offender, whereby the offender is said to have reacted to an action or behavior of the victim. *Precipitative victims* have some degree of responsibility for the victimization, because they have potentially made themselves vulnerable to offenders either by being in high-risk locations, acting inappropriately, or saying the wrong thing. *Biologically weak victims* have no responsibility for the victimization, as their age, disability, or other physical conditions make them targets for offenders. *Socially weak victims* also have no responsibility. Minorities, immigrants, or persons of the LGBTQ community fall into this category because they are thought to not be adequately integrated into society and are viewed as easy targets. *Self-victimizing victims* bear complete responsibility for their victimization. These are persons who engage in drug use, prostitution, or gambling. The final category of victim is the *political victim*. These victims have no responsibility for their victimization and are instead made victims because of their opposition to those in power.

The attempts to better understand the criminal interaction by the early victimologists certainly sparked a renewed interest in the victims of crime; however, their work did not address the harm and impact the victimization had on the victim. For example, what was not taken into consideration were the psychological, physical, and financial consequences of the crime and the process of recuperation needed to help the victim return to as close to normal as possible (Young, 1982; Kirchhoff, 2005). This trend of seeking to understand the interaction between offender and victim continued when the

**Functional responsibility:** the role victims play in not provoking others into victimizing or harming them, and the idea that victims should also do everything possible to prevent a victimization from occurring

first systematic study to provide empirical evidence of victim contribution in the commission of crime was conducted by Marvin Wolfgang.

## Marvin Wolfgang

In 1957, Marvin Wolfgang, investigating victim precipitation, analyzed data from all the homicide cases that occurred from 1948 to 1952 in Philadelphia. For a case to be considered victim precipitated, he argued that the "victim had to be the first to show and use a deadly weapon, to strike the first blow in an altercation—in short, [be] the first to commence the interplay or resort to physical violence" (Wolfgang, 1958, p. 252). After examining 558 cases, he found that 26% of the cases were victim precipitated. Moreover, from his analysis, he identified other factors that are typical in homicide cases. These are that often the victim and offender have a prior interpersonal relationship, the most common victims and offenders of homicide are male, that the victim may have a history of violent offending, and that alcohol was a common ingredient in victim-precipitated homicides.

One central concept that emerged from the early victimologists' exploration into the criminal interaction and has remained true is the link between offending and victimization and offenders and victims. Rather than all victims being thought of as innocent, victims were considered to be at least partially responsible for their victimization (Daigle &Muftic, 2016). However, the concept of victim precipitation has been criticized for having a preoccupation with victim blaming, an issue that society is still struggling to confront. Victim blaming impacts the way information and decisions made about innocence and guilt are evaluated and has been used to justify violent behavior (Zur, 1994).

# Theories of Victimization
. . . . . . . . . . . . . . . . . . . . . . . . . . . . . . . . . . . . . . . . . . . . . . . . . . . . . . . . . . .

During the 1960s and 1970s, a variety of paradigm shifts, along with social and political movements, were occurring, and new sources of information regarding the limitations of data compiled from police reports surfaced (see Chapter 1) (Wilcox, 2010; Saponaro, 2013). Realizing these limitations, a new approach to collecting data on victimization was developed. This approach entailed collecting large amounts of information through large surveys of the public on victimization (van Kesteren & van Dijk, 2010). Thus, surveys such as the National Crime Victim Survey (NCVS), the British Crime Survey (BCS), and the International Crime Victim Survey (ICVS) were developed and conducted on a regular basis (see van Dijk, van Kesteren, & Smit, 2008) (see Chapter 3). In comparison to police reports, these surveys allow researchers to estimate more accurately the incidence and generality of victimization in society. These surveys enabled measuring between reported and unreported incidences of victimization (van Dijk et al., 2008). The abundance of data these surveys collected on victims, along with a change toward a victim-oriented criminal justice system, was an ideal situation for the emergence of various theoretical perspectives on victimization to develop (Wilcox, 2010; Saponaro, 2013). A wide range of causal influences, from routine daily activities and lifestyles, to interpersonal dynamics, to broad-based social inequalities derived from this data was used to develop theoretical perspectives on victimization (see table below) (Wilcox, 2010).

| Table 2.1 Theoretical Perspectives in Victimology | |
| --- | --- |
| **Theory** | **Author/s** |
| Lifestyle-Exposure Theory | Hindelang, Gottfredson, and Garofalo (1978) |
| Routine Activity Theory | Cohen and Felson (1979) |
| The Opportunity Model | Cohen, Kleugel, and Land (1981) |
| The Differential Risk Model of Criminal Victimization | Fattah (1991) |
| The Social Learning Theory | Akers (1973) |
| Extended Low Self-Control Theory | Schreck (1999) |
| Extended Control Balance Theory | Piquero and Hickman (2003) |

## Lifestyle and Routine Activities

**Lifestyle-Exposure Theory:** refers to "lifestyle" as routine daily activities that include vocational (work, school, keeping house, etc.) and leisure activities (shopping and going to bars etc.). A person comes into contact through his or her lifestyle and/or behaviors with potential offenders. Therefore, a person who participates in activities away from the home, particularly at night, and with nonfamily members is more likely to be victimized

The Lifestyle-Exposure Theory (Hindelang, Gottfredson, & Garofalo,1978), Routine Activity Theory (Cohen & Felson, 1979), and Opportunity Model (Cohen, Kleugel, & Land, 1981) are theoretical explanations for understanding the social situations in which victimizations are believed to occur. These theoretical explanations use "testable propositions designed to explain why a person is victimized." This is done by proposing that a person's risk of victimization can be best understood by the extent to which his or her daily activities create opportunities for a motivated offender to commit crime (Daigle & Muftic, 2016, p. 26). The theories do not attempt to explain the motivation of offenders but rather the convergence in time and space between the perpetrator and the victim and their influences on victimization (Gottfredson, 1981).

According to Hindelang et al. (1978, p. 241), the **Lifestyle-Exposure Theory** refers to "lifestyle" as routine daily activities that include vocational (work, school, keeping house, etc.) and "leisure" activities (shopping, going to bars, etc.). A person comes into contact through their lifestyles and/or behaviors with potential offenders. Therefore, a person who participates in activities away from the home, particularly at night, and with nonfamily members is more likely to be victimized. Hindelang et al. (1978) pointed out that a person's lifestyle is structured by social constraints and role expectations; therefore, it is argued that the demographics of age, gender, race, marital status, and income greatly influence the lifestyle of individuals and their ability to engage in particular activities. The variance in lifestyle of the different demographic groups increases the probability of victimization. The demographic factors influence the prospect of an individual being in a certain location, at a particular time, and coming into contact with a potential perpetrator (Hindelang et al., 1978). For example, younger and single persons

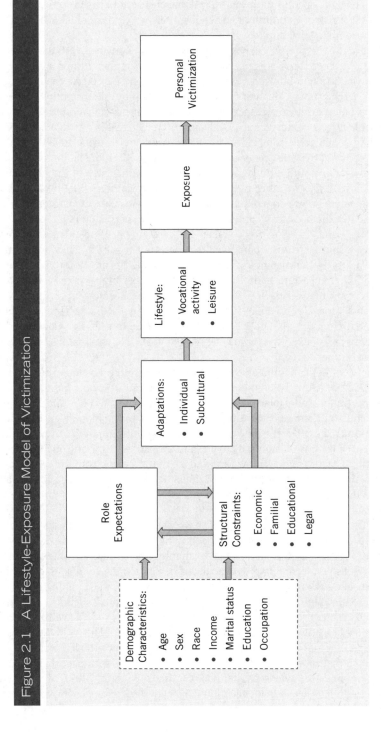

Figure 2.1  A Lifestyle-Exposure Model of Victimization

*Source:* Adapted from Hindelang, Gottfredson, and Garofalo (1978).

**Routine Activity
Theory:** this
theoretical perspective
argues not why
certain demographics
are susceptible to
criminal victimization
but rather why daily
routine activities
create the opportunity
for criminal
victimization (Cohen
& Felson, 1979). The
propositions of this
theory are that for
victimization to take
place, there must
be three elements:
(1) a motivated
perpetrator/s, (2)
suitable targets
(victim), and (3) the
absence of a capable
guardian at a given
place and time (Cohen
& Felson, 1979, p. 592)

are more likely to spend time away from home engaging in leisure activities that would place them at risk of victimization. Therefore, persons who are older and married are at a lower risk of victimization.

Similar to the lifestyle exposure theory is the **Routine Activity Theory**. This theoretical perspective argues not why certain demographic groups are susceptible to criminal victimization but rather why daily routine activities create the opportunity for criminal victimization (Cohen & Felson, 1979). The propositions of this theory are that for victimization to take place, there must be three elements: (1) motivated perpetrator/s; (2) suitable targets (victim); and (3) the absence of a capable guardian at a given place and time (Cohen & Felson, 1979, p. 592). Cohen and Felson (1979) assert that the absence of any of the three elements is sufficient to result in the failure of the successful completion or the committing of a victimization, particularly direct personal victimization. However, if the latter two elements (a suitable target [victim] and absence of a capable guardian) are combined, it may lead to an increase in victimization, without an increase in the necessary conditions that motivate perpetrators to become involved (Cohen & Felson, 1979, p. 589). Cohen and Felson (1979) postulated that prosperity in society would increase criminal victimization, not reduce it. They argued that with the increase of two-earner households, people would spend more time going to and from work and engage in more leisure activities, increasing their risk of victimization. Moreover, Cohen and Felson (1979) argued that advancement in technology of electronics and durable goods (e.g., televisions, microwaves, and cars) made them easier to steal, reuse, and resell, and become more desirable targets. For Cohen and Felson, victimization was linked to everyday activities rather than to social ills, such as poverty (Daigle & Muftic, 2016).

**Opportunity
Model:** takes from the
lifestyle-exposure and
routine activity theory
and expands on them
and identifies further
factors that may play
an integral role in
victimization. These
factors are exposure,
guardianship,
proximity of potential
perpetrators,
attractiveness of
potential targets,
and properties of
specific offences. The
inclusion of these
factors relocates
the prominence of
the theory from the
characteristics of the
perpetrator to
the characteristics
of the situation
(Saponaro, 2013)

Similar to both theories is the **Opportunity Model** developed in 1981. Cohen et al. (1981) developed this theory to better expound upon predatory victimization. The Opportunity Model takes from the Lifestyle-Exposure and Routine Activity Theory and expands on them and identifies further factors that may play an integral role in victimization. These factors are exposure, guardianship, proximity of potential perpetrators, attractiveness of potential targets, and properties of specific offences. The inclusion of these factors relocates the prominence of the theory from the characteristics of the perpetrator to the characteristics of the situation (Saponaro, 2013). In reality, this theory is the same as the two already mentioned and does no better in explaining why victimization occurs.

All three of the theories explained have been used to describe the variables that are said to influence the potential probability of victimization (Laub, 1990; Mawby & Walklate, 1994). This is done through examining the structural context of risk across spaces and also understanding what makes a person a more suitable target within such a context. For Zaykowski and Campagna (2014, p. 454), the combination of environment and vulnerability creates "opportunity" for a motivated offender. The theories of lifestyle-exposure, routine activities, and the opportunity model have been the prevailing theories of victimization for more than three decades. This is because researchers have found empirical support when testing for their propositions. For example, it has been shown that individuals' routine activities and lifestyles impact their risk of being involved in predatory offenses (Sherman, Gartin, & Buerger, 1989). More recent studies have indicated that individuals' routine activities and lifestyles increase their risk of being carjacked (Davis, 2001), sexually victimized (Fisher, Daigle, & Cullen, 2010), stalked, being victims of cybercrime (Halder & Jaishankar, 2011, 2016), and street robbery (Groff, 2007). Despite the evidence suggesting that social characteristics correlated with a higher-risk lifestyle make a person more vulnerable to being a victim of crime, the theories do not provide much support for violence that takes place within the family (Zaykowski & Campagna, 2014).

## The Differential Risk Model of Criminal Victimization

In an attempt to eradicate the limitations of the Lifestyle and Routine Activities theory, Ezzat Fattah developed the Differential Risk Model of Criminal Victimization in 1991. The intention of this theoretical perspective is to focus on not only the factors of lifestyle or the demographics of victims in criminal victimization but also on all relevant factors. Therefore, Fattah developed "a comprehensive scheme" consisting of 10 categories, which he argued influence the potential of being criminally victimized (Fattah, 2000, pp. 64-66):

1. Opportunities are linked to the characteristics of potential targets (persons, households, businesses) and the activities and behavior of those targets.

2. Risk factors are the sociodemographic characteristics such as age, gender, area of residence, and absence of guardianship.

3. Motivated offender: Perpetrators, even nonprofessional ones, do not choose their victims/targets at random but select them according to specific criteria.

4. Exposure to potential offenders and high-risk situations and environments enhances the risk of criminal victimization.

5. Associations: The homogeneity of the victim and perpetrator populations suggests that differential associations are as important to criminal victimization as they are to crime and delinquency. Therefore, individuals who are in close social and professional contact with potential perpetrators have a greater chance of being victimized than those who are not.

6. Dangerous times and dangerous places: Risks of criminal victimization are not evenly distributed in time and space—there are dangerous times such as evenings, early hours, and weekends. There are also dangerous places, such as places of public entertainment, where the risks of becoming a victim are higher than at work or at home.

7. Dangerous behaviors: Certain behaviors, such as provocation, increase the risk of violent victimization while other behaviors such as negligence and carelessness enhance the chances of property victimization. Other dangerous behaviors place those engaging in them in dangerous situations where the ability to defend and protect themselves against attack is greatly reduced.

8. High-risk activities increase the potential for victimization. Among such activities is the mutual pursuit of fun, as well as deviant and illegal activities.

It is also well known that certain occupations such as prostitution carry with them a higher than average potential for criminal victimization.

9. Defensive/avoidance behaviors: As many risks of criminal victimization could be easily avoided, people's attitudes to those risks can influence their chance of being victimized. It goes without saying that risk takers are bound to be victimized more often than risk avoiders.

10. Structural/cultural proneness: A positive correlation between powerlessness, deprivation, and the frequency of criminal victimization exists. Cultural stigmatization and marginalization also enhances the risk of criminal victimization by designating certain groups as "fair game" or as culturally legitimate victims.

Examining the 10 categories of the Differential Risk Model of Criminal Victimization, there is no doubt that Fattah has expanded on the previous theories (Life-Style Exposure, Routine Activities, Opportunity Model). However, the theory is not very different from the previous ones. Like its contributors, it tends to focus on a narrow and conventional understanding of criminal victimization (Mawby & Walklate, 1994; Spalek, 2006).

## Social Learning Theory

The opportunity theories mentioned above attempt to explain victimization through social structures. Psychological theories, on the other hand, attempt to explain victimization by examining the impact of individual pathology, culture, socialization, and learning on people. Ronald Akers (1973), applying the psychological theory of **social learning theory** to criminal behavior, argued that criminal behavior is learned behavior. The theory's premise is that individuals learn behavior by observing and imitating other people through the absorption of experiences and reinforcement. In other words, behavior that is either rewarded, or goes unpunished, develops into the observer's library of what is acceptable behavior (Akers, 1998). Akers (1998) outlined four main concepts in the process of social learning theory. These are (1) differential association, (2) definitions, (3) differential reinforcement, and (4) imitation. The concept of *differential association* places emphasis on the social interactions between people in peer groups such as those between families, neighbors, as well as those found in media content and the Internet (Nicholson & Higgins, 2017). These interactions shape the environment in which social learning of behavior occurs. Beyond the interaction within these groups is also the duration spent within these associations. Akers (1998) posited that the greater the amount of time and percentage of all time that is spent with certain people (delinquent or criminal others), the greater influence they will have on an individual's behavior. The next concept, *definitions*, relates to the individuals' own beliefs and attitudes as to whether or not it is acceptable to engage in criminal behavior. Definitions include the orientations, rationalizations, definitions of the situation, and other attitudes that label the commission of an act as right or wrong, good or bad, desirable or undesirable, and justified or unjustified (Nicholson & Higgins, 2017). Definitions do not work so much as direct motivators but rather as indicators that certain behaviors are likely to be rewarded or punished. Predictable reinforcement or punishment

**Social Learning Theory:** individuals learn behavior by observing and imitating other people through the absorption of experiences and reinforcement. In other words, behavior that is either rewarded, or goes unpunished, develops into the observer's library of what is acceptable behavior (Akers, 1998)

is what motivates behavior, regardless of whether motivation to participate in such an act is in line with someone's beliefs (Nicholson & Higgins, 2017). The third concept is *differential reinforcement*. This concept suggests that people are more likely to engage in a behavior based on certain desirable results involving rewards or punishment (Akers, 1998). People are more likely to engage in behaviors that are rewarded than engage in behaviors that are punished. Greater and more frequently occurring rewards such as status, monetary gain, or excitement associated with a behavior are positively correlated with a particular behavior. Conversely, behavior that is reinforced with a low frequency and severity of punishment is thought to deter individuals from engaging in such behavior (Akers, 1998). The final concept is *imitation*. The concept refers to behavior that is reinforced when individuals observe the behaviors modeled by others and also the consequences that follow others' behavior. For example, an individual may witness a criminal act and recognize the rewards the offender gained or the lack of punishment and feel encouraged to participate in the same behavior through imitation (Nicholson & Higgins, 2017).

Social learning theory, despite being used to explain criminal behavior, has been used to explain victimization. Social learning theory has been prominent in helping to understand violence within the family. The frequency and duration of violence in an individual's environment will influence the learning experience. When aggressive action brings desired results, violence becomes an acceptable means to an end. Therefore, social learning theory helps to explain the presence of the intergenerational transmission of violence. For example, children who grow up in abusive families may learn violent or abusive behaviors and imitate those behaviors later in life. Research has indicated the children who experienced abuse and or witnessed abuse in the home are at greater risk of being abusive themselves or ending up as the victim in an abusive relationship (Cappell & Heiner, 1990; Marshall & Rose, 1990; Dutton, 1995; Corvo & Carpenter, 2000). Although social learning theory has empirical support, critics of the theory have argued that the perspective does not acknowledge potential factors that can interfere with the process of transmitting values and why some people who experience abuse do not grow up to be abusers or victims.

## Extended Low Self-Control Theory

The General Theory of Crime was developed by Gottfredson and Hirschi in 1990. The main proposition of this theory is that **low self-control** is the most important predictor for delinquent and analogous behaviors (e.g., smoking, drinking, using illicit drugs, and/or engaging in risky behavior) (Gottfredson & Hirschi, 1990; Jones & Quisenberry, 2004). Why some people turn to criminal behavior and others do not is because offenders have a propensity or tendency to take advantage of opportunities for criminal behavior. This propensity to engage in criminal behavior results from a lack of direct control or guidance by parents or caregivers early in life. Gottfredson and Hirschi (1990) state that family and other institutions such as schools, neighborhoods, and the community play a crucial role in the development of an individual's self-control. They argue that self-control is not an inherent characteristic of an individual, but rather it is developed through social structures. Therefore, should self-control fail to be developed, an individual may exhibit six elements that increase his or her propensity to offend. These are

**Low Self-Control Theory:** low self-control is the most important predictor for delinquent and analogous behaviors (Gottfredson & Hirschi, 1990; Jones & Quisenberry, 2004). Why some people turn to criminal behavior and others do not is because offenders have a propensity or tendency to take advantage of opportunities for criminal behavior. This propensity to engage in criminal behavior results from a lack of direct control or guidance by parents or caregivers early in life

(1) impulsivity, (2) preference for simple tasks, (3) risk-seeking potential, (4) preference for physical activities, (5) self-centeredness, and (6) the possession of a volatile temper (Gottfredson & Hirschi, 1990, p. 89-90). *Impulsivity* refers to the need that persons with low self-control have to react immediately to situations to pursue immediate pleasure. The *preference for simple tasks* in persons with low self-control means that they lack persistence or diligence and seek tasks that provide easy opportunities and gratification. A person with low self-control will engage in *risk seeking* behaviors without thought of the consequences of such behaviors. A *preference for physical activities* in persons with low self-control means that they are less likely to act rationally or engage in mental activities. Low self-control will also be shown through *self-centeredness*. Here persons do not consider how their actions impact others, showing no empathy. The *possession of a volatile temper* in persons with low self-control often results in these persons reacting to situations with aggression or through other physical means.

Christopher Schreck recognized that the General Theory of Crime could also be used to explain victimization, not just offending. In 1999, Schreck developed the Extended Low Self-Control Theory. He argued that as there are often "parallels between victimization and offending [which] raise the possibility that a common underlying cause can influence the likelihood of both becoming an offender and a victim; low self-control can also explain the increase in the risk of criminal victimization" (Schreck, 1999, pp. 633-634). What Schreck (1999) takes from the General Theory of Crime is that low self-control and analogous behavior (e.g., the tendency to need immediate, easy, certain short-term satisfaction of desires) increases a person's vulnerability and risk of victimization (i.e., drinking influences a person's coordination and decision-making abilities) (Saponaro, 2013, p. 24). Schreck (1999) transforms the General Theory of Crime into one of vulnerability to crime. He further takes the six elements of low self-control that increase the propensity to offend and adapts them to victimization. These are (1) future orientation, (2) diligence, (3) risk seeking, (4) physical activity, (5) empathy, and (6) tolerance for frustration (Schreck, 1999, p. 636) (see Table 2.2). *Future orientation* implies that persons with low self-control live in the moment without considering the consequences of their actions, which places them in vulnerable situations. *Diligence* means that those with low self-control are inconsistent in their use of security and protective measures presenting themselves as attractive targets for offenders. Persons with low self-control engaging in *risk-seeking* behaviors can unintentionally place themselves in dangerous situations increasing their risk of victimization. *Physical activities* mean that persons with low self-control may react more quickly to a problem physically, which may lead to altercations and victimization. Persons with low self-control and who lack *empathy* are indifferent to others and often have fewer social relationships. This reduced guardianship can place the person in vulnerable situations. A *tolerance for frustration* implies that persons with low self-control are confrontational and hostile and create or engage in high-risk situations increasing the risk of victimization.

More recent developments have seen an integration of the extended low self-control theory and the routine activities theory (Schreck, Wright, & Miller, 2002; Holtfreter, Reisig, & Pratt, 2008). What has been found is that routine activities are important precursors to victimization; however, self-control influences the kinds of routines in which individuals engage. These findings indicate that self-control and opportunity influence victimization risk, and that future research should continue and perhaps extend a theoretical integration between the two theories (Holtfreter et al., 2008).

| Gottfredson & Hirschi (1990): General Theory of Crime | Schreck (1999): Extended Low Self-Control Theory |
|---|---|
| 1. *Impulsivity*: the need that persons with low self-control have to react immediately to situations to pursue immediate pleasure. | 1. *Future orientation*: implies that persons with low self-control live in the moment without considering the consequences of their actions, which places them in vulnerable situations. |
| 2. *Preference for simple tasks*: in persons with low self-control, it means that they lack persistence or diligence and seek tasks that provide easy opportunities and gratification. | 2. *Diligence*: means that those with low self-control are inconsistent in their use of security and protective measures, presenting themselves as attractive targets for offenders. |
| 3. *Risk-seeking potential*: a person with low self-control will engage in risk-seeking behaviors without thought of the consequences of such behaviors. | 3. *Risk-seeking*: persons with low self-control engaging in risk-seeking behaviors can unintentionally place themselves in dangerous situations increasing their risk of victimization. |
| 4. *Preference for physical activities*: in persons with low self-control, it means that they are less likely to act rationally or engage in mental activities. | 4. *Physical activity*: means that persons with low self-control may react more quickly to a problem physically, which may lead to altercations and victimization. |
| 5. *Self-centeredness*: low self-control will also be shown through self-centeredness. Here persons do not consider how their actions impact others, showing no empathy. | 5. *Empathy*: persons with low self-control and who lack empathy are indifferent to others and often have fewer social relationships. This reduced guardianship can place the person in vulnerable situations. |
| 6. *The possession of a volatile temper*: in persons with low self-control, it often results in these persons reacting to situations with aggression or through other physical means. | 6. *Tolerance for frustration*: a tolerance for frustration implies that persons with low self-control are confrontational and hostile and create or engage in high-risk situations increasing the risk of victimization. |

*Source:* Adapted from Schreck (1999).

## Extended Control Balance Theory

In the original Control Balance Theory, Charles Tittle (1995, p. 124) proposes that deviance, defined as behavior that the majority regards as unacceptable or that typically evokes collective response of a negative type, is caused by the amount of control that individuals exercise relative to the amount of control to which they are subject. According to Tittle (1995), two elements belong to the concept of control: (1) the degree of control an individual or group is subjected to, and (2) the degree of control an individual or group can exercise over others. Imposing excessive control over others (e.g., having a control surplus) and bearing the excessive control of others (e.g., having a control deficit) disrupts an individual's **control balance** and impacts his or her behavior (Delisi & Hochstetler, 2002). Being controlled and having the ability to control are continuous variables. Thus, it is argued that if the control ratio is balanced, then it is likely that an individual or group will conform to society's norms. If unbalanced, an individual or group may have a higher propensity to commit criminal behavior (Tittle, 1995; Akers & Sellers, 2009; Saponaro, 2013). Depending on the control ratio and the direction of the imbalance, Tittle (1995) postulates the types of deviant acts more likely to occur. These deviant acts include submission, defiance, predation, conformity, exploitation, plunder, and decadence. Persons with a control surplus are prone to commit autonomous acts of deviance, such as exploitation, plunder, and decadence. Those with a control deficit are prone to commit more repressive acts of deviance. These include submission, defiance, and predation. In the middle of this theoretical continuum is the control conformists, who are persons with a balanced control ratio (Tittle, 1995).

Alex Piquero and Matthew Hickman (2003), in exploring the validity of the control balance theory, developed the theory of Extended Control Balance, where they identified that control imbalances can be positively related to the probability of victimization. They reason that should there be a deficit in the control ratio, it is likely that an individual may become weak due to his or her inability to exercise control, which will make the individual passive, submissive, and vulnerable to victimization. Conversely, when there is a surplus in the control ratio, individuals are also at risk of victimization. The impunity, invulnerability, and "untouchability" these individuals exhibit may lead to victimization. Piquero and Hickman (2003) qualify this by arguing that overconfident individuals may seek out more risky situations to put themselves in, as they attempt to extend their control. To test the theory, Piquero and Hickman (2003) conducted a study on 253 urban undergraduate students to account for deviant victimization. Controlling for demographic variables (age, race, gender, and two lifestyle variables), they found persons with control ratio imbalances (both a surplus and deficit) were more likely to be victimized than those with a balanced control ratio (Piquero & Hickman, 2003). In particular, they found that persons with control imbalances were more susceptible to experience victimization by theft (Piquero & Hickman, 2003).

The extended control balance theory has also been applied to cases of domestic violence. Psychological abuse, a mechanism of control, can cause the victim to feel at greater risk for additional violence (Henning & Klesges, 2003). Financial control can cause the victim to feel powerless and unable to escape the abusive relationship (Wolf, Ly, Hobart, & Kernic, 2003). In both situations, the flow of control seems to be constantly in favor of the abuser, and there appears to be little that the victim can do to gain control in the relationship. When a victim is subject to the control of the abuser, whether it be psychological, physical, or financial abuse, the victim feels that there is an inability to gain control, and the reaction can be an increase in depression and hopelessness (Clements, Sabourin, & Spiby, 2004). This response, however natural, exacerbates the control imbalance and the potential for future violence against the victim (Piquero & Hickman 2003). Despite evidence to suggest that control ratio imbalances are a risk factor for victimization, relatively little research has been conducted to explore all the extensions of Piquero and Hickman's theory. More research is needed to better understand the usefulness of the theory in explaining victimization (Fisher et al., 2016).

# SUMMARY

Driven by research, theory has enhanced our understanding of victimization. No one theory, however, claims to have the answer, but researchers continue to consider the problems and seek to develop ways to address them. The early victimologists focused on expanding the criminological perspective to include victims. They identified the link between offending and victimization and offenders and victims. Rather than all victims being thought of as innocent, victims were considered to be at least partially responsible for their victimization (Daigle & Muftic, 2016). Their work developed the concepts of victim precipitation, victim facilitation, and victim provocation. However, these concepts impact the way information and decisions made about innocence and guilt are evaluated and has been used to justify violent behavior, leading to victim blaming.

Moving forward and resulting from a variety of social and political movements during the 1960s and 1970s, and a change toward a victim-oriented criminal justice system, data collected from police reports, and victim surveys allowed theoretical perspectives on victimization to develop. Today, routine daily activities and lifestyles, to interpersonal dynamics, to broad-based social inequalities are the prevailing explanations for victimization. These theories suggest that a risky lifestyle, poor social bonds, and interacting in certain geographical locations increases the risk of crime victimization. Social learning theory, on the other hand, argues that victimization may also be a process that is learned. Victims may have learned the motives, definitions, and behaviors that lead to and reinforce victimization.

Adapting the criminological theories of control balance theory and the general theory of crime to victimization has found that individuals with an unequal control-balance ratio or low self-control may be more prone to victimization. Through research and theory development we have gained an enormous amount of insight into the complexities of victimization, why it happens and who it happens to; however, much more work is needed to understand the social and policy implications of victimization and what efforts are made to return to as close to a normal life as possible by victims in the aftermath of crime.

# KEY WORDS

| | | |
|---|---|---|
| Control balance   32 | Low self-control   29 | Routine activity theory   26 |
| Facilitation   19 | Opportunity model   27 | Social learning theory   28 |
| Functional responsibility   22 | Precipitation   18 | Theories   18 |
| Lifestyle-exposure theory   24 | Provocation   20 | |

# INTERNET RESOURCES

**The Uniform Crime Report (ucr.fbi.gov)**

The Uniform Crime Reporting (UCR) Program has been the starting place for law enforcement executives, students of criminal justice, researchers, members of the media, and the public at large seeking information on crime in the nation. The program was conceived in 1929 by the International Association of Chiefs of Police to meet the need for reliable uniform crime statistics for the nation. In 1930, the FBI was tasked with collecting, publishing, and archiving those statistics.

**Crime Survivors for Safety and Justice (https://cssj.org)**

Crime Survivors for Safety and Justice is a program of Californians for Safety and Justice. Through policy advocacy, public education, partnerships, and support for local best practices, Californians for Safety and Justice promotes effective criminal justice strategies to stop the cycle of crime, reduce overreliance on incarceration, and build healthy communities.

**The Crime Report (https://thecrimereport.org)**

*The Crime Report* (TCR) is a multimedia information and networking resource based at John Jay College of Criminal Justice in New York. Published daily online, it provides comprehensive reporting and analysis of criminal justice news and research in the United States and abroad.

## CRITICAL THINKING QUESTIONS

1. Compare and contrast the differences between victim precipitation, victim facilitation, and victim provocation.

2. The early victimologists focused on expanding the criminological perspective to include victims. Describe how their concepts have impacted the way information and decisions made about innocence and guilt have been used to evaluate and justify violent behavior.

3. Describe the three propositions of Routine Activity Theory and why the absence of any of the three elements is sufficient to explain why a person may be victimized.

4. List the four concepts of social learning theory, and explain why the theory has been influential in understanding violence within in the family.

5. Discuss how a person with an unequal control-balance ratio or low self-control may be more prone to victimization.

# The Nature and Extent of Victimization

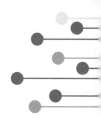

How do we know the prevalence of victimization and who are the typical victims? What are the shared characteristics among crime victims? There are many forms of statistical data compiled by government agencies, private groups, and researchers to address such questions. The most frequently cited sources of crime statistics in the United States are the Uniform Crime Report (UCR), the National Incident-Based Reporting System (NIBRS), and the National Crime Victimization Survey (NCVS). Currently, a transition from UCR to NIBRS is in progress, and the Federal Bureau of Investigation (FBI) is aiming to establish NIBRS as the crime-reporting standard by 2021 (Strom & Smith, 2017). Along with those large-scale databases, there are many survey studies focusing on specific victim groups to understand their challenges. This chapter begins with the available sources of crime victim data and highlights the strengths and weaknesses of those databases. Then, we look at the nature and extent of victimization as well as costs of victimization. Finally, we explore the help-seeking behaviors of victims and updates in the ongoing progress of new data collection for victim services.

## Primary Source of Crime Victim Data in the United States

### Uniform Crime Report (UCR)

The **Uniform Crime Report (UCR)** has so far provided the best view of crime trends in the United States since 1930 (Planty, Langton, & Barnett-Ryan, 2014). The UCR program measures crimes reported to local law enforcement departments and the number of arrests made by police agencies, which includes Part I and Part II offenses. Part I offenses include murder and nonnegligent manslaughter, forcible rape, robbery, aggravated assault, burglary, larceny-theft, motor vehicle theft, arson, and human trafficking (Planty et al., 2014). The human trafficking category was added in 2013 under the William Wilberforce Trafficking Victims Protection Reauthorization Act of 2008 (FBI, 2014a). Furthermore, the FBI announced a change in the definition of *rape* to clarify the scope of the offenses (FBI, 2014b). Under the new definition that went into effect in January 2013, *rape* is defined as "penetration no matter how slight, of the vagina or anus with any body part or object, or oral penetration by a sex organ of another person, without the consent of the victim" (FBI, 2014b). The Part II offenses consist of 21 additional crime categories including sex crimes, vandalism, and offenses against the family and children.

**Uniform Crime Report (UCR):** national crime data compiled by the FBI that includes crimes reported to local law enforcement departments and the number of arrests made by police agencies

The crime data compiled by the FBI are released as **Crime in the United States**, an annual report that is a valuable resource for understanding the number and rate of violent and property crime offenses in the nation and by state. Along with the crime statistics, the UCR program generates further annual reports such as the *Supplementary Homicide Report, Law Enforcement Officers Killed and Assaulted,* and *Hate Crime Statistics*. Those supplementary homicide reports include detailed information on homicides including victims' and offenders' age, sex, race, weapon type, victim-offender relationship, and the circumstances that led to the homicide (Rennison & Dodge, 2018).

Although the UCR has the most valuable official crime statistics in the United States, some potential problems in interpreting the data have been identified. The most serious shortcoming from a victimological standpoint is that the UCR counts only the crimes known to the police, and a significant number of crimes are unreported, the so-called dark figures of crime; more than half (52%) of all violent victimizations were not reported from 2006 to 2010. These victims thought the crime was a personal matter, that it was not important enough, and that nothing could be done, or feared retaliation (Langton, Berzofsky, Krebs, & Smiley-McDonald, 2012). Consequently, not only does the UCR fail to capture a substantial number of crimes occurring in the United States but also changes in victims' reporting behaviors given factors such as police mistrust could affect the overall crime rate. The other limitation of the UCR is the use of the hierarchy rule in which only the most serious offense is counted if a crime involved multiple offenses. Furthermore, the UCR program only collects limited categories of offenses. Although several modifications have been made to improve the data collection, for example, adding the human trafficking category and changing the definition of rape in 2013, other critical crimes such as stalking and cyberbullying are not collected yet. Finally, the recordkeeping and reporting practices of local police departments could affect the accuracy of the data.

## National Incident-Based Reporting System (NIBRS)

To address the limitations of the UCR and provide a more reliable source of crime statistics, the FBI launched the **National Incident-Based Reporting System (NIBRS)** as a more detailed crime reporting program. The NIBRS collects data on each reported crime incident and arrest for 46 specific crimes called Group A offenses as well as 11 lesser offenses from the arrest data (FBI, 2000). Some examples of offenses included in Group A but not in the UCR are kidnapping/abduction, pornography/obscene materials, and extortion/blackmail. Unlike the UCR, the NIBRS includes all offenses in a single incident and contains such detailed victim information as resident status, type of injury, and the relationship(s) of the victim to the offender (FBI, 2000).

Although the shift to the NIBRS could significantly improve the national crime statistics, the transition from the UCR to the NIBRS has lagged for the past two decades (Strom & Smith, 2017). One significant barrier to participating in the NIBRS is the lack of funding and technical support; in particular, the cost associated with converting to the NIBRS is a major concern for local agencies. Another barrier is the rigidity of the requirements for the NIBRS, which could create a significant burden for officers. Local agencies also are concerned that the transition from the hierarchal rules to the incident-based reporting might give the impression that the crime rate has increased in a jurisdiction. However, the empirical research indicates that the difference between the average estimate of the two systems for violent crime, property crime, and crime overall is marginal (Rantala & Edwards, 2000).

While the NIBRS is not yet nationally representative (FBI, 2015), the report released in 2014 contains detailed information on more than 5.4 million offenses from 6,520 law enforcement agencies, which represented 35.2% of all law enforcement agencies that participated in the UCR program. The comprehensiveness and accuracy of the NIBRS makes it possible to provide in-depth analysis of special crimes, for example, *Sex Offenses Reported via NIBRS in 2013*. The NIBRS recognizes six types of sex offenses: rape, sodomy, sexual assault with an object, fondling, incest, and statutory rape. Of all criminal incidents counted in the NIBRS in 2013, 1.4%, or 69,979, included at least one sex offense (U.S. Department of Justice—Federal Bureau of Investigation, 2015). As shown in Table 3.1, the sex offenses mostly occurred at a residential location, and the most likely victims of sex offenses were teenage females.

The NIBRS allows the provision of further details of such incidents. For example, sexual assault with an object was most often reported on Fridays, and the second most common days of the week were Tuesdays and Thursdays. By looking at all sex offenses combined, the most likely victims of sex offenses were teenage females. However, the disaggregated age data indicated that the most likely victim of sodomy is a 5-year-old male. (U.S. Department of Justice—Federal Bureau of Investigation, 2015). As more agencies participate in the program, the NIBRS data will become a crucial resource for victimological research and victim services.

### Table 3.1 Most Common Attributes for Six Sex Offenses

| | Rape | Sodomy | Sexual assaults with an object | Fondling | Incest | Statutory rape |
|---|---|---|---|---|---|---|
| Victim age | 15 years old | 5 years old | 15 years old | 14 years old | 14 years old | 15 years old |
| Victim sex | Female | Female | Female | Female | Female | Female |
| Offender age | 18 years old | 14 years old | 17 years old | 14 years old | 15 years old | 18 years old |
| Offender sex | Male | Male | Male | Male | Male | Male |
| Weapon used | Personal weapons | Personal weapons | Personal weapons | Personal weapons | — | — |
| Relationship | Acquaintance | Acquaintance | Acquaintance | Acquaintance | Child | Acquaintance |
| Location | Residence/ home | Residence/ home | Residence/ home | Residence/ home | Residence/ home | Residence/ home |

*Source:* U.S. Department of Justice—Federal Bureau of Investigation (2015). Sex Offenses Reported via NIBRS in 2013. Washington, DC: Author. https://ucr.fbi.gov/nibrs-sex-offenses-study-2013

# The National Crime
# Victimization Survey (NCVS)

The **National Crime Victimization Survey (NCVS)** is the most comprehensive nationwide household survey providing a detailed picture of crime victims and the consequences of crime, unreported crime, and victimization trends. The survey started in 1973 as the National Crime Survey (NCS), sponsored by the Law Enforcement Assistance Administration (LEAA), to address the unreported crime issues in the official crime statistics (Planty et al., 2014). Then, the U.S. Bureau of Justice Statistics officially took it over in 1992, changing the name of the survey to the National Crime Victimization Survey (NCVS) and redesigning the methodology and questions. Since then, supplements have been added periodically to obtain information in specific areas such as school crime and identify theft.

The NCVS is a self-reported survey interviewing persons age 12 or older that asks about the number and characteristics of victimization experienced during the previous six-month period. The U.S. Census Bureau serves as the primary data collection organization that conducts the interviews and processes the sample data. The sample consists of approximately 90,000 nationally representative households comprising nearly 160,000 persons (Bureau of Justice Statistics [BJS], 2015). The interviews continue every six months over three years per household. The survey uses a two-stage approach. The first stage is to screen whether an individual has experience with crime in the past six months. Then, in the second stage, detailed information is collected for each victimization experience identified during the first stage.

The NCVS provides comprehensive information on each victimization incident, including the offender's characteristics (e.g., age, sex, race, ethnicity, and the relationship to the victim), such situational factors as the time and location, whether a weapon was used, level of injury, the economic consequences of the crime, and whether the crime was reported and the reasons why. The methodology used does not ask the respondents about the specific type of crime experienced but rather collects detailed information about their experience and then classifies the data into such categories as personal crimes (e.g., rape, robbery, assault) and property crimes (e.g., burglary, motor vehicle, property theft) (BJS, 2015). Note that the survey does not measure some types of crimes, including homicide, kidnapping, verbal threats over the phone, and other forms of crime involving social media, arson, fraud, vandalism, drunk driving, and commercial entities. Other crimes such as public drunkenness, drug abuse, prostitution, illegal gambling, con games, and blackmail also are not measured. In increasing the scope of crime, The BJS attempts to collect much needed data on crime such as stalking, identify theft, and financial fraud on a periodic basis. For example, the first NCVS fraud supplement is currently under way (Langton, Planty, & Lynch, 2017).

The primary advantage of the NCVS is the inclusion of unreported crimes, or the so-called dark figures of crime, in the statistics, which makes it possible to provide a more complete picture of crime and victimization. Although the value of the NCVS is unquestionable, one must be aware of some limitations. As the information relies on the memory of the respondents, over- or underreporting could occur. As mentioned, the NCVS is not a good source to measure public order crime such as drug use, gambling, and prostitution. Furthermore, some segments are excluded from the survey; for example, by design, the NCVS excludes children under age 12. As it is a household survey, highly mobile individuals such as homeless persons, individuals in institutions (e.g., jails, prisons, and hospitals), and crimes against businesses are not included (Addington, 2008). Finally, unlike the UCR, which is published annually, the NCVS still takes a few years to publish the findings after the data are collected (Wellford, 2017).

A comparison of the NIBRS and the NCVS highlights the differences in methodology and the coverage of the data (Table 3.2).

Once the NIBRS becomes the national standard for crime reporting, it will provide a wealth of data and enhance the capabilities of crime statistics and criminological research. Equally important, the redesign of the NCVS will help improve the capabilities of the measurements that capture populations and crimes not measured in earlier versions. The continuous improvements of the NIBRS and the NCVS together will improve the quality, quantity, and time lines of crime data in the United States.

## Other Self-Report Surveys

The self-report method is an important research tool to understand the dynamics of victimization and victims by addressing certain crime categories that cannot be easily captured by the official statistics. Typically, a survey question asks about the prevalence of victimization within the past year or one's lifetime in a healthcare setting, shelters, mental health units, or at colleges or universities (Buzawa & Buzawa, 2003). The historical

### Table 3.2  Comparison of NIBRS and NCVS

| NIBRS | NCVS |
|---|---|
| Measuring crimes known to and recorded by law enforcement | Measuring crimes both reported and not reported to police |
| Incident-level data | Household-based self-report survey data |
| Includes crime against society or the public | Excludes drug-related offenses, prostitution, and weapon law violations |
| Includes all ages | Excludes crime against children under age 12 |
| Includes all individuals | Excludes institutionalized (jail and prison inmates) and transient individuals (homeless) |
| Includes crime against businesses, commercial entities, and religious organizations | Excludes crime against business and commercial establishments |
| Victim response to crimes and perspectives not measured | Includes help-seeking behaviors of victims and whether victims received assistance from victim service agencies |
| Public perceptions to police and crime not measured | Includes public perceptions (nonvictims) of the police and fear of crime |

landmark survey studies on family violence were conducted by Murray Straus and Richard J. Gelles (1988). They collected interview data from a nationally representative sample of 2,143 respondents in 1975 and 6,014 respondents in 1985. Analyzing the 1975 survey data, they found that about 4 in 100 couples admitted engaging in at least one serious outbreak of violence within the year. However, a 1985 survey showed such violence happened among 3 couples per 100.

The National Violence Against Women Survey conducted from November 1995 to May 1996 collected information from 8,000 women and 8,000 men about their experiences as victims of various forms of violence. The survey revealed that nearly 25% of female respondents and 7.6% of male respondents reported that they were raped and/or physically assaulted by a current or former spouse, cohabiting partner, or date at some time in their lifetime (Tjaden & Thoennes, 2000).

In the area of elder abuse, a National Institute of Justice telephone survey conducted in January 2008 found that 11% of persons age 60 and older reported some form of abuse in the previous year (Norman, 2010). Another national elder abuse study in the United States, conducted by Acierno et al. (2010), showed a similar result. Based on 5,777 samples collected via a computer-assisted telephone interviewing methodology, the authors found that the one-year prevalence of emotional abuse was 4.6%, 1.6% for physical abuse, 0.6% for sexual abuse, 5.1% for potential neglect, and 5.2% for financial abuse by a family member.

The quality of the self-report method has increased significantly since criminologist Austin Porterfield implemented a self-disclosure study comparing college students and juvenile delinquents in 1946 (Thornberry & Krohn, 2000). Self-report surveys ask sensitive questions while ensuring anonymity and capture victimizations that victims often did not consider to be a crime but rather family or interpersonal problems (United Nations, 2010). Yet, similar to other methodologies, the reliability and validity of the responses remains an issue. Some individuals could deny the victimization, and others could exaggerate the incidents. A retrospective study would involve errors of recall, which could result in over- or underreporting (Payne & Gainey, 2005). Additional methodologies for securing information from law enforcement officials, victims, and offenders could supplement the existing data and provide a comprehensive overview of crime.

## International Crime Statistics

We have discussed the crime statistics in the United States. But how could we know the victimization and crime rates relative to other countries? The UN Office on Drugs and Crime (UNODC, 2010) provides a global statistical series on crime and criminal justice, as well as homicide and other crime statistics, drug use and health consequences, drug prices, and drug seizures at the international level (www.unodc.org). The data and metadata for crime victimization surveys are available from 2004 to 2014. The International Classification of Crime for Statistical Purposes (ICCS) classifies criminal offenses and is available in multiple languages. The classification is based on generally accepted guidelines throughout the world relative to the designation of crime offenses. The ICCS is intended to provide a common database for enhanced international comparability assigning criminal offenses to hierarchical categories that have a certain degree of similarity.

The **International Crime Victim Survey (ICVS)** is the most comprehensive international resource for studying crime and victimization, crime reporting behaviors, victim satisfaction with the police, fear of crime, and public attitudes toward the criminal justice system (van Dijk, van Kesteren, & Smith, 2007). The survey uses standardized questions to make the findings internationally comparable rather than nation-specific surveys such as the National Crime Victimization Survey in the United States and the British Crime Survey (Lynch, 2006). The ICVS started in 1989 with the participation of 14 industrialized countries given the high demand for internationally comparable data. Since then, the survey has been carried out in 1992, 1996, 2000, and 2004/2005, collectively including more than 300,000 individuals age 16 or older who were randomly selected in 78 countries. The data are collected via phone using the computer-assisted telephone interviewing (CATI) technique or face-to-face methodology. The database is particularly beneficial as in many developing countries crime data are not available to the public and, even if available, the data are fragmented and not always reliable (van Dijk et al., 2007). Furthermore, because the surveys have been collected several times in many countries, the data can be used to compare crime trends across countries.

Yet, there are some limitations of the ICVS. First, the research that provides the data can be inconsistent. Second, the sample size is relatively small. Third, the ICVS focuses on individual crime rather than collective crime (e.g., corruption, organized crime). These concerns affect the comparability of equivalent data. Finally, although this concern is not limited to the ICVS, asking about victimization in the past 12 months or calendar year could result in the over- or underreporting of victimizations (van Dijk et al., 2007).

**International Crime Victim Survey (ICVS):** the most comprehensive large-scale crime and victimization surveys conducted in 78 countries by 2005

# The Nature and Extent of Victimization

How many people are becoming victims of crime each year in the United States? Who is more or less likely to become a victim of crime? As we have seen, both the official and self-report statistics attempt to make the best estimate of the number of victims and explain who the victims are and the victims' relationship to their offenders.

## Prevalence of Victimization

The NCVS estimates that 5.7 million violent victimizations and 15.9 million property crimes occurred in 2016 in the United States. Specifically, 1.3% of all persons age 12 or older experienced at least one violent crime, and a total of 8.8% of all households experienced at least one property victimization (Morgan & Kena, 2017).

When looking at the victimization trends, overall, the violent and property crime rates have declined over the past two decades; from 1993 to 2016, the rate of violent crime declined from 79.8 to 19.5 per 1,000, whereas the property crime rate declined from 351.8 to 113.9 per 1,000 households (Truman & Langton, 2015; Morgan & Kena, 2017). The UCR data also showed that reported crime has declined; the rate of fatal and nonfatal violent crime known to the police from 1993 to 2016 declined from 741.1 to 386.3 per 100,000. The rate of murder and nonnegligent cases known to the police decreased from

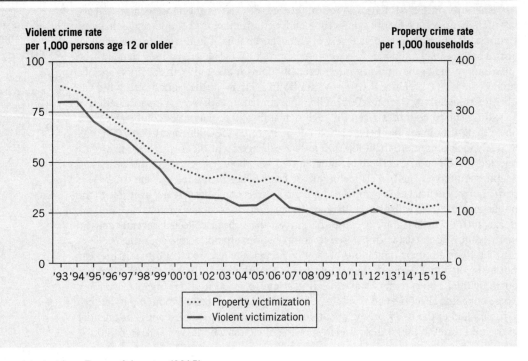

**Figure 3.1** Violent and Property Victimization, 1993–2016

Violent crime rate
per 1,000 persons age 12 or older

Property crime rate
per 1,000 households

•••• Property victimization
— Violent victimization

*Source:* Adapted from Truman & Langton (2015).

9.5 per 100,000 in 1993 to 5.3 per 100,000 in 2016. However, the number of active shooter events has dramatically increased over the past 15 years. The number of people killed or injured annually in active shooter incidents has increased by more than 100%, from 7 in 2000 to 134 in 2015 (National Center for Victims of Crime, 2017).

## Victim Characteristics

### Gender

It is generally understood that males have a higher violent crime victimization rate than females. However, the NCVS indicated that the gender differences have narrowed over time. For example, in 2005, the prevalence of violent crime for males age 12 or older was 1.7%, whereas that for women was 1.1%. In contrast, the 2016 data showed 1.41% for males and 1.26% for females (Truman & Langton, 2015; Morgan & Kena, 2018). One notable area where the gender difference is observed is the victim-offender relationship. In 2010, males experienced violent victimizations by strangers at nearly twice the rate of females. The rate of violence against males by strangers was 9.5 victimizations per 1,000 males in 2010 compared to 4.7 victimizations per 1,000 females (Harrell, 2012).

## Age

The victim data indicate that younger people are more likely to become victims of crime than older people. The NCVS of 2016 showed that those ages 25 to 34 had the highest rate of violent victimization among all age groups (ages 12–17, 30.9; 18–24, 30.9; 25–34, 31.8; 35–49, 22.9; 50–64, 16.1; and 65 or older, 4.4, per 1,000). Overall, the rate of violent victimization among the younger population has been declining, whereas it has been increasing slightly among older people. For example, the rate of total violence per 1,000 persons among those ages 18 to 24 declined from 61 in 2005 to 30.9 in 2016; the same rate for those ages 50 to 64 was 15 in 2005 and 16.1 in 2016 (Truman & Langton, 2015; Morgan & Kena, 2018).

Although the victimization rate of the elderly is much lower than any other age group, the aging trend would indicate more elderly victimization in the future. The baby-boomer generation, or the 76 million children who were born from 1946 to 1964, is reaching retirement age, and it is estimated that more than 20% of the U.S. population will be age 60 and older by 2030. Furthermore, a rapid increase is expected in those Americans age 85 or older (Himes, 2002). Financial abuse and exploitation is one of the most common and fastest growing forms of elder abuse (Mihaljcic & Lowndes, 2013). The extent of this form of abuse is greater than previously believed, and it is expected to increase with the rising number of older people in the population. Financial abuse accounts for 26% to 38% of all reported cases of elder abuse (Mihaljcic & Lowndes, 2013). The perpetrators of financial abuse could be family members, contractors, salespersons, attorneys, caregivers, insurance agencies, clergy, accountants, bookkeepers, or friends (Kemp & Mosqueda, 2005).

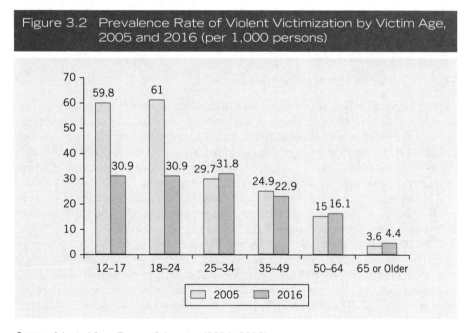

**Figure 3.2  Prevalence Rate of Violent Victimization by Victim Age, 2005 and 2016 (per 1,000 persons)**

*Source:* Adapted from Truman & Langton (2014, 2016).

## Race/Ethnicity

How does victimization vary across race and ethnicity? The NCVS data from 2016 displayed that there were no statistically significant differences in rates of serious violent victimization between Blacks and Whites (8.2 victimizations per 1,000 persons for Blacks and 6.3 for Whites). Hispanics have a similar rate (8.2 per 1,000), whereas American Indians or Alaska Natives have a much higher rate among all ethnic groups (13.3 per 1,000) (Morgan & Kena, 2017). However, Blacks were disproportionately represented as both homicide victims and offenders. The data from 1980 to 2008 indicate that the victimization rate for Blacks (27.8 per 100,000) was six times higher than the rate for Whites (4.5 per 100,000). The offending rate for Blacks (34.4 per 100,000) was almost eight times higher than the rate for Whites (4.5 per 100,000) (Cooper & Smith, 2011).

Ample research has demonstrated that the characteristics of neighborhoods affect the victimization rate. Regardless of race/ethnicity, individuals who live in disadvantaged areas have a higher risk for both stranger and nonstranger violence than those who are living in more advantaged communities, but certain minorities such as African Americans are more likely to live in challenging neighborhoods. For example, Blacks, Whites, and Latinos who live in disadvantaged areas have higher risk for both stranger and nonstranger violence than those who live in more advantaged communities (Krivo & Peterson, 2000; Lauritsen & White, 2001; Like-Haislip & Miofsky, 2011). Krivo and Peterson (2000) argue that "racial differences in disadvantage are so great that it is impossible to access what the effects for whites would be if they were as disadvantaged as the average African American in most urban areas" (p. 557). In fact, many differences among Blacks, Whites, and Latinos disappear when controlling for community and individual characteristics (Lauritsen & White, 2001). Black females experience 2.35 times more violence than White females, but such a difference is no longer significant when including such individual and neighborhood factors as family income, marital status, neighborhood socioeconomic disadvantage, and residential instability (Lauritsen & White, 2001).

## LGBTQ and HIV Affected Individuals

There is growing concern regarding the lack of attention to lesbian, gay, bisexual, transgender, and queer (LGBTQ) victims. Until recently, the availability of research in understanding the prevalence of victimization in the LGBTQ community was limited, which makes it difficult for victim advocates to address the issues in the community. In 2013, the UCR program first released statistics on crimes motivated by bias against sexual orientation (Weiss, 2017). According to the Hate Crime Statistics in 2016, 16.7% of victims of single-bias hate crime were targeted because of their sexual orientation. Of those victims, about two thirds (62.7%) were targeted because of the offenders' anti-gay bias (U.S. Department of Justice, Federal Bureau of Investigation, 2017).

The National Coalition of Anti-Violence Programs (NCAVP, 2017) has produced hate violence and intimate violence reports since 1998. According to the 2016 hate violence report, there were 77 total hate violence-related homicides of LGBTQ and HIV-affected people. The same report indicates that the perpetrators were not necessarily strangers; of 981 survivors, 52% of the victims knew their offenders, and nearly one third of the cases happened in a private residence. One major concern is the police response to survivors following incidents of violence; 31% of survivors experienced a

# Victim Assistance Programs

## National Coalition of Anti-Violence Programs (NCAVP)

The National Coalition of Anti-Violence Programs (NCAVP) is a national organization that addresses all forms of violence against and within LGBTQ and HIV-affected communities in the United States and Canada. With more than 50 members and affiliates, the NCAVP advocates for LGBTQ-inclusive policies and funding priorities for LGBTQ issues; conducts research and evaluations; supports the members and grassroots activities; and serves as a resource for training and technical assistance. The NCAVP provides community action toolkits and fact sheets that are particularly helpful for local communities to coordinate awareness campaigns and grassroots activities.

In 2017, the NCAVP mourned 37 LGBTQ victims whose lives were taken by violence. One of the victims was Bruce Garnett, who was an activist and advocate for LGBTQ rights in Virginia. Bruce was stabbed to death in his home on April 21, 2017.

hostile attitude by the police. Black survivors were 2.8 times more likely to experience excessive force from police than survivors who did not identify as Black.

The studies of same-sex intimate partner violence (IPV) from the National Violence Against Women Survey consistently found that the IPV among same-sex couples was more prevalent than that of different-sex couples (Tjaden & Thoennes, 2000; Messinger, 2011). By conducting a systematic review of 687 IPV studies, Badenes-Ribera, Bonilla-Campos, Frias-Navarro, Pons-Salvador, and Monterdi-i-Bort (2016) found that the most prevalent type of IPV among self-identified lesbians was emotional and psychological.

## Fear of Crime

**Fear of crime** is an emotional response to a sense of insecurity and being a victim of crime (Hanson, Sawyer, Begle, & Hubel, 2010). Fear of crime and actual crime rates are not necessarily correlated, and prior victimization is not a significant predictor of levels of fear (Cordner, 2010). In fact, some groups are more fearful than others regardless of their actual risk of victimization. For example, females are more fearful than males (Ferraro, 1996; Haynie, 1998; Craig, 2000). Also, the type of community (Akers, Greca, Sellers, & Cochran, 1987) is associated with one's sense of fear of crime. A study conducted by Hedayati Marzbali, Abdullah, Razak, and Maghsoodi Tilaki (2012) found that those with higher incomes were less fearful of crime as they could afford such deterrence methods as installing surveillance systems and increasing security (Hedayati Marzbali et al., 2012).

**Fear of crime:** an emotional response to a sense of insecurity and being a victim of crime (Hanson, Sawyer, Begle & Hubel, 2010)

As articulated in the "fear-victimization paradox" (Akers et al., 1987), it is a well-established fact that older people are more fearful of crime compared to their younger counterparts even though the actual crime victimization rate among the elderly is much lower than that of youngsters. In fact, elders are among the least likely to have experienced crime victimization. Bernat, Aleman, and Gitelson (2003) cited data from the U.S.

Department of Justice that indicate persons age 65 and older are about 20 times less likely to be violent crime victims than people aged 12 to 19. Articulated in the "fear-victimization paradox," it is a generally well-supported idea that despite the overall lower criminal victimization rate compared to other age groups, elderly people are more fearful of crime (Yin, 1980; Ferraro, 1995; Smith & Torstensson, 1997). However, one of the most comprehensive studies in this area (Kury, Obergfell-Fuchs, & Ferdinand, 2001), conducted in East and West Germany, cautioned that the relationship between age and fear of crime is more complex as many other factors such as gender, prior victimization experience, size of the community, one's habits and lifestyle, and confidence in the police are intricately intertwined.

Fear of crime could bring about significant changes in one's daily life. Garofalo (1981) explains behavioral changes of crime victimization by citing the study of DuBow, McCabe, and Kaplan (1979). First is avoidance, whereby a person removes one's self from or increases the distance from situations in which the perceived risk of victimization is high. Second is protective behavior or seeking to increase resistance to victimization, for example, better protecting a home with security devices. Third is insurance behavior or selecting behavior that seeks to minimize the costs of victimization. Fourth is communicative behavior, which means sharing information and emotions related to crime with others. Finally, participation behavior is "actions in concert with others which are motivated by a particular crime or by crime in general" (Garofalo, 1981, p. 72).

As seen, fear of crime can result in major changes in one's lifestyle, which can make one more cautious and reduce the likelihood of victimization. However, an excessive level of fear could decrease quality of life and might lead to a sense of distrust and alienation from social life. The policy implication would focus on reducing unreasonable fear among the citizenry while educating them on how to reduce the risk of victimization.

## Recurring Victimization

It is a fairly established fact that victimization is not evenly distributed throughout the population. Although most people and places do not experience crime victimization, those who are victimized consistently are at the highest risk of being victimized in the future. However, victimization patterns vary. **Recurring victimization** occurs when a person or place is victimized more than once by any type of victimization (Daigle, 2013). **Repeat victimization** occurs when the same victimization happens more than once to the same individual, household, place, business, vehicle, or other target (Grove & Farrell, 2011). **Near-repeat victimization** occurs when a place is victimized that is close by or near in proximity to a place that was victimized previously. **Polyvictimization** can be defined as a person who has experienced multiple victimizations of different kinds, such as sexual abuse, physical abuse, bullying, and/or exposure to family violence.

For instance, a study of female college students who attended postsecondary institutions in the 1996–1997 academic year found that college women who experienced victimization were a small number, but that group experienced a large number of victimizations. Of the women who experienced violent repeat incidents, less than 1% experienced 27.7% of all the violent incidents (Daigle, Fisher, & Cullen, 2008).

Researchers also have explored the time span to the next victimization and found that it occurs within a relatively short period. The previously mentioned study of

**Recurring victimization:** occurs when a person or place is victimized more than once by any type of victimization (Daigle, 2013)

**Repeat victimization:** occurs when the same victimization happens more than once to the same individual, household, place, business, vehicle, or other target (Grove & Farrell, 2011)

**Near-repeat victimization:** a victimization that occurs in a place that is close by or near in proximity to a place that was victimized previously

**Polyvictimization:** a person experiences multiple victimizations of different kinds, such as sexual abuse, physical abuse, bullying, and or exposure to family violence

college women showed that victims' heightened risk declines over time, specifically after the first month (Daigle et al., 2008). Similarly, a study of residential burglaries indicated that 25% of repeat burglaries occur within one week after the initial burglary, and 51% of subsequent burglaries occur within one month (Robinson, 1998). Johnson and colleagues (2007) similarly discussed that near-repeat victimization would happen within 200 meters of the burgled home with the greatest risk for a two-week period. However, after a relatively short period of high risk, the level of risk declined dramatically (Weisel, 2005).

There are two reasons for repeat victimization. One is the boost explanation, and the other is the flag explanation. The boost explanation explains that an offender gains important knowledge about the target by successfully performing the initial offense. For example, the burglar who entered the victim's residence could identify the location of valuable items in a house. The flag explanation focuses on the vulnerability of the victims and locations. College students are known to be more vulnerable than others because of their risky and careless behaviors. Many students communicate via social networking services (SNS) by posting their schedules online, their current locations, and other identifiable information that makes it easy for offenders to know their day-to-day routine with the utmost accuracy. Their lifestyle, such as walking to their destinations alone, being in parking lots, and attending parties, makes them more vulnerable.

Even though victims are vulnerable because of their poor judgment, we must be cautious not to blame the victims. Rather, the focus should be on educating about their possible revictimization and providing more resources and information for victim services. For example, a college campus could provide self-defense courses, and college prevention programs need to do more to specifically target those who are victims of crime. To prevent near-repeat victimization, the development of an emergency contact network in disseminating burglary information to a neighborhood in a timely manner would be crucial.

## Costs of Victimization

Crime imposes costs for individuals and society in various ways. Understanding the costs of victimization helps re-recognize the significance of victimization and raises important policy implications about allocating more resources for underserved victims and educating citizens about the significance of crime victimization. One of the most comprehensive analyses of costs of victimization conducted by Miller, Cohen, and Wiersema (1996) estimated that more than 49 million victimizations occurred annually from 1987 to 1990. When adding both tangible and intangible costs of victimizations, the total annual losses due to crime were $450 billion, which equals about $1,800 per U.S. resident in 1993 dollars. When converting the tangible costs of $105 billion into 2016 dollars, it became $157 billion (GAO, 2017).

As shown in Figure 3.3, the cost of crime includes not only costs borne by primary victims but also for family members and the workplace. In estimating the costs of crime, two types of costs, tangible and intangible, need to be integrated. **Tangible costs** include costs as a direct consequence of crime, for example, crime-incurred expenses such as property damage and loss and productivity. Productivity includes lost wages,

**Tangible costs of victimization:** costs as a direct consequence of crime, for example, crime-incurred expenses such as property damage and loss and productivity. Productivity includes lost wages, fringe benefits, and housework and loss of schooldays of victims and their families. Also, criminal justice costs such as police investigations and incarceration and costs in preventing future crime victimizations

## Figure 3.3 Examples of Costs of Crime and Elements to Categorize Costs.

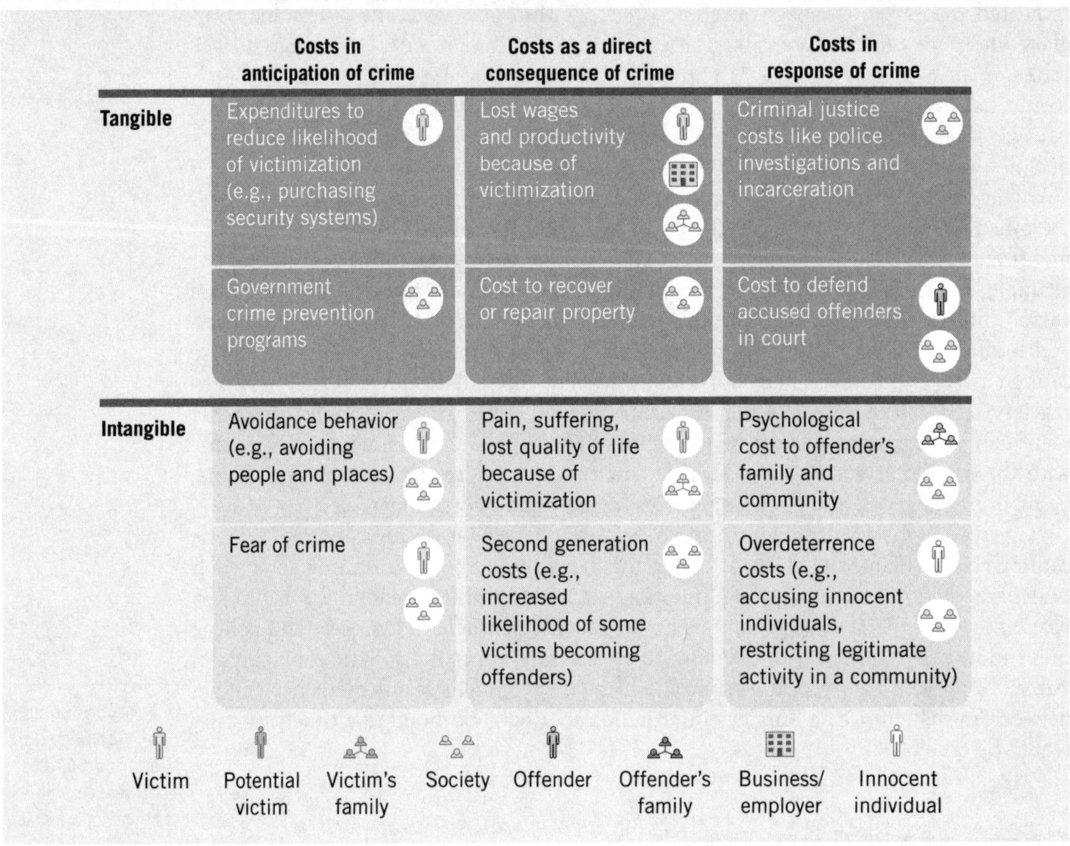

|  | Costs in anticipation of crime | Costs as a direct consequence of crime | Costs in response of crime |
|---|---|---|---|
| **Tangible** | Expenditures to reduce likelihood of victimization (e.g., purchasing security systems) | Lost wages and productivity because of victimization | Criminal justice costs like police investigations and incarceration |
| | Government crime prevention programs | Cost to recover or repair property | Cost to defend accused offenders in court |
| **Intangible** | Avoidance behavior (e.g., avoiding people and places) | Pain, suffering, lost quality of life because of victimization | Psychological cost to offender's family and community |
| | Fear of crime | Second generation costs (e.g., increased likelihood of some victims becoming offenders) | Overdeterrence costs (e.g., accusing innocent individuals, restricting legitimate activity in a community) |

Victim | Potential victim | Victim's family | Society | Offender | Offender's family | Business/ employer | Innocent individual

---

**Intangible costs of victimization:** costs such as pain, suffering, and reduced quality of life and fear of crime, as well as psychological costs to the offender's family and community, are more difficult to measure, but economists make efforts to use varied methods to place a dollar value on those losses (Cohen, Miller, & Rossman, 1994)

fringe benefits, and housework and loss of schooldays of victims and their families. Also, criminal justice costs such as police investigations and incarceration and costs in preventing future crime victimizations (e.g., purchasing security system and implementing crime prevention programs) are included in tangible costs.

**Intangible costs** such as pain, suffering, and reduced quality of life and fear of crime, as well as psychological costs to offenders' family and community, are more difficult to measure, but economists make efforts to use varied methods to place a dollar value on those losses (Cohen, Miller, & Rossman, 1994). For example, lost workdays could cost a victim due to unpaid workdays and affect society and the employer via lost productivity. Moreover, lost school days will also affect victims and society because of foregone wages, the absence of the pecuniary benefits of education, and the loss of social benefits due to lack of education. The death of a victim affects family members for loss of enjoyment, funeral costs, and the psychological impact of losing a loved one (GAO, 2017).

A study jointly conducted by UCLA scholars and the LAPD suggests the mathematical model correctly predicted the locations of crimes on 4.7% of its forecasts, whereas the human analysts were correct 2.1% of the time.

Beginning in 2011, the researchers analyzed when and where burglaries, theft from cars, and theft of cars occurred in the LAPD's Southwest division. Jeffrey Brantingham, a UCLA professor of anthropology and senior author of the study, commented that "not only did the model predict twice as much crime as trained crime analysts predicted, but it also prevented twice as much crime."

In the next phase, police officers in three LAPD divisions were deployed to 20 half-block areas based on the predictions of either the model or the human analysts and stayed in the locations as long as they deemed necessary. Neither the officers nor their commanders knew whether the assignments came from the computer or the human analysis. Across the three divisions, the computer model produced 4.3 fewer crimes per week, a reduction of 7.4%. In contrast, the human analysts only showed reduction of 2 crimes per week in each division. The researchers estimated that the computer model would save $9 million per year in Los Angeles, taking into account costs to victims, the courts, and society.

Human behavior and criminal behavior are complex, but Brantingham argues that "there are many aspects of human behavior that we can understand mathematically."

The research was funded by the National Science Foundation, the Air Force Office of Scientific Research, the Office of Naval Research, and the Army Research Office.

### Questions:

1. Do you think that police agencies should rely more on computer models to identify and target certain areas and persons to prevent future crime?

2. Are there any ethical concerns?

Wolpert, S. (2015). Predictive policing substantially reduces crime in Los Angeles during months-long test: UCLA-led study suggests method could succeed in cities worldwide. UCLA Newsroom. Retrieved from http://newsroom.ucla.edu/releases/predictive-policing-substantially-reduces-crime-in-los-angeles-during-months-long-test.

There are significant variations among researchers on estimating annual costs of crime ranging from $690 billion to $3.41 trillion and adjusted to 2016 dollars (GAO, 2017). McCollister, French, and Fang (2010) summed tangible costs for murder and associated criminal justice system costs and estimated the tangible cost to be $1,436,060 and the intangible cost to be $9,482,943. Roman (2011) calculated the cost of murder and nonnegligent manslaughter using civil jury awards at an estimated $1,623,696 per victimization.

As shown in Figure 3.4, under the victimization of violent crimes, even though the dollar value was almost 30 years ago, you still get the sense that the intangible costs for rape are far higher than the tangible ones as those victims suffer from loss of quality of life associated with fear, pain, and suffering. A more recent quality of life study indicates that crime victimization affects multiple areas of one's life, including parenting skills,

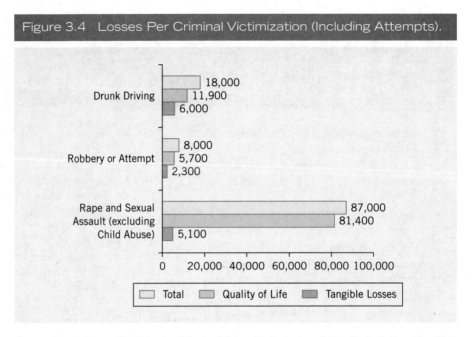

Figure 3.4  Losses Per Criminal Victimization (Including Attempts).

*Source:* Adapted from *The Extent and Costs of Crime Victimization: A New Look*, National Institute of Justice, Research Preview (1996).

impaired occupational functioning, higher rates of unemployment, and problematic intimate relationships (Hanson et al., 2010).

## Victim Reporting Behaviors

### Reporting to Police

The comparison between the UCR and the NCVS identified the existence of the dark figures of crime, or unreported crime. But what percentage of crime was not reported to the police, and why? The NCVS estimated more than half (58%) of violent victimizations were not reported to the police in 2016 (Morgan & Kena, 2017). More specifically, rape or sexual assault was less likely to be reported to the police (23% reported), whereas aggravated assault (58%) and robbery (54%) were more likely to be reported to the police. For this reason, more than a third (35%) of individuals who did not report thought the police would not or could not help, or they thought that the incident was not important enough to report (31%). In contrast, a greater percentage of victims of rape or sexual assault (28%) and aggravated assault (22%) noted that they did not do so because they were afraid of reprisal or getting the offender in trouble.

These were also the most common reasons cited for not reporting intimate partner violence victimization to the police (38%) (Langton et al., 2012).

In terms of the characteristics of victims, 55% of victimizations against men were not reported to the police, whereas 49% of those against women were not reported. Asian/Native Hawaiian/Other Pacific Islanders were less likely to report (66%) than other ethnicities (54% for White and 46% for Black). Younger people were less likely to report than older people (68% for ages 12–17 and 46% for age 65 or older). Less educated people and lower-income people were less likely to report than more educated ones. There is no difference between urban and rural residents regarding the reporting behavior, but urban residents were more likely than rural residents to mention that they did not report the case to the police because police would not or could not help. In contrast, rural residents were more likely to say that they dealt with the issue in another way or treated it as a personal matter rather than reporting the case to the police (Langton et al., 2012).

A notable trend is that the percentage of people who decided not to report to the police because they felt the police would not or could not help increased from 7% in 2005 to 20% in 2010. In a further breakdown of the reasons individuals did not report crimes, the percentage of individuals who stated that they believed the police would be ineffective or inefficient increased from 2% to 4%, and the percentage of individuals who thought the police would be biased increased from 1% to 3% (Langton et al., 2012).

A meta-analysis of 37 research studies on the effect of neighborhoods on crime found that a high level of social cohesion is correlated with higher crime reporting rates (Brisson & Roll, 2012). A particular focus needs to be on the underreporting of immigrants and minority groups. A study indicated that individuals whose parents or other family members are undocumented are less likely to report crime (Cavanagh & Cauffman, 2015). Another study found that although fear of deportation was a predictor in whether a woman would report domestic or intimate partner violence, another significant factor was her perception toward the police. If she felt that the police would use excessive force on the perpetrator, who would likely be a loved one, she was unlikely to report the case (Messing, Becerra, Ward-Lasher, & Androff, 2015). Reaching out to the immigrant community and finding ways to build trust with members of the community would help increase the reporting of cases (Davis & Henderson, 2003).

## Reporting to Victim Services Providers

Today, more than 20,000 service providers are recognized in the United States (Office for Victims of Crime, 2013), from criminal justice agencies such as the police and prosecutor's Offices to other public, private, and nonprofit agencies such as hospitals, religious groups, and social services to provide assistance and support to a myriad of victims. However, only a small proportion of crime victims have access to victim service programs. Less than 10% of violent crime victims seek help from victim services (Zaykowski, 2014).

Although victim service programs are widely available, most crime victims are not taking advantage of them. Discrepancies exist in access to the services, the types of crimes for which services are accessed, and the availability of services to certain populations. As might be expected, more people who report crimes to law enforcement receive victim services (14%) than those who do not report crimes (4%; Langton, 2011) given the fact that the police are one of the most common sources for accessing information about victim services. Still, less than a fifth of victims receive services. As shown in Figure 3.5, those cases for which victims receive assistance from victim service agencies are more likely to have follow-up actions by criminal justice agencies: police are notified of the crime, a formal complaint is signed, an arrest is made, and the victim receives contact from a non-law enforcement criminal justice authority, such as a prosecutor or a judge.

Although victims benefit from seeking assistance, many victims do not take action due to lack of knowledge or their own choice (Sims, Yost, & Abbott, 2006). Some of the factors that influence a decision to seek help are the victim's demographics, level of injury, relationship to the offender, mental and physical distress, and whether a weapon was involved. Female victims are more likely to seek help even though male

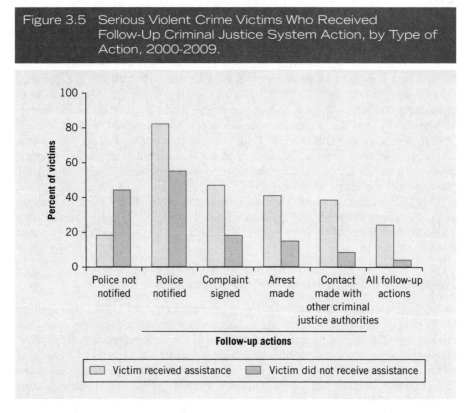

Figure 3.5   Serious Violent Crime Victims Who Received Follow-Up Criminal Justice System Action, by Type of Action, 2000-2009.

*Source:* Adapted from *The Extent and Costs of Crime Victimization: A New Look*, National Institute of Justice, Research Preview.

victims experience the same trauma as females (Tsui, Cheung, & Leung, 2010). Victims are more likely to receive assistance from public-sector agencies rather than private-sector ones. For victims of violent crime, more receive assistance in rural areas than in urban areas, however, the support for secondary victims is lacking in rural areas (Tsui et al., 2010). For domestic violence, in particular, services tend to be more widely available in well-to-do counties that host a prominent educational institution. Many subsets remain underserved in access to victim services. These include ethnic minorities, rural areas, persons suffering from substance abuse or mental health problems, victims of elder abuse, and those in the LGBTQ community, which could be influenced by cultural beliefs about the appropriateness of seeking such services or preference (Smith, Kilpatrick, Falsetti, & Best, 2002).

There are primarily two ways that victims seek support. One is from formal sources, whereby a referral is made by such professionals as law enforcement officers, mental health practitioners, and physicians. The other is through informal sources such as friends and family. In a large sample of assault victims participating in the National Violence and Threats of Violence Against Women Survey, 52% reported seeking support from family or friends in the previous year. In another study, 42% of college students reported turning to family or friends for support following experiences with intimate partner violence (Prospero & Vohra-Gupta, 2008). When research has explored the perceived satisfaction with support received from various formal and informal support networks, family and friends tend to receive more positive ratings (Becker, Skinner, Abel, Howell, & Bruce, 1982; Popiel & Susskind, 1985; Campbell, 2008). Informal support also has been linked to better psychological adjustment following rape compared to support from other sources, including mental health professionals, physicians, and the police (Ullman, 1996).

# Sources of Victim Services

## National Census of Victim Service Providers (NCVSP) and the National Survey of Victim Service Providers (NSVSP)

Today, various programs are available to victims, but there is a lack of information about organizational capacity such as their funding sources, staff and management expertise and diversity, and use of technology. Without knowing organizational capacity, the optimal service capacity and the best coordinated efforts to improve service delivery toward victims cannot not be achieved (Zweig & Burt, 2007). Vision 21 grew from a series of meetings sponsored by the Office for Victims of Crime (OVC) across the country to facilitate conversations about the victim assistance field and create the vision (Office for Victims of Crime, 2013).

In addressing the need for baseline data on the "types and amounts of funding, staff expertise, and diversity, salaries and benefits, the use of volunteers, access to staff-of-the-art technology, training, and technical assistance, effectiveness of collaboration and outreach initiatives, and the systematic use of strategic planning, evidence-based practice and program evaluation" (Office for Victims of Crime, 2013, pp. 33–34), the BJS, together with the OVC and the Office on Violence Against Women (OVAW), with the work of the BJS, the NCVS, and RAND Corporation, launched the National Survey of Victim Service Organizations (NSVSO) in 2014, which is the first nationwide attempt to survey victim service organizations.

The data collection process has two phases: the **National Census of Victim Service Providers (NCVSP)** and the **National Survey of Victim Service Providers (NSVSP)**. The NCVSP surveys victim service providers to better understand the field and includes such information as the type of organization and the types of victims served. The survey was sent to 21,000 victim service providers at the end of 2015. Following up on the NCVSP, the NSVSP will seek more specific information about victim service providers (Office for Victims of Crime, 2013).

The findings from those surveys will provide the OVC and other stakeholders with statistics that will measure the extent to which they are effectively reaching and serving victims. Enhanced statistical information from the NCVSP and NSVSP would help federal agencies make decisions to support effective programs and identify existing gaps in services. There are four areas that Vision 21 (Office for Victims of Crime, 2013) will address in the future.

**National Census of Victim Service Providers (NCVSP):** surveys victim service providers to better understand the field and includes such information as the type of organization and the types of victims served (Office for Victims of Crime, 2013)

**National Survey of Victim Service Providers (NSVSP):** follows up on the NCVSP, the NSVSP will seek more specific information about victim service providers (Office for Victims of Crime, 2013)

## Vision 21 Statements

- Victims of crime will be served through a national commitment to support robust, ongoing research and program evaluation that informs the quality and practice of victim services throughout the Nation. Evidence-based, research-informed victim service programs will become the standard of excellence in providing assistance and support to victims of all types of crime. (p. 1)

- Every state will establish wraparound legal networks that will help ensure that crime victims' rights are enforced and that victims of crime receive the broad range of legal services needed to help rebuild their lives in the aftermath of crime. (p. 9)

- All crime victims in the 21st century can readily access a seamless continuum of evidence-based services and support that will allow them to begin physical, emotional and financial recovery. (p. 17)

- As the 21st century progresses, the victim services field will integrate innovative technologies into its operations, fostering accountability, and operational efficiency and ensuring that victims of crime will have streamlined access to services regardless of location, socioeconomic status, and other traditional barriers. (p. 25)

- The victim services field will develop and institutionalize capacity to reach and serve all crime victims in need of help and support in the 21st century. (p. 33)

# SUMMARY

Crime statistics provide us with important information about crimes and victimization. Since 1930, the UCR has been considered the most reliable resource for crimes known to the police in the United States. However, the UCR limits its categories and has limitations in its methodology. The NIBRS addresses the weakness of the UCR by expanding the categories as well as the demographic information of victims and offenders and their relationship. It is anticipated that the NIBRS will become a national incident-report standard. The NCVS is a self-report survey that captures the dark figures of crime, or unknown victimizations, and provides a comprehensive picture of crime and victims. A shortcoming of the data is the possible under- or overreporting of cases due to the memory decay of the respondents. These major national statistics as well as rather smaller research findings tell us about who is more or less likely to report crime to the police and use victim services. Also, greater efforts are being made to calculate the costs of crime. With the emergence of addressing new crimes and strengthening of the service delivery, there is an urgent need to understand the service gaps and areas that lack services. As such, there is considerable progress in the effort to collect information from victim service entities, and in the near future, the findings from the NSVSO should tell us about the current organizational capacity of victim service entities. Such information could be used to transform victim services to be more accessible to victims.

# KEY WORDS

Crime in the united states   36
Fear of crime   45
Intangible costs   48
International crime victim survey (ICVS)   41
National census of victim service providers (NCVSP)   54

National crime victimization survey (NCVS)   38
National incident-based reporting system (NIBRS)   36
National survey of victim service providers (NSVSP)   54
Near-repeat victimization   46

Polyvictimization   46
Recurring victimization   46
Repeat victimization   46
Tangible costs   47
Uniform crime report (UCR)   35

# INTERNET RESOURCES

**Pew Research Center U.S. Politics and Policy (http://www.pewresearch.org)**

The Pew Research Center provides independent research in the areas of U.S. politics and policy, journalism and media, the Internet, science and technology, religion and public life, Hispanic trends, global attitudes and trends, social and demographic trends, and research methodology. Fact Tank is the Pew Research Center's real-time platform dedicated to finding news in the numbers. Pew Research Center makes its data available to the public for secondary analysis after a period of time.

**Inter-University Consortium for Political and Social Research (ICPSR) (https://www.icpsr.umich.edu/icpsrweb)**

The Inter-University Consortium for Political and Social Research is a social science data archive holding more than 10,000 studies. Currently, more than 700 universities, government agencies, and other institutions are members of the ICPSR, and students and researchers of the member institutions have full direct access to the data archive.

**Roper Center for Public Opinion Research** (https://ropercenter.cornell.edu)

The Roper Center for Public Opinion Research is the leading educational facility in the field of public opinion and holds data dating back to the 1930s and from more than 100 nations. Roper data are made available through a license to the institutions, and the students and researchers of the member institutions have access to hundreds of survey organizations from across the United States and around the world.

## CRITICAL THINKING QUESTIONS

1. If you were a victim advocate, how would you use the local crime statistics to educate community members?

2. Identify the groups of people who are at the greatest risk of violent victimization, and discuss the services needed to prevent victimization.

3. Explain the reasons why there is a gap between the fear of crime and actual crime rates. Why does the fear of crime raise an essential policy concern?

4. The statistics show that more than half of all the violent victimizations are not reported to the police. If you were a victim advocate, how would you explain the advantages of reporting the crime to the victims?

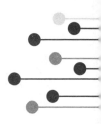

# CHAPTER 4

# Trauma and Recovery of Victims

For victims to recover from a traumatic event, like criminal victimization, it is crucial that they are provided with the proper support. Often victims will require immediate crisis intervention during the initial impact stage, along with support throughout the criminal justice process. Victim service providers, therefore, have to be trained and ready to deal with a variety of responses when trying to assist victims. This is because people respond to traumatic events differently. Criminal victimization is arguably experienced more seriously than an accident or similar misfortune, as it is difficult to accept that the suffering and loss being experienced is the result of the deliberate actions of another person (UNODCCP, 1999). The initial reactions following victimization may include shock, fear, anger, disorientation, helplessness, disbelief, and guilt (Norris & Krysztof, 1994; Shapland & Hall, 2007). These psychological, emotional, and social responses are normal reactions to such a traumatic event. Victims' reactions depend on a number of factors: the context in which the victimization occurred, that is, the location of the incident, time of day it occurred, or the relationship to the offender; the victims' coping styles; and their resources (National Center for Victims of Crime [NCVC], 2012). The psychological responses can be either short-term or long-term (Hanson, Sawyer, Begle, & Hubel, 2010); however, if such crisis intervention is not received, the long-term effects can greatly affect the victims' recovery process. Trained victim service providers should inquire about the victims' welfare by asking if they feel safe, assuring victims that they are safe if that is true, and determining if they are in need of medical attention. It is essential for victim service providers to have an understanding of the impact of victimization and the variety of reactions victims may experience in order to assist in their recovery (Peterson & Walker, 2003). A victim's life may never be the same, but he or she can regain some form of control over his or her life and a sense of confidence (NCVC, 2012).

## Physiological Impact of Victimization

The physiological reaction in response to a perceived harmful event, or when a person's physical survival is threatened, is known as the flight-fight-or-freeze response (Barlow, 2002; Bracha, 2004; Schmidt, Richey, Zvolensky, & Maner, 2008). This response is triggered to assist in determining whether fleeing from the situation, fighting, or freezing increases the chances of survival. The freeze response is an added dimension to the more common flight-or-fight response. Freeze responses may occur when an individual perceives there to be little immediate chance of escaping or winning a fight or when immobility increases the chance of surviving (Schmidt et al.,

It was a Wednesday evening, at 8:00PM; Denise and her son Steven had finished dinner with her parents and were preparing to leave to go home. Approaching her car, Denise noticed another car driving slowly past the house. Not paying much attention to the suspicious car, Denise and Steven proceeded to say goodbye to her father and started her car to leave. Suddenly, as she was leaving the driveway, the suspicious car she noticed earlier came speeding down the road and pulled in front of her, blocking her exit. Within seconds, a man had got out of the passenger side of the car with a gun, threatening Denise's father to stay back and not move. The man then approached Denise's window, pointing the gun at her head and demanding that she get out of the car. Denise opened the car door to get out, and as she was doing so, the man grabbed her arm and pulled her out the car. At this time, Steven was still in the passenger seat of the car. The man then got in the car and threatened Steven with the gun. With the gun pointed at his head and his hands in the air, Steven was unable to unlatch his safety belt to get out the car. The man, frustrated at the time it was taking Steven to get out the car, hit Steven on the head with the butt of the gun and unlatched the safety belt himself. While this was happening, Denise and her father could do nothing more than watch as all this was transpiring. Once unlatched, Steven exited the car. The driver of the suspicious car then pulled away, allowing the man in Denise's car to drive away with her car and all of her and Steven's personal belongings. They had just been carjacked.

Feeling shocked and scared, Denise, Steven, and Denise's father went inside and called the police. She also explained to her mother, who was inside at the time, what had just happened. The police and emergency personnel arrived. The emergency personnel examined Steven's head and were able to treat his injury at the scene. The police took their statements and questioned them for about an hour, asking for details about what happened, the offenders, and what type of car they were driving. The police officers left them with assurances that they would do everything they could to apprehend the carjackers. They also gave Denise information on victim assistance programs in the area where they could go to get further assistance following their victimization.

During the days and weeks that passed, Denise worked to file an insurance claim, cancel and replace her credit cards, and replace her driver's license and some of the essential items Steven needed for school, as those items were all in the car when they were carjacked. Neither of them followed up on the victim assistance programs. Denise, in particular, found it very hard to forget about the man and what had happened. In fact, she missed a week of work. She also found it difficult to sleep, experiencing night terrors and feeling very anxious. She began avoiding driving at night and also wanted someone to serve as a lookout every time she arrived or left her house. Denise also began to notify her family every time she was about to drive, with the idea that if she did not arrive somewhere in a certain amount of time, her family should worry and call the police. Three months after the carjacking, Denise was encouraged by a friend who had a similar experience to contact a victim assistance program to get help.

2008). Simply knowing when to attack, flee, or freeze from situations that are perceived as harmful can be extremely complicated. Often the clarity of action to take is missing, for example, in situations such as domestic abuse or bullying (Peterson & Walker, 2003). Moreover, often stressors may be triggered by psychological events. For example, in response to victimization, frustrations in working with the criminal justice system, disruptions in life routines, and possible intrusions by the media may evoke both immediate and long-term reactions. Stress involves an intersection between psychological and physiological responses, the number of stressors faced today (i.e., pressure on the job, mortgage payments, children, health insurance) add to the varied reactions and coping styles of victims (Peterson & Walker, 2003; Regehr, LeBlanc, Barath, Balch, & Birze, 2013). What is good to know is that even with all the stressors facing each of us, better medication, nutrition, and counseling is available to help people live better lives.

## Definitions of Stress and Trauma

To better understand the trauma and recovery of victims, it is important to have the key concepts of stress and trauma defined, as these terms are often used interchangeably in the literature (Boss, 2002). Puleo and McGlothlin (2014) explain that in Western culture, the word *stress* is generally used to describe emotional reactions ranging from feelings of mild irritation and frustration to being overwhelmed with fear. *Trauma* typically refers to the damage done to the biopsychosocial world of the individual as the result of a stressor or multiple stressors (Peterson, 2003). While the definitions may seem rather obvious, they have important distinctions within the context of providing assistance to victims.

## Stress

From the biological perspective, **stress** is any demand made on a person that causes a reaction either biologically or psychologically. Stress causes changes in hormonal patterns, such as increased production of adrenalin and cortisol, which over time, may

**Stress:** any demand made on a person that causes a reaction either biologically or psychologically

deplete the body's energy resources, impair the immune system, and lead to illness (Dickerson & Kemeny, 2004; Puleo & McGlothlin, 2014). Everyone has some form of stress. Not all stress is bad stress, however. Some stress is needed for us to develop and even grow stronger. For example, working to solve a puzzle or problem is stressful but not overly so, and solving the puzzle or problem teaches individuals new ways to do things. Traveling is stressful but also exciting and enjoyable to many people. A good physical workout is stressful on the body but also enables us to feel good afterward and helps our bodies to grow stronger (Peterson & Walker, 2003).

Han Selye (1956) described two types of stress: (1) eustress, or positive stress, which is the result of changes in our environment that are perceived positively, and (2) distress, or negative stress, which is often harmful to the individual and caused by changes in the environment that are perceived negatively. Selye (1956) argued that distress tends to cause more biological damage to a person than eustress, which seemingly contributes to a person's well-being. Therefore, how a person perceives stress has an effect on how he or she will adapt (Selye, 1956; Regehr, Hill, & Glancy, 2000). Psychological distress often results in an inability to cope with the demands or pressures around us, and if severe enough, can potentially lead to psychological disorders such as anxiety, depression, and posttraumatic stress disorder (PTSD) (Regehr et al., 2000, 2013; Peterson & Walker, 2003).

Stress is therefore defined as "the demand, either physically or psychologically, that is outside the norm and that signals a disparity between what is optimal and what actually exists" (Peterson & Walker, 2003, p. 68). It is a part of life, and it is normal and impossible to avoid. There are events that may take place in a person's life that are stressful. Being injured in a skiing accident is stressful and so is losing your job; however, they are not the same types of stress and people respond differently in each situation, though some of the responses may overlap (Peterson & Walker, 2003). The degree of stress depends on the perceptions of, and meaning attributed to, the stressor event. Any form of stress has the potential to change some aspect of our life, but increased stress does not necessarily lead to a crisis. Often, stress is managed, and the individual or family can arrive at a new steady state (Jannoff-Bulman, 1992; Puleo & McGlothlin, 2014).

## Trauma

**Trauma:** the result of severe distress and causes damage. Some stressors may be single incidents of relatively short duration, whereas others may occur over longer periods of time, resulting in prolonged exposure to the threatening stressor (Collins & Collins, 2005)

Stressors that involve trauma are powerful and overwhelming, and they threaten perceptions of safety and security (Puleo & McGlothlin, 2014). **Trauma** is therefore the result of severe distress and causes damage. Some stressors may be single incidents of relatively short duration, whereas others may occur over longer periods of time, resulting in prolonged exposure to the threatening stressor (Collins & Collins, 2005). According to the *Diagnostic and Statistical Manual of Mental Disorders* (DSM-V) (American Psychiatric Association, 2013), a traumatic event involves the threatened or actual death or serious injury, or a threat to the well-being of oneself or to another person. Traumatic events may be human caused accidents or catastrophes, such as the Deepwater Horizon disaster which led to the largest oil spill in U.S. waters. An uncontrollable blowout caused an explosion on the oilrig that killed 11 crewmen and ignited a fireball visible from 40 miles away. The fire was inextinguishable, leading to the rig sinking and the well gushing at the seabed, affecting much of ocean life in the area. The multiple terrorist attacks on September 11, 2001; the Boston Marathon Bombing on Patriots Day, April 15, 2013; and mass shootings such as those at Columbine High School in Littleton, Colorado, Sandy Hook Elementary School in Newtown, Connecticut, and the Pulse Club Shooting in Orlando, Florida, are all examples of acts of deliberate human actions, as are the numerous homicides and sexual assaults that occur in the United States each year. Other traumatic events include natural disasters, which include Hurricane Katrina that struck the Gulf Coast of the United States, leaving a wake of death and destruction in New Orleans, and the 2011 earthquake and tsunami that resulted in tens of thousands of deaths in Japan.

Traumatic events fracture and shatter the very basic assumptions people have about themselves and the world they live in (Jannoff-Bulman, 1992). This is because we develop theories about how the world works. For example, we trust that most people will act in benevolent ways. We expect that more good will happen to us than bad and never expect someone to steal our car, or be sexually assaulted, or kill someone we love. We know these things happen but assume that they will never happen to us. When they do, it is often not just a recovery from the specific acts of a violent crime that is needed but a recovery that involves a reorganization and understanding of ourselves and the world around us (Jannoff-Bulman, 1992; Peterson, 2003).

## Responses to Trauma

Victimization causes many emotional responses that are normal: anger, rage, anxiety, fear, depression, and so forth (Kirchhoff, 2005). Most victims respond to traumatic events within a normal range of reactions to abnormal events, whereby the individual's baseline is not disrupted to the point that causes impairment or dysfunction. While others may become significantly distressed and impaired and develop psychological disorders such as acute stress disorder (ASD) and posttraumatic stress disorder (PTSD) (Andrews, Brewin, Rose, & Kirk, 2000). The risk of psychological disturbance tends to increase with the magnitude or intensity of the traumatic stressor and with the degree to which the event was human caused and intended to harm (Kirchhoff, 2005; Puleo & McGlothlin, 2014).

Reactions to traumatic events typically include physical, behavioral, cognitive, and emotional responses, which tend to occur in stages, but ultimately are temporary. The intensity of the reactions usually subsides over time. Physical responses involve the automatic nervous system that prepares the body to fight, flight, or freeze and may include heart palpitations, shortness of breath, nausea, muscle tension, headaches, and fatigue (Bracha, 2004). The physical problems created by stress will vary from person to person, but victimization can disrupt any of the body's systems and increase the risk of stress-related illness. Often victims want to regain control over their lives quickly and minimize an illness and not seek medical assistance. Victim service providers should support and encourage victims regarding concerns about health and assist them to obtain the appropriate medical care (Peterson, 2003). Behaviorally, victims may experience sleep and dietary changes, social withdrawal, and purposeful avoidance of and attention to reminders of the traumatic event. Changes in relationships may also occur, along with an increased consumption of alcohol or mood-altering substances. These reactions may appear normal to victim service providers but present great distress for victims. Providing referrals for further counseling and evaluation may be necessary to help victims deal with these changes in behavior (Jannoff-Bulman, 1992; Peterson, 2003). The cognitive reactions victims may experience include rumination, preoccupation with the traumatic event, forgetfulness, and difficulty concentrating. A common indictor of cognitive problems for victim service providers to be aware of is the failure to follow a conversation by either diverting it or tuning out.

While many victims return to a healthy level of functioning, others experience consequences that greatly affect their ability to function. Mentioned above, the two most common psychological disorders victims experience are ASD and PTSD (Andrews et al., 2000). These two disorders are similar in their symptomology. According to the DSM-V, the diagnostic criteria for ASD and PTSD include hyperarousal (hypervigilance, difficulty concentrating, exaggerated startle responses, sleep disturbances), re-experiencing (flashbacks, nightmares, intrusive thoughts), and avoidance (attempting to avoid reminders of the traumatic event, inability to recall components of the event, detachment, disassociation, restricted effect), which cause distress and impair important areas of daily functioning. ASD is diagnosed if these symptoms appear within one month of the traumatic event. If these symptoms are experienced for more than one month, then PTSD may be diagnosed. If the symptoms persist for more than three months, PTSD is considered chronic (American Psychiatric Association, 2013).

PTSD can be debilitating and greatly impact a victim's ability to recover to a state of normal functioning. It is difficult to know how many crime victims experience PTSD. There are many events that can trigger PTSD symptoms. Entering the criminal justice system is one such example. Having to identify objects, people, or items related to the traumatic event, often many months later, can trigger a reaction. Anniversaries of the trauma or holidays near the date can have the same impact. Research has indicated that between 25% and 28% of crime victims experience PTSD (Resnick & Kilpatrick, 1994; Kilpatrick & Acierno, 2003). Victims of sexual assault, aggravated assault, or family violence and family members of homicide victims are more likely to develop PTSD (Black et al., 2011). High exposure to the criminal justice system almost doubles the victims' chances of suffering from PTSD. The negative psychological responses to victimization should be evaluated closely and taken seriously by victim service providers who should be distinctively aware of the symptoms of PTSD.

## Resources

Resources: traits, characteristics, or abilities to meet the demands of a stressor event that can be available at the individual, family, or community level

Availability and access to resources following victimization can greatly reduce the effect of trauma. McCubbin and Patterson (1982) describe **resources** as traits, characteristics or abilities to meet the demands of a stressor event that can be available at the individual, family, or community level. There are two types of important resources: those that are available and used to settle the initial reactions to the stressor and those that are acquired, developed, or strengthened subsequent to a crisis situation (McCubbin & Patterson, 1982). Individual resources include education, health, employment, and

**Table 4.1   DSM-V Diagnostic Criteria for Posttraumatic Stress Disorder**

**Posttraumatic Stress Disorder**

**Diagnostic Criteria**                                                                          309.81(F43.10)

**Posttraumatic Stress Disorder**

**Note:** The following criteria apply to adults, adolescents, and children older than 6 years. For children 6 years and younger, see corresponding criteria below.

A.  Exposure to actual or threatened death, serious injury, or sexual violence in one (or more) of the following ways:

 1.  Directly experiencing the traumatic event(s).

 2.  Witnessing, in person, the event(s) as it occurred to others.

 3.  Learning that the traumatic event(s) occurred to a close family member or close friend. In cases of actual or threatened death of a family member or friend, the event(s) must have been violent or accidental.

 4.  Experiencing repeated or extreme exposure to aversive details of the traumatic events(s) (e.g., first responders collecting human remains: police officers repeatedly exposed to details of child abuse).

    **Note:** Criterion A4 does not apply to exposure through electronic media, television, movies, or pictures, unless this exposure is work related.

B.  Presence of one (or more) of the following intrusion symptoms associated with the traumatic event(s), beginning after the traumatic event(s) occurred:

 1.  Recurrent, involuntary, and intrusive distressing memories of the traumatic event(s).

    **Note:** In children older than 6 years, repetitive play may occur in which themes or aspects of the traumatic event(s) are expressed.

 2.  Recurrent distressing dreams in which the content and/or affect of the dream are related to the traumatic event(s).

    **Note:** In children, there may be frightening dreams without recognizable content.

 3.  Dissociative reactions (e.g., flashbacks) in which the individual feels or acts as if the traumatic event(s) were recurring. (Such reactions may occur on a continuum, with the most extreme expression being a complete loss of awareness of present surroundings.)

    **Note:** In children, trauma-specific reenactment may occur in play.

 4.  Intense or prolonged psychological distress at exposure to internal or external cues that symbolize or resemble an aspect of the traumatic event(s).

 5.  Marked physiological reactions to internal or external cues that symbolize or resemble an aspect of the traumatic event(s).

*(Continued)*

Table 4.1   (Continued)

**Posttraumatic Stress Disorder**

Diagnostic Criteria                                                                        309.81(F43.10)

C.  Persistent avoidance of stimuli associated with the traumatic event(s), beginning after the traumatic event(s) occurred, as evidenced by one or both of the following:

1.  Avoidance of or efforts to avoid distressing memories, thoughts, or feelings about or closely associated with the traumatic event(s).

2.  Avoidance of or efforts to avoid external reminders (people, places, conversations, activities, objects, situations) that arouse distressing memories, thoughts, or feelings about or closely associated with traumatic event(s).

D.  Negative alterations in cognitions and mood associated with the traumatic event(s), beginning or worsening after the traumatic event(s) occurred, as evidenced by two (or more) of the following:

1.  Inability to remember an important aspect of the traumatic event(s) (typically due to dissociative amnesia and not to other factors such as head injury, alcohol, or drugs).

2.  Persistent and exaggerated negative beliefs or expectations about oneself, others, or the world (e.g., "I am bad," "No one can be trusted," "The world is completely dangerous," "My whole nervous system is permanently ruined").

3.  Persistent, distorted cognitions about the cause or consequences of the traumatic event(s) that lead the individual to blame himself/herself or others.

4.  Persistent negative emotional state (e.g., fear, horror, anger, guilt, or shame).

5.  Markedly diminished interest or participation in significant activities.

6.  Feelings of detachment or estrangement from others.

7.  Persistent inability to experience positive emotions (e.g., inability to experience happiness, satisfaction, or loving feelings).

E.  Marked alterations in arousal and reactivity associated with the traumatic event(s), beginning or worsening after the traumatic event(s) occurred, as evidenced by two (or more) of the following:

1.  Irritable behavior and angry outburst (with little or no provocation) typically expressed as verbal or physical aggression toward people or objects.

2.  Reckless or self-destructive behavior.

3.  Hypervigilance.

4.  Exaggerated startle response.

5.  Problems with concentration.

6.  Sleep disturbance (e.g., difficulty falling or staying asleep or restless sleep).

F.  Duration of the disturbance (Criteria B, C, D, and E) is more than 1 month.

G.  The disturbance causes clinically significant distress or impairment in social, occupational, or other important areas of functioning.

H.  The disturbance is not attributable to the physiological effects of a substance (e.g., medication, alcohol) or another medical condition.

*Specify* whether:

**With dissociative symptoms:** The individual's symptoms meet the criteria for post-traumatic stress disorder, and in addition, in response to the stressor, the individual experiences persistent or recurrent symptoms of either of the following:

1.  **Depersonalization:** Persistent of recurrent experiences of feeling detached from, and as if one were an outside observer of, one's mental processes or body (e.g., feeling as though one were in a dream; feeling a sense of unreality of self or body or of time moving slowly).

2.  **Derealization:** Persistent or recurrent experiences of unreality of surroundings (e.g., the world around the individuals is experienced as unreal, dreamlike, distant, or distorted).

    **Note:** To use this subtype, the dissociative symptoms must not be attributable to the physiological effects of a substance (e.g., blackouts, behavior during alcohol intoxication) or another medical condition (e.g., complex partial seizures).

*Specify* if:

**With delayed expression:** If the full diagnostic criteria are not met until at least 6 months after the event (although the onset and expression of some symptoms may be immediate).

**Posttraumatic Stress Disorder for Children 6 Years and Younger**

A.  In children 6 years and younger, exposure to actual or threatened death, serious injury, or sexual violence in one (or more) of the following ways:

1.  Directly experiencing the traumatic event(s).

2.  Witnessing, in person, the event(s) as it occurred to others, especially primary caregivers.

(APA, 2013)

individual psychological characteristics, whereas family resources include attributes of cohesion and adaptability and shared interests. Community resources include external supports such as social networks, victim assistance organizations, and law enforcement (UNODCCP, 1999). Assisting the victim to identify or reach out to resources provided by victim service providers can improve their daily functioning following a traumatic event.

## Perception

The perception and interpretation of a traumatic event to an individual is important in understanding the different manifestations of reactions. How a victim reacts to such an event depends not only on the available resources but also the meaning he or she attaches to it. Puleo and McGlothlin (2014) write that meanings attributed to stressor events are subjective, and the factors that contribute to reactions include ambiguity (i.e., when facts cannot be obtained, or information is missing), denial, and the belief and value systems of the individual. Often following victimization, victims' perception of the world and the role people play in it changes. Questioning the senselessness and absurdity of a world in which human beings can be so cruel to one another greatly affects their reaction and ability to recover (Lerner, 1980; Hafer & Bègue, 2005). Victim support providers need to be nonjudgmental, supportive, and open in their responses to the interpretations and meanings ascribed to stressors by victims.

## Coping

**Coping:** the thoughts and acts that people use to manage the internal and external demands posed by a stressful or traumatic event (Peterson, 2003)

**Coping** refers to the thoughts and acts that people use to manage the internal and external demands posed by a stressful or traumatic event (Peterson, 2003). It is a process where any behavioral or cognitive action is taken in an effort to manage stress. If the stressor is perceived as challenging or threatening (as opposed to irrelevant), the individual then determines what responses are possible and what their potential outcomes might be (Lazarus, 1993). There are two major categories of coping strategies: problem-focused strategies and emotion-focused strategies.

Problem-focused strategies are aimed at taking control of the stress. This involves changing or modifying aspects of the environment that are thought to be the causes of stress (Carroll, 2013). These efforts include seeking information or assistance, defining the problem, generating possible solutions and discussing their consequences, putting into place a plan of action, and finally acting upon it. Problem-focused strategies can be directed at the challenges and stress that come with being a victim of crime and are subsequent to the crime. These include dealing with media and the criminal justice system (Peterson, 2003; Puleo & McGlothlin, 2014). Emotion-focused coping strategies are used in the management of unchangeable stressors (DeGraff & Schaffer, 2008). Rather than changing the problem, as in problem-focused coping, this strategy involves the reappraisal process of the stressful situation, attempting to change the meaning of a stressor, or creating emotional distance from it and taking control over one's emotions (Carver, 2011). Using this strategy has assisted victims of crime dealing with emotions such as depression and anger (Folkman & Moskowitz, 2004). Depending on the type of stressor, a combination of these two types of strategies may be necessary in assisting a victim's recovery.

The effectiveness of any strategy is dependent on the context of the traumatic event. This means that any particular strategy the individual employs to cope with the trauma can be either adaptive or maladaptive (Kirby, Shakespeare-Finch, & Palk, 2011). Some responses that are typically viewed as maladaptive include increased drug and alcohol consumption (self-punishment) and avoidance, which are generally recognized as being detrimental to recovery. Adaptive coping incorporates efforts to seek support from resources (family, community, etc.), to understand and express emotions in dealing with the incident, and to incorporate problem-solving activities to relieve the source of stress (Lazarus & Folkman, 1984). Better adjustment in the aftermath of trauma comes from the identification of coping abilities that encourage the engagement of resources and problem-solving skills.

## Resilience

**Resiliency** is defined as a person's ability to maintain a balanced state in the face of challenges. In other words, it is the ability to "bounce back" after being traumatized, where the person is able to process and make sense of the disruption in his or her life, identify his or her resources, and successfully handle the crisis (Bonanno, 2004, 2005). Some victims are able to deal with their traumatic event without seeking professional help or ever coming to the attention of victim services (Gannon & Mihorean, 2005). People who are able to adjust to challenges are likely to have improved ability to cope. This may be emotional or behavioral adaptability or finding the positive elements in negative events (Bonanno, 2005; Tugade & Fredrickson 2007). Research on resilience has found that a variety of factors can operate to ensure resilience. These factors include social support, being socially competent, and being able to apply cognitive skills to solving problems. People who have social support and high-quality relationships show greater resiliency than those who have fewer social resources (Bonanno, 2005; Haskett, Nears, & Ward, 2006). While the decision regarding where to go for support lies with the victims, those who use their support systems are more likely to seek professional help, especially if they feel positively supported (Norris, Kaniasty, & Thompson, 1997). Social support and networks provide resources such as information that are important in dealing with adversity. People who are socially competent tend to have better communication skills, show empathy and caring, and demonstrate the ability to connect to others. Thus, social competency improves resiliency by helping the person meet any required needs (Haskett et al., 2006).

Finally, cognitive skills such as intelligence and problem-solving skills help the person to effectively examine and choose between different options in dealing with stress. Greater cognitive skills allow for people to generate more options and make them less likely to choose options with negative effects (Haskett et al., 2006; Gewirtz & Edleson, 2007).

> **Resilience:** a person's ability to maintain a balanced state in the face of challenges. In other words, it is the ability to "bounce back" after being traumatized, where the person is able to process and make sense of the disruption in his or her life, identify his or her resources, and successfully handle the crisis (Bonanno 2004; 2005)

## Reducing and Preventing Trauma

As previously mentioned, reactions to victimization differ all the time and from person to person, with numerous factors influencing these reactions: past experiences, general well-being, perception and meaning attributed to victimization, resources, and coping abilities. The longer the victim experiences any distress, the greater the potential for both psychological and physiological harm (Sorenson, 2002). It must be the goal of the victim service provider to assist in reducing stressors and to be alert to any signs of emotional or physical distress. The victim service provider must be prepared to deal with these reactions and those that may emerge in the aftermath of victimization and also to prepare

# Victim's Assistance Programs

## Connecting Mental Health & Education, Inc.

Connecting Mental Health & Education's aim is to provide therapy to all clients in need, especially those in grave danger. This includes therapy for those who suffer from depression, anxiety, or symptoms of post-traumatic stress resulting from abusive and criminal injustices. They focus on domestic violence (DV), child abuse, spousal abuse, and elder abuse. See http://www.connectingmentalhealth.com for more information.

the victim to deal with these (UNODCCP, 1999). There are a variety of ways to help reduce and prevent trauma. However, victim service providers need to be aware that some of the methods used to reduce stress and trauma are not equal in their effectiveness or efficiency and that service providers are not always able to assist victims. Therefore, victim service providers are encouraged to develop professional networks with police personnel, medical professionals, teachers, community leaders, religious leaders, and social service agencies who can offer further assistance to victims (UNODCCP, 1999).

Some of the options used to reduce and prevent trauma by victim service providers are trauma specific counseling, normalization, education (effects of trauma, legal advice, and injury), and developing the crisis story. Trauma-specific counseling is designed to treat only the crime that happened and any consequences or issues that arises in its aftermath. This does not mean that pre-existing issues should be ignored but rather that only once trauma-specific support has been initiated and addressed can other issues be dealt with (Jennings, 2004). Normalization involves reassuring victims that their traumatic reactions are common and to be expected (Young, 1993). To assist victims with normalization, introducing them to other stories of victims who have experienced similar crises often helps them to learn about the commonality of pain and emotional reactions. Education is a key component in reducing trauma and preventing trauma. Providing materials describing victims' reactions to trauma is valuable. This information may be ignored immediately following an event; however, in the following days, such information will be welcomed as the victims begin to reconstruct their lives. Education concerning physical injuries and where to get medical assistance is vital for victims. For example, such information aids the victim in better understanding the time and process needed for forensic examinations, along with how physical injuries may qualify them for victim compensation. Providing victims with information regarding legal implications is just as important. Information on what to expect from the criminal justice system informs victims of their options and steps that are taken to investigate, prosecute, and resolve the case (UNODCCP, 1999; Litz, Gary, Bryant, & Adler, 2002). Lastly, because recounting the crisis may be too painful and lead to re-experiencing negative emotional reactions, it is necessary for victims to develop a crisis story that aids them in avoiding these reactions. Victim service providers should let victims tell the stories they want to and not push for too much information. This can be done by assuring victims that what they are feeling is not uncommon and that they can stop telling their stories at any point and come back to them later (Young, 1993).

Most victim service providers recognize the fact that they may not be able to alleviate the continuing stresses of victims, but by providing the necessary reassurance, counseling, and education, they will help them to cope better with life's crises.

## Stages of Recovery

Recovery is arguably the most important goal for victim service agencies. A recovered victim is one who has come to terms with having been victimized and who acknowledges what was lost. Having gone through this process, the victim is able to establish meaning from his or her experience and integrate what has been learnt to continue a functional life (Masters et al., 2017). Discussed already, working with someone who has experienced a traumatic event can be challenging, as everyone reacts differently. Despite the different reactions most victims go through, a three-phase process: impact stage, recoil stage, and the recovery achievement stage (Tyhurst, 1957; Office for Victims of Crime, 2001) have been commonly associated with victim recovery. Along with these phases, safety, remembrance and mourning, and self-care are identified as important concepts in the stages of recovery.

### Victim Recovery

Based on research investigating individual patterns of responses to community disasters, J. S. Tyhurst (1957) identified three common phases victims go through following a traumatic event: impact stage, recoil stage, and recovery achievement stage. The impact stage follows the traumatic event and is when victims often experience shock, fear, anger, disbelief, numbness, and anxiety. Some victims are vulnerable to greater emotional reactions as they feel they are unable to protect themselves during this stage, while others may be able to react in a more rational manner. At this stage, victims' primary concerns are the basic needs of food, shelter, warmth, and safety. It is at this stage that victim service providers should ensure the victims' safety and identify the appropriate interventions by providing emotional and practical support, along with making referrals to mental health services should this be necessary to assist with long-term recovery (Herman, 1997; Masters et al., 2017). These first steps are essential to victim recovery.

In the recoil stage, the victims' reactions can vary from anger, rage, and helplessness to self-blame and even shame for what happened. Victims may ask in this stage *"why me?"* or *"why did I not do something different?"* These feelings can consume victims' every thought and greatly affect their ability to function normally in their daily lives. These feelings can cause negative physiological reactions, too. Headaches, stomachaches, insomnia, and lowered energy levels are common physical reactions to the preoccupation victims may have with the traumatic event (UNODCCP, 1999; Masters et al., 2017). Victims during this stage may require more extensive assistance from trained specialists such as psychiatrists' or psychologists. Victim service providers greatly assist victims in this stage by providing information about the victims' situation, accompanying victims' through the criminal justice system, and ensuring that they receive the necessary services to help them function more effectively. The treatment option for victims may be either short term or long term. Short-term treatment options assist victims who have minor disorders, health issues, and problems managing stress. Long-term treatment usually addresses more severe reactions to trauma such as PTSD, anxiety disorder, and depression (Andrews, 1990; Yeager & Roberts, 2015). Reducing these symptoms of trauma assists victims with recounting and recalling the traumatic event without producing reactions characterizing the recoil stage (Herman, 1997).

The recovery achievement stage is marked by a renewed sense of empowerment and feelings that the traumatic event has become an integrated part of one's life story. Regardless of what may seem to be a setback, triggered by anniversaries and other reminders, victims in this stage are usually able to function with little or no disruption. Victims are also able to put into perspective that traumatic events, while not normal, do happen, and by overcoming the adverse consequences, they have a more positive self-perception and willingness to continue and possibly help others with similar distress (Herman, 1997; Van Camp, in press). Every victim deserves the opportunity to recover, and victim service providers are in the best position to assist victims in achieving this goal.

## Safety

Following criminal victimization, victims often state that their feelings of safety and security have been shattered. According to Bryant-Davis (2005), **safety** is a sense of protection, well-being, and security. It is the feeling people experience when they are not in danger. If people are safe, they feel comfortable expressing themselves, their thoughts, and their feelings. Feeling safe means that the person is less likely to be anxious and tense (Bryant-Davis, 2005). Because traumatic events produce distress and anxiety, along with endangering the victim physically and emotionally, it is not uncommon to feel afraid. Being afraid may affect victims' interactions with people, places, or social environments. Regaining feelings of safety and security is crucial for recovery. Moreover, being educated to identify possible unsafe situations or persons from safe ones is just as important. Victim service providers have to maximize every opportunity to increase victims' physical and emotional safety. This can be done by honestly assessing the victims' safety, and if they are not safe, determining the best steps they can take to increase their safety (Bryant-Davis, 2005). Depending on the traumatic experience, the victims may not feel that they are worthy of protection and safety. It is important for victim service providers to encourage and improve the victims' self-worth and make sure the interventions taken are focused on empowerment and increasing their perceptions of safety and security. It is impossible for victim service providers to prepare for all possible variations when working with victims, but they should have a strategy for safety planning and revisit it as circumstances change. Assisting with planning and assuring the safety of victims, family, and friends is important to ensuring that loved ones stay safe and recover effectively (UNCG, 2013).

**Safety:** a sense of protection, well-being, and security. It is the feeling people experience when they are not in danger

## Remembrance and Mourning

Most people remember events in their lives from childhood through to adulthood, and positive and negative events are usually a part of a person's memory. Traumatic events can remain embedded in victims' contemporary experiences. Victims need to be able to confront their memories without becoming overwhelmed (Bryant-Davis, 2005). The more victims are able to do this, the more power the victims will gain over their memories and ability to function without disruption. As victims recall these memories, so too, they begin to confront them and work through the pain and begin to experience a decrease in anxiety (Foa & Rothbaum, 2001). Remembering transforms the victim's experience of the trauma. With the support and guidance of victim service providers and other resources, the memory goes from unbearable to bearable. Crisis intervention therapy and cognitive-behavioral therapy are individual therapies that have shown to best assist victims, effectively transform their memories, and improve a sense of self and empowerment (Foa & Rothbaum, 2001; Allen, 2005). Remembering and speaking the truth to traumatic experiences is a way for victims to move forward (Herman, 1997). Victim service providers can best assist victims in this regard by providing basic education on coping and self-care strategies and a list of available resources to where victims can get the type of assistance that deals with traumatic memories.

Mourning is experiencing grief for and recognizing the losses one has endured. It requires acceptance of the loss and capability to confront feelings of sadness (Bryant-Davis, 2005). Many victims try to avoid this process and deny the impact of the trauma, as it may reveal weakness or show that the event or perpetrator has power over them. It is healthy for people to mourn and allow themselves to feel a range of emotions. Like remembrance, it is important for people to confront these feeling, as by doing so, the person learns strategies to lessen emotional reactions (Young, 1991; Foa & Rothbaum, 2001). Victim service providers should develop strategies for surviving families and friends for coping through the mourning process and promoting growth to avoid remaining in despair. By learning and understanding that healthy expressions of sadness are necessary, people can move forward while still holding onto the lasting memories of loved ones.

## Self-Care

**Self-care** is the opposite of self-harm. When a victim engages in self-care, they are expressing to others that they value their health and are finding ways to move on from the traumatic event. Self-care activities are important for every human being (Herman, 1997). Victim service providers should encourage the value of self-care particularly within the context of trauma recovery from a violation that affects a victim's sense of self-worth. Empowerment is key to self-care and should be done through the acknowledgment of barriers to resources, as well as strategies to assist in these barriers being overcome (Bryant-Davis, 2005). Self-care activities that should be encouraged include the following:

- Set aside time to rest and sleep (if the victim cannot sleep he or she should seek help)

- Eat regularly and healthy

- Maintain good and regular hygiene (cleaning one's body, teeth, hair, clothes, and living environment)

- Communicate with family and friends

- Try to be physically active

**Self-care:** is the opposite of self-harm. When victims engage in self-care they are expressing to others that they value their health and are finding ways to move on from the traumatic event. Self-care activities are important for every human being (Herman, 1997)

# Victim's Assistance Programs

## Mental Health America

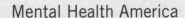

Mental Health America is the nation's leading community-based nonprofit dedicated to addressing the needs of those living with mental illness and to promoting the overall mental health of all Americans. Their work is driven by their commitment to promote mental health as a critical part of overall wellness, including prevention services for all; early identification and intervention for those at risk; and integrated care, services, and support for those who need it, with recovery as the goal. See http://www.mentalhealthamerica.net for more information.

- Take time to engage in enjoyable activities (reading, listening to music, watching a movie)
- Schedule regular preventative visits to support services and the doctor or go to the hospital when experiencing physical or emotional distress

## SUMMARY

The initial reactions following victimization may include shock, anger, disbelief, and helplessness. These psychological, emotional, and social responses are normal reactions to such an event. It is crucial that victims are provided with the proper support, as these events can fracture and shatter the very basic assumptions people have about themselves and the world they live in. Crisis reactions tend to occur in stages but are often temporary with the intensity of the reactions usually subsiding over time. While many victims return to healthy levels of functioning, others may experience psychological disorders, such as ASD and PTSD. The stressor itself does not only determine how victims' and their families respond and adapt to traumatic events but also how the entire situation is perceived and the availability of resources. Recovery is arguably the most important goal for victim service agencies. A recovered victim is one who has come to terms with having been victimized and acknowledges what was lost. Having gone through this process, the victim is able to reestablish feelings of safety and security and find meaning from the experience that is integrated into his or her life story. Victim service providers need to be aware of the physical and emotional reactions of victims and be able to respond in proactive ways providing crisis intervention, strategies for recovery, and referrals to needed resources.

## KEY WORDS

Coping  66
Resilience  67
Resources  62

Safety  70
Self-care  71

Stress  59
Trauma  60

# INTERNET RESOURCES

**The National Organization for Victim Assistance (http://www.trynova.org)**

NOVA is a private, nonprofit, 501(c)(3) charitable organization. Its mission is to champion dignity and compassion for those harmed by crime and crisis. It is the oldest national victim assistance organization of its type in the United States and is the recognized leader in this noble cause. This website contains information about victim assistance.

**The American Mental Health Counselors Association (http://www.amhca.org)**

The American Mental Health Counselors Association (AMHCA) is the leading national organization for licensed clinical mental health counselors. AMHCA strives to be the go-to organization for licensed clinical mental health counselors for advocacy, education, leadership, and collaboration. Our organization provides the backbone of resources needed for clinical mental health counselors to thrive in today's world.

**Coping with Trauma and Grief (https://victims ofcrime.org/help-for-crime-victims/coping-with-trauma-and-grief)**

The National Center for Victims of Crime includes information on coping with trauma and grief. Furthermore, it provides links to resources for victims, including information about PTSD and resiliency.

**The National Center for PTSD (http://www.ptsd .va.gov/)**

The National Center for PTSD is dedicated to research and education on trauma and PTSD. The website publishes the latest research findings to help those exposed to trauma and those working with trauma victims.

# CRITICAL THINKING QUESTIONS

1. List and discuss the three physiological reactions to traumatic events.

2. What are the ways people cope following a victimization? Discuss the two types of copying strategies used to help victims.

3. What are some steps victim services can take to reduce the impact of trauma?

4. Critically discuss the stages of recovery.

5. Why is self-care not only important for victims but also for victim service personnel, too?

# Understanding the Criminal Justice System and Victim Assistance

The structure of the criminal justice system in the United States is generally divided into law enforcement, courts, and corrections. Throughout the stages, victims interact with many different professionals. Those professionals include, but are not limited to, law enforcement officers, medical examiners, prosecuting and defense attorneys, judges, correctional officers, parole and probation officers, and victim advocates. The next three chapters will provide an overview of the criminal justice system and how professionals can assist crime victims at each stage. Chapter 5 addresses the investigative process and available resources for victims. It discusses victim interaction with the police and the ways that victim services assist crime victims on their initial entry into the criminal justice system. Chapter 6 covers the court process. We explore the role of the prosecution and the judiciary in how victims' rights are protected, victims' opportunities to participate in trials, and the importance of victim services programs to support the process. Chapter 7 highlights corrections, prison violence, and services available to victims. It addresses how victims' rights and interests are addressed in the postsentencing stage. Some of the key discussions in this chapter include the victim notification process, victim impact panels, and the victim-offender reconciliation process. The chapter also covers prison violence and offenders becoming victims in facilities. Finally, Chapter 8 discusses the juvenile justice system and restorative justice.

Before getting into the details of each stage, let us look at the overall process in the U.S. criminal justice system and review the important terms used in the system. Please note that criminal justice processes differ significantly by jurisdiction, and presented here is a general overview of the system. Also, the extent of a victim's involvement in the criminal justice system can vary depending on the nature and type of the crime. Therefore, please consult with your local criminal justice agencies for further detailed information in your area.

| Law Enforcement | Arrest | Police exercise authority to take a suspect into custody. |
|---|---|---|
| | Investigation | The police investigation process includes determination of whether a crime has been committed, the identification of the perpetrator, apprehending the perpetrator, and providing evidence to support a conviction in court. |
| Courts | Booking | An arrestee is taken to the police station or jail, and personal information, alleged charge(s), fingerprints, and photographs are recorded. |
| | Initial appearance | Most states have a statutory requirement that the suspect must be taken before a magistrate or a judge within a reasonable time period. The individual is informed about the charge(s) against him or her and of his or her constitutional rights. |
| | Preliminary hearing/Grand Jury | In this hearing, it is determined whether there is probable cause to believe the suspect committed the offense in the complaint. Some states require grand juries of 12 to 23 citizens to determine whether sufficient evidence exists. |
| | Arraignment and plea | The defendant appears before a court for an arraignment. The defendant is notified of the formal charges and informed again of his or her rights. The defendant makes an admission of denial or guilt. When the plea is not guilty, a trial date is set. |
| | Trial | The defendant has an option to have a bench trial, whereby guilt is determined by a judge, or a jury trial. The prosecutor must prove his or her case beyond a reasonable doubt. After the defendant pleads guilty or is found guilty at the trial, the judge sets a date for sentencing. |
| | Sentencing | The judge determines the sentence, or the jury makes a recommendation. In some jurisdictions, the judge must follow the jury's recommendation. The defendant may appeal to a higher court. |
| Corrections | Incarceration | The most common formal sanction is incarceration, or the confinement of the convict. Jail is a municipal facility and usually houses those sentenced to less than one year of incarceration. Prison is a state or federal facility for housing those who are sentenced to more than one year. There are also private prisons run by the private sector. |
| | Release | Parole is the early conditional release of a prisoner from incarceration. Those who receive an early release are supervised by parole officers. The parole officers conduct surveillance and assist offenders in readjusting to the community. |

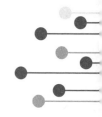

# The Investigative Process and Victim Assistance

One of the common expressions of crime victims is that "*I never thought it could happen to me.*" But they might also feel that "*this isn't what I expected*" (Bard & Sangrey, 1986, p. 4). In fact, the unfamiliar process of the criminal justice system often makes victims and their family members feel overwhelmed and intimidated. Victims might also feel that their concerns and voices are ignored, and as a result, they feel that they are revictimized by the system. To better support victims, we must understand the gaps between what victims expect from the system and how the system actually operates. This chapter addresses the first stage in the criminal justice system, which is police operations and the investigation of crime, and discusses how victims interact with the relevant professionals. This chapter also covers the victim assistance and human services agencies that help victims in crisis.

## Policing in America

Police operations in the United States are mostly localized, but there are also federal and state agencies. Federal law enforcement agencies are in charge of enforcing federal laws. The most common sworn officers at the federal level are at the Federal Bureau of Investigation (FBI), the U.S. Secret Service, and the Drug Enforcement Administration (DEA). State law enforcement agencies are defined by state law. State police agencies are commonly known as the "highway patrol." Beyond enforcing motor vehicle laws on state highways, some state agencies offer crime lab services for local police departments. Police departments mainly cover urban areas, whereas sheriff's Offices provide law enforcement services in counties in rural areas and operate jail facilities. Sheriff's Offices also provide court security and enforce child support orders. Besides traditional law enforcement duties, police departments perform other duties such as developing strategies to prevent crimes and providing services to citizens and crime victims. Due to those wide variety of duties, there are many types of professionals working within police departments. Those police officers who have arrest powers and carry a firearm and a badge are called sworn officers or peace officers, and the professionals who do the administrative work in law enforcement agencies are called civilians (Masters et al., 2017).

Since the 1980s, the **community-oriented policing (COP)** strategy has been adopted in many police agencies throughout the United States. Beyond traditional law enforcement practice, the COP addresses prevention, problem-solving, community engagement, and partnerships to address crime and social disorder. Under the COP model, the police officers assigned to a specific neighborhood actively engage in community meetings and events and build trust with community members. Through

**Community-oriented policing (COP):** addresses prevention, problem solving, community engagement, and partnerships to address crime and social order beyond traditional law enforcement practice

the interactions with community members, the officers become more aware of local problems such as social disorder and fear of crime so that they can put more resources in the needed areas and resolve problems with community members. The COP not only improves the citizen-police relationship but also enhances community resiliency to crime (Fisher-Stewart, 2007).

Ample studies have shown the effectiveness of the COP in citizens' perceptions and fear of crime (Trojanowicz, 1985), attitudes toward the police (Thurman, 1995), and reducing different types of crime (Clarke & Goldstein, 2003; Sampson, 2004; Zanin, Shane, & Clarke, 2004). However, not all strategies in the COP necessarily work for reducing crime. One study showed that foot patrols, community meetings, storefront Offices, and newsletters do not reduce crime, but that door-to-door contact with residents does reduce crime (Mastrofski, 2006). The meta-analysis of prior research on community-oriented policing showed that community policing improves perceptions of police legitimacy, but its impact on crime prevention is limited (Gil, Weisburd, Telep, Vitter, & Bennett, 2014). Tillyer's study (2018) focusing on the impact of COP on arrests indicated that creating a COP unit alone would not influence arrests. However, when the agencies actively engaged in COP, included COP in their mission statement, and partnered with the community with COP efforts, the likelihood of arrest in violent crime incidents increased. Prior studies showed that the overall impact of COP in reducing crimes is rather limited, yet positive interactions with the police would no doubt increase citizens' confidence in the police.

## Victims' Initial Contact With the Police

When a crime is reported to the police, a police officer will arrive at the crime scene, make an initial investigation, and write a report. The officer's initial contact with the victim is particularly important, as it could affect a trustful relationship thereafter. Victims feel comforted and reassured if officers arrive quickly, listen carefully, and appear to be concerned (Bard & Sangrey, 1986). There are three things that the officer should know about the victim. First, the initial reactions of victimization are helplessness and fear. Therefore, the officer could remind the victim that he or she is no longer in danger by saying "you are safe now" or "I am here now." Second, victims have swirling emotions of feeling self-blame, anger, shame, sadness, and denial. The officer could help the victim by showing his or her readiness to listen to the victim's stories and show sympathy by saying "what you are feeling is completely normal." Third, victims are concerned about their involvement and role in the criminal justice system. The officer could briefly explain the criminal and medical procedures and provide a list of resources available to the victims (National Sheriffs' Association, 2008).

A student whose purse was snatched recalled her emotional moment and explained how the officers' attitude helped to calm her.

> I hadn't been hurt and there wasn't very much money in the purse, but I just couldn't stop crying. . . . I was still crying when the cops came, and they were just terrific about it. They sat down with me and listened to the whole story. By the time I finished telling it I had finally gotten myself under control. And you know, I'll never forget those guys (Bard & Sangrey, 1986, p. 118).

Subsequent to the initial interview, the officer could provide the victim with the necessary transportation. The officer could take the victim to a secure location, which might be the home of a friend or a family member depending on the victim's preference, or it could be a shelter or a hospital. If the case involves intimate partner violence, the officer will ensure the safety of any children involved, as well. A physically injured victim who needs immediate medical attention will be taken to an emergency room.

After that, the police interaction with the victim differs depending on the extent, nature, and type of the crime. If it is a minor property crime, the officer will ask questions and file an initial report. The victim may have little contact with the officer thereafter. The victim could check on the progress of the investigation by the case identification number and the name of the responding officer. In some instances, victims could get a copy of the police report, if desired. A police report usually consists of the fact sheet that includes basic information on the location and general nature of the crime. More details are in the narrative report, which records statements through the interviews of the victim and other persons. A supplemental form will include information about suspects and additional witnesses or victims. Most local police departments will provide victims with a copy of the fact sheet, but further details are restricted due to the investigation and respective policies (Villmoore & Benvenuti, 1988). But again, the practice differs by jurisdiction, and individuals should confirm the procedures within their local police department.

If a crime is of a serious nature, the involvement of the victims in the investigation process is more intense. They will likely be questioned several times by detectives. Victims are anticipated to cooperate with the police investigation, especially if they request the reimbursement of their crime-related out-of-pocket expenses from the government. For example, the California Victims of Crime Compensation Program notes that those victims who are willing to receive financial reimbursement are generally expected to cooperate with law enforcement during the investigation and prosecution of the crime (CalVCB, https://www.victims.ca.gov/victims/eligibility.aspx). Further details of compensation programs will be discussed in Chapter 6.

The police investigation involves determining whether a crime has been committed, identifying the perpetrator, apprehending the perpetrator, and providing evidence to support a conviction in court by constructing a **modus operandi (MO)** or developing a description of the way particular criminals operate (Bard & Sangrey, 1986). During the investigative interview, detectives might ask the victim questions that seem irrelevant or unnecessarily personal. The victim should feel free to ask the officer about anything that he or she does not understand or about the reasons behind the questions.

**Modus operandi (MO):** a term used by law enforcement to develop a description of the way particular criminals operate. Sometimes referred to by its initials, MO

Even if victims attempt their best efforts to explain the situation, their explanation could appear inconsistent and redundant. This is because people in crisis are off balance and are sometimes confused about what exactly happened. Possibly, their memory might return a few days later or even weeks after the interview. The police appreciate any additional information, even if victims might think it trivial, as the information could help develop a good MO to apprehend a suspect (Bard & Sangrey, 1986).

Educating the citizens about the importance of preserving evidence would significantly help police investigations. For example, when one encounters a crime, he or she could write a memo about whatever is remembered about the crime. It is important to be specific about who, when, where, and what happened. Second, a person should keep any clothes or other property that might help resolve the crime. In the case of a physical assault, a victim should not take a shower or change clothes before the police arrive. Third, one could ask a friend or a family member to take pictures of one's injuries, the crime scene, and any damaged property due to the crime. Finally, one could obtain estimates for repairs or replacement of the property damaged or stolen by the crime (North Carolina Bar Association, 1996).

Several outcomes are possible after the investigation. In reality, most reported crimes do not result in an arrest. For a variety of reasons, the police might decide that there are no legal grounds on which to pursue the victim's complaint. Or, they might be unable to accumulate enough evidence to make an arrest. If the police have successfully apprehended a suspect, the victim might be asked to identify the suspect by looking at photographs or a lineup. Lineups usually are held soon after an arrest or an arraignment. Both the prosecuting attorney and the defense attorney might be present at the lineup. Victims sometimes are asked to visit the crime scene and explain what happened there.

The most difficult ending of this stage for the victims is if the case is closed without a suspect being arrested. The victims might be disappointed and become frustrated that justice has not been served. By definition, justice has to do with getting what one deserves, for example, a person who did a bad thing should be punished. Bard and Sangrey (1986) noted that justice for crime victims has a further implication in which they feel that they deserve to get special consideration from criminal justice personnel. The frustrations and challenges caused by this kind of outcome could be softened by providing sufficient information to the victims. For example, the family and friends of the victim can help ease this sort of pain by encouraging the victim to keep his or her expectations about the outcome of the investigation realistic from the beginning. The police could be honest about what they think the probability of an arrest is in a specific case. The nationwide figures and local statistics showing the arrest rate for a particular crime in the victim's own area might also be used as a general guideline. Above all, victim advocates could take a critical role in easing the frustration and emotional turmoil of victims.

## Role of Victim Advocates

The criminal justice system agencies tend to be large, structured hierarchies with many policies and procedures, which makes it difficult to make a personalized response (Bard & Sangrey, 1986). The goal of the criminal investigation is to establish probable cause and arrest a suspect. Detectives who try to achieve that goal consider the victim's statement as important evidence (Martin, 2005). It is normal for the police to treat a victim in such a manner, yet a victim might feel that the process is aggressive, intimidating, and repetitive. As such, victim advocates could intervene in the relationship between victims and detectives to ease the tension.

Victim advocates are trained professionals who offer victims information, support, and help finding resources and assist victims with paperwork. To become a victim advocate, in most cases, a high school diploma/GED and a valid state driver's license are required. Candidates also must pass a criminal background check. Preferred qualifications include a bachelor's degree in social or behavioral science, sociology, or criminal justice or criminology. However, qualifying experience involving the provision of social services, counseling, or crisis intervention in a recognized social service program might be substituted for the required education. Other preferred qualifications often include being bilingual; direct experience in the field of victim services; and having general knowledge of the criminal justice system and community resources; crisis intervention techniques; related laws, regulations, and procedures; and current issues in the fields of domestic violence and victimology. Also, the nature of the job requires good communication skills, observing the rules of confidentiality, being able to relate to persons of various social and economic backgrounds, and flexible working hours.

In California, the following are mandatory services for all types of crimes (Villmoare & Benvenuti, 1988, p. 125).

- Interpreter services

- Field visits, when necessary

- Crisis counseling for emotional trauma

- Emergency assistance obtaining urgently needed items such as temporary shelter, food, transportation, clothing, and medical care, including prescription medicine, eyeglasses, and dentures

- Information about and referral to community resources

- Assistance filing claims with the Victims of Crime Program

- Assistance obtaining the release of property held as evidence

- Information and assistance for witnesses and victims attending a hearing including, when necessary, accompaniment to the hearing

- Information on case status and case disposition

- Notification of friends and relatives concerning the crime and the victim's condition

- Intervention with employers to provide information about the crime and to minimize the loss of pay arising from the crime or the need to serve as a witness

Although many states allow victims to have support persons at a police interview, such practice depends on officers' preference and familiarity with victim advocacy services (Hazelwood & Burgess, 2008). If a referral to services is heavily dependent on an officer's decision, it is particularly important to know how the officer values victim assistance. A survey conducted by Hatten and Moore (2010) indicated that officers find victim assistance programs to be valuable and an important resource for the community. Yet, an officer's intention to contact a victim advocate is influenced by the nature of the crime. Hatten and Moore (2010) found that if a victim is under the influence of a controlled substance, the officer is less likely to contact an advocate. Also, many officers seem to be influenced by gender; in the case of male victims, officers rarely contact an advocate.

# Different Types of Victim Services

The following sections list resources for victims who need immediate attention following victimization.

## Hotlines

**Hotline:** a 24-hour toll-free telephone line and online services for victims to get information on resources, a local shelter, and advocacy services

Most local and national victim agencies provide a **hotline** or a 24-hour toll-free telephone line and online services for victims to get information on resources, local shelters, and advocacy services. They provide immediate short-term counseling, but for long-term counseling and interventions, a hotline worker will make a referral (Masters et al., 2017). Hotlines are a critical lifeline for victims. In 2016, domestic violence hotline workers nationwide received more than 14 calls on average every minute (National Network to End Domestic Violence, 2011). Some hotlines are subdivided to help a specific type of victim. Table 5.1 shows some examples of national hotline services.

## Crisis Intervention

**Crisis intervention:** provides immediate assistance by addressing the internal and external difficulties of individuals in crisis

*Crisis* is defined as "a perception or experiencing of an event or situation as an intolerable difficulty that exceeds the person's current resources and coping mechanisms" (James & Gilliland, 2005, p. 3). The goal of **crisis intervention** is to provide immediate assistance by addressing the internal and external difficulties of individuals in crisis. The six-step model of crisis intervention includes (1) defining the problem, (2) ensuring client safety, (3) providing support, (4) examining alternatives, (5) making plans, and (6) obtaining commitment (James & Gilliland, 2005). The first three steps are the listening stage, and the last three steps are the acting stage.

Crisis intervention is becoming critical in police work. A study conducted by Luckett and Slaikeu (1990) indicates that a vast majority of calls involve crisis intervention for those who are in emotional disturbance. In response to the need of law enforcement collaboration with mental health and crisis intervention agencies, the Memphis Police Department developed the Crisis Intervention Team (CIT) in 1988 (Teller, Munetz, Gil, & Ritter, 2006). Many police departments followed and have adopted the CIT model in their department. The police are the first responders on the scene, and police officers who have received training in crisis intervention are particularly beneficial in controlling a situation before it gets worse. It is important to note that helping professionals including police officers might experience burnout and compassion fatigue. Managing their own stress and self-care will be discussed in Chapter 13.

## Child Protective Services (CPS)

**Child Protective Services (CPS):** a specialized component of the child welfare system, responsible for supporting and intervening for those children alleged to be abused, neglected, or exploited, and their families (McDaniel & Lescher, 2004)

**Child Protective Services (CPS)** is a specialized component of the child welfare system, responsible for supporting and intervening for those children alleged to be abused, neglected, or exploited and their families (McDaniel & Lescher, 2004). CPS is legally mandated by U.S. federal and state laws that outline the definitions of child abuse and neglect and the reporting responsibilities and procedures (Muscat, 2010). Also, some

## Table 5.1 Direct Services for Crime Victims—Toll-Free Numbers

| | |
|---|---|
| Americans Overseas Domestic Violence Crisis Center | 866-USWOMEN (866-879-6636) |
| Childhelp USA National Hotline | 800-4-A-CHILD (800-422-4453) |
| Disaster Distress Helpline | 800-985-5990 |
| Mothers Against Drunk Driving | 877-MADD-HELP (877-623-3435) |
| National Domestic Violence Hotline | 800-799-7233 |
| TTY Hotline | 800-787-3224 |
| National Teen Dating Abuse Helpline | 866-331-9474 |
| TTY Hotline | 866-331-8453 |
| National Organization of Parents of Murdered Children | 888-818-POMC (888-818-7662) |
| National Runaway Safeline | 800-RUNAWAY (800-786-2929) |
| National Suicide Prevention Lifeline | 800-273-8255 |
| Rape, Abuse & Incest National Network (RAINN) | 800-656-HOPE (800-656-4613) |
| Safe Phone Helpline (sexual assault support for the DoD community) | 877-995-5247 |
| Sexual Assault Support and Help for Americans Abroad | 886-USWOMEN (866-879-6636) |
| StrongHearts Native Helpline (domestic violence and dating violence support for Native Americans) | 844-7NATIVE (844-762-8483) |

*Source:* Office for Victims of Crime. https://www.ovc.gov/help/tollfree.html

local departments of social services outline regional policies and procedures (McDaniel & Lescher, 2004).

The CPS casework process is systematic and involves seven basic steps (Comstock & McDaniel, 2004). The first step is intake, which involves receiving a report or a referral. CPS screens the documents and assesses the appropriateness and urgency of the referral. During the intake, CPS will gather as much information as possible and document the information. The next step is investigation, which starts when the CPS worker contacts the child and family. CPS assesses if there is any indication of abuse or neglect and risk to the child. CPS staff makes a home visit and looks at the conditions of the home, as well as observes the relationship between the parent or the guardian and the child and other family members. The gathered information is documented. The third step is family assessment, whereby CPS works with the family to identify the family problem and determines ways to minimize the risk. The fourth step is service planning. In this stage, information about formal and informal services and resources is provided to the family, and the changes that need to occur to keep the child safe are specified. That process is followed by service provision, which involves the arrangement of services provided by other agencies and individuals. The sixth step is monitoring family progress and evaluating the case plan. CPS contacts all the service providers and has a discussion with family members to determine if the plan should be terminated or revised. The final stage is case closure, which includes the evaluation of the goal attainment and the decision to terminate or continue the services. The record of the rationale for case closure is documented. Please note that cases will be closed when the risk of maltreatment has been reduced or eliminated or the agency does not have a sufficient basis to move forward. However, family needs would still be apparent beyond the scope of the CPS system. In such circumstance, every effort should be made to help the family receive services through appropriate community agencies.

There are multiple roles for the CPS staff: (1) case manager to oversee the process; (2) collaborator to work with other service providers, family members, and community resources; (3) treatment provider and advocate to support the child and family members; and (4) administrator to keep the records of the work (Comstock & McDaniel, 2004). The partnership with law enforcement is particularly critical for CPS. The CPS workers determine which cases should be reported to law enforcement and conduct joint investigations with law enforcement to minimize the number of interviews with an alleged child victim (Comstock & McDaniel, 2004).

A number of studies have indicated that female caregivers who are involved with the CPS experience higher rates of intimate partner violence (IPV). Furthermore, those females have a much higher risk of substance abuse and depression (Flanagan, Sullivan, & Connell, 2015). Prior studies indicated that CPS workers significantly underestimate IPV victimization, substance abuse, and depression of female caregivers (Marcenko, Lyons, & Courtney, 2011; Bunger, Chuang, & McBeath, 2012), and further training opportunities might be helpful. Also, stronger referral strategies to victim service agencies would be helpful in enhancing the well-being of those females and their children (Flanagan et al., 2015). More details of the child welfare system and children in both the welfare system and juvenile justice system will be discussed in Chapter 8.

## Adult Protective Services

**Adult Protective Services (APS):** social service agencies that respond to the abuse and neglect of older adults, individuals with disabilities, and others who are at risk for mistreatment and neglect

**Adult Protective Services (APS)** responds to the abuse and neglect of older adults, individuals with disabilities, and others who are at risk for mistreatment and neglect (Stelle, 2010). APS is a statutorily based social services program funded by state and local governments. APS programs differ significantly by state or even by county in terms of the definition of elder abuse, client eligibility, the availability of resources, and the nature of reporting and investigation (Mosqueda et al., 2015). Because of such variations, a client eligible for services in one state might not receive similar services in another state (Jackson, 2017). APS is operated by the principle that adults have a right to make decisions for themselves. As such, state statutes generally require that an individual must consent before receiving the services, except in the case that a person lacks capacity or is in an emergency situation (Jackson, 2017). This could cause a dilemma for the APS caseworkers, as intervening in certain situations against victims' will could result in better outcomes rather than respecting a decision to decline services (English, 2012).

APS caseworkers are often the first responders to reports of suspected cases of abuse or neglect of vulnerable adults (Stelle, 2010). The investigative process follows the process of receiving a report of suspected abuse, provision of support, and monitoring of the individual and interventions. A report of suspected abuse could be made by mandated reporters or by community members. Then, APS caseworkers contact the victim and assess issues of competency, risk of harm, and the victim's desire for intervention. Given the gathered information about the risks, service needs, and the individual's physical and mental conditions, APS caseworkers develop a comprehensive service plan. They also coordinate with community resources such as mental health care services, legal services, and home-based services such as home health care or home modification programs. After placing clients in services, APS caseworkers monitor and evaluate the progress and may make some modifications depending on the risk and need of the clients.

There are some similarities and distinctions between APS and victim services (Jackson, 2017). Both APS and victim service agencies respond to individuals with needs, including victims of crime and victims of elder abuse. As such, there is considerable overlap among the types of services available to victims (Jackson, 2017). However, there are some significant differences in their origins and legality. APS was formed by federal policies, and APS practice is bound by state statute. In some instances, APS has an obligation to impose involuntary interventions with court approval. Those situations include older adults who lack the capacity to make decisions or in emergency situations (Jackson, 2017). APS takes proactive measures by visiting the victims and conducting face-to-face interviews in determining the situations. In contrast, nonprofit-based victim services are completely voluntary. Those service agencies are generally grounded in the empowerment philosophy and wait for victims to access their services (Jackson, 2017). In terms of the profile of workers, Balaswamy (2004) found that community-based agency workers had significantly fewer years of experience than APS caseworkers, and they were less professional (Sullivan, 2011).

A major concern in both fields is a lack of evidence-based practice, and more empirical research on the effectiveness of the interventions is necessary. Above all, collaborative efforts and cross-training, for example, integrating elder abuse themes into domestic violence training, would be beneficial to both agencies (Jackson, 2017). Different types of collaboration and service delivery models will be discussed in Chapter 14.

## Informal Supports (Family, Friends, Neighbors, and Bystanders)

Often, the important supporters for a victim in crisis are family members, friends, neighbors, and bystanders. Remember from Chapter 3 that more than half of violent victimizations are not reported to the police, and fewer than 10% of violent crime victims seek help from victim services. Rather, victims are more likely to use informal networks to ease the aftermath of a crime (Davis & Ullman, 2013). According to Davis, Lurigio, and Skogan (1999), 40% of victims across samples in four cities had been assisted by their families or friends. The most common forms of informal support include emotional support, household logistic support, and long-term assistance. Particularly, friends and family members would be a great help for taking victims to a doctor, watching children, and being cordial and listening to their stories. Those people could also encourage victims to seek help from formal services (Davis & Ullman, 2013).

It is a frequent occurrence for people who support victims also to experience some challenges. The most common problem is secondary traumatic stress caused by being exposed to another person's trauma. It is a well-known fact that helping professionals suffer from secondary trauma, but this is also true for friends, relatives, and neighbors. A study conducted by Friedman, Bischoff, Davis, and Person (1982) indicated that more than 80% of supporters of victims showed some form of secondary victimization. The same study also indicated that supporters developed a greater fear of crime. Some felt increased suspicion of people, and others felt less safe at home or on the street. Further discussion of secondary traumatic stress and compassion fatigue and the importance of self-care will be discussed in Chapter 13.

**Bystanders**, individuals who are neither victims nor perpetrators, also play a crucial role in intervening and helping victims. Research has shown that the decision to intervene in a situation is affected by situational factors and the characteristics of the victims. Latané and Nida (1981) found that bystanders were less likely to give aid if other bystanders were present. Nicksa (2014) found women tend to report sexual assault, physical assault, and theft to police more than men. However, Katz, Pazienza, Olin, and Rich (2015) did not find gender differences in intent to help in a party rape situation. The role of bystanders is particularly important in a bullying situation as bullying is more likely to occur in front of other students. Alarmingly, a study of 587 seventh- and eighth-grade students indicated that half of the students said that they did nothing when they last witnessed some of their peers being bullied, and 40% of the bystanders did not consider the bullying any of their business (Pergolizzi et al., 2009). Efforts to promote social support from peers and teachers on campus and to create schoolwide bullying prevention strategies and educate the students on the possible contributions of bystanders would be beneficial to enhance the role of bystanders in preventing school bullying.

**Bystanders:** individuals who are neither victims nor perpetrators but they saw or know about a crime that happened to someone else

## Specific Types of Victims and Law Enforcement

We have seen a wide variety of services offered to victims who need immediate attention. Yet, victims are not a unified group, and it is important to review the distinct needs and challenges of specific types of victims. This section will review the experience of victims of IPV, rape victims, bereaved victims, and hate crime victims with law enforcement and victim advocates and explore their challenges. Please note that more detailed discussions of victim assistance in victims of family violence, sexual assaults, and cyber-crime will be discussed in Part III, Impact of Crime on Victims.

# Intimate Partner Violence Victims' Experience With Law Enforcement

As seen in the case study on the following page, the response to IPV in the criminal justice system was long ignored. IPV was treated as a private matter, the police response to spousal abuse was reluctant, and complaints were likely to be ignored (Gelles & Cornell, 1990). The tumultuous decade of the 1970s changed all that. Building on the success of the civil rights movement, women's organizations began to push for their rights. In the mid-1970s, the newly formed National Organization of Women (NOW) and other organizations such as the National Coalition Against Domestic Violence, the National Organization of Victims' Assistance (NOVA), and the National Clearinghouse for the Defense of Battered Women exerted political pressure to force changes in laws (Wallace, 1998). Consequently, the U.S. Attorney General's Task Force on Family Violence recommended treating domestic violence as a crime and using an arrest-preferred response by law enforcement agencies, which was followed by the passage of the 1984 Family Violence Prevention and Services Act (Kakar, 1998).

A landmark study on the effects of police arrests was conducted by Sherman and Berk in 1984. Based on their experiment, they concluded that arresting certain domestic violence offenders was the preferred police response to deter future violence. Even though the study was criticized because of its methodological concerns and generalizability, it became the most cited study in the field and had immediate nationwide policy implications (Buzawa et al., 2017). State and local governments responded by changing laws to make arrest mandatory when probable cause exists. Although mandatory arrest and arrest-preferred policies became popular among policy makers, researchers have raised concerns about an overemphasis on the effectiveness of specific deterrence (Buzawa et al., 2017).

One new direction is to create a specialized domestic violence (DV) unit in police departments. An evaluation study of the DV unit in Charlotte, North Carolina, indicated that the unit, which aims to reduce recidivism by conducting intensive investigation and victim assistance, was associated with lower recidivism rates after controlling for the effects of arrest and jail time (Exum, Hartman, Friday, & Lord, 2014). Nonetheless, there is a debate over the effectiveness of victim assistance as to whether helping with restraining orders and developing safety plans actually empower victims (McDermott & Garofalo, 2004).

The evaluations of police attitudes and behavior toward domestic violence victims showed mixed results. Some research indicated the changes are positive (Stewart, Langan, & Hannem, 2013) and that victims viewed police as supportive, understanding, kind, and respectful (Erez & Belknap, 1998). Especially when the intervention was effective, the victim was particularly pleased with the police response.

> They were pretty nice; like they actually told him to leave the house and not to come back for a couple of days. So they did a good job with that. Like he actually left. . . . like if I would have said it he would have come back home. (Stewart et al., 2013, p. 277)

However, other studies reported victims' negative interactions with police (Stewart et al., 2013; Li, Levick, Eichman, & Chang, 2015). For example, an evaluation of mandatory arrest policies showed an unintended consequence. One area is the increased

# CASE STUDY
## Thurman v. City of Torrington (1984)

*"This is Tracy Thurman. My husband is outside again . . . he is threatening to kill me."* Tracy called the police department and urged that her abusive husband, Charles, be arrested for violation of a restraining order. When a single police officer finally arrived at the scene approximately 25 minutes after she called, Tracy had been stabbed in the chest, neck, and throat. Furthermore, Charles kicked Tracy in the head twice, once in front of their child, in the presence of the officer. Even after three more police officers arrived at the scene, they did not stop Charles from wandering about the crowd and continuing to threaten Tracy. Finally, when Charles approached Tracy again, the officers arrested him and took him into custody. Prior to the incident, Tracy had attempted multiple times to contact the police for protection, bur her voice was never taken seriously by the police. The court found deliberate police indifference and violation of

the equal protection of the law guaranteed to Tracy. The jury awarded Tracy and her son $2.3 million.

The Thurman case had a significant effect on police practice in responding to similar situations (Buzawa, Buzawa, & Stark, 2017). To avoid high-priced liability, some departments adopted pro-arrest policies. As a result of several lawsuits against police departments before and after Thurman, police departments adopted a mandatory arrest policy and began treating domestic violence as a crime, making arrests when probable cause exists without consideration of marital status.

### Questions:

1. *How has the police response changed over the past 30 years?*

2. *How would this case be handled if it happened today?*

---

number of dual charges and the female-partner-only arrests (Durfee, 2012). In some cases, the women attempted to defend themselves from male aggressors, and that resulted in an arrest. In other cases, women acted out after receiving chronic verbal and emotional abuse from their partner (Li et al., 2015). In most cases, the experience with law enforcement negatively affected women. Women who experienced an arrest not only lost faith in the police, while suffering the humiliation of the arrest and jail experience, but also experienced the loss of a job or a future job opportunity.

Victims who repeatedly have contacted the police felt that the police response to them is unfavorable. For example, a woman who called the police after a physical fight regretted the response from the officer: "[The officer] was like, 'You know, we're getting really sick and tired of coming up here. If we get called once more time, we're taking your child and you both are going to jail'" (Li et al., 2015, p. 410). Other concerns occurred when women had limited opportunity to explain their situation. Police officers who presume immigrant victims have limited language capability are more likely to communicate with White witnesses (Yen, 2000). In cases involving domestic violence with immigrant wives and White husbands, the police were inclined to take statements from the American husbands and thus failed to make proper interventions (Yen, 2000).

Although the police response to domestic violence has improved significantly since the 1980s, the need to train officers on sensitivity toward victims and cultural competency remains. More discussions of cultural competency are found in Chapter 13.

## Rape Victims

All rape victims are offered a medical exam. A **rape kit**, or sexual assault kit (SAK), is a package of items used for gathering and preserving multiple pieces of evidence. The evidence needed for an investigation is as follows (Daigle, 2013, p. 114):

**Rape kit, or sexual assault kit (SAK):** a package of items used for gathering and preserving multiple pieces of evidence from a sexual assault victim

- Foreign material swabbed from patients' bodies, including blood, semen, and saliva

- Foreign material dislodged from one's mouth with dental floss

- Loose hairs, possibly belonging to the assailant, captured by swabs, tweezers, or a towel placed under the patient during the exam

- Blood and urine samples from victims that might reveal traces of drugs or other substances slipped to the victim

A disturbing fact is that 200,000 or more untested kits remain in the police departments (Lovrich et al., 2004; Strom & Hickman, 2010). For these reasons, law enforcement agencies perceive DNA evidence as not helpful or necessary to the task of investigating a reported crime because (1) an offender had not yet been identified, (2) there are questions about the usefulness of such evidence, (3) there is no specific request from the prosecutors to test the evidence, and/or (4) there were no charges filed against an identified offender. Also, in the case of the perpetrator as a nonstranger, the identity of the offender is not in question, and as such, criminal justice stakeholders have questioned the usefulness of testing those kits. Yet, DNA can help link offenders across crimes by being uploaded into the CODIS (Combined DNA Index System) and the federal DNA criminal database. Therefore, it is important to train law enforcement personnel on the uses of DNA evidence throughout all phases of criminal proceedings, and further assistance on improving the availability, accessibility, and affordability of DNA forensic testing is crucial (Campbell, Feeney, Pierce, Sharma, & Fehler-Cabral, 2016).

In understanding the dynamics of rape cases, the interactions among law enforcement, victims, and victim advocates must be explained. Rape victim advocates are often the first responders as the first action rape victims are likely to take is to call a local rape hotline. Also, when a victim is taken to the emergency room, hospital personnel immediately call a local crisis center (Maier, 2008). The role of victim advocates is critical as the victim experience in the hospital is often traumatic and harmful. Rape victims feel a further loss of control and dignity during the administration of the rape kit, medical exam, and police questioning (Maier, 2008). In fact, an interview with rape victim advocates indicates that one fifth of victim advocates stated that the police and medical practitioners revictimize rape victims (Maier, 2008).

# CASE STUDY
## About One Third of Wisconsin's Untested Rape Kits Involve Possible Child Victims

Wisconsin Department of Justice officials recently released the figures of untested rape kits. In 2014, the authorities estimated about 6,000 rape kits were never sent to state labs for testing. Among those, the largest group was those for children under the age of 10, followed by those ages 18 to 29. About 62% of the child rape kits are scheduled for testing within two years, but the remaining ones are not scheduled for testing. The reasons for their not being scheduled for testing are similar to those for adult cases. In most cases, a person already has been convicted. Some of the other reasons are a lack of victim consent and indications that no crime happened. Attorney General Brad Schimel, who oversees the Department of Justice, believes the kits could be legally tested without victim consent—but that would violate privacy rights.

Police practice also affects the backlog. Many kits were never sent to labs because police declined to pursue investigations or because prosecutors declined to pursue charges. Those two scenarios explain nearly 42% of Wisconsin's rape kit backlog, including more than 1,000 kits involving possible child victims and more than 900 kits involving possible crimes against young adults.

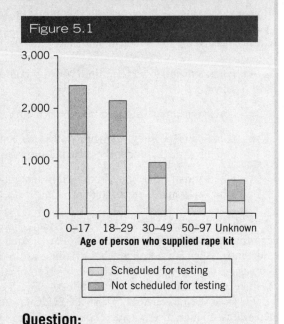

Figure 5.1

## Question:

1. *How might the victims feel if they found out that their rape kits had never been tested and had been sitting in a warehouse for many years?*

Long (2017) notes that police officers' view of rape is multifaceted. Given the effects of trainings and reforms to laws that changed the police response to rape victims, police officers no longer believe rape myths. However, the personal feelings of the officers toward rape victims rest on their own beliefs about rape (Long, 2017). It is generally considered that female police officers are more appropriate to respond to rape cases, but the research shows mixed results. Some studies show that female officers are more sympathetic to rape victims (Aderden & Ullman, 2012) and enthusiastic about working with advocates and rape victims (Rich & Seffrin, 2013). However, Wentz and Archbond (2012) found that there is no difference between female and male officers in terms of stereotypical beliefs about rape. The studies of gender difference of officers' attitudes toward rape victims indicate that female officers are worse or no better than male officers in treating rape victims (Martin, 2005; Aderden & Ullman, 2012). Therefore, Long (2017) suggests much research is necessary to examine the influence of the gender of officers on the ways that rape victims are treated.

Rape victims might experience trauma at the hospital due to long waits and experiences with doctors and nurses. Long waits are particularly problematic as victims are not able to eat or drink, use a bathroom, or change clothes for preserving evidence. A pelvic exam conducted by a male emergency room doctor is a traumatizing experience for female victims who were raped by men (Maier, 2008). A study indicated that Sexual Assault Nurse Examiner (SANE) nurses are better able to serve rape victims than non-SANE doctors as victims receive more prompt care from SANE nurses (Crandall & Helitzer, 2003; Martin, 2003).

In reflecting their experience with police officers and medical examiners, victim advocates suggest that the automatic presence of an advocate in the emergency room is important as victims might not be adequately informed about available services by nurses or doctors. Victim advocates could empower victims by expressing they believe victims, stressing that the crime committed against them was not their fault, and allowing victims to make their own decisions (Maier, 2008).

## Bereaved Victims

**Bereaved victims,** or family members and friends who lost a significant other to homicide, experience substantial distress because the loss is so sudden, and they cannot stop imagining the throes of dying and severe fear that the loved one experienced in his or her last moments. Also, bereaved victims often feel guilty as they mourn, thinking that they could have done something to save the victim's life (Zinzow, Thompson, & Rheingold, 2013). The anniversary of the day of death, holidays, birthdays, or any other days that are related to the memories of the loved one are a particularly hard time for bereaved victims.

> The empty chair. It's there at the table, and everything else . . . the turkey, family members, the Christmas tree, presents, everything else disappears. All you see is that empty chair. (Front Range, http://www.colorado-pomc.org)

Research indicates that homicide survivors are more likely to have higher post-traumatic stress disorder (PTSD) symptoms than victims of other interpersonal violence (Zinzow, Rheingold, Byczkiewicz, Saunders, & Kilpatrick, 2011). Parents whose children died by homicide are significantly more impacted by PTSD outcomes than parents who lost their children from accidents or suicide. The same study also reported that marital satisfaction of parents bereaved by homicide is lower than other groups (Murphy, Johnson, Wu, Fan, & Lohan, 2003). A study of a nationally representative sample of adolescents of homicide survivors in the United States showed that homicide survivors were at risk for depression, drug use, and alcohol abuse; therefore, the authors suggest the need for awareness, assessment,

**Bereaved victims:** family members and friends who have lost a significant other to homicide

# Victim Assistance Programs

## Colorado Front Range, Chapter of the Parents of Murdered Children

The Parents of Murdered Children (POMC) is a national organization dedicated to providing support and assistance to all survivors of homicide victims. Dan Levey, POMC's executive director, has been serving as an advocate for victims' rights since 1996, when his brother Howard was murdered. As of 2017, POMC had local chapters in 21 states. These local chapters hold monthly meetings and provide support for the families and friends of those who have died by violence. For example, Front Range, a chapter in Colorado, supports persons who survive the violent death of someone close; provides contact with similarly bereaved persons and establishes self-help groups that meet regularly; provides information about the grieving process and the criminal justice system; communicates with professionals in the helping fields about the problems faced by those surviving a homicide victim; and increases society's awareness of these problems. Front Range publishes a newsletter every other month in which it announces the meeting schedule and in memoria of the names of victims and birthdays remembered. See http://www.colorado-pomc.org for more information.

and treatment of the significant mental health needs of homicide survivors within clinical and criminal justice settings (Rheingold, Zinzow, Hawkins, Saunders, & Kilpatrick, 2012).

Telling someone about the death of a loved one is not an easy task. When a murder occurs, such a painful message is delivered in person by medical personnel, coroners, or medical examiners; law enforcement officers; spiritual leaders; social service workers; or victim advocates (Masters et al., 2017). In many cases, detectives accompany a victim service counselor to make the notification to the next-of-kin (Goodrum, 2007). To support the victims in crisis, victim advocates will provide emotional support and information about how the death occurred, accompany parties to identify the victim, and assist with funeral arrangements (Masters et al, 2017).

There is a stark contrast in the approach to the case between detectives and bereaved victims. Detectives will act as professionals, pursuing a murder case in an orderly manner, with a systematic, objective, and unemotional manner. Normally, given prior experience, detectives often first suspect the victim's relatives, bereaved victims, friends, and acquaintances. In contrast, bereaved victims are emotional and feel shock, distraught, and disbelief (Goodrum, 2007).

The bereaved victims can also encounter further emotional difficulties. The first challenge is over the body of the murdered victim. Bereaved victims are usually emotionally upset and want to see the body of the loved one immediately. Seeing and touching the body is a basic social psychological function in the bereavement process (Goodrum, 2007). For example, a mother whose 19-year-old son was deceased expressed the following:

> I really wanted to go into my house and see my son. I at least [wanted to] say goodbye to him [for] the last time. But no, they wouldn't let you. . . .

I guess they have to follow policy or whatever, but it's hard because [I] didn't get to see my [son]. He was frozen [when I finally saw him at the funeral home], so that makes it harder. That makes it a lot harder. (Goodrum, 2007, p. 739)

However, detectives perceive the body as critical evidence and attempt to maintain the integrity of the murder scene. As such, they will limit bereaved victims' contact with the deceased's body. A murder detective explained his duty as follows:

Our sole responsibility is to find who committed that crime. . . . I don't [usually] talk to the [bereaved victim] right off the bat. . . . My priority when I get to the scene is to make sure that the scene is being preserved properly. (Goodrum, 2007, p. 741)

Another challenge is the victim's desire to get information about the case from law enforcement. Bereaved victims want to be informed about the case, the manner of the death, and the status of the murder investigation. Law enforcement and victim advocates feel that balancing the demands of victims for case information and law enforcement's obligation to solve the murder is not easy. Also, some victims are frustrated when they provide information about the death, suspects, and evidence, but the detectives dismiss such information as unimportant. To reduce some of the tension between victims and law enforcement, victim advocates could carefully explain the investigative procedures and the reasons why some of the information cannot be released to the victims.

## Hate Crime Victims

A **hate crime** is defined as "a criminal offense that is motivated by personal prejudice and directed at others because of their perceived race, ethnicity, sexual orientation, gender, gender identity, religion or disability" (Office for Victims of Crime, 2017, p.1). According to the FBI Hate Crime Statistics in 2016, there were 7,615 victims of hate crimes reported to the police. The statistics show that more than half (58.9%) of the hate crime victimization was due to the offenders' race/ethnicity/ancestry bias. The second most common motivation for hate crime was religious bias, which accounted for 21.1% of the total, and the third bias category was sexual orientation–related bias (16.7%). Nearly two thirds (62%) of hate crime offenses were committed against persons, and 36.9% were against property. About 1% were victims of crimes against society (U.S. Department of Justice, Federal Bureau of Investigation, 2017).

The impact of hate crime on victims is much more severe than of similar crimes without bias in several ways. First, as the perpetrators have attacked the victims on the basis of their core, immutable identity, the aftermath for the victims involves more severe crisis. Research indicates that hate crime victims experience more distress (Herek, Gillis, & Cogan, 1999) and fear (McDevitt, Balboni, Garcia, & Gu, 2001) than those who were attacked in similar non-hate-motivated crimes. Second, the hate-crime

**Hate crime:** a criminal offense that is motivated by personal prejudice and directed at others because of their perceived race, ethnicity, sexual orientation, gender, gender identity, religion or disability (Office for Victims of Crime, 2017, p.1)

victims feel increasingly vulnerable due to the fact that the offenders hate something that the victim cannot change. Third, the victims are fearful of a repeat attack and retaliation after reporting such a crime. This is a particular concern among LGBTQ persons whose identity becomes readily visible after reporting a crime (Herek et al., 1999). In addition to direct victimization, victims might also experience secondary victimization by interacting with criminal justice professionals, media, neighbors, and co-workers. Hate crimes could possibly increase intergroup tensions, which might result in a retaliatory attack, and the community itself could suffer from stigma, fear, and insecurity through bias crimes (National Center for Hate Crime Prevention, Education Development Center, 2000).

The role of law enforcement officials is critical as they protect vulnerable groups and individuals from further victimization. When interviewing the victims, the officer must be particularly sensitive to using appropriate terminology and words. The victims might be intimidated if the officers' attitude is victim-blaming or intrusive or if officers use personal value judgments. When interviewing the victims, the officers must be cautious to avoid questions such as "Are you gay?" or "Was this a bias crime?" but rather ask the reasons why this happened to the victim and why the perpetrator was motivated to attack the victim.

When assisting victims of hate crimes, victim advocates must acknowledge the significant nature of the crimes on victims and address the victims' feelings and trauma. The safety of victims is paramount, and victim advocates should assist in creating a safety plan for the victims. When referring victims to service agencies, advocates must be conscious about the cultural background of the victims and select culturally appropriate services. Advocates should familiarize themselves with the laws and medical and legal systems in the jurisdiction. Most important, hate crimes affect the entire community. Victim advocates could take the lead in organizing a community response, raising public awareness, and showing support for both the victims and the community.

The following is a list of culturally appropriate counseling guidelines:

- Provide appropriate emotional support services to victims

- Identify potential issues in interviewing victims

- Use interpreters and translators

- Understand the victim's cultural history of oppression

- Observe differences in cultural considerations of time and space

- Recognize the importance of spiritual values

- Work effectively with the family and friends of the victim

- Understand the role of the victim assistance professional

- Understand the role of institution or agency

(*Source:* National Center for Hate Crime Prevention, Education Development Center, 2000)

# SUMMARY

In this chapter, we studied police operation and victims' involvement with the initial stage of the criminal justice system. The role of police is to respond to calls, investigate cases, and apprehend suspects. But, we also learned that police do crisis intervention for those who are in emotional disturbance. Nowadays, many police departments have a CIT to work with local mental health agencies in responding to those individuals in crisis more effectively. As a first responder, in the initial contact with a victim, particular attention needs to be paid to victims who are helpless and frightened, emotionally overwhelmed, and concerned about their involvement in the criminal justice system.

This chapter also covered a wide variety of victim assistance and human service agencies. There is significant overlap in the services provided between nonprofit-based victim assistance and CPS and APS. However, some distinctive differences must be understood. Although CPS and APS are involuntary interventions, the interventions conducted by nonprofit-based victim assistance are all voluntary. The functions of CPS and APS are statutorily regulated. For better coordination, agencies should understand that functions and cross-training would be particularly beneficial.

Many challenges remain for victims who interact with the criminal justice system. This chapter highlighted the distinct needs and concerns of victims of intimate partner abuse, rape victims, and bereaved victims. To some extent, the conflicts between victims and police are inevitable as their goals and perceptions about the case are completely different. The goal of the police is to solve the case and apprehend the suspect, whereas the case is more personal for victims, and sometimes they have unrealistic expectations for criminal justice agencies. The role of victim advocates is particularly critical to fill the gaps and explain to victims the role and processes of the criminal justice system while emotionally supporting those in crisis.

# KEY WORDS

Adult protective services
  (APS)  84
Bereaved victims  91
Bystanders  86

Child protective services
  (CPS)  82
Community-oriented policing
  (COP)  77
Crisis intervention  82

Hate crime  93
Hotlines  82
Modus operandi (MO)  79
Rape kit  89

# INTERNET RESOURCES

**Federal Law Enforcement Training Centers (FLETC) Victim-Witness Program (https://www .fletc.gov/victim-witness-program)**

The FLETC Victim-Witness Program is designed to serve as a resource for federal law enforcement officers who assist victims of crime. The website provides useful links to national and international Internet resources to assist victims of crime primarily for federal law enforcement officers but is also beneficial for anyone who works with crime victims.

**Office of Community-Oriented Policing Services (COPS Office) (https://cops.usdoj.gov)**

The Office of Community-Oriented Policing Services (COPS Office) has been dedicated to advancing community policing since 1994 as a component of the U.S. Department of Justice. The website provides information on grant programs that aim to enhance community policing efforts, useful resources on community policing topics, and training opportunities for law enforcement and communities.

**National Organization for Victim Assistance (NOVA) (https://www.trynova.org)**

The National Organization for Victim Assistance (NOVA) is the oldest national victim assistance organization in the United States that provides victim advocacy, education, and credentials. NOVA responds to the plight of people, for example, offering free educational webinars to anyone affected by the Las Vegas shooting on coping with common reactions to such a traumatic event.

## CRITICAL THINKING QUESTIONS

1. Discuss victims' involvement in the early stage of the criminal justice system. What are some reasons why victims would feel revictimized?

2. The community-oriented policing model would create a good relationship between community members and the police. Identify some of the community issues in your neighborhood and how the COP model could resolve those issues.

3. Identify some challenges of bereaved victims. If you were a victim advocate, how would you assist those victims?

4. Discuss why the impact of hate crime on victims is much more severe than that of similar crimes without bias. If you were a bystander of a hate crime, what would you do?

# The Court Process and Victim Assistance

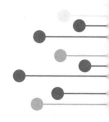

Adjudication is the stage in which victims are granted many rights. A majority of states recognize that the victims have the right to be treated with dignity, respect, and sensitivity throughout the criminal justice proceedings, but that right is particularly relevant to the sentencing stage in which victims make a statement about how the crime has affected their lives. In most states, victims have the right to be informed about court dates, the time, the location, and available services. Victims also have the right to apply for compensation and receive restitution from offenders to recover financial losses caused by the crime. This chapter discusses the criminal justice trial proceedings in the United States and how victims can exercise their rights. Note that the procedures and practices of the court system and the scope of victims' rights differ by state. Therefore, it is impossible to account for all the differences. Yet, in addressing each stage of the common court process, we can evaluate the controversial issues around victims' rights and determine in which areas victims can be better supported.

## The Court Process

### Booking

After an arrest is made, the suspect is taken to a police station or jail for booking. **Booking** is the official process of recording the suspect's information and taking him into custody. Fingerprints and photographs of the suspect are taken, and personal information and criminal history of the arrestee are documented. In the case of minor offenses such as traffic violations, a citation might be issued rather than holding a person in detention. After the booking process is completed, the case is referred to the prosecutor. The prosecutor, who is sometimes called the district attorney, decides what charge(s) will be brought against the accused. In determining specific charges, the prosecutor gathers evidence of the crime, which includes the arrest report, and makes inquiries of the arresting officers and detectives. The prosecutor might also interview the victim and other witnesses to get further information about what happened at the crime scene. The prosecutor has considerable discretion in determining what crimes to charge, whether the crime would be a misdemeanor or a felony, or whether to charge at all. A crime victim does not have the right to drop the charges once a criminal prosecution has begun. The **victim and witness assistance programs** offered by the prosecutor's office will be discussed later in this chapter.

**Booking:** an arrestee is taken to the police station or jail, and personal information, alleged charge(s), fingerprints, and photographs are recorded

**Victim and Witness Assistance Programs:** programs that provide information on rights and services to victims and witnesses, and encourage victims to participate in the criminal justice system to the extent they wish

## Initial Appearance

**Initial Appearance:** the defendant's appearance before a magistrate or a judge in a reasonable period after his or her arrest

Once the arrestee is formally charged, he or she is brought before a magistrate or a judge usually within 48 hours. This first adjudication step is called an **initial appearance** whereby the defendant is informed of the charge(s) against him or her and notified of his or her constitutional rights. In most misdemeanor cases, the defendant is asked to make a plea at this point. A plea is a statement of formal denial or admission of guilt. To plead guilty means that a person admits to all the charges. When the defendant pleads guilty, a sentence will be handed down by the judge or magistrate in most misdemeanor cases. Common sentences for misdemeanor cases are jail time, fines, community service, program placement, or probation. There is also an option for *nolo contendere*, which means that the defendant does not admit to the charges but will not dispute them in criminal court. When a defendant pleads not guilty, the judge will set a trial date (Masters et al., 2017).

## Bail Hearing

**Bail:** the money or equivalent property put up to secure the release of the defendant while he or she is awaiting the trial

**Bail** is the money or equivalent property put up to secure the release of the defendant while he or she is awaiting the trial. The purpose of bail is to ensure the defendant will appear before the court and to protect the public. Those defendants who do not have sufficient money to pay the bail may use a bail bond agent, who charges a percentage to act as a surety for their bail. In most states, defendants can be released on their own recognizance, which is a written promise to appear in court.

The prosecutor makes recommendations to the judge as to whether bail should be granted and, if so, the appropriate amount. In doing so, the prosecutor might ask the victim to determine the level of injury and the potential risks to him or her if the defendant is released. Yet, the judge has the authority to make the final decision. The judge will take into consideration the seriousness of the crime, prior criminal history, and the probability of the defendant returning to court, as well as other factors, in setting the amount (Villmoare & Benvenuti, 1988).

In most states, victims have the right to be informed when the defendant is released prior to trial, but only a few states allow victims to attend, be heard, and or be consulted during the proceedings. To ensure the victims' and public safety, some jurisdictions use an electronic device to monitor the location of the defendant in the community. Such technology is mostly used in cases of stalking, domestic violence, and sexual assault (Rennison & Dodge, 2018).

## Plea Bargaining

**Plea bargain:** a negotiated agreement among the defendant, the prosecutor, and the court

The criminal proceedings are more extensive and complicated for a serious felony crime case. But, keep in mind that nearly 90% of felony cases are settled with a plea bargain rather than going to trial (Fishe, 2000). A **plea bargain** is a negotiated agreement among the defendant, the prosecutor, and the court. When the defendant agrees to plead guilty, certain charges against the defendant may be reduced or dropped. Or in another circumstance, the defendant might agree to plead guilty in exchange for a certain type of sentence. Plea bargaining has pros and cons for the victims. On one hand, a plea bargain reduces court congestion and makes it possible for a speedy trial. It also reduces the burden on victims as they no longer need to go to court to provide testimony, and it assures the conviction of the defendant. On the other hand, many victims feel uneasy and that an injustice has occurred knowing that the charges have been reduced or dropped for the crimes committed against them (Villmoare & Benvenuti, 1988).

The level of involvement of victims in the plea bargaining process differs by state. In at least 22 states, the prosecutors are required to consult with victims about plea bargaining. Some states, such as Georgia and Illinois, allow victims to submit a written victim impact statement before entering a plea bargain agreement. In Arizona, victims are permitted to be present and heard during any settlement discussions (Crime Victims' Institute Sam Houston State University Criminal Justice Center, 2005). Yet, victims do not have the right to control or stop the negotiation or to veto the agreement (National Center for Victims of Crime, 2002a).

## Preliminary Hearing/Grand Jury

Unless the defendant pleads guilty, various pretrial activities happen before the trial. The next step is to determine whether there is enough evidence to hold a person for trial. Depending on the jurisdiction, it is processed by a preliminary hearing or a grand jury. A **preliminary hearing** is a common practice in the United States (Masters et al., 2017). In a preliminary hearing, a judge determines whether there is sufficient evidence or if probable cause exists to believe that a crime has been committed by the defendant. If the judge fails to find probable cause, the case will be dismissed. If the judge finds probable

> **Preliminary hearing:** a hearing that determines if sufficient evidence exists to allow charges to be passed against the defendant

## CASE STUDY
### Ariel Castro Agreed to Plead Guilty in a Deal to Avoid the Death Penalty

Ariel Castro, who was accused of kidnapping and three counts of rape for holding three women captive in his home for nearly a decade, agreed to plead guilty in a deal to avoid the death penalty. He was sentenced to life in prison without the possibility of parole, but one month into his sentence, he committed suicide in his jail cell. Three women, ages 14, 16, and 20 years old, disappeared separately from 2002 to 2004 in Cleveland, Ohio. They were held captive in his home for about a decade. During that time, the women were chained in the basement, repeatedly assaulted, and raped. When they attempted to

escape, he severely punished them. He starved one woman until she had a miscarriage. On May 6, 2013, one woman escaped while Castro was away from home and went to a neighbor's house to call 911. "Help me, I've been kidnapped, and I've been missing for 10 years. And I'm here. I'm free now."

### Question:

1. *Assess the pros and cons of the pre-bargaining outcomes in the Ariel Castro case. Do you agree to the use of plea bargaining in heinous crimes like this?*

cause, the case moves to a trial. Then, the prosecutor issues a formal accusation of a crime based on the findings of the preliminary hearing.

All the defendants in federal felony cases are entitled to a grand jury, but the practice of a grand jury in state cases varies; in some states, grand juries are required to be seated in certain circumstances. In other states, prosecutors have discretion to decide whether a grand jury is used (Masters et al., 2017). A grand jury, which consists of a group of citizens, hears the evidence presented by a prosecutor and determines whether sufficient evidence exists to hold a person for trial but does not determine if the defendant is guilty. If a grand jury finds that probable cause exists, it produces an indictment, which is a document formally listing the charges against the defendant.

## Arraignment

Once the indictment or information is filed, the defendant is arraigned in court. In this hearing, the defendant is formally informed of the specific charges against him or her. Then, he or she is asked to enter a plea. Similar to the previously mentioned misdemeanor cases, the defendant enters a plea of guilty, not guilty, or *nolo contendere*. Many felony cases are resolved at the **arraignment**.

**Arraignment:** the defendant appears before a court and is notified of the formal charges and informed of his or her rights. Then, the defendant makes an admission of denial or guilt

## Trial

A trial could take place as a bench trial or a jury trial. In a bench trial, a judge acts as the fact finder and makes a ruling on guilt or innocence. In a jury trial, a judge is the "arbiter of the law," who decides issues of law, and the jury is the "trier of fact," which determines whether the evidence establishes guilt (Villmoare & Benvenuti, 1988).

The major players in a bench trial are the judge, the prosecutor, and the defense attorneys. The judge has significant authority during the trial to ensure the functionality of the courtroom and oversee the trial proceedings. The judge is responsible for determining appropriate conduct, deciding whether evidence may be introduced, ruling on various motions the attorneys make, and ensuring correct procedure (Rennison & Dodge, 2018).

The prosecutor is the representative of the state or of the United States in prosecuting the criminal. The prosecutor is known as the most powerful figure in the criminal justice system due to his or her enormous discretion, including the discretion as to whether to drop charges against the defendant. The decision to drop charges either before or during a trial is called *nolle prosequi,* which means to "be unwilling to pursue" in Latin (Masters et al., 2017). Most of the time, the prosecutor is the primary contact for the victim (Villmoare & Benvenuti, 1988). The extent of the prosecutor's interactions with victims depends on the circumstance of the crime, the significance of the victim as a witness in the case, and individual prosecutors. The prosecutors usually explain the court proceedings and review the testimony to be provided by the witnesses. In addition, a victim assistance center will help find various services for victims and witnesses, such as transportation and child care, and escort victims and witnesses to the courtroom. More detailed services offered to victims and witnesses will be discussed later in this chapter.

The defense attorney represents the rights and interests of the defendant. The Sixth Amendment of the U.S. Constitution requires that those who are accused of a crime have a right to be represented by an attorney. As such, criminal defendants who cannot afford an attorney have a public defender or free, court-appointed counsel. The defense attorney is not prohibited from communicating with the victim. Although the victim is not obligated to discuss the case with the defense attorney, the defense attorney has a right to cross-examine the victim (Villmoare & Benvenuti, 1988).

Criminal defendants have a right to have their cases tried before a jury. In most jurisdictions, jurors must be U.S. citizens age 18 or older who are proficient in English and who are physically capable of sitting through the trial (Masters et al., 2017). Death penalty trials and federal cases require 12 jurors, but the number of jurors in state cases could differ; it could be 12 members or six members. The first step in a jury trial is to assemble the venire, or the pool of potential jurors, from the community. In the jury selection, called *voir dire,* prospective jurors are questioned in court under oath by the judge, the prosecutor, and the defense attorney. Jurors who might be biased against the prosecution or the defendant, for example, a relative of the victim, would be excused from the pool. During the trial, jurors are instructed by the judge on the law that they must follow. After all the evidence is presented to the jurors, the judge reminds the jurors again to be objective and impartial (Rennison & Dodge, 2018). Jurors are removed from the courtroom to select a jury foreperson, deliberate, and reach a verdict.

Any victim could be requested to testify at these hearings. Those victims and witnesses who are required to appear in court are informed in advance by a **subpoena**, which is a written order stating the time and place of appearance. Victims should know that not obeying a subpoena is a violation of a court order and makes them subject to immediate arrest. A victim subpoenaed to appear as a witness should consult with the prosecutor or a victim assistance center for assistance. The victim will be sworn to tell the truth and directed to sit in the witness chair. The victim will be questioned by the prosecutor, and then the defense attorney cross-examines the victim (Masters et al., 2017).

**Subpoena:** a written order stating the time and place of appearance

As a witness, victims should adhere to the following advice (Villmoare & Benvenuti, 1988):

*Tell the truth.* If a witness is telling the truth, he or she should have nothing to fear from an aggressive cross-examination. If the witness does not know an answer or does not remember, he or she should say so.

*Pay attention to the questions.* A witness should clearly understand a question before attempting to answer it and can ask for clarification.

*Pause briefly to think about the answer before responding.* The witness should take a second to collect his or her thoughts to ensure that the answer is correct and not misleading in any way. Any incorrect statement that might be made inadvertently should be corrected as soon as the mistake is realized.

*Provide only the information that is requested.* Do not elaborate or attempt to add color or detail beyond what is specifically asked for. Should an attorney object to a question, the witness should not respond until the judge has stated his opinion as to the objection.

*Remain calm.* In some situations, the attorney might become argumentative or attempt to elicit an emotional response from a witness. This is typically a ploy to get a witness to overreact. The witness should refrain from showing anger.

Finally, it is recommended that witnesses should not look at the prosecuting attorney or any other specific person in the courtroom.

## Sentencing

The last stage of the adjudication process is sentencing. Sentencing could happen right after the trial or it could be scheduled for a later date. The victim has the right to be notified of all sentencing proceedings—the date, time, and location, and final sentence or disposition (Office of Victims of Crime, n.d.).

There are five primary goals in sentencing: retribution, incapacitation, deterrence, rehabilitation, and restoration. In most cases, a sentence encompasses multiple goals (Masters et al., 2017). The notion of **retribution** is that punishment is "justifiable" or deserved given the seriousness of the crime that the offender committed. While retribution focuses on a crime that already has happened, **deterrence** is future oriented: The goal is to prevent a future crime by sending a message that crime does not pay. **Incapacitation** is to disable offenders from committing a future crime, mostly through imprisonment. The goal of **rehabilitation** is to teach offenders skills and to address the needs of the offenders so that they will not commit crime in the future. **Restoration** is most closely related to crime victims and their family. As the crime already has happened and cannot be undone, the focus is on restoring the harm done to victims, family, and friends of victims and the community. Restoration could be achieved by paying restitution or by doing community service (Rennison & Dodge, 2018).

Research indicates that victims are not necessarily punitive toward their offenders. According to the National Survey of Victims' Views, which consists of a nationally representative sample of 3,165 people across the country, of more than 800 victims who were identified and interviewed, 6 in 10 victims prefer shorter prison sentences and more spending on prevention and rehabilitation to prison sentences (Alliance for Safety and Justice, 2016). The same study also shows that 1 in 3 victims prefer holding people accountable through options beyond just prison, such as rehabilitation, mental health treatment, drug treatment, community supervision, or community service. However, such views might not be consistent across all types of crime victims. A study of 174 adult crime victims (rape and nonsexual assault) conducted in Germany found low support for rehabilitation among the victims (Orth, 2003).

## Victim Involvement in the Court Process

### Victim Impact Statements (VISs)

One of the crucial rights of crime victims is to participate in the criminal justice proceedings. The idea of **victim impact statements** (VISs) was first formulated in 1976

**Retribution:** sentencing goal that considers punishment as justifiable or deserved given the seriousness of the crime that the offender committed

**Deterrence:** sentencing goal that discourages offenders and the general public from committing crime

**Incapacitation:** sentencing goal that disables offenders from committing a crime, mostly through imprisonment

**Restoration:** sentencing goal that focuses on restoring the harm done to victims, family, and friends of victims and the community

**Rehabilitation:** goal is to teach offenders skills and to address the needs of the offenders so that they will not commit crime in the future

by James Rowland, who was the chief probation officer in Fresno County, California (Schuster & Propen, 2010). He advocated that victims should have a voice in court, and his notion was quickly accepted by other jurisdictions. Following the Federal Omnibus Victim and Witness Protection Act, which made it possible to consider victim impact statements in federal criminal cases in 1982, many states followed by passing their own VIS laws. Now all 50 states have some form of VIS laws to address when and how to submit VISs (National Center for Victims of Crime, 2002b).

The format of the VIS can be a written statement, a sworn or unsworn oral presentation, or even a prerecorded audio or video statement, and it commonly addresses the harm or trauma, the economic loss or damage to victims as a result of the crime, and a victim's reaction to the proposed sentence or disposition (Schuster & Propen, 2010). A VIS can be submitted by the direct victims or by family members and friends who are indirectly affected by the crime (Daigle, 2013). According to the National Crime Victim Law Institute (2010), in many states, including Alabama, Kentucky, and Arizona, the VISs are submitted to the probation officer for the presentence investigation report (PSI). Other states, for example, Wisconsin, have statutes that specify the victim must present a statement in court or submit a written statement to be read in court (Wis. Stat. Ann. $972.14(3)(a)). In Texas, a VIS must be presented after the sentence is pronounced (Tex. Code Crim. Proc. Ann. Art 42.03).

VISs have potential benefits for crime victims in many ways. Under the adversarial system, victims are not considered a party to the proceedings (Ashworth, 2002), therefore victims are likely to feel that they are marginalized from the system. VISs give an opportunity for the court to acknowledge the victim with dignity (Erez & Roberts, 2013). Victims would feel more ownership over the case by speaking in their own words about their experience with victimization, and it could increase satisfaction with the criminal justice process (Englebrecht & Chavez, 2014). Erez (1990) noted that VISs help victims recover from the trauma associated with victimization and the court experience. VISs also provide judges and prosecutors with additional information that can be helpful in determining a sentence and setting the amount of restitution (Erez & Rogers, 1999).

Although VISs have been widely accepted as one of the important instruments to enhance victims' participation within the criminal justice system, the premises of VISs have been debated. Davis and Smith (1994) found that a VIS had no impact on victims' satisfaction with the criminal justice process or its outcome. Furthermore, victims were even dissatisfied if their recommendations were not reflected in sentencing (Davis, Henley, & Smith, 1990). Lens et al. (2015) found that a VIS had no direct therapeutic effects but that feelings of anger and anxiety were stabilized after delivering a VIS. Bandes (1999) asserts that making a VIS can be a traumatizing experience for victims. There is disagreement as to whether victim participation at the sentencing stage increases the severity of sentences. An early study by Erez and Tontodonato (1992) found that defendants in cases in which a VIS was presented were more likely to be sentenced to prison rather than probation. Similarly, some studies have found that a VIS increases the severity of the sentence (Paternoster & Deise, 2011; Myers, Roop, Kalnen, & Kehn, 2013). Yet, others found no or marginal effects (Davis & Smith, 1994; Erez & Roeger, 1995; Erez & Laster, 1999). There are also some concerns regarding the emotionality of the statements presented in court (Ewick & Silbey, 1995; Reisner & Nelligan, 2002; Schuster & Propen, 2010; Booth, 2012).

**Victim impact statements (VIS):** the format of the VIS could be a written statement, a sworn or unsworn oral presentation, or even a prerecorded audio or video statement, and it commonly addresses the harm or trauma, the economic loss or damage to victims as a result of the crime, and a victim's reaction to the proposed sentence or disposition (Schuster & Propen, 2010)

# Victim Impact Statement

Your honor, members of the audience, and defendant,

It is both an honor and privilege to be standing in front of you today. The fact that I made it out of this modern-day hell alive is truly a blessing. The more I reflect on the pain and suffering I had experienced, the more I realize how much of a responsibility I carry to deliver this impact statement. You see, the burden rests on my shoulders because there are those victims who have suffered far greater crimes than I have, and yet, didn't receive the opportunity to speak. And to those victims and their families, I say that justice isn't exactly justice. When someone like myself is victimized, there isn't a parade filled with gifts waiting on me for my return. I entered a second victimization: the return to normalcy. It's a near impossible task, but with the right people, it gets easier each day.

*******

Education played the largest factor in my journey to freedom. Something that I cherished all my life was taken away from me, spit on, and came with a constant reminder from the defendant that "I was never good enough" and that "my family never loved me." The fact that I was able to successfully complete school was one of the most rewarding accomplishments of my life because the defendant instilled in me that I would never be able to complete this feat. As proud as I am, I want to stress that those who experienced the trauma at the same level as mine may have not received the same opportunities that I had. It is for this reason that I believe federal funding needs to be given to community colleges to provide an incentive for those victimized in trafficking to pursue a degree in criminal justice. As great as a trend it is to see trafficked victims to pursue a degree in cosmetology, or social service, more education among criminal justice employees needs to be done in order to better serve our members of the community looking to return to normalcy, just as much as we victims strive to. I also believe that training among private corporations is necessary in order for

employees at all areas of management to be able to identify the signs of abuse.

I know many of you, including your honor, are probably thinking the same thing: Well, if Suleman can speak so eloquently (and look good doing it), why do we need to worry about what happens to the defendant or if he should even be sentenced? Well, let me tell you why:

This man is what we call a "generational trafficker." What this means is that this individual goes out of his way to attack people at different points in their life, as well as different time periods. No, this man is not a time traveler, but his actions absolutely reflect that. When we take myself and my family out of the equation, we still have 4 more people victimized in this country. I know we can't speculate here, but there's a safe bet that this man victimized additional people back in his home country.

By waiting weeks for victim advocates to contact me regarding the status of the case, or answering questions on specific incidents during the victimization at inappropriate times, I have learned the art of patience and discretion, something absent with the individuals I have dealt with throughout this process. As thankful as I am for everyone who helped me in this process, I want to stress that we should all learn a lesson from this specific case, as it serves as a time-stamp for where our community stands on the subject of trafficking. However, I want to say my true patience exists from the actions of the defense . . . seeing defense attorneys coming and going to pick up a paycheck from the defendant, which in-turn derives from the victims he's enslaved, truly disappoints me. I guess it is ironic that I have been able to withstand every question asked toward me while on the record, as I am technically paying for these men to yell and object to things I have to say. But that subject is for another time. I guess I'm beating around the bush. You see, the issue isn't defense attorneys profiting off of trauma, my concern relies within the court system to grant motions for continuances without regard for defendants who are held without bail. This is completely contradictory and something I feel we as a society should explore further. The message you send to taxpayers is this: "this individual is way too dangerous to put on the streets, but I'm not going to resolve this no-bail situation because I don't see it as a priority right now." Ouch.

********

Yes, I've driven myself toward contemplating suicide on many occasions since I escaped. There have been many days where I let you win and get the better of this situation. But it came to a point where I realized that I no longer live for myself, but I live to serve others, especially the people you victimized, because we both know it never started and ended with just me. You did a phenomenal job in breaking me. You found a way to pinpoint every weakness I had and succeeded in isolating me from all aspects of human contact. The fact that I had to beg to use my own passport to complete the hiring process for a job that I worked at to give you every paycheck is supreme control. You effortlessly did everything in your power to kill me, yet, miraculously, I'm still alive. I'd give you a participation trophy for trying, but it's probably considered contraband for the place you're heading. You see, I spent years asking myself why I didn't escape sooner, why couldn't I have been able to read your next move, or even why couldn't I have trusted people to help me. I learned over the years that I've spent too much time asking the wrong questions. It isn't the "why" that matters. There's no logical justification to any of this. Instead, we as a society should be asking ourselves "How can we prevent these crimes from happening?"

I hope the court makes an example out of you to show former, current, and future victims of crime what pure evil truly looks like. I had to sit here for the last few months, answering question after question, helping to decipher what was reality, and what was the fiction that you created. I am hoping that my time here helped to clarify all of this. I am well aware that you did everything you possibly could to hold out, by electing to not take a plea deal, and waste the court's time claiming innocence. But through the hell you put me through, I'm resilient and immune to your destruction.

For those who were directly involved in helping me through my victimization, I think it can be understood that I don't wish those injuries and mental trauma on my worst enemy, because it is a death sentence. As professional as I have remained throughout these proceedings, I want to be clear that my kindness should not be taken for weakness. If there's anything I have learned from coming back to normalcy, it is this: "Success is the best revenge."

I once again would like to thank everyone who made it out here today to hear me speak. I know it must have not been easy considering the time that had to be taken off to listen to something that happened four years ago. I'd also like to thank anyone who reads this transcript. Access to information is really the right start to implement change no matter who we are or where we come from.

*The statement is reprinted with permission from Suleman Masood.*

## Victim Impact Statements in Death Penalty Cases

The use of VISs in death penalty cases has been even more controversial. But before discussing the constitutional issues of VIS in capital cases, it is important to know how the proceedings of capital cases differ from noncapital criminal trials. In a capital case, prosecutors are required to file a notice of their intent to seek the death penalty in the case. During *voir dire*, attorneys ascertain whether prospective jurors are suitable to serve on death penalty cases. The trial is bifurcated—one trial determines guilt, and a second trial establishes the penalty (Rennison & Dodge, 2018). In determining the penalty, jurors are instructed to assess the mitigating factors and aggravated factors. Mitigating factors could be the defendant's circumstances, for example, his or her adverse upbringing, being a victim of abuse, or suffering from mental illness. It could be the fact that he or she had a respectable life. Aggravating factors are related to the nature of the crime; was it heinous, cruel, or did it involve torture? After assessing those factors, jurors provide a recommended sentence to the judge. In some states, a judge must follow the recommendation of the jury (Rennison & Dodge, 2018). Defendants who receive the death penalty usually pursue criminal appeals, which makes it longer to resolve the case.

The permissibility of the VIS in the sentencing stage in death penalty cases has been contested in court. In *Booth v. Maryland* (1987), the U.S. Supreme Court ruled that the Eighth Amendment prohibits capital sentencing juries from considering victim impact evidence. In *Booth,* the trial judge allowed the jury to consider a VIS that indicated how the victims were well respected from the family and community and how the murder affected the victim's family. The Supreme Court reversed the death sentence and held that it is impermissible to allow a jury access to such evidence in the sentencing phase of a death penalty proceeding (Wallace, 2007). The Court stated that victim impact evidence might be "wholly unrelated to the blameworthiness of a particular defendant." Justice Powell commented that such evidence would impose a constitutionally unacceptable risk that the jury might impose the death penalty in an arbitrary and capricious manner (Englebrecht & Chavez, 2014). *South Carolina v. Gathers* (1989) followed the rationale of *Booth.* During the sentencing phase, the prosecutor made a closing argument in which he referred to the information from a witness and portrayed the victim as a religious, civic-minded citizen (Lee & Slowinski, 1990). The Supreme Court noted that references to the qualities of the victim were similar to the *Booth* decision as such evidence was likely to inflame the jury and violate the defendant's Eighth Amendment right.

However, in *Payne v. Tennessee* (1991), the Court reversed the *Booth* decision and noted that the victim's character and the harm caused to the victim could be considered in a sentencing decision. This case happened in 1987 when Pervis Tyrone Payne murdered Charisse Christopher and her 2-year-old daughter, Lacie, when Charisse resisted his sexual advances. Charisse was stabbed 41 times by a butcher knife, and Lacie also had numerous knife wounds. Her 3-year-old son, Nicholas, was also wounded but survived. During the penalty phase, witnesses urged the jury not to impose the death penalty by referring to the defendant's background, reputation, and mental state. The prosecution called Charisse's mother, who cared for Nicholas, to testify over the defendant's objection.

> He (Nicholas) cries for his mom. He doesn't seem to understand why she doesn't come home. And he cries for his sister Lacie. He comes to me many times during the week and asks me, Grandmama, do you miss my Lacie. And I tell him yes. He says, I'm worried about my Lacie. (Schuster & Propen, 2010, p. 64)

Payne was sentenced to death, and the case was appealed to the U.S. Supreme Court. The Court stated that the *Booth* decision was wrong in stating that this kind of evidence leads to the arbitrary imposition of the death penalty. In the majority of cases, victim impact evidence serves entirely legitimate purposes (Wallace, 2007). *Payne* found that victim impact evidence would help inform courts with a "quick glimpse" of the life of the crime victim (Englebrecht & Chavez, 2014).

Nonetheless, opinions differ in terms of the impact of a VIS on the decision making of jurors. For example, in their experimental study of mock jurors, Nadler and Rose (2003) found that "severe emotional jurors" gave more punitive sentences than less or not informed jurors. Paternoster and Deise (2011) hypothesized that jurors might not necessarily act in a punitive manner, but the stories shared by families and friends would personalize the victim to jurors, and they are more likely to feel empathy and sympathy. As a result, they might help family members in some ways. To test the hypothesis, the researchers conducted a randomized controlled experimental study and found that those who viewed a VIS were significantly more likely to think that a sentence of death "would help the victim's family find closure or help them recover from their loss" (p. 154). Similarly, other studies indicate that information about the crime victim might influence jurors' view of the victim as well as sentencing outcomes (Greene, Koehring, & Quiat, 1998; Sundby, 2003).

As observed, it has to be admitted that there are some continuing debates relative to VISs (Englebrecht & Chavez, 2014). Particularly, substantive research has not been done on generating when, what, and how a VIS should be presented. To take some examples, should a VIS be more constrained even if it would result in taking away a victim's sense of ownership of the case? Should prosecutors and victim advocates advise victims to avoid certain topics or censor the statement before presenting? When would be the best timing to present a VIS? Also, such as in death penalty trials, the sentencing phase can be years after the incident. Then, the question is whether such a long duration undermines the potential benefit to the victim.

## Restitution

A judge can order **restitution** as a part of the sentence in any criminal case (Rennison & Dodge, 2018). The most common form of restitution is financial, which requires the offender to make payments to the victim for crime-related losses. Those would include medical expenses, lost wages, lost or damaged property, and funeral expenses (Herman & Waul, 2004). In reality, restitution usually does not fully reimburse the victims because of the offender's socioeconomic status. In fact, Herman and Waul (2004) noted that this is the least addressed area in victim rights in the criminal justice system and that more systemwide changes in ways to enforce payments are necessary. For example, with a comprehensive evaluation of the offender's assets at the time of sentencing, one could develop a better payment schedule. Victims could work with the probation or parole officers to discuss compliance with the payments and the possibility of charging perpetrators with a violation of their probation or parole conditions for nonpayment or extending probation or parole while a certain amount of restitution is unpaid (Office of Victims of Crime, 2002). The restitution agreement is more likely to reach the goals of restorative justice, which will be discussed in Chapters 7 and 8.

## Victim Compensation Programs

One of the important rights of crime victims is to be compensated for crime-related financial losses. A victim **compensation** program started in California in 1965, and variations of the program are now operational in all 50 states, the District of Columbia,

**Restitution:** the most common form of restitution is financial, which requires the offender to make payments to the victim for crime-related losses. Those would include medical expenses, lost wages, lost or damaged property, and funeral expenses (Herman & Waul, 2004)

**Compensation:** victims are recompensed for crime-related financial losses. The money for the program comes mostly from court fees and fines that are collected from convicted criminals (Herman & Waul, 2004). In addition to the state funds, the federal government supplements the money through the Victims of Crime Act (VOCA) by the Office for Victims of Crime (OVC) the Virgin Islands, and Puerto Rico, making financial compensation available for victims of crime (Lonsway, 2017). The money for the program comes mostly from court fees and fines that are collected from convicted criminals (Herman & Waul, 2004). In addition to the state funds, the federal government supplements the money through the Victims of Crime Act (VOCA) by the Office for Victims of Crime (OVC). To be eligible for VOCA funds, states are required to cover all U.S. citizens who are victims of any crime committed within the state borders as well as in a federal jurisdiction such as a national park, a military base, or on tribal lands (Office for Victims of Crime, 2002).

Victims may be compensated for various expenses, including medical care costs, mental health treatment costs, funeral costs, and lost wages (Daigle, 2013). However, there are some important eligibility criteria for victims to receive the funds. Most states require victims to report the crime to law enforcement within a specified time frame. This requirement is particularly challenging for the victims of sexual assault, as most of those victims do not report the case to the police. Furthermore, an additional requirement expects victims' cooperation with criminal justice professionals during the investigation and prosecution, which makes it even harder for sexual assault victims to access the compensation fund. Another common requirement that is challenging for victims is that they must be innocent of any criminal activities. Those victims who were involved in a crime during the use of illegal drugs, driving under the influence of drugs or alcohol, or participating in the sex trade might be excluded from eligibility. Victims cannot receive compensation if they have received reimbursement from other sources such as health insurance and auto insurance (National Center for Victims of Crime, 2003).

Those eligibility criteria are among the reasons that the compensation programs are underused. For example, about one fifth of claims were denied from 1998 to 2002 (Herman & Waul, 2004). But the other major reason for the program being underutilized is simply that victims do not know about the program. As such, victim advocates should inform victims about the programs and assist them with the application. Furthermore, they could help victims to appeal adverse decisions made by the crime compensation board (Lonsway, 2017).

Figure 6.1 shows the compensation paid to victims in FY2015-16 in California.

## Civil Justice System

A civil trial is significantly different from a criminal trial. In civil cases, a person who starts the process is called the plaintiff, and the other party is called the defendant. Civil cases only require a preponderance of evidence in determining if the facts show in favor of one party or the other, which is a much lower standard than criminal cases that require proof beyond a reasonable doubt to convict the defendant. Also, the Fifth Amendment's self-incrimination clause does not apply to civil cases, and the plaintiff may call the defendant to the stand to testify during the plaintiff's case. In civil cases, only nine of 12 jurors must agree for a verdict to be reached, whereas in criminal cases, most states require a unanimous verdict.

There are several reasons why victims pursue civil litigation. As a matter of course, many want to recover monetary compensation for both economic and noneconomic losses. But many cases are filed by victims who are unsatisfied with the outcome of a criminal trial in which the defendant received a lesser sentence than they believe to be required for a "moral victory" (Villmoare & Benvenuti, 1988, p. 93). In fact, victims can

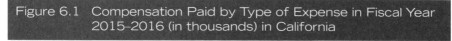

Figure 6.1 Compensation Paid by Type of Expense in Fiscal Year 2015-2016 (in thousands) in California

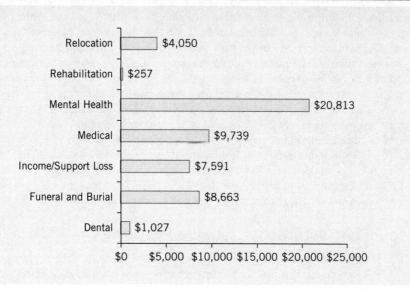

succeed in a civil suit against the defendant even if the defendant is not convicted of the criminal charges due to the different weight of evidence needed for criminal and civil cases. Victims might desire to be in control of the proceedings through a civil lawsuit when they feel mistreated in the criminal justice system (Wallace, 2007). Let us look at the historical case of O. J. Simpson's trial. After O. J. Simpson was found not guilty for the deaths of both his exwife, Nicole Brown Simpson, and a restaurant waiter in 1995, the families of the two victims filed a civil lawsuit against Simpson. The jury found Simpson responsible for both deaths, and the families were awarded a total of $33.5 million in damages. Even though they are unlikely to receive all the money, Ron Goldman's father commented that "the jury decision of last Tuesday was the only decision important to us, to find the killer of my son and Nicole responsible. The money is not an issue. It never has been. It's holding the man who killed my son and Nicole responsible" (Ayres, 1997).

Even though civil lawsuits have a lower standard of burden of proof compared to criminal trials, as seen in the O.J. Simpson case, whether the victims will actually receive the compensation is highly uncertain. Most convicts could be in jail or prison serving their sentences, and even if they are released, they might have little income and few assets. Victims should keep in mind the relative costs for the trial such as hiring attorneys, paying court filing fees and expert witness fees, and making the decision to file the lawsuit after carefully balancing the likely costs and benefits (Villmoare & Benvenuti, 1989). It might happen that victims could be sued by the perpetrator in return for their filing a civil lawsuit or reporting the crime. This type of harassing lawsuit has become more common, especially in the university setting. Often, lawsuits are used to attempt to get victims and their families to give up their lawsuits, and there is a need in this area for considerable improvement (Lonsway, 2017).

# Assisting Victims of Crime

Victim advocacy can take place at the individual level or the system level. Advocacy on an individual level refers to victim advocates who work with individual victims to protect their interests and provide emotional support. Remember from Chapter 5, common areas of individual advocacy include personal support, employer and landlord intervention, property return, intimidation protection, and referrals. Another important area is to support financial recovery by assisting with insurance claims, restitution, and compensation paperwork. Support is also needed for court-related services such as court orientation, notification, transportation, child care, escort to court, and assisting with the victim impact statement (Lonsway, 2017). In contrast, system advocacy addresses systemic issues and improving the overall response or outcome for victims. For example, system advocacy might include engagement in legislative advocacy to enact laws that protect victims and their rights and collaboration with other professionals to provide advocacy services throughout the criminal justice process (Lonsway, 2017). This chapter focuses on individual advocacy, and system advocacy and collaborative efforts are addressed in Chapter 14.

## Victim and Witness Assistance Programs

The first victim assistance program was created by Carol Vittert in St. Louis, Missouri, in 1972. The program, called "Aid for Victims of Crime," was a community-based program in which Ms. Vittert received a list of the victims from the police, and she and her friends visited those victims' homes to help. Two years later, the first system-based program was created in district attorneys' Offices in Milwaukee and Brooklyn. These programs were funded by the Federal Law Enforcement Assistance Administration (LEAA), which aims to enhance crime prevention efforts (Davies, 2010).

A decade after the first victim assistance program was established, the **Victim and Witness Protection Act of 1982 (VWPA)** was enacted. The goals of the legislation are

> (1) to enhance and protect the necessary role of crime victims and witnesses in the criminal justice process; (2) to ensure that the Federal government does all that is possible within limits of available resources to assist victims and witnesses of crime without infringing on the constitutional rights of defendants; and (3) to provide a model for legislation for state and local governments. (U.S. Department of Justice, https://www.justice.gov/usao-wdla/programs/victim-witness)

Every U.S. Attorney's Office has a Victim/Witness Assistance Program to assist victims of federal crimes. The program provides information on rights and services to victims and witnesses of federal crimes, as well as encourages the participation of victims in the criminal justice system to the extent that they wish, in accordance with federal law. Although each district could differ in how each program is run, the following services are commonly offered:

- Information on court proceedings and case status
- Emotional support during the trial
- Referral to appropriate community resources

**Victim and Witness Protection Act of 1982:** the goals of the legislation are (1) to enhance and protect the necessary role of crime victims and witnesses in the criminal justice process; (2) to ensure that the federal government does all that is possible within limits of available resources to assist victims and witnesses of crime without infringing on the constitutional rights of defendants; and (3) to provide a model for legislation for state and local governments. (U.S. Department of Justice, https://www.justice.gov/usao-wdla/programs/victim-witness)

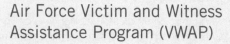

# Victim Assistance Programs

## Air Force Victim and Witness Assistance Program (VWAP)

Did you know that victim and witness assistance is available for military survivors?

The Air Force Victim and Witness Assistance Program (VWAP) is governed by the Administration of Military Justice. The program is designed to ensure that all victims and witnesses of crime in an offense investigated or prosecuted by U.S. Air Force authorities receive the assistance and protection to which they are entitled. The program uses a multidisciplinary approach, in which victims and witnesses receive information and such services as emergency medical services, social services, legal assistance, and restitution and other relief and reasonable protection from a suspected offender. These services are coordinated with local civilian agencies, the District Attorney, the U.S. Attorney's Office, hospitals, and shelters. See http://www.usafa.af.mil/Leadership/Judge-Advocate/VWAP for more information.

- Crisis intervention

- Acting as a liaison with investigative agencies

- Providing transportation, lodging, parking, and court related services

Also, judicial circuits and counties in states offer victim/witness programs. For example, in California, each county works directly with the California Victim Compensation Program (CalVCP) to assist victims (https://victims.ca.gov/victims/localhelp.aspx). Those local victim/witness programs are commonly housed in district attorneys' Offices helping victims apply for compensation, guiding victims through the criminal justice system, and providing for victims' needs. Many of the services for victims in prosecutors' Offices are legislatively mandated by state law through the Crime Victim's Bill of Rights. Examples of services that crime victims receive include, but are not limited to, the following:

- Stabilizing lives (e.g., crime-scene cleanup; referral to services such as TANF, shelters, and food stamps; employer and school intervention)

- Meeting emotional and physical needs (e.g., 24/7 victim advocacy; emotional support to the victim and family members; assisting with victim impact statements; providing transportation)

- Meeting security and safety needs (e.g., prompt victim protection; assisting with temporary protective orders; notification of court schedule and the status of the offender)

- Assisting with the criminal justice system (e.g., coordinating the victim's need to attend trials; emotional support to the victim and family during the trials; compensation and restitution).

## Comprehensive Legal Services

Comprehensive legal services for victims of crime include legal advocacy, civil legal services, and victim rights enforcement. Legal advocates assist victims in obtaining orders of protection or civil no contact orders. Civil legal services include assisting victims in divorce, custody and visitation, and child and spousal financial support matters. Victim rights enforcement includes protecting victim rights, for example, filing a motion to quash a subpoena that seeks a victim's personal information including medical, educational, and computer records.

According to a victim service provider survey conducted in Illinois, the type of legal service needed for victims depends on the recovery phases (immediate 0–3 months, intermediate 3–6 months, or long-term 6–12 months). In the immediate phase, 32% of victims need criminal justice advocacy, but the percentage declines for the intermediate (24%) and long-term phases (21%). Civil legal assistance is most needed in the immediate phase (18%) and slightly declines thereafter (15% for intermediate and 11% for long term). In contrast, victim compensation is most needed at the intermediate stage (15%) followed by long term (9%). Only 4% indicated that it is needed at the immediate stage. The needs of victims also depend on the crime type. For example, a majority of victims of domestic violence identified a need for legal advocacy during intake (Vasquez, 2017).

The national evaluation of the legal assistance for victims (LAV) program showed that overall the local agencies receiving LAV funding were satisfied with pro bono programs in which private attorneys provided services free of charge. However, the survey indicated that there is a shortage of pro bono attorneys for domestic violence cases and in rural areas. Especially, pro bono attorneys were reluctant to take on domestic violence cases due to the complexity of the cases and the need for immediate attention. The report indicated a need for better legal services for low-income domestic violence victims (Institute for Law and Justice, 2005).

## Advocates as Expert Witnesses

**Expert witnesses:** can talk about opinions given their specialized area of knowledge, research, and experience

In addition to advocacy services, victim advocates could testify in court as **expert witnesses**. Expert witnesses can talk about opinions given their specialized area of knowledge, research, and experience. In many cases, expert witness educate the court (Masters et al., 2017). The rape myth still exists in society, and jurors often are preoccupied by stereotypical ideas about rape victims. For example, if a case does not fit the jurors' ideal of true victims, they might doubt the credibility of the victim's testimony. Victim advocates could educate jurors about the reality of rape cases and the common reactions of victims.

An advantage in using victim advocates as expert witnesses is that they are mostly accessible and cooperative and might not need to be paid for their services. Their testimony would be effective as their experience is in the field and working with victims. However, there are several concerns about using advocates as expert witnesses. As victim advocates work directly with victims, their testimony could be viewed as biased. Also, when both a victim advocate and a victim serve as witnesses, they are not allowed to communicate with each other and, as a result, the victim might not be able to receive sufficient support. Therefore, it is recommended that when a victim advocate testifies in court, he or she should not be the one who is directly working with the victim of the case (Lonsway, 2017).

## Court-Appointed Special Advocate (CASA)

The Child Abuse Prevention and Treatment Act (CAPTA) is key federal legislation enacted in 1974 concerning the representation of the interests of children who are abused or neglected in judicial proceedings. In response to the law, the first **court-appointed special advocate** (CASA) program was created in Seattle. The idea of the program was developed originally by a Seattle Superior Court judge, David Soukup, who was greatly challenged to make a decision on behalf of neglected and abused children without enough information. As such, he explored the possibility of having appointed community volunteers who could speak up for the best interests of these children in court. After successfully recruiting 50 volunteers, the CASA was officially launched in 1997. Since then, the movement has grown, and there are nearly 1,000 CASA/GAL (guardian ad litem) programs in 49 states, helping more than 251,000 abused and neglected children find safe, permanent homes (National Court Appointed Special Advocate Association, 2017). These advocates not only represent the children but also work with their families and assist them with the court proceedings (Leung, 1996). Specifically, trained child advocates' major roles are fact finder, legal representative, case monitor, mediator, information source, and resource broker (Duquette, 1990).

> **Court-appointed special advocates (CASA):** help abused and neglected children find safe, permanent homes (National Court Appointed Special Advocate Association, 2017). Those advocates not only represent the children but also work with their families and assist them with the court proceedings (Leung, 1996)

The evaluation studies of CASA indicated that overall, CASA-trained volunteers performed comparably to specialized staff attorneys in terms of assessing children's needs and advocating children's interests (Poertner & Press, 1990; Abramson, 1991). Also, when CASA volunteers were involved, children as well as parents and guardians received more services than those cases with staff attorneys. Yet, there is more room to assess the impact of CASA on the court outcomes. The evaluation conducted by Poertner and Press (1990) found that there was no difference between cases with CASA and staff attorneys in terms of time to final disposition, reentry into the judicial system, and the percentage of cases with final disposition to the abuser.

## SUMMARY

The materials in this chapter presented the role of the prosecution and the judiciary in how victims' rights are protected, victims' opportunities to participate in trials, and the importance of victim service programs to support the process. This chapter also discussed current controversies about victim participation in the sentencing stage. The VIS is one way to enhance victims' participation in the adversarial system, but research findings still showed mixed results about the effectiveness of the VIS in the victim recovery process and satisfaction with the criminal justice system. A more controversial issue is the permissibility of VIS at the sentencing stage. VISs bring emotion into the courtroom: Although the expression of compassion and grief are mostly appreciated, some argue excessively emotional statements could undermine the integrity of the

process. Victim advocates play major roles in supporting victims in an unfamiliar court process and guide victims in order to lessen pains and struggles during the court proceedings. Even though there are many programs and services offered to victims during the court stage, not all victims take advantage of those services because they are simply unaware, or the eligibility criteria is an obstacle for them to take action. In some cases, services simply might not be available, for example, there is a lack of availability of pro bono attorneys for low-income domestic violence victims and victims in rural areas. Furthermore, even if a judge orders restitution or a victim is awarded compensation from a civil lawsuit, the challenge remains as to whether they can actually receive such money because of the offenders' socioeconomic status.

# KEY WORDS

Arraignment   100
Bail   98
Booking   97
Compensation   107
Court-appointed special advocate
   (CASA)   113
Deterrence   102
Expert witness   112

Incapacitation   102
Initial appearance   98
Plea bargain   98
Preliminary hearing   99
Rehabilitation   102
Restitution   107
Restoration   102

Retribution   102
Subpoena   101
Victim and witness assistance
   programs   97
Victim and witness protection act
   of 1982   110
Victim impact statements   103

# INTERNET RESOURCES

**Victim Support Services (http://victimsupportservices
.org/help-for-victims/victim-impact-statements)**
   Victim Support Services in Washington State is
the oldest victim assistance organization. The website
explains the purpose of the victim impact statements
and highlights some important guidelines for making
a statement. The website also includes sample victim
impact statements.

**Office for Victims of Crime (https://www.ovc.gov/
map.html)**
   The website provides the U.S. Resource Map of
Crime Victim Services & Information. Click on your
state or territory to find victim compensation and

assistance, victim notification programs, other victim assistance programs through the online directory,
and information on reporting crime victims' rights
violations.

**California Victim Compensation Board (https://
victims.ca.gov/victims)**
   The California Victim Compensation Board provides financial assistance for victims of violent crime.
The website includes a short video with an overview
of the program, eligibility, what expenses might be
covered, and how to apply the compensation. Non-
English compensation applications are available
through the website.

# CRITICAL THINKING QUESTIONS

1.  Victims sometimes have unrealistic expectations
    of the criminal justice system and become even
    more dissatisfied with the system when their
    recommendations are not accepted. If you were a
    victim advocate, how would you advise them of
    the realities?

2.  Discuss the differences between criminal and
    civil trials. What are some reasons that victims
    pursue civil lawsuits?

3.  Find a video of a victim presenting a victim impact
    statement in court. Learning from the statement,
    identify unmet needs of victims of crime, and
    discuss the areas that need to be addressed.

4.  Some argue that victim impact statements bring
    emotionality to the courtroom, which could
    generate tension and conflict and undermine
    the integrity of the process. Do you agree or
    disagree?

# Corrections, Prison Violence, and Victim Assistance

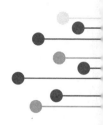

The later stages of the criminal justice system include institutional and community corrections. A sentenced offender could be housed in a correctional facility or placed in a community while serving time. Although incarceration has been widely acknowledged as a popular method of punishment in the United States, a majority of nonviolent and low-risk offenders are, in fact, sentenced to community corrections (Rennison & Dodge, 2018). The primary scope of this chapter is to explain the correctional system and how victim advocacy and services are offered under the correctional system. It also discusses how the system ensures the safety of victims and the public when offenders are released into the community.

Victim services in corrections have advanced significantly since the American Correctional Association (ACA) Task Force developed a set of recommendations to address the needs of victims in response to the murder of Lisa Bianco, who was killed by her exhusband upon release from prison on a work furlough in 1989 (National Center for Victims of Crime, 1997). Crime victims have the right to be notified upon offenders' release or escape from prison. Victims might have an opportunity to attend parole hearings or provide a victim impact statement to a parole board. Victims can also support offenders' rehabilitation by serving as a speaker on victim impact panels and participating in the victim-offender reconciliation process.

The issue of inmates becoming a victim within correctional settings is the secondary scope of this chapter. Research increasingly points to a high prevalence of violence and victimization among incarcerated inmates. Yet, challenges remain for victim advocates to serve this population. This chapter reviews the key elements of victimization in prison and the impact of victimization on their postincarceration life and explores how advocacy could meet the needs of the population.

## Correctional Systems

### Institutional Corrections

**Institutional corrections** refers to detaining individuals in secure facilities. Prisons in the United States are operated by local, state, federal, and private agencies. In contrast, jails are usually operated at a local level. Overall, the goals of institutional corrections are to preserve public safety, reduce the risk of repeat criminal behavior through incarceration, and make offender behavioral change (National Center for Victims of Crime, 1997).

### Jails

**Jails** generally hold individuals who are awaiting trial or awaiting transfer to other facilities after a conviction and misdemeanor offenders serving sentences of one year or less.

**Institutional corrections:** housing individuals in secure facilities, usually jails or prisons

**Jails:** local facilities generally hold individuals who are awaiting trial or awaiting transfer to other facilities after a conviction and misdemeanor offenders serving sentences of one year or less

However, in some jurisdictions, jails might also hold inmates whose sentences are longer than one year. Jails in the United States are operated by municipalities and counties. The Bureau of Justice Statistics estimates that, on average, 740,700 inmates were housed in county and city jails in 2016. The size of the jails varies considerably by jurisdiction. Although 20% of jails hold more than 2,500 inmates, about 8% of jails hold less than 100 inmates. A vast majority of jail inmates are male (85.5%). However, the proportion of women in the jail population increased from 11.4% as of midyear 2000 to 14.7% as of midyear 2014. About 69.7% of individuals housed in jails in the end of year 2016 had a felony charge (Kaeble & Cowhig, 2018).

Mental health issues among incarcerated inmates appear to be a significant policy concern. In reviewing 28 scholarly pieces published from 1989 to 2013, Prins (2014) noted that prevalence estimates of mental illness in correctional settings were 3 to 12 times higher than community samples. Furthermore, the prevalence of serious psychological distress and history of mental health problems is much higher among jail inmates than prison inmates. Nonetheless, a limited number of inmates has received adequate mental health treatment in jails (Rich, Wakeman, & Dickman, 2011). A study of 261 jail inmates in facilities outside of Washington, DC, showed that 18.5% of the inmates who have some mental health and/or substance dependency problems did not participate in any of the formal treatment programs or other services (Meyer, Tangney, Stuewig, & Moore, 2014). Men are less likely to participate in the program than women: 25.4% of men who needed the treatment did not participate in the program whereas for women that was only 3.2%. As to why those inmates do not participate in the programs, Meyer et al. (2014) explained that many inmates tend to believe that they are not eligible for such programs even though their length of stay is sufficient to qualify for the programs. Other common responses were skepticism about the effectiveness of the programs, stigma concerns, a lack of motivation, and the absence of available programs. Mental health is one of the significant predictors of recidivism (Carr, Baker, & Cassidy, 2016), and addressing the needs of inmates while incarcerated and beyond would help close the revolving door and ultimately create a safer community.

## Prisons

**Prisons:** facilities that usually hold felony offenders who have been sentenced to one year or more

**Prisons** usually hold felony offenders who have been sentenced to one year or more. In 2016, 1,505,400 prisoners were incarcerated in state and federal prisons (Kaeble & Cowhig, 2018). Federal prisons are operated by the Federal Bureau of Prisons. The population in federal prisons peaked in 2013 and started to decline thereafter (Federal Bureau of Prisons, 2017). Similar to federal prisons, the prison population in many states has been stable or modestly declining due to recent policy changes in shortening of sentences or sentences to community corrections for those less serious offenders (Rennison & Dodge, 2018). Some states have contracted private agencies to operate their prisons. For example, Hawaii, Tennessee, Montana, New Mexico, and Oklahoma housed at least 20% of their prison population in privately operated facilities as of year-end 2016 (Kaeble & Cowhig, 2018).

Most prison inmates are male; females make up only 7.4% of the sentenced federal and state prison population as of year-end 2016. The imprisonment rate for Black males is much higher than that of White and Hispanic males. The aggregate counts of prisoners collected annually from administrative databases in state departments of corrections showed that 41.3% were Black males, whereas 39% were White males, and 16.6% were

Hispanic males in 2016. When calculated per 100,000 U.S. residents age 18 or older, Blacks were incarcerated at 1,608 per 100,000, Whites at 274, and Hispanics at 856 in 2016 (Kaeble & Cowhig, 2018).

In the prison system, inmates are classified by their risk level and the need to be housed in an appropriate security-level facility. The federal system uses a five-level security system: minimum security, low security, medium security, high security, and administrative maximum. State prisons also use similar security levels, but those vary by state (Rennison & Dodge, 2018). Minimum-security prisons house mainly nonviolent offenders who are considered to have little or no physical risk to other inmates. Medium-security prisons hold those who are convicted of less serious crimes such as theft and assault. Maximum-security prisons are the most secure facilities in many states. Inmates who are housed in maximum-security prisons are serving long sentences for violent crimes such as murder, rape, and child abuse. Finally, **super-maximum (supermax) prisons** have the highest level of security to hold the most dangerous offenders.

## Solitary Confinement

In 2013, approximately 25,000 prisoners were held in long-term **solitary confinement** in supermax prisons (Rennison & Dodge, 2018). Those inmates housed in supermax include Ramzi Yousef, who was convicted of leading the 1993 attack against the World Trade Center; Ted Kaczynski, who is known as the Unabomber; and Eric Rudolph, the so-called Olympic Park Bomber (CNN, 2015). Supermax inmates are locked in their small cells alone for 23 hours per day and spend one hour in a recreation space, which is only slightly larger than their prison cell. Inmates have little contact outside of guards and prison staff. Food is slid through a small hole in the door. On average, inmates stay in that condition for three years, but some stay as long as 20 years (Rennison & Dodge, 2018).

Long-term isolation creates anxiety, depression, anger, cognitive disturbances, perceptual distortions, obsessive thoughts, paranoia, and psychosis (Reyes, 2007). Some argue that solitary confinement "manufactures madness" by denying the basic human need to interact with others (Masters et al., 2017). In 2012, a federal class-action suit was filed against the supermax prison in Florence, Colorado, alleging the isolation, deprivation, and neglect of prisoners who are seriously mentally ill. During the trial, a dozen prisoners testified as to the self-harm behaviors of the inmates. "One man ate his finger while guards watched and laughed. Others cut their faces and put flies in the wounds, self-castrated, or pushed objects into their urethras" (Washington Lawyers Committee, 2017). After more than four years of litigation, a settlement with the Federal Bureau of Prisons was reached (Washington Lawyers Committee, 2017). Because of the settlement, most inmates with serious mental illness cannot be put in solitary confinement; other inmates must be provided access to programming and have their condition and care monitored. Concern for the human rights of prisoners in the United States associated with solitary confinement calls for system reform advocacy.

## Capital Punishment and Death Row Inmates

According to the Bureau of Justice Statistics (Snell, 2017), there were 2,881 inmates under sentence of death in 33 states at the end of 2015. Among those, five states (California, Florida, Texas, Alabama, and Pennsylvania) held 60% of all inmates on

**Supermax prison:** the prison with the highest level of security that holds the most dangerous offenders

**Solitary confinement:** inmates are locked in their small cells alone 23 hours a day and spend one hour in a recreation space, which is only slightly larger than their prison cell. Inmates have little contact outside of guards and prison staff

# CASE STUDY
## Hunger Strike at Prison

On July 11, 2011, to protest the repeated use of solitary confinement, about 400 prisoners at California's Pelican Bay State Prison started a hunger strike. Most of the prisoners had been in solitary confinement for more than 5 years and some for more than 20 years. The prisoners had five central demands: (1) Eliminate group punishments for individual rules violations; (2) Abolish the debriefing policy, and modify active/inactive gang status criteria; (3) Comply with the recommendations of the U.S. Commission on Safety and Abuse in Prisons (Gibbons & Katzenbach, 2006) regarding an end to long-term solitary confinement; (4) Provide adequate food; and 5) Expand and provide constructive programs and privileges for indefinite security housing unit inmates. By framing the protest around basic human rights and disciplined tactics for resistance, the protest led to a broader discussion of supermax prisons and the use of such extreme punishments as solitary confinement.

## Questions:

1. Do you think that solitary confinement is inhumane, or it is necessary for certain individuals?

2. What kind of basic rights should solitary-confined inmates have?

death row as of December 31, 2015. Between January 1, 2016, and December 31, 2016, five states executed 20 inmates. Those states were Georgia (9), Texas (7), Alabama (2), Florida (1), and Missouri (1). Among 2,979 death row inmates in 2013, 98% were male, and only 2% were female. The average age of death row inmates is 47, and only 42% are high school graduates. Fewer than 10% have a college degree. A majority has never married (54.8%) (Snell, 2014).

Abundant empirical research has supported the effect of a victim's race on the outcome of capital cases (Gross & Mauro, 1989; Pierce & Radelet, 2011; Radelet & Pierce, 2011; Girgenti, 2015). Girgenti (2015) found that the odds of a defendant likely receiving a death sentence in a White victim case are 2.5 times greater than in a Black victim case after controlling for relevant variables. Known as the "White female victim effect," the interaction of gender and race has shown an effect on death sentences (Holcomb, Williams, & Demuth, 2004). However, a recent study by Girgenti (2015) did not find the gender of victims to be a significant factor on death sentencing outcomes.

## Death Row Inmates and the Murder Victim's Family

Dialogue between a death row inmate and a victim family member rarely occurs. Looking at Texas as an example, only a few formal dialogues were documented. Yet, some forms of communication possibly have occurred over the telephone, in letters, and through third parties (Barrile, 2014). Little known is whether such communication facilitates any meaningful changes in the survivors' mind-set. In a study of 52 family members of murder victims for which the capital case of the offender ended in an execution in Texas and Virginia, a clear majority of survivors believed that the punishment fit the severity of the crime and the suffering and loss of the victim. Among those survivors, nearly one half heard an apology from the offender during a face-to-face meeting, a telephone conversation, or in writing. Among those, few forgave the offender. Only 15% noted that forgiveness occurred, and 23% accepted the offender's remorse when it was offered (Barrile, 2014). The author noted that forgiving the offender has substantial meaning for the survivors. Forgiveness helped their emotional well-being by reducing anger, hatred, and obsessive ruminations about the offender and the crime. Nonetheless, most survivors still support the death penalty. Barrile (2014) explains survivors' contradictory feelings using the term "forgive-but-die sentiment." On one hand, survivors are willing to forgive the offender. On the other hand, they believe capital punishment must still be imposed as it fits the seriousness of the crime and the offender would remain a threat so long as he or she is alive.

## Witnessing Executions

In general, victims have a choice to view executions of their loved one's murderer. In Virginia, Governor George Allen began allowing surviving family members of capital-murder victims to witness executions in 1994 (Green, 2015). In Texas, the first witnessed execution happened in 1996. The process starts with the family members being informed about the schedule of the execution and being asked if they want to witness it. In the Texas case, once a family member decides to view an execution, he or she can bring close friends of the deceased or surviving relatives, but the number is limited to five witnesses per victim. They wait in an adjacent room during the actual execution. Before viewing an execution, the witnesses learn about the protocol and watch a video to know what the prison and the execution chamber look like and what to expect. After the execution, victim services staff will make follow-up contact a few weeks after the execution to offer additional assistance as needed (Masters et al., 2017).

Survivors' feelings about witnessing an execution vary. A study of survivors who witnessed an execution found that relief was one of the most common themes expressed by them (Gross & Matheson, 2003). In another study, interviews with 27 survivors and their families of the Oklahoma City bombing found that "closure" is identified as a common theme. Those who attended the execution felt that justice was done and that the process was completed (Madeira, 2010). Similarly, a story of a son whose father was murdered felt double relief after witnessing the execution. He no longer had to worry about the offender being out of prison, and the legal process was over. Notably, some survivors who witnessed an execution became even angrier recalling the suffering of their loved one (Green, 2015). Witnessing the execution can help bring closure for survivors, but it does not necessarily heal and mediate their anger.

Sentencing allows offenders to serve their sentences without incarceration. As such, it is sometimes referred to as community supervision (Bureau of Justice Statistics, n.d.). Community corrections programs include probation, parole, community service, mediation, sex registers, house arrest, work release, and treatment programs (Masters et al., 2017).

**Community corrections:** sanctions that allow offenders to serve their terms in a community setting outside of jail or prison.

Some offenders are required to attend court-ordered programs. The community corrections sanction is considered more cost-effective than incarceration. For example, estimates suggest that the yearly incarceration cost per inmate is about $30,000, whereas the yearly probation cost per offender is $700 to $1,000 (Rennison & Dodge, 2018).

## Probation

**Probation:** commonly used as an alternative to incarceration where offenders can live under supervision in the community

**Probation** is commonly used as an alternative to incarceration where offenders can live under supervision in the community. In some jurisdictions, the offenders are sentenced to a short-term incarceration sentence immediately followed by probation, which is referred to as a split sentence (Bureau of Justice Statistics, n.d.). Although the level of supervision differs by offender, offenders are usually required to fulfill certain conditions under the supervision. Examples of such conditions include the payment of fines, fees, or court costs and participation in treatment programs. Failure to comply with any conditions can result in incarceration. A probation officer is responsible for monitoring the progress of probationers in completing the sentence. An officer might visit the offender at home or at work to monitor compliance with the rules.

Approximately 4.65 million adults were on probation, parole, or some other form of postprison supervision by the end of 2015. Probationers accounted for 81% of all adults under community supervision, which is four times more than the parole population. The majority of probationers are male, but the percentage of females on probation increased from 2005 (23%) to 2015 (25%) (Kaeble & Bonczar, 2016).

Some important rights for victims include ensuring safety while offenders serve their community corrections sentences and notification of changes in and violations of conditions of probation and the termination of the sentence. Correctional agencies are obliged to protect victims from intimidation, harassment, and/or harm by offenders under their supervision. Victims of crime would benefit from understanding how probation and parole work.

## Parole

**Parole:** the conditional release of a prison inmate ending their term under the supervision of parole officers

**Parole** is the conditional release of a prison inmate. When inmates follow prison rules and show positive behavior during incarceration, they can be conditionally released from prison before ending their term under the supervision of parole officers. Parole officers provide supervision, and support services help offenders reintegrate into the community. Parole release is determined by a parole board. Although practices vary by state, parole board members usually consist of individuals who have experience in criminal justice system fields and are appointed by the state's governor. The minimum eligible parole date for inmates serving life terms with possibility of parole is set by statute, but that date could be reduced if the inmate accumulates good-time credits. Some inmates are not eligible for parole because they are serving life sentences without the possibility of parole (Masters et al., 2017).

### Victim Participation in the Parole Process

There are 12 basic rights and services that parole authorities should provide to crime victims before, during, and after the parole process (National Center for Victims of Crime, 1997):

1. Information about the parole process (including parole hearings), available in written, audio, and/or video formats in languages commensurate with victim populations in the agency's state

2. Notification (upon request and in writing) of upcoming parole proceedings at least 60 days in advance of any hearing

3. Designation of professionals or volunteers to accompany victims to parole hearings

4. Procedures to keep victims and offenders separate by sight and sound at parole hearings, if victims so desire (in states where victim presence at the parole hearing does not require offender presence at the same time)

5. Waiting areas for victims that are separate by sight and sound from the offender and his or her family and friends

6. Acceptance of victim impact statements before or during parole hearings in person by the victim (allocution), written, audiotaped, and/or videotaped, and in measures that are commensurate with the victim's age, cognitive development, and culture (multilingual)

7. Confidentiality of victim information and victim impact statements from the offender and his or her counsel before, during, and after parole hearings

8. Timely notification of the outcome of any decisions resulting from parole hearings

9. Notification of parole violations and relevant hearings to both the victim of the original offense that resulted in incarceration as well as the victim of the offense for which the revocation hearing is being conducted

10. Information for victims about parole supervision, conditions of parole, the name of the parole agent, and who to contact within the parole authority for additional information or resources

11. Training for all staff involved in parole proceedings about basic victimology theory, along with an overview of state law, policies, and victim services relevant to the agency

12. Training for all state and local victim service providers about the parole process and related victims' rights

Participating in and providing input at parole hearings is a critical component for victims who wish to participate in the criminal justice system. Those victims who felt that they were excluded from the criminal justice process particularly appreciate the opportunity to have input at parole hearings (Parsonage, Bernat, & Helfgott, 1992).

There is a shortage of empirical studies relevant to victim participation at parole hearings and its impact on outcomes. Among those limited studies, an experimental study conducted by Parsonage et al. (1992) found that parole cases in which victim testimony was proffered had higher refusal rates than cases without victim testimony on the Pennsylvania Parole Board. Another study of victim participation at parole hearings in Alabama found a similar result (Morgan & Smith, 2005). The researchers found that regardless of written or oral input, victim participation is the second strongest predictor of parole dispositions. Furthermore, the study indicated that the more actions (e.g., written or oral protests) that are taken, the more likely the parole will be denied. However, a study conducted by Caplan (2010) with a representative sample of parole-eligible adult inmates in New Jersey found that victim input was not a significant predictor of parole release when controlling for other variables. Nonetheless, institutional behavior, crime severity, and criminal history were significantly associated with parole release (Caplan, 2010).

Considering the substantial impact of victim input in parole decisions, Moriarty (2005) raised some concerns about fairness in the process for offenders. The author argues that there should be a balance between an offender's rehabilitation and the safety and sense of security of the public and victims. For example, victims could be updated on the status of an offender's behavioral changes from prison programs so that the public would not have unrealistic fear toward offenders after their release from prison (Moriarty, 2005).

## Other Alternatives to Incarceration Programs

**Day Reporting Centers (DRCs):**
a one-stop center that addresses the criminogenic needs of the participants by providing comprehensive programs

**Day Reporting Centers (DRCs)** are one-stop centers for offenders who must report and participate in various programs. The common components of a DRC include an educational program, mental health services, substance abuse treatment, electronic monitoring, probation supervision, and case management. The eligible offenders are referred to the DRC, where they are closely monitored and report regularly for drug and alcohol screening and receive intensive case management, substance abuse and mental health treatment, life skills, prosocial skill development, career guidance, and job training. The effectiveness of the DRCs on recidivism showed mixed results. A study conducted by Carr et al. (2016) showed those who were admitted to a DRC and completed the program were less likely to recidivate than probationers in the same district who share similar characteristics. Other studies also show positive outcomes (Ostermann, 2009; Champion, Harvey, & Schanz, 2011). However, a randomized study conducted by Boyle, Ragusa-Salerno, Lanterman, and Marcus (2013) found that men who were referred to a DRC had no significantly better outcomes than those on traditional parole supervision. As the DRCs include multiple components and operate differently, further exploration of why some programs work whereas others do not is needed.

**Electronic Monitoring (EM):** an intermediate sanction in which offenders are monitored through a GPS tracking device

The other popular alternative sanction is **electronic monitoring** (EM) in which offenders are monitored though a GPS tracking device. The EM program has been used to reduce jail and prison populations in a cost-effective way. It is also expected to suppress crime during the monitored period. Yet, the effectiveness of the programs on recidivism is unknown. One challenge is that EM is commonly used with other programs such as house arrest and the DRCs, therefore the true effect of EM is difficult to measure. Also, EM has been used for offenders with different risk levels, and low-risk offenders could be successfully completing their probation and parole terms without being monitored by the device. Renzema and Mayo-Wilson (2005) suggest that EM itself would not reduce recidivism but might bring about a better result in conjunction with other promising programs.

Other alternative programs include house arrest in which an offender is required to stay in his or her own house and community service whereby the offender works in the community; for example, a DUI offender gives speeches to schoolchildren about the dangers of drunk driving or cleans up the streets and public spaces. Community service sanctions can be ordered by a judge. Also community service is one of the common outcomes of restorative justice programs. More discussion of restorative justice programs occurs later in this chapter and in the next chapter.

# Victim Services and Programs in Correctional Settings

## Victim Services Officers

Some correctional facilities have victim services officers to provide advocacy services to prison employees. Corrections settings are a stressful environment where the perception of fear among officers is high, especially among female officers (Gordon & Baker, 2017). A study of correctional employees in France found that correctional employees overall demonstrated a high level of posttraumatic stress disorder (PTSD) symptoms, burnout, and stress (Boudoukha, Altintas, Rusinek, Fantini-Hauwel, & Hautekeete, 2013). The authors noted, in particular, that violent interactions with inmates, including witnessing incidents, led to experiencing high levels of PTSD. Victim services officers can assist with those officers in crisis to provide immediate intervention and referrals for long-term counseling. Victim services offered in correctional facilities are not limited to prison employees. In some facilities, services are offered to visitors who are emotionally or physically abused during a visit and to inmates who are physically and sexually abused by staff or fellow inmates. In some instances, victim services officers could assist victimized inmates in writing grievances in a situation such as a lack of access to medical or mental healthcare, improper service provision, and failure to respond to an incident in a timely manner (Masters et al., 2017).

## Restorative Justice (RJ) Programs in Prisons

Restorative justice (RJ) programs are often found in community settings as an alternative to the traditional criminal justice system. However, there is growing interest in implementing such programs inside prisons. Although more core components of RJ concepts will be discussed in Chapter 8, RJ addresses crime in such a way that victims, offenders, communities, and criminal justice professionals engage in dialogue and repair the harm caused by the crime (Zehr & Mika, 1998). Here, one must be aware that there are some contradictions between RJ and imprisonment. The focus of RJ is on the crime victim and to repair harm and reconcile the damaged relationship. In contrast, prisons focus on offenders and crime. Although the advantage of RJ is its flexibility, the prison system is highly structured, and incarceration isolates offenders from the community and the victim. Political and financial interests also make it difficult to implement RJ in prisons. For those reasons, the traditional model of RJ will not be fully developed inside prisons. However, there are some promising practices that have been implemented throughout the world. In Canada, prisoners can participate in projects that support the needs of the community, for example, repairing wheelchairs and making park benches, which provides prisoners the opportunity to compensate communities for their criminal behavior and helps them integrate into the community. In victim-offender mediation (or dialogue) programs, actual or surrogate victims and offenders have face-to-face or indirect meetings facilitated by a trained community volunteer or a prisoner (Dhami, Mantle, & Fox, 2009).

An examination of RJ programs in prison showed some positive indicators. Dhami et al. (2009) summarized several RJ program evaluations conducted in different prisons and found positive outcomes. Those include a pilot Sycamore Tree Project in one prison that helped offenders to understand the impact of crime and become aware of the victim's needs. A study of the Inside Out Trust in 15 prisons showed that both prisoners and staff viewed community work as having a positive impact on inmates as those programs connect inmates to the outside community and teach them new skills. The evaluation of victim-offender mediation programs in Texas and Ohio found that 60% of the victims and families interviewed indicated that the meeting had helped with healing and improved their feelings about the offender. Although there are many promising RJ prison programs, some studies have shown the limitations of the programs. For example, RJ in prisons does not necessarily improve empathy, communication, and conflict resolution skills (Petrellis, 2007). Structural problems, such as overcrowding, staff shortages, and poor living conditions, make it harder to implement RJ in prison (Guidoni, 2003).

## Impact of Crime on Victims Classes (ICVCs)

**Impact of Crime on Victims Classes** (ICVCs) are mostly operated in state prisons in the United States to enhance adult offender acceptance of responsibility for their previous criminal conduct, understand the impact of crime on victims, develop personal safety skills, learn about healthy relationships with others, and contribute to their communities in a way to prevent future victimization (Carson, Chenault, & Matusiak, 2016). ICVCs are technically not a true restorative justice program as many of the participants are serving a life sentence and have little chance to be reintegrated into their home communities. Nonetheless, the program uses the concept of reintegrative shaming to enhance inmate integration into the prison community (Carson et al., 2016). The reintegrative shaming theory, which is presented by John Braithwaite, explains that fear of being shamed by family, friends, and significant others deters an individual from committing crime, and such an informal social control is more effective than the formal control of a criminal justice authority (Van Camp, 2017).

These classes use a curriculum in which trained facilitators, who are usually staff or inmates, facilitate the discussion. For the study conducted by Carson et al. (2016), the facilitators were exclusively inmates who had taken the class as students, a second time as observers, and then as cofacilitators before leading the class. Videotapes of victims or a victim impact panel are sometimes incorporated into the curriculum. Evaluation of the ICVCs showed some positive outcomes but in limited areas. After examining a sample of

# CASE STUDY
## Forgiveness Given to Conor McBride

Perhaps one of the most powerful examples of restorative justice is the McBride case, in which a restorative justice program was used to facilitate dialogue in a murder case in Florida. In 2010, Conor McBride shot to death his girlfriend, Ann Grosmaire. Both were 19 years old and had been in a relationship for three years. When the Grosmaire family heard the devastating news and went to the hospital, Ann was on the verge of death but kept asking for forgiveness for Conor. Even though the Grosmaires had a good relationship with Conor prior to the incident, they were unwilling to forgive him. Things started to change when they learned that Cornor would receive at least a life sentence in prison for first-degree murder. The Grosmaires did not want to keep Conor in prison for the rest of his life and learned about an alternative way to handle the case, which was a restorative justice program. Yet, in Florida, the program had never been used for such a serious crime.

Both the McBrides and the Grosmaires continued to support each other through the difficult time and advocated to make the restorative justice meeting happen. Then, a little more than one year after the incident, a restorative justice program became a reality. The sessions took place in a similar format as a usual victim-offender mediation, with the only difference being that attorneys were present with both parties. Both parties expressed how the incident had affected them and Conor told

his story and explained how it happened. Conor admitted he had temper issues. It was hard for both the Grosmaires and the McBrides to accept that it was not an accident but rather that Conor had lost his mind at that time, picked up the gun, and shot at Ann. The Grosmaires and the McBrides reached an agreement that 10 to 15 years in prison would be appropriate for him. Two weeks later, the Leon County assistant state attorney, Jack Campbell, who handles high-profile murder cases, gave Conor a choice between 25 years of imprisonment or 20 years of imprisonment plus 10 years of probation. Conor chose the latter.

Forgiveness played an important role in the process. The Grosmaires said they did not forgive Conor for his sake but for their own. "Forgiveness for me was self-preservation," Kate Grosmaire said (Tullis, 2013). Forgiveness also helped Conor not only for reducing his sentence but also because, with the Grosmaires' forgiveness, he could accept responsibility and not be condemned. Yet, Kate Grosmaire notes that forgiving him does not change the fact that her daughter is no longer with them.

### Discussion:

1. Do you agree or disagree that restorative justice programs should be used for violent crimes such as murder, robbery, and rape?

Source: Mahajan, B. (2017). Victim offender mediation: A case study and argument for expansion to crimes of violence. *The American Journal of Mediation, 10*, Retrieved from http://www.americanjournalofmediation.com/pg1.cfm.

probationers and parolees who participated in the ICVC program, Jackson, Lucas, and Blackburn (2009) found that the program had no influence on an offender's shame, guilt, or empathy levels, but participants were more likely to hold themselves accountable for their actions. Carson et al. (2016) concluded that, overall, the impact of the ICVC programs on reducing institutional misconduct was limited.

## Other Victim-Offender Programs in the United States

Probation and parole agencies can provide victims with information on programs such as restorative justice through which victims and offenders jointly participate. Under the restorative justice model, offenders, victims, and the community are considered important parties to resolve a conflict. The principles of restorative justice programs will be discussed in Chapter 8: Juvenile Justice System, Restorative Justice, and Victim Assistance. Below are some examples of restorative justice programs implemented in the United States:

*Community reparation boards,* consisting of community members appointed by the Department of Corrections, provide a sentencing option for nonviolent offenders to make reparation to victims and the community. Reparative activities include restitution, community work services, mediation/dialogue, cognitive skills development sessions, victim empathy programs, and decision-making programs.

*Community/neighborhood impact statements* provide an opportunity for citizens whose lives are detrimentally affected by crime, such as drug- and gang-related illegal activities to inform the court about how such crimes affect their quality of life.

*Family group conferencing* involves the youthful offender and his or her family; the victim and his or her family or designated representative; and a representative of the juvenile justice system. The outcome of family group conferencing is the formulation of a plan that includes victim input and restitution and helps offenders learn new skills that will help them to avoid future reoffending.

*Victim/offender dialogue* (also called mediation) is a structured, voluntary meeting between a victim and an offender with a trained facilitator to discuss the impact of the crime and to develop an arrangement that attempts to hold the offender accountable and to make amends to the victim, as well as provide the offender with educational opportunities.

*Restorative community service* performed by offenders can improve the quality of life for both the community and victims. Examples include work crews that clean graffiti, direct service to the victim if he or she chooses, and improving safety measures (such as locks) for elderly citizens' homes.

*Community work service programs* provide opportunities for offenders to work, develop new skills, and be paid so they can, in turn, fulfill their restitution obligations.

# Victim Involvement in Correctional Programs

## Victim Impact Panel (VIP)

A **Victim Impact Panel** (VIP) consists of three or four speakers who have been seriously injured or whose friend or family member was killed by a drunken driver and who share their personal stories about how the accident affected their lives to a group of driving while intoxicated (DWI) offenders in a nonblaming manner. Those panels run usually biweekly or monthly. The concept of a VIP was first introduced by Mothers Against Drunk Driving (MADD) in 1982. You will find the story of how MADD was created in a box later in this chapter. To take full advantage of the program, the NHTSA (2005) recommended a wide range of consideration when selecting speakers. The recommendations include

# Victim Assistance Programs

## Mothers Against Drunk Drivers (MADD)

On May 3, 1980, a 13-year-old girl, Carime Anne Lightner, was killed by a drunk driver, Clarence Busch. She was hit from behind, thrown 125 feet, and left on the road to die. Clarence Busch did not stop to render aid and kept the accident secret until his wife discovered damage to his car. He was out on bail from another hit-and-run drunk driving crash and had three prior convictions for drunk driving in four years. Busch was prosecuted but sentenced to only two years for vehicular manslaughter. He was given the usual time off for good behavior and was placed at a work camp and a halfway house, where he owned a car and drove to and from work and home on weekends. His full license was returned to him upon his release just 18 months later.

Another tragedy happened shortly after his release; Busch hit another girl while drinking and driving with a blood alcohol concentration (BAC) of 0.20.

Through the experience of the way her daughter's case was handled, Carime's mother, Candace Lightner, learned that the significance of a DWI was not recognized by the criminal justice system. Ms. Lightner launched Mothers Against Drunk Drivers (MADD) from her home in 1980, which became an organization in 1984. The efforts of Ms. Lightner and MADD made remarkable changes on public perceptions and the ways that the criminal justice system responds to drunken driving.

See http://wesavelives.org/caris-story/ for more information.

---

contacting the potential speakers after they have completed both civil and criminal proceedings. It also recommended giving speakers sufficient time to prepare their stories. Describing their own tragedy is an extremely emotional process, and the coordinator should provide them with enough professional assistance and resources. Most victims would be able to present only a few times due to the extremely sensitive nature and personal commitment of the panel. Video presentations could be used for supplemental support, but live presentations are more powerful than videotaped presentations. Although it is an emotional challenge for the presenters, those who participated in such panels valued the process as they felt that they could do something to prevent further DWIs (NHTSA, 2005). A study of victims who participated in a VIP found that 82% of the respondents felt that the participation helped them in their recovery, but 8% mentioned that they felt that the experience had been harmful to them (Mercer, 1990).

The positive effects of a VIP on DWI recidivism is well recognized as shown in the 10 promising sentencing practices for a DWI offender (NHTSA, 2005). Earlier studies examining the impact of a VIP indicated that participation in a VIP changed the offender's attitude toward drunken driving (Sprang, 1997) and showed a lower recidivism rate than the comparison group (Shinar & Compton, 1995; Fors & Rojek, 1999). However, other researchers have shown some reservations about the effectiveness of the program on recidivism. For example, Rojek, Coverdill, and Fors (2003) found the positive effect of a VIP on recidivism, but their further analysis indicated that the impact of a VIP diminished in about two years. In a study of the effect of a VIP for male and female DUI offenders, C'de Baca, Lapham, Liang, and Skipper (2001) found that a VIP referral does not have a statistically significant impact on first-time male and female DWI/driving under the influence (DUI) offenders after controlling for various risk factors. The same authors also found that female repeat offenders who were referred to VIPs were more likely to be rearrested compared to their male counterparts. The authors explained that VIPs are designed to influence DWI/DUI offenders on an emotional level, and for that reason, female offenders who confront victims could feel shame and guilt and possibly aggravate alcohol consumption and reoffending.

Today, VIPs have been used not only in DWI/DUI cases but also in other types of crime such as domestic violence and property-related crimes (National Institute of Justice, 2007). These programs are mostly tied to sentencing options such as diversion or accompanying a probation sentence whereby offenders are court ordered to attend the panels. Furthermore, VIPs are introduced in a wide variety of settings including prison, jail, treatment programs, defensive driving schools, and youth education programs and at training for juvenile and criminal justice professionals to better understand the significance of victimization on crime victims (National Institute of Justice, 2007).

## Victim Notification

One of the crucial rights for victims is to be informed about the status of offenders. A federal crime victim is entitled to be notified in certain circumstances through the Department of Justice **Victim Notification System** (VNS). The VNS is a free computer-based system through which federal crime victims can access information on an offender's custody and release status. Victims who have an ID number and a PIN can access the information via the VNS website at https://www.notify.usdoj.gov/index.jsp.

The Victim Information and Notification Everyday (VINE) system allows crime victims to obtain information about particular criminal cases and the status of offenders who are in county jails or state prisons. Victims can check an offender's custody status via notifications by phone, e-mail, text message, or teletypewriter (TTY) device. The information is available 24 hours a day by phone at 1-888-2NV-VINE (1-888-268-8463) or at https://www.vinelink.com/#/home.

According to a survey study conducted by Irazola, Williamson, Niedzwiecki, Debus-Sherrill, and Sun (2015), overall 63% of service providers and 76% of victims who have used the automated notification system indicated high satisfaction with the system in their jurisdiction. Among those who were registered for the system, 94% noted that they would encourage other victims to register for and use the service. Some benefits of automated notification for crime victims and service providers are that the system increases a victim's sense of safety (91%), assists victims in making decisions about their safety (88%), helps victims feel empowered (79%), and enhances victims' participation in their cases. Some challenges using automated notification systems are delayed or outdated notifications, inaccurate notifications, not enough or too many notifications, and difficulty using the website or registering for the system.

### Community Notification and Sex-Offender Laws

#### Megan's Law

Federal sex-offender registration started in 1994 when Congress passed the Jacob Wetterling Crimes Against Children and Sexually Violent Offender Registration Act.

> **Victim Notification System (VNS):** a free computer-based system through which federal crime victims can access information on an offender's custody and release status

The law was advocated for by the parents of Jacob Wetterling, who was abducted by an armed stranger in rural Minnesota when he was 11 years old in 1989. His body parts were discovered in 2016 (Ellis & Sanchez, 2016). Speculating that a previously convicted sex offender was responsible for the crime, Jacob's parents urged states to take preventive measures to protect children from sexual predators. The act mandates that states adopt laws requiring released sex offenders to register with law enforcement agencies (Lewis, 1996).

Two years later, another tragedy happened to a 7-year-old girl in New Jersey. Megan Kanka was lured into the house of Jesse Timmendequas, where she was sexually assaulted and murdered. Timmendequas had two prior convictions for sex crimes with young children and lived just across the street from the Kankas' residence. Megan's parents lobbied to pass a law that makes sex-offender registration information available to the public so that the citizens could take preventive measures to increase the safety of children. New Jersey enacted the law in 1996, which is named "Megan's Law," after the victim. In 1996, President Bill Clinton signed the federal Megan's Law and an amendment to the Jacob Wetterling Act. Those laws together became a federal requirement for states to pass statutes for sex-offender registration and community notification. All 50 states have some form of a law to this effect.

Megan's Law is one of the most well-known laws that ensures public safety (Levenson, D'Amora, & Hern, 2007). Overall, Megan's Law gained popularity as it is assumed that sex-offender registration and community notification make citizens feel safer. However, in a survey of those who attended community notification meetings in Wisconsin, Zevitz and Frakas (2001) found that, overall, citizens felt the meeting was informative, but many attendees still felt anxious and frustrated. Indeed, 67% of those attendees who came expecting to place blame on public officials or to prevent or remove the resident sex offender left feeling more concerned than before.

A survey of sex offenders indicated that two thirds of the respondents noted that the notification unfavorably affected not only the offenders but also the lives of parents, siblings, and offspring. Those offenders also felt that obstacles in finding a place to live and the visibility of them in the community made it harder to reenter the community. Another study found that because of the obstacles to reentry and threats and harassment by community members, the majority of sex offenders released from prison expressed depression, shame, and hopelessness (Levenson et al., 2007).

The impact of the law on the recidivism of sex offenders has shown mixed results. Some earlier research studies comparing the reoffending rate of sex offenders pre- and postnotification law inception found no impact of the law on recidivism (Schram & Milloy, 1995; Adkins, Huff, & Stageberg, 2000). However, after controlling for demographic characteristics and criminal history, Barnoski (2005) found that the five-year sexual recidivism rates were significantly lower for the prenotification groups than the postnotification counterparts. Finally, a methodologically rigorous study conducted by Duwe and Donnay (2008) found that broad community notification significantly reduced the risk of sexual reoffending in all three measures studied (i.e., rearrest, reconviction, and reincarceration). However, after controlling for the effect of the independent variables, community notification did not show a statistically significant impact on general reoffending. The authors concluded that community notification could reduce recidivism but that the law makes it harder for sex offenders to reenter the community.

## Jessica's Law

The Jessica Lunsford Act was named after a 9-year-old girl who was abducted and murdered by a convicted sex offender who had a lenient sentence for a previous sex crime in Florida. The act aims to protect young children from sexual offenders by increasing the severity of punishment: a mandatory minimum sentence of 25 years in prison and lifetime electronic monitoring (LEM) for adult offenders who have been convicted of lewd, unchaste, or licentious acts against a victim younger than 12 years old. Furthermore, the sexual battery or the rape of a child younger than 12 years old is punishable by life imprisonment with no chance of parole. Other states followed Florida and enacted their own version of "Jessica's Law." Currently, more than 40 states have some form of Jessica's Law. For example, in California, Proposition 83, which is California's version of Jessica's Law, was approved with the overwhelming support of the voters in 2006. The law increases the legal penalties for sex offenses, requires LEM for felony registered sex offenders, and prohibits registered sex offenders from residing within 2,000 feet of any school or park (Takahashi, 2017).

Increasing the penalties and strengthening the supervision for those who commit sexual offenses are assumed to deter offenders from committing other crimes and to protect children whom they might victimize. However, research has found the deterrence effects of Jessica's Law are not as intended. A study of resident restrictions of sexual offenders in Colorado found that residential restrictions of supervised sex offenders did not have any effect on the sex offender's reoffending (Griffin & Wooldredge, 2013). Several reports also indicate that residency restrictions and notification laws adversely affected their reentry to the community. In California, many registered offenders became homeless due to residency restrictions, and such an unstable living arrangement makes them more prone to recidivate (Zucker, 2014). A report in Minnesota showed that residency restrictions forced offenders to move to rural remote areas that have few employment opportunities, a lack of social support, and limited availability for medical treatment, counseling, and other rehabilitative social services (Minnesota Department of Corrections, 2003). Fear of sex crimes became the driving force for strict laws. Without changes in public thinking about sex offenders, offender reentry remains challenging.

# Prison Violence and Victimization in Prison

## Violent Victimization in Prison

There is minimal attention to the issue of offenders being victimized while incarcerated. Nonetheless, research has indicated that violent victimization occurs in prison at a much higher rate than in the general population. As for reference, self-reported violent crime victimization was experienced by about 1% of the total population (Truman & Morgan, 2016). Even looking at those who live in lower-income communities, the violent victimization rate is 1.5% (Teplin, McClelland, Abram, & Weiner, 2005). Although the definition, environment, and time period differ by researcher, prison research indicates that those inmates who experienced a physical assault during the past 6 to 12 months of the study period ranged from a low estimate of 5.8% to a high of 21% (Teasdale, Daigle, Hawk, &

Daquin, 2016). An examination of the nationally representative sample of prisons and prisoners in the United States indicated that both individual factors (e.g., sex, race, type of offense, and mental disorders) and institutional factors (e.g., proportion of males, violent offenders, multiracial offenders, and the number of major infractions occurred in the facility) affect one's risk of being physically assaulted in prison (Wooldredge & Steiner, 2012).

In connection to prison violence, researchers have expressed increasing concerns about the high prevalence of PTSD among incarcerated inmates. When looking at the general population in the United States, the lifetime prevalence of PTSD is 6.8% (Kessler & Wang, 2008). In contrast, a study of nonviolent inmates in a **detention facility** for the Iowa Department of Corrections found rates of existing PTSD to be 10% for men and 23.2% for women (Gunter et al., 2008). Similarly, another study of male prison and jail inmates in New England indicated that 21% of the study sample met the criteria for current PTSD (Gibson et al., 1999). Most of those offenders will return to the community sooner or later, and trauma experienced while incarcerated could affect their transition to the community and recidivism. As such, it is important to understand prison violence and the impact of victimization on offenders.

> **Detention Facility:** a secure facility that places juveniles during juvenile court proceedings. It is sometimes called detention center or juvenile hall

## Sexual Victimization in Prison

A high prevalence of sexual victimization in prisons and jails has received public policy attention. In addressing sexual victimization issues in correctional settings, the Prison Rape Elimination Act (PREA) of 2003 was established to "provide for the analysis of the incidence and effects of prison rape in Federal, State, and local institutions and to provide information, resources, recommendations and funding to protect individuals from prison rape" (National PREA Resource Center, n.d.). The efforts to collect data from federal and state prisons, local jails, and other special facilities, including the U.S. Armed Forces, Indian tribes, and the U.S. Immigration and Customs Enforcement (ICE), is a significant step to improving the quality of care needed for the population.

According to the National Inmate Survey (NIS) conducted from February 2011 to May 2012, among the sample of 92,449 inmates age 18 or older and 1,738 inmates ages 16 or 17, an estimated 4.0% of state and federal prison inmates and 3.2% of jail inmates reported experiencing one or more incidents of sexual victimization by another inmate or facility staff within 12 months of the study period (Beck, Berzofsky, Caspar, & Krebs, 2013). Narrower analyses of specific groups of inmates showed that females, Whites, and those with higher education are more likely to be victimized than their counterparts. Above all, the most vulnerable populations are transgender inmates. As shown in Table 7.1, nearly 40% of transgender inmates in federal and state prisons reported sexual victimization in 2011–2012.

There is a strong linkage between sexual victimization and psychological distress among inmates. The NIS estimated that 6.3% of inmates who have serious psychological distress reported sexual victimization by another inmate. In contrast, among prisoners who do not have any indication of mental illness, only 0.7% reported their sexual victimization (Beck et al., 2013).

## Impact of Victimization on Postincarceration

There is relatively limited research on how victimization while incarcerated affects life after release. Yet, learning from the consequences of victimization in general, it is not

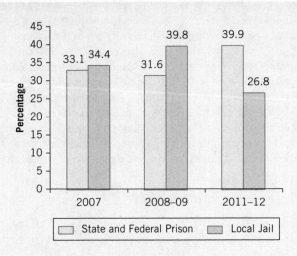

surprising that victimization during incarceration negatively affects offenders' reentry to the community. A study of formally incarcerated individuals who had coercion experiences in prison found that they are likely to have lower well-being and show trauma symptoms after release (Listwan, Colvin, Hanley, & Flannery, 2010). Not only their own victimization but also vicarious victimization cannot be overlooked. Daquin, Daigle, and Listwan (2016) examined the influence of witnessing different types of victimization while incarcerated on offender reentry. The authors found that witnessing sexual assaults has the most significant impact on reentry as such experience increases the risk of subsequent arrest and parole violation. The authors also found that negative consequences are not limited to violent crime, but even witnessing a theft increases the risk of maladoptment into the community. The findings suggest that reentry programs should expand the scope of trauma treatment programs for vicarious victims.

## Victim Advocates for Sexually Assaulted Inmates

Prison rape asserts masculinity and signifies power over those inmates who are in a weaker position (Jacobs, Fleisher, & Krienert, 2009). Sexual assaults in prison are not only a devastating fact for victims but also raise serious health concerns due to higher infection rates of HIV and AIDS than in the general population (Mariner, 2001). A potential dilemma for serving advocates of rape victims in corrections comes from the fact that those victims are convicted criminals. Rape crisis advocates might have reserved feelings related to assisting those offenders who might have hurt or even sexually assaulted someone in the past. Furthermore, a correctional institution has a complex set of rules and regulations, which might prevent advocates from providing the adequate assistance that they could usually offer to an individual in crisis. In times of trouble to make an ethical decision, victim advocates always refer to the basic guideline for human rights, which states that "all victims who reach out should be provided with help for past or present sexual assault" (Pennsylvania Coalition Against Rape, 2006, p. 5). Also, it is important for victim advocates to reflect their own values with the mission and policies of their agencies before visiting a prison (Pennsylvania Coalition Against Rape, 2006).

One commonly used intervention program for crime victims is formulating support groups. However, coordinating and facilitating meetings within correctional institutions necessitates specific considerations. First, one might avoid using terms such as *victims* or *sexual assaults* in the name of support groups in correctional settings as those terms are attached to stigma. Suggested terms would relate to health and wellness, safety, or prevention. Second, for the program to be successful, collaboration with prison staff to maintain the safety and security of the inmates is crucial. Furthermore, collaborating with allied professionals on substance abuse, domestic violence, poverty, and other issues might help advocates get their programs into prisons. Third, those who coordinate the program should carefully assess the readiness of the candidates, that is, whether an individual is ready to share his or her experience with others. Other areas of concern are relevant to the program design and operation. The coordinator should carefully assess how the program design would maximize the benefits to the participants. For example, whether the membership would be closed or open, the frequency of meetings, the development of the rules and goals, safeguards, trust issues among the members, and how to empower the group members to become active leaders in the facilities are questions that must be addressed (Pennsylvania Coalition Against Rape, 2006).

## SUMMARY

This chapter outlined victim involvement in institutional and community corrections. Sooner or later, most individuals incarcerated in jails and prisons are released to the community and might live in the same neighborhood as their victims. In the past, victims had no idea if those offenders were returned to the community. Corrections departments have become aware of the need for victim services in correctional settings and opportunities for victims to assist those offenders in becoming law-abiding citizens. An example is the VIP for DUI offenders, which helps offenders realize the consequences of their actions relative to the victims and their family members. The safety and security of victims and citizens have been ensured by victim and community notification programs. Furthermore, victims have the right to be informed of probation and parole hearings and might be allowed to express their concerns to the parole board. Restorative justice programs give the victim an opportunity to facilitate a dialogue with the offender. As seen in the case of Conor McBride, dialogue and forgiveness can happen in the most serious violent cases.

It should also be recognized that many incarcerated inmates are, in fact, victims of violent crime and suffer from PTSD and other health-related issues. However, few victim services and limited advocacy are available to them. Furthermore, there is increasing concern for the basic human rights of inmates in solitary confinement and the limited reentry opportunities for sex offenders. Much work remains to understand how to support these populations that lack resources and a voice.

## KEY WORDS

Community corrections   119
Day reporting centers
  (DRCS)   122
Electronic monitoring (EM)   122
Impact of crime on victims
  classes (ICVCS)   124

Institutional corrections   115
Jails   115
Parole   120
Prisons   116
Probation   120
Solitary confinement   117

Supermax prison   117
Victim impact panels
  (VIPS)   126
Victim notification system
  (VNS)   128

## INTERNET RESOURCES

**Innocence Project (https://www.innocenceproject.org)**
    The Innocence Project was started 25 years ago by Barry Scheck and Peter Neufeld to identify wrongful convictions using DNA technology. This Web site provides statistics, stories of exonerated individuals, and the latest activities of the project.

**Justice Policy Institute (http://www.justicepolicy.org)**
    The Justice Policy Institute, a national nonprofit organization, researches, analyzes, and identifies effective programs and policies and supports people working for justice reform. The Web site includes reports, briefs, and fact sheets, as well as links to criminal and juvenile justice related news.

**European Forum for Restorative Justice (http://www.euforumrj.org)**
    The European Forum for Restorative Justice comprises volunteer members from at least six different European countries and aims to help establish and develop victim-offender mediation and other restorative justice practices. This Web site highlights some of the innovative projects and upcoming events and conferences.

## CRITICAL THINKING QUESTIONS

1. Those who are in supermax prisons are the most dangerous criminals who have committed the most heinous crimes. Do you agree or disagree with keeping them in solitary confinement without any human contact for many years?

2. What are some distinct factors for victims of violent crime in correctional settings? Should those victims be provided the same resources as victims of crime?

3. How do you balance the safety of victims with the offender's rehabilitation in parole hearings?

4. What are some unintended consequences of Megan's Law and Jessica's Law?

# Juvenile Justice System, Restorative Justice, and Victim Assistance

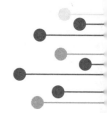

This chapter provides an overview of the juvenile justice system in America as well as the shortcomings and challenges of the system, particularly the unmet needs of juvenile victims and juvenile offenders who have had adverse childhood experiences. Knowing that there is a significant victim-offender overlap in juvenile cases and many youths are in both the child welfare and juvenile justice systems, the chapter addresses how social workers and juvenile justice case workers collaboratively address the needs of youthful offenders. One distinct feature of this chapter is addressing the complex trauma of abused youths. In recent years, there has been a growing interest in applying trauma-informed care in the juvenile justice system. This evolving approach could offer better solutions in responding to trauma-related youth behaviors and providing youth with a safer environment. Yet, to make systemic changes happen, continuing education for all the stakeholders in gaining knowledge on child trauma and the essential elements of trauma-informed care is needed. This chapter summarizes the framework and the core components of the trauma-informed juvenile justice system and explains the steps by juvenile facilities to implement core domains in their policies, protocols, and programming.

The secondary focus of this chapter is the application of restorative justice in the juvenile justice system. As endorsed in the 1996 National Juvenile Justice Action Plan, the philosophy of restorative justice is well-suited to the framework of the juvenile justice system. This chapter explains how the principles of restorative justice differ from the traditional criminal justice system and why restorative justice could produce better solutions for victims, offenders, and community members. Besides victims of heinous violent crimes committed by juveniles, a majority of victims of juvenile offenses are themselves juveniles and family members. As such, the restorative justice approach could be a better solution for many juvenile cases. The summary of some promising restorative justice programs, as well as a case study, explain the transformation of the restorative justice themes into practice. However, as you will see, more comprehensive evaluation is necessary to optimize the benefits of such programs.

Note that not all juvenile offenders are the victims of child abuse and neglect. Also, there are juvenile offenders who commit heinous crimes. In 2010, about 0.8% of all petitioned delinquency cases were waived to criminal court, and half of those waived cases involved serious person offenses (Puzzanchera & Addie, 2014). Keep in mind that the overviews of juvenile offenders and victims of juvenile crimes covered in this chapter are not exhaustive.

## Historical Overview of the Juvenile Justice System

Until the beginning of the 19th century, children who broke the law were treated in the same ways as adult offenders in the United States. The reformatory movement started with the rapid urbanization and industrialization of New York and other cities, which generated greater concern for youths who lacked adequate parental supervision. To provide appropriate care for wayward youths who committed vagrancy or petty crimes, the New York House of Refuge was established in 1825. Jane Addams, the founder of Hull House in Chicago and a Nobel Peace Prize recipient in 1931, had a significant influence on progressive social movements. Addams and other activists helped to establish various social programs, including the Immigrants' Protective League; the Juvenile Protective Association, which was the first juvenile court in the United States; and the Juvenile Psychopathic Clinic, later called the Institute for Juvenile Research (Harvard University Library (n.d.). With the passage of the Illinois Juvenile Court Act of 1899, the first juvenile court in the United States was established in Cook County, Illinois (Siegel & Welsh, 2015).

The basic philosophy of the early juvenile justice system was to serve the best interests of the child. Therefore, the emphasis of the system was on rehabilitation and treatment rather than punishment. The doctrine of ***parens patriae*** (Latin for "parent of his country") was used as the rationale for the state to act as a parent when a child's parents failed to provide appropriate parental supervision. Because of that, juvenile court hearings were informal, and the consideration of due process protections of adjudicated juveniles was absent (Sickmund & Puzzanchera, 2014).

However, during the 1950s and 1960s, professionals and scholars started to question the effectiveness and fairness of the juvenile justice process as many juveniles were held in facilities on the pretense of treatment. To reduce an overinstitutionalized juvenile population, Congress passed the Juvenile Justice and Delinquent Prevention Act in 1974, which provided funds to states to improve the protection of juveniles in the system. The main scopes of the act were to deinstitutionalize status offenders (e.g., truancy, running away from home, violating curfew, underage use of alcohol), to separate juvenile offenders from adult offenders, and to reduce overrepresentation of the minority population in the system. At around the same time, the U.S. Supreme Court began to grant due process rights to juveniles. Through a series of landmark cases, juvenile delinquents gained constitutional protections similar to those for adult offenders (Siegel & Welsh, 2015).

In the mid-1980s to the mid-1990s, the violent crime arrest rates for juveniles surged (Puzzanchera, 2014). Riding the tough-on-crime trend, the focus of the system shifted from rehabilitation to the accountability of juveniles. Consequently, the number of cases judicially waived to criminal court peaked in 1994, and that number was 124% greater than that in 1985 (Hockenberry & Puzzanchera, 2015). However, the number of judicially waived cases started to decline thereafter; there was a 50% decline from 1994 to 2001. A possible explanation of the drastic change is legislative revisions in many states whereby certain serious offenses were removed from juvenile court jurisdiction, and prosecutors were allowed to file cases directly in criminal court (Hockenberry & Puzzanchera, 2015). Continuing reform in the system to adapt to changes over time, the contemporary juvenile justice system aims to balance between public safety and the rehabilitation of juveniles (Sickmund & Puzzanchera, 2014).

The age criteria of the juvenile justice system in some states also has changed over time. Since 1975, five states made changes raising or lowering its upper age limit. As of 2016, 42 states set the upper age for juvenile court jurisdiction as 17, seven states as 16, and two states as 15. However, many states have statutory exceptions, which exclude

**parens patriae:** the doctrine that gives the state the authority to act as the parent when a child's parents fail to provide appropriate parental supervision

certain juvenile offenders from juvenile court jurisdiction (Office of Juvenile Justice and Delinquency Prevention, 2017). Although most states do not have a minimum age for juvenile court jurisdiction, some states have set that age—from 6 in North Carolina to 10 in other states (Masters et al., 2017).

# Rights of Victims of Juvenile Crime

In the past, juvenile court hearings were closed to the public and juvenile records were kept confidential. Consequently, victims were rarely informed about court decisions and the status of juveniles. However, riding the wave of the victims' rights movement in the criminal justice system, victims' rights in the juvenile justice system have been gradually recognized since the 1980s. Most states now grant victims of juvenile delinquency some or all the rights guaranteed to victims of adult crime (Henning, 2009). The general provisions of victim rights for juvenile crimes recognize the right to notice of the juvenile's transfer, release, discharge, or escape from detention; the right to receive adequate protection from harm or threat; the right to receive information on juvenile justice procedures; the right to notice of relevant court proceedings and any schedule changes; and the right to receive a speedy trial and restitution. Juvenile statutes often include an additional obligation on the youth's parents to pay restitution to the victims of the child's conduct. Victims have the right to attend all public court proceedings involving the juveniles, subject to the approval of the judge. Finally, in most states, victims can submit a victim impact statement during the disposition hearing (Henning, 2009).

Some critics argue that much of the emphasis on victim rights in juvenile cases could deter the primary goal of the juvenile justice system, which focuses on the rehabilitation of juveniles (Rennison & Dodge, 2018). For example, the victim impact statement is one of the crucial rights granted to victims. However, presenting the statement at the disposition hearing might result in a harsher disposition, which is contradictory to the goal of juvenile justice. Alternatively, as will be discussed later in this chapter, restorative justice programs could bring better outcomes for the offender and the victim (Henning, 2009).

Furthermore, the complexity of the juvenile justice system presents a major challenge for victims participating in the system. The National Center for Victims of Crime (2013) conducted a series of focus groups and identified five unmet needs of victims of juvenile offenders. First, victims felt there is lack of understanding among juvenile professionals about the victimization experience and the harm to victims. Second, victims would like to receive more information about services, the court proceedings, and the rights and roles of victims in that process. Third, victims want to more actively participate in juvenile justice proceedings and receive better guidance about how they can access quality victim services. Fourth, victims support rehabilitation and restitution and believe more restorative justice options and practices could be used. Lastly, victims expect professionals to understand the special challenges facing victims. These challenges include the trauma and vulnerability of victims, the lack of opportunities for receiving restitution, and the aftermath of relationships where the victim and the youth offender knew each other. Confidentiality in the system is a particular obstacle for many victims.

# Victims of Juvenile Crimes

The statistics show a significant overlap between the age groups of juvenile offenders and victims. According to the National Incident-Based Reporting System (NIBRS), from 1997 to 1998, a majority of the victims of violent offenses committed by juveniles were themselves younger than 18 (see Table 8.1). Furthermore, almost all victims of juveniles knew their offender, and only 7% of victims of nonfatal violent crimes by juveniles was an adult who was a stranger to the offender (McCurley & Snyder, 2004). Among those adult victims (age 30 or older) of juvenile aggravated assault, 37% were parents and stepfathers, and for simple assault juvenile cases, a majority included family members.

Considering a significant victim-offender overlap in juvenile cases, it is reasonable to imagine that those offenses are likely to occur within the sphere of everyday life. More than half (55%) of juvenile violent crimes that involved juvenile victims occurred in a residence, and 18% in a school (Sickmund & Puzzanchera, 2014). Especially, school violence cannot be overlooked as the Centers for Disease Control and Prevention's Youth Risk Behavior Survey (YRBS) showed that more than 3 in 10 high school students were in physical fights, and one in 25 was injured (Sickmund & Puzzanchera, 2014). Besides the physical violence, one of the growing areas of concern is cyberbullying among juveniles, and that topic will be covered in Chapter 12.

As seen, many victims of juvenile crimes are fellow juveniles and family members, and the crimes occur within close proximity of home or school. Also, as outlined later in this chapter, you will find that child victimization and abuse have a strong linkage to problem behaviors and delinquency. Therefore, focusing on the unmet needs of youthful offenders would be critical in reducing further youth crimes and victimization. But before discussing the underlying issues of juvenile delinquents, let us review the juvenile justice process and child welfare system and how those two systems are interrelated.

| Table 8.1 Proportion of All Victims Victimized by Juvenile Offenders | | | | |
|---|---|---|---|---|
| | **Victim Age** | | | |
| **Offense** | **<18** | **<12** | **12–17** | **18+** |
| Total offenses | 51% | 47% | 53% | 9% |
| Sexual assault | 36 | 44 | 30 | 5 |
| Robbery | 59 | 80 | 56 | 13 |
| Aggravated assault | 55 | 49 | 56 | 11 |
| Simple assault | 55 | 49 | 56 | 9 |

# Juvenile Justice Process

The juvenile justice system uses more neutral terminology to distinguish it from the adult criminal justice system as shown in Table 8.2 below.

Although the process might differ significantly by jurisdiction, Figure 8.1 explains the common procedural stages in the juvenile justice system.

## Police Investigation

Juvenile delinquents are usually referred to the juvenile justice system by law enforcement officers. However, in some instances, juveniles can be referred by parents, school officials, probation officers, or other adults. When an officer encounters a juvenile delinquent act, he or she has greater latitude in deciding how to handle the case. After assessing the nature of the offense and other factors such as prior contact with the police and the attitude and demeanor of the child, an officer might give a warning and let the child leave with his or her parents or guardian, refer the child to a social welfare agency, or take the child to a local juvenile facility. In 2010, 23% of all juvenile cases handled by the police resulted in release without further action; 68% were referred to juvenile court; and less than 10% were referred for criminal prosecution or other agencies (Sickmund & Puzzanchera, 2014).

## Prosecution and Intake

When an officer determines further intervention is necessary, the child usually is taken to a juvenile detention center. However, in rural areas that do not have a juvenile facility, the child might be held in a jail. To determine whether to remand the child to a facility, a detention hearing occurs within 24 hours or the time frame otherwise specified by state law. The purpose of the hearing is to determine if there is sufficient grounds to continue

| Table 8.2 | Comparison of the Terminology Used in the Two Systems |
|---|---|
| **Juvenile Justice System** | **Adult System** |
| **Delinquency** | Crime |
| **Custody** | Arrest |
| **Detention facility (juvenile hall)** | Jail |
| **Adjudicatory hearing** | Trial |
| **Disposition** | Sentence |
| **Residential placement** | Incarceration |
| **Aftercare** | Parole |

**Custody:** placing juveniles in a secure environment.

**Detention facility (juvenile hall):** A secure facility that places juveniles during juvenile court proceedings. It is sometimes called detention center or juvenile hall.

Figure 8.1 Juvenile Justice System Case Flow

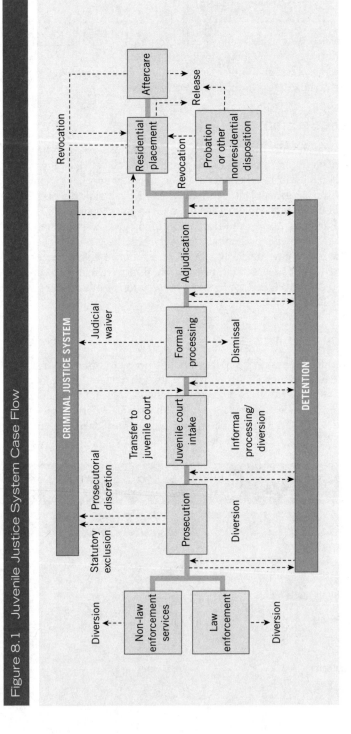

*Source:* Herz et al. (2012, p. 63).

detention of the juvenile. Most states allow detaining youth prior to trial if they are considered a danger to the community (Siegel & Welsh, 2015).

Once a juvenile is taken into custody, his or her case is screened by the juvenile court system. The possible outcomes are the case being dismissed, diverting the child to a community agency, petitioning the child to the juvenile court, or filing a petition and holding the child in detention. If juveniles admit to committing a delinquent act and voluntarily agree to comply with specific conditions such as victim restitution, school attendance, and a curfew, the cases are mostly handled informally. That is, after a juvenile has met the conditions to which he or she agreed, the case will be dismissed. However, if a juvenile fails to comply with the agreement, the case is referred to formal processing (Siegel & Welsh, 2015).

## Adjudication Hearing

In a formal juvenile process, two types of petitions are possible: a delinquent petition requesting an **adjudicatory hearing** (i.e., trial) or a petition requesting a waiver hearing to transfer the case to adult court. The juvenile, his or her family, and an attorney appear before a judge, or a jury, who determines the facts of the case. Similar to adult offenders, juveniles have the right to counsel, freedom from self-incrimination, the right to confront and cross-examine witnesses, and access to procedures concerning rules of evidence, the competence of witnesses, pleadings, and pretrial motions. If the juvenile court finds the juvenile committed a delinquent act, the court must convene a disposition hearing (Siegel & Welsh, 2015).

**Adjudicatory hearing:** the stage of juvenile court proceedings where the judge finds whether the allegations in the petition can be sustained

## Disposition Hearing

In most jurisdictions, the **disposition hearing** is separate from the adjudication hearing. Probation staff members prepare the predisposition report, which is similar to the presentence report in adult cases, and present it to the presiding judge at the disposition hearing. In some states, the predisposition report is mandatory, and in other states it is required only if there is a possibility that the child might be institutionalized (Siegel & Welsh, 2015). After considering all recommendations, the juvenile court judge orders a disposition. The primary factors the judge considers for a disposition are the age of the offenders, the circumstances and gravity of the offense, and prior delinquent history (Villmoare & Benvenuti, 1988).

**Disposition hearing:** juvenile court proceedings in which a judge decides the most appropriate placement of an adjudicated juvenile

## Disposition

A wide variety of disposition options are available to juvenile court judges. Examples include restitution or fines, house arrest and electronic monitoring, therapy, probation, psychiatric treatment, day treatment and reporting centers, residential treatment facilities, and secure confinement (Rennison & Dodge, 2018). Probation is the most commonly used sanction by juvenile courts. Most juveniles receive blended dispositions with some sort of supervised probation and additional requirements such as counseling or restitution to the victim. Some innovative dispositions found in restorative justice practices will be discussed later in this chapter.

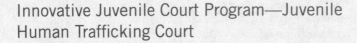
## Innovative Juvenile Court Program—Juvenile Human Trafficking Court

Minors who become human trafficking victims are a growing occurrence in Fresno County. In 2017, the Fresno County Superior Court started a pilot program with a three-year, $383,651 grant from the Judicial Council of California. The juvenile human trafficking court will function as a normal court but will take in juveniles who were involved in or forced into acts of prostitution and other human trafficking offenses, victimized in the child welfare system, or at high risk of exploitation. The court's focus is to use court-imposed mental health treatment programs and support services to help children recover from the exploitation and trauma of being in the sex trade and keep them out of such situations in the future. Some of the grant funding will also be used to provide professional education to workers in the court system and related agencies on working with youth who have been victims of human trafficking.

Gangs view prostitution as "low-hanging fruit," as women can make as much as $10,000 in a day. Unlike guns or drugs, women can be sold over and over again. "The greed, the lack of humanity—they live off the flesh of another," Miiko Anderson, the Fresno County deputy district attorney assigned to the human trafficking unit, said.

Appleton, R. (2017, November 28). To break the cycle of children sold for sex, the legal system is trying something new. *Fresno Bee*. Retrieved from https://www.fresnobee.com/news/special-reports/human-trafficking/article186937063.html.

---

**Residential placement:** placement for youth in residential facilities that might be publicly or privately operated and could be a prison- or a home-like setting

**Aftercare:** upon release from an institution, a juvenile is often ordered to a period of aftercare, which is similar to adult parole

In 2010, about one fourth of the cases in which the juvenile was adjudicated as delinquent resulted in **residential placement** (Hockenberry & Puzzanchera, 2015). Such residential facilities might be publicly or privately operated and can be a prison- or a home-like setting. Upon release from an institution, the juvenile is often ordered to a period of **aftercare**, which is similar to adult parole. If the juvenile does not follow the conditions of aftercare, he or she might be recommended to return to the same facility or another one.

## Specialized Court Programs

Besides the traditional juvenile justice court system, many attempts have made to create specialized court programs for juveniles. Juvenile drug court programs have gained popularity to intervene more effectively with juveniles who have substance abuse issues. Substance abuse issues are prominent among juveniles; for example, in 2000, nearly 17% of juvenile arrests were due to substance-related offenses (Belenko & Logan, 2003). In the Monitoring the Future study, among high school seniors, 44% of males and 38% of females reported alcohol use in the past 30 days, and 28% of males and 18% of females said they had five or more drinks in a row in the previous two weeks (Sickmund & Puzzanchera, 2014). Addressing the prevalence of substance abuse issues among juveniles, the drug court programs integrate substance abuse treatment and criminal justice supervision. Even though those programs have been welcomingly adopted in many jurisdictions, the meta-analysis of the programs indicated that juvenile drug courts were no more effective than traditional court processing for reducing recidivism or drug use (Tanner-Smith, Lipsey, & Wilson, 2016). The authors note that the lack of positive outcomes is in part due to the low-quality research studies currently available even though particular drug court configurations could be effective. More evaluation research would be necessary to determine how the court programs could affect changing the behaviors of youth. Other innovative court programs include teen court, in which juvenile offenders are tried and sentenced by a jury of peers (Logalbo & Callahan, 2001), and juvenile mental health courts that address the special mental health needs of juveniles (Heretick & Russell, 2013).

## Child Welfare System

There is a significant overlap between the criminal justice system and the child welfare system. Especially children who are the victims of child maltreatment are crucial witnesses of crimes in the criminal justice system. At the same time, they receive protection and services from the child welfare system. The research indicates that the perpetrators of violent crimes with juvenile victims are usually family members. According to NIBRS data in 2009 and 2010, of overall violent crime cases known to law enforcement, 28% of males and 35% of females from birth to age 17 were victimized by family members (Sickmund & Puzzanchera, 2014). Even though parents have fundamental rights to make decisions concerning the care, custody, and control of their children without government interference, if the parents' care does not meet reasonable standards or a child's life is in danger, the state can step in and remove a child from the home and place him or her in a secure environment. Figure 8.2 shows the process of the child welfare system for how reported child maltreatment cases are handled by the system.

**Figure 8.2  Case Flow of Children in the Child Welfare System**

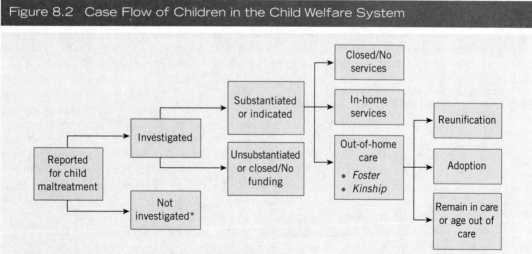

*Nearly half of all states have policies that allow for "alternative response"—no requirement that determination of maltreatment has or has not occurred. Despite the variability among states, these differential responses address the service needs of families who may be at risk and avoid labeling the caregiver as a perpetrator of maltreatment. The screening and investigation functions are altered by the presence of alternative response systems in the child welfare agency.

*Source:* Herz et al. (2012, p. 63).

## Screening and Investigation

All states have statutes that require professionals who frequently come in contact with children to report suspected child maltreatment to an appropriate agency. For example, mandatory reporters in California include teachers, social workers, physicians, nurses, clergy members, athletic coaches, and commercial film and photographic print or image processors (Child Welfare Information Gateway, 2015). The child welfare service agencies screen those cases, and about 67% are moved onto investigation or assessment (U.S. Department of Health and Human Services, 2004). At an initial investigation, a case worker assesses if a child is in imminent danger. If the maltreatment is a one-time incident and the child is at no risk of danger in the future, the case will be closed.

Many states now use a **differential response** (DR) or two-track system. There are some variations in operating the DR, but under the two-track system the cases are classified into an investigative response (IR) or an alternative response (AR). An IR addresses the most serious at-risk cases, and forensic evidence and formal investigation are implemented. An AR is used for moderate- or low-risk cases, which do not require a formal investigation but for which community services are provided for the families. As of 2014, 20 states and the District of Columbia had statewide DR programs, another seven states had regional or county implementation of DR, at least eight states were in various stages of actively planning DR initiatives, and nine states were in the planning stages (Child Welfare Information Gateway, 2014).

In an emergency, investigators can take the child into custody and place him or her in a secure environment. In some jurisdictions, police and child protection staff make an independent investigation, and the other jurisdictions conduct coordinated investigations as part of a multiagency team. Medical examinations provide the critical evidence needed to substantiate a crime or child maltreatment. Overall, 10% to 25% of all reported sexual abuse cases receive medical exams (Finkelhor, Cross, & Cantor, 2005). In some states, certain types of child maltreatment cases reported to the child welfare system are automatically referred to police or prosecutors. Other states allow more discretion as to whether cases are reported to the police or prosecutors (Finkelhor et al., 2005).

## Substantiation of Child Maltreatment

The determination of child maltreatment requires a preponderance of evidence or that there is enough information and facts that a reasonable person would believe that child maltreatment has occurred. The national statistics indicate that about 30% of all reported cases were substantiated in 2004 (Finkelhor et al., 2005). Some reasons that reported maltreatment cases are not substantiated include failure of the family or other informants to cooperate with the investigation, lack of sufficient evidence, allegations made outside the jurisdiction or authority of the agency, and/or an agency's inability to investigate adequately due to insufficient resources. False allegations were less than 1% of all cases (Finkelhor et al., 2005).

## Provision of Services

The child protection system offers counseling, parent education, and family support to prevent future maltreatment. According to the U.S. Department of Health and Human Services, those services are usually offered 7 to 8 weeks after an investigation begins

(Finkelhor et al., 2005). Family members and children might also receive services from other agencies such as mental health services.

## Court Hearing

When child maltreatment is substantiated, an advisement hearing is held. During the hearing, the court reviews the facts of the case and determines if the removal of the child is justified. Also, the parents are notified of the charges against them (Siegel & Welsh, 2015). If the parents deny the petition, a pretrial conference is held. About three fourths of the cases that go to a pretrial conference are settled, and the parents accept a treatment plan. The treatment plan includes the type of services that the child and the child's family will receive, reunification goals, and alternative placement options in case the reunification goals are not met.

## Out-of-Home Placement

The most serious intervention is to remove a child from his or her home. Approximately 6% of cases investigated for suspected child maltreatment involved removal from the home in 2002 (Finkelhor et al., 2005). During 2015, 269,509 children entered the foster care system, and the median length of stay in the system was 13.5 months. Children removed to live with their relatives tend to stay for longer periods of time (Child Welfare Information Gateway, 2017). Children of ages 1 to 5 were 31% of the foster care population. The median age of children in foster care in 2010 was 9.2. Minority youth were overrepresented in the foster care population. Although in the U.S. child population, 44% are minority, minorities accounted for 58% of the foster care population (Sickmund & Puzzanchera, 2014).

## Reunification

The ultimate goal of the child welfare system is to reunify the family. Under the Adoption and Safe Families Act of 1997, families generally receive 15 to 18 months of family reunification services. In cases where reunification never happens, even after receiving those services, parental rights are terminated, and the child enters post permanency planning services (Child Welfare Information Gateway, 2017). Several factors affect a successful reunification. Overall, research suggests that social and economic factors such as family income, level of education of the parents, and children's health and disability status are related to the outcome of reunification (Hines, Lee, Osterling, & Drabble, 2007). The other relevant factor is marital status: When mothers are married, reunification is more likely to happen (Courtney, 1994; Wells & Guo, 1999). Age of children entering the child welfare system has mixed findings. Although some studies found younger children are less likely to be reunified (Courtney, 1994; George, 1990), another study found that not to be the case (Hines et al., 2007).

# Youth in the Juvenile Justice and Child Welfare Systems

Ample studies have shown a strong linkage between a history of childhood maltreatment and juvenile delinquency (Courtney, Piliavin, Grogan-Kaylor, & Nesmith, 2001;

Courtney & Heuring, 2005; Jennings, Piquero, & Reingle, 2012). The term **crossover youth** is used to describe youth who experience maltreatment and engage in delinquency (Abbott & Barnett, 2015). **Dually involved youth** refers to those youth who are simultaneously involved in the child welfare and juvenile justice systems (Cutuli et al., 2016). According to a national report of juvenile offenders and victims in 2014, two thirds of youth who entered the juvenile justice system in Seattle experienced some form of child welfare involvement (Sickmund & Puzzanchera, 2014). Moreover, youth with an extensive history of child welfare involvement were three times more likely to be involved in the juvenile justice system than those who had no child welfare involvement. Of those juveniles with no child welfare experience, the recidivism rate for a new offense within two years was 34%, whereas for juveniles with extensive child welfare involvement, the rate was 70% over the same period (Sickmund & Puzzanchera, 2014).

Many factors contribute to the crossover risk of children. Researchers agree that placement instability increases the likelihood of juvenile justice involvement (Jonson-Reid & Barth, 2000; Stewart, Livingston, & Dennison, 2008; Goodkind, Shook, Kim, Pohlig, & Herring, 2013). In general, placing a child with relatives is considered a preferred option because kin placement allows family connectedness to be maintained, reduces the trauma associated with placement, and increases placement stability (Ryan, Hong, Herz, & Hernandez, 2010). However, a comparison of the juvenile delinquent involvement for those youth who were in kinship placement and nonkin placement indicated that Hispanic males and females were better off by being placed in relatives' homes, whereas African American and White male youth in kin placement had a much higher risk of juvenile justice involvement than when placed in nonkin homes (Ryan et al., 2010). Youth placed in congregate care facilities (e.g., group homes, maternity homes, residential treatment facilities) have much higher risk of juvenile justice involvement than other types of placement (Ryan et al., 2010; Goodkind et al., 2013; Cutuli et al., 2016).

Researchers consistently found that the crossover risk of African American youth is much higher than that of White youth and other ethnic groups even after controlling for mediating factors (Ryan & Testa, 2005; Huang, Ryan, & Herz, 2012). A study of individuals born from 1985 to 1994 whose families received in-home services from the child welfare system and/or who were placed in out-of-home care in Allegheny County, Pennsylvania, indicated that African American youth are more than twice as likely as White youth to have juvenile justice involvement (Cutuli et al., 2016).

Across studies, boys in the child welfare system were found to be at higher risk of juvenile justice involvement than girls (Dishion & Patterson, 2006; Moffitt, 2006; Puzzanchera, Adams, & Sickmund, 2010; Cutuli et al., 2016). However, caution is necessary as the pathway of girls who are getting into the juvenile justice system is quite different from that of boys (Bender, 2010). Bloom, Owen, and Covington (2003) suggested that substance abuse, victimization, trauma history, and mental health conditions lead to female pathways to offending, and programs for female offenders need to target such issues. Owen, Wells, and Pollock (2017) echo this argument in describing the pathways that women travel to crime as related to their multiple marginalization and a social and human capital deficit or their lack of connection to conventional institutions, such as family, school, and work.

*Crossover youth:* youth who experience maltreatment and engage in delinquency

*Dually involved youth:* youth who are simultaneously involved in the child welfare and juvenile justice systems (Cutuli et al., 2016)

A girl who had been involved in the system remarked:

I was locked up 10 different times within a two-year period. Inside juvie, I met other girls like myself who were there for prostitution, running away, and truancy. All of us were from the same neighborhoods, poor families, and seemed to have the same disposition of trauma, anger mixed with hopelessness. We were not violent girls. We were girls who were hurting. Being confined to a tiny cement room was one of the hardest things I have ever had to experience. Being locked up, all I could do was reflect on my life but it didn't seem to help. I became even more withdrawn and angry. (Saar, Epstein, Rosenthal, & Vafa, 2015, p. 2)

Although the reasons are inconclusive, some researchers suggest that the increasing rate of girls' involvement in the juvenile justice system over the past two decades is considered not a result of those girls getting more violent or committing more delinquent activities but rather those girls being potentially referred to the system due to aggressive enforcement policies for nonserious offenses (Saar et al., 2015). Especially, girls are disproportionately entering the system with status offenses. For example, in 2013, 37% of female youths were detained for status offenses and technical violations compared to 25% of their male counterparts. When looking at simple assault and public order offenses, excluding the possession of weapons, 21% of female youths with those charges were detained in a juvenile facility compared to 12% for male youths (Sickmund, Sladky, Kang, & Puzzanchera, 2015). Another notable gender difference is that justice-involved female youth have reported higher levels of exposure to sexual assault and interpersonal victimization, whereas justice-involved boys have reported higher rates of witnessing violence (Cauffman, Feldman, Waterman, & Steiner, 1998; Wood, Foy, Layne, Pynoos, & James, 2002; Ford, Chapman, Hawke, & Albert, 2007). A report prepared by the Georgetown Law Center indicated that the sexual abuse rate for justice-involved girls is four times higher than that of boys (Saar et al., 2015).

Those juvenile delinquents with adverse childhood experiences are the most vulnerable population. The **Crossover Youth Practice Model** (CYPM) is designed to target that population and enhance the efficiency and effectiveness of the systems to better address the needs of youth in the two systems (Center for Juvenile Justice Reform, 2015).

**Crossover Youth Practice Model (CYPM):** a model designed to achieve the efficiency and effectiveness of the welfare and justice systems to better address the needs of crossover youth

## Crossover Youth Practice Model (CYPM)

The Crossover Youth Practice Model was developed by the Center for Juvenile Justice Reform (CJJR) at the Georgetown University McCourt School of Public Policy to minimize the involvement of maltreated youth in the juvenile justice system (Center for Juvenile Justice Reform, 2015). This research-based approach assists child welfare, juvenile justice, and related agencies in adopting policies and practices that aim to improve the lives of youth and families. The CYPM is implemented in three phases as discussed below.

Phase I attempts to identify crossover youth at the earliest time, for example, arrest and juvenile intake. The CYPM suggests that an intake process should include a validated screening process to determine if a youth is involved in the child welfare system. The communication between the juvenile justice (JJ) case worker and the child welfare (CW) social worker is essential. For example, sharing the client database between the child welfare and juvenile justice systems helps to identify crossover youth in a timely manner. The model recommends that youth, family members, the CW social worker, the JJ intake worker, attorneys, and other service providers come together to explore ways to divert youth from the system.

Phase II focuses on youth who are formally prosecuted. The CW social worker and the JJ case worker jointly work with the youth and the family to make an assessment and create a case plan. An assessment includes prior behavioral patterns, family stability, the needs of the youth and the family, criminogenic factors, and other needs including education and mental health. After a comprehensive assessment, an integrated case plan is developed. A case plan includes evidence-based interventions and services that address the specific needs of the youth. An agreement on the plan by the youth and his or her parents should occur after the youth and the parents fully understand the plan and any expected changes.

Phase III addresses the youths who are in the disposition process. The focus of this stage is ongoing case management and planning for case closure. At this stage, the CW social worker and the JJ case worker determine which agency should be the main point of contact for the family and who will have primary responsibility for other tasks. Yet, continuing communication between the professionals is expected. Efforts to find ways to keep youth connected with family and professionals who are specialized in mental health, employment, housing, healthcare, and education help provide ongoing necessary support.

An evaluation study of the CYPM conducted by Haight, Bidwell, Choi, and Cho (2016) indicated that the CYPM youth were less likely to recidivate than the control group even after controlling for location, time, and other key factors. As the model is relatively new, more comprehensive evaluation is needed to identify when, for whom, and under what conditions the CYPM is most effective (Haight et al., 2016).

# Trauma-Informed Juvenile Justice System

## Complex Trauma in Children

Children and adolescents who are exposed to domestic violence or have experienced chronic child abuse and neglect often confront lifelong problems beyond diagnoses of posttraumatic stress disorder (PTSD). In addressing the need for a more comprehensive picture of complex trauma of maltreated children, Cook, Blaustein, Spinazzola, and Kolk (2003) reviewed the relevant literature and identified seven primary domains of impairment observed in traumatized children. Those domains are (1) attachment, (2) biology, (3) affect regulation, (4) dissociation, (5) behavioral control, (6) cognition, and (7) self-concept as shown in Table 8.3.

**Attachment:** When the caregiver of the child is the cause of trauma, children demonstrate insecure and disorganized attachment problems. The key features of disorganized attachment are (1) increased susceptibility to stress, (2) an inability to regulate emotions without external assistance, and (3) altered help-seeking.

## Table 8.3   Domains of Impairment of Children Exposed to Complex Trauma

**Domains of Impairment in Children Exposed to Complex Trauma**

| I. Attachment | III. Affect regulation | V. Behavioral control |
|---|---|---|
| Problems with boundaries | Difficulty with emotional self-regulation | Poor modulation of impulses |
| Social isolation | Difficulty labeling and expressing feelings | Self-destructive behavior |
| Interpersonal difficulties | Problems knowing and describing internal states | Aggression toward others |
| Difficulty attuning to other people's emotional states | Difficulty communicating wishes and needs | Pathological self-soothing behaviors |
| Difficulty with perspective taking | | Sleep disturbances |
| | | Eating disorders |
| | | Substance abuse |
| | | Excessive compliance |
| | | Oppositional behavior |
| | | Difficulty understanding and complying with rules |
| | | Reenactment of trauma in behavior or play (e.g., sexual, aggressive) |
| II. Biology | IV. Dissociation | VI. Cognition |
| Sensorimotor developmental problems | Distinct alterations in states of consciousness | Difficulties in attention regulation and executive functioning |
| Analgesia | Amnesia | Lack of sustained curiosity |
| Problems with coordination, balance, body tone | Depersonalization and derealization | Problems with processing novel information |
| Somatization | Two or more distinct states of consciousness | Problems focusing on and completing tasks |
| Increased medical problems across a wide span (e.g., pelvic pain, asthma, skin problems, autoimmune disorders, pseudoseizures) | Impaired memory for state-based events | Problems with object constancy |
| | | Difficulty planning and anticipating |
| | | Problems understanding responsibility |
| | | Learning difficulties |
| | | Problems with language development |
| | | Problems with orientation in time and space |

*(Continued)*

Table 8.3 (Continued)

**Domains of Impairment in Children Exposed to Complex Trauma**

| | | | |
|---|---|---|---|
| VII. Self-concept | | | |
| Lack of continuous, predictable sense of self | | | |
| Poor sense of separateness | | | |
| Disturbances of body image | | | |
| Low self-esteem | | | |
| Shame and guilt | | | |

**Biology:** Trauma further interferes with the development of brain functioning. The integration and communication of the right and left hemispheres of the brain are disrupted with stress, and children are prone to react with extreme helplessness, confusion, withdrawal, or rage. Traumatic experiences during middle childhood and adolescence increase the risk for disruptions in self-regulatory abilities.

**Affect Regulation:** Child trauma not only affects child core regulatory systems but also affects the capacity to self-regulate behavioral and emotional expressions and to communicate their wishes and needs to others. Those include deficits in the capacity to identify internal emotional experiences, difficulties with the safe expression of emotions, and impaired capacity to modulate emotional experience.

**Dissociation:** *Dissociation* is the "failure to integrate or associate information and experience in a normally expectable fashion" (Putnam, 1997, p. 7). Dissociation is associated with biological alternations in the brain. When trauma is chronic, a child is more likely to rely on dissociation to manage the experience.

**Behavioral Control:** Chronic childhood trauma is associated with both under- and overcontrolled behavior patterns. Children could become aggressive to others, abuse substances, or comply with rules excessively. Sexually abused children might engage in sexual behaviors to achieve acceptance and intimacy.

**Cognition:** Neglected infants and toddlers demonstrate delay in language development and deficits in overall IQ. Children and adolescents who experience trauma demonstrate deficits in attention, abstract reasoning, and executive functioning. In elementary school, maltreated children are more likely to avoid challenging tasks and are overly reliant on teachers' guidance. By middle school and high school, maltreated children are more likely to exhibit higher incidences of disciplinary referrals and suspensions (Eckenrode, Laird, & Zahn-Waxler, 1993).

**Self-Concept:** Children normally consolidate a stable and integrated sense of identity. However, traumatized children are more likely to have a sense of self as defective, helpless, deficient, and unlovable. Children tend to self-blame for negative experiences if they already feel powerless and anticipate rejection.

## Impact of Complex Trauma in Juvenile Facilities

As seen, exposure to violence during childhood affects one's sense of security while being confined in detention facilities. Those juveniles who have cumulative complex traumas are more likely to overreact to perceived threats (Pickens, 2016). Sometimes, trauma-experienced youth often display extremely aggressive reactions to protect themselves from being designated as weak or as a failure. Other times, such youth might physically and emotionally isolate themselves from others. Those traumatic stress reactions could be triggered by certain activities, for example, a song about mothers during the Mothers' Day weekend that might lead to recalling harsh memories and result in completely withdrawing from any activities. Alternatively, an enforcement of disciplinary action might retraumatize children. For example, a child who refuses to take a shower or substantially delays taking a shower is generally considered to have a defiant attitude toward officers and staff in the facility. However, having a shower could be a trauma reminder for some children if their parents used a cold or hot shower as a method of punishment or the child might have been sexually abused while taking a shower. If such is the case, punitive ways to control the behavior not only interfere with recovery but also might make the trauma worse (Pickens, 2016).

Managing youth trauma-related aggressive behavior becomes a burden for juvenile detention officers and counselors. Furthermore, when interacting with youth with severe trauma, staff could develop vicarious trauma or become burned out and decrease their ability to perform their duty (Saakvitne, Pearlman, & Abrahamson, 1996). To create a safer environment for both youth and detention staff and addressing the complex trauma of children, a major adjustment in the juvenile justice system would be necessary.

## Trauma-Informed Care (TIC)

Increased awareness of the pervasive trauma of juvenile delinquents has brought attention to rethinking the policies, procedures, and services in juvenile facilities. According to the American Association of Children's Residential Centers (2010), trauma-informed care is defined as

> an approach to organizing treatment that integrates an understanding of the
> impact and consequences of trauma into all clinical interventions as well as
> all aspects of organizational function. A core concept of trauma-informed care
> is a universal precaution: Presume that every person in the treatment setting

has likely been exposed to abuse, neglect, persistently overwhelming stress or other traumatic experiences. (Branson, Baetz, Horwitz, Hoagwood, & Kendall-Tackett, 2017, p. 636)

Yet, there is no consensus on the definition of TIC among scholars (Branson et al., 2017). Table 8.4 shows the core domains of TIC for juvenile justice as summarized by Branson et al. (2017).

## Clinical Services

Clinical service domains include initial screening and then comprehensive mental health assessment for youth who screen positive; evidence-based trauma-specific mental health interventions; and services and programs that address the needs of diverse groups of youth and that reduce disparities related to race/ethnicity, gender sexual orientation, developmental level and socioeconomic status. Only evidence-based trauma-informed treatment should be used with youth and families.

## Agency Context

Agency context domains contain service planning and referrals that prioritize youth and family preference; staff training and education on child development, family dynamics, trauma, work-related traumatic stress reactions, and PTSD; promoting a physically and psychologically safe environment among youth, families, and staff; and creating written policies and procedures that incorporate the principles of a TIC. Training needs to be ongoing so that new information and science about trauma are included.

| Table 8.4 Core Domains of a TIC for Juvenile Justice | |
|---|---|
| **Area of focus** | **Domains within this area** |
| Clinical Services | Screening and assessment |
| | Services and interventions |
| | Cultural competence |
| Agency Context | Youth and family engagement/involvement |
| | Workplace development and support |
| | Promoting a safe agency environment |
| | Agency policies, procedures, and leadership |
| System Level | Cross-system collaboration |
| | System-level policies and procedures |
| | Quality assurance and evaluation |

## System Level

System-level domains include cross-system collaboration to coordinate care across child welfare, education, healthcare, and behavioral and mental health systems and to develop an information-sharing system among those agencies; development of system-level policies to minimize the contact of youth in juvenile justice; and data collection and evaluation of the process and the impact of implementing TIC. Collaboration also includes the family court system, which generally lacks a connection to the aforementioned social service agencies.

The concept of trauma-informed care has shed new light on the juvenile justice system. However, there is still disagreement as to the definitions and domains within this area of focus. Branson et al. (2017) suggest that prospective evaluation research could determine which practices or policies would produce positive outcomes for youth and staff and enhance the overall efficiency of communication and collaboration among relevant agencies.

# Balanced and Restorative Justice for Juveniles

Crime should never be the sole, or even primary business of the state if real differences are thought in the well-being of individuals, families and communities. The structure, procedures, and evidentiary rules of the formal criminal justice process coupled with most justice officials' lack of knowledge and connection to (the parties) affected by crime, preclude the state from acting alone to achieve transformative changes. (Bazemore, 1998, p. 351)

## Overview of the Restorative Justice Principle

The primary goal of restorative justice is to restore the relationship between victims, offenders, and communities and to establish peace among those three stakeholders. Zehr (1990) defined *restorative justice* as a framework that focuses on repairing the harm done to victims and the community through a process of negotiation, mediation, victim empowerment, and reparation. Although the philosophy of restorative justice has existed in the indigenous traditions of community justice (Maruna, 2013), the introduction of restorative justice to the juvenile justice system in the United States is fairly new. In the late 1970s, some communities recognized restorative justice as an alternative way to handle juvenile property crime cases (Umbreit, 2001). Since that time, restorative justice has gained popularity across many states. The 1996 National Juvenile Justice Action Plan recommended "balanced and restorative justice" endorsing adaptation of restorative justice as a framework of justice reform. The balanced approach addresses three primary goals: offender accountability to the victim and the community, offender rehabilitation and reintegration, and enhancing community safety and security (Bilchik, 1997).

Restorative principles are incorporated in many state statutes and codes (Pavelka, 2016). For example, a California statute, the 2005 Welfare and Institutions Code, Section 1700-1705 Article 1. General Provisions and Definitions, includes restorative

*Restorative justice:* a framework that focuses on repairing the harm done to victims and the community through a process of negotiation, mediation, victim empowerment, and reparation (Zehr, 1990)

justice-related language—"community restoration, victim restoration, and offender training and treatment." The New Jersey legislative statement (P.L. 2002 Title 2A:4A-21) requires the Juvenile Justice Commission "to incorporate into the juvenile justice system the principle of balanced and restorative justice." Furthermore, many national and international organizations, including the United Nations, the American Bar Association, the National Organization for Victim Assistance, and the National Council of Crime and Delinquency, have endorsed restorative justice and its principles (Pavelka, 2016).

As shown in Table 8.5, restorative justice is distinguished from traditional retributive responses to crime. Under traditional criminal justice, crime is considered an act against the state and a violation of the law. In contrast, restorative justice considers offenders, victims, and the community all to be important stakeholders of justice processes. The focus of the traditional criminal justice system is the offender's accountability, which is defined by punishment. In contrast, restorative justice emphasizes the future, and accountability is defined as assuming the offender will take responsibility and take action to repair the harm of the offense. The traditional criminal justice system is formal, and sentencing options are limited. In contrast, restorative justice is informal, and resolution could be anything from an apology letter to community service or restitution (National Center for Victims of Crime, 1999, pp. 45–46).

## Programs Using a Restorative Justice Approach

Restorative justice is not a specific program but rather a set of values and a process (Kramer, 2003). Restorative justice embraces a wide variety of programs, including restorative justice conferences/family group conferences, victim-offender mediation (VOM), circles, victim impact panels, and restorative panels (Bazemore & Maruna, 2009). Below are some programs that have been commonly used to respond to juvenile crimes.

### Restorative Justice Conferences and Family Group Conferences

Restorative justice conferences and **family group conferences** are similar in design and application. Such conferences are coordinated with a trained facilitator whereby the offender(s), the victim(s), their families, other affected individuals, and anyone who supports the victim and the offender are the common participants in the conference. Those supporters include people from schools, churches, and community-based organizations. Police officers could serve as facilitators or become participants of the conference. Conferencing allows victims, parents, and others to express their concerns and the impact of crime on them, which helps youth become aware of the consequences of their wrongdoing and makes them more accountable. Consequently, those youth are more likely to complete the tasks to which they agreed (McGarrell, 2001).

### Victim-Offender Mediation (VOM)

**Victim-offender mediation (VOM)** brings a victim and an offender together with a trained mediator to discuss the offense for which they were involved. The mediator usually has a separate premediation session with the offender and the victim, which is an essential step to make the mediation successful (Umbreit, 1994). During the session,

**Family group conferences:** an informal meeting coordinated with a trained facilitator whereby the offender(s), the victim(s), their families, other affected individuals, and anyone who supports the victim and the offender are the common participants in the conference

**Victim-offender mediation (VOM):** a trained mediator coordinates a meeting of a victim and an offender to discuss the offense for which they were involved and facilitate a dialogue. The mediator usually has a separate premediation session with the offender and the victim

**Table 8.5   The Shift From "Retributive Justice" to Restorative Justice**

| Retributive Justice | Restorative Justice | Implications for Victims |
| --- | --- | --- |
| The criminal justice system controls crime. | Crime control lies primarily in the community. | The community—including victims and their allies—participates in and directly benefits from deterrence. |
| Offender accountability is defined as taking punishment. | Accountability is defined as assuming responsibility and taking action to repair harm. | Offenders are held directly accountable to victims. |
| Crime is an individual act with individual responsibility. | Crime has both individual and social dimensions of responsibility. | Prevention, intervention, and breaking the cycle of violence are important considerations. |
| Crime is an act against the state, a violation of the law, and an abstract idea. | Crime is an act against another person in the community. | The individualization of the victim and breaking the cycle of violence are important considerations. |
| Punishment is effective: a. Threat of punishment deters crime. b. Punishment changes behavior. | Punishment alone is not effective in changing behavior and is disruptive to community harmony and good relationships. | The victim is individualized as central to the crime and the criminal justice system process, with the community duly noted as being affected by crimes. |
| Victims are peripheral to the process. | Victims are central to the process of solving a crime. | Restorative justice principles are "victim-centered." |
| The offender is defined by deficits. | The offender is defined by his or her capacity to make reparation. | Reparations to the victim and to the community are a priority. |
| The focus is on establishing blame, on guilt, and on one's past (did he or she do it?). | The focus is on problem solving, liabilities/obligations, and the future (what should be done?) | A central goal is to deter future criminal action through conflict resolution, problem solving, and fulfilling obligations to the victim and to the community. |
| The emphasis is on adversarial relationships. | The emphasis is on dialogue and negotiation. | Victims are active participants in determining appropriate reparations. |
| An imposition of pain is used to punish and deter or prevent crime. | Restitution is a means of restoring both parties; the goal is conciliation/restoration. | Restitution holds the offender accountable and is meaningful to both him or her and the victim. |
| The community is on the sideline, represented abstractly by the state. | The community is the facilitator in the restorative process. | Just as the community is negatively affected by crime, it is positively affected by the restorative justice process. |

*(Continued)*

| Table 8.5 (Continued) | | |
|---|---|---|
| **Retributive Justice** | **Restorative Justice** | **Implications for Victims** |
| The response is focused on the offender's past behavior. | The response is focused on harmful consequences of the offender's behavior; the emphasis is on the future. | Crime deterrence in the future focuses on victim and public safety. |
| There is a dependence on proxy professionals. | There is direct involvement by participants. | Victims and their allies are directly involved in the criminal and juvenile justice and restorative justice processes. |

a victim talks about his or her experience and the impact of the offense. The offender might explain the reasons why he or she committed the offense and answer the victim's questions. After a full discussion of the case, the parties discuss the agreement and create a plan. A common agreement is to write an apology letter, determine monetary payments, perform community service, and participate in supportive groups or services (Kramer, 2003). Evaluation of VOM indicated that victims were significantly less fearful of being revictimized (Bazemore & Umbreit, 2001).

## Circles

**Circles** are methods of dialogue whereby any member of the community who has an interest in the case can participate. The root of circles is found in aboriginal and Navajo traditions. In 1991, Judge Barry Stuart of the Yukon Territorial Court introduced the sentencing circle as a means of sharing the justice process with the community (Bazemore & Maruna, 2009). Circles operate on the principles of respect, equality, and consensus-based decision making. With a skilled facilitator, all parties are given a voice and can speak freely. The stronger connectedness of people in the community is a critical element of the program.

**Circles:** one of the restorative justice practices where the community members who has an interest in the case uses a circle to discuss the case to deal with the harm created by the offender, of healing the victim, and of restoring the community

## CASE STUDY
### Restorative Justice in Practice

A high school student received an anonymous text message that said, "I will stab you." She was scared and confused and immediately called her mother. The mother, who was out of town, was panicked to get the call from her daughter. While driving back to town, her mind went blank and she felt helpless. In addition to the victim and her family, the incident was also a significant threat to school security. Assuming a possible weapon was on campus, the school could have done a lockdown and multiple police agencies would have responded to protect the students at the school, which would have cost thousands of dollars.

After all, the school's quick response to the incident revealed that the message was sent from three of the victim's classmates. They got a new app that allowed them to send an anonymous text message and wanted to try that without thinking about the consequences. Those students had no idea about the effect their joke would have on the victim, the victim's family, the school, and themselves. The seriousness of the case called attention to those students who could have received suspension for the rest of the semester, which may have delayed their graduation. However, knowing those students had no prior school suspensions and violations, the case was assigned to a family conference program.

Before the family conference, the case manager visited each family and explained the mediation process. After the victim, the classmates, and their parents agreed to participate in the meeting, the family conference was held. During the conference, the three students explained that they did not have any intention to hurt the victim and thought the text message was a joke. They appeared uncomfortable facing the victim and remorseful. Each apologized to the victim about their careless action in hurting the victim and the victim's family. Then, their parents made sincere apologies to the victim and her parents about their children's inconsiderate behavior.

The victim listened silently to those remarks in tears. When the case manager asked her about a possible resolution, she said that 15 hours of community service would be appropriate. Her mother added that she still cares about her classmates even after the incident and did not want to be too harsh on them. Then, one parent suggested that community service could be talking to incoming freshman students about how their thoughtless action resulted in

affecting the life of the victim, family, and other people. After everyone expressed their thoughts, the meeting moved to reaching agreements. The agreement included 15 hours of community service, which included the presentation to incoming students. The students also promised that they would never send any offensive text message to her or anyone else, and if they observed someone doing such an act, they would try to stop it. The meeting was closed with the following remark "The trust was broken, but here is the opportunity to rebuild the trust."

Without the active involvement of the victim and the offenders in the conference, it seems unlikely that the victim's and her mother's feelings would have been discovered. Although a school suspension might have held the three students accountable for their action, they probably would have never thought about how their action deeply affected the victim and her family. Including the victim and the three students in the conference and providing an opportunity for dialogue produced good outcomes: The victim will feel safer in school, the three students understood the consequences of their behavior and were provided with an opportunity to make amends to those harmed by their action, and incoming freshman students will have an opportunity to learn a lesson from their story.

Reedley Peace Building Initiative (RPBI), Reedley, CA (http://rpbi-reedley.org/)

## Question:

1. *Recall that some of the cases resulted in school suspension when you were in high school. Discuss how the case could be handled differently if a restorative justice program was used.*

## Program Evaluation

Overall, restorative justice programs bring a high level of satisfaction to the participants (Umbreit & Coates, 1992; Strang, 2002). For example, an experimental study conducted in Indianapolis indicates that more than 90% of victims who participated in the process showed satisfaction with the way the case was handled, whereas only 68% of the nonparticipating control group indicated so. Also, 95% of victims who attended a conference agreed that they had an opportunity to express their views. Furthermore, an examination of the rearrest rate for those who completed the conference and the control group (i.e., completed other diversion programs) indicates that the conference group had a lower arrest rate than the control group over six months, but there was no statistically significant difference between the two groups over 12 months (McGarrell, 2001). Another study indicated a significantly long-term impact on female offenders compared to their male counterparts (Rodriguez, 2007).

Although flexibility and the multiple objectives of restorative justice are unique themes, those make it difficult to collect reliable data to assess the impact of the programs (Presser & Van Voorhis, 2002). Some researchers suggest that more rigorous evaluation is essential to determine how well the specific components of the programs lower recidivism and increase victim satisfaction. Others recommend that a comprehensive program evaluation would include the impact of the programs on victims' psychosocial coping outcomes and trauma reduction (Adler School Institute on Public Safety and Social Justice, 2011).

## SUMMARY

The juvenile justice system has recognized victims' rights in the system. However, some argue that the inclusion of victims' rights might conflict with the rehabilitation of juvenile offenders. One way to consolidate juveniles' and victims' rights is the "balanced and restorative justice for juveniles" approach in which the focus is on how to restore the harm to victims while holding the juveniles accountable for their act. Many restorative justice programs, including victim-offender mediation, family conferencing, and circles, appear promising, but questions remain about how effective the programs are at crime reduction and helping victims' recovery process.

Increased awareness of complex trauma has propelled the juvenile justice system to explore the ways to meet the needs of the youth in the child welfare and juvenile justice systems. Research has indicated the impact of child abuse and neglect is far more complex than the diagnosis of PTSD involving diverse issues including child attachment, biology, affect regulation, dissociation, behavioral control, cognition, and self-concept. However, the current juvenile justice practices do not necessarily recognize the risk of those youths on further trauma exposure in detention facilities. Research has indicated that minority and female youth are particularly vulnerable as they have experienced adverse effects from involvement in these systems. The trauma-informed juvenile justice system is a new approach to addressing youth's complex trauma and creating a safer environment. While the importance of the approach is well-recognized by professionals and scholars, it is still in the developmental stage and systemwide efforts to unify definitions and develop research-based practices and policies are necessary.

## KEY WORDS

Adjudicatory hearing   141
Aftercare   142
Circles   156

Crossover youth practice model
    (CYPM)   147
Crossover youth   146

Custody   139
Detention facility
    (juvenile hall)   139

## INTERNET RESOURCES

**National Association of Youth Courts (https://www.youthcourt.net)**

The National Association of Youth Courts provides informational services, delivers training and technical assistance, and develops resource materials on how to develop and enhance youth court programs in the United States. The website includes links featuring information about youth/teen court programs by state.

**Monitoring the Future (http://www.monitoringthefuture.org)**

Monitoring the Future (MTF) has collected information on the behaviors, attitudes, and values of American secondary school students, college students, and young adults. This website includes recent survey results, publications, and links to information on other research, health, and education issues.

**Fight Crime: Invest in Kids (https://www.strongnation.org/fightcrime)**

The website provides research findings and resource materials promoting solutions that steer kids away from crime. For example, its most recent study about an epidemic of opioid misuse discusses how early care and education programs can support young children affected by their parents' substance abuse.

## CRITICAL THINKING QUESTIONS

1. What are some possible theoretical and practical conflicts between victims' rights and juvenile justice?

2. What are some reasons for children with adverse childhood experiences to become involved in the juvenile justice system? How should the juvenile justice system address the needs of those children?

3. What is trauma-informed care? What are some advantages of adapting a trauma-informed approach for the juvenile justice system?

4. What are the strengths and limitations of the restorative justice model? In what ways do restorative and retributive justice differ?

PART

III

# Impact of Crime on Victims

# Victim Assistance for Family Violence

## Child Abuse and Elder Abuse

Like victimization, violence within the family is not a new phenomenon; in fact, it is a problem that is age-old (Maryniak, 2000). A place of safety, love, support, and care are often terms used to describe family, but child abuse, sibling abuse, abuse of parents, intimate-partner violence, and elder abuse affect millions of people on a daily basis (World Health Organization, 2012). However, it is only in modern times that society has begun to define family violence as a social problem and create laws and develop programs to assist and protect those from violence in the home. The path to recognizing violence within the home and to protect those affected has not always been clear. The rise of the women's movement and children's movement in the 1960s and 1970s (see Chapter 1), along with a key publication by Dr. C. Henry Kempe, Silverman, Steele, Droegemueller, and Silver (1962) on battered child syndrome, was invaluable in bringing violence within the home into the public view. Research on family violence has helped to shed light on this problem and how pervasive it is worldwide. While we will never know the true extent to which violence within the family occurs, considerable progress has been made to better understand and address its occurrence. Barnett, Miller-Perrin, and Perrin (2011) write that many nongovernmental organizations, medical professionals, criminal justice authorities, researchers, lawyers, lawmakers, and the media have all combined their efforts to assist those in need and continue to educate the public on its occurrence and raise awareness. To better understand the phenomena of family violence, it is important to first describe what family violence is and then examine the forms it takes and the assistance offered to the victims.

## What Is Family Violence?

**Family violence:** any assault, battery, sexual assault, sexual battery, or any criminal offense resulting in personal injury or death of one family or household member by another who is related to the victim either biologically or legally through marriage or adoption

On a daily basis, we are confronted with stories or reports of family violence through television dramas, newspapers, magazines, radio, and even through politics. These stories become the discussion points at social gatherings, where still today, people assume that if it's that bad the victim will seek help, simply leave the relationship, report to a teacher, colleague, or friend. However, the reality is never that simple (Gosselin, 2014; LaViolette & Barnett, 2014). Family violence is a complex issue with no easy answers or a "magic-bullet-solution" for intervention and prevention. Even trying to define family violence presents a problem. In the United States, the legal definition of family violence varies according to state and federal law. Therefore, it is vitally important that all those who serve victims of crime have a comprehensive understanding of the legal criminal and civil definition of family violence in their respective states (Palmer & Edmunds, 2003). **Family violence** is generally defined, unless indicated otherwise, as,

Any assault, battery, sexual assault, sexual battery, or any criminal offense resulting in personal injury or death of one family or household member by another who is related to the victim either biologically or legally through marriage or adoption. A crime is considered family violence if the victim was the offender's current or former spouse; parent or adoptive parent; current or former stepparent; legal guardian; biological or adoptive child; current or former stepchild; sibling; current or former step sibling; grandchild; current or former step- or adoptive-grandchild; grandparent; current or former step- or adoptive-grandparent; in-law; or other relative (aunt, uncle, nephew). (Durose et al., 2005, p. 4)

The literature on family violence refers mostly to women and children, but the reality is that family violence occurs to all members of a family, including males, who come from every walk of life, rich or poor, and from every race and creed (Gosselin, 2014).

Family violence can include neglect, physical abuse, sexual abuse, psychological abuse, and financial abuse. These common terms are defined in the following sections.

## Neglect

**Neglect** is defined as failure or refusal of a parent, guardian, or other caregiver to provide for a child's basic needs. The abuse includes harm due to the action or inaction of the caregiver. There are four types of neglect (Erickson & Egeland, 2002):

1. Physical (failure to provide necessary food or shelter, or lack of appropriate supervision)

2. Medical (failure to provide necessary medical or mental health treatment)

3. Educational (failure to educate a child or attend to special education needs)

4. Emotional (inattention to a child's emotional needs, failure to provide psychological care, or permitting the child to use alcohol or other drugs)

**Neglect:** failure or refusal of a parent, guardian, or other caregiver to provide for a child's basic needs. The abuse includes harm due to the action or inaction of the caregiver

## Physical Abuse

Physical abuse is often the most recognizable form of abuse. It is defined as the use of force or threat of force that results in an injury or a pattern of injuries that are nonaccidental. Physical abuse can be as emotionally traumatizing as it is physically traumatizing (Gosselin, 2014; Network for Victim Assistance (NOVA), 2016). The abuse may include, but is not limited to, the following:

- Pushing, shoving, slapping, punching, kicking, or choking the victim

- Welts, burns, or bites

- Holding, tying down, restraining, or strangling the victim

- Shaking a child or adult

- The inability to provide care to an infant or child or disabled, injured adult

- Intentional infliction of exposure to a (deadly) disease, such as a sexually transmitted disease (STD), HIV, AIDS, or other communicable infections.

## Sexual Abuse

Sexual abuse is any nonconsensual sexual contact of any kind. It includes but is not limited to the following (Malley-Morrison & Hines, 2004; National Center for Victims of Crime (NCVC), 2016):

- Rape (including marital rape)

- Unwanted touching

- Sodomy

- Exposure to pornography

- Treating one in a sexually demeaning manner (e.g., catcalling)

- Voyeurism

- Coerced nudity

## Psychological Abuse

Psychological abuse is intended by the perpetrator to instill fear, anguish, degradation, and pain in order to control the victim. Psychological abuse can be inflicted verbally and physically. Psychological abuse often precedes or accompanies physical abuse as a way to control the victim (Palmer & Edmunds, 2003). Psychological abuse may include the following:

- Verbal abuse (e.g., name calling, humiliation, constant criticizing)

- Physical and social isolation

- Threats of harm

- Deprivation of resources to meet basic needs

- Forced violation of one's moral principles

## Financial Abuse

Financial abuse is the making or attempt to make an individual financially dependent by maintaining total control over financial resources, withholding one's access to money, or forbidding one's attendance at school or employment (NCVC, 2016). Financial abuse can include the following (National Network to End Domestic Violence, 2017):

- Forbidding the victim to work

- Not allowing the victim access to a bank account

- Withholding money or giving "an allowance"

- Misusing "protective" legal instruments (e.g., powers of attorney)

- Stealing the victim's identity, property, or inheritance

These are the forms of abuse victim service providers are likely to encounter when assisting victims of family violence. Family violence is categorized into three groups; however, this chapter will only focus on two of the categories: child abuse and elder abuse. Intimate partner violence will be addressed separately in Chapter 10.

# Victim Assistance
# for Child Abuse Victims

The protection of children is a global concern. In the United States, child abuse is one of the most serious concerns. It was revealed in 2015 that 4 million children were referred to child protective services (CPS) for suspected maltreatment (U.S. Department of Health and Human Services (USDHHS), 2017). CPS responds to alleged maltreatment determined by the definitions of child abuse and neglect in the statutes and policies of each state. Alleged maltreatment is either screened in or screened out. The following are reasons a report may be screened out (USDHHS, 2017):

- The report did not concern child abuse and neglect.

- The report did not contain enough information for a CPS response to occur.

- A response by another agency was deemed more appropriate.

- Children in the referral were the responsibility of another agency or jurisdiction (e.g., military installation or tribe).

- Children in the referral were older than 18 years.

When reports are screened in, an investigation is initiated in which CPS will make a determination about the alleged child maltreatment. The two most common outcomes following an investigation are reports being substantiated or unsubstantiated. Substantiated reports conclude that the allegation of maltreatment or risk of maltreatment was supported or founded by state law or policy, meaning that a child was found to have been the victim of abuse or neglect. Unsubstantiated reports conclude that there was not sufficient evidence under state law to suspect that the child was maltreated or at-risk of being maltreated (USDHHS, 2017).

In 2015, approximately 3.4 million children received an investigation or alternative response from CPS. Of the 3.4 million children, 683,000 were substantiated reports.

From these reports, the most common forms of abuse children suffered were neglect (75.3%) and physical abuse (17.2%). However, it is not uncommon for a victim to experience more than one form of abuse at the same time. Often a child who is being sexually or physically abused may be experiencing psychological abuse or neglect, too. The most tragic outcome of child abuse is death. It was estimated nationally in 2015 that 1,670 children died from abuse and neglect. A sad reality of child abuse is that the majority (78.1%) of perpetrators were parents of the victims, with 6.3% of perpetrators being related to the victim in some way (USDHHS, 2017).

Child abuse and neglect is an important societal concern, and the statistics in the United States reflect its magnitude. The ramifications for those affected are an ongoing challenge to our society. This means that there is a great need to provide assistance to this vulnerable population. However, a critical first step in establishing effective responses and victim services is having a consistent definition of child abuse and neglect.

## Definitions of Child Abuse and Neglect

The federal government provides minimum standards for a definition of child abuse and neglect; however, each state writes its own laws using these minimum standards. A challenge to addressing the problem of child abuse and neglect in society is finding a consistent definition. Some of the discernable differences in definitions across the states have pertained to injury outcomes, which are difficult to define clearly. For example, in cases of physical abuse, the definitions focus on harm done to the child, injuries which are visible and may be evidenced (injury outcomes); whereas, with neglect and psychological abuse, the harm is not always visible (Miller-Perrin & Perrin, 2012). Having varying definitions of the problem greatly affects the determinations of its scope, as it influences how data on child abuse and neglect are collected. It also affects how the characteristics of the problem are described, programs are developed, who is obligated to report, and how people are trained to address the problem (Boyce & Maholmes, 2013). Section 3 of the Child Abuse Prevention and Treatment Act (CAPTA) defines **child abuse** and neglect as,

> At a minimum, any recent act or set of acts or failure to act on the part of a parent or caretaker, which results in death, serious physical or emotional harm, sexual abuse or exploitation, or an act or failure to act, which presents an imminent risk of serious harm. (Peterson, Joseph, & Feit, 2014)

The laws on child abuse and neglect place emphasis on two components of behavior that threaten the safety and security of children. These are acts of omission or commission. Acts of omission pertain to neglect and its varying forms (e.g., physical, psychological, medical, and educational) regardless of the intended consequences. Acts of commission, on the other hand, refer to abuse. These are the deliberate and intentional verbal and physical actions that cause harm or threat of harm to the child (Baker & Festinger, 2011; Gosselin, 2014; Peterson et al., 2014).

**Child abuse:** the definition of child abuse and neglect contained in Section 3 of the Child Abuse Prevention and Treatment Act (CAPTA) (Peterson, Joseph & Feit, 2014) is "At a minimum, any recent act or set of acts or failure to act on the part of a parent or caretaker, which results in death, serious physical or emotional harm, sexual abuse or exploitation, or an act or failure to act, which presents an imminent risk of serious harm"

Reflecting on her childhood and the abuse she experienced for eight years, Monica describes how she first became aware of her abuse and that what she was experiencing was wrong. As is so often the case with child abuse, victims may not be aware that they are being abused, as they may not understand what is appropriate and inappropriate behavior, along with the fact those who are committing the abuse are the ones they rely on the most for support and care. In Monica's case, she was 8 years old when her elementary class participated in a child abuse prevention program called "Speak Up Be Safe." To this point, Monica recalled that nothing seemed strange about her childhood—however, after she had watched the video and participated in the program, she began to realize that something at home was not right. Monica's mother was a nurse and worked long and awkward hours, meaning that her father was her primary caregiver. Each night after eating and going to bed, Monica's father would come into her room and touch her. After this realization, she knew she needed to tell an adult she trusted. The next day, Monica went to speak to her soccer coach. She cannot recall exactly what she told her coach, but she remembers that she explained about the inappropriate behavior. Her coach told her that she would talk to her parents. Monica does not know what the coach said to her parents, but she said "nothing changed—I imagine my dad talked his way out of it; he talked his way out of many things in his life. He was very manipulative."

Monica said that she spoke to a trusted adult, but the abuse did not stop. She remembers feeling very vulnerable. The abuse continued for a couple more years before she decided to disclose to her mother what was happening. Her mother called the police, and Monica had to sit through a forensic interview. Her dad was taken into custody, and her mother asked him to leave, but it was not long before he was

back home. The police never followed through on the investigation, and soon after returning home, her dad moved them out of state. It was at this point that she recalls that her father had also become verbally and physically abusive toward her mother and one of her brothers. Monica's abuse by her father continued for a couple more years. She disclosed a third time to her mother, but her mother was now not working nor was she mentally or physically strong enough to leave her father. After a sleep over, it came out that her father had molested one of Monica's friends. Monica's friend immediately told her parents and the school who called child protective services (CPS). They opened up an investigation—but her father immediately moved them to another state. At this point, Monica said she felt so confused and scared. She kept thinking that when she was 18, she could move out of her house and be free from that monster.

A few weeks after settling into her new school, Monica was called to the office. When she got there, a lady was waiting to speak to her. The lady was from CPS. CPS had tracked her down after they had moved so abruptly. Her dad was arrested and eventually sentenced to 12 years in prison with lifetime probation, which Monica had requested. Her dad served his time, but once he was released, he tracked her down and began to harass her. He was arrested for harassment and breaking the terms of his probation and resentenced to 10 years in prison. Despite the fact that she confided in people, and her abuse continued, Monica feels strongly that the child abuse program she participated in as a child was greatly beneficial. She feels that more of these programs need to be implemented in schools, and she says that "sometimes schools are the only place where kids feel safe outside their homes, and if they can identify that something is wrong and is not right, they may be able to get help at a young age."

*(Continued)*

(Continued)

The names and length of this story have been edited from the original. This story is taken from ChildHelp.org. (https://www.childhelp.org)

## Questions:

1. Discuss what makes it difficult for children to report cases of child abuse.

2. In a case like Monica's, list and discuss what multiservice programs you would recommend.

3. Discuss the challenges in identifying cases of child abuse and what you think could be done to improve mandated reporting.

## Signs and Symptoms of Child Abuse and Neglect

Child abuse and neglect have been described as leading public health problems in the United States. To address this societal concern, it has been identified that certain people are in a unique situation to recognize and intervene on behalf of children and families who are impacted. These are called mandatory reporters. **Mandated reporting** is the legislative requirement that certain professionals must report cases of suspected child abuse or neglect for investigation to a designated authority within a specified amount of time (USDHHS, 2015). Social workers, teachers (and other school personnel), physicians (nurses and other health care workers), counselors, childcare providers, medical examiners or coroners, law enforcement officers, and members of the clergy are required by law to make a report when they have reason to suspect child maltreatment. Recognizing high-risk situations and the signs and symptoms of maltreatment helps to prevent serious injuries and relieves the victims of the responsibility to seek help for themselves (Pietrantonio et al., 2013). Importantly, any concerned person can make a report of suspicions of child abuse or neglect and assist in protecting a child from harm.

Despite the advantages of identifying high-risk situations, it has been widely recognized that the knowledge to identify and attitudes about duties to report child abuse and neglect are poorly understood (Narayan, Socolar & Claire, 2006; Anderst & Dowd, 2010). Improving the knowledge and fostering more positive attitudes of the duty of protecting children is argued to produce more effective reporting (Matthews et al., 2017). Therefore, enhancing identification and coordination between educational, legal, medical, and victim service responses is of paramount importance.

Abusive behavior comes in many forms; therefore, it is important that mandated reporters and victim service providers be aware of the common signs of abuse and neglect. According to the U.S. Department of Health and Human Services (2015), the following signs may signal the presence of child abuse or neglect:

The child

- Shows sudden changes in behavior or school performance

- Has not received help for physical or medical problems brought to the parents' attention

**Mandated reporting:** is the legislative requirement that certain professionals must report cases of suspected child abuse or neglect for investigation to a designated authority within a specified amount of time (USDHHS, 2015)

- Has learning problems (or difficulty concentrating) that cannot be attributed to specific physical or psychological causes
- Is always watchful, as though preparing for something bad to happen
- Lacks adult supervision
- Is overly compliant, passive, or withdrawn
- Comes to school or other activities early, stays late, and does not want to go home
- Is reluctant to be around a particular person
- Discloses maltreatment

The parent

- Denies the existence of—or blames the child for—the child's problems in school or at home
- Asks teachers or other caregivers to use harsh physical discipline if the child misbehaves
- Sees the child as entirely bad, worthless, or burdensome
- Demands a level of physical or academic performance the child cannot achieve
- Looks primarily to the child for care, attention, and satisfaction of the parent's emotional needs
- Shows little concern for the child

The parent and child

- Rarely touch or look at each other
- Consider their relationship entirely negative
- State that they do not like each other

Signs of physical abuse when the child

- Has unexplained burns, bites, bruises, broken bones, or black eyes
- Has fading bruises or other marks noticeable after an absence from school
- Seems frightened of the parents and protests or cries when it is time to go home
- Shrinks at the approach of adults
- Reports injury by a parent or another adult caregiver
- Abuses animals or pets

Signs of physical abuse when the parent or other adult caregiver

- Offers conflicting, unconvincing, or no explanation for the child's injury, or provides an explanation that is not consistent with the injury
- Describes the child as "evil" or in some other very negative way
- Uses harsh physical discipline with the child
- Has a history of abuse as a child
- Has a history of abusing animals or pets

Signs of neglect when the child

- Is frequently absent from school
- Begs or steals food or money
- Lacks needed medical or dental care, immunizations, or glasses
- Is consistently dirty and has severe body odor
- Lacks sufficient clothing for the weather
- Abuses alcohol or other drugs
- States that there is no one at home to provide care

Signs of neglect when the parent or other adult caregiver

- Appears to be indifferent to the child
- Seems apathetic or depressed
- Behaves irrationally or in a bizarre manner
- Is abusing alcohol or other drugs

Signs of sexual abuse when the child

- Has difficulty walking or sitting
- Suddenly refuses to change for gym or to participate in physical activities
- Reports nightmares or bedwetting
- Experiences a sudden change in appetite
- Demonstrates bizarre, sophisticated, or unusual sexual knowledge or behavior
- Becomes pregnant or contracts a venereal disease, particularly if under age 14
- Runs away

- Reports sexual abuse by a parent or another adult caregiver

- Attaches very quickly to strangers or new adults in their environment

Signs of sexual abuse when the parent or other adult caregiver

- Is unduly protective of the child or severely limits the child's contact with other children, especially of the opposite sex

- Is secretive and isolated

- Is jealous or controlling with family members

Signs of psychological maltreatment when the child

- Shows extremes in behavior, such as overly compliant or demanding behavior or extreme passivity or aggression

- Is either inappropriately adult (parenting other children, for example) or inappropriately infantile (frequently rocking or head-banging, for example)

- Is delayed in physical or emotional development

- Has attempted suicide

- Reports a lack of attachment to the parent

Signs of psychological maltreatment when the parent or other adult caregiver

- Constantly blames, belittles, or berates the child

- Is unconcerned about the child and refuses to consider offers of help for the child's problems

- Overtly rejects the child

This list of the signs of abuse or neglect is not all-inclusive, and attention must be paid to other behaviors that may seem unusual or concerning. It is important for mandated reporters and victims service providers to act in a timely manner if a child is suspected to be the victim of abuse. While reporting child abuse can be difficult and uncomfortable, remember that most children in such situations are unable to help themselves (Matthews et al., 2017).

## Effect of Child Abuse on Victims

The effects of abuse on a child vary depending on the circumstances of the abuse or neglect, personal characteristics of the child, and the child's environment. While some effects can be severe and long lasting, it is important to note that children can and do go on to live healthy and productive lives (McGregor, 2008). Research conducted over the last three decades indicates that child abuse and neglect has more of an adverse effect on those who have experienced it than those individuals who have no such experience (Teicher & Samson, 2016). When discussing the effects of child abuse, researchers and advocates focus on these three elements: physical, psychological, and behavioral effects.

Physical abuse can include cuts, bruises, burns, kicking, punching, strangling, and shaking. The effects of this abuse can cause broken bones, hemorrhaging, or in severe cases, death. The pain from this abuse may eventually pass; however, the suffering it causes a child can be long lasting. According to Casanueva, Stambaugh, Tueller, Dolan, and Smith (2012), child abuse and neglect can have a multitude of long-term effects on physical health. These include seizures, paralysis, and mental and developmental delays. The longer the abuse continues, the greater the effect it has on the child (Casanueva et al., 2016; Teicher & Samson, 2016). Physically abused children are also susceptible to developing psychological disorders (Mullen, Martin, Anderson, Romans, & Herbison, 1996; Teicher & Samson, 2016). Numerous research studies conducted with abused children have found that they are more likely to have low self-esteem and develop and have to deal with excessive fear, anxiety, and aggressive behavior that adversely effects their lives at home, school, and in other social environments. Some of the psychological disorders associated with child abuse and neglect are eating disorders, depression, anxiety disorders, posttraumatic stress disorder (PTSD), attention deficit/hyperactivity disorder (ADHD), and conduct disorder (Briere & Elliott, 1994; Coates & Gaensbauer, 2009; Cecil, Viding, Fearon, Glaser, & McCrory et al., 2017). Psychological disorders may cause a person to develop unhealthy coping strategies such as smoking, abusing alcohol or drugs, or overeating. Such behaviors can lead to long-term physical health problems, such as sexually transmitted diseases, cancer, and obesity (Herrenkohl, Hong, Bart Klika, Herrenkohl, & Jean Russo, 2013; Yang, et al., 2013; Messman-Moore & Bhuptani, 2017).

There is an ongoing body of research that has focused on the behavioral effects of child abuse that indicates that the victimization of children has grave social consequences. Among other things, child abuse appears to have a significant effect on criminal behavior. Different types of abuse have been associated with the increased risk of delinquent behavior and adult and violent criminal behavior (Currie & Tekin, 2006; Widom, 2017). It is argued that children who have either witnessed or experienced abuse learn to use violent behavior or justify violent behavior as appropriate (Sousa, Bart Klika, Herrenkohl, & Packard., 2016). However, not all victims of child abuse and neglect use or go on to use violent behavior or commit criminal acts. Many children affected by child abuse and neglect are resilient, able to heal, and go on to thrive (McGregor, 2008). Resilience has been broadly defined as the capacity to adapt successfully to disturbances that threaten functioning or development (Masten, 2014). It is important to note that resilience is not an inherent trait in children but results from a mixture of protective factors that cause a child to have positive or negative reactions to adverse experiences. Protective factors can be found within the family and or community and can impact the ways in which children and teens process and understand the exposure to violence (Afifi & Macmillan, 2011; USDHHS, 2015).

While the priority is to prevent child abuse and neglect from occurring, it is equally important to respond to those children and adults who have experienced abuse and neglect. Our understanding of the effects of child abuse and neglect has greatly increased, along with the programs and organizations that have developed to assist these victims and help reduce the impact of trauma. One of the most important developments designed to address and respond to the impact of trauma has been trauma-informed care. **Trauma-informed care** "is a strengths-based framework that is grounded in an understanding of and responsiveness to the impact of trauma, that emphasizes physical, psychological, and emotional safety for both providers and victims, and that creates opportunities for victims to rebuild a sense of control and empowerment" (Hopper, Bassuk, & Olivet, 2009). The importance of this approach has become especially evident in victim assistance and the responses to the many children and families who have experienced some form of past trauma.

## Effective Responses to Child Abuse and Neglect

Our society faces few challenges more important than responding to child abuse and neglect. Mentioned above, while the priority is to prevent child abuse and neglect from occurring, it is equally important to respond to those who have experienced such trauma. The physical, mental, and developmental ramifications abuse and neglect have on children can greatly affect their productivity over a lifespan, along with presenting challenges for effective responses from public systems, such as child welfare, social services, law enforcement, the juvenile justice system, and the education system (Currie & Tekin, 2006; Klain & White, 2013; Widom, 2017). Given the impact that exposure to abuse and neglect has on children, providing effective services and making decisions that are in the best interest of a child is challenging. Safety, well-being, and growth are the key elements needed to be taken into account when considering effective responses. Today, all programs and services tasked with responding to children do so from a trauma-informed perspective. Trauma-informed interventions require that practitioners have an understanding of the impact of trauma on child development and are trained to know how to effectively minimize its effects without causing additional trauma. Such trauma-informed practices present an excellent opportunity for programs to assist in the recovery from trauma and help children to regain a sense of balance in their lives (Klain & White, 2013).

Most of the programs developed are designed to assist with multiple forms of abuse and include interventions that look to use multiservice interventions, enhance parenting skills, and reduce the effects associated with maltreatment. While these programs and interventions are presented as the most effective ways to address the need to assist children and families, it is important to note that their efficacy remains controversial (O'Reilly, Wilkes, Luck, & Jackson, 2010; Kuhn & Laird, 2014).

### Multiservice Interventions

Because most children who experience abuse and neglect come from homes that have a multitude of problems or deficits, research has suggested that no one intervention technique or method can be successful, and that successful intervention requires a multiservice approach (Gaudin, 1993; O'Reilly et al., 2010). Multiservice intervention programs provide a broad range of services that include supportive community services from

**Trauma-informed care:** a strengths-based framework that is grounded in an understanding of and responsiveness to the impact of trauma, that emphasizes physical, psychological, and emotional safety for both providers and victims, and that creates opportunities for victims to rebuild a sense of control and empowerment (Hopper et al., 2009)

multiple sources (child welfare, law enforcement, the courts, schools, hospitals, health departments, and mental health agencies) and a combination of individual, family, and group counseling methods, behavioral skills training to eliminate problematic behavior, individual and group parenting education, and family therapy (Gaudin, 1993). These programs are able to use interdisciplinary coordination to greatly facilitate therapeutic and supportive services with ongoing problem solving to assure the child's safety and that all efforts made have the best chance of succeeding.

## Home Visitation Programs

Home visitation programs for parents is a widespread early-intervention initiative aimed at preventing child abuse and neglect (Council on Child and Adolescent Health, 1998; Howard & Brooks-Gunn, 2009). It has been identified that many families have insufficient knowledge of parenting skills and an inadequate support system of friends, extended family, or professionals to help with the vital tasks of raising a child (Gaudin, 1993). According to Gaudin (1993), concern about the amount of children abused and neglected and placed in out-of-home care has produced an increased emphasis on the use of intensive in-home, family-focused models of service. Home visitation programs attempt to identify high-risk parents in a community and provide them with the parental education, social support, and resources from public and private community services (Gaudin, 1993; Howard & Brooks-Gunn, 2009). These programs are aimed at treating the family as a whole and are believed by researchers and policy makers to be a beneficial and cost-effective strategy for providing services to families and children.

## Group Counseling Programs

The effects of child abuse and neglect can be long lasting, and it is important to have programs that respond to the trauma experienced. A child's disclosure of abuse and neglect, a challenging economic climate, or overwhelmed parents with limited resources to provide the basic needs for their child are just some examples of the vulnerability and imbalance that many families encounter (Benedetti, 2012). One of the most common treatment options to address the effects of child abuse and neglect are group counseling programs. These programs set out to reduce the child's sense of isolation or stigma through exposure to other victims of abuse, develop self-protective strategies, and teach relaxation techniques, along with developing a better understanding of family violence (Kolko & Swenson, 2002).

## Legal Support for Victims of Child Abuse

Child victims occupy as much time and attention and resources within the criminal justice system as offenders. But the matter of child victims in the justice system has not been addressed so systematically (Finkelhor, Paschall, & Hashima, 2001, p 11). State criminal codes and statutes treat children differently from adults. Crimes committed against children are specifically stated offenses, such as neglect and rape without force (Gosselin, 2014). The majority of states in the United States have extended the statute of limitations for crimes against children, specifically child sexual abuse. The statute of limitations refers to the time that is allowed by law in which a case may be prosecuted

......................................................................................

## Multiservice Intervention Programs

*Project 12-Ways.* Project 12-Ways offers 12 different services to neglectful families including emergency financial assistance, transportation, homemakers, recreational opportunities, weight loss programs, and parent groups as well as behavioral techniques for teaching parenting and home management skills. See http://project12-ways.siu.edu/about/index.php for more information.

*The Family Support Center.* The multiservice program addresses the need for short-term crisis and respite care for children at risk for abuse or neglect. Their services include in-home instruction on nutrition, home and money management, and child care skills from trained parent aides; parent support groups; employment preparation; and facilitation of connections with community services. See http://www.familysupportcenter.org for more information.

## Home Visitation Program

Healthy Families America. Healthy Families America (HFA) is a family support program that embodies an infant mental health approach, with the belief that early, nurturing relationships are the foundation for lifelong, healthy development. The signature program of Prevent Child Abuse America, HFA is one the leading family support and home-visiting programs in the country. Currently, HFA has a presence in 38 states and serves nearly 100,000 families annually with services that are proven to improve family self-sufficiency, improve early-learning in children, and reduce child maltreatment. See http://www.healthyfamiliesamerica.org for more information.

## Group Counseling Programs

*Alliance for Children.* Alliance for Children offers both individual and group counseling free of charge to families referred to the counseling program. The program focuses on teaching children to learn healthy ways of coping in order to decrease the traumatic symptoms of child abuse and neglect. Alliance for Children believes that with the support of a protective caregiver and effective treatment, a child can recover without long-term effects. Counseling sessions are offered in both English and Spanish. See http://www.allianceforchildren.org for more information.

*Family Nurturing Center.* Family Nurturing Center is a nonprofit social service agency dedicated to ending the cycle of child abuse by promoting individual well-being and healthy family relationships. Their services and programs focus on the education, prevention, and treatment of all forms of child abuse and neglect. They offer individual and family (group) counseling to children with a history of abuse/trauma (including physical abuse, sexual abuse, emotional abuse/neglect and witness to domestic violence). See http://www.familynurture.org for more information.

after the illegal act occurs. A few states have no time limitation for the prosecution of sexual offenses against children. In all states, there is no statute of limitations for the prosecution of murder (Wistrich, 2008; Gosselin, 2014).

The key federal legislation addressing child abuse and neglect is the CAPTA (please see table for other child legislation acts). The act was originally enacted in 1974 but has been amended several times and was most recently amended and reauthorized in 2010, by the CAPTA Reauthorization Act of 2010. The act provides federal funding to states in support of prevention, assessment, investigation, prosecution, and treatment activities, along with providing grants to public agencies and nonprofit organizations, including Indian Tribes and tribal organizations, for demonstration programs and projects (USDHHS, 2017). Additionally, CAPTA provides funding to support research, evaluation, technical assistance, and data collection activities on child abuse. Importantly, CAPTA also sets forth a minimum definition of child abuse and neglect.

Under CAPTA and its recent provisions, victims of child abuse and neglect are now allowed special courtroom procedures (not in all states, however). These special courtroom procedures do not require special statutes in order to be implemented and are believed to be more sensitive to the needs of children who have to go through this process. Examples of some of the criminal justice provisions include the following (Davidson, 2011; Petersen, Joseph, & Feit, 2014):

- Using alternatives to live in-court testimony of child victims (e.g., closed circuit television (CCTV))

- Setting limits on challenges to the competency of child witnesses

- Providing privacy protections for child victims and witnesses

- Allowing child victim impact statements

- Appointing a guardian ad litem for a child victim or witness

- Allowing testifying children to have an adult support person with them

- Establishing a procedure to ensure a speedy trial of child victim cases

While it may seem rational to arrest and prosecute an offender of child abuse and neglect, the decision to do so is not a simple one. Each decision to arrest and prosecute is done on a case-by-case basis by the investigating team, with the final decision to prosecute made by the district attorney. In each situation, the final decision to prosecute is based on the following factors (Gosselin, 2014):

- Age of the child

- Seriousness of the offense

- Reluctance to testify

- Evidence

- Probability of successful prosecution

This can be a great source of frustration for all those who work with child victims and understand the effects of child abuse. CAPTA and the work that it has produced are understood best in the context of politics, cultural events, and societal changes. CAPTA has been instrumental in attempting to respond to the occurrence and effects of child maltreatment and finding ways to prevent it; however, more evidence-informed services need to be made available to families through local child welfare agencies and other key public and private partners. Collaboration among agencies and programs providing child abuse and neglect prevention and treatment services are the hallmark of the work needed to move forward (USDHHS, 2015).

## Education and Outreach

Talking about victimization, particularly child abuse, is never pleasant. It can be embarrassing and make people feel very uncomfortable. However, if left, the effects on individuals, communities, and society as a whole can be severe. Child abuse exploits and degrades children. It causes serious short-term and in some cases long-term damage to their development (Casanueva et al., 2012; Herrenkohl et al., 2013). Having child abuse a part of the public discourse is vitally important, as it raises awareness about the problem and allows responsible agencies to take action to create knowledgeable, responsible, and protective communities to keep children safe. To accomplish this, we must initiate and promote research, training, and public education to strengthen protective factors that raise awareness about the risk factors for abuse while also directly addressing those risk factors (Ekstrand, 1996; Overlein, 2010). Therefore, it is important for advocates, lawyers, law enforcement, researchers, and victim assistance organizations to disseminate accurate information to the public and policy-makers about the problem.

Education and outreach is a way to keep the problem of child abuse in the public discourse and possibly reduce the number of those who are abused. Too often, cases of child abuse go unreported, as those who are tasked to protect children don't recognize the signs and symptoms of abuse or don't know how to respond. Many, too, are afraid to get involved, fearing the consequences of reporting or not understanding the legal implications of reporting (Pietrantonio et al., 2013). Therefore, it is important for teachers, parents, and all those who work with children to be educated on the signs and symptoms of child abuse, and more importantly, to educate children on abuse and who to reach out to should they have any concerns.

To facilitate educating all those who work with children and disseminating information about the problem of child abuse, many community education and outreach programs have been developed. These programs include parent education, home visitation, parent support groups, health fairs, and a variety of family-based community events. Such prevention efforts help to develop parenting skills; better understand the benefits of nonviolent discipline techniques; where additional support can be found; and how a child's emotional, physical, and developmental needs can be affected by abuse. Other initiatives including media campaigns—such as using local radio and television stations to broadcast events and provide information on assistance programs; hosting an awards breakfast/dinner honoring those key individuals and organizations working to prevent child abuse; having kids' parades, local hero days, or candlelight vigils for child abuse victims; and disseminating multilingual child abuse prevention materials—have also been effective in raising awareness of child abuse and the assistance available (USDHHS, 2004).

# Human Trafficking of Children

Trafficking in persons is a pressing social concern with a number of implications for those assisting victims. Law enforcement, medical professionals, victim service personnel, and social workers play an instrumental role in the area of identification, exit from trafficking, rehabilitation, and restoration (Cole, 2009; Hodge, 2014). **Human trafficking** is

> the recruitment, transportation, transfer, harboring or receipt of persons, by *means* of the threat or use of force or other forms of coercion, of abduction, of fraud, of deception, of the abuse of power or of a position of vulnerability or of the giving or receiving of payments or benefits to achieve the consent of a person having control over another person, for the *purpose* of exploitation. Exploitation shall include, at a minimum, the exploitation of the prostitution of others or other forms of sexual exploitation, forced labor or services, slavery or practices similar to slavery, servitude or the removal of organs. (United Nations, 2000)

Human trafficking is a factor in almost every country and affects every demographic. However, one common factor across all forms of trafficking is the victims' vulnerability to exploitation. Traffickers frequently prey on the most vulnerable people in some of the poorest nations, where they are forced to serve the interests of traffickers through the application of physical and psychological coercion (United Nations, 2000; Hodge, 2014). It is difficult to provide accurate and reliable data on human trafficking locally, nationally, and globally. Over the years, the advocacy of survivors has expanded the understanding of the crime, and together with research and program evaluations, a better understanding of its occurrence and who it affects has emerged. Additional efforts and resources for research, data collection, and evaluation are needed to identify those actions most effective to prevent this victimization (United Nations, 2000).

It is estimated by the International Labor Organization (ILO) that 21 million people are trafficked globally. Of this figure, roughly 26% are children (ILO, 2017). Traffickers prey on those who lack security and opportunity, coerce or deceive them to gain control, and then profit from their compelled service. Arguably, the most vulnerable population in society is children. It is important for governments and communities to develop effective strategies to increase awareness and prevent human trafficking. It is equally important that those working in victim assistance organizations be familiar with human trafficking and knowledgeable of the relevant legal statutes and available resources to be able to assist victims (Logan, Walker, & Hunt, 2009). Victims, specifically children, are likely to be unaware of the options available to them; by informing them of the services available, practitioners may be able to encourage their escape (Clawson, Dutch, Solomon, & Grace, 2009; Macy & Graham, 2012).

## Labor Trafficking of Children

Despite families and communities cherishing their children, the sad reality is, children can be easily used as commodities in situations where families are desperate and can be sent off to work when families feel they have no other financial options to survive (United Nations, 2000). Traffickers manipulate vulnerable families and children into working long hours in substandard conditions for little or no wages. Child trafficking generally implies that someone has organized the movement of a child with the immediate or ultimate aim of their exploitation and kept the child in bondage through a combination of fear, intimidation, abuse, and psychological coercion (Hodge, 2014; Todres, 2016). A child can be a victim of labor trafficking, regardless of the location or whether or not consent for the exploitation was given. While children are able to engage in certain forms of work, there are legal prohibitions and widespread condemnation against forms of slavery or slavery-like practices (United Nations, 2000). One form of work children are subjected to is peddling. Peddling is a form of child labor, where children often go door to door or stand on street corners or in parks selling cheap goods, regardless of weather conditions and without access to food, water, or facilities. Child labor trafficking also occurs in the context of domestic service, agricultural work, and hospitality industries (e.g., restaurants and hotels) (Greenbaum, 2016; Todres, 2016; Hannan, Martin, Caceres, & Aledort, 2017); It is important to remember that child victims of labor trafficking may also be sexually abused or simultaneously victims of sex trafficking (Hannan et al., 2017).

It is estimated that there are 5.5 million child victims at any given point in time (ILO, 2017). It is not always easy to identify children who are victims of labor trafficking, but there are some key indicators to be aware of. According to the U.S. Department of Homeland Security Blue Campaign (2017), these are some common indicators to help recognize a child who is a victim of human trafficking:

- The child appears to be disconnected from family, friends, community organizations, or houses of worship.

- The child has stopped attending school.

- The child appears to be disoriented or confused or shows signs of mental or physical abuse.

- The child appears to be fearful, timid, or submissive.

- The child shows signs of having been denied food, water, sleep, or medical care.

- The child is living in unsuitable conditions.

## Sex Trafficking of Children

While anyone can be a victim of sex trafficking, we know that kids who are homeless or runaways and youth interacting with the child welfare system are more vulnerable to this form of trafficking. Research has found that 50% to 90% of child sex trafficking victims have been involved in the child welfare system (USDHHS, 2015; U.S. Department of State, 2016; Hannan et al., 2017). Like labor trafficking, vulnerability and instability create opportunities for traffickers to reach out and bond with children forming relationships that can be used against the child to initiate sexual activity. Moreover, the Internet and social media have made it easier for children to be lured in, bought, and sold online (Leary, 2014). The massive online commercial sex market has made it increasingly more difficult for law enforcement to find children and identify their traffickers. The common forms of commercial sexual exploitation victims have been found to engage in are mail order brides, pornography, prostitution, stripping, and working for phone sex companies (Women's Support Project, 2014). An increasing concern is that research has found that traffickers are targeting younger victims because they are worried that older children may already have sexually transmitted diseases like HIV or AIDS (Adams, Owens, & Small, 2010).

All children under the age of 18 who are coaxed into commercial sex are victims of sex trafficking (U.S. Department of State, 2016). Children cannot consent to sex trafficking, so there is no need to demonstrate "force, fraud, or coercion," as is necessary for labor trafficking. Therefore, a key difference between child labor trafficking and child sex trafficking is that force, fraud, or coercion is present in child labor trafficking, whereas any child involved in a commercial sex act with or without the use of force is considered a sex trafficking victim (Walts, 2011). As with labor trafficking, children who are victims of sex trafficking are not always easy to identify, but there are some common indicators to help recognize these victims. The U.S. Department of Homeland Security Blue Campaign (2017) lists these indicators:

- Has an excess amount of cash in their possession (and is reluctant to explain its source)
- Has hotel keys and key cards
- Lies about age/false ID
- Has inconsistencies when describing and recounting events
- Has a presence or fear of another person (often an older male or boyfriend who seems controlling)
- Has a high number of reported sexual partners at a young age
- Has sexually explicit profiles on social networking sites
- Is not enrolled in school or has repeated absence from school
- Has a prepaid cell phone

Victims of child sex trafficking have been found to suffer from high rates of PTSD, memory loss, aggression, fear, depression, anxiety, hostility, anger, sexually transmitted diseases/infections (STD/STI), physical injuries, and emotional and psychological trauma from engaging in unwanted sex (Greenbaum, 2016). Therefore, being able to create a safe space for victims to recover is vital, along with an environment that strengthens a victim's resolve from being lured back into that life and revictimized.

In general, victims of human trafficking are difficult to identify and assist, with child victims arguably being a more challenging population to identify and treat. There are NGOs and agencies that attempt to combat and assist these victims. However, because many of them attempt to address all forms of trafficking, it is difficult to provide comprehensive services to one particular form and assist victims in stabilizing their lives (U.S. Department of State, 2016). But there are programs to assist these child victims. The Central Valley Against Human Trafficking (CVAHT) in California, the Salvation Army Trafficking Outreach Program and Intervention Techniques (STOP-IT) in Illinois, and Safe Horizon's Street-work in New York offer services to minors who are victims of both sex and labor trafficking. CVAHT provides assistance to victims of all forms of human trafficking. Along with partner organizations, CVAHT provides emergency shelter, transitional housing, case management, immigration services, transportation, and referrals to other agencies for victims. STOP-IT is an antitrafficking organization that features a drop-in center and individualized case-management services to connect clients with basic needs such as housing, education, and employment. Similarly, Street-work serves street-involved youths, including those who may have been trafficked, by offering a drop-in center and access to housing, food, and other necessities. The effectiveness of these programs is yet to be comprehensively evaluated; however, they have been made more accessible to child victims through targeted outreach and provided the help for victims to escape and receive the assistance (Gibbs *et al.*, 2014).

# Victim Assistance for Victims of Elder Abuse

While known to exist, it has only been since the last half of the 20th century that efforts have been made to define, successfully criminalize and prosecute offenders, and provide assistance to those affected by elder abuse and neglect (Barnett et al., 2011; Goodrich-Liley, 2017). In 1978, the first national investigation into elder abuse and neglect occurred, highlighting the scope of the problem, along with indicating the potential for the problem to increase in the coming decades (Olinger, 1991). The concern for the increase in the problem of elder abuse and neglect is due in large part to the rapidly increasing aging population. According to the U.S. Census Bureau, the population of persons over 65 and older was at 40.5 million in 2010, but by 2030, that population group will reach over 72.1 million (Administration on Aging, 2017). By 2050, senior citizens will outnumber children ages 14 and under for the first time in history. With an aging population, there is an increased need for care and support, along with a considered effort to address the issues of vulnerability and dependency that increase as persons get older.

Similar to other forms of family violence, elder abuse and neglect is seriously underreported, with less than half of the cases reported being substantiated, which means that not enough evidence is provided or available to support the charge of abuse or neglect. When a case is not substantiated, this does not mean, however, that abuse did not occur but rather that the evidence provided did not meet the criteria to pursue legal charges (Tatara, Kuzmeskus, Duckhorn, & Bivens, 1998). It is very difficult to estimate the actual incidence and prevalence of elder abuse and neglect in society. In 1998, the National Elder Abuse Incidence Study (1998) estimated that approximately 450,000 people are abused (National Center on Elder Abuse, 1998). However, more recent studies estimate that 2.1 million older adults are victimized by physical, psychological, and other forms of abuse and neglect every year, with only every 1 out of 6 cases reported to authorities (American Psychological Association [APA], 2012). Older adults are also susceptible to financial abuse, with one in every 20 persons over the age of 60 likely to be a victim (Acierno, Hernandez-Tejada, Murry, & Steve, 2009; Takahashi, 2017).

After living in Miami for 20 years, Helen's daughter, Cindy, and her husband, Robert, decided to move back to California. Robert had recently closed his stationary company after it had not been doing well for a number of years. Helen offered for Cindy and Robert to come and live with her. Helen's husband had passed away two years earlier. She had just turned 81 years of age and was becoming more and more dependent on assistance. Helen had had two hip replacements, as well as open heart surgery. She lived on a large property that had a cottage at the back. Helen offered to move to the cottage and for Cindy and Robert to move into the house with their two kids. Helen was so excited as she thought this would be a great opportunity to spend time with her daughter and her grandchildren.

Once Cindy and Robert arrived, Robert immediately started looking for work. They decided that it would be better for Cindy to stay at home and look after the kids, as childcare was very expensive, and she would only be working to cover the cost of having someone else look after her children. Robert struggled to find a permanent job, and over the course of a year, had worked for three different companies. The lack of permanent work and a steady income meant they had to ask Helen to help them cover some of their expenses. Helen gladly offered to assist them. But soon, Helen realized that Robert had stopped looking for work and found it easier to have Helen just cover their expenses. Helen became concerned that she was now covering all of their expenses. While she was happy to help her daughter's family, she was also aware that she only had a limited amount of resources and growing medical expenses. She decided to speak to Cindy and Robert. When she did, Cindy immediately left the room and left her with Robert. Robert did not seem to understand and became angry

with her. He said, "your husband left you lots of money—it's time you started to help your family." Helen tried to explain to him that she only had a limited amount of money and needed it to help her with her medical expenses. Robert did not accept this and told her to think of her grandchildren.

Two more months went by. Helen was growing more and more concerned. She was still covering all of their expenses. She decided to miss two doctors' appointments thinking that she was fine and would rather save the money. She also decided to cut back on her eating to try and save more money. One night, Robert came to her cottage drunk and demanded that she give him money so he could start another business. Helen, surprised and scared, immediately said she would see what she could do. The next morning, however, she went to the house to speak to Cindy and Robert. Again, when she started to speak, Cindy left the room. Robert, again, became angry, and this time started to call her names and told her she was not allowed to see her grandchildren unless she gave him the money. Helen, frightened and feeling vulnerable, gave Robert the money to start his business.

Helen continued to cover Cindy and Robert's expenses for six more months. During this time, Helen did not go to the doctor and became more and more withdrawn. She also became very weak and was constantly scared of Robert and his behavior. Trying to save her money, she started to miss her weekly bridge meetings with her friends. One night, Cindy came to her cottage crying. Cindy explained to her that they had no money and that Robert had taken her money for the business and spent it and had never even tried to start the business. This was the first time Cindy had actually come and spent time with her mom since moving back. Over the next couple of weeks, Cindy would come and have coffee with Helen every day. Helen was still not going to her doctors' appointments and felt very weak. She also began feeling constantly tired.

After not going to her bridge meetings for more than two months, her friends called her and insisted that she come to bridge, saying that it would be good for her to get out. Helen agreed and arranged for her friend to fetch her and to take her to the bank so she could draw some money. When she got to the bank, the banker said, "Mrs. Cummings, it's so good to see you two days in a row." Helen immediately replied, "you must have me confused with someone else." The banker laughed and replied how he had assisted her and her daughter with signing her accounts over to her daughter. Helen began to panic and said that she really did not have any recollection of being in the bank with her daughter the previous day. The banker commented that she did look very tired when she came and offered to show her the video footage of her and her daughter. After seeing the footage, Helen's friend recommended she go to the doctor to have a health check-up. She also took Helen to the local community center to get advice from the community resource officer. After her health check-up, the doctor found that Helen had high levels of temazepam (a sleeping medication) detected in her blood. Her daughter, Cindy, had been lacing her coffee every time she came to visit her. Cindy and Robert wanted to get her to sign over all her accounts and eventually

the property to them. The community resource officer put Helen into contact with a local elder abuse victim assistance organization that was able to assist her with the bank to get her accounts back into her name. They also assisted her in getting the police involved to remove Cindy and Robert from her property. Helen could not believe that her own daughter had tried to steal from her—especially after all she had done for them. During this time, her health had suffered, and she was living in constant stress. Even though she was able to get her bank accounts back, Helen had to sell her house that she had lived in for 40 years to recuperate from her losses. She finds it hard to talk about what happened to her, as she feels ashamed. She has not spoken to or seen her daughter and grandchildren since this happened.

## Questions:

1. In addition to suffering emotional, verbal, and financial abuse, what other form of abuse was Helen suffering from?

2. Financial abuse is very common among cases of elder abuse. If you were a victim advocate, what would you do to assist Helen?

3. List and describe the importance of education and outreach for elder abuse for community organizations, like the bank, to be aware of possible cases of elder abuse.

The response to elder abuse and neglect as compared to other forms of family violence is not as well established (McNamee & Murphy, 2006). Adult protective services (APS) are in every state to assist in the protection of older adults and work in conjunction with other agencies to ensure their protection. Every state has some form of provision in its legislation authorizing states to protect and provide services to vulnerable adults; however, not every state has mandatory reporting of elder abuse. Two states, Colorado and North Dakota, rely on voluntary reporting to identify cases of elder abuse and neglect (Office for Victims of Crime, 2012). In one of the largest and most rigorous national studies of state level APS conducted, the 2011 Survey of State Adult Protective Services in 2009 found that 292,000 cases of alleged abuse were reported based on estimates in 33 states (Government

Accountability Office GAO], 2011). It is argued that the number of investigations into elder abuse and neglect is set to increase given the changing elder demographics, which greatly impacts the services needed to assist them. This is because despite elder abuse and neglect being in the public eye and it receiving more and more attention, there is a noticeable lack of intervention initiatives and services available to victims (Wolfe, 2003).

## Defining Elder Abuse and Neglect

There is no standardized definition of elder abuse, which is a problem because it affects the process in determining who is a victim of abuse and the services available to that person. According to the National Clearing House on Abuse in Later Life (NCALL) (2017), older adults are persons who have attained the age of 50. The National Center for Elder Abuse (2017) refers to adults as aged 60 and above. The Bureau of Justice Statistics (2012) differentiates older crime victims as being aged 65 and above. The Older Americans Act (1965) uses the age of 60. The conundrum of having a definitive age for elder abuse victims is further complicated when individual states define the age of older adults differently. Similarly, states apply different criteria to determine when an older victim is eligible for protective services or receives special protections under criminal statutes (Gaboury, Seymour, & Heisler, 2012).

> In most states statutes require both a specific age and vulnerability or impairment because of a physical or mental (cognitive) disability. However older adults may be defined, elder abuse generally consists of various forms including physical abuse, sexual abuse, psychological abuse, neglect, and financial exploitation. (Gaboury et al., 2012, p. 4)

**Elder abuse:** elder abuse and neglect is the intentional actions causing harm or creating serious risk of harm, whether or not harm is intended, to a vulnerable elder by a caregiver or other person who stands in a trusted relationship, or failure by a caregiver to satisfy the elders basic needs or to protect the elder from harm (Bonnie & Wallace, 2003, p. 40)

Confinement, abandonment, or abduction, may be additional categories of abuse and neglect and may be included in a state's definition under another form such as physical abuse, neglect, or psychological abuse. Therefore, it is imperative for victim service personnel to be aware of their state's statutes to see how older adults are defined under criminal and protective services laws (Falk, Baigis, & Kopac, 2012; Gaboury et al., 2012).

Because there is no standardized definition of elder abuse and neglect, including at the federal level, a general definition is provided:

> **Elder abuse** and neglect is the intentional actions causing harm or creating serious risk of harm, whether or not harm is intended, to a vulnerable elder by a caregiver or other person who stands in a trusted relationship, or failure by a caregiver to satisfy the elders basic needs or to protect the elder from harm. (Bonnie & Wallace, 2003, p. 40)

## Signs and Symptoms of Elder Abuse and Neglect

Understanding the signs and symptoms of elder abuse and neglect is imperative for addressing the problem and making sure that those who are unable to speak for themselves receive the needed assistance. For victim service personnel, working with older victims of crime and abuse can be challenging due to the complexities of the criminal justice system and because much of the abuse and neglect of elderly people occurs out of public view, goes undetected, and is seldom reported (Gaboury et al., 2012). As with cases of child abuse, limited knowledge of how to identify cases of abuse and neglect, along with attitudes about the duties, leaves many victims left without support (Narayan et al., 2006; Anderst & Dowd, 2010; Matthews et al., 2017).

Research on elder abuse and neglect has indicated that both men and women are susceptible to victimization, but women appear to be at greater risk. Martin et al. (2006) argue that because women tend to live longer than men, they are at a greater risk to develop a physical illness or cognitive impairment (e.g., dementia, Alzheimer's disease), which may require institutionalization in care homes or the dependency on family and friends. Shared living arrangements have also been found to increase the risk of victimization. If the abuser is dependent on the elderly individual for food, housing, or financing, this may increase the potential for abuse (Bonnie & Wallace, 2003). Moreover, if the elderly individual is dependent on care, but that care is beyond the capacity of the caregivers' ability to help, the risk for abuse increases (Namkee & Mayer, 2000; Pillemer, Burnes, Riffin, & Lachs, 2016). Social isolation is another factor to consider in the abuse of the elderly. Abusers may limit the elderly person's contact with friends and family or other social networks to limit support and avoid detection (Pillemer et al., 2016).

The National Center on Elder Abuse (NCEA) (2015) lists the following signs and symptoms of abuse and neglect, which indicate an older adult is being victimized:

Neglect

- Lack of basic hygiene, adequate food, or clean and appropriate clothing
- Lack of medical aids (glasses, walker, teeth, hearing aid, medications)
- Person with dementia left unsupervised
- Person confined to bed is left without care
- Home cluttered, filthy, in disrepair, or having fire and safety hazards
- Home without adequate facilities (stove, refrigerator, heat, cooling, working plumbing, and electricity)
- Untreated pressure "bed" sores (pressure ulcers)

Psychological/Emotional Abuse/Neglect

- Unexplained or uncharacteristic changes in behavior, such as withdrawal from normal activities, unexplained changes in alertness, and self-neglect
- Caregiver isolates elder (doesn't let anyone into the home or speak to the elder)
- Caregiver uses threatening, belittling, or controlling behavior
- Behavior from the elderly person mimics dementia, such as rocking, sucking, or mumbling to oneself

Physical/Sexual Abuse

- Inadequately explained fractures, bruises, welts, cuts, sores, or burns
- Unexplained sexually transmitted diseases

Financial Abuse/Exploitation

- Lack of amenities victim can afford
- Vulnerable elder/adult "voluntarily" giving uncharacteristically excessive financial reimbursement/gifts for needed care and companionship
- Caregiver has control of elder's money but is failing to provide for elder's needs
- Vulnerable elder/adult has signed property transfers (power of attorney, new will, etc.) but is unable to comprehend the transaction or what it means

## Effects of Elder Abuse on Victims

The effects of elder abuse and neglect are not as well researched as those on child abuse and intimate partner violence. Nonetheless, we do know that abuse and neglect has a multitude of negative impacts that affect the physical, psychological, and financial well-being of older adults. Research on older adult victims has revealed that they suffer from the same types of crimes as those of other ages and circumstances but are particularly vulnerable to victimization by family and friends and those they rely on for assistance (Comijs, Penninx, Knipscheer, & van Tilburg, 1999; Bonnie & Wallace, 2003; Namkee & Mayer, 2000; Martin et al., 2006; Pillemer et al., 2016). Victimization at the hands of family members or friends appears to compound the effects on older adults and increases their sense of vulnerability. Away from the home, most elder abuse and neglect occurs in the community or in institutional (facility) settings. These include retirement communities, assisted-living facilities, or nursing homes, where older adults either live independently, semi-independently, or with extensive care services provided (e.g., bathing, dressing, feeding, and assistance with medical care) (Gaboury et al., 2012). Older adults are also at an increased risk of repeated victimization, as most abusers are known to and trusted by the victim and are often persuaded by those trusted individuals to avoid contacting law enforcement or other agencies (Lachs & Pillemer, 2004).

The effects of elder abuse and neglect are divided into four categories: physical abuse, neglect, psychological abuse, and financial abuse. The most common forms of physical abuse recorded result from hitting, punching, shoving, slapping, restraints, forced feeding, and the susceptibility to new illnesses as a result of sexual abuse and the contraction of sexually transmitted diseases. Older adults who experience physical abuse are at an increased risk of death earlier than those who have not experienced it (Dong et al., 2009; Gaboury et al., 2012). Neglect occurs when a caregiver is unable or unwilling to provide the necessary care for an adult for whom he or she is responsible. This may result from caregivers being inexperienced, as a result of the caregiver having a disability that affects the care he or she can provide, or the willful desire to inflict physical or psychological distress on a person

(Robinson, de Benedictis, & Segal, 2012). The effects of neglect can include poor hygiene, poor hydration and nutrition, and unsafe or unsanitary living conditions. The effects of neglect on older adults can lead to feelings of shame, guilt, or embarrassment (Robinson et al., 2012). Neglected older adults have also been found to lose interest in life, become withdrawn, and have an increased suicidal ideation. The forms of psychological abuse that are willfully inflicted on victims are the most difficult to identify. They can include threats of harm, intimidation, abandonment, and humiliation (Pillemer et al., 2016). As a result of psychological abuse, many victims experience feelings of fear, anger, and despair, and are at an increased risk of developing PTSD (Comijs et al., 1999; Pillemer et al., 2016). The prevalence of financial abuse of older adults is extremely high. Mentioned above, one in every 20 persons over the age of 60 is likely to be a victim (Acierno et al., 2009). The loss of financial resources is devastating to any person but is arguably more traumatic for older adults who are unable to replace that money. Financial abuse includes the inappropriate use of an older person's financial resources and property rights. The effects can include anguish, despair, self-blame, and homelessness (Acierno et al., 2009).

Victim assistance personnel are vital aids in supporting older victims and helping them through these challenging periods. Being able to assist in keeping them safe and improving their living conditions are key to their well-being and may require extra preparation and attentiveness by the advocate due to the victims' age and needs.

## Effective Responses to Elder Abuse and Neglect

Responding to elder abuse and neglect requires that both the public and professionals recognize what constitutes abuse, what needs to be done to detect it, and what is the best way to counter it (Goodrich-Liley, 2017). Not having a standardized definition of elder abuse and neglect (as discussed previously) greatly affects how APS and other agencies respond to vulnerable older adults. Unlike child abuse and intimate partner violence, there exist very few agencies that specialize in responding to and assisting elderly victims of crime. Research into service provisions for elderly crime victims has identified the following gaps: age appropriate counseling groups, lack of knowledge about resources with victim assistance personal assisting elderly victims, lack of community support for programs, and advocacy training and services (Beaulaurier, Seff, Newman, & Dunlop, 2005; Klein, Tobin, Salomon, & Dubois, 2008). However, those working with elderly victims have argued that their missions, jurisdictions, and patients include all adults, regardless of age, and that it is important to recognize that there are many overlapping issues that face both older and younger populations, which is why it is a good reason to provide seamless services across ages instead of conditioning resources on age (NCEA, 2014). On the other hand, it is just as important to not assume that the needs, wishes, priorities, and considerations that affect older victims are the same as younger victims. This is why multidisciplinary programs have been created to address the issue of elder abuse and neglect and to help those affected. Multidisciplinary programs or teams vary from state to state but generally consist of groups of professionals from diverse disciplines who come together to provide assessment and consultation in abuse cases. They include APS, members from the criminal justice system, mental health professionals, victim advocates,

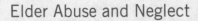

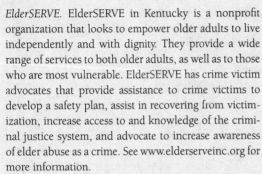

## Elder Abuse and Neglect

*ElderSERVE.* ElderSERVE in Kentucky is a nonprofit organization that looks to empower older adults to live independently and with dignity. They provide a wide range of services to both older adults, as well as to those who are most vulnerable. ElderSERVE has crime victim advocates that provide assistance to crime victims to develop a safety plan, assist in recovering from victimization, increase access to and knowledge of the criminal justice system, and advocate to increase awareness of elder abuse as a crime. See www.elderserveinc.org for more information.

*Volunteers in Victim Assistance.* Volunteers in Victim Assistance (VIVA) in Nevada assists a wide variety of victims by providing crisis intervention, family and group counseling, hospital visitations, criminal justice support, and advocacy to help victims in their struggle to move from victim to survivor. By assisting victims, VIVA helps to integrate these people back into society as whole and to support them to be productive people. See www.victimassistance.us for more information.

*NYC Elder Abuse Center.* The NYC Elder Abuse Center in Brooklyn is a collaborative initiative bringing together government and nonprofit organizations to develop innovative responses to the problem of elder abuse and to provide practitioners with pertinent and relevant information to make their interventions more efficient and effective. New York City is fortunate to have more than one temporary shelter option for abused older adults with trained victim assistance advocates offering both short- and long-term housing options. See www.nyceac.com for more information.

clergy, and financial institutions (e.g., banks, credit unions, and mortgage lenders). The goal of these teams is to assist with ensuring victims' safety and mental health, filling police reports, assisting with short-term emergency housing in cases of caregiver abuse, filing victim compensation claims, and overcoming conflicting goals and gaps with different agencies. The following section will focus on safety planning programs for elder crime victims, medical care, and shelter programs.

## Safety Planning Programs

When someone is being abused and seeking assistance, it is important to develop a safety plan that can help victims regain a sense of control over the situation, feel safer, and prepare for emergency situations (Gaboury et al., 2012). Safety plans never guarantee a person's safety, but they are vital in the assistance process. Assistance programs help to develop personalized safety plans and encourage the older person to work through the plan by thinking about his or her safety, recording important numbers and documents, and considering all accessible ways to leave, if and when necessary. This can be particularly challenging for older adults as their mobility may rely on the assistance of others.

## Medical Care Programs

Depending on the elderly victim's mental or physical health condition, the victim may need medical assistance. Because older adults do not usually self-report instances of elder abuse, the responsibility for identification, reporting, and intervention rests largely with healthcare professionals, social service agencies, and police departments. Programs that offer assistance with medical care will admit the patient to a hospital, obtain a court protective order, place the victim in a safe home, and only permit the return home if the patient has the capacity to make an informed decision or refuses intervention (NCEA, 2015).

## Shelter Programs

Older victims may live in the same home as their abuser, rely on a caregiver for care, or live in a residential facility, where it may be necessary to move a victim for his or her safety and to meet the elder's continuing care needs (Gaboury et al., 2012). Similar to intimate partner shelters, facilities that cater to elderly crime victims focus on providing a safe haven for victims of abuse. They generally offer short-term care where they have access to nursing and therapeutic staff. Such shelters also look to establish community partners, which provide residences with an opportunity to maximize and expand those connections so that they can be more permanently placed in a facility that is appropriate for their needs (Reingold, Solomon, & Levin, 2014).

## Legal Support for Victims

Social change is rarely easy or quick. Recognition and action at local, state, and national levels has been slow in coming. Progress has been made at the federal level with the enactment of the Elder Justice Act in 2010. The act is Congress's first attempt to provide comprehensive legislation to address elder abuse, neglect, and exploitation. The act has strengthened laws protecting elders, along with providing resources to detect, treat, intervene in, and better understand the problem. Some of the provisions of the act include mandated reporting of any suspected crime against an elder in a long-term care facility (Colello, 2017). The act also imposes additional mandatory individual reporting requirements on owners, managers, and even contractors of care facilities and requires facilities to develop internal policies for addressing elder abuse and neglect, along with providing annual training to staff. Failure to comply with reporting requirements could mean a civil monetary penalty of up to $300,000 and exclusion from participation in any federal health care program. Individual employees also face fines for failing to report a suspected crime (Colello, 2017). Other provisions include developing grant programs that aim to improve outreach for elder abuse and justice, enhancing workforce and electronic health record technology, funding to improve adult protective services programs, and establishing and training a long-term care ombudsman. "A long-term care ombudsman is an advocate for the elderly who investigates complaints and responds to requests for assistance from older adults living in long-term care facilities, as well as from those living in residential care or assisted living facilities" (Goodrich-Liley, 2017, p. 319). To date, however, most of the provisions set out in the act have not received the federal funding promised (Colello, 2017). Congress awarded $4 million in 2015 and $8 million 2016. Unfortunately, the authorization for these funds expired in 2014. This has resulted in government not substantially developing and expanding the services for vulnerable older adults to address the prevention, detection, and treatment of elder abuse (Colello, 2017).

## Education and Outreach

Discussed previously, social change rarely happens easily or quickly. And while on a national level positive change has occurred with the enactment of the Elder Justice Act, the fact that much of the funding promised to address the problem has not been forthcoming has greatly impacted the ability of agencies to effectively implement education and outreach programs. Thus, it has become increasingly important for victim service organizations and personnel focusing on older adults to work collaboratively with other agencies. This has led much of the outreach for elder abuse and neglect to become more general in its scope, trying to reach a broad audience. However, special efforts still need to be made to reach individuals who are isolated, disabled, and who have low literacy levels, or where cultural barriers exist (Stein, 2017). Similar to intimate partner violence outreach programs (see Chapter 10), organizations focusing on older adults provide workshops, trainings, and classes to educational institutions, as well as care facilities, medical professionals, law enforcement, businesses (including financial institutions), civic groups, and faith-based organizations. These efforts so far have helped to inform the public of the problem and influence policy makers, although not enough. Sadly, elder abuse and neglect is a pervasive problem, where major gaps exist in funding, policy implementation, research, education, and training. Without the full implementation of the Elder Justice Act and the much-needed support to improve APS program services, training, and education, many elderly will remain vulnerable and, worst of all, become victims (Chen & Dong, 2017).

## SUMMARY

On a daily basis, we are confronted with stories or reports of family violence through television dramas, newspapers, magazines, radio, and even through politics. The family is thought to be a place of safety, love, support, and care, but child abuse and elder abuse affect millions of people on a daily basis (World Health Organization, 2012). Family violence is a complex issue with no easy answer or "magic-bullet-solution" for intervention and prevention. While we have become more aware of family violence occurrence in society, and the effects it has on victims and the community, we will never truly know the extent to which it pervades society. Research on all forms of family violence has indicated that the effects on victims can be short- and long-term, with victims potentially suffering devastating physical, psychological, financial, and social consequences. Given the impact of family violence, victim assistance organizations have responded with programs and services using trauma-informed interventions. Trauma-informed interventions present an excellent opportunity for programs to assist in the recovery from trauma and help victims to regain a sense of balance in their lives (Klain & White, 2013). Most of the programs developed are designed to assist with multiple forms of abuse and include interventions that look to use multiservice interventions, enhance parenting skills, and reduce the effects associated with victimization. While these programs and interventions are presented as the most effective ways to addressing the need to assist children and families, it is important to note that their efficacy remains controversial.

Improving the knowledge of and fostering more positive attitudes toward the duty of protecting those within the family structure is imperative to addressing the problem of family violence. Abusive behavior comes in many forms; therefore, it is important that social workers, teachers (and other school personnel), physicians (nurses, and other healthcare workers), counselors, childcare providers, medical examiners or coroners, law enforcement officers, and members of the clergy are aware of the common signs of abuse and neglect. Recognizing high-risk situations and the signs and symptoms of maltreatment helps to prevent serious injuries and relieves the victims of the responsibility to seek help for themselves. Enhancing identification and coordination between educational, legal, medical, and victim service responses is of paramount importance.

Key legislation addressing each component of family violence has been enacted, which has improved criminal codes and statutes that protect victims, assist in providing compensation and restitution, and funding for research and the development of assistance organizations. While much has been done to protect children, much still needs to be done in the area of elder abuse.

A vital component of any assistance organization and a condition of the funding they receive is education and outreach. Many education and outreach programs for family violence include parent education programs, including initiatives such as media campaigns, using local radio and television stations to broadcast events to provide information on assistance programs; hosting an awards breakfast/dinner honoring those key individuals and organizations working to prevent child abuse; or having kids' parades, local hero days, or candlelight vigils for victims, along with disseminating multilingual prevention materials to raise awareness of the assistance available. Social change is rarely easy or quick. Action at local, state, and national levels can be slow in coming; therefore, it is imperative for victim assistance organizations and personnel to establish reliable resources and networks in the community that can facilitate effective responses to family violence.

## KEY WORDS

Child abuse   166
Elder abuse   184
Family violence   162

Human trafficking   178
Mandated reporting   168

Neglect   163
Trauma-informed care   173

## INTERNET RESOURCES

**The Child Protection Services (www.childwelfare .gov/aboutus)**

The Child Welfare Information Gateway promotes the safety, permanency, and well-being of children, youth, and families by connecting child welfare, adoption, and related professionals as well as the public to information, resources, and tools covering topics on child welfare, child abuse and neglect, out-of-home care, adoption, and more.

**The Blue Ribbon Project (www.blueribbonproject .org)**

The Blue Ribbon Project: Supporting Victims of Child Abuse and Youth in Foster Care is designed to be a community outreach program assisting to both prevent of child abuse and support abused and neglected children. The Blue Ribbon Project understands that victims of child abuse carry a burden throughout their lives, and the effects of abuse last a lifetime. The project offers a variety of functional outreach programs that directly serve abused and neglected children in the community, youth in foster care, as well as adult survivors of abuse and neglect. Through our dedication to these children, we remain committed to achieving our vision of raising awareness around child abuse in our communities and acting as advocates for those affected by child abuse and neglect.

**The National Center on Elder Abuse (www.ncea .acl.gov)**

The National Center on Elder Abuse provides the latest information regarding research, training, best practices, news, and resources on elder abuse, neglect, and exploitation to professionals and the public. First established by the U.S. Administration on Aging (AoA) in 1988 as a national elder abuse resource center, the NCEA was granted a permanent home at AoA in the 1992 amendments made to Title II of the Older Americans Act. The NCEA is one of 27 Administration on Aging–funded resource centers. Research shows that as many as two million elders are abused in the United States. The Administration on Aging recognizes that as a government, as a society, and as individuals, we must increase our efforts to ensure that all older adults age with dignity and honor.

## CRITICAL THINKING QUESTIONS

1. List and discuss some of the signs and symptoms of child abuse and neglect.

2. Describe the types of programs developed to effectively respond to victims of child abuse and neglect.

3. What are the advantages of using trauma-informed care when working with victims?

4. Discuss the importance of medical care programs for victims of elder abuse.

5. Describe some of the problems with defining elder abuse.

# 10

# Victim Assistance for Intimate Partner Violence

Discussed in the previous chapter, acts of family violence pervade our everyday lives through stories or reports on television, in newspapers and magazines, on radio, and even through politics. Family violence has been recognized as a social, legal, and public health problem, which is extremely complex and has no simple solution (Berns, 2004; LaViolette & Barnett, 2014). The victims of family violence come from every walk of life. The violence experienced not only impacts the victim but also poses dangers for and impacts immediate family members as well. Family violence covers a broad range of acts, with the legal criminal and civil definition of family violence varying according to state and federal law (Palmer & Edmunds, 2003). Despite the lack of definitional consensus, family violence can be categorized into three groups. In Chapter 9, the focus was on child abuse and elder abuse. In this chapter, the focus will be on the third category, intimate partner violence (IPV). The overwhelming majority of victims of IPV are women, but men are victimized, too (Bartholomew, Regan, Oram, & White, 2008; Godbout et al., 2017). To gain a better understanding of IPV, it is important to define it, describe the effects it has on victims, and explore the types of assistance offered to those who suffer its consequences.

## Victim Assistance for Intimate Partner Violence Victims

Historically called "domestic violence, battering, or spousal abuse," IPV has been acknowledged internationally as a public health, social policy, and human rights concern. Intimate partner violence occurs in heterosexual and same-sex relationships, with both men and women suffering from this form of violence. Data from the 2011 National Intimate Partner and Sexual Violence Survey (NISVS) estimates that over 10 million women and men in the United States experience physical violence each year by a current or former intimate partner. It is also estimated that an average of 1 in 5 women and 1 in 7 men are likely to experience some form of intimate partner violence over the course of their lifetime, highlighting the magnitude of IPV in society (Black et al., 2011; Breiding, Basile, Smith, Black, & Mahendra, 2015). Many factors contribute to IPV (individual, relationship, community, and societal), and preventing it requires a clear understanding of these factors and how to identify various opportunities for prevention (Capaldi, Knoble, Shortt, & Kim, 2012).

Much of the social and legal visibility IPV receives today is a result of the women's movement in the 1960s and 1970s (see Chapter 1). The women's movement was instrumental in bringing to light the violence that women and children were experiencing behind closed doors. The advocacy of this movement sought to change the way the criminal justice system responds to victims of this violence, and established shelters to protect and provide assistance to victims. In the 1970s, the first three shelters and hotlines for victims were established (Young & Stein, 2004). Today, over 5,000 shelters and service programs exist in the United States (Gosselin, 2014). Many of these shelters and programs assisting victims of IPV provide services like housing, crisis counseling, legal assistance, employment, and job training (Lyon, Lane, & Menard, 2008). While the amount of attention and services offered to victims has dramatically increased, the ramifications for those affected is an ongoing challenge to victim service organizations and society as a whole.

## CASE STUDY
### 'You Can Either Have Your Friends and Your Family, Or You Can Have Me'

I was 21 when we met, and living with my mother and my two brothers. I had tons of friends, a decent job, and I took classes at night. Soon after I started dating him, my family told me they disapproved. They saw something in him that I couldn't see. But I had this Bonnie-and-Clyde type of attitude. You guys just don't like him because I love him, I thought. Get over it. The first time he slapped me, I said: "This is not going to be me." My mother had been a victim of domestic abuse, and I grew up in Trinidad watching her being beaten by my dad. This is not my future, I swore. He came back with apologies and purple roses—my favorite color. I accepted the apology. I thought it meant he wasn't going to do it again. I was wrong. Over the next month, he became more violent, punching and slapping me in private. I didn't tell anyone about the abuse. I didn't want them to know they were right. One day, he got in an altercation with my brother, and the cops were called. This is the moment he asked me to choose between my family or him. I felt like he loved me, and he was the only person who was on my side. Everyone else was against us. So I picked him. I moved out of my family's home and became

temporarily homeless. We lived in a motel for a week, and when the money ran out, we lived in his car. He warned me not to call my family. He said if I reached out, they would come get me, and we would be separated. He said if I contacted them, it would be the end of our relationship. On top of that, I was ashamed to call my family. I felt I would be judged. Everyone warned me [about him], and I didn't listen. For about a month, I was homeless. He would take me to different apartments to wash up so I could go to work. I was masking all of this like it was normal. Finally, I was able to save up enough money to rent a studio apartment. He would stay most days and nights there. Once we had our own space, the abuse accelerated. Punching, kicking, strangling. Often for hours. He would say: "You know how much I love you, right? Your family doesn't love you like I love you. Where are they right now? They aren't looking after you like I am." In my mind, I thought I could handle the abuse, I'd be fine. Mentally, you become so messed up that you start to think you are part of the problem. We stayed together for two years, and (The names and length of this story have been edited from the original for length and clarity.)

I fell out of contact with everyone who was important to me. I wasn't on speaking terms with my family. I lost touch with my friends. I dropped out of school because it caused too many problems for me to be around other people. He used to pick me up from class. If I was standing near a man—even a security guard—when he arrived, there would be trouble. It was easier not to go. Work was the only time I was allowed to be out of his sight, but even then, he would constantly call me or show up randomly. If he called and I didn't answer the phone, he would go crazy. He was jealous of my coworkers. He'd question the length of my dresses when I got dressed for work. Why I was wearing a particular pair of underwear that day. The accusations were never-ending. One night he beat me so bad I thought I might die. He held a knife over my neck and threatened to kill me. He pummeled me for five hours, punching and kicking and strangling me. He would stop and then start again. Then he just fell asleep, because he was tired. I felt like something had been broken inside, physically and emotionally. As he slept, I crawled out of bed and took a cab to the emergency room. It was the first time I'd ever sought help. There, alone in the ER, I hit my breaking point. I realized I could have died in that apartment and no one would have known, because I had no contact with my mother or my brothers, or even my best friend. I was completely isolated. After I was released from the hospital, I went home and had my locks changed. I didn't hear from him for two weeks. He eventually called me asking to see me. I said no, that we were done for good. He didn't like that. One night, he tried to break into my apartment. He was banging, and I could feel his body pressing on my door. He was attempting to pry it open with a crowbar. I tried to call the police on my landline, but he had preemptively cut my telephone line in the basement. I believe he had every intention to kill me. Luckily, I had a prepaid phone stowed away. My hands shook as I unwrapped it to call 911. Once he heard me talking to dispatch, he took off. When the cops arrived, I was too scared to open the door. After that, the stalking began. He would leave derogatory notes on my car: Anybody who f$#Ks Lovern knows that I had her first, they are getting leftovers. I filed a restraining order. Once he was out of my life, I was ready to restart it. The first person I told about the abuse was my best friend. She was dumbfounded, and she encouraged me to tell my mom. That was a difficult call. Two years had passed. I was so far removed. I thought I was going to be shamed and judged. She had been worried about me for so long. It was hard to open up about what I had experienced. But together, we started the work of rebuilding our relationship. Over time, my extended family found out what happened. They never asked me about it—they just understood. I was welcomed back without question at Thanksgivings and family get-togethers. I was no longer alone. Re-entering public life took some getting used to, after such extreme isolation. For a long time, I didn't trust myself to look guys in the eye, especially men who were talking to me. I would hear his voice. No one is going to love you how I love you, he'd say. No one is going to want you like I want you. But my own voice got louder the longer I was away from him, and in time, I started to be myself again. The smiley-faced social butterfly I once was started to re-emerge. It was OK to make eye contact with strangers, to have dinner with friends, to dress the way I saw fit, to not have to be on the clock constantly. Looking back, I wish I had sought help—if not from family and friends, then from someone else. I now know that no matter how it feels, you are never alone. You can break free if you trust yourself.

This story is taken from an article published in the *Huffington Post* in 2014: "Why Didn't You Just Leave? Six Domestic Violence Survivors Explain Why It's Never That Simple," by Melissa Jeltsen (https://www.huffingtonpost.com/2014/09/12/why-didnt-you-just-leave_n_5805134.html).

*(Continued)*

(Continued)

## Questions:

1. What made it challenging for Lovern to leave her abusive relationship?

2. You are a victim advocate helping Lovern. Develop a safety plan for her, and discuss what you have included in it.

3. Compile a list of services in your community that help victims of intimate partner violence. Which one of these services would you recommend for Lovern to go to for help to recover from her traumatic experience?

## Defining Intimate Partner Violence

Intimate partner violence (IPV) occurs in all settings and affects persons of all races, education levels, and ages (World Health Organization, 2012). IPV is defined as any "physical, sexual, or psychological harm committed by a current or former spouse, opposite-sex cohabitating partner, same-sex cohabiting partner, date, or boyfriend or girlfriend" (Breiding et al., 2015, p. 11). IPV can take on many forms but is generally categorized into four defining harms: physical, sexual, psychological, and economical abuse (Tong, 1984; Breiding et al., 2015). Physical violence refers to nonsexual physically violent actions that may include pushing, shoving, punching, slapping, strangling, kicking, pulling hair, and restraining the partner. Sexual violence includes forcing a partner to perform any sexual act without freely consenting or being unable to consent or refuse. Psychological abuse includes the use of verbal and nonverbal communication with the intent to harm another person mentally or emotionally, ultimately to gain control over that person. Psychological abuse can include threats of harm, name calling, criticizing, humiliating, and, in cases of same-sex relationships, threatening to disclose sexual orientation to family, friends, or employers. Research suggests that psychological abuse often precedes physical and sexual violence or cooccurs with other forms of violence (Follingstad, Rutledge, Berg, Hause, & Polek, 1990; O'Leary, 2015). Stalking is another form of psychological abuse used in cases of IPV. Stalking is a "pattern of repeated, unwanted, attention and contact that causes fear or concern for one's own safety or the safety of someone else (e.g., family member, close friend)" (Breiding et al., 2015, p. 14). Economical abuse may involve a partner creating financial dependency by restricting a person from working, getting that person fired or released from their place of employment, or making that person ask for money or taking the money they have earned (Tong, 1984; Gosselin, 2014; Breiding et al., 2015).

Stated earlier, many factors contribute to IPV (individual, relationship, community, and societal). According to the World Health Organization (2012) these are the most consistent factors associated with IPV:

Individual Factors

- Young age
- Low level of education

- Witnessing or experiencing violence as a child

- Harmful use of alcohol and drugs

- Personality disorders

- Acceptance of violence (e.g., feeling it is acceptable to beat a partner)

- Past history of abusing partners

Relationship Factors

- Conflict or dissatisfaction in the relationship

- Male dominance in the family

- Economic stress

- One partner having multiple partners

- Disparity in educational attainment (e.g., where one person has a higher level of education than the other)

Community and Societal Factors

- Gender-inequitable social norms (especially those that link notions of manhood to dominance and aggression)

- High levels of poverty

- Low social and economic status of women

- Weak legal sanctions against IPV (particularly within marriages)

- Lack of women's civil rights, including restrictive or inequitable divorce and marriage laws

- Broad social acceptance of violence as a way to resolve conflict

- Armed conflict and high levels of general violence in society

World Health Organization (2012), http://www.who.int/en

Better understanding IPV and the forms of violence victims suffer, along with the risk factors that influence its occurrence, are vital for policy makers, researchers, public health practitioners, victim advocates, service providers, and media professionals seeking to help victims and to find sustainable ways to prevent IPV.

## Signs and Symptoms of Intimate Partner Violence

IPV and abuse is used to gain and maintain control over the victim. Abusers use a variety of tactics to obtain control, such as fear, guilt, shame, intimidation, and violence

(Mick, 2006; LaViolette & Barnett, 2014). Abusers' behavior often alternates between violent, abusive behavior and apologetic behavior, where they make sincere promises to change. This may lead abusers and victims to hide, overlook, excuse, or deny that there is a problem (LaViolette & Barnett, 2014; Eriksson & Mazerolle, 2015), making identifying and assisting those in IPV relationships difficult. Noticing and acknowledging the warning signs and symptoms of IPV are the first steps to ending it, making the training of teachers, health care professionals, counselors, and victim assistance personal imperative in recognizing and accurately interpreting signs and symptoms associated with IPV (Brandl, Herbert, Rozwadowski, & Spangler, 2004). While the following is not an inclusive list of all the signs and symptoms of IPV, these are the most commonly identified by research.

Typical physical signs include contusions or minor lacerations to the head, face, neck, breast, or abdomen (Breiding, Chen & Black, 2014). These are often distinguishable from accidental injuries, which are more likely to involve the periphery of the body. Persons in an abusive relationship are also more likely to have multiple injuries compared to accident victims. When this pattern of injuries is seen in victims, particularly in combination with evidence of an old injury, physical abuse should be suspected (Gagnon & DePrince, 2017). In addition to physical signs and symptoms, IPV victims may also exhibit psychological signs of abuse such as depression and anxiety (Mega, Mega., Mega, & Moore, 2000; Peterson & Walker, 2003). As a result of prolonged stress, victims may manifest various physiological symptoms that generally lack a more common medical explanation. For example, they may complain of backaches, headaches, and digestive problems. These victims may also complain of fatigue, restlessness, insomnia, or loss of appetite (Peterson & Walker, 2003).

The Office on Women's Health lists these additional signs and symptoms that may be indicators of a person in an abusive relationship (Office on Women's Health, 2015). The person

- seems afraid or anxious to please his or her partner;
- does everything his or her partner says and does;
- checks in often with his or her partner to report where he or she is and what he or she is doing;
- talks about his or her partner's temper, jealousy, or possessiveness;
- has frequent injuries, with the excuse of "accidents";
- is prevented from working, going to school, or attending social occasions, without explanation;
- is forced to dress in clothing designed to hide bruises or scars (e.g., wearing long sleeves in the summer or sunglasses indoors);
- has low self-esteem and is depressed, anxious, or suicidal;
- is restricted from seeing family and friends and rarely goes out in public without his or her partner; and/or
- has limited access to money, credit cards, or transportation (e.g., a car).

# Effects on Victims

Intimate partner violence has numerous direct and indirect effects on victims. Like child abuse, the effects are influenced by a number of factors including the frequency, severity, and type of IPV experienced. While the effects of IPV can be short term, research suggests that the influence of abuse can persist long after the violence has stopped (Heise & Garcia-Moreno, 2002). When discussing the effects of IPV, researchers and advocates focus on these elements: physical health, mental health, sexual and reproductive health, and the economic effects. The physical health damages that result from IPV include injuries caused as a result of direct violence. These injuries include bruises and welts, lacerations, fractures, and broken bones or teeth (Breiding et al., 2014; Breiding et al., 2015). The physical health effects of IPV, however, go beyond the physical injuries. IPV victimization is also commonly associated with a number of ailments that often have no identifiable medical cause and are thought to be the result of prolonged stress. These conditions include gastronomical problems, fatigue, hypertension, diabetes, high cholesterol, and heart disease, especially among women (Black & Breiding, 2008; Becker-Dreps et al., 2010; Breiding et al., 2015). Research also suggests that IPV victimization can be linked to victims engaging in unhealthy behaviors, such as smoking, excessive drinking, and substance abuse (Peterson, 2003; Charbone-Lopez, Kruttschnitt, & Macmillan, 2006).

The mental health effects of IPV may be severe and long lasting. Anxiety, depression, eating and sleeping disorders, posttraumatic stress disorder (PTSD), and low self-esteem are among the psychological damages caused by IPV (Black & Breiding, 2008; Coker et al., 2011; Breiding et al., 2015). The mental health effects for victims who have been physically or sexually abused are particularly significant, as they are more likely to experience PTSD later in life (Cook, Dinnen, & O'Donnell, 2011). Evidence also suggests that IPV victims report higher rates of suicidal ideation and attempted suicide. Suicidal ideation and attempted suicide were significantly higher among women who had experienced physical or sexual violence than those who had not (Heise & Garcia-Moreno, 2002; Garcia-Moreno, Henrica, Watts, Ellsbery, & Heise, 2005; Chang, Kahle, & Hirsch, 2015).

There are a host of sexual and reproductive health effects that result from IPV. Importantly, while men are victimized by IPV, too, women are the most frequent victims of sexual violence. A women's sexual and reproductive health can be affected directly through forced sexual intercourse, which may result in sexually transmitted infections (such as HIV) or indirectly when a partner interferes with a women's ability to use contraceptives (Heise, Moore, & Toubia, 1995; Chisholm, Bullock, & Ferguson, 2017). Unwanted pregnancies may also result from sexual violence or the inability to use contraceptives. As such women may seek out or be forced to have an abortion or unsafe abortion, which may lead to reproductive health complications later in life (Campbell & Soeken, 1999; Chisholm et al., 2017). Violence also occurs during, before, and after pregnancy. In the United States, it is estimated that between 50% and 70% of women who are abused before pregnancy are also abused during pregnancy. Additionally, it is estimated that among women whose pregnancies were intended, 5.3% reported abuse during the pregnancy, compared with 12.6% for women whose pregnancies were mistimed, and 15.3% for women whose pregnancies were unwanted (Parson, Goodwin, & Peterson, 2000; Saltzman, Johnson, Gilbert, & Goodwin, 2003; Chisholm et al., 2017).

In addition to the physical, mental, and sexual health effects, IPV can have significant economic effects on victims. Victims may be forced to not work by their partners or may be fired as the abuse affects their ability to fulfill their work responsibilities (LaViolette & Barnett, 2014). It is estimated that nearly a quarter of employed women report that IPV has affected their work performance at some point in their lives. Moreover, it is estimated that each year 8 million days of paid work is lost in the United States because of IPV (Rothman, Hathaway, Stidsen, & Vries, 2007). Losing financial independence greatly affects victims' choice to stay or leave an abusive relationship as they become financially dependent on their abusive partner. This subsequently leads to many victims becoming homeless when they do leave an abusive relationship, forcing them to find temporary housing from friends or family or use women's shelters or homeless shelters (Brush, 2011; LaViolette & Barnett, 2014). The economic effects of IPV do not only affect the individual but also society more generally. In a study by Max, Rice, Finkelstein, Bardwell, and Leadbetter (2004), IPV was estimated to cost the United States, $8.3 billion annually. This figure was reached by combining medical costs ($5.8 billion) and loss of productivity estimates ($2.5 billion). However, these costs are substantially underestimated for they do not include the cost of the criminal justice system and other social services interventions associated with IPV (Basile & Black, 2011).

Better understanding the effects IPV has on victims can greatly affect how we address the problem in society and assist those in need. As in cases of child abuse, trauma-informed care has become particularly useful and has been implemented in most programs and organizations assisting victims of IPV.

## Effective Responses to Intimate Partner Violence

As discussed previously and in Chapter 1, it was not more than 40 years ago when assistance to those victimized by IPV was nonexistent. The women's movement in the 1960s and 1970s was instrumental in drawing attention to the problem of abuse in the home. Today, our knowledge of the problem and all those who are victimized (including men and members of the LGBT community) has increased significantly, and now over 5,000 shelters and service programs exist in the United States to assist victims of IPV (Black et al., 2011; Gosselin, 2014; Brown & Herman, 2015). Most shelters in the United States today provide **multiservice interventions** to victims of IPV. These services include 24-hour hotlines, counseling, support groups, transitional housing programs, safety planning, financial education, employment training and assistance, legal advocacy, and programs specifically designed for children (O'Reilly, Wilkes, Luck, & Jackson, 2010; Sullivan, 2011). Most of the victim assistance organizations also focus on raising awareness among policy makers, law enforcement, social services, and the education system to better understand the need for an appropriate response to IPV. The following sections focus on safety planning programs, transitional housing, and legal advocacy programs.

**Multiservice intervention:** includes 24-hour hotlines, counseling, support groups, transitional housing programs, safety planning, financial education, employment training and assistance, legal advocacy, and programs specifically designed for children (O'Reilly et al., 2010; Sullivan, 2011)

### Safety Planning Programs

Safe Horizon is a victim assistance organization in New York City that assists victims who have experienced domestic violence, child abuse, sexual assault, stalking, human trafficking, youth homelessness, and other victimizations. Their safety-planning program involves devising safety plans unique to each survivor, as each situation is different and requires a different approach to increasing safety for the survivor. Safe Horizon also offers a confidential hotline to assist survivors to develop a plan. See https://www.safehorizon.org for more information.

### Transitional Support Housing

The Marjaree Mason Center provides emergency and longer-term safe housing, along with a wide variety of support services for victims of domestic violence in Fresno County, California. The center operates two confidentially located safe houses and ensures that victims of domestic violence, male or female, are provided a safe place to reside while their traumatic situation is

addressed, and while they attain the support needed to return to the community safely. The safe houses ensure that each family has its own private rooms, so families are not separated during their stay. All safe houses feature large communal kitchens and play areas for children. See https://mmcenter.org for more information.

### Legal Advocacy

CONNECT is a leading, nonprofit training, educational, and advocacy organization dedicated to preventing interpersonal violence and promoting gender justice. CONNECT aims to build individual and community partners to help change beliefs, behaviors, and institutions that perpetuate violence to create safe families and peaceful communities. CONNECT's legal advocates provide victims of interpersonal violence with basic and in-depth information and advocacy concerning the police, district attorney, criminal and family court, probation and parole, and social services such as shelter, housing, public assistance, and immigration. See http://www.connectnyc.org for more information.

### Safety Planning Programs

Shelters for victims of IPV have saved many lives. They have done this by assisting victims who face a multiplicity of problems. For example, victims wonder if they will ever feel safe again. Where will they live? Should they get assistance from the police? Shelters help victims with all these issues and many more, but one of the primary issues they help victims with is **safety planning**. Safety planning for victims is generally done with a victim advocate, who helps to assess a victim's current situation and create an individualized plan that helps to increase his or her safety (Campbell, 2001). Safety plans are critical for victims in abusive relationships and who are looking to leave their partners. They involve, amongst other things, discussing and agreeing on a safe place to go when they do leave their partner, opening and/or hiding money in a separate account, getting a second set of keys made for the house or car, having a packed bag with clothes and important documents ready to go when needed or left with someone the victim trusts, practicing getting out of the house safely, avoiding rooms with no exits and/or weapons

**Safety Planning:** involves, amongst other things, discussing and agreeing on a safe place to go and preparing for other safety contingencies when victims leave their partners (e.g., bathrooms, kitchen), teaching children to not get in the middle of a fight, and memorizing emergency numbers (Campbell, 2001; Parker, Gielen, Castillo, Webster, & Glass, 2016).

## Transitional Support Housing Programs

Due to the high rate of economic abuse and the risk of homelessness when victims leave abusive relationships, transitional housing programs provide victims and their children with private, low-cost living space for a set period of time (Baker, Holditch-Niolon, & Oliphant, 2009). **Transitional housing** programs may provide assistance for 90 days, or in some cases depending on the organization, up to two years. Victims are usually placed in apartment-style facilities or in a communal house at no cost to the family or individual. In some cases when there is no housing space available, vouchers for a motel stay or hotel room may be given to victims and their families. Only organizations who have this financial support to do so offer these vouchers, and they are usually only for a couple of nights and under strict conditions (Martin & Stern, 2005; Baker et al., 2009). How each program is run and the conditions for which housing is provided varies according to each organization. For example, some programs may require victims who are in temporary housing to also participate in economic and empowerment programs. These programs assist in teaching financial literacy (i.e., the knowledge and skills necessary to make sound financial decisions and acquire resources) and to develop economic self-efficacy (i.e., the ability to independently meet their daily needs) (Miller-Perrin, Perrin, & Renzetti, 2018, p. 217). Research suggests that financial instability, the threat or actual experience of poverty, and economic dependence on an intimate partner, along with the mental health impacts of IPV, are among the primary factors that lead victims to returning to their abusive partners, increasing the risk of revictimization (Black & Breiding, 2008; Breiding et al., 2015; Miller-Perrin et al., 2018).

**Transitional housing:** programs that may provide assistance for 90 days, or in some cases depending on the organization, up to two years. Victims are usually placed in apartment-style facilities or in a communal house at no cost to the family or individual

## Legal Advocacy Programs

Legal advocacy programs provide technical support to victims of IPV on issues such as custody, visitation rights, divorce, child support, protection orders, landlord/tenant issues, and other matters. Legal advocate programs typically also provide court accompaniment to victims. Most programs can provide assistance to victims by phone or in individual meetings, along with providing referrals to community partners who are able to assist with family law, criminal law, and immigration (Sullivan, 2011; Fitzpatrick, 2014). Importantly, legal advocates are not attorneys and cannot give legal advice. They only assist victims in navigating the complicated criminal justice system and provide information to help victims to make informed decisions.

Research conducted on victim services for IPV victims has established that most victims are satisfied with the services they receive and acknowledge an increased understanding of the criminal justice system and their rights, along with feeling more hopeful and positive about their future. There is little doubt that the availability and type of services offered to victims of IPV today is far superior than it was 40 years ago; however, there is still a need for more research and evaluation of the services and programs offered to improve the needs of those who find themselves in abusive relationships and need help.

## Legal Support for Victims

For many years, the incidence of IPV was largely ignored or condoned by the legal and criminal justice system in the United States. Fortunately, much has changed, and legal remedies for violence against women, men, and members of the LGBT community have proliferated in the United States (Goldfarb, 2008; Modi, Palmer, & Armstrong, 2014). Arguably the most important piece of legislation to be passed was the Violence Against Women Act (VAWA) in 1994. According to Ake and Arnold (2018, p. 3-4), the passing of the VAWA "unmistakably signaled that domestic violence was finally being taken seriously on a national scale" and was seen as a symbol of national commitment to eradicate the problem. The VAWA has been modified and reauthorized several times to enhance its coverage and its effectiveness in addressing the problem in society (Sacco, 2015). Some of the modifications to the act included enhanced federal domestic violence and stalking penalties, added protections for abused foreign nationals, and newly developed programs for elderly and disabled women. Additionally, VAWA has enhanced legislation for repeat stalking offenders, added additional protections for battered and trafficked foreign nationals, created programs for sexual assault victims and American Indian victims of domestic violence and related crimes, and created programs designed to improve the public health response to domestic violence (Goldfarb, 2008; Sacco, 2015). Moreover, the VAWA made it a federal crime to cross state lines in order to commit domestic violence or to violate a protection order, mandated restitution awards in federal sex crime cases and interstate domestic violence cases, required states to give full faith and credit to protection orders issued in other states, expanded the rape shield protections in the Federal Rules of Evidence, and reformed immigration law to help immigrant women escape their abusers (Goldfarb, 2008; Sacco, 2015). The VAWA also provides approximately $1.62 billion in federal funds to support a broad range of programs, including training of police, prosecutors, and judges; support of women's shelters, community domestic violence projects, and rape prevention programs; creation of national toll-free domestic violence hotlines; and research and data collection. The funding provided for these programs is also used to stimulate collaboration between government agencies and nongovernmental organizations, along with improving outreach by organizations to victims and the community (Goldfarb, 2008; Modi et al., 2014; Sacco, 2015).

## Education and Outreach

Because we want to help families and individuals thrive in our communities, it is imperative that we confront the issues that affect them the most. **Intimate partner violence** too often shatters the lives of people from all walks of life. On an international and national level, attention to intimate partner violence has taken on several forms; from the implementation of various laws and their subsequent amendments, to formal hearings and task forces on family violence, to media portrayals in television, movies, and documentaries (DePrince, Belknap & Gover, 2012). On a local level, many victim assistance organizations have consciously implemented education and outreach components in their organizations that take action to increase the knowledge of IPV, its consequences, and the support that is offered in their communities (Goolkasian, 1986; DePrince et al., 2012). It is argued that well-coordinated policies and protocols that maximize the legal sanctions and available community resources with early coordinated victim outreach improves criminal justice outcomes and increases victims' safety and empowerment (DePrince et al., 2012).

**Intimate partner violence:** any "physical, sexual, or psychological harm committed by a current or former spouse, opposite-sex cohabitating partner, same-sex cohabiting partner, date, or boyfriend or girlfriend" (Breiding et al., 2015, p. 11). IPV can take on many forms but is generally categorized into four defining harms: physical, sexual, psychological, and economic abuse (Tong, 1984; Breiding et al., 2015)

Typical outreach programs for IPV include workshops, trainings, and classes for students in educational institutions (elementary, middle, and high schools, colleges), as well as for medical professionals, law enforcement, businesses, civic groups, and faith-based organizations. Education and outreach works to create a culture in our communities that is intolerant of domestic and sexual violence, along with helping to eliminate barriers to services (Ellis & Hart, 2003). Programs also actively tailor their presentations to specific audiences to be culturally aware, addressing any attitudinal barriers that exist (Ellis & Hart, 2003).

Research into the effectiveness of education and outreach programs for IPV has shown positive results on decreasing women's reluctance to work with prosecutors and increasing women's likelihood of being encouraged to take part in the prosecution of their abusers. In addition, women who received outreach reported decreased PTSD symptom severity, depression, and fear one year later. Although there were no effects of outreach on revictimization or social support levels, women receiving outreach were more prepared to leave their abuser (DePrince et al., 2012). While these findings are very positive, more research is needed into the effectiveness of education and outreach programs, along with their effect on minority groups such as men and the LGBT community.

## Why Victims Find It Challenging to Leave Abuse Relationships

Despite the difficulties, hardships, and trauma victims in abusive relationships experience, the most challenging decision they have to make is whether to stay or leave. If victims remain with their abusers, they are criticized and often blamed for the victimization. If they choose to leave the abusers, they may face criticism for a lack of commitment to the relationship or the welfare of their children or spouse (LaViolette & Barnett, 2014). The reality is that most people do not understand the dynamics of an abusive relationship and the important fact that most relationships do not start with one partner abusing the other. Yet, many people will ask questions like "why does she stay?" or make comments such as "I would not put up with abuse" or that "I would leave if my partner was abusing me" (LaViolette & Barnett, 2014). The reality is that leaving an abusive relationship is not that simple. There are a variety of factors that may make it challenging for victims to leave an abusive relationship, including the following:

- Love
- Normalization of abuse
- Fear

- Isolation
- Economic dependence
- Children

As stated previously, most relationships do not start with one partner abusing the other. Most relationships begin because people have an interest in one another and develop feelings for each other. Researchers have frequently noted that victims, particularly women, tend to blame themselves for the abuse they experience and often believe that if they just try harder, or *love* more, the abuse will stop (Fraser, 2005, p. 17; Power, Koch, Kralik, & Jackson, 2006). Some victims believe that their abuse is part of the destiny of true love and that they must maintain love despite the challenges it brings (Hayes & Jeffries, 2013). For some victims, the thought of existing outside an intimate relationship is often more painful than staying in an abusive one (Fraser, 2005, p. 17).

The **normalization of abuse** occurs when the victim doesn't recognize the violence as unacceptable or rationalizes the abuse as being deserving. Normalizing the abuse makes it very difficult for victims to seek and obtain help (Bostock, Plumpton, & Pratt, 2009). The services available to help victims in abusive relationships are dependent upon the victims being able to leave the abuser, but there are many hardships and dangers that are attached to leaving (Ooms, 2006). While the majority of people assume leaving is the safest option, in reality, more victims are killed trying to leave their abusive partners than at any other point (Browne, 2004). Therefore, *fear* is a very important factor to consider. In addition to the fear victims may feel for their safety and that of their children, victims may also feel fear about making major life changes and the possibility of losing custody of their children.

> **Normalization of abuse:** when the victim doesn't recognize the violence as unacceptable or rationalizes the abuse as being deserved

Another challenge victims encounter when considering whether to leave an abuser is *isolation* from family and friends (Bostock et al., 2009). Research has found that abusers will often isolate victims from sources of support and deprive them of their independence (Bostock et al., 2009; LaViolette & Barnett, 2014). Being isolated from a support system reduces the perception of the victims that they can and will be helped should they seek it. Another form of deprivation of independence is preventing victims from working, which makes them *economically dependent* on the abuser. According to the National Coalition Against Domestic Violence (NCADV, 2017), most victims either fear leaving an abusive relationship or return to the relationship for financial reasons. As long as victims remain economically dependent upon their abusers, it is exceedingly difficult for them to put a stop to the abusers' control and successfully leave the relationship (Conner, 2014). Another common factor influencing a victim's decision to leave or stay is children. Often victims feel that if they choose to leave the relationship, their children will be worse off, as some feel that it is not good for children to be raised by a single parent. Others fear that they may lose their children completely in a custody battle. In other instances, the abuser may harm or threaten to harm the children should the victim leave (LaViolette & Barnett, 2014).

Beyond these factors, victims may choose to stay with their batterers for many other reasons. It is vitally important that victim assistance personnel are cognizant of these factors that influence a victim's decisions to leave or stay.

## SUMMARY

IPV is a complex issue with no simple solution. While we are consistently reminded of its occurrence in society, and the effects it has on victims and the community, we will never truly know the extent to which it pervades society. The devastating physical, psychological, financial, and social consequences it has on victims means that victim assistance organizations play a pivotal role in helping victims to leave abusive relationships and recover. Most of the programs developed to help victims of IPV include multiservice interventions such as safety planning programs, transitional housing programs, and legal advocacy programs.

Improving the knowledge of effects of IPV, along with acknowledging that leaving an abusive relationship is not that simple, will help in addressing the problem and reducing the stigma surrounding it. As stated in Chapter 9, abusive behavior comes in many forms; therefore, recognizing high-risk situations, along with the signs and symptoms of abuse will help to prevent serious injuries and relieve the victims of the responsibility to seek help for themselves.

Key legislation addressing IPV has been enacted, which has improved criminal codes and statutes that protect victims. However, while we have done much to help victims of IPV, millions of people are still affected each year and remain in vulnerable situations.

## KEY WORDS

Intimate partner violence   203
Multiservice intervention   200

Normalization of abuse   205
Safety planning   201

Transitional housing   202

## INTERNET RESOURCES

**The National Resource Center for Domestic Violence (www.nrcdv.org)**

For more than 20 years, the National Resource Center on Domestic Violence (NRCDV) has been a comprehensive source of information for those wanting to educate themselves and help others on the many issues related to domestic violence. Through its key initiatives and special projects, NRCDV works to improve community response to domestic violence and, ultimately, to prevent its occurrence. Its comprehensive technical assistance, training, and resource development are a few examples of the many ways in which NRCDV broadly serves those dedicated to ending domestic violence in relationships and communities.

**The Office on Women's Health (www.womens health.gov)**

The Office on Women's Health was established in 1991 within the U.S. Department of Health and Human Services (HHS). OWH coordinates women's health efforts across HHS and addresses critical women's health issues by informing and advancing policies, educating health care professionals and consumers, and supporting model programs.

**The Center: The Lesbian, Gay, Bisexual, & Transgender Community Center (www.gaycenter.org)**

The Center offers a wide spectrum of programs to ensure that all LGBT community members have the tools they need to lead happy, healthy lives, by offering health and wellness programs, arts, entertainment and cultural events, parenthood and family support services, and connections to the community and other needed resources.

## CRITICAL THINKING QUESTIONS

1. List and discuss some of the signs and symptoms of intimate partner violence.

2. Define intimate partner violence (IPV), and describe the factors that contribute to it.

3. How has the Violence Against Women Act helped to protect victims of IPV?

4. Discuss the importance of safety planning for victims of IPV.

5. List and discuss the factors that make it challenging for victims to leave an abusive relationship.

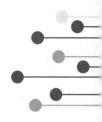

# CHAPTER 11

# Victim Assistance for Sexual Victimization

Sexual assault is a pervasive societal problem. It is dehumanizing and devastating, and it affects people from all walks of life. Many victims of sexual victimization suffer tremendous physical, psychological, financial, and social consequences that greatly impact their lives (Parkhill et al., 2016). Similar to other forms of victimization, the effects of sexual violence have been linked to personal health problems (e.g., headaches, poor sleeping patterns, sexually transmitted diseases, and unintended pregnancies) and psychological disorders, such as posttraumatic stress disorder (PTSD; Nickerson et al., 2013; Parkhill et al., 2016). According to the National Sexual Violence Resource Center (2015), it is estimated that nearly 1 in 5 women and 1 in 71 men will have experienced rape at some point in their lives, with 1 in 20 women estimated to experience some other form of sexual violence during their lives. Powerful social movements, along with the knowledge that many victims are reluctant to report and engage with the criminal justice system, have led authorities to enact laws that counter traditional barriers to victim cooperation and offer them much needed assistance. The Violence Against Women Act (VAWA) in 1994, which has been reauthorized several times (2000, 2005, 2013), is such a multifaceted effort by authorities to support actions that prevent sexual violence against women and men, increase awareness through research and outreach, and expand services for victims (Neill Christensen & Williams, 2017). Neil et al. (2017) argue there is a critical need to provide comprehensive and compassionate evidence-based interventions to victims of sexual violence that support recovery and foster public policy and advocacy. Thus, it is important for victim service providers to know what constitutes sexual violence and its facts. This will ultimately allow them to establish relationships that consist of support, acceptance, and empathy that help victim recovery.

## What Is Sexual Victimization?

Sexual violence can take many different forms, however, generally speaking, it covers a wide range of victimizations that include any sexual act, attempt to obtain a sexual act, unwanted sexual comments or advances, or acts to traffic, or any other acts directed against a person's sexuality using coercion, by any person regardless of their relationship to the victim, in any setting, including but not limited to home and work (Jewkes, Sen, & Garcia-Moreno, 2002). The specific laws for sexual crimes vary by state. All states prohibit sexual victimization, but the exact definitions of the crimes within the category of sexual victimization differ from state to state. Each specific law shares some basic elements, but the structures, wording, and scope of the offenses may vary considerably (Calhoun, McCauley, & Crawford, 2006). Stated above, sexual victimization can take an enormous toll on victims,

I was sexually assaulted in the workplace on a routine basis. I was 17 when I got my first job at a local coffee shop. An older male coworker, who I initially thought was a sweet older man, who treated me kindly and always offered to guide me while I was learning the job, one day began to make inappropriate comments to me about the things he wanted to do to my body. At first I could not believe what I was hearing—I knew it was wrong but thought it was a once off strange comment—but it was not—it happened all the time. This made me feel very uncomfortable, but I was still young and had no idea of who to speak to or what to do. I decided to speak to my manager—whose response was "Oh just ignore him! He's harmless." I decided to ask him myself to please stop making the comments, but he just ignored me and continued. One day, my harasser followed me home—this terrified me. I decided to speak to the owner of the store, who took direct actions and scolded my boss and fired the harasser. This made the workplace feel very awkward for a while, but things got better and I was able to continue to work there for another two years.

After completing my studies, I started my dream job as a marketing consultant. I was so happy to be working in the field I studied. However, almost immediately upon starting my job, my boss began touching me. He would constantly rub my shoulders or put his hands on me. I really did not like this and spoke to one of my colleagues. She did not seem to think this was a problem and replied, "it could be worse, he could be doing other stuff." The touching continued, which was followed with inappropriate jokes and constant staring at my chest. What I hate more than anything, he would not do this in front of anyone else—so I thought no one would believe me. I decided to speak to another manager at his level, who showed some understanding, and who also told me to document

everything. I appreciated his advice but still felt as if this would not stop my boss's behavior or make me feel more comfortable. I took my notes to human resources (HR), but this was a big mistake. The notes were good, but often HR's interest is to protect the company not always the staff. They did not investigate the matter properly and thought that I was more of the problem. As I was the only woman to complain, HR thought I was a liar. They decided to move me from his team and took away all my clients. I was left just answering phones and doing filing. I felt so isolated, as my colleagues deemed me to be a trouble maker. Every time I would see him in the office, he would just smile at me and look me up and down. I tried my best to ignore him and work my way back up to doing what I was doing. One day I was working late, and he came into my office—no one was around—he put his hands on my shoulders and said, "I am not angry with you or what you did, and if you come for a drink with me, I will put you back on my team— come on Sweetcheeks, let's go." I felt so anxious and panicked. I grabbed my things and said I had to go. That night I just felt that things would never improve, and I would always feel uncomfortable working at the company. A week later, I handed in my resignation. After the exit interview, the HR lady walked with me to the car and said you are not the first lady to leave because of this man, and she was so sorry she could not do more to help me. This made me feel so angry and helpless. I am back working at the coffee shop and have been unable to find a job in my field again. All the while, this man still works for the company, and I can only imagine how many women he has harassed.

## Questions:

1. Discuss the barriers victims experience when reporting sexual harassment.

2. How important was it for the victim to document her harassment, and do you think it would have helped her to receive outside assistance?

3. What impact do you think the harassment had on the victim, and do you think that it may affect her wanting to report this type or any victimization in the future?

and it is imperative for victim service providers to have a compressive understanding of sexual victimization and its different forms to be able to effectively assist victims.

## Rape

Throughout most of history, rape was not even viewed as a crime because women were considered to be the property of their fathers and husbands. When it initially became an offense, rape was only considered a crime in terms of a property violation of another man. The punishment that was delivered was to the man who damaged the husband's property. The woman, too, would often be punished, regardless of her lack of complicity in the assault. Over the years, powerful social movements have forced lawmakers to recognize the powerlessness of women in society in the face of male domination and the violence they are often exposed to. The original definition of rape was "the carnal knowledge (i.e., vaginal penetration) of a female, forcibly and against her will" (Calhoun et al., 2006, p. 98). This definition of rape was rather narrow, as it only included forcible male penetration of the female vagina. Moreover, it assumed that only females could be the victims of rape. Today, we know males are not only raped in prison but in the broader community, too (Scarce, 1997; Javid, 2014). The definition also placed an enormous emphasis on force, when in reality, most victims know their assailants, and often incidents of rape are the result of coercion or social pressure, not physical violence (Buchhandler-Raphael, 2011; Wilson & Miller, 2015). As a consequence, more contemporary definitions of rape have developed, and while they differ by state, most share some commonalities. For example, rape can now be perpetrated by and against both males and females. Most states also now include husbands from the definition of rape. Definitions also include contact between the mouth and penis, vulva, or anus, or penetration of another person's genitals or anal opening with a finger, hand, or object. Also, contact or penetration must occur without the consent of the victim or when the victim is unable to give consent because of temporary or permanent mental or physical incapacity. The ability of the victim to give consent must be determined in accordance with the individual state's statutes; however, physical resistance is not required on the part of the victim to demonstrate lack of consent (U.S. Department of Justice, 2017).

According to Daigle and Muftic (2016), there are four different forms of rape: forcible rape, drug and alcohol facilitated rape, incapacitated rape, and statutory rape.

- *Forcible rape*: Penetration achieved by violence or the threat of violence without the free consent of the victim (Daigle & Muftic, 2016).

- *Drug or Alcohol Facilitated Rape*: Victims are given, without their knowledge or consent, drugs or alcohol that may impair their ability to guard themselves from

**Forcible rape:** penetration achieved by violence or the threat of violence without the free consent of the victim (Daigle & Muftic, 2016)

**Drug or alcohol facilitated rape:** occurs when victims are given without their knowledge or consent drugs or alcohol that may impair their ability to guard themselves from being assaulted. Drugs commonly given to victims include Rohypnol ('roofies'), Gamma-Hydroxybutyric (GHB), and Ketamine, which impair the motors skills of the victim and possibly cause loss of memory (Lee & Jordan, 2014) being assaulted. Drugs commonly given to victims include rohypnol ("roofies"), gamma-hydroxybutyric (GHB), and ketamine, which impair the motor skills of the victim and possibly cause loss of memory (Lee & Jordan, 2014).

- **Incapacitated Rape**: The victim cannot consent because of self-induced consumption of drugs, alcohol, or any other intoxicant (Daigle & Muftic, 2016).

- **Statutory Rape**: A relationship between a juvenile and an adult that is illegal under the age of consent status but does not involve the degree of coercion or manipulation sufficient to qualify under criminal statutes as a forcible sex crime (Lee & Jordan, 2014). The minimum age of consent that most states set is between 14 and 18; however, the legal definitions and terminology for statutory rape vary between states.

## Other Forms of Sexual Victimization

While rape undoubtedly receives the most attention, there are other forms of sexual victimization, which occur in the workplace, in educational institutions, and in many other social environments. The different forms include sexual coercion, unwanted sexual contact, and noncontact sexual abuse (Daigle & Muftic, 2016). Like rape, these various forms of sexual victimization can have devastating effects on a victims' psychological health, physical well-being, and vocational development (Diehl, Glaser, & Bohner, 2014).

- **Sexual Coercion**: Unlike using physical violence or the threat of physical violence to have sexual intercourse, sexual coercion is instead the act of using psychological manipulation, threat of nonphysical punishment, or pressuring or pestering for sex (Daigle & Muftic, 2016). Sexual coercion generally exists in environments where there is an imbalance in power and control, where offenders exploit behaviors or status that make people vulnerable to victimization through fear, obligation, and guilt or the ability to recognize sexually aggressive behavior (Kalra & Bhugra, 2013).

- **Unwanted Sexual Contact**: It may involve the intentional touching, either directly or through the clothing, of any part of a person's body without his or her consent, or of a person who is unable to consent or refuse. Furthermore, unwanted sexual contact can include the perpetrator making a person touch them (Centers for Disease Control and Prevention, 2017).

- **Noncontact Sexual Abuse**: It does not involve any physical contact between the perpetrator and the victim. The noncontact occurs without the victims consent, or when they are unable to consent or refuse, and includes sending unwanted pornographic images or videos via text messaging or e-mail or verbal sexual harassment (e.g., making sexual comments) (Centers for Disease Control and Prevention, 2017). Some acts of noncontact sexual abuse can occur without the victim's knowledge, where comments or pictures are posted on social networking sites or the Internet (Daigle & Muftic, 2016).

Again, it is essential for victim service providers to be familiar with both state and national legislation, along with local law enforcement agency procedures regarding cases of sexual victimization. Being able to accurately explain policies and procedures to a person following a trauma is crucial to managing his or her emotions and reducing stress.

## Victim Assistance for Victims of Sexual Violence

· · · · · · · · · · · · · · · · · · · · · · · · · · · · · · · · · · · · · · · · · · · · · · · · · · · · · · · · · · · · · · · · ·

To reiterate the point, sexual victimization is an enormous problem. It is estimated that a sexual victimization occurs every 98 seconds in the United States (Rape, Abuse and Incest National Network [RAINN], 2016). Within one year, approximately 213,000 people are raped or victimized by some form of sexual violence (Neill et al., 2017). These estimates highlight the need for victim assistance that not only aids the victims with coping with the trauma of victimization, but also guides him or her through the complexities of the criminal justice system. Discussed in Chapter 1, assistance to victims of crime was not always readily available; this was even more so for victims of sexual violence. The first rape crisis centers were established in the 1970s and only available in a limited number of cities. Gradually, as the women's movement grew and sexual victimization became more of an issue on the national agenda, so did the responses to the problem increase and improve. These responses included support for victims during criminal investigations, prosecutions, sentencing, appeals, and other stages of the criminal justice process, but more important, more sophisticated crisis intervention programs were developed to assist victims (Young, 1989). Today, these responses are enshrined in numerous laws that help to ensure that victims are protected and have an opportunity to actively participate in the criminal justice system, along with insurances that those who are most at risk of sexual victimization have access to vital information on its occurrence and that efforts are being made to prevent it (Fisher, Daigle, & Cullen, 2008). For example, the enactment of Title IX in 1972 and the Jeanne Clery Act in 1990 (discussed more below) requires that colleges and universities report rape and other crimes in an annual report, as well as provide assistance and awareness training to students, staff, and faculty. Furthermore, the laws that have been enacted ensure that funding is made available for state compensation programs. Grant assistance programs also provide funding for the development of victim assistance organizations and for research to be conducted to evaluate programs to better help victims. In conjunction with these responses, many prevention programs have been established. For example, Take Back the Night and Denim Day USA are nonprofit organizations who host events across the country and use network activism through many of the social media platforms to raise awareness and show support and commitment to ending sexual violence.

However, despite the efforts that have been made to improve responses to and assistance for victims, sexual violence is still grossly underreported. Many researchers argue that one of the most prominent factors influencing victims reporting and ultimately accessing services are preconceived notions or myths of sexual victimization (Burt, 1980; Hayes, Lorenz, & Bell, 2013; Hill, 2014). "Myths" regarding sexual victimization are connected to a history of patriarchy and can be defined as false, prejudicial, or

*Unwanted sexual contact:* may involve the intentional touching, either directly or through the clothing of any part of a person's body without his or her consent, or of a person who is unable to consent or refuse. Furthermore, unwanted contact sexual can include the perpetrator making a person touch them (Center for Disease Control and Prevention, 2017)

*Noncontact sexual abuse:* does not involve any physical contact between the perpetrator and the victim. The noncontact occurs without the victims' consent or when they are unable to consent or refuse and includes sending unwanted pornographic images or videos via text messaging or e-mail or verbal sexual harassment (e.g., making sexual comments) (Center for Disease Control and Prevention, 2017). Some acts of noncontact sexual abuse can occur without the victim's knowledge, where comments or pictures are posted on social networking sites or the Internet (Daigle & Muftic, 2016)

stereotyped beliefs and misperceptions about rape and other forms of sexual violence. According to Lee and Jordan (2014), these myths fall into three categories: blaming the victim, excusing the perpetrator of responsibility for the crime, and justifying the assault. Such beliefs tend to be more prevalent among males in society and greatly affect how women and other vulnerable groups react to such victimization (Hayes et al., 2013). As a consequence, many women, and in fact many men and members of the LGBTQ community, too, do not report sexual victimization because of myths, stigma, and fear of the reaction from the criminal justice system and professionals (Kassing & Prieto, 2003; Nagoshi et al., 2008; Hill, 2014). The following is a list of the common myths that pervade our society and impact victims, as well as the behavior of friends, family, medical services, victim services, social services, and law enforcement personnel. Along with each of these myths are facts about sexual violence in society.

*Myth:*     Most rapes are committed by strangers.

*Fact:*     Approximately 7 out of 10 rapes are committed by someone known to the victim (RAINN, 2016).

*Myth:*     If victims of sexual assault do not fight back, they must have thought the assault was not that bad or they wanted it.

*Fact:*     Many survivors experience tonic immobility or a "freeze response" during an assault where they physically cannot move or speak (TeBockhorst, O'Halloran, & Nyline, 2014).

*Myth:*     If a woman drinks and goes home with a man, or wears skimpy clothing, it is her fault she got raped.

*Fact:*     It is never a victim's fault. No one asks or deserves to be raped. Rape is a violent attack and a crime in which the perpetrator controls the victim (RAINN, 2016).

*Myth:*     A lot of victims lie about being raped or give false reports.

*Fact:*     Only 2% to 8% of rapes are falsely reported, the same percentage as for other felonies (Lonsway, Archambault, & Lisak, 2009).

*Myth:*     People with disabilities are at low risk for sexual assault.

*Fact:*     People with disabilities are victims of sexual assault twice as frequently as people without disabilities (U.S. Department of Justice, 2014).

Therefore, in attempting to address sexual violence in society, it is crucially important to increase public knowledge about this crime, shifting societal awareness away from myth to fact and increasing the understanding of its impact on victims (Neill et al., 2017). For victim service providers who may have been subjected to these myths growing up, it may be difficult to recognize the extent to which these beliefs are not true. Thus, being cognizant of these myths and informed of the facts of sexual violence allows service providers to be more sensitive to the needs of victims (Lee & Jordan, 2014).

# Rape Trauma Syndrome

In 1974, Ann W. Burgess and Lynda L. Holmstrom conducted a study on 146 patients admitted to an emergency ward of a city hospital. Of the 142 patients, 92 had been victims of rape. From their analysis of the rape victims, they found that many shared a consistent series of reactions following the event. The phrase they used to describe these series of reactions was *rape trauma syndrome* (Burgess & Holmstrom, 1974). While reactions to victimization vary from individual to individual and may be influenced by a number of factors—for example, the interpretation and meaning attached to the incident by the victims, their age, life experience, and support systems (Janoff-Bulman, 1992; Kirchhoff, 2005)—there are common psychological, physical, and behavioral reactions experienced by victims. Importantly, there is no one way to respond to rape, but by understanding what reactions are common, Burgess and Holmstrom (1974) argued that specific therapeutic techniques in crisis intervention could be applied to better assist victims.

From their research, Burgess and Holmstrom (1974) described two distinct phases of victims response to sexual assault: (1) the acute phase and (2) a long-term reorganization phase. In the acute phase, victims may feel shock, fear, anger, and anxiety, which may be visually noticeable from the victim's reactions or masked by a composed or subdued behavior (Burgess & Holmstrom, 1974). The victim may also feel humiliation, embarrassment, and self-blame. Physical reactions to the victimization can include physical trauma, pain, general soreness and tension, gastrointestinal irritability, and genitalia disturbances (Burgess & Holmstrom, 1974; Fanflick, 2007; Tannura, 2014). The long-term reorganization phase typically begins two to six weeks after the attack and is a period in which victims attempt to regain a sense of control over their lives. This period is characterized by motor activity, such as changing residences, changing telephone numbers, or visiting family members. Burgess and Holmstrom (1974) found that rape trauma syndrome has commonalities consistent with PTSD, such as intrusive thoughts, decreased social engagement, impaired memory, sleep disturbances, and hypervigilance. Rape-related phobias, such as fear of being alone or fear of having people behind one, and difficulties in sexual relationships also are prominent (Giannelli, 1997; Tannura, 2014).

# Effective Responses to Victims of Sexual Victimization

Interventions to prevent and respond to sexual violence in society are crucial. Detailed earlier in the chapter is the extent to which sexual violence pervades our society. However, despite the number of victimizations that are recorded each year, it is important to remember that many incidents go unreported, meaning that many victims don't get access to needed services. In identifying the most effective way to respond to victims of sexual assault, two facilities play a key role in providing intervention and evaluation services for victims (Lee & Jordan, 2014). These are emergency rooms in hospitals and crisis centers.

Emergency rooms are typically the first place victims will present themselves after having been victimized. Here they can be treated for a variety of health concerns (e.g., sexually transmitted infections, HIV/AIDS, pregnancy), as well as be examined by a Sexual Assault Nurse Examiner (SANE Nurse). SANE nurses are specially trained forensic nurses who provide first-response medical care and crisis intervention to victims of sexual violence either in hospitals or clinic settings. Using a victim-centered approach, SANE practitioners help to preserve the victim's dignity, enhance medical evidence collection for better prosecution, and promote community involvement and concern with crime victims and their families (Ledray, 1999; Campbell, Patterson, & Lichty, 2005). SANE programs have been found to be extremely effective in responding to victims. They have been found to provide better healthcare provisions to victims than hospitals who did not have a SANE program (Campbell et al., 2006). The quality of the forensic evidence collected by SANEs has been found to contain less errors than those collected by doctors or non-SANEs (Sievers, Murphy, & Miller, 2003). Other research has shown statistically significant increases in case progression through the criminal justice system, along with successful prosecution with SANE cases (Crandall & Helitzer, 2003; Campbell et al., 2005). More importantly, victims have reported that they were kept informed of the procedures by nurses with expertise, treated with respect, and made to feel safe (Ericksen et al., 2002; Campbell, Greeson, & Fehler-Cabral, 2013).

The second type of treatment facility for victims of sexual violence is crisis centers. Typically located away from emergency rooms, crisis centers are self-contained units that provide a multitude of services to victims of sexual violence. Most crisis centers have 24-hour hotlines that allow for victims to make an initial contact for assistance. Crisis centers also make use of trained on-call volunteers or crisis counselors to assist victims who present themselves at the crisis center, police department, or emergency room. The function of crisis counselors is to support victims during the reporting process or any further dealings with the criminal justice system, as well as to support them through any medical examinations (Lee & Jordan, 2014). It is pivotal that volunteers and crisis counselors have a comprehensive understanding of the policies and procedures of medical examinations, so as best to guide and assist victims during this vulnerable time (Schopper, 2017). Crisis centers also provide short-term and long-term counseling, assist victims with legal advocacy, help victims develop safety plans, and offer education programs (Lee & Jordan, 2014; Schopper, 2014). Many crisis centers work closely with SANE programs, and while both seek to provide compassionate and empowering care, their roles are distinct (healthcare versus advocacy). It is important that both understand what it is they are trying to achieve and make sure that their roles are clearly defined to eliminate any potential conflict when assisting victims (Townsend & Campbell, 2018).

While emergency rooms and crisis centers are the most prevalent places victims take themselves, or are taken, police departments are another point of entry for victims of sexual violence (Lee & Jordan, 2014). Today, many police departments provide officers with specific training for working with these victims. Because of the role SANEs, crisis centers, and police departments play in effectively responding to victims of sexual violence, many communities have developed sexual assault response teams (SARTs). SARTs are multidisciplinary, collaborative teams made up of rape crisis center advocates, medical/forensic examiners, police, and prosecutors but may also include other groups that work with victims or are a part of the criminal justice system. SARTs seek to improve victims' help-seeking experiences and increase offender accountability (Greeson, 2014). According to Greeson (2014), the underlying concept of a SART is to bring practitioners from different disciplines together in a coordinated way to ensure that victims receive consistent information, support, and services. SARTs have been found to improve professional relationships among system personnel, as well as streamline team decision making about responses to sexual violence (Greeson & Campbell, 2013). Research has also found that SARTs have improved legal outcomes, shortening the time between victimization and a report being made by the victim and increasing the level of victim participation and satisfaction in the criminal justice system (Nugent-Borakove et al., 2006; Greeson, 2014 ). The following sections include examples of crisis centers and SANE and SART programs around the country.

## Education and Outreach

Because sexual violence is a societal problem stemming from systemic gender inequalities, oppression, and stereotypes; media representations of men and women; homophobia; and a lack of accountability for perpetrators (Katz, 2006), education and outreach programs are essential components of every assistance organization. By recognizing the behaviors that influence, perpetuate, and condone sexual violence, education and outreach programs can focus on questioning cultural norms, strengthening protective factors, challenging harmful attitudes, and exploring intervention strategies (Katz, 2006; Cissner, 2009). According to Olivet, Bassuk, Elstad, Kenney, and Jassill (2013, p. 53), there are three essential aspects of education and outreach programs. The first, education and outreach means going to where people are, rather than waiting for them to seek services at a specific place. Second, by educating and doing outreach, social services are able to assist and raise awareness of services to those most at risk and those who are marginalized or live in rural areas. Lastly, education and outreach is essential because it is probably the best tool we have in combating societal problems.

Typical education and outreach programs for sexual violence include workshops and trainings in educational institutions (elementary, middle, and high schools, colleges) as well as for medical professionals, law enforcement, businesses, civic groups, and faith-based organizations. However, research into one-session educational and awareness programs used by most assistance organizations has revealed that they have limited long-lasting effects on risk factors or behavior for sexual violence (DeGue, 2014). Although these one-session programs increase awareness of the issue, it is unlikely that such programs are sufficient to change behavioral patterns that are developed and continually influenced and reinforced across the lifespan (DeGue, 2014). While these types of programs are low cost and appealing in educational and other settings, they may actually detract from other programs that may be more effective. Comprehensive educational and community- or organization-level programs may have the greatest potential for population-level impact and reducing sexual violence (DeGue et al., 2012; Tharp et al., 2013).

Education and outreach programs focus on a wide audience: medical professionals, law enforcement, businesses, civic groups, and faith-based organizations.

## Sexual Assault

### Crisis Center

*Santa Barbara Rape Crisis Center*: The Santa Barbara Rape Crisis Center is a private, nonprofit agency that has provided counseling, crisis intervention, and support services to victims of sexual violence and their families. See http://www.sbrapecrisiscenter.org/index.html for more information.

### SANE Program

*The Michigan Department of Health & Human: Services Sexual Assault Nurse Examiner (SANE) Program*: The MDHHS SANE program operates out of many hospitals across the state. The purpose of the SANE program is to assist victims with medical concerns, administer a sexual assault evidence collection kit, and take care of overall physical health of a victim. The program requires examiners to provide medication to prevent STIs, medication to prevent pregnancy, a physical examination and wellness check to make sure victims are not hurt or injured, and/or a sexual assault evidence collection kit. They also help victims by assisting with the billing of hospital visits. See http://www.michigan.gov/mdhhs/0,5885,7-339-71548_7261_7272_7714_78103–,00.html for more information.

### Bystander Intervention

*The Red Flag Campaign*: The Red Flag Campaign uses a bystander intervention strategy to address and prevent sexual assault, dating violence, and stalking on college campuses. The campaign encourages friends and other campus community members to say something when they see warning signs ("red flags") for sexual assault, dating violence, or stalking in a friend's relationship. See http://www.theredflagcampaign.org.

*Green Dot Campaign*: The Green Dot Campaign's strategy is to capitalize on inherent human good. The campaign focuses on reducing power-based personal violence and addressing other social issues that impede

progress toward safe and equitable communities. We believe all individuals are capable of positive action, collectively mobilizing a force powerful enough to create lasting societal change. We accelerate individual impact by inspiring hope for change, providing realistic tools to act, and helping overcome personal, relational, and cultural barriers. See https://alteristic.org.

### SART Program

*Florida Council Against Sexual Violence: Sexual Assault Response Teams*: The FCASV SART believes that victims are entitled to be treated in a dignified, sensitive, and competent manner, which requires allied professionals to work together. The FCASV SART believe that by providing a coordinated, multidisciplinary, victim-centered approach to sexual assault investigations and service provision, responders can help minimize the trauma that victims experience and encourage others to come forward and seek help. SARTs benefit communities by:

- Ensuring victims have the best and most comprehensive services available

- Helping bring perpetrators to justice

- Providing a forum for discussion and problem solving for service providers, investigators, and prosecutors

- Assisting communities in creating coherent and effective protocols

- Informing professionals about emerging technologies in forensic science, including toxicology and biology (DNA) where there are continuing advances and improvements in the techniques and processes being employed

- Improving communication and fostering a good working relationship amongst agencies

See https://www.fcasv.org for more information.

Education and outreach on college and university campuses, however, is of particular importance given the problem of sexual violence at these institutions. According to DeGue (2014), educational institutions can best effect change and implement sexual violence prevention strategies using the best available research evidence on sexual violence prevention efforts. DeGue (2014) points out that providing awareness-raising educational sessions, presentations, or courses to specific student groups that may be at higher risk for sexual violence victimization and perpetration, such as incoming freshmen and athletes, is important. However, one-session education and awareness programs, often used by institutions because they are timely and cost effective, have been shown to be insufficient in affecting change in behavioral patterns that are developed and continually influenced and reinforced across the lifespan (DeGue, 2014). Therefore, the success of sexual violence education and outreach efforts on college campuses is dependent on identifying and implementing effective strategies.

Common prevention strategies and other program activities being implemented by colleges and universities include social media campaigns designed to raise awareness and change social norms related to sexual violence, such as the Red Flag Campaign, the White Ribbon Campaign, and Walk a Mile in Her Shoes campaign. Other common programs include bystander interventions, such as Green Dot and Bringing in the Bystander. The ultimate objective of education and outreach programs is to help create comprehensive and effective responses to sexual violence and to advocated that it is not to be tolerated.

## Human Trafficking

Discussed in Chapter 9, human trafficking is a factor in almost every country and affects every demographic. One common factor across all forms of trafficking is the victims' vulnerability to exploitation. Traffickers frequently prey on the most vulnerable people in some of the poorest nations, where they are forced to serve the interests of traffickers through the application of physical and psychological coercion (United Nations, 2000). To restate, *human trafficking* is "the recruitment, transportation, transfer, harboring or receipt of persons, by *means* of the threat or use of force or other forms of coercion, abduction, fraud, deception, abuse of power, or of a position of vulnerability, or of the giving or receiving of payments or benefits to achieve the consent of a person having control over another person, for the *purpose* of exploitation. Exploitation shall include, at a minimum, the exploitation of the prostitution of others or other forms of sexual exploitation, forced labor or services, slavery or practices similar to slavery, servitude or the removal of organs" (United Nations, 2000).

Research on human trafficking and program evaluations has enabled us to have a much better understanding of its occurrence and who it affects. However, given the very nature of its occurrence, we will never truly know the extent to which it pervades society and how many people are affected (United Nations, 2000). The International Labor Organization (ILO) estimates that 21 million people are trafficked globally. In the United States, reports on human trafficking seem to be increasing every year. According to the Polaris Project (2016), there were 8,042 cases of human trafficking identified, which is a 35% increase from 2015. The increase in the number of cases identified is attributed to the growing awareness of the problem, along with available resources in communities

(Polaris Project, 2016). Despite the sustained antitrafficking efforts, much work remains. Millions of individuals are affected by traffickers who exploit their vulnerabilities. The broader effects of human trafficking on society must still be addressed. Governments must work in partnership with NGOs, victims, community and religious leaders, and the private sector to develop targeted strategies to prevent and address the factors that drive trafficking in these communities (U.S. Department of State, 2016). Human trafficking can take on many different forms; however, the following section will only address the issues of sex trafficking.

## Sex Trafficking

**Sex trafficking** refers to when a person is coerced, forced, or deceived into prostitution—or maintained in prostitution through one of these means after initially consenting (U.S. Department of State, 2016). Sex trafficking may occur within debt bondage, as women and girls are forced to continue in prostitution through the use of unlawful "debt" purportedly incurred through their transportation, recruitment, or even their crude "sale"—which exploiters insist they must pay off before they can be free (U.S. Department of State, 2016). Despite the prevalence of sex trafficking in the United States being unknown, we do know that many women, children, and men are sold for sex against their will in cities and towns across the United States. In 2014, the illicit sex economy was estimated to generate around $290 million in revenue depending on the city (Dank et al., 2014).

Victims of sex trafficking are typically runaways and homeless youth or victims of domestic violence, sexual assault, war, or social discrimination (U.S. Department of State, 2016). Sex traffickers (also referred to as "pimps") prey on the vulnerability of persons and communities exploiting disadvantaged homes or exploiting victims through promises of love, food, money, or shelter (Epstein & Edelman 2013; Polaris Project, 2016). Approaches to trafficking persons include "gorilla pimping" and "Romeo pimping." Gorilla pimping, involves the trafficker kidnapping or using violence and intimidation to force the victims to comply (Kennedy, Klein, Bristowe, Cooper, & Yuille, 2007). The Romeo pimp, on the other hand, controls the victim primarily through psychological manipulation. This is done through courtship techniques to romance victims by showering them with gifts and a promise of a better life. Following this manipulation phase, the Romeo pimp will then introduce the idea of selling sex (Kara, 2009). Although Romeo pimps may shower their victims with affection and gifts (especially during the recruitment phase), the threat of violence is always said to be present (Kara, 2009). Others victims are lured in with false promises of a job, such as being beauticians, models, or dancers, while others are trafficked by their parents or families and forced to sell sex. Victims may find themselves in these situations for days, weeks, or even years. Leaving a trafficked situation is not easy, as many victims are psychologically abused, forced to developed drug addictions, feel guilt and shame, have established emotional attachments to the pimp, or have physical threats placed against them or their families (Kennedy et al., 2007; Kara, 2009; U.S. Department of State, 2016).

In 2000, the United States enacted the Trafficking Victims Protection Act (TVPA), which has been reauthorized several times, most recently in 2013. The act establishes human trafficking and related offenses as federal crimes and attaches severe penalties to those who violate them. It also mandates restitution to be paid to victims of human trafficking. The act additionally created the Office to Monitor and Combat Trafficking in Persons,

**Sex trafficking:** when a person is coerced, forced, or deceived into prostitution—or maintained in prostitution through one of these means after initially consenting (U.S. Department of State, 2016)

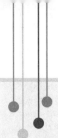

# Victim Assistance Programs

## Human Trafficking

### Run 2 Rescue

Run 2 Rescue in Riverside, California, is a Christian organization that aims to reach, rescue, and restore victims of human trafficking. The organization aims to identify victims, assist them out of bondage, and place them in a safe living environment. By working with local, state, and federal agencies, they actively work to change laws to make it harder for the pimp/trafficker to sell another human being in the commercial sex industry. See http://run2rescue.com/vision.php.

which oversees the implementation of the act, and monitors its progress, requiring the Trafficking in Persons (TIP) report to be published each year. The TVPA also established the T-visa and U-Visa for victims of human trafficking and crime who are willing to assist law enforcement and government in investigation and prosecuting criminal activity. The visas allow victims and their families to become temporary U.S. residents and to possibly apply to become permanent residents after three years (Kagan, 2015; Department of State, 2016).

While the government and communities have begun to build better responses to the needs of this vulnerable population, services are still desperately needed to help those who often lack access to services (Deshpande & Nour, 2013). Sex trafficking is a critical health issue with broader social implications that require both medical and legal attention. Challenges facing victim assistance organizations assisting sex trafficking victims are screening and identifying victims, training and technical assistance with multisector professionals, increasing outreach to those at risk for trafficking, and connecting them to service delivery systems (Alvarez & Alessi, 2012). As discussed in Chapter 9, because many assistance organizations attempt to address all forms of trafficking, it is difficult to provide comprehensive services to one particular form and assist victims in stabilizing their lives (U.S. Department of State, 2016). Many of the assistance organizations offer emergency shelters, transitional housing, case management, immigration services, transportation, and referrals to other agencies for victims.

## Victim Assistance for Sexual Violence Victims on College Campuses

Sexual violence on college campuses has been receiving more attention lately. Schools are not the safe havens they once appeared to be (Fisher, Daigle, & Cullen, 2010); college students are at higher risk for sexual violence than their noncollege-bound peers (Karjane, Fisher, & Cullen, 2005). Sexual violence on college campuses is certainly not a new phenomenon. Research on the problem has revealed that rates of sexual harassment, rape, and sexual assault in higher education have not changed over the past three decades (Sanday, 2007; Rosenthal, Smidt, & Freyd, 2016). The increase in attention to the problem of sexual violence on college campuses has Congress enacting several laws requiring institutions of higher learning to notify students about crime on campus, publicize their prevention and response policies, maintain open crime logs, and ensure that victims of sexual violence know their rights and that they are protected (Karjane et al., 2005). The following sections will review the nature and extent of sexual violence on college campuses, along with the responses to the problem.

## Extent of Campus Sexual Victimization

One subpopulation that has been found to be at an elevated risk for sexual violence is college students. Research has indicated that a sizable percentage of men and women are sexually assaulted during their college years (Fisher, Cullen, & Turner, 2000; Krebs, Lindquist, Warner, Fisher, & Martin,2007; Krebs, Lindquist, Warner, Fisher, & Martin, 2009; Fisher et al., 2010; Krebs et al., 2016). College women, as compared to their noncollege peers and the general population, are disproportionately sexually victimized more and by men (Krebs et al., 2007; Krebs et al., 2009). College men also experience sexual violence, however (Krebs et al., 2007; Krebs et al., 2016). In a study of nine U.S. colleges, it was found that the prevalence rate for completed sexual assault experienced by undergraduate women was 10.3%, and the prevalence rate for completed rape among undergraduate women was 4.1%. For men, the study showed 3.1% experienced completed sexual assault, and 0.8% experienced rape.

According to Fisher, Reyns, and Sloan (2016, p. 249), "in the language of lifestyle-routine activities theory, college campuses bring together potential offenders in proximity to a large pool of suitable targets, often with little or no guardianship." Research attempting to better understand sexual victimization on campuses has focused on whether colleges affect victimization risk or whether victimization risks are linked to other factors, such as students' lifestyles. Fisher et al. (2016) write that what emerged from these studies was that college students, especially college women, are more at risk for specific types of victimization on campuses than they are off campus, suggesting that the college campuses increase victimization for these types of offenses. Other factors that have been investigated to better understand the occurrence of sexual victimization are substance use and college lifestyles. It is important to note, however, that by investigating substance use, such efforts should not be construed as victim blaming or as attempts to attribute responsibility for the incident to the victim. Instead, such an investigation is done for the purposes of better developing prevention programs by knowing as much as possible about factors that place certain individuals at greater risk for victimization (Krebs et al., 2007). Mustaine & Tewksbury (2002) found that going to parties and consuming alcohol or engaging in buying and selling drugs are predictors of sexual victimization, along with belonging to clubs or organizations and being a member of an athletic team (Lackie & deMan, 1997; Tyler, Hoyt, & Whitbeck, 1998; Mustaine & Tewskbury, 2002; Forbes, Adams-Curtis, Pakalka, White, 2006). In a study by Forbes et al. (2006), it was found that college men who had participated in aggressive sports (including football, basketball, wrestling, and soccer) in high school used more sexual coercion (along with physical and psychological aggression) in their college dating relationships than men who had not. This group also scored higher on attitudinal measures thought to be associated with sexual coercion, such as sexism, acceptance of violence, hostility toward women, and rape myth acceptance (Forbes et al., 2006).

Collecting information that advances our understanding of sexual violence assists us in attempting to prevent this form of victimization and better meets the needs of victims. However, the rate of reporting on college campuses is low. Less than 5% of completed or attempted rapes are reported to law enforcement officials (Fisher, Daigle, Cullen, & Turner, 2003). Common barriers to reporting identified by victims include the following (Fisher et al., 2003):

- Not having proof that the incident occurred

- Fear of retaliation by the perpetrator

- Fear of hostile treatment by the authorities

- Uncertainty that the authorities would consider the incident serious enough

- Not knowing how to report the incident

- Desire to prevent family and others from learning about it

The reluctance to report sexual violence may also be related to the victim's perceptions of the event, along with campus policies on drug and alcohol use (Karjane et al., 2005), as victims fear violating these policies and facing possible adjudication. According to Karjane et al. (2005), a large percentage of institutions (84%) offer confidential reporting to students; however, less than half offer anonymous reporting. Preventing sexual violence of all types requires a shift in our understanding of the problem and the way we react to those who perpetrate sexual violence and those who suffer its consequences. Change doesn't happen overnight, but change does happen.

## Campus Responses to Sexual Violence

Sexual violence on college campuses is a significant problem. The consequences and reporting (or nonreporting) of victimization incidents, and strategies for preventing and reducing the risk of sexual violence and effectively responding to victims, is of paramount importance (Krebs et al., 2007). According to Eisenburg, Lust, Hannan, and Porta (2016), the consequences of sexual victimization for students can be severe and include physical injury, which may be extensive enough to require medical treatment or hospitalization; unwanted pregnancy and sexually transmitted diseases (STDs), including HIV; and psychological harm that may require treatment and affect students' academic achievement as well as their capacity to contribute to the campus community. The effects of sexual violence can go beyond those of the individual and have negative effects on colleges and universities. The American Association of University Professors (AAUP) (2012) argues that sexual violence on campuses harms and undermines the institutions' educational mission, which is to provide a safe and hospitable learning environment necessary for learning and teaching. It, too, casts doubt on campus authorities to end campus violence. Furthermore, institutions found to be in violation of basic preventive measures or acting in a responsible manner to reported cases of sexual violence may be fined and or lose funding.

Given the problem of sexual violence on college campuses, Congress has stepped in and enacted laws requiring institutions of higher learning to notify students about crime on campus, publicize their prevention and response policies, maintain open crime logs, and ensure that victims of sexual violence know their rights and that they are protected (Karjane et al., 2005). The two noticeable pieces of legislation enacted by Congress are Title IX in 1972 and the Clery Act in 1990. (Both these acts will be discussed in more detail in the sections below.) In order to meet the intent of the federal laws, many colleges and universities have established a sexual assault response policy. This is a formal statement by the institution to recognize and deal with the problem of sexual violence on campus. The policy is implemented to address issues of reporting; training and prevention programming; resources for victims; and investigation, adjudication, and campus sanctions (Karjane et al., 2005; Fisher et al., 2010; AAUP, 2012). Not all policies formulated by colleges and universities include the same language and procedures, however. Research has shown that while schools comply with the federal law, they do so unevenly (Karjane et al., 2005). For example, it was found that most schools comply with the requirement to report crime data, but only about a third do so in a way that is fully consistent with federal laws. This is because definitions and classifications for sexual victimization differ according to the state, jurisdiction, investigatory agency, and institution. The inconsistency in definitions confuses efforts to address campus sexual victimization and its recording. A way to encourage victim reporting—anonymous reporting—was only found to be an option for victims at just half of the nation's schools. Additionally, fewer than half the schools studied provided services to inform students how to file criminal charges (Karjane et al., 2005). This leads to the identification of another complex issue in the response to sexual violence at colleges and university campuses, bringing offenders to justice by a dual jurisdiction of campus administration and law enforcement (AAUP, 2012). Sexual violence at colleges and universities is potentially subject to two parallel but not fully commensurate systems of investigation and adjudication: the campus disciplinary process, which seeks to determine whether the institution's sexual misconduct policy was violated, and the criminal justice system, which seeks to determine whether the alleged attacker is guilty of a criminal act. Most reports of sexual violence are handled administratively. A perpetrator found in violation of campus policy may be disciplined in a variety of ways, including suspension or expulsion. However, if the campus does not consider the incident a crime, it will not be recorded in the college or university's crime report. Campus authorities are often reluctant to refer incidents to the criminal justice system and thereby yield control of the proceedings, opening them to public as well as media scrutiny (Karjane et al., 2005; AAUP, 2012).

To counter many of the issues that affect responses to sexual violence on campuses, the AAUP (2012) provides a set of recommendations for colleges and universities to include in their sexual assault response policies. Reporting remains a problem in general for sexual victimization; therefore, response policies should provide clear and explicit guidelines for reporting an incident by staff, faculty, and students, along with consistent definitions of the forms of sexual violence explaining why these actions violate codes of conduct and may be considered criminal offenses. This requires having clear procedural guidelines for the investigation of an incident, adjudication, and the sanctions to be imposed for violating the sexual misconduct policy. Then, procedures on reporting in the policy should not deter a victims' ability to make informed choices about how to proceed with an incident and should include statements on confidentiality and anonymous reporting (AAUP, 2012). All members of the campus community (staff, faculty, students) are argued to share in the responsibility for combating the problem of sexual violence on campus. Therefore, response policies should include provisions for training personnel and providing counseling services to victims in times of need. Moreover, response policies should include provisions to educate the campus community on prevention and security measures, healthy relationships, the meaning of consent, and strategies for bystander intervention (Karjane et al., 2005; Katz, 2006; AAUP, 2012). Finally, the sexual assault response policy should be made widely accessible to the campus community through all modes of communication available.

Ensuring that colleges and universities have robust policies and procedures to deal with sexual violence increases the effectiveness of the response to victims and the broader campus community. Moreover, it strengthens the mission to provide a safe and hospitable learning environment, along with creating a culture of respect.

## Title IX Sexual Violence Guidance

In 1972, Congress passed **Title IX**, which is a civil rights law that prohibits discrimination on the basis of sex in any educational program or activity that receives federal funding. This includes most schools, including private institutions and grades K-12 (Marcotte & Palmer, 2016). The law specifically aims to address sexual harassment, sexual violence, or any discrimination based on race, gender, religion, or national origin that may deny a person access to educational benefits or employment in educational institutions (AAUP, 2016; Marcotte & Palmer, 2016). The women's movement of the 1960s and 1970s was instrumental in the passing of this law. While drawing attention to many other issues in society, the women's movement called attention to gender discrimination in access to educational programs and employment. Prior to Title IX, many colleges and universities either set quotas for the admission of women or prohibited them from attending altogether. Additionally, women faculty were more frequently denied tenure than their male counterparts, and in some cases, were required to take pregnancy and maternity leave or prohibited from entering faculty clubs (United States Department of Justice, 2012; AAUP, 2016).

Since its enactment, Title IX has improved access to educational and employment opportunities, helping to ensure that no educational or employment opportunities are denied to persons based on their race, gender, religion, or national origin (United States Department of Justice, 2012). However, the success of Title IX in addressing sexual violence on college and university campuses has arguably been less successful. High-profile cases have brought into question how campus administrations have failed to punish gross and repeated acts of sexual violence (Fisher et al., 2010; AAUP, 2016). Under Title IX, schools are expected to proactively prevent and respond to claims of sexual harassment, sexual violence, and other forms of gender-based violence and retaliation. Once cases are reported, the school's Title IX coordinator should ensure that complaints are resolved promptly and appropriately. Coordinators are expected to initiate a prompt and impartial processes of investigating, monitoring outcomes, assisting in adjudicating cases, working closely with law enforcement, helping schools identify patterns, and assessing the effects of sexual violence on the campus community (U.S. Department of Education Office for Civil Rights, 2015). To further substantiate the requirements of Title IX, the U.S. Department of Education's Office of Civil Rights released a "Dear Colleague Letter" in 2011 (DCL) to remind schools of their responsibilities to take immediate and effective steps to respond to sexual violence. The DCL clarified the requirements that schools have to initiate a prompt and equitable investigation if the school is aware of an allegation of sexual violence. The standard of proof to be used in investigations must

**Title IX:** a civil rights law that prohibits discrimination on the basis of sex in any educational program or activity that receives federal funding. This includes most schools, including private institutions and grades K-12 (Marcotte & Palmer, 2016)

be a preponderance of evidence, which is a lower burden of proof than the beyond a reasonable doubt standard used for sexual assault cases in the criminal justice system (Marcotte & Palmer, 2016). If the investigation process results in a finding that sexual violence did occur, the institution must take immediate actions to address the issue and prevent its reoccurrence. The letter also clarifies the rights of the victim to file a complaint with the Office for Civil Rights (within 180 days) should he or she feel that any of the steps in the investigation were not done adequately (U.S. Department of Education, Office for Civil Rights, 2015; Marcotte & Palmer, 2016). However, on September 22, 2017, the U.S. Department of Education issued another "Dear Colleague Letter," withdrawing the statements of policy and guidance reflected in the 2011 letter. The 2011 letter is argued to be well intentioned but criticized for placing undue pressure upon colleges and universities to adopt procedures that deprive both the accused to a fair investigation process and victims to an adequate resolution of their complaints (U.S. Department of Education Office for Civil Rights, 2017). One of the major criticisms of the 2011 letter is that the preponderance of evidence is too low of a standard to determine guilt and has the potential to have persons being falsely accused of sexual violence.

The goal is to make our educational institutions safe places to learn, where students feel treated equally. It is still too early to evaluate the effects of rescinding the guidelines of the 2011 DCL letter; however, the move to do so seems to be a retreat in the steps taken by the Education Department to address the issue of sexual violence on campuses. The Education Department should instead take responsibility to counsel schools on achieving fair processes, not abandon processes that may not seem perfect or being perfectly enforced.

## Jeanne Clery Act

The Clery Act was named after Jeanne Clery, who was raped and murdered in her dorm room by a fellow student on April 5, 1986. During the investigation of her murder, it was established that the university had failed to report 38 violent crimes that had previously occurred on campus. As a result, Jeanne Clery's parents advocated for a law that would require colleges and universities to disclose campus crime information (Wood & Janosik, 2012). The Jeanne Clery Disclosure of Campus Security Policy and Campus Crime Statistics Act (Clery Act) was enacted in 1990. The act has been amended several times and most recently updated in 2013. The act requires colleges and universities (both public and private) who receive federal funds to report campus crime statistics to the Department of Education (DOE). Specifically, the act requires the campuses to report security policies and provide data on alcohol- or drug-related offenses, weapons violations, hate crimes on campuses and the surrounding areas, homicide, robbery, vehicle theft, arson, burglary, aggravated assault, and all sexual offenses. Campuses are additionally required to report the compiled crime data for the prior three years to the DOE (Gregory & Janosik, 2003; Wood & Janosik, 2012). According to Wood and Janosik (2012), the Clery Act is a consumer protection law, which provides data to current and prospective students and their families to heighten their awareness of the problems being encountered on campuses so that they can make informed decisions about enrollment. In response to the mass shooting at Virginia Tech in 2007, the Clery Act requires colleges and universities to disseminate timely warnings and emergency notifications to staff, faculty, and students about incidents on campus and the immediate areas (Fisher et al, 2016).

In coordination with Title IX, the Clery Act additionally requires campuses to provide counseling services and assistance to victims with changing academic courses, transportation, living or work situations, and notifying local law enforcement (Dunn, 2014; Janosik & Plummer, 2005). Campuses who fail to adhere to the requirements of the act may be subject to fines or lose federal funding.

The Clery Act has received both significant praise and significant criticism from the higher education community (Wood & Janosik, 2012). The act has greatly assisted in raising awareness of the problem and making institutions accountable to the communities they serve. At the same time, however, confusion about issues of reporting, classification, and location determination of crimes has plagued the process of addressing sexual violence on campuses (Wood & Janosik, 2012; Dunn, 2014). Colleges and universities aiming for comprehensive compliance with federal law need to go further and incorporate a better understanding of research on campus sexual violence, along with working toward consistent classifications and definitions, to ensure resulting policies and procedures adequately address and prevent instances of sexual violence (Dunn, 2014).

## SUMMARY

Sexual violence includes a wide range of victimizations, such as any sexual act, attempt to obtain a sexual act, unwanted sexual comments or advances, or acts to traffic, or any other acts directed, against a person's sexuality using coercion, by any person regardless of their relationship to the victim, in any setting, including but not limited to home and work (Jewkes et al., 2002). Sexual violence has tremendous physical, psychological, financial, and social consequences that greatly impact the lives of victims (Parkhill et al., 2016). Similar to other forms of victimization, the effects of sexual violence have been linked to personal health problems (e.g., headaches, poor sleeping patterns, sexually transmitted diseases, and unintended pregnancies) and psychological disorders such as PTSD and rape trauma syndrome (Nickerson et al., 2013; Parkhill et al., 2016). Numerous laws have been enacted to protect and help victims, along with affording them an opportunity to actively participate in the criminal justice system (Fisher et al., 2008). All states prohibit sexual victimization, but the exact definitions of the crimes within the category of sexual victimization differ from state to state. Each specific law shares some basic elements, but the structures, wording, and scope of the offenses may vary considerably (Calhoun et al., 2006). Therefore, in attempting to address sexual violence in society, it is crucially important to increase public knowledge about this crime, shifting societal awareness away from societal stereotypes and increasing the understanding of its impact on victims (Neill et al., 2017). For victim service providers, it is vitally important to be cognizant of what informs and affects people's access to services and the needs of victims (Lee & Jordan, 2014).

One subpopulation that has been found to be at an elevated risk for sexual violence is college students. Two noticeable pieces of legislation to address the issue of sexual violence on campuses are Title IX in 1972 and the Clery Act in 1990. They require that colleges and universities report all forms of sexual violence and other crimes in an annual report, as well as provide assistance and awareness training to students, staff, and faculty. Campuses who fail to adhere to the requirements of the act may be subject to fines or lose federal funding.

Education and outreach programs are essential components to addressing the issues of sexual violence in society. However, the most effective change is achieved when all resources are used, along with evidence-based research on prevention efforts.

# KEY WORDS

Drug or alcohol facilitated
   rape   209
Forcible rape   209
Incapacitated rape   210

Noncontact sexual abuse   210
Sex trafficking   218
Sexual coercion   210

Statutory rape   210
Title ix   223
Unwanted sexual contact   210

# INTERNET RESOURCES

**The Only with Consent (http://onlywithconsent.org)**
   Only with Consent is dedicated to stopping sexual violence through consent and health education. They exist to provide resources to young people so that they can make healthy choices. By upsetting rape culture and generating consent culture, they aim to help create a safe space for people across the world. Their goals are to educate people of all ages about consent and encourage all people to take action. They are creating age-appropriate educational curriculum that can be used in schools across the country. This will open up dialogue around consent, which is the first and most important step toward creating consent culture. All people, regardless of their age, gender, gender identity/expression, sexuality, religious beliefs, marital status, socioeconomic class, race, clothing choices (or lack thereof), mental state of mind, or developmental abilities, have the right to not have their personal space violated verbally or physically.

**End Rape on Campus (http://endrapeoncampus.org)**
   End Rape on Campus (EROC) works to end campus sexual violence through direct support for survivors and their communities; prevention through education; and policy reform at the campus, local, state, and federal levels. They envision a world in which each individual has an educational experience free from violence, and until then, that all survivors are believed, trusted, and supported. EROC directly assists student survivors and their communities. Their work includes, but is not limited to, establishing support networks, filing federal complaints, and mentoring student activists. They help students organize for change on campus as well as work with administrators to ensure best practices are in place and enforced. Though they are not mental health or legal professionals, they are able to connect survivors to their growing network of mental health professionals and lawyers as needed.

# CRITICAL THINKING QUESTIONS

1. Discuss the differences in the different forms of rape.

2. How would you go about educating the public on sexual violence and helping to dispel its myths?

3. Discuss the importance of SANEs and how they have contributed to the effective response to victims of sexual violence.

4. Less than 5% of completed or attempted rapes are reported to law enforcement officials. Discuss some of the common barriers to reporting, and identify ways these can be addressed.

5. How does the Clery Act work to provide better services and protection to victims of sexual violence on college campuses?

# CHAPTER 12

# Victim Assistance for Cyber-Crime

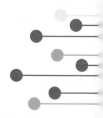

More and more, we hear about cyber-crime. In today's networked society, the demand for new technology and Internet connectivity not only on computers and phones, but also in virtually all modern services, while providing a range of benefits, has also provided new opportunities for criminal activities to emerge (Roberts, 2009; Ngo & Paternoster, 2011). In particular, the online domain has become an arena for seemingly countless forms of victimization, such as identity theft and cyber-harassment (Halder & Karuppannan, 2009; Roberts 2009; Fisher, Reyns, & Sloan, 2016). Cyber-crime and victimization can be either property based or person based depending on the target and involves the process of victimizing others through the use of information and communication technologies (Halder & Karuppannan, 2009; Roberts 2009; Fisher, et al., 2016). Research on victims of cyber-crime has found that the effects can be severe, resulting in psychological distress, anger and depression, lower job and academic performance, loss of employment, social relationship problems, and in some cases death (Beran & Li, 2005; Dehue, Bolman, & Vollink, 2008; McLoughlin, Meyricke, & Burgess, 2009; Sahin, Aydın & Sarı, 2011; DePaolis & Williford, 2015). It is difficult to provide a prevalence rate of cyber-crime given its varying forms; and like other forms of victimization, it is underreported. However, continued research into the prevalence, types, and impacts of cyber-crime is important in order to better inform victim service provision and to effectively address the needs of current and future cyber-crime victims (Roberts, 2009).

## What Is Cyber-Crime?

Cyber-crime has economic, public health, and national security implications. However, the term *cyber-crime* is complicated and not easy to define. In fact, there is no single definition of the term that covers all the acts mentioned in the different state, national, and international legal approaches that aim to address it (Gercke, 2012; Finklea & Theohary, 2015). Broadly defined, **cyber-crime** is a term used to denote the use of computer technology to engage in unlawful activity (Brenner, 2007). Cyber-crime does not require physical proximity between the victim and perpetrator for the consummation of an offense. Furthermore, cyber-crime is unbounded; in other words, it is not constricted to a geographical location. The victim and perpetrator can be in different cities, states, or countries. All a perpetrator needs is a device that provides him or her access to the Internet. A large portion of cyber-crime is automated, meaning that perpetrators can commit thousands of crimes quickly and with little effort. While one-to-one victimization does occur, it is not the typical form of cyber-crime (Brenner, 2007; Finklea & Theohary, 2015). Brenner (2007) points out that a large percentage of cyber-crime has been a migration of traditional crimes or "real world" crimes into cyber-space.

*Cyber-crime:* the use of computer technology to engage in unlawful activity (Brenner, 2007)

For example, fraud, theft, forgery, and extortion are crimes that can all be facilitated through cyber-space. While this greatly affects the individual, the individual is not the target but rather their property and personal information is the target.

While one-to-one victimization may not be the typical form of cyber-crime, the Internet provides ample opportunity for offenders to select and victimize individuals. Cyberbullying, cyber-stalking, and sexual exploitation are all forms of one-to-one victimization perpetrated online. The almost unlimited opportunities to remain connected through mobile devices, online forums, social networking sites, and video or photo sharing sites has made online harassment extremely common with devastating effects on those victimized. Moreover, with the option for such communication to be anonymous, and the ability of perpetrators to assume false identities or aliases, many barriers to offending have been removed, and it is difficult to address (Fisher et al., 2016). This, too, has made it difficult to develop and implement programs to assist victims of cyber-crime. The following sections will focus specifically on Internet fraud, cyberbullying, cyber-stalking, and child sexual exploitation and on what is being done to assist those who are affected by such crime. For those working in victim assistance, cyber-crime poses a particular challenge, as there are limited resources to assist those affected.

## Internet Fraud

Fraud is not a new phenomenon, and its definition and outcomes on victims have not changed; only the method of perpetration has evolved to include online capabilities, creating new opportunities for fraudsters to target people (Lee, 2003; Pratt, Holtfreter, & Reisig, 2010). This new platform for fraud allows for anonymity and operates in real time, which means prospective victims can be targeted more easily and quickly, and even affected more than once, as fraudulent electronic transactions can be repeatedly processed within a short period of time (Lee, 2003; Pratt et al., 2010). There are multiple forms of Internet fraud, ranging from viruses that attack computers with the goal of retrieving personal information, to e-mail schemes that lure victims into wiring money to fraudulent sources, to online dating romance scams where the end goal for the victim is typically that they will be in a committed relationship rather than simply in receipt of large sums of money (Singleton, 2013; Whitty, 2015a). The forms of Internet fraud are constantly evolving; therefore, it is important for victim assistance personnel to know that these forms of victimization exist and can be devastating to those affected by them.

**Internet fraud:**
any fraudulent scheme in which one or more components of the Internet, such as websites, chat rooms, or e-mail, are used to defraud victims or to otherwise take advantage of them (Rose, 2005)

According to Button and Cross (2017), the use of the Internet for criminal purposes is one of the most critical challenges facing law enforcement in general. Internet fraud does not have the traditional boundaries as seen in traditional crimes, and traditional methods of detecting and investigating fraud do not always work in this virtual environment (FBI, 2016; Button & Cross, 2017). The full extent of the fraud being committed on the Internet is unknown. This is because often victims of fraud are unsure of how or where to report what they see or what they have experienced; or when they do report, it is not reported to one central repository (FBI, 2016; Button & Cross, 2017). This is further complicated with fraud through the criminal use of the Internet taking many different forms. This has all made defining Internet fraud increasingly difficult. For the purposes of this chapter, we will only look at the forms of fraud that effect individuals and not businesses or organizations. **Internet fraud** is therefore defined as any

In February 2013, I came home after work on a Friday and received a phone call. I had gotten a call the day before as well from a major credit card company asking me to call them, and I initially thought that that was fraudulent. I thought, "Oh sure, I'm going to call this credit card company and talk to them about my account." [Sarcastically] I thought it didn't seem legit. I cross-checked the phone number, and sure enough, it was to a major credit card company's fraud department. They said someone had tried to obtain a credit card using my name, address, and Social Security number and asked if had I signed up for a card. I told them I had not. It was more serious than I thought. I just thought someone had stolen my credit card and had gone out to eat and purchased some items. There was no relaxing from that point on. It's been almost two years, and it's still like it just happened. I went to Equifax, Experian, and Transunion, and you're supposed to answer four security questions, which should be easy if it's you: Which of these four addresses have you lived at? Which of these employers have you worked for? I couldn't get to two of my reports because she had infiltrated my credit history to the point that her information overrode mine. I can't even tell you what that felt like—like someone had taken over my life. I finally got into the third credit report by guessing questions. As I scrolled down, there was account after account that wasn't mine, inquiry after inquiry after inquiry.

Overwhelming doesn't come close to how I felt. It wasn't like, "Oh well, I'll deal with this tomorrow." And that was only that one report. The reports don't contain the same activity, so I could only imagine what the other two reports showed. I had to call each credit bureau and company trying to ascertain when an account was opened or when an inquiry was made and tell them this was identity theft. Since it was Friday night and these Offices are typically open Monday to Friday from 9 to 5, when I'm at work, I resolved what I could at that moment. Because I wasn't able to get my other credit reports online, I had to order them by mail and include my birth certificate, Social Security card, and utility bills. I found out I was a victim pretty early on—after she'd been using my information for six months. But still, she attempted to open up in the neighborhood of 50+ accounts. So I can only imagine how many accounts would have been opened if I hadn't found out as early as I did.

I placed a fraud alert on my credit reports and eventually froze them. With an alert, you get calls, and the next day I got multiple calls. I would get a call from Discover: Someone just called, it sounds fraudulent, you have a flag, did you just call? No.

I don't know who she is. I had never heard of her in my life. She lives a town over from me. She was using my maiden name and a 10-year-old address—so perhaps at some place in my community I trusted, like a school or a doctor's office or employer, she came across that information. I can only make assumptions and jump to conclusions at this point. I tried as part of the police investigation to find out where she got the information. She never had to say where she got it as part of the plea, which is infuriating because I'm sure I'm not the only victim from the place where she accessed my info. But if this continues to pop up in the future, I can say, this person was convicted in this case against me. But the companies aren't interested in pursuing her. She has nothing. So the companies continue to come to me.

*(Continued)*

(Continued)

All companies have different ways in which they have you prove that you are who you say you are. When you are a victim of identity theft, you are put in the position of having to prove who you are to a greater extent than the criminal had to in order to get goods and services. You're treated like you're trying to get out of paying for something. I hold the companies just as responsible as the criminal. I think there's a lot more due diligence they can extend at the onset. A number of companies were able to flag and say this is identity theft, but a number of companies allowed it to happen.

The government isn't much help either. You're bounced around from agency to agency: If you're an identity theft victim, here are the 400 steps you have to do. I think people don't really understand what identity theft is. I could have put myself in that category before. People think it's credit card identity theft—someone went to Target and bought something, so why are you all upset about this? In that case, you call your credit card company and say this is a fraudulent charge, fill out some papers, and get on with your life. That wasn't the case for me. I had to prove who I am, I had to go through court, I had to go through grand jury, I had to give testimony. I am very fortunate in my case that I had someone to point to. Sometimes, people aren't as fortunate. It's the most time-consuming, upsetting, emotional event you have to go through. Somebody went in and so easily removed my information and had their information override mine on this all important, encompassing document—my credit report. You're told from a young age to establish credit responsibility so down the road, you can make a big purchase like a vehicle or home. Meanwhile, some lunatic has barely any information about me and gets access to all these goods and services—yet I have to go fill out all these affidavits and turn in my utility bills and all my personal data to remove this fraudulent charge. The companies didn't ask anywhere near that when they extended the credit. But now that it affects their bottom line, they turn around and make me do all this.

## Questions:

1. Discuss how the impact of being a victim of cyber-crime differs from being a victim of traditional crime.

2. In order to help a victim of identity theft, what should a victim advocate do to best assist the victim?

3. Given the extent to which we use the Internet, what more do you think needs to be done to make people aware of the risks of identity theft?

This story is shortened from the original published in Forbes in 2014: "Someone Had Taken Over My Life': An Identity Theft Victim's Story" by Laura Shin. (https://www.forbes.com/sites/laurashin/2014/11/18/someone-had-taken-over-my-life-an-identity-theft-victims-story/#1283461225be)

fraudulent scheme in which one or more components of the Internet, such as websites, chat rooms, or e-mail, are used to defraud victims or to otherwise take advantage of them (Rose, 2005). Understanding and using the Internet to combat Internet fraud is essential for law enforcement, but it is equally important to assisting victims effected by the criminal activity.

Although there are countless forms of Internet fraud, the four major categories of Internet fraud are described in the next sections of this chapter, followed by some of the most common schemes used to take advantage of victims.

# Identity Theft

**Identity theft** is a crime that involves the illegal access and use of an individual's personal or financial information without permission (Bailes et al., 2013; Finklea, 2014). Typical information stolen and used are name, date of birth, address, Social Security number, and credit card information. This form of Internet fraud can result in financial loss and seriously damage a victim's credit history, which may require substantial effort to rectify. Identity theft often sets in motion, or makes a victim more vulnerable to, other types of crime. Finklea (2014) argues that identity theft can both facilitate and be facilitated by other crimes. For example, identity theft may make possible crimes such as bank fraud, document fraud, or immigration fraud, and it may be aided by crimes such as theft in the form of robbery or burglary. Common ways in which victims' information is stolen are as follows (Bailes et al., 2013, p. 5):

- **Credit card skimming**: stealing a victim's credit card information during a legitimate transaction

- **Dumpster diving**: searching through trash to find personal information to steal

- **Hacking**: electronically breaking into personal computers, databases at financial institutions, and online retailers to steal personal information

- **Stealing a wallet or purse**: using someone's driver's license, personal checks, or credit or debit cards directly

- **Phishing**: using spam e-mail or the phone to pose as a legitimate organization to lure victims into revealing bank or brokerage account information, passwords or PINs, Social Security numbers, or other types of confidential information

**Identity theft:** a crime that involves the illegal access and use of an individual's personal or financial information without permission (Bailes et al., 2013; Finklea, 2014)

# Investment Fraud

Investment fraud generally refers to a wide range of deceptive practices that sell something, for example, a company, product, or security that either does not exist or will not live up to the financial return being promised (Blanton, 2012). According to Blanton (2012), fraudsters use fake or dubious investment companies to sell securities purportedly backed by a "hot" new consumer product, technology, or business opportunity. They will also capitalize on news events such as natural disasters or stock market declines, going to great lengths to create an appearance that the company or the product they are touting is real or is doing well to be a worthy investment. Investment fraud may involve stocks, bonds, commodities, foreign currency, or real estate (Blanton, 2012; Bailes et al., 2013). Types of investment fraud vary, but some of the common schemes are as follows (Bailes et al., 2013, p. 6):

- **Market manipulation or "pump and dump" scam**: A fraudster deliberately buys shares of a very low-priced stock of a small, infrequently traded company and then spreads positive, usually false, information to build (or "pump") interest in the stock. Believing they're getting in early on a promising investment, unknowing investors create buying demand, resulting in a rapidly increasing stock price. The fraudster then sells (or "dumps") his or her shares at the higher price and vanishes, leaving many people caught with worthless shares of stock when it becomes apparent there was no basis for the positive outlook for the promoted company.

- **Ponzi scheme**: A person known as a "hub" attracts money from new investors and uses it to pay so-called "returns" to earlier-stage investors, rather than investing or managing the money as promised. Like pyramid schemes, Ponzi schemes require a steady stream of incoming cash to stay afloat. But unlike pyramid schemes, investors in a Ponzi scheme typically do not have to recruit new investors to earn a share of the "profits." Ponzi schemes tend to collapse when the fraudster at the hub can no longer attract new investors or when too many investors attempt to get their money out—for example, during turbulent economic times.

## Mortgage and Lending Fraud

Being scammed out of your home can be financially and emotionally devastating and has been a significant contributor to the nation's financial woes, wreaking havoc from residential neighborhoods to global financial centers (Wagner, 2010). Mortgage fraud includes situations in which homebuyers or lenders falsify information to obtain a home loan. False information can include overvalued appraisals, guarantees of low interest rates, inflated income, and the fraudulent use of someone's name without the knowledge of that individual (Wagner, 2010; Bailes et al., 2013). This form of fraud destabilizes financial service sectors by reducing the value of mortgage-backed securities, potentially causing enormous investor losses (Wagner, 2010). Common mortgage schemes include the following (Bailes et al., 2013, p. 7):

- **Appraisal fraud**: a loan officer fraudulently overvalues an appraisal to make a sale.

- **Mortgage rescue and loan modification scam**: an advance-fee scam where homeowners are lured with promises to save them from foreclosure or lower their mortgage payments—in exchange for an advance or monthly fee. Sadly, many of these homeowners never get the relief they have been promised.

- **Reverse mortgage scam**: while they can be useful products, reverse mortgages have been associated with high fees and aggressive marketing as an easy way for retirees to finance lifestyles—or to pay for risky investments—that can jeopardize their financial futures. In some cases, a victim pays an advance fee to obtain a reverse mortgage that is never provided.

- **Loan origination scheme**: the perpetrator originates a loan using false information (e.g., misrepresenting the buyer's income or employment).

## Mass Marketing Fraud

Mass-marketing fraud refers to fraud schemes that use the Internet to contact, solicit, and obtain money, funds, or other items of value from multiple victims in one or more jurisdictions (Anderson, 2016). Mass-marketing fraud has a substantial impact on economies and markets, and for victims, the risks extend well beyond the loss of personal savings or funds to include physical threats or risks, loss of their homes, and psychological damage (Whitty, 2015**b**; Anderson, 2016). Common mass marketing schemes include the following (Bailes et al., 2013, p, 8-9):

- **Foreign lottery schemes**: promises of winnings from a fraudulent foreign lottery with the requirement that the "winner" pay an advance fee to cover taxes, before the winnings can be released.

- **E-mail schemes**: an offer received by mail, telephone, or e-mail for the "opportunity" to share a percentage of millions of dollars that the scammer purports to be transferring out of a country; the victim is scammed out of an advance payment that was required before receiving his or her "share."

It is impossible to list all the forms of Internet fraud, as those who perpetrate them are continually creating new, inventive scams as ways of defrauding and taking advantage of victims. For victim assistance personnel, knowing the exact scam is not as important as understanding the impact these crimes have on victims and the resources needed to assist in their recovery.

## Extent of Internet Fraud

In the United States, it is estimated that 75% of the population has access to the Internet at home (United States Census Bureau, 2016). People use the Internet for a variety of reasons, such as to send and receive e-mails, to obtain news, for entertainment, to manage their finances, and to buy and sell goods and services (Reisig, Pratt, & Holtfreter, 2009). In 2015, sales from e-commerce of U.S. retailers totaled $340.4 billion, up 14% from a revised $298.7 billion in 2014 (United States Census Bureau, 2017). Given the amount of revenue e-commerce generates, it is easy to see why the Internet is fertile territory for fraud. According to the FBI's *Internet Crime Report* (2016), approximately 280,000 complaints are made each year to the Internet Crime Complaint Center (IC3) (2016). In 2016, it was reported that victim losses totaled $1.3 billion, as a result of internet fraud (IC3, 2016).

According to the Identity Theft Resource Center (ITRC) (2017), the number of U.S. data breaches tracked in 2016 reached an all-time high of 1,093, which is an increase of 40% of the number reported in 2015. The ITRC defines a data breach as an incident in which an individual's name plus a Social Security number, driver's license number, medical record, or financial record (credit/debit cards included) is potentially put at risk because of exposure. Identity theft can go undetected for a significant period of time. Singleton (2013) writes that most identity theft goes undetected for at least one month, with a small amount remaining undetected for as long as two or more years. On average, victims spend 200 hours re-establishing their identity (Singleton, 2013).

The IC3 reported that in 2016, 16,878 people were victims of identity theft, 15,895 were victims of credit card fraud, and 19,465 were victims of phishing scams.

While fraud is common knowledge, many people cannot identify the red flags of fraud because they do not know what to look out for when engaging in financial activity (FINRA Investor Education Foundation, 2013). For example, it is thought that most investment fraud results from a lack of an understanding of reasonable returns on investments, which leaves people vulnerable to fraudulent pitches promising unrealistic or guaranteed returns. Playing on this vulnerability, fraudsters use deceptive practices and provide misleading information to coax investors into purchasing goods, stocks, bonds, real estate, and or to join Ponzi schemes (Bailes et al., 2013). The Internet has increased the ability of fraudsters to reach more people quickly and reduce the costs of entry for fraudulent investment, and by not being aware of the pitfalls in investment opportunities, victims stand to lose substantial amounts of money (Lee, 2003; Pratt et al., 2010; FINRA Investor Education Foundation, 2013). In 2016, 2,197 people reporting being victims of investment fraud, 12,574 were victims of real estate schemes, and 81,029 people reported being victims of nonpayment/nondelivery schemes (IC3, 2016).

Mass-marketing includes a number of different schemes, including lottery schemes, e-mail schemes, and telemarketing fraud. Mass-marketing fraud is a type of fraud that exploits multiple mass communication techniques (e.g., e-mail, Instant Messenger, bulk mailing, social networking sites, and telemarketing) to identify and contact victims (Button, Lewis, & Tapley, 2014). Researchers have found that many victims that fall for mass-marketing fraud are actually aware of some of the scams, but this awareness does not necessarily prevent them from becoming victims (Lea, Fischer, & Evans, 2009; Whitty & Buchanan, 2012). Lea et al. (2009) actually argue that detailed knowledge of a scam may increase a person's vulnerability to becoming a victim. People often develop an "illusion of invulnerability," which leads them to overlook certain factors or details of a scam. Mass-marketing schemes can be devastating to those who are affected. Often victims of mass-marketing fraud are blamed for their victimization and viewed as stupid or naïve. None of which is true. Being blamed by family and friends greatly affects victims' recovery, especially when the recovery of the lost funds is unlikely. Just under 26,000 people reported being victims of e-mail schemes, and 4,231 people reported being victims of lottery/sweepstakes in 2016 (ITC3, 2016).

Again, it is important to mention that we will never know the true extent of Internet fraud and its varying forms. This is because only a fraction of it is reported. There are many reasons why people do not report Internet fraud; these include feeling that little can be done to catch those responsible and recover lost funds and not knowing where to report or who to report to. However, the main reason why people don't report Internet fraud is because they feel embarrassed. How society reacts to victims and victimization greatly affects the victims' reaction to their victimization and can potentially limit their access to needed victim assistance.

# Effective Responses to Victims of Cyber-Crime

Given that so much of what we do relies on Internet access (e.g., e-mail, banking, entertainment, shopping), it is important to consider that virtually anyone can fall prey to

Internet fraud. Fraudsters do not discriminate on factors such as a person's age, finances, educational level, gender, race, culture, ability, or geographic location. In fact, they often rely on certain factors to target victims. Age is one such factor. The fastest growing age group online is the 50-and-older age group (Blanton, 2012; FINRA Investor Education Foundation, 2013). With older adults spending more time online, with more assets than younger adults available to them for discretionary uses such as investment opportunities, it makes them an attractive group for online fraudsters to seek-out (IC3, 2016). Research has also determined that older adults often lack the ability to make effective financial decisions, as they are more likely to suffer from dementia and other types of cognitive impairments, which increases their susceptibility to Internet fraud (Agarwal, Driscoll, Gabaix, & Laibson, 2010). Other factors that increase a person's risk of becoming a victim of Internet fraud include behavioral factors such as impulsivity, clicking on pop-ups, opening e-mails from unknown sources, selling products on online auction sites, and downloading applications (Shadal, Pak, & Sauer, 2014). Certain life experiences have also been found to increase a person's risk of becoming a victim, including being in debt or worrying about debt, having a weaker social network of friends and family and feeling isolated, and having experienced more negative life events (e.g., death of loved one or friend, serious injury) (Shadal et al., 2014). Another factor that has been linked to Internet fraud is lack of knowledge about Internet safety, for example, not knowing that banks do not send e-mails to customers asking them to click on a link to verify personal information, and that a privacy policy does not always mean the website will not share a person's information with other companies (Shadal et al., 2014).

Irrespective of the factors that place people at risk of Internet fraud, it is important to not blame them for falling prey to fraudsters who actively use deceptive tactics to victimize them. It is equally important to note that these victims suffer financial and psychological harm and may even experience health problems related to the victimization (Button et al., 2014). According to Whitty (2013), the psychological impact can sometimes outweigh the financial impact and include feelings of shame, guilt, embarrassment, depression, suicidal ideation, grief, anxiety, and loss of trust (Whitty & Buchanan, 2012; Whitty, 2013; Button et al., 2014).

Therefore, it is extremely important for victim assistance personnel to recognize the different types of Internet fraud and understand the impact it has on victims. Helping victims to identify the type and extent of the fraud is crucial to getting them the needed assistance. Bailes et al. (2013) write that victim assistance personnel need to first listen and let victims tell the whole story. Once through, then they can try to help victims piece together a chronological, fact-based account of the fraud. In assisting victims of Internet fraud, the victim assistance personnel must also help victims manage their expectations. Very rarely in cases of Internet fraud is financial recovery possible. Bailes et al. (2013) points out that victims may seek assurances that their assets are recoverable, and victim assistance personnel need to guard against providing false hope, which could lead to further trauma if the end result is loss. Providing victims with the following information is recommended (Bailes et al., 2013, p. 20-21):

- Recovery requires that victims work with regulatory, criminal justice, or social service agencies to address their problems.

- Encourage victims to report any financial fraud, no matter how small, as it helps law enforcement, regulators, and government agencies put a stop to the fraud and prevent the further victimization of more consumers. Reporting is also recommended if the victim is looking for financial recovery.

- Inform victims that some agencies do not communicate with victims beyond the initial reporting.

- Provide victims with a list of available resources that can assist in their financial recovery.

- Explain to victims that full financial recovery is difficult to achieve even when criminal prosecution results in a restitution order.

- Explain to victims that recovery is not only about finances, but it is also about the victim facing any psychological trauma caused by the crime and potentially seeking help to process feelings and restore mental health.

Given the extent to which the Internet has become a part of our lives and the increase in the use of the Internet as a tool to defraud people, many local, state, and national organizations have been formed to provide assistance to victims.

Recovery from Internet fraud often requires that victims take many steps to address the problem. Victim assistance personnel can greatly assist victims to assess what happened and identify the most appropriate resources for reporting and recovery (Bailes et al., 2013).

## Education and Outreach

The Internet has changed and continues to change society, presenting consumers with exciting new means for them to purchase goods, to communicate more effectively, and to access sources of information that were previously difficult to access in order to make better-informed purchasing and investment decisions. However, to avoid the pitfall of fraud on the Internet and to encourage trust in the consumer that the Internet is safe, businesses, government, and consumer groups must actively engage in education and outreach to raise awareness of Internet fraud. Similar to education and outreach programs for traditional crimes, successful Internet fraud awareness raising programs require knowing and understanding who is affected and how and strategizing how best to reach them. Beyond raising awareness about a specific topic, outreach and education programs should motivate individuals to take action or make changes to improve their safety (Jacobson, McDuff, & Monroe, 2015). Given that the Internet has the potential to connect and reach a large amount of people quickly and has the ability for information to be permanently accessible, education and outreach programs can actively reduce the number of fraud victims. Typical Internet fraud education and outreach programs provide information on the types of fraud being committed and the evolving ways in which people are being scammed (Button & Cross, 2017). Providing consumers with this form of information not only empowers them but also indicates to them that businesses are actively working to address the problem and its evolving nature. Moreover, awareness programs should guide consumers on how to access services and support should they suspect that they have been a victim and provide clear information of what processes will follow a report. Education and outreach are essential in locations were fraudsters actively solicit victims.

# Victim Assistance Programs

## Identity Theft

*Federal Bureau of Investigation Internet Crime Complaint Center (IC3)*: The IC3 provides the public with reliable and convenient reporting mechanisms to submit information to the FBI concerning suspected Internet facilitated criminal activity and to develop effective alliances with law enforcement and industry partners. The IC3 analyzes information and disseminates it for investigative and intelligence purposes to law enforcement and for public awareness. See www.ic3.gov.

*Scam Victims United*: Scam Victims United offers support and resources to victims through message groups and networking with other victims. This provides a safe environment in which they can share their stories with others who have been through the same experience without worry of blame or judgment. Scam Victims United also works with government officials to advocate for tougher laws for consumer protection from these types of scams and encourages legitimate businesses who are unknowingly being used by the people running these scams to assist in warning people and finding ways to protect their customers. See www.scamvictimsunited.com.

*Fraud.org*. Fraud.org is a project of the National Consumer League (NCL), a nonprofit advocacy organization based in Washington, DC. In response to the growth in telemarketing and Internet fraud, Fraud.org provides anti-fraud advocacy, consumer education, and direct consumer counseling support. Fraud.org has helped millions of consumers protect themselves and love ones against malicious scams. See http://www.fraud.org.

## What Is Cyber-Bullying and Stalking?

The increasing ability for people to share their lives with friends and family through digital platforms, such as chat rooms, blogging websites, video sites (e.g., YouTube), and social networking sites (e.g., Facebook, Instagram, Twitter), has transformed the ways of sharing personal information and who is able to access that information (Dooley, Pyzalski, & Cross, 2009; Luxton, June, & Fairall, 2012). Having an online presence creates a kind of permanent public record, which may be accessible to schools, employers, colleges, clubs, or anyone interested in researching an individual now or in the future. The ability to be connected 24/7, while convenient, has also exposed us to potentially dangerous interactions placing our safety and psychological well-being at risk. This has led to a growing problem of what is known as cyberbullying and cyber-stalking (Southworth, Finn, Dawson, Fraser, & Tucker, 2007; Dooley et al., 2009; Kraft & Wang, 2010; Luxton et al., 2012; von Marees & Petermann, 2012). Cyberbullying and cyber-stalking can be devastating not only for those directly affected but for the friends and family of the victims, too. Cyberbullying and cyber-stalking have distinctive characteristics, which highlights the concern for those affected: the immediate and continuous access to digital services can make it difficult for those experiencing either of these victimizations to find relief from the harassment. As most of the information communicated online is permanent and public, the harassment can affect other areas of the victims' lives (if not reported or removed). Then, because much of the harassment is not seen or overheard by others, it can be hard to recognize and get access to needed help (U.S. Department of Health and Human Services, 2017).

## Defining Cyber-Bullying and Cyber-Stalking

**Cyber-harassment:** encompasses all of the events of traditional harassment but extends the victimization to include electronic devices to communicate messages that annoy, torment, or terrorize a victim (Southworth et al., 2007; Hazelwood & Koon-Magnin, 2013; Fisher et al., 2016)

**Cyberbullying:** the willful and repeated harm inflicted through the medium of electronic text, in which hurtful content is disseminated to the victim (Hinduja & Patchin, 2008; Benzmiller, 2013)

**Cyber-stalking:** the repeated pursuit of an individual using electronic or Internet-capable devices (Reyns, Henson, & Fisher, 2012, p. 1)

**Cyber-harassment** encompasses all of the events of traditional harassment but just extends the victimization to include electronic devices to communicate messages that annoy, torment, or terrorize a victim (Southworth et al., 2007; Hazelwood & Koon-Magnin, 2013; Fisher et al., 2016). As cyber-harassment has become more of a significant problem in society, researchers have focused on two particular forms of cyber-harassment, cyberbullying and cyber-stalking.

Bullying is a complex relational behavior that takes many forms. The debate as to whether cyberbullying is a new phenomenon or simply an extension of traditional bullying continues, but what is irrefutable is that it has many of the same consequences as for those affected by traditional bullying. In fact, online bullying potentially magnifies the harm (Benzmiller, 2013). Benzmiller (2013, p. 933), argues that the "defining characteristics of cyberbullying overlap with the criteria of traditional bullying, in that the perpetrator intends to hurt the victim, the victim perceives the interaction as hurtful, the harmful interactions are repetitive, and there is a power imbalance. Both traditional bullying and cyberbullying are rooted in aggression, but in cyberbullying, the aggression may or may not be directed toward a target known to the perpetrator in the offline world." **Cyberbullying** has therefore been defined as the willful and repeated harm inflicted through the medium of electronic text, in which hurtful content is disseminated to the victim (Hinduja & Patchin, 2008; Benzmiller, 2013). While anybody can be a victim of cyberbullying, it is particularly prevalent among school children, members of the LGBTQ community, persons with disabilities, and socially isolated youth. As with traditional bullying, those affected by cyberbullying are likely to avoid places at school or school itself, experience psychological distress (e.g., depression, anxiety, reduced self-esteem), develop alcohol and drug problems, and contemplate or attempt actual self-harm (Randa & Reyns, 2014).

Due to the Internet's provision of anonymity, cyber-stalking is proliferating and becoming a social concern (Hazelwood & Koon-Magin, 2013). **Cyber-stalking** is "the repeated pursuit of an individual using electronic or internet-capable devices" (Reyns, Henson, & Fisher, 2012, p. 1). It includes a variety of behaviors that involve repeated threats or harassment (which may be perceived as unwelcome and intrusive) through the use of electronic mail or other computer-based communication that would make a reasonable person afraid or concerned for his or her safety (Southworth et al., 2007; Reyns et al., 2012). A variety of cyber-stalking behaviors have been identified and include monitoring e-mail communication either directly on the victims' computer or through software programs that monitor communication; sending e-mails that threaten, insult, or harass victims; disrupting e-mail communications by flooding victims' e-mail boxes with unwanted mail or by sending virus programs; using the victims' e-mail identity to send false messages to others or to purchase goods and services; and using the Internet to seek and compile personal information for use in harassment (Southworth et al., 2007, p. 843). Cyber-stalking can make victims feel intimidated, stressed, or anxious. Its repetitive nature means victims often feel that they have lost a sense of control over their lives, never knowing when the stalker may appear or contact them again. The fact that the stalker can access the victim at any time from any distance undermines the victim's sense of security and can lead to a constant feeling of fear for the victim (Hazelwood & Koon-Magin, 2013).

# Extent of Cyber-Bullying and Cyber-Stalking

Discussed above, while many of the defining characteristics of cyberbullying are similar to traditional bullying, there are several characteristics that distinguish this form of victimization from its traditional form. Specifically, cyberbullying allows perpetrators to maintain anonymity and the capacity to post messages to large audiences. These distinguishing characteristics also suggest that persons who may not be vulnerable to in-person bullying could, in fact, be targets of cyberbullying. (Hinduja & Patchin, 2008; Schneider, O'Donnell, Stueve, & Coulter, 2012; Benzmiller, 2013). High-profile cases of suicide among youth victims of cyberbullying have raised concerns about its prevalence and the impact it has on those affected.

Among youths, reports have indicated that 93% of teens are active users of the Internet, and 75% own a cell phone, which is up from 45% in 2004 (Lenhart, Purcell, Smith, & Zickuhr, 2010). The Cyber-Bullying Research Center, who has been collecting data from middle and high school students since 2002, surveying over 20,000 students across the United States, indicates that on average, about 28% of students have reported being a victim of cyberbullying at some point in their lifetime (Patchin & Hinduja, 2016). In an earlier study, Hinduja and Patchin (2007) found that one in five of students (20%) who had been victimized by cyberbullying had seriously thought about suicide, and almost all of those who thought of suicide (19%) also attempted it. There are many different ways in which victims are bullied online, such as being sent harassing e-mails or instant messages; having obscene, insulting, or slanderous messages posted to social networking sites; or having dedicated webpages developed to promote and disseminate defamatory content. However, the most common form of cyberbullying victimization reported was receiving hurtful e-mails. Of those surveyed, 18.3% complained about receiving such e-mails (Hinduja & Patchin, 2007). Cyberbullying tends to vary by gender as well. It was found in a study that the male to female ratio of victimization within a person's lifetime was different (16.6% for males vs. 25.1% for females); more females reported being victims of online harassment (Hinduja & Patchin, 2010). However, it is important to bear in mind that males may be less likely to admit that they have been bullied. The length of time that students are bullied varies considerably. In a study conducted by Limber, Olweus, and Luxenberg (2013), 23% of students who reported being bullied indicated that the bullying only lasted one to two weeks. However, alarmingly, 51% reported the bullying lasted for six months or more, with 39% reporting that the bullying lasted longer than one year. It is no wonder that bullied students are driven to despair given the 24/7 nature of cyberbullying (Limber et al., 2013).

Cyberbullying is not limited to schools; it is a problem in the work place, too. The danger of cyberbullying in the workplace is that it follows the victims home, with the harassment continuing after working hours. With an increase in the number of employees that take home laptops or work from mobile devices (e.g., tablets and smartphones), perpetrators can be constantly harassing victims. According to Namie (2014), 27% of Americans have suffered abusive conduct at work, with 72% of Americans aware that bullying takes place within the workplace. In a study conducted by Coyne et al. (2017), eight out of 10 people had experienced some form of cyberbullying behavior in the first six months after starting a job. The results also showed that between 14% to 20% experienced some form of cyberbullying behavior on a weekly basis.

Although there is no comprehensive, nationwide data on the extent of cyber-stalking in the United States, Baum, Catalano, and Rand (2009) found, in analyzing data from the Supplemental Victimization Survey, that approximately one in four stalking victims reported some form of cyber-stalking, such as e-mails (83%) or instant messages (35%). Besides these data on cyber-stalking, most of the research has relied on information collected from college students. According to Fisher et al. (2016), while estimates of the figures on cyber-stalking differ according to the respective definitions used by researchers of cyber-stalking, studies have indicated that as many as 40% of college students have been cyber-stalked at some point (Reyns et al., 2012). The most common forms of cyber-stalking are e-mail (82%), instant messaging (29%), blogs or bulletin boards (13%), Internet sites about the victim (9%), and chat rooms (4%) (Baum et al., 2009). Victims of cyber-stalking may experience anxiety, insomnia, social dysfunction, and severe depression at a higher prevalence than the general population (Baum et al., 2009).

Most states now have legislation in place that requires business, schools, and college campuses to establish antibullying and stalking policies that help to address this form of harassment and provide assistance to victims (Schneider et al., 2012).

## Effective Responses to Victims of Cyber-Bullying and Cyber-Stalking

Cyberbullying and cyber-stalking are two of the unwelcome by-products of the Internet and the advancement in communication technology. Despite the prevalence of which these victimizations affect society, lawmakers both at the state and federal level have struggled to effectively address these issues (Donegan, 2012). Donegan (2012, p. 37), writes that "unfortunately, it has taken a number of high profile cases to force lawmakers to come to terms with the harsh reality of the situation and attempt to mold laws to deal with such issues." One of the major factors affecting the enactment of legislation is the assumed infringement on a person's First Amendment rights and the concern of limiting what people could do or say on or off school or work premises. Because most of cyberbullying and cyber-stalking occurs off campus or work premises using home computers or other devices and a nonschool or work Internet connection, administrators are often reluctant to get involved (Donegan, 2012; Notar, Padgett, & Roden, 2013). To legally intervene in cases, specifically cases of school cyberbullying, administrators need to show that the misbehavior substantially or materially disrupted learning and interfered with the educational mission or school disciplinary code or threatened other students. Basically, educators must show that they had to stop day-to-day school activities to address the behavior that occurred off-site or to respond to school-based consequences of that behavior (Notar et al., 2013). This can be very challenging to do.

Attempting to take action, the federal government has defined the requirements for off-campus behavior, such as cyberbullying, to be regulated by schools or organizations. The laws that have been enacted by states have included specific language addressing cyberbullying and electronic harassment that may make schools and districts more vulnerable to lawsuits when they fail to initiate the policies and protections required to keep students and employees from being victimized. By including off-campus discipline in their statutes, states are attempting to mitigate the risks associated with the ubiquitous presence of social media in their lives and move toward greater accountability for bullying in general (Notar et al., 2013).

With specific regard to cyber-stalking, it was in 2006 when the federal government responded to the problem by amending the Violence Against Women Act (2000), to make cyber-stalking a part of the federal interstate stalking statute. In addition to the change in federal legislation, many states have begun to amend their laws to include prohibitions against harassing a person through electronic, computer, or e-mail communications (Goodno, 2007; Gray, Citron, & Rinehart, 2013). However, despite the changes made to federal and state legislation, critics argue that the changes made to state statutes do not address all aspects of cyber-stalking. For example, some states have attempted to amend existing stalking statutes to cover cyber-stalking by simply adding the wording "via electronic communications." While some states have simply inserted the general phrase "electronic communications" into existing statutes, others have identified specific types of communications, for example, e-mails, computer communications, or communications on the network. While amending current stalking statutes to include electronic communications is a step in the right direction, many argue that this is not enough and more needs to be done (Gray et al., 2013), because it has resulted in inconsistent definitions, requirements, protections, and penalties for those affected and in need of assistance.

Cyber-stalking and cyberbullying are crimes that can mentally and physically affect the victim, and there can be dangerous consequences to such harassment. These victimizations have resulted in tragic events including suicide and self-harm, and can totally disrupt a victim's life and peace of mind. Cyberbullying and cyber-stalking present a range of physical, psychological, and financial trauma for the victim, who may begin to develop or experience the following behaviors (Lenhart, Ybarra, Zickuhr & Price-Feeney, 2016):

- Low self-esteem

- Withdrawal from family and spending a lot of time alone

- Reluctance to let parents or other family members anywhere near their phones, laptops, or tablets

- Finding excuses to stay away from school or work

- Not engaging with friends or being excluded from social events

- Losing weight

- Fresh marks on the skin that could indicate self-harm and dressing differently to hide any marks

- A change in personality (anger, depression, crying, withdrawn)

Given the effects cyberbullying and cyber-stalking can have on victims, victim assistance personnel need to be aware of state and federal laws, along with being knowledgeable about what advice to give to victims of these crimes. For example, victim assistance personnel should advise victims that it is important to keep all evidence of the bullying

# Victim Assistance Programs

## Cyberbullying and Cyber-stalking

**STOMP Out Bullying**: STOMP Out Bullying is a national nonprofit dedicated to changing the culture for all students. It works to reduce and prevent bullying, cyberbullying, sexting, and other digital abuse; educates against homophobia, LGBTQ discrimination, racism, and hatred; and deters violence in schools, online, and in communities across the country. The organization promotes civility, inclusion, and equality. It teaches effective solutions for responding to all forms of bullying, as well as educating kids and teens in school and online. It provides help for those in need and at risk of suicide and raises awareness through peer mentoring programs in schools, public service announcements by noted celebrities, and social media campaigns. See http://www.stompoutbullying.org/ for more information.

**FightCyberstalking.org**: FightCyberstalking.org is an online resource site for cyber-stalking victims. The organization provides information on reporting a cyber-stalker, online privacy tips, and tips for safer socializing on social media. See https://www.fightcyberstalking.org for more information.

and harassment (e-mail, text messages, posts, comments). If there are ways for the victim to determine who exactly is making the comments, they should try to document it. Then, assistance personnel should advise victims to contact the service or content provider through which the bullying is occurring (e.g., mobile phone company, Facebook) to obtain assistance (Cyberbullying Research Center, 2017). Moreover, assistance personnel need to be aware of what resources are available in the community to refer victims to.

## Education and Outreach

Young or old, the Internet has been fully embraced as a tool for work and for socializing. The extent to which our lives are influenced by the Internet, and the potential for it to be used as a tool to harass others, has meant that education and outreach has never been more important.

Willard (2007) writes that schools, businesses, and community members can all help to inform people of the dangers of the Internet. Education and outreach is not the only way to curb cyberbullying and cyber-stalking, but it is certainly one of the best ways people can be informed about how to prevent it, the legal consequences, ways to empower and activate bystanders, and most importantly, how to detect and assist those who are being effected (Willard, 2007; Chisolm, 2014). Given that cyberbullying and cyber-stalking are old forms of victimization perpetrated through new forms of technology, education and outreach programs should target law enforcement, mental health professionals, and faith-based organizations that may otherwise not be aware of the extent to which people are affected by these forms of victimization. Public libraries and community technology centers are also key locations for programs to target.

Education and outreach at schools and colleges is arguably the most important. Research has indicated that cyberbullying and cyber-stalking are particularly prevalent on school and college campuses (Baum et al., 2009; Hinduja & Patchin, 2010; Reyns et al., 2012; Limber et al., 2013). Therefore, educating and empowering children and young adults to independently prevent and address these concerns is a means to reducing this growing problem. Education and outreach programs can include developing and making classes that address online safety and digital citizenship part of the curriculum and peer education and leadership programs. Awareness and prevention messages can be incredibly powerful when they come from peers. Holding on-campus contests to increase awareness and education about online safety can also be incredibly powerful. Moreover, information can be provided to students and parents through newsletters and workshops. Actively engaging students and parents in a meaningful way through education and outreach programs is key to helping address the problem and ensuring that those who are affected know where to get help.

## What Is Cyber Child Sexual Exploitation?

Fast-paced technological innovation and widespread and increasing accessibility to the Internet are facilitating child sexual exploitation nationally and transnationally (Hughes, 2002). According to a UNODC report in 2015, children are gaining increased access to information and communication technologies (Internet, mobile phones, tablets, etc.) earlier and earlier, which exposes them to opportunities for abuse and exploitation (Malby, Jesrani, Banuelos, Holterhof, & Hahn, 2015). The advancement and accessibility of the Internet through communication devices enables sexual predators to stalk children, where they can easily buy, sell, and exchange millions of images and videos of sexual exploitation. It also allows predators to do so anonymously and in the privacy of their own homes. Children are at a particular risk for sexual exploitation, as they often do not fully understand the threats associated with using the Internet or are not sufficiently aware that, once shared, control over such material is effectively waived (Hughes, 2002; Malby et al., 2015). Coupled with the accessibility of the Internet is the growing market and demand for pornographic material. Hughes (2002) writes that as a result of the huge market on the Internet for pornography and the competition among pornographic sites, the material offered has become rougher, more violent, and degrading, which in turn has increased the demand to exploit and abuse children (Hughes, 2002). Differences in the definition of the child have led to varying responses to child sexual exploitation by the legal systems and law enforcement agencies who frequently lack the human and financial resources and technical capacity to investigate this form of digital victimization.

### Defining Cyber Child Sexual Exploitation

The benefits of the Internet and globalization have brought with them an unanticipated set of social problems. Among these problems is cyber child sexual exploitation (Estes & Weiner, 2001). According to the National Coalition to Prevent Child Sexual Exploitation (NCPCSE) (2012), the production and distribution of abusive images of children on the Internet is a multibillion-dollar industry. Since 2002, more than 51 million images and videos of pornography depicting children have been discovered and reviewed by the National Center for Missing and Exploited Children to identify individuals who have been victimized (NCPCSE, 2012). Ospina, Harstall, and Dennett (2010, p. 5) write that *child sexual abuse* is an umbrella term that encompasses all forms of sexual abuse, violence, and exploitation directed toward children and youth through which an individual (usually an adult) can achieve sexual gratification or financial gain. Specifically, **cyber child sexual exploitation** is defined as:

> Situations in which these abusive practices occur or are facilitated through the use of the internet or other file-sharing and mobile communication technologies. Where a person, usually an adult, achieves sexual gratification, financial gain or advancement through the abuse or exploitation of a child's sexuality by abrogating that child's human right to dignity, equality, autonomy, and physical and mental wellbeing, i.e. trafficking, prostitution, prostitution tourism, mail-order bride trade, pornography, stripping, battering, incest, rape and sexual harassment. (Estes & Weiner, 2001; Ospina et al., 2010; Malby et al., 2015; Acar, 2016)

Both child sexual abuse and exploitation involve an offender taking advantage of a child's lack of power and status (Malby et al., 2015).

Misuse of the Internet to exploit children generally constitutes a violation of criminal laws; however, age specifications vary among state laws and impact who is defined as a victim (Ospina et al., 2010). As discussed in Chapter 9, the federal government provides minimum standards for a definition of a child and the varying forms of abuse; however, each state writes its own laws using these minimum standards. Therefore, a challenge to addressing the problem of child abuse and exploitation in society is finding a consistent definition.

Children can be abused and exploited on the Internet in a variety of different ways. According to Ospina et al. (2010), each type of exploitation that takes place online involves directly or indirectly, sexual contact between the abuser and the child. Using a typology of Internet-based child sexual exploitation developed by Gallagher, Fraser, Christmann, and Hodgson (2006) in the United Kingdom, Ospina et al. (2010, p. 7-8) detail the different ways in which children are sexually exploited online.

## Internet-Initiated Grooming

Some types of sexual offending require an offender to use charm and manipulation to coerce a victim into a sexual relationship (Winters & Jeglic, 2017). In these cases, an offender will initiate contact with a child online and begin a nonsexual relationship at first to gain the child's affection or interest and trust, which is referred to as "grooming." **Grooming** is often characterized as seduction, a slow and gradual process of active engagement and a desensitization of the child's inhibitions, where the offender gradually gains power and control over the child (Ospina et al., 2010; Winters & Jeglic, 2017). Offenders pretend to care, listen, and show genuine understanding of what the child is experiencing, with the aim of ultimately using the trust gained and information given to exploit the child. After a close bond is established, the offender lures the child into sexual

---

**Cyber child sexual exploitation:** situations in which these abusive practices occur or are facilitated through the use of the Internet or other file-sharing and mobile communication technologies. Where a person, usually an adult, achieves sexual gratification, financial gain, or advancement through the abuse or exploitation of a child's sexuality by abrogating that child's human right to dignity, equality, autonomy, and physical and mental well-being

**Grooming:** often characterized as seduction, a slow and gradual process of active engagement and a desensitization of the child's inhibitions, where the offender gradually gains power and control over the child (Ospina et al., 2010; Winters & Jeglic, 2017)

interactions, which may include anything from exposure to pornographic material and requests of visual material of the child or youth in sexually seductive poses, to phone conversations, or face-to-face meetings, with the subsequent risk of direct physical sexual abuse (Ospina et al., 2010; Winters & Jeglic, 2017).

## Internet-Based Child Pornography

Internet-based child pornography is where an individual has either taken, made, distributed, showed, or possessed inappropriate images on the Internet, or alternatively, has exposed a child to pornographic or sexually abusive images via the Internet (Ospina et al., 2010). "Pictures of children can also be digitally transformed (or 'morphed') into pornographic material and distributed across the Internet without the children's knowledge until they begin to surface online" (Ospina et al., 2010, p. 8). According to Cooper, Delmonico, and Burg (2000), three attributes of the Internet contribute to and facilitate the consumption of child pornography: (1) accessibility: there are an enormous number of websites dedicated to child pornography that are accessible 24/7; (2) affordability: gaining access to the material online does not demand substantial financial resources; and (3) anonymity: the Internet enables there to be no personal contact with others to consume pornographic material. Of great concern to the victim is the permanency of the online abuse. Digital material is very difficult to erase, which means images of the victims can be distributed indefinitely leading to repeated, long-term victimization of the child (Martin, 2015).

## Internet-Initiated Incitement or Conspiracy to Commit Child Sexual Abuse

Exploitation of children can also take place through illicit activities that are initiated through the Internet. The most common forms of child commercial sexual exploitation online are sex trafficking, child pornography, and child sex tourism (Women's Support Project 2014). Websites will advertise products and illicit services such as sex-for-hire services with minors and even arrange child sex tour packages, where information is provided about countries that have less stringent laws on child sexual abuse (Ospina et al., 2010).

The ways in which the Internet can be used to commit crime against children continue to change, which means that there is still much to be learned about child sexual exploitation, its impacts on children, and what can and must be done to combat this form of victimization. The importance of gaining a better understanding of this form of victimization has become especially evident in the responses to the many children and families who need assistance to safely navigate the Internet.

## Extent of Cyber Child Sexual Exploitation

While cyber child sexual exploitation is defined as a national and global health problem, the total number of victims is unknown, as there is no common database tracking such information (Estes & Weiner, 2001; Greenbaum, 2014). Moreover, children and young people rarely report their experiences of this abuse, and professional identification levels vary considerably across the country. Research also often trails the development of new technology and the methods in which children are being exploited, which often reflects conservative estimates of the extent of online victimization.

The U.S. Department of Justice, Bureau of Justice Statistics (BJS) reported on the federal prosecution of child sex exploitation offenders from 2004 to 2013. In the period 2004 to 2013, a total of 37,105 suspects were investigated and referred to the U.S. attorneys for commercial sexual exploitation of children (Adams & Flynn, 2017). According to Adams and Flynn (2017), the number of suspects referred for child sex trafficking and the production and possession of child pornography grew exponentially in the period 2004 to 2013. For the production of child pornography, the number of suspects referred increased 195% from 2004 to 2013 (from 218 to 643 suspects). For child sex trafficking, the number of suspects referred grew 111% (from 488 to 1,031). The number of suspects referred for the possession of child pornography increased by 28% from 2004 to 2013.

In a study conducted by Wolak, Finkelhor, Mitchell, and Ybarra (2008), they found that 9% of all 10- to 17-year-olds receive unwanted sexual requests while on the Internet. Over a period of a year, one in 25 children received an online sexual solicitation where the solicitor tried to make offline contact. Jones, Mitchell, and Finkelhor (2012) found in another study that 23% of all 10- to 17-year-olds experience unwanted exposure to pornography. In a report published by the National Institute of Justice (NIJ) in 2007, it was found that more than 90% of children who are commercially sexually exploited had been previously sexually abused. Most alarmingly, the report also found that 75% of child pornography victims are living at home when they are photographed. Meaning that parents are often the ones responsible for the abuse and exploitation (NIJ, 2007).

Given that an enormous number of children are at risk of becoming victims of online child sexual exploitation each year (Estes & Weiner, 2002, 2003, 2005), very little research exists on the impact such victimization has on the individual and its long-term consequences. Malby et al. (2015) argues that the use of the Internet and the advancement in communication devices may increase the harm suffered by children who are abused and exploited. With a large portion of victims being sexually exploited also experiencing sexual abuse (NIJ, 2007), research suggests that a "layering of harm" can occur when images or videos of abuse are distributed online.

> Sexual abuse constitutes the first layer of harm, and the production of an image or video, which exacerbates the negative effects of the abuse represents a separate, second layer of harm. Each subsequent viewing or distribution of that material serves to re-victimize and exacerbate the psychological damage to the abused. (Malby et al., 2015)

Gallagher (2007) also notes that in cases of contact sexual abuse, most children also suffer physical abuse, psychological abuse, and/or neglect. Research on the effects of abuse on children found that they are more likely to have low self-esteem and to develop and have to deal with excessive fear, anxiety, and aggressive behavior that adversely affects their lives at home, in school, and in other social environments. Some of the psychological disorders associated with child abuse and neglect are eating disorders, depression, anxiety disorders, posttraumatic stress disorder (PTSD), attention deficit/hyperactivity disorder (ADHD), and conduct disorder (Briere & Elliott, 1994; Coates & Gaensbauer, 2009; Cecil, Viding, Fearon, Glaser, & McCrory, 2017). Psychological disorders may cause a person to develop unhealthy coping strategies such as smoking, abusing alcohol or drugs, or overeating. Such behaviors can lead to long-term physical health problems, such as sexually transmitted diseases, cancer, and obesity (Herrenkohl, Hong, Bart Klika, Herrenkohl, & Jean Russo, 2013; Yang et al., 2013; Messman-Moore & Bhuptani, 2017).

As stated previously, little is known about the effects of cyber child sexual exploitations, and although it is likely that many of the psychological and social impacts are similar to those of victims of contact sexual abuse, the extent to which the Internet intensifies victimization is yet to be fully researched (Bryce, 2011).

# Effective Responses to Child Sexual Exploitation

While any child can be a victim of sexual exploitation, we know that perpetrators look to exploit particular vulnerabilities of children, as well as the communities they live in. For example, we know that those in our society who have less power and access to resources are often victimized and exploited at higher rates (Gallagher, 2007; Hodge, 2014; Malby et al., 2015). Perpetrators take advantage of this imbalance of power and often try to identify victims with social, emotional, and basic needs that they can use in the grooming process. Perpetrators, too, often rely on the fact that those around them often ignore their actions, allowing them to continue (Gallagher, 2007; Malby et al., 2015). For victims, the relationship with the perpetrator can be complex. Often the perpetrator is a parent or guardian (NIJ, 2007). Children abused by parents or guardians may not identifying themselves as victims, and in some cases, blame themselves for their victimization, which limits their access to needed resources.

To address the increase in sexual exploitation over the Internet, the U.S. federal government, along with the majority of states, have included within their criminal codes guidelines for offenses related to the sexual exploitation of children. However, as stated earlier, due to the lack of consistent definitions, requirements, protections, and penalties, many discrepancies exist in the criminal codes that cover all the substantive offenses (United States Congress, House Committee on Energy and Commerce, 2007). At the federal level, the United States has four primary law enforcement agencies that investigate the sexual exploitation of children over the Internet. These agencies are (1) the Federal Bureau of Investigation (FBI); (2) Immigrations and Customs Enforcement (ICE); (3) the U.S. Postal Inspection Service (USPIS); and (4) the Internet Crimes Against Children (ICAC) Task Forces (Wolak, Finkelhor, & Mitchell, 2012). Currently, agents from each of these law enforcement agencies are assigned to the National Center for Missing and Exploited Children (NCMEC) and assist in investigating cases. Additionally, the Department of Justice (DOJ) initiated Project Safe Childhood, which is an initiative to help coordinate efforts between state, local, and federal law enforcement authorities when investigating online crimes against children. The initiative requires each U.S. Attorney to designate a Project Safe Childhood coordinator to partner with local federal

# Victim Assistance Programs

## Child Sexual Exploitation

*The Mayo Clinic Child and Family Advocacy Center*: The Mayo Clinic Child and Family Advocacy Center is a partner in the National Plan to Prevent the Sexual Abuse and Exploitation of Children developed by the National Coalition to Prevent Child Sexual Abuse and Exploitation. The Center offers an efficient, child-centered response to child abuse. A multidisciplinary team that includes law enforcement, victims' advocates, health care providers, mental health practitioners, prosecuting attorneys, and child protection officials works together to investigate cases of child abuse and care for victims. The center is designed to create a sense of safety and security for child victims and to put their needs first. See www.mayoclinic.org.

*Prevent Child Abuse America*: Prevent Child Abuse America is a nonprofit organization dedicated to promoting services that improve child well-being in all 50 states and developing programs that help to prevent all types of abuse and neglect. Prevent Child Abuse America is also a partner in the National Plan to Prevent the Sexual Abuse and Exploitation of Children developed by the National Coalition to Prevent Child Sexual Abuse and Exploitation. See www.preventchildabuse.org.

law enforcement agents in order to increase federal involvement in child pornography cases and to train state and local law enforcement on how to investigate cases, along with educating local communities on the problem. These agencies and NCMEC also work with several U.S.–based Internet service providers to terminate websites that contain images of child pornography (United States Congress, House Committee on Energy and Commerce, 2007; Wolak et al., 2012).

The DOJ through the Office for Victims of Crime has also made funds available to victim service organizations to provide trauma-informed care and culturally competent services to victims of sexual exploitation and sex trafficking. The funding for these services requires victim services organizations to work with law enforcement agencies to develop multidisciplinary plans to combat the sexual exploitation and sex trafficking of minors and provide residential care for victims (Development Services Group, Inc., 2014). The resources offered to victims of sexual exploitation and sex trafficking include education for at-risk children, training for victim assistance personnel and other professionals, direct care and support for victims, programs designed to prevent online sexual exploitation and sex trafficking, hotlines, and outreach and education initiatives (Clayton, Krugman, & Simon, 2013). While it is not easy to always identify victims of sexual exploitation and sex trafficking, victim assistance personnel need to prepare themselves to identify risk factors for past or ongoing victimization among the children in their care.

## Education and Outreach

Education and the empowerment of children and young adults are crucial elements in preventing and addressing the concerns of online sexual exploitation. However, given the evolving form of online exploitation, all organizations serving children and youth should incorporate regular trainings about child sexual abuse and online exploitation, and its prevention, into ongoing, regular in-service education for all staff and volunteers, including older youth who supervise younger children in these settings (National Coalition to Prevent Child Sexual Abuse and Exploitation, 2012). Additionally, education and outreach programs focusing on online sexual exploitation need to focus on identifying and reducing factors that fuel the demand for children to be sexually exploited. The National Coalition to Prevent Child Sexual Abuse and Exploitation (2012) posits that educating the general public and professionals in the field about the demand for sexual abuse and exploitation of children helps them to see the powerful role that prevention can play in countering the demand and lessening the normalization of sexual harm. Collaborating with local, state, and national organizations who actively use research to develop advanced comprehensive prevention programs that are culturally relevant is vital when implementing education and outreach programs. Using evidence-based prevention programs through continuing research demonstrates that victim assistance organizations understand the problem and are aware of what needs to be done to effectively respond to it by having knowledge of its characteristics and consequences, along with policy and practice challenges (Ospina et al., 2010). The main education program employed by organizations serving children and young adults is the one developed by the National Center for Missing & Exploited Children funded by the U.S. Department of Justice, Office of Juvenile Justice and Prevention. This interactive, educational program provides age-appropriate resources to help teach children and teens how to be safer on and offline. The program focuses on safety skills, which include teaching youth how to practice good digital citizenship by avoiding and reporting inappropriate content, protecting personal information, preventing cyber bullying, and learning how to recognize and prevent other potential Internet risks, even personal exploitation, and how to report victimization to a trusted adult (NCMEC, 2017).

## SUMMARY

In today's networked society, abusive online conduct such as cyberbullying, cyber-stalking, and the sexual exploitation of children can cause serious damage, including severe psychological distress, loss of employment, and even physical violence or death. The prevalence of this conduct suggests that more effective means are necessary to redress online wrongs and to protect victims. The almost unlimited opportunities to remain connected through mobile devices, online forums, social networking sites, and video or photo sharing sites has made the varying forms of cyber-crime extremely common. The ability for such communication to be anonymous and the ability for individuals to assume a false identity or alias means that barriers to offending have been removed, and the offenses are difficult to address. This, too, has made it difficult to develop and implement programs to assist victims of cyber-crime. For those working in victim assistance, cyber-crime poses a particular challenge as there are limited resources to assist those affected. It is difficult to provide a prevalence rate of cyber-crime given its varying forms, as like other forms of victimization, cyber-crime is underreported. However, cyber-crime has additional elements that make it difficult to obtain an accurate prevalence rate. Cyber-crime does not require physical proximity between the victim and perpetrator for the consummation of an offense. Cyber-crime is also unbounded, in other words, it is not constricted to geographical location. The victim and perpetrator can be in different cities, states, or countries. All a perpetrator needs is a device that provides him or her access to the Internet. A large portion of cyber-crime is automated, meaning that perpetrators can commit thousands of crimes quickly and with little effort.

Young or old, the Internet has been fully embraced as a tool for work and for socializing. The extent to which our lives are influenced by the Internet, and the potential for it to be used as a tool to harass others, has meant that education and outreach has never been more important. Schools, businesses, and community members play an instrumental role in helping to inform people of the dangers of the Internet. Education and outreach programs that focus on addressing what drives the demand for the varying forms of cyber-crime can be greatly effective in preventing cyber-crime and lessening the normalization of its effects.

With specific regard to cyber-crime, the U.S government and many states have begun to amend their laws to include prohibitions against harassing a person through electronic, computer, or e-mail communications and to include criminal codes for offenses relating to the sexual exploitation of children. However, the lack of consistent definitions, requirements, protections, and penalties means that many discrepancies exist in the criminal codes that cover all the substantive offenses (United States Congress, House Committee on Energy and Commerce, 2007), and that affects how the criminal justice system responds to these victimizations.

While it is impossible for victim assistance personnel to recognize all the different types cyber-crime, it is important to understand the effects it has on victims and the community. Helping victims of cyber-crime requires personnel to not provide false hope in the recovery of assets in Internet fraud cases, and in cases of cyberbullying, cyber-stalking, and online sexual exploitation, helping victims piece together a chronological, fact-based account of their victimization. Victim assistance personnel can greatly assist victims to assess what happened and identify the most appropriate resources for reporting and recovery.

## KEY WORDS

Cyber child sexual
    exploitation  244
Cyberbullying  238

Cyber-crime  227
Cyber-harassment  238
Cyber-stalking  238

Grooming  244
Identity theft  231
Internet fraud  228

## INTERNET RESOURCES

**The Internet Crimes Against Children Task Force Program (www.icactaskforce.org)**

The Internet Crimes Against Children Task Force Program is a national network of 61 coordinated task forces representing over 4,500 federal, state, and local law enforcement and prosecutorial agencies. These agencies are continually engaged in proactive and reactive investigations and prosecutions of persons involved in child abuse and exploitation involving the Internet.

**The Cyberbullying Research Center (www.cyber bullying.org)**

The Cyberbullying Research Center is dedicated to providing up-to-date information about the nature, extent, causes, and consequences of cyberbullying among adolescents. Cyberbullying can be defined as "Willful and repeated harm inflicted through the use of computers, cell phones, and other electronic devices." It is also known as "cyber bullying," "electronic bullying," "e-bullying," "sms bullying," "mobile bullying," "online bullying," "digital bullying," or "Internet bullying." The Center also explores other adolescent behaviors online including sexting, problematic social networking practices, and a variety of issues related to digital citizenship.

**The Gundersen National Child Protection Training Center (www.gundersenhealth.org)**

Gundersen National Child Protection Training Center (Gundersen NCPTC) and its programs work to end all forms of child maltreatment through education, training, and prevention, while advocating for and serving children, adult survivors, and communities. Gundersen NCPTC prepares current and future child protection professionals to recognize and report the abuse of children. As leaders in the field since 2003, more than 100,000 child protection professionals have been trained in all 50 states and 17 countries on topics pertaining to child abuse investigations, prosecutions, and prevention.

## CRITICAL THINKING QUESTIONS

1. Discuss the different types of Internet fraud and why it is becoming a growing concern for law enforcement and victim service organizations.

2. What steps do victim assistance personnel take to help victims of Internet fraud? What expectations do they need to manage following such a victimization?

3. What are the differences between cyberbullying and cyber-stalking and cyber-exploitation?

4. Critically discuss the steps taken to address the sexual exploitation of children online.

5. How best can education and outreach be used to assist in combating sexual exploitation online?

PART

# IV

# New Directions in Victim Assistance

CHAPTER

# 13

# Professionalism and Ethics in Victim Assistance

*Vicki is an undergraduate intern who works as a hotline advocate at the local crisis center. Having majored in criminology and obtained a victim services certificate from the school, she started to feel that the center underestimates her skills and knowledge. She also has been frustrated to see a lack of attention to the women who contact the center. Even though many women suffer from trauma, the center is currently understaffed and has not been providing adequate services to them. Vicki decided to do online counseling services in addition to her normal duty as a hotline advocate without telling any staff in the center.*

Is Vicki's decision ethical? If you were Vicki, what would you do? We make many ethical decisions in our daily lives. Sometimes we make a decision consciously and at other times unknowingly. Recall the occasions that you made a difficult decision. How do you know if you made the right choice? Thinking about Vicki's case, you might feel that her decision was not appropriate, but can you explain the reasons why it was wrong? Was there a better way to handle the issue? Learning how to make the best decision in a challenging situation is the central purpose of this chapter.

It begins by presenting important terms necessary to understand professional ethics. After learning the eight steps to resolving an ethical dilemma, you will have an opportunity to practice those steps through hypothetical scenarios. This chapter also highlights the potential risks for those who work in the fields of human services such as victim advocates, police officers, and other professionals. You will find that those professionals are particularly vulnerable to psychological distress, and therefore they need to learn common risk indicators and how to manage those risks. Self-care is crucial for all helping professionals as it reduces stress and enhances well-being.

## Ethics in Victim Assistance

### Defining Terms

***Ethics*** is the "science of morality" (Homan, 1991, p. 1), which addresses what is the right thing to do and how we ought to behave. ***Normative ethics*** deals with moral duties or the set of considerations as to how one should act. ***Applied ethics*** is the application of ethical principles to specific issues in private or public life. ***Professional ethics*** is a specific type of applied ethics focusing on the ethical rules that govern specific professional standards (Pollock, 2010).

***Values*** are defined as elements of desirability, worth, or importance (Pollock, 2010). Consider the following values: happiness, health, pleasure, beauty, honesty, love, justice, fairness, and wealth. Everyone prioritizes certain values more than others. For example,

---

*Sidebar definitions:*

***Ethics:*** the "science of morality" which addresses what is the right thing to do and how we ought to behave

***Normative ethics:*** deals with moral duties or the set of considerations as to how one should act

***Applied ethics:*** the application of ethical principles to specific issues in private or public life

***Professional ethics:*** a specific type of applied ethics focusing on the ethical rules that govern specific professional standards (Pollock, 2010)

***Values:*** elements of desirability, worth, or importance (Pollock, 2010)

an individual who believes that success is more important than pleasure might focus more on his or her professional career and have less leisure time. Another critical factor is that not all values are moral values. For example, although pleasure and happiness are important in our lives, those are not necessarily tied to moral behavior. In contrast, certain values such as respect, responsibility, and humility are to be used as a basis for ethical decision making. Ethically, moral values should take priority over nonmoral values when they come into conflict. There are also social values such as democracy and the public good, which are considered necessary to achieve a good society (Williams & Arrigo, 2012). In evaluating your personal values, you might also consider how those values are related to larger professional and societal values and how they would influence your response to challenging situations.

## Laws and Ethics

Most laws tell us what we cannot do in public and for some occasions in private, but there are other laws that encourage good behavior. For example, all states and the District of Columbia have some form of **Good Samaritan laws**. Good Samaritan Laws protect passersby, bystanders, and healthcare providers who are willing to assist those who need immediate assistance from liability if unintended consequences result from their assistance (Legal Resource Library, http://resources.lawinfo.com/personal-injury/what-are-good-samaritan-laws.html).

Keep in mind that ethical standards are not necessarily written down in the form of laws or other rules, but there is significant overlap between ethical standards and laws (Banks, 2009). For example, both one's morality and actual laws tell us that we should not kill an innocent human being or steal someone's property. Yet, the interpretation of those laws has differed over time. Under the Nuremberg laws enacted by the Nazi regime in Germany, Jews were not considered legally as fully human (Williams & Arrigo, 2012). Similarly, laws promoting apartheid in South Africa and Jim Crow laws in the United States, which were lawful, clearly violate the ethical standards of today.

Besides laws, the activities of the private and public sectors are governed by regulations. *Regulations* usually come from federal or state governments. *Standards* are often used as a basis for accreditation in the private or the public sector. Noncompliance of regulations and standards could result in sanctions, which would likely be a fine. *Guidelines* are usually recommendations rather than directives among professional groups (Pollock, 2010).

## Codes of Ethics

A *code of ethics* is a set of professional rules that regulates the behavior of the individual. It is common for organizations to have a value system and a code of ethics to educate and guide the behavior of those who work in a profession. Examples of a code of ethics in the criminal justice system are the Law Enforcement Code of Ethics and the Canons of Police Ethics adopted by the International Association of Chiefs of Police (IACP), which is a preface to the mission and a commitment that law enforcement agencies make to the public they serve (International Association of Chiefs of Police, http://www.theiacp.org/

**Good Samaritan laws:** protect passersby, bystanders, and healthcare providers who are willing to assist those who need immediate assistance from liability if unintended consequences result frnm their assistance (Legal Resource Library, http://resources.lawinfo.com/personal-injury/what-are-good-samaritan-laws.html)

*Regulations:* usually come from federal or state governments. Noncompliance of regulations could result in sanctions, which would likely be a fine

*Standards:* a basis for accreditation in the private or the public sector. Noncompliance of standards could result in sanctions, which would likely be a fine

*Guidelines:* are usually recommendations rather than directives among professional groups

*Code of ethics:* a set of professional rules that regulate the behavior of the individual

codeofethics). The American Correctional Association Code of Ethics expects its members to maintain honesty, respect for the dignity and individuality of human beings, and a commitment to professional and compassionate service (American Correctional Association, www.aca.org). The American Jail Association Code of Ethics for jail officers aims to professionalize those who work in detention and correctional facilities (American Jail Association, https://members.aja.org/ethics.aspx). The American Bar Association (ABA) Model Rules of Professional Conduct were adopted in 1983 and serve as a model for the ethics rules of lawyers in most states (American Bar Association, https://www.americanbar.org/groups/professional_responsibility/publications/model_rules_of_professional_conduct.html).

## Ethical Codes in Victim Assistance

Until the 1950s, there were no ethical codes for human services professionals (Hook, 2005). Things started to change in the 1950s, when the state and local chapters of the National Association of Social Work (NASW) started to create codes of ethics. The NASW consolidated local and national codes of ethics and adopted the NASW Code of Ethics in 1960. The code has been modified several times to address the specific needs of individuals. Yet, as the area of victim services grew, the need for specific counseling protocols for victim assistance providers emerged. As such, in 1999, the National Victim Assistance Standards Consortium (NVASC) was formed by the Office for Victims of Crime at the U.S. Department of Justice, and standards of ethics for those who work in the victim services fields were crafted to support them in everyday workplace decision making.

The standards of ethics include a set of guiding values including competence, integrity, professional responsibility, respect for people's rights and dignity, concern for others' welfare, and social responsibility (Hook, 2005). Competent service providers should understand the needs of clients and make appropriate decisions using available resources in the community; be honest about their qualifications and treat their clients fairly; maintain professional standards of conduct and not compromise their professional responsibilities; respect the fundamental rights and dignity of victims; respect the victims' right to privacy, confidentiality, and self-determination; be actively concerned with the welfare of those they serve; and educate themselves about their professional, legal, and social responsibilities, as well as support the interests of victims and be committed to social justice.

With those guiding values, the NVASC developed ethical standards of professional conduct. The full version can be found in the Appendix.

## NVASC Ethical Standards of Professional Conduct

### Section 1: Scope of Service

Section 1 covers the scope of service. It starts with the statutory and constitutional rights of the victim at both the state and federal levels. For example, in 1984, California was the first state to provide confidential privilege to rape victims' communication with their counselors (Arabian, 2009). By 2009, a majority of states had adopted some form of similar protection for counselors of rape victims (Arabian, 2009). Even though the communications between rape and domestic violence victims and advocates are protected by law in most states (National Center on Protection Orders and Full Faith & Credit, 2014), service providers should continually check state statutes regarding whether they can be subpoenaed in court to testify about their clients.

This section also covers professional boundaries and alerts the provider not to mislead the title, role, and responsibilities to his or her clients and to maintain professional behavior, a professional appearance, and professional competence. Using one's position to obtain special favors, privileges, advantages, gifts, or access to services that are unrelated to the agency's interests or that serves one personally should be avoided. Also, one must always be clear with clients about any fees associated with a service.

## Section 2: Coordinating Within the Community

Section 2 talks about the relationship with the community. The service provider must respect different opinions, and when making public statements, one should clarify if the opinions are personal, on behalf of one's agency, or representing overall professionals in the field. Knowledge should be shared not only with other practitioners but also with volunteers and interns. A team approach is highly valued in the field of victim assistance, and professionals share with and listen to their colleagues. Along with attaining the goals of agencies, one could actively take part in community activities and advocate to improve justice systems and victim services.

## Section 3: Direct Services

Section 3 discusses the issues related to providing direct services to the victims. Victims have basic civil rights and other rights protected by state statutes and guidelines. For example, the victim retains (1) all basic civil rights in the professional relationship; (2) the right not to be discriminated against in the provision of services on the basis of race/ethnicity, language, sex/gender, age, sexual orientation, disability, social class, economic status, education, marital status, religious affiliation, residency, or HIV status; and (3) the right to know any exceptions to the confidentiality privilege.

One challenge of a provider arises when a provider disagrees with the victim's preference in handling the situation. What one could do is to provide information about available resources and options so that the victim is fully informed to make a decision. Building a trust relationship is crucial to advocate for victims effectively.

Note that the provider should encourage victims to make their own decisions, but when the victim's decision conflicts with state and federal laws, regulations, and agency policies, one could take the following steps to resolve the issue.

1. Verbally inform the victim about the conflict.

2. Consult with a colleague or a supervisor.

3. Possibly refer to alternative agencies for further services or resolution of the conflict.

Information on confidentiality and exceptions should be provided to the victim at an early stage. These are the possible exceptions:

1. Consulting with other professionals, supervisors, or consultants

2. Written consent of the person who provided the information

3. Death/Disability, with the written consent of a personal representative

4. When communication reveals intended commission of a crime and/or a harmful act

5. Medical emergency, or the victim is unable to release the necessary information

6. Mandated reporting of abuse of a child or a vulnerable adult

7. When a person waives confidentiality by bringing public charges against the provider

8. Minor victims, according to state laws

Previous relationships between a provider and a victim such as a business partner or a familial or personal relationship would create a potential conflict of interest. The professional relationship should be terminated when the service is no longer relevant to the victim's needs. It is strongly discouraged to terminate a relationship if the purpose is to pursue a business or personal relationship with the victim. It is sometimes difficult to avoid dual relationships; one's client could be a neighbor or even the child of a friend. If one cannot avoid a personal or business relationship, the provider should consult with his or her supervisor. Sexual relationships with victims are the most serious violations of the ethical standards. Finally, the provider should be aware that he or she could be traumatized by listening to the stories of the victims.

## Section 4: Administration and Evaluation

Section 4 mentions that a provider must report clear violations of ethical standards to the appropriate authorities. (Please see Appendix for the full version of NVASC Ethical Standards of Professional Conduct.)

Now, let us consider the case of the hotline advocate at the beginning of this chapter. The NVASC Ethical Standards of Professional Conduct 1.2 indicate that Vicki's actions are beyond the scope of her role specified in her title. Vicki could have communicated with her colleagues and supervisor to improve the system and collaborate with other agencies to support victims. She could also have advocated for better services for crime victims and taken a leadership role in the community (The NVASC Ethical Standards of Professional Conduct, Section 2).

| | |
|---|---|
| *Ethical dilemmas:* situations where one has to make a moral decision from two or more choices | # Ethical Dilemmas and Ethical Decision Making |

*Ethical dilemmas* arise when one has to make a decision from two or more choices. In reality, sometimes there is no clear-cut right or wrong answer from among those choices, and competing obligations and interests could be involved. For example, Linzer (2004) highlights the ethical dilemma of a social worker whose elderly abused clients choose to remain in an abusive environment even though better options are offered. Such refusal leads to conflicts among the ethical principles of "autonomy, beneficence and paternalism, and nonmaleficence, and ambiguity over determining decision-making capacity" (p. 166). How would you balance these conflicts and resolve the case?

Ethical decisions should be made in systematic and logical ways. Let us begin our discussion of the analytical steps, which are explained in *Ethics in Victim Services* by Melissa Hook (2005). Please note that the following case example was modified for this textbook, and further detailed discussions of the ethical decision-making process and other examples can be found in Hook's book.

*Ana Lopes works at a local nonprofit family resource center. Her new client, Vanessa Martinez, lives with her parents, two younger sisters, grandparents, uncles, and aunts in a rural area. All family members except for Vanessa and her two sisters are undocumented. They work in the field and share scarce resources. Vanessa mentioned to Ana that her uncle had been inappropriately touching her for several weeks. When Ana suggested that Vanessa should report the case to the police, Vanessa was upset and said that was not an option as it could create a risk of deportation not only for her uncle but also for other family members.*

If you were Ana, what would you do?

Among the many ethical decision-making models, we will use one for resolving ethical dilemmas in victim services. When making a decision in such a difficult case, follow these eight analytical steps.

1. Assess the facts.
2. Identify the relevant ethical standards.
3. Assess the practical concerns that affect the decision-making process.
4. Consider the possible courses of action.
5. Consider the consequences of the possible courses of action.
6. Consult with a peer or a supervisor.
7. Select the best option and action.
8. Evaluate the outcomes.

(Hook, 2005, p. 71)

## Step 1: Assess the Facts

The first step is to assess all the facts that led to the ethical dilemma.

- The provider's 19-year-old client has been molested by her uncle.
- The client's uncle is an undocumented immigrant.
- The uncle's behavior has been escalating.
- The client does not want to report the case to the police.

## Step 2: Identify the Relevant Ethical Standards

The next step is to review the relevant ethical standards per the NVASC Ethical Standards of Professional Conduct. In this scenario, the following standards would apply.

> *3.2. The VA provider recognizes the interests of the person served as a primary responsibility.*

> *3.4. The VA provider respects the victim's right to self-determination.*

## Step 3: Assess the Practical Concerns That Affect the Decision-Making Process

List the practical considerations in the case. In this scenario, the major ethical dilemmas are as follows:

- The possible deportation of the client's uncle and other family members could break her family apart.

- The uncle's behavior needs to be stopped to ensure a secure environment for Vanessa.

## Steps 4 and 5: Consider the Possible Courses of Action and the Consequences of the Possible Courses of Action

List the possible courses of action and consider the potential positive and negative outcomes. These are a few examples.

*Report the case to police:* Vanessa would no longer be afraid of her uncle. It might also stop his inappropriate behavior with other victims. It could lead to deportation of all family members.

*Give a warning to her uncle:* Vanessa could give the uncle a chance to correct his behavior without reporting the case to the police. The awareness of the consequences might cause him to change his behavior. Vanessa would no longer be molested but might still feel insecure living with her uncle.

*Encourage Vanessa to leave the house:* Vanessa would no longer be molested, and the uncle could still help support her family. Yet, he might start to molest her siblings as another target. Leaving on her own might violate the cultural expectation of her.

*Hold a family conference:* One could take a restorative justice approach by inviting a mediator and holding a family conference. Vanessa would feel that her voice was heard, and her uncle would know how his behavior affected her. However, the solution might be inclined to protect the family rather than focusing on the best interests of Vanessa.

As you can see, none of the decisions is perfect, and there are pros and cons with each decision. Also, the outcomes might differ depending on the parties' legal status, income, geographic location, and family relationship. Perhaps, the decision that Ana made might not be the best one from the professional's standpoint. However, as stated in the NVASC Ethical Standards of Professional Conduct 3.4, the victim advocate must respect the victim's right to self-determination and provide better resources to help him or her make the best decision.

After examining the facts, you discuss the case with your colleagues and supervisor (Step 6) and select the best option and action (Step 7). Finally, do not forget to evaluate the outcomes (Step 8), which will be useful resources for future inquiry.

Now, it is time for you to consider the following situations.

## Situation 1

You are a case manager at a local rape counseling services center. When reviewing the backgrounds of new case files, you realize that one of your clients, Angelica Rodrigues, is a daughter of your neighbor. Angelica is known to the community for her drinking and delinquent activities, and you have made several complaints to her parents in the past. Once, you even reported the case to the police. Supposedly, her boyfriend is a member of MS-13. The file indicates that she was severely raped by her boyfriend and other gang members, which requires immediate attention. You have some reservations about reaching out to her, but the center recently lost another case manager, and you are the only person who could handle the case. What would you do?

## Situation 2

You are a housing manager of the family resident units at a local domestic violence shelter. One night, you find that one female client, Mai Lee, has been smoking marijuana at the facility, which is a violation of the shelter's policy, and that might result in her being expelled from the facility. Mai begged you not to report the case to the director as she has four children and no place to go. Also, she is terrified that her exhusband might take advantage of the incident to get custody of her children. What would you do?

## Situation 3

You are a victim advocate who is a mother of a seven-year-old boy. Today is your son's birthday, and you plan to visit his grandparents and have a birthday dinner with them. When you are about ready to leave, you get a phone call from a teenage girl who was sexually assaulted by her boyfriend. She is extremely vulnerable and does not know what she should do. Given your experience, the case needs immediate attention, but all the other advocates already left for the day, and you are the only person remaining at the center. At the same time, your family is anxiously waiting for you at home. What would you do?

## Situation 4

You realize that one of the victim advocates in your center who started work a few months ago has been depressed. She has had a hard time keeping up with her work schedule, and you have covered her shift several times. One day, she started to cry in front of you and mentioned that she was overwhelmed by listening to the horrific stories of her clients. The following morning, you notice her breath smells like alcohol. What would you do?

## Special Considerations in Victim Services

### Multicultural Competency

Many crime victims are reluctant to reach out for services because they feel that service providers do not have adequate resources to address their specific cultural and personal needs.

> When I called the hotline, I was ready to get help to improve my relationship with my husband. However, no one was available who could speak my language. I had to wait for someone to call me back, but I was worried that my husband might pick up the phone. So I didn't give my number.

> I wish I could have talked with someone who understood that I can't leave my relationship and don't want to. I really was hoping that my husband and I could receive counseling. Instead, I'm now being told to move to a shelter with my children. How will this work for us? I can't find a job, I don't have a car, my family is far away.

> I should have never said anything.

> (Quotes from Purnell, Teng, & Warrier, 2012, p. 4).

**Multicultural competence:** gaining knowledge, understanding, supporting, and appropriately responding to victims across different languages and cultures

**Multicultural competence** in victim services involves understanding and appropriately responding to victims with a distinct combination of cultural variables. In 1995, the American Counseling Association (ACA) revised its ethical standards to require that counselors not discriminate based on race, ethnicity, culture, class, religion, spirituality, disability, marital status, gender, age, and/or sexual orientation (Hook, 2005). The development of multicultural competency in victim services starts with service providers comprehending and identifying with their own racial orientation. Knowing and appreciating one's own culture helps a provider recognize how culture affects victims' behavior and decisions. Ultimately, that knowledge and understanding must be used to develop and implement culturally appropriate interventions to assist victims from different cultures (Hook, 2005).

Culture is "a dynamic process characterized by the shared values, beliefs, expectations, and practices across the members and generations of a defined group" (Cruickshank & Collins, 2012, p. 340). Culture is stable in the sense that traditions, norms, and customs are transmitted from generation to generation. Nonetheless, culture is evolving. Consider the term for lesbian, gay, bisexual, transgender, queer, and questioning (LGBTQ) individuals. The initial term was LGB in the 1980s, *T* was added in the early 1990s, and *Q* was introduced in the last decade. Now, many believe that more options will be added (Marc, 2004). With the fluidity of definitions, the identities of LGBTQ individuals are multifaceted, and they could experience additional layers of racism and discrimination. Warrier et al. (2002) cited a story of a colleague who was a Latina lesbian; she indicated that when she is in the lesbian community there is pressure to "whitewash her Mexican heritage" (p. 668).

One good example is victim services for LGBTQ individuals in domestic violence situations. Given the underlying assumption of females as victims, the protocols for health centers have not fully prepared methodologies to support LGBTQ individuals. A gay male victim of intimate partner abuse traditionally is less likely to be screened for intimate partner abuse than a female victim (Warrier et al., 2002). Yet, some promising changes have been observed such as the Fenway Community Health case in which a protocol was created to screen all patients regardless of gender for domestic violence and for follow up with gender-neutral verbal questions. The site also reviewed its internal policies to improve outreach to the gay community in advertising job openings and now offers sensitivity training for staff who are working with LGBTQ patients (Warrier et al., 2002). The intake form for the clinics and the shelters should ask preferred pronoun (he or she) and add transgender options to male/female. However, it is not recommended to use the term "other" as this term gives an impression that the client's identity is not worth listing. The intake form for children should include the labels "parent/guardian" rather than using mother and father to make the form inclusive to same-sex parents (Sheedy, 2016).

Another area for which a culturally competent response is necessary is with the Asian and Pacific Islander (API) community. The significant gap between the official records and self-reported surveys in family violence of Asian American families is well known. Studies show that 41% to 61% of Asian women experience some form of violence by an intimate partner during their lifetime (Yoshihama, 1999; Raj & Silverman, 2002). Yet, victim advocacy for Asian Americans is limited due to the myth that API victims refuse social support or any government assistance and choose to rely on their own ethnic network (Nopper, 2014). A more accurate picture of Asian communities indicated that abused women are hesitant to seek any advocacy services because there is intense stigma and shame attached to disclosing family secrets to others among Asian families (Vang & Bogenschutz, 2011). A good resource for API service providers is the A-Z Advocacy Model for Asian Pacific Islander Survivors (Dabby, 2017). The model explains how culturally specific work could be operationalized by API serving programs and provide positive help-seeking experiences to API survivors. Supportive responses from advocates who share similar cultural background preserve all important pride in community. Consider a battered woman who sought refuge and was placed in a shelter in Minnesota and just wanted to eat rice, reflecting how rice is critical for the Asian culture and is "a life preserver in troubled times and something more" (Boyd, 2010).

Another example is Native American communities, which suffer from geographical isolation, oppression, and economic adversity. According to a National Institute of Justice report in 2001, "Violence Against American Indian and Alaska Native Women and Men," more than 4 in 5 American Indian and Alaska Native women (84.3%) have experienced violence in their lifetime, including sexual violence and physical violence by an intimate partner. Looking at the Navajo Nation, cases of domestic violence skyrocketed in 2008, almost doubling from 2007 (Navajo Nation Human Rights Commission, 2016). Along with a high prevalence of violence, the Navajo community also suffers from a lack of shelter services for Navajo domestic violence victims. As of 2016, the Navajo Nation had

# Victim Assistance

## My Sister's House

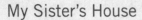

My Sister's House in Sacramento is one of only a few shelters specifically serving Asian women victims and their children. The facility was created in 2000 to develop a culturally appropriate space for victims of domestic violence and violence against women in immigrant and refugee communities, specifically those from Southeast Asian countries.

Currently, the agency offers an emergency shelter and a transitional house and an antitrafficking shelter in a culturally appropriate environment. Also, the Women to Work program provides health information and referrals, transportation, clothing, child care and housing assistance, employment and career guidance, legal assistance, and counseling.

The agency also organizes a day-long training institute to educate social service and law enforcement providers from around the state about working with Asian and Pacific Islander survivors of domestic violence and human trafficking.

In 2004, the Sacramento Regional Community Foundation honored My Sister's House with the James and Susan K. Lennane Award for Innovation.

See http://www.my-sisters-house.org/ for more information.

only three women's shelters (Navajo Nation Human Rights Commission, 2016). This is a problem because if a victim has to leave the reservation to seek shelter services, it is a challenge as it means she will be separated from her extended family. Even if she decides to seek services outside the reservation, she will face further cultural challenges. For example, the healing ceremony in Navajo uses tobacco and herbs such as sweet grass, sage, or cedar. However, the shelter staff who lack understanding of the Navajo culture might consider that those women were using illegal drugs or violating the shelter rules. Also, Native women have a tradition to respect the spirits of their children and not address child misbehavior in public. Those traditions could be misinterpreted in a way that Navajo women are neglecting children. Moreover, the shelter might not have staff who understand the native language (Warrier et al., 2002). Since 2012, there has been an ongoing investigation of the extent and nature of gender violence in the Navajo Nation and efforts to support the creation of laws and policies that would "return the Navajo Nation to Navajo principles" (Navajo Nation Human Rights Commission, 2016, p. 21). Yet, challenges remain.

These are only a few examples, and all other subgroups of survivors can face unique barriers including Islamophobia that makes Muslim survivors hesitant to seek help; refugees escaping from civil war coping with the triple traumas of war, escape, life in refugee camps, and resettlement; and victims with limited English proficiency struggling to establish their credibility. It is important that victim assistance agencies understand the extent of regional and cultural diversity and build the capacity to advocate for that.

## Volunteers

Volunteers play critical roles in victim assistance. Using volunteers would not only reduce the cost of services but also bring about enthusiasm, compassion, and empathy.

Conversely, volunteers gain personal growth through work. Sympathy, empathy, pride, a desire to help, and willingness to learn about the field are some of the reasons to motivate volunteers to do victim assistance (Ellemers & Boezeman, 2010; Ottoni-Wihelm & Bekkers, 2010; McNamee & Peterson, 2016). Another study found that a sense of duty is connected to religious values (Starnes & Wymer, 2000). Sustained volunteerism is related to satisfaction with the experience and commitment to the organization (Grube & Piliavin, 2000; Davis, Hall, & Meyer, 2003). A survey of volunteers serving victims of sexual abuse indicated that those volunteers who have a higher level of satisfaction showed higher levels of intent to remain. Also, those who received higher levels of training and social support showed a higher level of satisfaction (Hellman & House, 2006).

The roles of volunteers differ by service. Volunteers could take on all kinds of cases or the tasks could be clearly divided among the offered services. There is no clear-cut or best model, but volunteers demand respect and sufficient support (Wardell, Lishman, & Whalley, 2000). The professionalization of volunteers might be critical for the quality of services, but some scholars alert that the nature of volunteers, in terms of flexibility and personal and attentive care, should be a critical component of volunteerism and that the overprofessionalization of volunteer work might pollute the "voluntary spirit" (Roose, Verschelden, Vettenburg, & Vanthuyne, 2012).

# Challenges in Serving Victims

## Understanding Stress

> I took a day off once and went to the grocery store, and I was stopped and asked if I was a sexual assault nurse. This woman sat in the middle of the grocery store and told me the story of how her son was sexually assaulted by a school teacher. I was just trying to get away for a day, but it seems to follow me everywhere. I cried. I saw [my] stress, the tremendous weight loss. I felt bad for her and helpless at the same time because her son won't go to law enforcement. I work out of my home so my office is here. It is hard to get away. (Maier, 2011, p. 166)

Health care and human service professionals who genuinely try to meet the needs of their clients often marginalize their own risks. The work-related negative consequences in such professions have been described as burnout and compassion fatigue (Najjar, Davis, Beck-Coon, & Doebbeling, 2009). Both burnout and compassion fatigue affect professionals by creating feelings of helplessness, loneliness, anxiety, and depression (Conrad & Kellar-Guenther, 2006). However, there are some notable differences between them. Although burnout occurs through excessive and prolonged job stress (Cherniss, 1980), compassion fatigue arises from a closer relationship between a service provider and his or her client (Gallagher, 2013). Burnout is an accumulative process over an extended time, whereas compassion fatigue could happen from "a single exposure to a traumatic incident"

(Conrad & Kellar-Guenther, 2006, p. 1073). Unlike burnout, compassion fatigue is often associated with feelings of fear and sadness (Pearlman & Saakvitne, 1995). Nonetheless, untreated compassion fatigue can contribute to burnout (Conrad & Kellar-Guenther, 2006).

## Stress and Burnout

> I still take about 100 hours each month on call. Plus I am about 40 hours in the ER each week. And my pager is with me at all times. The police call me, the DA calls me, the nurse who is on-call calls me. I got called the other night at 2 o'clock in the morning because they were having a problem. I am pretty much 24-7! (Quote from a director of the Sexual Assault Nurse Examiners, Maier, 2011, p. 167)

**Burnout:**
a progressive syndrome of emotional exhaustion, depersonalization, and diminished personal accomplishment caused by overwork or stress (Brown, O'Brien, & Deleon, 1998)

By definition, **burnout** is a progressive syndrome of emotional exhaustion, depersonalization, and diminished personal accomplishment (Brown, O'Brien, & Deleon, 1998). Exhaustion reflects the stress dimension of burnout, that is, putting emotional and cognitive distance from the work overload. Depersonalization is an attempt to distance oneself from his or her clients. Exhaustion or depersonalization interferes with job effectiveness. Those who are exhausted and depersonalized find it difficult to gain a sense of accomplishment (Maslach, Schaufeli, & Leiter, 2001). A high level of burnout can have harmful effects on a professional's physical and mental well-being (Green et al., 2014). Research has shown a high prevalence of burnout among social workers due to excessively large caseloads and overwork, experience with an unsupportive public and hostile clients, and organizational environments that seem unfair and dysfunctional (Conrad & Kellar-Guenther, 2006). The followings are the risk factors of burnout.

### Risk Factors

Burnout occurs as a result of a complex interplay between individual and organizational factors (Green et al., 2014). Maslach and Leiter (1997) listed six external factors that influence burnout.

1. Workload and its intensity, time demands, and complexity

2. Lack of control of establishing and following day-to-day priorities

3. Insufficient reward and the accompanying feelings of continually having to do more with less

4. The feeling of community, in which relationships become impersonal and teamwork is undetermined

5. The absence of fairness, in which trust, openness, and respect are not present

6. Conflicting values, in which choices that are made by management often conflict with their mission and core values (p. 120)

Please take the stress screener text (Mental Health America) and understand your stress.

http://www.mentalhealthamerica.net/stress-screener

The American Psychological Association's Stress in America poll in 2007 found that one third of people in the United States experience extreme levels of stress. Furthermore, nearly one in five found that they are experiencing high levels of stress 15 or more days per month. As seen in the discussion of this chapter, that affects your mental and physical health. Controlling stress is a learned behavior, and stress could be managed by changing unhealthy behaviors.

The followings are the tips offered by the APA.

**Understand how you experience stress.** Everyone experiences stress differently. How do you know when you are stressed? How are your thoughts or behaviors different from times when you do not feel stressed?

**Identify your sources of stress.** What events or situations trigger stressful feelings? Are they related to your children, family, health, financial decisions, work, relationships, or something else?

**Learn your own stress signals.** People experience stress in different ways. You may have a hard time concentrating or making decisions; feel angry, irritable or out of control; or experience headaches, muscle tension, or a lack of energy. Gauge your stress signals.

**Recognize how you deal with stress.** Determine if you are using unhealthy behaviors (such as smoking, drinking alcohol, and over/under eating) to cope. Is this a routine behavior, or is it specific to

certain events or situations? Do you make unhealthy choices as a result of feeling rushed and overwhelmed?

**Find healthy ways to manage stress.** Consider healthy, stress-reducing activities such as meditating, exercising, or talking things out with friends or family. Keep in mind that unhealthy behaviors develop over time and can be difficult to change. Don't take on too much at once. Focus on changing only one behavior at a time.

**Take care of yourself.** Eat right, get enough sleep, drink plenty of water, and engage in regular physical activity. Ensure you have a healthy mind and body through activities like practicing yoga, taking a short walk, going to the gym, or playing sports that will enhance both your physical and mental health. Take regular vacations or other breaks from work. No matter how hectic life gets, make time for yourself—even if it's just simple things like reading a good book or listening to your favorite music.

**Reach out for support.** Accepting help from supportive friends and family can improve your ability to manage stress. If you continue to feel overwhelmed by stress, you may want to talk to a psychologist, who can help you better manage stress and change unhealthy behaviors.

http://www.apa.org/helpcenter/stress-tips.aspx

## Question:

1. *What is your level of stress? Identify some stressors in your life. Learning from the APA tips, what kind of changes would you make to manage your stress?*

In a stressful organizational climate such as one with a high level of role overload and role conflict, staff turnover has been associated with burnout (Glisson et al., 2008). Yet, the relationship between caseload size and burnout shows mixed results. Although some studies show the relationship (Acker & Lawrence, 2009), a more recent study found that caseload size was not related to any of the burnout components (Green et al., 2014).

Individual factors related to burnout include the external locus of control, a lack of self-esteem, and maladaptive coping styles (Maslach et al., 2001). Those early in their careers are more susceptible to burnout than their older, more experienced counterparts (Maslach et al., 2001). Studies consistently have found that service providers' own history of victimization has been linked to greater levels of PTSD-like symptoms. Especially, law enforcement and mental health professionals who have a history of abuse during childhood have reported significantly higher levels of trauma survivor–like symptoms than those professionals who were never abused as a child (Follette, Polusny, & Milberk, 1994). Police officers and prison guards are more likely to show high levels of cynicism and inefficiency (Schaufeli & Enzmann, 1998).

## Compassion Fatigue

**Compassion fatigue:**
a traumatic stress reaction apparent among the healthcare and human services professions such as law enforcement officers, hotline workers, nurses, ministers, counselors, and victim advocates who provide direct services and assistance to their clients (Joinson, 1992; Conrad & Kellar-Guenther, 2006)

**Compassion fatigue** is a traumatic stress reaction apparent among the healthcare and human services professions such as law enforcement officers, hotline workers, nurses, ministers, counselors, and victim advocates who provide direct services and assistance to their clients (Joinson, 1992; Conrad & Kellar-Guenther, 2006). The essential factor of this emotional response is empathy or a "central focus and feeling with and in the client's world" (La Monica, 1981, p. 398). Empathetic individuals might absorb the traumatic stress of those they help. As a result, they experience symptoms similar to their clients such as difficulty sleeping, difficulty concentrating, social withdrawal, poor judgment, and addictive behavior (Gallagher, 2013). Morrissette (2004) called this phenomenon "the pain of helping," referring to it as the psychological injury of the helping professionals.

McHolm (2006) identified two different types of compassion fatigue. One is when service providers personally absorb the client's trauma or pain. The other is similar to PTSD; for example, while listening to horrifying stories and graphic descriptions, service providers could reexperience a traumatic event (Figley, 1995).

Anger is an interesting component for victim advocates as it could be a stressor or a valuable coping mechanism. On one hand, victim advocates of sexual assault victims expressed that anger is the most difficult part of their job (Figley, 1995). On the other hand, some of the counselors of domestic violence victims noted that the feeling of anger can be a coping mechanism to protect them from a feeling of sadness (Iliffe & Steed, 2000). In fact, interviews with victim advocates for rape victims indicated that the emotions of fear and anger were indicators of growth and motivation for the advocates to continue with their work (Wasco & Campbell, 2002). A survey of domestic violence shelter workers found that they feel most stressed when learning an abused woman returns home even though future abuse is suspected, managing the anger at the perpetrators of domestic violence, and "dealing with the overwhelming pain and horror of domestic violence" (Brown et al., 1998).

## Case Study

C.R. has been a family physician for six years and has been caring for a 34-year-old woman diagnosed with cervical cancer. Her disease is advanced, and she suffers from severe pain. After she is transferred to a local hospital, it takes a while for C.R. to visit her. When she finally decides to visit her patient, the patient thanked C.R. for her ongoing support and care. C.R. felt distressed to hear these words.

C.R. suppressed tears and only nodded in response. After her patient passed away, C.R. began to wonder whether she was able to take care of those who are terminally ill. One day, her medical office assistant asked her about taking on another patient with an advanced disease, and C.R. was surprised at her "immediate gut reaction of distress and fear." (summary of quote, Gallagher, 2013, p. 265)

## Compassion Satisfaction

**Compassion satisfaction** refers to the level of satisfaction and pleasure derived by helping others through one's work and by contributing to the well-being of others and to the greater good of society (Conrad & Kellar-Guenther, 2006; Măirean, 2016). Research has shown that those healthcare providers who have higher levels of compassion satisfaction have healthy coping mechanisms and the resources to prevent the development of compassion fatigue (Makic, 2015). Research found that compassion satisfaction and burnout are inversely related (Conrad & Kellar-Guenther, 2006). Another study found that those child welfare workers who engaged in higher levels of trauma-informed self-care (e.g., setting realistic goals, a team approach, safety training, continuing education) experienced higher levels of compassion satisfaction and lower levels of burnout (Salloum, Kondrat, Johnco, & Olson, 2015).

A study of domestic violence advocates indicated that a shelter's culture is highly related to job satisfaction. Having a supportive shelter culture helped advocates manage the challenges of shelter life. Also, management and executive staff have an important role in shaping their experience. For example, one staff member noted:

> [The executive director] sets the examples for all of us. The way she treats me transfers to how I treat my clients. So, if I love my job, and love the work atmosphere, and love the staff, then it just continues into what I do with clients. (Merchant & Whiting, 2015, p. 474)

> **Compassion satisfaction:** the level of satisfaction and pleasure derived by helping others through one's work and by contributing to the well-being of others and to the greater good of society

## Self-Care

Self-caring is recognized as critical to any helping professionals who provides services and advocacy through which they might experience secondary trauma, burnout, and other health-related concerns. Self-care not only ameliorates work-related stress but also allows practitioners to handle their health and well-being holistically and enhance their personal and professional lives (Lee & Miller, 2013). Self-care is caring for oneself or "any activity that one does to feel good about oneself" (Richards, Campenni, & Muse-Burke, 2010, p. 255) concerning such areas as physical, psychological and emotional, social, spiritual, leisure, and professional (Lee & Miller, 2013). Professional self-care has distinguished elements from personal self-care, but many times those are interrelated. For example, personal self-care might be marginalized by bringing one's work home at night. Professional self-care could be diminished when a person experiences poor personal relationships in private (Bressi & Vaden, 2017).

The strategies for personal self-care focus on promoting one's well-being. Examples of personal care strategies include understanding disrupted schemas; maintaining an appropriate work-life balance; undertaking personal psychotherapy; identifying healing activities, for example, yoga and meditation; and attending to spiritual needs. Examples of professional care include consulting with experienced senior colleagues about case management, developing and maintaining professional networks, having a realistic tolerance of failure, and setting work and personal goals. The organization could also enhance the professional self-care of workers by developing a comfortable environment and creating a culture of support and respect within the workplace (Najjar et al., 2009).

Below are examples of how to design and implement a professional self-care plan.

### Table 13.1  Designing and Implementing a Professional Self-Care Plan

| Support Structure | Brainstorm strategies that will build this structure to strengthen your professional self-care. | Design a plan to implement the strategy. Strategies should be concrete, relevant, attainable, and easy to evaluate. |
|---|---|---|
| **Workload and Time Management** | | |
| | Take small breaks throughout the workday. Contain the amount I talk about work when I'm not at work. | After seeing each client, I will take a two-minute break to focus on my breathing. After 6:30 p.m., I will not engage in work-related conversations. |
| **Attention to Professional Role** | | |
| | Recognize the client is the authority in his or her life. Identify my specific role when working in multidisciplinary teams. | Each time I meet with a client, I will notice if I want to direct a client's choices and reframe the situation for myself according to social work values. At the start of each multidisciplinary team meeting, I will initiate the practice of having all participants identify their unique role and expertise within the group. |

| Attention to Reaction to Work | |
|---|---|
| Attend to sad feelings related to the experiences of the children of families to whom I provide services. Attend to instances when my work brings up my own trauma history or past stressors. | When I am feeling sad, I will find an appropriate way to honor this sadness (e.g., journal, supportive colleague) and remind myself of the clients' resilience. I will attend therapy once a week. |
| **Professional Social Support and Advocacy** | |
| Seek out regular supervision. Advocate for my own needs in my workplace. | I will initiate scheduling a regular 45 minute, one-on-one, supervision session with my assigned supervisor (e.g., Wednesday at 3:30 p.m.). I will contact appropriate personnel regarding organizational support for continuing education opportunities. |
| **Professional Development** | |
| Read materials relevant to professional development. Attend a conference twice a year. | Each week, I will read one scholarly article that relates to my practice. At the start of each year, I will identify two conferences to attend. |
| **Revitalization and Generation of Energy** | |
| Make my workspace pleasant. Remind myself of my passion for my work with something tangible. | I will identify three ways to try and make my workspace pleasant for me and try them for one month before reassessing their usefulness. When I am feeling discouraged, I will revisit a particular meaningful memento that reminds me of successful work with a client. |

## ABCD formula

The underlying premise of professional ethics is to be a good person. When making a difficult decision, a person of goodwill could rationally apply an ethical system and come up with a good solution. Here is a simple "ABCD formula" that you can recall whenever you have to make a decision (Goodman, 2013).

Actions

Beliefs

Conduct

Discipline

**Actions:** Your daily actions and activities will influence your decisions. Maintain a healthy lifestyle. Eat well, exercise regularly, and manage your stress. Do not lie or cheat, and do your best.

**Beliefs:** Beliefs are not just about religion. Believe in yourself, your agency, your profession, your family, and your friends. Believe in the laws, policies, and procedures of your agency. Believe that you can make change possible for victims every day.

**Conduct:** Consider how your conduct would be felt by your mom, dad, wife, husband, daughter, and son. Are they proud of you? Would your actions not shame or embarrass them?

**Discipline:** If you are unable to resist the temptation of immediate gratification from the possible benefits in your job and you cannot establish professional boundaries with your clients, you might do better to consider an alternative career.

Goodman's ABCD formula notes that managing stress is critical for sound ethical decisions.

## SUMMARY

In this chapter, we studied ethics, morals, and values, and how those concepts determine our behavioral choices as a profession. We learned that a code of ethics is a set of professional rules that ensure an individual in a particular profession responds to perceived situational demands. The professionals in the victim assistance fields could refer to the Ethical Standards of Professional Conduct developed by the NVASC as a guide for their professional activities. To resolve an ethical dilemma, we applied eight steps to help analyze a dilemma systematically.

We also studied the importance of self-care in victim assistance. Those professions working in human services can feel stress and burnout. Compassion fatigue is a psychological injury of those helping professionals who absorb the traumatic stress of those they help. Consequently, they can also suffer from PTSD symptoms. In reverse, those who develop sustainable healthy coping mechanisms and have the resources to prevent the development of compassion fatigue could successfully develop compassion satisfaction and experience lower burnout. Goodman's ABCD formula (i.e., actions, beliefs, conduct, and discipline) is a handy guideline for any profession.

## KEY WORDS

Applied ethics   254
Burnout   266
Code of ethics   255
Compassion fatigue   268
Compassion satisfaction   269
Ethical dilemmas   258

Ethics   254
Good samaritan laws   255
Guidelines   255
Multicultural competence   262
Normative ethics   254

Nvasc ethical standards of
   professional conduct   256
Professional ethics   254
Regulations   255
Standards   255
Values   254

# INTERNET RESOURCES

**Mental Health America (http://www.mentalhealth america.net)**

Mental Health America, a nonprofit organization founded in 1909, has been promoting overall mental health in America. Its website offers online mental health screening tools such as a work health survey, an addiction test, and a PTSD test. It also includes information on various treatment options including online therapy.

**Immigration Advocates Network (https://www .immigrationadvocates.org)**

The Immigration Advocates Network website includes information on immigration news, training opportunities, and resources. It also offers a specific link for professional resources to an advocate, organizer, or service provider at a nonprofit organization or to become a member of specific immigrants' rights organizations and pro bono attorneys representing low-income immigrants.

# CRITICAL THINKING QUESTIONS

1. List the three personal values that you feel are the most important. What are some reasons those values are important to you? How would those values be related to professionalism in victim services?

2. Discuss examples of the codes of ethics in criminal justice. In what ways might they help improve professionalization in victim assistance?

3. Identify some of the cultural barriers in your community. Then, discuss how multicultural competency in victim services could help remove those barriers.

4. Why would human service providers be at risk for compassion fatigue? What are the indicators, and what are some strategies for coping?

# Collaborative Responses to Victims

Collaborative efforts in responding to crime victimization help in the delivery of improved services to address the multiple needs of victims. For instance, domestic violence victims generally need not only temporary shelter but also additional resources including counseling, job training, childcare, transportation, medical care, and financial assistance (Grossman, Lundy, George, & Crabtree-Nelson, 2010). Collaborative responses to victims could lessen the burden of victims while enhancing the efficiency of investigations; for example, child forensic interviewing is known to be best conducted within a multidisciplinary team context (Jones, Cross, Walsh, & Simone, 2005; Cronch, Viljoen, & Hansen, 2006). Furthermore, such efforts would help agencies deliver services more efficiently. By sharing information and resources, professionals would be educated about available resources within other agencies, thereby reducing duplication in service delivery (Brandl et al., 2007).

With the evolution of victim services beginning in the 1960s, collaborative approaches have been used at the local, state, and national levels (Brandl et al., 2007). Even though much has been accomplished, victim services face new challenges with emerging crimes such as victims of civil war, financial fraud targeting the elderly, online stalking and bullying, and the urgent need to address human trafficking. The efforts of reaching out to underserved victims, marginalized populations, and hidden or underreported victimization require further collaborative ways to work with entities beyond the scope of traditional networks. By closely examining the strengths and challenges of existing working relationships, professionals could better achieve optimal outcomes by enhancing their capabilities to serve victims.

## Collaborative Approaches

Historically, much of the effort to support crime victims was conducted exclusively within specific disciplines and boundaries. As such, law enforcement practice was to receive calls, respond, interview parties, and possibly make arrests. Then, cases were handed to prosecutors whereby the decision to prosecute was made. Even though prosecutors relied on other agencies and individuals to gather evidence, these relationships were case specific. Victim advocates assisted clients, but their services and options were client selected, and they did not necessarily seek out other disciplines to meet victims' needs (Brandl et al., 2007).

Over time, however, professionals recognized that this "silo-like" approach limited their ability to meet the needs of the complex situations of victims, often causing duplication of effort and frustration among victims. For example, in child abuse cases, victims were repetitively interviewed—by an initial responder, an investigator, a healthcare provider, a child protective service worker, and prosecutors. Those multiple interviews by different entities not only created trauma for children but also led to questions about the reliability of testimony (Newlin et al., 2015). Another development was in the area of intimate partner violence; by the late 1980s, service providers realized that without the coordination of health, social, and other services in the criminal justice system, the safety of victims could not be secured (Henning & Feder, 2005).

The advantages of collaborative efforts with a team of representatives from law enforcement, healthcare, the prosecution, and child welfare services minimizing the number of forensic interviews has been stressed by researchers (Pence & Wilson, 1994; Cronch et al., 2006; Cheung & McNeil Boutté-Queen, 2010; Duron & Cheung, 2016). In the case of domestic violence, law enforcement partnering with a victim advocate in handling cases results in better serving the victims' needs and improving the collection of evidence (Muellemen & Feighny, 1999; Camacho & Alarid, 2008).

The most informal way to connect with other agencies is through networking, whereby agencies and community groups share information via meetings and social networking services (SNS). Such networking could take the form of membership or be open to the public. More formalized ways to connect include the 3Cs, or Cooperation, Coordination, and Collaboration, which is a commonly used model in the for-profit sector (Simonin, Samali, Zohdy, & Laidler-Kylander, 2016).

## Cooperation

The most often cited definition of cooperation is from Fairchild, who defined *cooperation* as "the process by which individuals or groups combine their effort, in a more or less organized way for the attainment of a common objective" (Sharma, 2007, p. 372). Cooperation is a rather informal relationship built on trust, whereby two or more people jointly work together to pursue common goals over a relatively short time frame (Simonin et al., 2016). In such a scenario, the resource investment of each group would be limited, and no organizational changes would occur. As such, authority remains with individual organizations. An example of cooperation can be seen in the way that many organizations offer various resources to the victims of a natural disaster. This type of working arrangement could be a starting point in developing further relationships among the relevant organizations.

**Cooperation:** the process by which individuals or groups combine their efforts, in a more or less organized way, for the attainment of a common objective (Sharma, 2007, p. 372)

## Coordination

"**Coordination** entails formal relationships around specific efforts or programs. Organizational resources are made available to partner organizations and rewards are shared" (Simonin et al., 2016). A relationship under coordination is more formal than cooperation, in which more precise task assignments and specific protocols could be established among the entities. There is some shared risk, yet the function and most of the authority of the organizations does not change significantly (Seymour, 2000). A successful example is "coordinated community response" to domestic violence. In Minnesota, in implementing a coordinated community response program, the basic infrastructure of the agencies involved in domestic violence case processing has been modified, and written

**Coordination:** formal relationships around specific efforts or programs. Organizational resources are made available to partner organizations and rewards are shared. (Simonin et al., 2016)

procedures, policies, and protocols governing the intervention and prosecution of criminal domestic violence assault cases were developed. All participating agencies agreed to identify, analyze, and find solutions to their collective intervention goals (Thomas et al., 2011). Further details of the coordinated community response will be discussed later in this chapter.

## Collaboration

**Collaboration:**
a durable and pervasive relationship between two (or more) organizations that results in a new structure and shared mission.

"**Collaboration** usually involves a more durable and pervasive relationship between two (or more) organizations that results in a new structure and shared mission" (Simonin et al., 2016). Collaboration will produce something new through the relationships of organizations. Often, collaborations aim to achieve specifically defined and measurable objectives and outcomes (Simonin et al., 2016). However, given such a sophisticated working relationship, collaborations require extensive time and energy to develop a formal structure and follow the established protocols (Seymour, 2000). Resources are pooled or jointly secured for a longer-term effort. An example of a fruitful collaboration is the Industry Employment Initiative (IEI), an Australian-based response to chronic unemployment that includes the CEOs of Social Ventures Australia, the Brotherhood of St. Laurence, Jesuit Social Services, and Mission Australia. The contributions of each organization are directed toward a collective effort to address the affected disadvantaged populations. In working collaboratively beyond an individual organization, there is strength and effectiveness that could not otherwise be achieved (Simonin et al., 2016).

### Table 14.1   Elements of the 3Cs

|  | Cooperation | Coordination | Collaboration |
|---|---|---|---|
| **Nature of relationship** | Informal arrangement | Semiformal partnerships | Formalized partnerships |
| **Commitment** | Low commitment | Moderate commitment | High commitment |
| **Time frame** | Short term | Longer term | Long term |
| **Resource investment** | Resources are separate, and investment is minimal. | Resources are acknowledged and possibly available for a specific project. Investment is moderate. | Resources are pooled or jointly secured. Major investment by each organization. |
| **Authority and accountability** | Rests solely with individual organizations | Retained by original organizations, but some sharing of leadership and control | Transfer to new unit |
| **Involvement** | Network and share information | Some joint planning | Joint planning and delivery |

As you can see, cooperation requires the least involvement and investment for an organization, whereas collaboration is the most complex and sophisticated relationship. Other forms of relationships include partnerships, coalitions, and multidisciplinary teams, which are often used in nonprofits and government agencies.

## Partnership

A **partnership** is "a collaborative relationship between entities to work toward shared objectives through a mutually agreed division of labor" (World Bank, 1998, p. 5). Having shared leadership via transparent decision-making processes, a partnership makes it possible to build consensus and resolve conflicts among agencies. A success-ful partnership must have a clear understanding of individual members' accountability and responsibilities regarding the division of labor and receive communication from members through an effective feedback system, consequently improving the coordi-nation of policies, programs, and service delivery, and resulting in better outcomes (Compassion Capital Fund National Resource Center, 2010).

The development of a partnership could have four stages: forming, storming, norming, and performing. The initial stage of building the partnership is forming. That is followed by open and frank discussions as to the purpose and goals of the partner-ship, or storming. As agreement on the purpose and goals coalesces, norming occurs. And the final stage is performing, or the partnership actually carrying out the defined purpose and goals (Compassion Capital Fund National Resource Center, 2010). The criminal justice partnership often takes place with the university, criminal justice, and community sectors coming together to develop an innovative research project to resolve community issues.

> **Partnership:** a collaborative relationship between entities to work toward shared objectives through a mutually agreed division of labor (World Bank, 1998, p. 5)

## Coalition

A **coalition** is a grouping of organizations aligned to achieve a set of goals. The partici-pating organizations have determined that their collective efforts can be more effective than individual approaches. There are multiple types of coalitions: a formal coalition, a semiformal coalition, an informal coalition, and group networks. In a formal coalition, the organization would apply for and operate under 501(c)(3) status, a federal structure for nonprofit entities. With a semiformal coalition, the member groups might provide resources to the organization on an in-kind basis perhaps sharing the leadership roles. The informal coalition is probably the most prominent structure, whereby a convening group coordinates the organization on behalf of the member groups and takes respon-sibility for administration and leadership. Group networks are less formalized and typi-cally serve as an informational hub, with member groups sharing information on issues of relevance to the coalition.

A coalition serves many functions relative to drawing attention to the common objectives of the collective membership through enhanced communication, education, and calls to action. The collaborative engagement typically makes the coalition more efficient and effective in achieving its objectives than any member group could be it on its own (Grobman, 1999). The Coalition Against Trafficking in Women (CATW) (http://www.catwinternational.org) is a New York–based nongovernmental organization that

> **Coalition:** a grouping of organizations aligned to achieve a set of goals. The participating organizations have determined that their collective efforts can be more effective than individual approaches

## California Elder Justice Coalition (CEJC)

*"Promoting policy and practice that improve the lives of vulnerable and abused adults in California."*

The California Elder Justice Coalition (CEJC) is the only multidisciplinary statewide network for elder justice. It was developed in 2008. Its goals are to provide a voice from the field to guide elder justice policy development; create a critical mass that is needed to elevate elder justice into the consciousness of policy makers; provide policy makers, advocates, and stakeholders with streamlined, nonpartisan, and interdisciplinary information; explore problems and promising solutions; and provide opportunities for information sharing and consensus building (http://www.elderjusticecal.org).

The CEJC consists of a wide variety of partnerships of criminal justice agencies and social services at the state and national levels, including prosecutors, departments of aging and adult services, disability rights organizations, public and private agencies, and researchers.

Since the CEJC was established, it has actively coordinated conferences and affected elder policies. Some examples are as follows:

*Hosted California's first elder justice summit in 2010 and the From Policy to Practice Elder Justice Summit in 2013.

*Produced *Improving California's Response to Elder Abuse, Neglect, and Exploitation: A Blueprint.*

*Explored leading issues through special projects and events, including the development of the Educating Elder Justice Professionals about Long-Term Services and Supports Action Plan.

*Represented California's elder justice network and stakeholders at state and national policy forums and hearings.

(California Elder Justice Coalition. (2016). From blueprint to benchmarks: Building a framework for elder justice (p. 75). Retrieved from https://www.ccoa.ca.gov/docs/Publications/CCoAPublications/CEJC_From_Blueprint_to_Benchmarks_2016.pdf)

---

**Multidisciplinary Team (MDT):** multidisciplinary teams include, but are not limited to, personnel with a background in law enforcement, child protective services, juvenile counseling and adolescent mental health, and domestic violence (Wasserman, 2005). Under a multidisciplinary team, each discipline provides information relevant to the case, and the ultimate decision is made by one person

works to end human trafficking and the commercial sexual exploitation of women and children worldwide. The activities of the CATW include drafting and advocating for new policy and legislation at the local, national, and international levels to prevent women and girls from becoming victims of human trafficking; raising awareness about the root causes of human trafficking; serving as expert witnesses in court; and conducting seminars and briefings with parliamentarians and lawmakers (Coalition Against Trafficking in Women, 2014).

## Multidisciplinary Teams

A **multidisciplinary team (MDT)** approach can be seen originally in federal legislation, or Public Law 101-630, the Indian Child Protection and Family Violence Prevention Act, which mandated the establishment of MDTs. Section 3209(e) of the act states that each multidisciplinary team established under this section shall include, but not be limited to, personnel with a background in law enforcement, child protective services, juvenile counseling and adolescent mental health, and domestic violence

(Wasserman, 2005). The difference between *multiple* disciplinary and *inter*disciplinary is that under a multidisciplinary team, each discipline provides information relevant to the case, and the ultimate decision is made by one person. In contrast, under an interdisciplinary team, professionals from a wide variety of disciplines such as physicians, nurses, social workers, pharmacists, chaplains, and others share information and decisions are made collectively (Nerenberg, 2008).

# Five Steps of Collaborative Processes

We have seen various ways that agencies and professionals work together. The next level is to understand the steps to create a team and make it workable. Brandl et al. (2007) illustrate the five steps of team processes that lead to a team's success. These stages are planning, formation, performing the work, evaluation, and sustaining the efforts. One must be of aware what has to be done at each stage and who should be involved in those processes.

## Planning

Collaborative efforts could emerge for various reasons. The planning stage includes identifying a shared vision, conducting a needs assessment, and determining the purpose. The first task is to create a vision, which represents the comprehensive ideas of what the team wants to achieve. The discussion about vision can help the organizations better understand the needed resources and changes to achieve the vision. The second step is to conduct a needs assessment. This would include collecting information about the case examples, trends, and analysis of the target population. Another way to gather information is to conduct focus groups or surveys to get input from the target population. Once the base data are collected, the next step is to call a meeting to invite people to share the findings. The discussion might be on the gaps between services and needs, which could lead to possible changes in the participating organizations' work to address the gaps. The meeting could also address possible types of collaboration and who should be on the team in order to achieve the goals.

## Formation

The second stage is formation, which involves selecting key persons, defining team goals, developing collaborative agreements, and setting policies and procedures. The selection of the team members should be based on the vision and purpose of the team, which is determined at the initial stage. Such members would be derived from, but not limited to, criminal justice agencies, health services, social services, and victim advocates. In addition, certain professions with particular skill sets and expertise could become ad hoc members for specific cases. Once key members are identified, the team must define members' roles, clarify goals, establish processes, and establish standards and methods to proceed. The team structure could be formal or informal. The formal group requires selecting leaders, establishing operating rules, formalizing procedures, and operating as

Figure 14.1   Five Steps of Collaborative Processes

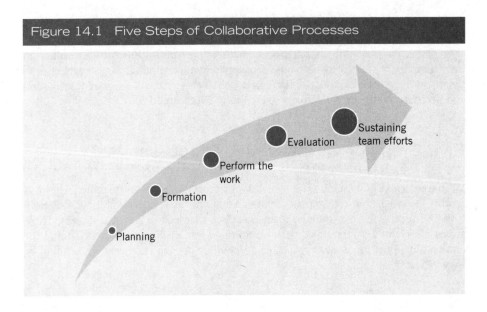

a permanent body. Collaborative agreements could be written in the form of a memoran-
dum of understanding (MOU), which is a common practice. A study of MDTs indicates
that more than half of the respondents had developed an MOU (Nerenberg, 2008). At
this point, it is important for the members to clarify the roles of each member and
develop policies and procedures. The members will build relationships and trust and
should be aware of the resources available to them.

## Perform the Work

After the formation stage, the actual work can begin. Relevant cases will be discussed in
detail, and the team will develop the intervention plans. Yet, the team should have set
boundaries and limits and determine how to make, record, and monitor any decisions that
are adopted. The members should establish a regular meeting time and location. Also, it is
important to decide how and who will create the agenda, how and to whom materials will
be exchanged, and how members will communicate during and between meetings. The use
of technology, such as a website, e-mail, virtual storage, Facebook, teleconferencing, and
webinars could enhance the level of communication among members, but an appropriate
level of confidentiality must be respected. The decision-making process needs to be clarified in the by-laws. For example, a decision could be made by a formal vote or arrived at by
consensus. If a vote is taken, the decision could be based on unanimity or a majority vote.

## Evaluation

Evaluation is important for the team to know whether the collaborative efforts are actually working. Also, evaluation will help improve the program and discover unintended
side effects. There are two types of evaluation. One is process evaluation, which is an

assessment of whether a program was implemented as intended, and the other is an outcome (impact) assessment, which determines whether a program has achieved its intended results. Before conducting an outcome assessment, an Evaluability Assessment (EA) must be completed. An EA is "the systematic process that helps identify whether program evaluation is justified, feasible, and likely to provide useful information" (Juvenile Justice Evaluation Center, 2003, p. 5). Other useful research could include a client satisfaction survey, which identifies the areas that need additional services. It is always a good idea to seek the external reviewers to assess if the program is working. One way is to partner with universities.

## Sustaining Team Efforts

It is inevitable that teams lose interest and processes slip over time. As seen in a prior stage, an evaluation study is one of the best ways to rethink the purpose of a collaboration, its accomplishments, and areas that needed to be addressed. Furthermore, sustaining team efforts might require new members, innovative ideas, and trainings. Trainings and workshops by new members could help educate existing members and motivate them on keeping involved with the processes. Disseminating the findings in public meetings and via a website would help the public be aware of the efforts and attract volunteers to join the efforts.

# Advantages of Collaborative Working Relationships

Victims, professionals, organizations, and society could benefit from collaborative working relationships. Victims will be able to access more information and have multiple needs addressed in the early stages of intervention. It could reduce victims' burden of duplicate and repetitive interviews. This is particularly beneficial for child victims. For example, many MDTs conduct joint forensic interviews whereby an interviewer talks to the child and other investigators watch via a one-way mirror or a closed-circuit TV (Jones et al., 2005). Reducing the number of forensic interviews helps child victims perceive the investigative experience as less harmful (Cronch et al., 2006) and is particularly beneficial for child victims who have been severely traumatized (Faller, Cordisco Steele, & Nelson-Gardell, 2010). The proper interventions with victims ultimately improve the quality of life of the victims and reduce revictimization (Brandl et al., 2007).

Collaboration would be beneficial for the professionals in criminal justice agencies and for victim advocates. By collaborating with other agencies, professionals could gain knowledge beyond their own discipline and, in return, they could educate other members regarding their expertise in the field. Collaborative work also helps reduce burnout, territorial disputes, and workload disparities by sharing information and getting feedback from others (Brandl et al., 2007). It could increase the safety of professionals partnering with law enforcement when they make home visits and house calls. Furthermore, having the participation of multiple agencies makes it difficult for perpetrators to retaliate against a particular individual (Quinn & Heisler, 2004).

Collaborative work also benefits the organizations. First, it could enhance organizational efficiency and cost saving by the creation of economies of scale and shared resources. The opinions from experts in different fields could result in better conclusions while reducing unnecessary time and money to investigate cases (Brandl et al., 2007). Furthermore, it could improve the acquisition of information. For example, physicians could make accurate assessments and proper intervention plans with input from victim advocates and social service workers. In terms of elder abuse cases, adult protective services can better address the needs of clients by obtaining information from a wide variety of agencies. Those agencies would include medical and mental health professionals, victim advocates specializing in domestic violence and sexual assault, law enforcement, prosecution officials, and civil lawyers (Brandl et al., 2007). Ultimately, collaboration helps advance organizations' stated missions more successfully.

Finally, the broader societal benefits cannot be ignored. Effective interventions would reduce recidivism, thereby providing protection to the public. Medical costs would be reduced when medical professionals improve the health profile of victims and safety plans, resulting in less repeated hospitalization. Also, new ideas and innovative programs could emerge through networking and shared information, and, ultimately, those could become a driving force to improve public policy and social and systems change (Brandl et al., 2007).

## Challenges to Successful Working Relationships

In establishing fruitful working relationships, it is important to understand the challenges to achieving such success.

Seymour (2000) outlines these challenges as follows:

1. *Lack of a shared vision or mission.* Working together toward a common goal that is clearly enunciated and understood by all parties enhances the likelihood of successfully achieving that goal.

2. *Lack of agreement about the problem or issue to be addressed.* All of the stakeholders need to be on the same page relative to the concern being addressed.

3. *Lack of incremental successes on the pathway to an ultimate goal.* Often, a larger goal can seem unattainable without indicators of smaller successes en route to the ultimate goal.

4. *Egos.* Stakeholders must be cognizant of the need to participate collaboratively, without a single party or faction trying to control or dominate the effort.

5. *Lack of diversity among group members working toward a common goal.* Diverse and differing viewpoints are an asset to collaborative efforts. If all the parties are identical, then the opportunity for innovation is greatly reduced.

6. *Not having the "right players" at the table*. It is important to have representation from all of the stakeholders to a particular issue.

7. *Lack of understanding and implementation of change management techniques*. Many collaborative efforts are instigated to encourage some type of change. Once that change is identified and implemented, it should be refined and institutionalized.

8. *Lack of resources*. An adequate allocation of resources must be provided to sufficiently address the problem at hand.

9. *Lack of measures to evaluate success*. The objectives should be measurable and monitored.

10. *Lack of understanding about victim trauma, rights, and needs*. With respect to victim trauma, rights, and needs, sufficient understanding of each element and training with respect to addressing the concerns must be sufficiently addressed.

Working to minimize the impact of these challenges on collaborative efforts will ultimately benefit the effectiveness of the relationships.

## Service Delivery Models

There are various service delivery models that have different origins, ideologies, and approaches. These models have some similarities and distinct features. The models also differ in terms of their focus and goals. Knowing the benefits and limitations of each model helps organizations better craft services and interventions. Three prominent victim-service models—the domestic violence prevention model, the public health model, and the family preservation model—are highlighted below.

## Domestic Violence Prevention Model

The domestic violence prevention model is rooted in the domestic violence movement, which coincided with the rise in influence of national grassroots women's advocacy organizations such as the National Coalition Against Domestic Violence, the National Organization of Victim's Assistance (NOVA), and the National Clearinghouse for the Defense of Battered Women. These organizations exerted political pressure to make changes in laws and played a prominent role in the passage of the Violence Against Women Act (VAWA) as part of Title VII of the Violent Crime Control and Law Enforcement Act (Pub. L. No. 103-322) in 1994 (Wallace, 1998).

The federal government moved to turn the VAWA legislation into a functioning grants program. The Office of Justice Programs within the Department of Justice administers these grants as the STOP (i.e., Services, Training, Officers, and Prosecutors) Violence Against Women program (Urban Institute, 1999). Grants have been used to train law enforcement officers and prosecutors; develop, train, or expand specialized units of law enforcement officers and prosecutors; develop and implement more effective police and prosecution policies, protocols, orders, and services; develop, install, or expand data collection and communication systems; develop, enlarge, or strengthen victim service programs; develop, enlarge, or strengthen programs to address stalking; and develop, enlarge, or strengthen programs to help Indian tribes (Urban Institute, 1999).

Domestic violence interventions operate under an empowerment model (Nerenberg, 2008), which addresses the power imbalance observed at both the micro and macro levels. The microlevel approach addresses the needs and problems of individuals, whereas the focus of the macro level is group and institutional changes. Specifically, at the micro level, the focus is on empowering victims in the following ways:

- *Education:* Help victims understand the nature of domestic violence.

- *Support groups:* Facilitate a help-seeking process and develop support groups in which members could learn from each other's experiences and expand social support networks.

- *Safety plans:* Develop safety planning—for example, where to go in an emergency—and develop a list of resources.

- *Shelters:* Provide a safe place to stay.

- *Counseling:* Provide counseling to reduce fear and self-blaming and address posttraumatic stress disorder (PTSD).

- *Advocacy:* Provide assistance with victims' rights, and meet the needs for their daily life, as well as support court-related needs and services including civil order protection.

- *Financial resources:* Achieve financial self-sufficiency.

Macro strategies address underlying gender inequalities and discrimination. Such approaches address advocating for equal rights, the end to discrimination, and adequate resources. They also include a stronger police response to domestic violence. Criminal justice responses include mandatory arrest policies, no-drop policies, evidence-based prosecution, vertical prosecution, and allowing evidence to be admitted under exceptions to the hearsay rule (Nerenberg, 2008).

The changing perspectives on domestic violence were greatly influenced by the feminist movement. Even though intimate partner abuse is the leading cause of injuries to females (Campbell, 2002; Jewkes, 2002), the response in the criminal justice system was long ignored. Domestic violence was treated as a private matter; therefore, criminal justice agencies tended not to get involved in such issues. As a result, the police response to spousal abuse was reluctant, and complaints were likely to be ignored (Gelles & Cornell, 1990). The movement raised awareness of domestic violence as a serious crime and of the role of gender and power relationships in adequately understanding the root causes of domestic violence.

Yet, the challenge remains to see domestic violence through a feminist lens. Yllö (2005) argues that the feminist perspective fails to note that the issues surrounding domestic violence are intertwined with gender, race/ethnicity, and class, therefore requiring a much more diverse perspective. Another area that has been given insufficient attention is partner violence within the LGBTQ community, which has been understudied despite the fact that violence among same-sex couples is as serious as that among heterogeneous couples (Tjaden & Thoennes, 2000; Messinger, 2011). Also, the issue of women's violence toward men has been raised by the prominent scholar Murray Straus. Straus (2005) cited family conflict studies that showed approximately equal rates of assaults reported by women and men. However, the available resources for men are significantly limited.

## Public Health Model

The public health model offers three approaches—primary, secondary, and tertiary preventions—aimed at reducing diseases and other health risks and social problems. **Primary prevention** focuses on preventing or eliminating diseases or injuries before they happen. This can be done with education about healthy lifestyles. **Secondary prevention** is done by the early detection and treatment of disease or an injury. An example is regular checkups to identify and treat disease for those who have risk factors. **Tertiary prevention** stops problems that are already present, softens the impact of an ongoing illness or injury that has a lasting effect, and reduces the likelihood of recurrence.

These preventive steps are used in the criminal justice and juvenile justice systems. For example, primary prevention programs address juveniles before they manifest themselves as criminals. Examples of such programs are child skills training, after-school recreation, juvenile mentoring programs, and job training. Secondary prevention programs provide counseling services for youth and adults who are at risk for violating the law. Finally, tertiary prevention programs would mandate aftercare programs for those who are being released from prison or a detention center (Siegel & Welsh, 2012).

The public health model originated with the Broad Street pump incident, which was an outbreak of cholera that occurred in London in 1854. This violent and sudden attack caused the deaths of 127 people living in or around Broad Street in its first three days. The death toll reached 500 within 10 days. A physician, Dr. John Snow, identified the source of the outbreak as polluted water from the Broad Street pump and convinced city leaders to remove the pump handle. Unlike his colleagues, who were focusing on treating the cholera patients, Dr. Snow's approach was "preventive intervention" by figuring out the cause of the epidemic and addressing the problem for the entire community (Nerenberg, 2008).

Another important milestone has been advances in epidemiology. Epidemiology is "the study of the distribution and determinants of health-related states or events (including disease), and the application of this study to the control of diseases and other health problems" (World Health Organization, n.d.). Researchers use different statistical analyses to describe the patterns, characteristics, and risk factors associated with disease. Such discoveries help health practitioners develop new methods of prevention. For example, preventions could include educating the public about how the diseases are transmitted and providing immunizations for at-risk groups. The discovery of the relationship between lung cancer and smoking led to antismoking campaigns. Later, a public health approach was applied to social problems including domestic violence (Dahlberg & Krug, 2002).

**Primary prevention:** the efforts that focus on preventing or eliminating diseases or injuries before they happen. This can be done with education about a healthy lifestyle.

**Secondary prevention:** an intervention that addresses the early detection and treatment of a disease or an injury. An example is a regular checkup to identify and treat disease for those who have risk factors

**Tertiary prevention:** an intervention that addresses the problems that are already present, softens the impact of an ongoing illness or injury that has a lasting effect, and reduces the likelihood of recurrence

The public health model is a good approach for crime prevention. Also, successful campaigns have become the driving force behind changes to the social system. One good example of a successful public health campaign is Mothers Against Drunk Drivers (MADD), which successfully changed public perceptions about drunken driving as a crime rather than an accident (Masters et al., 2010). Founded by a mother whose daughter was killed by a drunk driver, MADD supports drunk and drugged driving victims and survivors and advocates for laws and policy changes, which have resulted in increased penalties for drunk drivers. Yet, preventive approaches are politically vulnerable as such programs are more likely to be terminated when resources are scarce (Nerenberg, 2008).

## Family Preservation Model

The term *family preservation* was introduced specifically to designate a particular kind of intervention, an Intensive Family Preservation Services (IFPS) program that follows a model invented in Washington State in the mid-1970s (Wexler, 2005). In general, the family preservation model assumes that the most effective way to prevent child abuse and neglect is to work with families rather than removing children from their homes or separating them from family members (Kelly & Blythe, 2000). The theory of the family preservation model is based on the family system theory, which assumes that each member of a family is interdependent and will respond to expected roles, which are determined by relationship agreements (Nerenberg, 2008). Under this model, practitioners assist families in understanding their dynamics and changes by discussing problems, family duties, and tasks. Practitioners develop service plans to reduce stress, resolve conflict, support families, and monitor risk by building on family strengths (Nerenberg, 2008). Advocates of family preservation argue that the approach is not only more humane but also safer than foster care most of the time (Wexler, 2005).

For family preservation to be safe and effective, careful screening is required. For example, Nerenberg (2008) summarized the criteria developed by Bergeron as follows (p. 71):

- Small caseloads

- Several clients within a family

- Providing intensive, short-term treatment to families within their homes to develop a complete picture of the abusive situation, build trust, and avoid contributing to the families' stress

- A "strengths perspective," which assumes that clients and their families have the ability to change and are important partners in developing solutions

- The use of informal and formal services to reduce family stress, increase caregivers' skills, and manage conflict, including providing or connecting families with appropriate community services

- Ongoing monitoring of the abusive home to ensure abuse is not recurring

- Education in caregiving and conflict management skills

- Flexible and creative practice approaches that use experimentation and improvisation

The benefit of applying the family preservation model is its flexibility. It acknowledges the critical role of each family member in resolving conflicts, which is particularly important for rural areas where resources are scarce. The goal of the model is to keep families together; it can be more humane and less costly than foster care. Furthermore, Wexler (2005) said that family preservation is more child-centered and is safer than foster care for "*most* children *most* of the time" (emphasis in the original; p. 317). The author argues that foster care programs create not only emotional harm to children but also result in increased deaths of children. "Foster care panics" refer to a series of incidents that occurred in Illinois in 1993, New York City in 1996, and Florida in 1999, whereby deaths increased among children "known to the system" (i.e., existence of a record of the child in the CPS database; Wexler, 2005, p. 320).

Yet, some prominent scholars such as Gelles (2005) have expressed concerns about the family preservation approach. He indicated that the model is well intended, but, in reality, if a family has abused or neglected a child, it is difficult to help such a family and assure the safety of a child. In his view, "child safety, child welfare, a child reaching his or her developmental potential, and permanency" (p. 337) are the priorities over a child-centered perspective.

## Examples of Collaborative Efforts

There is no doubt that collaboration is an essential component in assisting crime victims. The Vision 21 strategic initiative sees effective collaboration in the 21st century as moving beyond informal partnerships and increasingly multijurisdictional linkages (U.S. Department of Justice, Office of Justice Programs, Office for Victims of Crime, 2013). An example of such a new model can be observed in Massachusetts where the Building Partnerships for the Protection of Persons with Disabilities Initiative (BPI) aims to protect individuals with disabilities (U.S. Department of Justice, Office of Justice Programs, Office for Victims of Crime, 2013). Other well-established collaborations are the Coordinated Community Response (CCR), the Sexual Assault Response Team (SART), the Domestic Violence Fatality Review Team (DVFRT), and the One-Stop Centers.

### Coordinated Community Response (CCR)

The **Coordinated Community Response (CCR)** is an intervention strategy that was developed by the Domestic Abuse Intervention Project (DAIP) in Duluth, Minnesota, during the 1980s. CCR programs involve collaboration between community and criminal justice agencies to coordinate victim advocacy to support victims and their families and hold batterers accountable. Participating agencies include law enforcement

**Coordinated Community Response (CCR):** collaboration between community and criminal justice agencies to coordinate victim advocacy to support victims and their families and hold batterers accountable. Participating agencies include law enforcement agencies, advocates, healthcare providers, child protection services, local businesses, the media, employers, and clergy (Home of Duluth Model, http://www .theduluthmodel. org/about.html)

agencies, advocates, healthcare providers, child protection services, local businesses, the media, employers, and clergy (Home of Duluth Model, http://www.theduluthmodel.org/about.html).

The collaboration is particularly important for victims of intimate partner violence (IPV), who face multidimensional challenges. Previous studies found that victims of IPV suffer from multiple psychological difficulties including depression (Anderson, Saunders, Yoshihama, Bybee, & Sullivan, 2003), anxiety (Coffey, Leitenberg, Henning, Bennett, & Jankowski, 1996), substance abuse (Lipsky, Caetano, Field, & Larkin, 2005; Nathanson, Shorey, Tirone, & Rhatigan, 2012), and posttraumatic stress disorder (PTSD; Lawyer, Ruggiero, Resnick, Kilpatrick, & Saunders, 2006; Nathanson et al., 2012), as well as physical injuries (Shorey, Tirone, & Stuart, 2014). As a result of victimization, the healthcare costs for IPV victims are much higher than those for nonvictims (Rivara et al., 2006). Furthermore, the victims of IPV tend to lack resources, particularly adequate residential arrangements (Williams, 1998) and, consequently, economically depend on the abusers (Johnson, 1992).

Traditional efforts to address the challenges of the victims of IPV were temporary shelters and counseling, which were not adequate to meet the needs of the victims. Given the urgent necessity of community coordination, the U.S. Congress in 1995 passed legislation to help fund nonprofit organizations in establishing collaborative projects (Post, Klevens, Maxwell, Shelley, & Ingram, 2010). In response to this legislation, the Centers for Disease Control and Prevention funded six CCR projects in 1996, and additional funding was provided for a total of 10 projects in 1999 and 2000 (Post et al., 2010).

Theoretically, comprehensive and seamless services to the victims of IPV would ultimately reduce or eliminate overall intimate partner violence (Shorey et al., 2014). However, an assessment of the impact on IPV showed that there was no significant impact of CCRs on IPV rates in any of the 10 sites after controlling for age, marital status, income, and education (Post et al., 2010). Other studies also failed to demonstrate positive outcomes for victims (Shorey et al., 2014). For these reasons, Kreuter, Lezin, and Young (2000) explain that collaborative mechanisms might not be suitable for carrying out planning and implementation tasks; perhaps the expectations for change in health status or systems are unrealistic within the time and resource constraints, or it is possible that health status or system changes occur, but it might be difficult to demonstrate scientifically the existence of the cause-effect relationship. Yet, specific components of the CCR show some positive outcomes, and there is a need for further research to determine how the effectiveness of CCRs is associated with the essential processes or factors of a collaborative effort and the external conditions (Post et al., 2010).

## Sexual Assault Response Team (SART)

A **Sexual Assault Response Team (SART)** serves sexual assault victims by building, expanding, formalizing, and maintaining strong interagency responses to sexual violence. SART models could be a more informal cooperative partnership to a more formalized coordinated and multidisciplinary response at the local, regional, state, tribal, or territory levels (National Sexual Violence Resource Center, 2011). Core members typically include victim advocates, law enforcement officers, forensic medical examiners, forensic laboratory personnel, and prosecutors. Additional team members could

---

**Sexual Assault Response Team (SART):** serves sexual assault victims by building, expanding, formalizing, and maintaining strong interagency responses to sexual violence. SART models could be a more informal cooperative partnerships to more formalized coordinated and multidisciplinary responses at the local, regional, state, tribal, or territory levels (National Sexual Violence Resource Center, 2011)

include dispatchers, emergency medical technicians, correctional staff, culturally specific organization representatives, sex offender management professionals, policy makers, federal grant administrators, faith-based providers, and civil and victims' rights attorneys (Office of Justice Programs, 2011).

For example, the North Carolina Coalition Against Sexual Assault adopted SARTs and **Sexual Assault Nurse Examiners** (SANEs) throughout the state in 1997. SANEs are the trained nurses who conduct a forensic exam and provide comprehensive care to sexual assault victims. To encourage the reporting of rape cases and remove the barriers to prosecuting such cases, the program provides internal information-sharing and training, raises community awareness of available resources, enhances community commitment to victims/survivors of sexual assault, develops the CCR/SART response protocols, and partially reviews cases (North Carolina Coalition Against Sexual Assault, http://www.nccasa.org/projects/sart).

The evaluation of the SART program indicated that SART members believe the SART increases the level of communication and information exchange. For example, an evaluation of the SART team in an urban hospital emergency department indicated that the SART program resulted in improved healthcare for survivors of sexual assault and improved relations with the Special Victims Unit, the police, and the prosecutor's office (Moreno-Walton, Ryan, Nunez, & Alexander, 2012). Regarding the improvement in relationships among responders in three pilot sites in Illinois, the responders first shared their responses to sexual assault, then exchanged information on their respective systems, and finally developed a collective methodology for improved responses. However, another study suggested that SARTs did not make a difference in conviction rates (Greeson & Campbell, 2013).

Existing research suggests that providing technical assistance on effective collaborative practices is a key to making collaborations successful (Roussos & Fawcett, 2000). As such, many state and national organizations provide resources such as trainings, written materials including toolkits and manuals, and technical assistance to help communities effectively develop and maintain SARTs.

## Domestic Violence Fatality Review Team (DVFRT)

The **Domestic Violence Fatality Review Team (DVFRT)** represents the collective efforts of multiple agencies and multidisciplinary organizations to prevent future domestic violence fatalities, ensure the safety of domestic violence victims and their children, and hold the perpetrators accountable (Websdale, 2001). The teams review and analyze domestic violence homicide cases to uncover basic knowledge about causes. Other cases that might be reviewed by the team include deaths due to suicides, accidents, injuries, pregnancies, HIV, women killing men, kidnappings, child deaths, deaths of prostitutes, sexual assault murders, homeless women, and "near misses" to broaden their knowledge and capabilities (Wilson & Websdale, 2006).

The first DVFRT was created after the tragic murder of Veena Caron by her husband, Joseph Caron, in 1990. Even though Veena had obtained a restraining order, Mr. Caron violated the order and made several attempts to kidnap his son at school. Eventually, he killed Veena at the school in front of teachers and schoolchildren and then committed suicide. The incident created alarm as to the absence of a coordinated response to domestic

**Sexual Assault Nurse Examiners (SANE):** trained nurses who conduct a forensic exam and provide comprehensive care to sexual assault victims

**Domestic Violence Fatality Review Team (DVFRT):** the collective efforts of multiple agencies and multidisciplinary organizations to prevent future domestic violence fatalities and ensure the safety of domestic violence victims and their children and hold the perpetrators accountable (Websdale, 2001)

violence, and in 1991, the Commission on the Status of Women of San Francisco asked for a multiagency, multidisciplinary public investigation of the case. The major findings from the investigation were four major service gaps for battered women: access, communication/coordination, data collection, and training (Commission on the Status of Women City and County of San Francisco, 1991). Given the recommendations, a coordinated interprofessional response system to domestic violence was created, which became a national model for more than 82 DVFRTs nationwide (Wilson & Websdale, 2006).

As of 2012, about half of the states had an active statewide team (Florida State University Institute of Family Violence Studies, 2012). However, the memberships, collaborations, and goals differ by states. For example, in Nevada, a bill was introduced in 2011 to start a domestic violence fatality review team in response to the high fatality rate in the state. The Review Team in Minnesota was founded by Watch, a nonprofit court monitoring organization. In New York, the Office of the Prevention of Domestic Violence has partnered with the National Fatality Review Initiatives to conduct examinations of domestic violence–related homicides. The Texas Council on Family Violence has collaborated with the Houston Police Department to host a review of domestic violence–related fatalities (Florida State University Institute of Family Violence Studies, 2012).

The National Domestic Violence Fatality Review Initiative has good resources such as reports, videos, and webinars for organizations interested in learning more about the DVFRTs. Yet, there is a need for empirical research on the intermediary process indicators and long-term outcomes of the DVFRT process (Storer, Lindhorst, & Starr, 2013).

## One-Stop Centers (Family Justice Center)

**One-stop centers,** or family justice centers, allow crime victims to receive various services, including health, welfare, counseling, and legal services in one location. In the United States, the President's Family Justice Center Initiatives funded $20 million in federal grants to create such centers for victims of domestic violence, sexual assault, and elder abuse (U.S. Department of Justice, 2007). One of the prominent centers is the San Diego Family Justice Center (https://www.sandiego.gov/sandiegofamilyjustice center), where more than 25 agencies provide services in one location. Those men, women, children, and family members who are affected by family violence can visit the center to receive safety, protection from their abuser, legal help, counseling, food, clothing, spiritual support, medical assistance, and other free services from the center's professionals and volunteers (San Diego Family Justice Center, 2018). The San Diego Family Justice Center is located downtown near the location of the collaborative agencies, but in other regions, a possible location for a center is in health facilities.

The following best practices have been identified through program evaluation, focus groups, and client feedback surveys (U.S. Department of Justice, 2007, p. 2):

1. Colocated, multidisciplinary services for victims of family violence and their children increases safety and support.

2. Pro-arrest/mandatory arrest policies in family justice center communities increases accountability for offenders.

3. Policies incidental to arrest/enforcement reduce revictimization of victims.

**One-stop centers:** also referred to as family justice centers, allow crime victims to receive various services, including health, welfare, counseling, and legal services in one location

4. Victim safety/advocacy must be the highest priority in the family justice center service delivery model.

5. Victim confidentiality must be a priority.

6. Offenders must be prohibited from onsite services at centers.

7. Community history of domestic violence specialization increases the success of collaboration in the family justice center model.

8. Strong support from local elected officials and other local and state government policy makers increases the effectiveness and sustainability of family justice centers.

9. Strategic planning is critical to short-term and long-term success in the family justice center service delivery model.

10. Strong/diverse community support increases resources for victims and their children.

## CASE STUDY
### Female Workers Face Rape, Harassment in U.S. Agriculture Industry

The research conducted by FRONTLINE, Univision, the Investigative Reporting Program at the UC Berkeley Graduate School of Journalism, and the Center for Investigative Reporting revealed sexual violence and harassment against female agricultural workers are prominent throughout the United States, yet financial desperation and tenuous immigration status made those females remain silent and accept such working conditions. Even if they want to file a complaint, legal services for low-income clients are limited in rural areas. For example, in California's Central Valley, which is a largely agricultural region, there are only a handful of private and legal aid organizations that would take on these cases. Furthermore, of those females who made complaints, 85% experienced retaliation such as being demoted, fired, or further harassed while their supervisors remained on the job. A regional attorney in San Francisco for the U.S. Equal Employment Opportunity Commission noted that female agricultural workers describe the fields as "the fils de calzon," or "fields of panties," and "the green motel."

Yeung, B., & Rubenstein, G. (2013, June). Female workers face rape, harassment in U.S. agriculture industry. *The Center for Investigating Reporting*. Retrieved from https://www.pbs.org/wgbh/pages/frontline/social-issues/rape-in-the-fields/female-workers-face-rape-harassment-in-u-s-agriculture-industry.

### Question:

1. Learning from successful collaborative efforts in helping victims of domestic violence and other victims, how could local victim advocate agencies support female agricultural workers? Who should be at the table for such a discussion?

# SUMMARY

Numerous collaborative efforts have resulted in better services for victims, more organizational efficiency in service delivery, and better training for practitioners and criminal justice professionals regarding available resources beyond their disciplines. To make a collaboration successful, one must know the various ways to collaborate, including the 3Cs, or cooperation, coordination, and collaboration. Further relationships include partnerships, coalitions, and multidisciplinary teams. Five steps are necessary for a successful collaboration: planning, formation, performing the work, evaluation, and sustaining. Furthermore, one should know the advantages and challenges of

collaboration and the different models to support victims. In this chapter, we have discussed the domestic violence prevention model, the public health model, and the family preservation model. Each model has a different historical background, advantages, and challenges. Some existing collaborative approaches are the CCR, the SART, and the DVFRT. Furthermore, the CEJC has been addressing emerging issues in elder abuse. Yet, many of the programs have been operated under different settings, and there is a need to conduct empirical research to carefully evaluate the effectiveness of the programs and develop best practice models to address the needs of victims.

# KEY WORDS

Coalition  277
Collaboration  276
Cooperation  275
Coordinated community response (CCR)  287
Coordination  275

Domestic violence fatality review team (DVFRT)  289
Multidisciplinary team (MDT)  279
One-stop centers  290
Partnership  277
Primary prevention  285

Secondary prevention  285
Sexual assault nurse examiners (SANE)  289
Sexual assault response team (SART)  288
Tertiary prevention  285

# INTERNET RESOURCES

**National Crime Prevention Council (https://www .ncpc.org)**

The National Crime Prevention Council, founded in 1982, has provided tools that communities can use to learn crime prevention strategies, engage community members, and coordinate with local agencies. The website includes useful resources for homes and neighborhoods, as well as school safety.

**Sane Program Development and Operation Guide (https://www.ovcttac.gov/saneguide)**

The website under the Office for Victims of Crime (OVC) provides a blueprint for nurses and

communities that would like to start a Sexual Assault Nurse Examiner (SANE) program. The guide includes how to develop a partner-centered, trauma-informed SANE program.

**GRANTSPACE (https://grantspace.org)**

The website includes useful resources for non-profit organizations that need to fund-raise, write grants, and collaborate. It provides collections of sample documents, such as cover letters, letters of inquiry, letter of proposals, and proposal budgets. Some of the on-demand trainings are free, and others are available for nominal fees.

# CRITICAL THINKING QUESTIONS

1. Select one of the emerging crime issues in your community, and discuss how the local agencies and community organizations could collaboratively address the issues. Discuss the pros and cons of different collaborative approaches.

2. There is an inherent tension between preserving family and ensuring the safety of an abused or neglected child. Describe the possible scenarios of positive and negative outcomes.

3. Assume you are the director of a local domestic violence shelter. What are some challenges in developing a collaborative relationship with the police department to prevent domestic violence? How would you overcome those obstacles?

4. With the development of technology, there are many new and innovative ways to provide resource information to victims. How could technology improve service delivery, and what are some challenges of using technology?

# 15

# Challenges in
# Victim Services

C rime, and in particular violent crime, is one of the most persistent areas of public concern and attention. The American public receives daily doses of its occurrence and the impact it has on people's lives through stories in print, on television, and in social media (Danis, 2003). While crime and its impact are well documented today, this was not always the case. The plight of crime victims in the United States to be recognized and have access to services following victimization emanates from the energy and growth of social movements during the 1970s. These movements were led and inspired by persons who had personally suffered the effects of victimization and were supported by others who showed empathy and provided insight into advancing the services needed to assist those who had been affected by crime (Young & Stein, 2004). The framework for the acknowledgement and advancement in services offered to victims has also developed from the study of victimology. Victimology, as a scientific discipline, has drawn its knowledge from research from a variety of backgrounds, such as law, social work, nursing, psychology, and medicine (Mawby & Walklate, 1994; Kirchhoff, 2005, 2010; Fattah, 2010). The significance of these social movements and the advancement of victimology have greatly impacted our understanding of the recovery of individuals who have suffered the emotional and psychological trauma, physical injuries, or financial losses of crime. Additionally, the advocacy of these social movements and victim assistance organizations today have changed the way victims are treated in the criminal justice system and the support offered to them. The progression of victims' rights and legislative policy has prompted an increase in services offered to victims at both the state and federal level and within the community. Victim assistance now encompasses a broad range of services designed to aid victims from the commission of the crime until after the case disposition and beyond (Young & Stein, 2004). Services to victims include crisis intervention, family counseling, education, vocational training, legal assistance, and assistance with victim compensation claims (Kuhn & Laird, 2014; Dussich, 2015). Although the developments in victimology and victim assistance have been useful, the lessons learned from victims indicate that there is still much more room for growth and improvement.

## Looking Ahead

Every year, millions of individuals in the United States become victims of crime. Those that are affected have countless needs, which may include medical treatment and counseling. Moreover, the victimization they experience can have a lasting impact on a victim psychologically, physically, and economically (Rutledge, 2011). To survive the aftermath of a crime, individuals and their families may need a variety of social and mental health services. As described above, victim services provide a variety of services from crisis intervention to assistance with the criminal justice system. The availability and types of services available to victims and their families has grown dramatically over the last 40 years. The availability of public funding has also allowed many private and nonprofit agencies to develop and expand their services, encouraging local and state criminal justice agencies to maintain units of crime victim personnel (Danis, 2003; Dussich, 2015). States have even enacted laws requiring all law enforcement and prosecutors' Offices to designate a coordinator of crime victim assistance. As the field has developed and victims' rights and services have been codified, required, and accepted in the criminal justice system, so has the field evolved in terms of expectations, standards, and training (Bostaph & Throndyke, 2017). **Victim assistance** has been described as a "fully-fledged advocacy and service field dedicated to meeting the physical, financial, and psychological needs of victims and their families" (OVC, 1998). According to Underwood (2003), this description provides a mission statement for victim assistance as a profession, a profession that is not restricted to one standard of practitioner, one type of organization, one type of crime victim, or one level of service. However, despite the many advances the field has made regarding services and the standardization of these services, moving forward, victim assistance still faces the issue that many victims receive little or no assistance, with many organizations struggling to only provide baseline services for victims. While many victim assistance organizations want to progress, many argue that there is inadequate funding and a lack of research data to support the efforts and changes needed to progress. In order for victim services to continue to progress, the U.S. Department of Justice, Office of Justice Programs released a report titled *Vision 21 Transforming Victim Services* (2013), detailing recommendations to be considered for the field to progress.

**Victim assistance:** a fully-fledged advocacy and service field dedicated to meeting the physical, financial, and psychological needs of victims and their families (OVC, 1998)

## Improving Strategic Planning

Improving **strategic planning** has been identified as one of the most crucial elements in the field of victim assistance. Research suggests that programs able to address high-level questions of mission, vision, and goals have the greatest social impact (Backer, 2001; Mckinsey & Company, 2001). This is challenging for victim assistance programs who often struggle to just stay open and are often not in a position to define and carry out strategic plans. Boardman and Vining (2000) reiterate this point by stating that many nonprofits are faced with the reality of simply trying to make ends meet at a time when competition for government funds is fierce and continuously increasing. However, research on improving programs for crime victims has continuously shown that many programs lack a comprehensive strategy for assisting crime victims, which often results in a lack of unification and coordination leading to missed opportunities for funding (Taylor, 2015). The *Vision 21: Transforming Victim Services* report (U.S. Department of Justice, Office of Justice Programs, 2013) argues that victim assistance has paid a price for its less-than-unified strategic efforts. Strategic planning is invaluable to identifying more diversified sources of funding. Victim assistance and advocacy groups at the local, state, and national levels need to unite their strategic planning efforts to forge a strong and cohesive national network of victim assistance. There is no one best method for strategic planning in victim assistance, but for certain, strategic planning is crucial for

**Strategic planning:** address high-level questions of mission, vision, and goals having the greatest social impact (Backer, 2001; Mckinsey & Company, 2001)

programs' survival and making sure that those who provide the services and those who need are in the best position to do so (Giffords & Dina, 2004).

## Focusing on Evidence-Based Research

While tremendous advancements have been made in providing services for victims and gaining support for programs by the criminal justice system and policy makers, victim assistance organizations need to turn their attention toward improving their use of practices that have been proven to be effective and reliable for the broad array of victims they serve. Using **evidence-based practices** means using data and research to inform and guide programs that will improve outcomes for individuals, agencies, and communities (Gibel, Carter, & Ramirez, 2016). Most victim assistance organizations focus on providing services to victims and trying to raise awareness in their communities, but do very little, if any, in the way of evaluating the efficacy of their programs. The evaluation of programs and services needs to become an integral part of these organizations. Conducting continual assessment will not only better inform the strategic plan of the organization but also ensure that the programs offered are victim-centered, evidence-based, and accountable (U.S. Department of Justice, Office of Justice Programs, 2013; Gibel et al., 2016).

**Evidence-based practices:** using data and research to inform and guide programs that will improve outcomes for individuals, agencies, and communities (Gibel, Carter, & Ramirez, 2016)

## Integration of Technology

To address the needs of crime victims, numerous and diverse programs have been developed, offering a wide variety of resources specific to individuals' needs. In order to try and compile a comprehensive list of the different types of services and rights offered to victims by state, the Office of Victims of Crime has an interactive website that identifies and categorizes services across the country. While this is one example of the integration of technology to better inform people of the services available, more needs to be done to improve access to information about services, which are often difficult to find (Lim, Greathouse, & Yeung, 2014). In today's networked society, where the demand for new technology and connectivity provides a range of benefits, the field of victim assistance, too, needs to develop a technology infrastructure to increase the profile, accessibility, and responsiveness of programs. It is argued that doing so would resolve some of the issues faced by crime victims and the organizations that serve them (U.S. Department of Justice, Office of Justice Programs, 2013; Lim et al., 2014).

Lim et al. (2014, p. 1-2) detail some of the ways victim assistance agencies could better use technology. To increase access to information, a comprehensive online database of resources needs to be developed, where people can find services that are best suited to their needs and location. Technology, too, can improve an agency's efficiency. Given that many victim service personnel are overloaded and duplicate many of each other's responsibilities, using an electronic case management system instead of a paper system could make internal processes more efficient, along with the sharing of records. Such a system could also be used more broadly, where information can be shared between agencies to improve their effectiveness, ultimately helping to find the right services for victims. While the use of new technology is of paramount importance to the advancement of the field, agencies also need to understand their obligations to confidentiality in accordance with federal and state laws, making sure that information is transferred

# Victim Assistance Programs

## VINE

VINE is a solution that lets victims of crime and other concerned citizens access timely and reliable information regarding offenders. It is offered free of charge to registrants, is completely confidential, and features multiple language support.

Offering peace of mind, the VINE service lets victims call a toll-free number, visit the website, or use the VINELink™ mobile app to anonymously check on an offender's custody status. See https://www.vinelink.com for more information.

securely. Maintaining confidentiality is paramount to preserving the safety, privacy, and trust of those seeking services.

## Funding for Victim Assistance Programs

Stated above, a common challenge for victim assistance programs is often just staying open. Developing strategic plans, using evidence-based practices, incorporating new technologies, and improving the overall accessibility to programs for crime victims all rely heavily on funding. Funding opportunities for programs are not only competitive but complex to apply for and are generally only available for short periods of time (Taylor, 2015; Gibel et al., 2016). As a consequence of limited resources and short funding periods, many programs have reported that they only focus on short-term projects that can be completed within funding periods, as they feel it would not be responsible to start offering services and programs to the community without a guarantee of their continuity (Newmark, 2006). The *Vision 21: Transforming Victim Services Report* (U.S. Department of Justice, Office of Justice, 2013) recommends that agencies and key constituencies need to work together with Congress to revise the funding formula for programs to expand assistance to more crime victims and strengthen the administrative framework to effectively manage funding. By working together to identify ways in which common concerns regarding funding can be addressed, victim service programs and criminal justice system stakeholders may also find ways to maximize the use of existing resources. Addressing funding for assistance programs will strengthen the capacity of organizations to address what we now understand about the impacts of crime on victims, which are often complex and require more sustainable long-term programs. Working to address these recommendations will be challenging and compelling, but it is an important step in prioritizing the needs and goals of victim assistance organizations and those they look to help as the field moves forward and continues to grow.

While these recommendations detail a way for victim services to progress more broadly, the field also must become more knowledgeable about the reach and impact of human trafficking and terrorism, which are crimes not new to the field of victim services but that are becoming increasingly in need of more dedicated services to assist those affected. The next sections will discuss what needs to be done to address the service gaps for these crimes.

# Victim Assistance
# for Human Trafficking Victims

Discussed in more detail in Chapters 9 and 10, human trafficking is a global public health concern. Taking place in virtually every country in the world, it generates billions of dollars in profit at the expense of millions of innocent victims (National Sexual Violence Resource Center [NCVRC], 2012), many of whom suffer from a range of physical and psychological issues resulting from inhumane living conditions, poor sanitation, inadequate nutrition, poor personal hygiene, brutal physical and emotional attacks at the hands of their traffickers, dangerous workplace conditions, occupational hazards, and a general lack of quality health care (CdeBaca & Sigman, 2014; Greenbaum, 2014). Victim assistance organizations play a critical role in responding to victims of human trafficking. By working with local, state, and national law enforcement agencies, many organizations can provide a wide variety of services that include providing safety, food and shelter, training and education, and legal services (NCVRC, 2012). As our knowledge of the problem continues to grow, so does the realization that we need more services to help those that are trafficked. Human trafficking has transformed the nature of crime victimization, which is requiring the field of victim services to respond with programs and practices that are informed and adequate to meet the needs of such a hidden population, who even when receiving help remain vulnerable. This is particularly important when working with undocumented persons who often do everything in their power to avoid contact with the criminal justice system and agencies associated with it for fear of arrest or deportation. For those victims who do receive help and enter the system, too often they encounter a process that is confusing, overwhelming, and at times even traumatizing, doing little to protect against the risk of future victimization (U.S. Department of Justice, Office of Justice, 2013).

Therefore, victim assistance organizations and personnel need to be effectively trained to assist victims of varying cultural backgrounds and who have endured varying levels of trauma. They also need to assist human trafficking victims by being adequately informed on the options for legal assistance for victims, in particular, providing victims information about T-visas and U-visas. A T-visa is a nonimmigrant visa that allows a foreign victim of human trafficking to remain in the United States for up to four years. According to the Department of Health and Human Services (2012), there are several benefits of the T-visa. These include providing foreign victims legal nonimmigrant status in the United States for a period of four years, employment authorization, the possibility of adjusting status to lawful permanent resident, and having immediate family members obtain nonimmigrant status as T-visa derivatives. The U-visa is set aside for victims of certain crimes who have suffered mental or physical abuse and who are helpful to law enforcement or government officials in the investigation or prosecution of criminal activity. Victims who apply for the U-visa receive the same benefits under the same rules that apply to refugees (Broder & Neville, 2015). Information and assistance regarding these visas are crucial for victims of human trafficking who are vulnerable and often encounter language barriers, are separated from family and friends, lack an understanding of U.S. laws, and fear deportation. Other forms of assistance needed to help human trafficking victims are housing, health care, and employment training.

There is little doubt that human trafficking is one of the most prominent human rights issues of our time. While the U.S. government has made progress to improve the antitrafficking response for victims, more needs to be done to ensure services that support the victim in regaining control of their lives and empowering them to make informed decisions about the options available to them.

## Victim Assistance for Victims of Terrorism

Human-caused events such as acts of terrorism are deliberately planned and perpetrated for political, sociocultural, revenge-motivated, or hate-based reasons (Bruce, 2013). Those who are affected—victims, surviving families, and communities—cope not only with the resulting deaths, injuries, and destruction but also with the horrific knowledge that their losses were caused by intentional human malevolence (U.S. Department of Health and Human Services, 2005). The threat of terrorism has increased in recent years in the United States and abroad. These traumatic events also impact first responders, media personnel, government officials, and others whose job-related responsibilities bring them in contact with the disaster's tragic impact. The reality of such violent acts is leading responsible agencies to develop programs and initiatives that support victims of domestic and international terrorism. Stated already, the field of victim services has made tremendous advancements in assisting those affected by crime. However, despite the advancement in services, very little has been done to develop services to assist victims of terrorism. According to the Office for Victims of Crime (2004), when a major disaster is caused by deliberate human acts, sudden and unexpected threat, horror, and destruction inevitably impact innocent and unsuspecting people in the course of their daily routines. The resulting deaths and destruction of property require the development of innovative programs and approaches for assisting victims and their families. Moreover, when rescue and recovery efforts extend over weeks and months, family members endure prolonged uncertainty and an ongoing threat of possible future attacks, which contribute to heightened anxiety and a sense of vulnerability (U.S. Department of Health and Human Services, 2005).

The psychological, physical, and financial effects resulting from an act of terrorism can be significant. The aftereffects of such violence are arguably more severe and longer lasting when the disaster results in a significant number of fatalities, seriously injured victims, and destroyed businesses and homes (U.S. Department of Health and Human Services, 2005; Ruben & Wessley, 2013). Following such violence, many victims and families require a physical need for warmth, safety, rest, food, and shelter; psychological first aid; the need for accurate and timely information about the safety and well-being of loved ones, friends, and coworkers; and the ability to connect with support systems. As a consequence of these reactions, victim service organizations need to be able to cater to these concerns and needs of victims. This requires that organizations develop and implement effective policies and strategies, along with training personnel to respond to such violence that occurs without warning and poses an extreme threat to life and trauma. Responding to the lack of services for victims of terrorism, funding through the Victims of Crime Act (VOCA) has been made available to assist organizations in developing such strategies to assist victims. Funding has been provided to organizations to better assist in disseminating information about resources and services in the community and to provide assistance with compensation claims that help the victims with out-of-pocket expenses, including medical and mental health services, lost wages, and burial expenses (OVC, 2004; Gilbert, 2017). However, despite the move to improve these needed services, many organizations still fall short of assisting with these victims' needs (Gilbert, 2017).

Another challenge victim assistance organizations are faced with when dealing with acts of terrorism is the unfortunate social reactions to minority groups. As many acts of terrorism are perpetrated by specific groups defined by their culture, religion, nationality, politics, or ethnicity, often, already disenfranchised groups are stereotyped and blamed for the violence. This may result in anger and people motivated to act aggressively toward these groups. Such social reactions to these groups following an act of terrorism greatly impacts their ability to access effective and compassionate services. Often victims from these groups fear drawing more attention to themselves or their communities and are deterred from reporting the crime to law enforcement or seeking services (Hook, Murry, & Seymour, 2005). Therefore, it is important that victim assistance organizations work to foster community healing through respectful and equal treatment of all who seek services and actively work to collaborate with community groups developing effective outreach and tools for service providers who serve minority groups.

Discussed already, given the increased threat of acts of terrorism, it is crucial for victim assistance organizations to implement strategies to deal with such events. Understanding the unique issues faced by victims and having effective plans in place that clarify the assistance roles and responsibilities prior to an act of terrorism will greatly assist in victims having access to needed services more quickly in times of great distress.

## International Collaboration and Victim Assistance

As the number of people who live or travel overseas for business, study, or vacation increases, so does the vulnerability to crime increase. As we have become more global and mobile, it is no longer possible to confine victim assistance to the borders of a particular country. Crime and victimization have become transnational, and countries must look beyond their national boundaries to share information, technology, and resources to assist victims and deal with emerging forms of transnational and international crimes (OVC, 1998; Letschert & Groenhuijsen, 2011). While victim-related policies and practices vary by country, there is much to be gained from sharing and exchanging experience at the international level. Globally, interest in the victims' movement is still relatively new, and international recognition of victimology is growing. The growth in

# Victim Assistance Programs

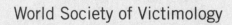

## World Society of Victimology

The World Society of Victimology (WSV) is a not-for-profit, nongovernmental organization with special category consultative status with the Economic and Social Council (ECOSOC) of the United Nations and the Council of Europe. Brought together by a mutual concern for victims, its worldwide membership includes victim assistance practitioners, social scientists, social workers, physicians, lawyers, civil servants, volunteers, university academics of all levels, and students. The purpose of the WSV is to advance victimological research and practices around the world, to encourage interdisciplinary and comparative work and research in this field, and to advance cooperation between international, national, regional and local agencies, and other groups who are concerned with the problems of victims. See http://www .worldsocietyofvictimology.org for more information.

the recognition of victims has been assisted by global initiatives from international organizations such as the United Nations, the World Health Organization, the International Migration Office, Doctors Without Borders, and Amnesty International to name only a few. However, while there is greater awareness of the needs of victims, much still needs to be done to ensure that victims around the world receive consistent and appropriate services. To do this is far from easy, as no victim is like another victim, and they all have different needs.

Therefore, in advancing the access to services for victims, international standards for victim assistance and victims' rights need to be established by encouraging the adoption of the United Nations Declaration of the Basic Principles of Justice for Victims of Crime and Abuse of Power (Dussich & Mundy, 2006). Moreover, standards for those who work with victims need to be established and improved upon, by providing international technical assistance and victim-related training materials, along with developing a database on evidence-based programs (U.S. Department of Justice, Office of Justice, 2013; Gibel et al., 2016). Lastly, as a result of crime, many victims suffer physical and psychological harm and financial loss; compensation programs provide desperately needed financial assistance to help victims pay for some of the costs resulting from crime such as uninsured medical and mental health counseling expenses, lost wages, and funeral expenses. Countries and states within the United States are encouraged to develop or reexamine their compensation and assistance programs to ensure that provisions are made for compensation, restitution, and other assistance in cases involving foreign nationals (U.S. Department of Justice, Office of Justice, 2013; Miers, 2014).

Danieli, Rodley, and Weisaeth (1996, p. 1) write "that traumatic events cause drastic and often tragic changes in people's lives," and while much is being done internationally to alleviate the plight of different kinds of victims, all too often these efforts, whether governmental or nongovernmental, are fragmented and carried out in relative isolation from each other. It is hoped that by using widely dispersed sources of information, governments and nongovernmental organizations can effectively help to reduce victimization and its impact.

# SUMMARY

Victim assistance plays a pivotal role in the aftermath of crime. Following victimization, many victims and their families may need a variety of social and mental health services. Victim assistance organizations help to provide such services that include crisis intervention, supportive counseling, resource mobilization, filing compensation claims, information about the criminal justice system, and employment education (Danis, 2003), all of which help the victim to recover and return to a life as close to normal as possible. The development and advocacy of victim assistance, along with the progression of victims' rights and legislative policy, have led to an increase in services offered to victims at both the state and federal level (Young & Stein, 2004). Moreover, the availability of public funding has meant that many private and nonprofit agencies have been able to develop and expand their services to those in need. As the field has developed, so has its acceptance in the criminal justice system (Bostaph & Throndyke, 2017). However, despite the many advances the field has made regarding services, victim assistance still faces the issue that many victims receive little or no assistance, and many organizations struggle to stay open. Moving forward, addressing issues of planning, using evidence-based research, integrating technology, and improving funding will strengthen the capacity of organizations to provide services to victims and become more sustainable.

Lastly, as crime and victimization have become transnational, countries must look beyond their national boundaries to share information, technology, and resources to assist victims (OVC, 1998; Letschert & Groenhuijsen, 2011). The reach and impact of such crimes as human trafficking and terrorism have transformed the nature of crime victimization, requiring the field of victim services to respond with programs and practices that are informed and adequate to meet the needs of these victims. While the victims' movement is still relatively new, and international recognition of victimology is growing, victim-related policies and practices can gain from sharing and exchanging experience at the international level.

# KEY WORDS

# INTERNET RESOURCES

### The Office for Victims of Crime (www.ovc.gov)

The Office for Victims of Crime (OVC) administers the Crime Victim Fund, which is financed by fines and penalties paid by convicted federal offenders, not from tax dollars. The OVC channels funding for victim compensation and assistance throughout the United States, raises awareness about victims' issues, promotes compliance with victims' rights laws, and provides training, technical assistance, publications, and products to victim assistance professionals.

### Victim Support Europe (www.victimsupport.eu)

Victim Support Europe was founded in 1990 and has been working for over 25 years for a Europe, and a world, where all victims have strong victims' rights and services, whether they report the crime or not. Victim Support Europe works toward this mission through advocacy to improve EU and international laws, through research and knowledge development, and through capacity building at the national and local level.

# CRITICAL THINKING QUESTIONS

1. Discuss the importance of victim assistance organizations for victims of crime.

2. How has victim advocacy shaped or changed laws and policies to better improve services for victims of crime?

3. What challenges do victim assistance organizations face going forward?

4. Explain the importance of using evidence-based practice.

5. Describe the role new technologies can play in improving the services offered to victims.

# Appendix

The National Victim Assistance
Standards Consortium (NVASC)
Ethical Standards

## Section 1: Scope of Service

1.1: The Victim Assistance (VA) provider understands his or her legal responsibilities, limitations, and the implications of his/her actions within the delivery setting and performs duties in accord with laws, regulations, policies and legislated rights of persons served.

1.2: The VA provider accurately represents his or her professional title, qualifications, and/or credentials in relationships with persons served and in public advertising.

1.3: The VA provider maintains a high standard of professional conduct.

1.4: The VA provider achieves and maintains a high level of professional competence.

1.5: The VA provider who provides a service for a fee informs a person served about the fee at the initial session or meeting.

## Section 2: Coordinating within the Community

2.1: The VA provider conducts relationships with colleagues and other professionals in such a way as to promote mutual respect, public confidence, and improvement of service.

2.2: The VA provider shares knowledge and encourages proficiency in victim assistance among colleagues and other professionals.

2.3: The VA provider serves the public interest by contributing to the improvement of systems that impact victims of crime.

# Section 3: Direct Services

3.1: The VA provider respects and attempts to protect the victim's civil rights.

3.2: The VA provider recognizes the interests of the person served as primary responsibility.

3.3: The VA provider refrains from behaviors that communicate victim blame, suspicion regarding victim accounts of the crime, condemnation for past behavior, or other judgmental, anti-victim sentiment.

3.4: The VA provider respects the victim's right to self-determination.

3.5: The victim assistance provider preserves the confidentiality of information provided by the person served or acquired from other sources before, during, and after the course of the professional relationship.

Exceptions

- Consulting with other professionals, supervisors, consultants (all bound)

- Written consent of person who provided the information

- Death/disability, written consent of personal representative

- When communication reveals intended commission of crime, harmful act

- Medical emergency, victim unable to release necessary information

- Mandated reporting of abuse of child or vulnerable adult

- When person waives confidentiality by bringing public charges against the provider

- Minor victims, according to state laws

Confidential privilege refers to legal rights of confidentiality:

- Attorney-client privilege

- Psychotherapist-patient

In a courtroom, privilege permits client/patient to "own" the information that has been communicated. Only the client can waive the privilege, which gives consent for the information to be used in court.

In some states, right of confidential privilege is extended to domestic violence and sexual assault service providers to protect communication with the victims they serve.

3.6: The VA provider avoids conflicts of interest and discloses any possible conflict to the program or person served, as well as to prospective programs or persons served.

- Nothing to compromise the best interest of the persons or agency served
- Previous relationships
- Providers who survive a crime, do not bring it into counseling relationship with another victim. It transfers the focus from the victim to the provider.

3.7: The VA provider terminates a professional relationship with a victim when the victim is not likely to benefit from continued services.

- Service no longer relevant to his or her needs

3.8: The VA provider does not engage in personal relationships with persons served, which exploits professional trust or which could impair the VA provider's objectivity and professional judgement.

- If there is a potential for loss of objectivity, conflict of interest, or the exploitation of a victim seeking help, the mixing of personal and professional roles is not appropriate.
- If a provider cannot avoid a personal or business relationship with a client, the provider should seek counsel and supervision from colleagues regarding his or her objectivity regarding the case.

3.9: The VA provider does not discriminate against a victim or another staff member on the basis of race/ethnicity, language, sex/gender, age, sexual orientation, (dis)ability, social class, economic status, education, marital status, religious affiliation, residency, or HIV status.

3.10: The VA provider furnishes opportunities for colleague VA providers to seek appropriate services when traumatized by a criminal event or client interaction.

## Section 4: Administration and Evaluation

4.1: The VA provider reports to appropriate authorities the conduct of any colleague or other professional (including oneself) that constitutes mistreatment of a person served or that brings the profession into dishonor.

*From the book* Ethics in Victim Services *by Melissa Hook, 2005 published by Victims' Assistance Legal Organization.*

# Glossary

**Adjudicatory hearing:** The stage of juvenile court proceedings where the judge finds whether the allegations in the petition can be sustained

**Adult Protective Services (APS):** Social service agencies that respond to the abuse and neglect of older adults, individuals with disabilities, and others who are at risk for mistreatment and neglect.

**Aftercare:** Upon release from an institution, a juvenile is often ordered to a period of aftercare, which is similar to adult parole.

**Applied ethics:** the application of ethical principles to specific issues in private or public life.

**Arraignment:** The defendant appears before a court and is notified of the formal charges and informed of his or her rights. Then, the defendant makes an admission of denial or guilt.

**Bail:** The money or equivalent property put up to secure the release of the defendant while he or she is awaiting the trial.

**Bereaved victims:** family members and friends who have lost a significant other to homicide.

**Booking:** An arrestee is taken to the police station or jail, and personal information, alleged charge(s), fingerprints, and photographs are recorded.

**Burnout:** a progressive syndrome of emotional exhaustion, depersonalization, and diminished personal accomplishment caused by overwork or stress (Brown, O'Brien, & Deleon, 1998).

**Bystanders:** Individuals who are neither victims nor perpetrators but they saw or know about a crime that happened to someone else.

**Child abuse:** The definition of child abuse and neglect contained in Section 3 of the Child Abuse Prevention and Treatment Act (CAPTA) (Peterson, Joseph & Feit, 2014) is "At a minimum, any recent act or set of acts or failure to act on the part of a parent or caretaker, which results in death, serious physical or emotional harm, sexual abuse or exploitation, or an act or failure to act, which presents an imminent risk of serious harm."

**Child Protective Services (CPS):** a specialized component of the child welfare system, responsible for supporting and intervening for those children alleged to be abused, neglected, or exploited, and their families (McDaniel & Lescher, 2004).

**Circles:** One of the restorative justice practices where the community members who has an interest in the case uses a circle to discuss the case to deal with the harm created by the offender, of healing the victim, and of restoring the community.

**Coalition:** a grouping of organizations aligned to achieve a set of goals. The participating organizations have determined that their collective efforts can be more effective than individual approaches.

**Code of ethics:** a set of professional rules that regulate the behavior of the individual.

**Collaboration:** a durable and pervasive relationship between two (or more) organizations that results in a new structure and shared mission.

**Community corrections:** Sanctions that allow offenders to serve their terms in a community setting outside of jail or prison.

**Community-oriented policing (COP):** Addresses prevention, problem solving, community engagement, and partnerships to address crime and social order beyond traditional law enforcement practice

**Compassion fatigue:** a traumatic stress reaction apparent among the healthcare and human services professions such as law enforcement officers, hotline workers, nurses, ministers, counselors, and victim advocates who provide direct services and assistance to their clients (Joinson, 1992; Conrad & Kellar-Guenther, 2006).

**Compassion satisfaction:** The level of satisfaction and pleasure derived by helping others through one's work and by contributing to the well-being of others and to the greater good of society

**Compensation:** victims are recompensed for crime-related financial losses. The money for the program comes mostly from court fees and fines that are collected from convicted criminals (Herman & Waul, 2004). In addition to the state funds, the federal government supplements the money through the Victims of Crime Act (VOCA) by the Office for Victims of Crime (OVC).

**Control Balance Theory:** proposes that deviance, defined as behavior that the majority regard as unacceptable or that typically evokes a collective response of a negative type, is caused by the amount of control that individuals exercise relative to the amount of control to which they are subject.

**Cooperation:** the process by which individuals or groups combine their efforts, in a more or less organized way for the attainment of a common objective (Sharma, 2007, p. 372).

**Coordinated Community Response (CCR):** involve collaboration between community and criminal justice agencies to coordinate victim advocacy to support victims and their families and hold batterers accountable. Participating agencies include law enforcement agencies, advocates, healthcare providers, child protection services, local businesses, the media, employers, and clergy (Home of Duluth Model, http://www.theduluthmodel.org/about .html).

**Coordination:** formal relationships around specific efforts or programs. Organizational resources are made available to partner organizations and rewards are shared. (Simonin et al., 2016).

**Coping:** the thoughts and acts that people use to manage the internal and external demands posed by a stressful or traumatic event (Peterson, 2003).

**Court-appointed special advocates (CASA):** help abused and neglected children find safe, permanent homes (National Court Appointed Special Advocate Association, 2017). Those advocates not only represent the children but also work with their families and assist them with the court proceedings (Leung, 1996).

**Crime in the United States:** an annual report released by the FBI that is a valuable resource to understand the trend, the number, and rate of violent and property crime offenses in the nation and by state.

**Crisis intervention:** provides immediate assistance by addressing the internal and external difficulties of individuals in crisis

**Crossover youth:** Youth who experience maltreatment and engage in delinquency.

**Crossover Youth Practice Model (CYPM):** a model designed to achieve the efficiency and effectiveness of the welfare and justice systems to better address the needs of crossover youth.

**Custody:** placing juveniles in a secure environment.

**Cyber-bullying:** the willful and repeated harm inflicted through the medium of electronic text, in which hurtful content is disseminated to the victim (Hinduja & Patchin, 2008; Benzmiller, 2013).

**Cyber child sexual exploitation:** Situations in which these abusive practices occur or are facilitated through the use of the Internet or other file-sharing and mobile communication technologies. Where a person, usually an adult, achieves sexual gratification, financial gain, or advancement through the abuse or exploitation of a child's sexuality by abrogating that child's human right to dignity, equality, autonomy, and physical and mental well-being, for example, trafficking, prostitution, prostitution tourism, mail-order bride trade, pornography, stripping, battering, incest, rape and sexual harassment (Estes & Weiner, 2001; Ospina et al., 2010; Malby et al., 2015; Acar, 2016).

**Cyber-crime:** the use of computer technology to engage in unlawful activity (Brenner, 2007).

**Cyber-harassment:** encompasses all of the events of traditional harassment but extends the victimization to include electronic devices to communicate messages that annoy, torment, or terrorize a victim (Southworth et al., 2007; Hazelwood Koon-Magnin, 2013; Fisher et al., 2016).

**Cyber-stalking:** the repeated pursuit of an individual using electronic or Internet-capable devices (Reyns, Henson, & Fisher, 2012, p. 1).

**Day Reporting Centers (DRCs):** A one-stop center that addresses the criminogenic needs of the participants by providing comprehensive programs.

**Detention facility (juvenile hall):** A secure facility that places juveniles during juvenile court proceedings. It is sometimes called detention center or juvenile hall.

**Deterrence:** Sentencing goal that discourages offenders and the general public from committing crime.

**Differential response (DR):** Two-track system where the case is classified into an investigative response (IR) or an alternative response (AR).

**Disposition hearing:** Juvenile court proceedings in which a judge decides the most appropriate placement of an adjudicated juvenile.

**Domestic Violence Fatality Review Team (DVFRT):** the collective efforts of multiple agencies and multidisciplinary organizations to prevent future domestic violence fatalities and ensure the safety of domestic violence victims and their children and hold the perpetrators accountable (Websdale, 2001).

**Drug or alcohol facilitated rape:** occurs when victims are given without their knowledge or consent drugs or alcohol that may impair their ability to guard themselves from being assaulted. Drugs commonly given to victims include Rohypnol ('roofies'), Gamma-Hydroxybutyric (GHB), and Ketamine, which impair the motors skills of the victim and possibly cause loss of memory (Lee & Jordan, 2014).

**Dually involved youth:** youth who are simultaneously involved in the child welfare and juvenile justice systems (Cutuli et al., 2016).

**Elder abuse:** Elder abuse and neglect is the intentional actions causing harm or creating serious risk of harm, whether or not, to a vulnerable elder by a caregiver or other person who stands in a trusted relationship, or failure by a caregiver to satisfy the elders basic needs or to protect the elder from harm (Bonnie & Wallace, 2003, p. 40)

**Electronic Monitoring (EM):** An intermediate sanction in which offenders are monitored through a GPS tracking device.

**Ethical dilemmas:** Situations where one has to make a moral decision from two or more choices.

**Ethics:** the "science of morality" which addresses what is the right thing to do and how we ought to behave.

**Evidence-based practices:** using data and research to inform and guide programs that will improve outcomes for individuals, agencies, and communities (Gibel, Carter, & Ramirez, 2016).

**Expert witnesses:** can talk about opinions given their specialized area of knowledge, research, and experience.

**Facilitation:** when the victim, often unknowingly, makes it easier for offenders to target him or her or set in motion the events that lead to the victimization

**Family group conferences:** an informal meeting coordinated with a trained facilitator whereby the offender(s), the victim(s), their families, other affected individuals, and anyone who supports the victim and the offender are the common participants in the conference

**Family violence:** Any assault, battery, sexual assault, sexual battery, or any criminal offense resulting in personal injury or death of one family or household member by another who is related to the victim either biologically or legally through marriage or adoption. A crime is considered family violence if the victim was the offender's current or former spouse; parent or adoptive parent; current or former stepparent; legal guardian; biological or adoptive child; current or former stepchild; sibling, current or former step sibling; grandchild; current or former step- or adoptive-grandchild; grandparent; current or former step-or adoptive-grandparent; in-law; or other relative (aunt, uncle, nephew) (Durose et al., 2005, p. 4)

**Fear of crime:** an emotional response to a sense of insecurity and being a victim of crime (Hanson, Sawyer, Begle & Hubel, 2010).

**Forcible rape:** penetration achieved by violence or the threat of violence without the free consent of the victim (Daigle & Muftic, 2016).

**Functional responsibility:** the role victims play in not provoking others into victimizing or harming them, and the idea that victims should also do everything possible to prevent a victimization from occurring

**Good Samaritan laws:** protect passersby, bystanders, and healthcare providers who are willing to assist those who need immediate assistance from liability if unintended consequences result from their assistance (Legal Resource Library, http://resources.lawinfo.com/personal-injury/what-are-good-samaritan-laws.html).

**Grooming:** often characterized as seduction, a slow and gradual process of active engagement and a desensitization of the child's inhibitions, where the offender gradually gains power and control over the child (Ospina et al., 2010; Winters & Jeglic, 2017).

**Guidelines:** recommendations rather than directives among professional groups

**Hate crime:** a criminal offense that is motivated by personal prejudice and directed at others because of their perceived race, ethnicity, sexual orientation, gender, gender identity, religion or disability (Office for Victims of Crime, 2017, p.1).

**Hotline:** a 24-hour toll-free telephone line and online services for victims to get information on resources, a local shelter, and advocacy services.

**Human trafficking:** the recruitment, transportation, transfer, harboring, or receipt of persons, by means of the threat or use of force or other forms of coercion, of abduction, of fraud, of deception, of the abuse of power or of a position of vulnerability or of the giving or receiving of payments or benefits to achieve the consent of a person having control over another person, for the purpose of exploitation. Exploitation shall include, at a minimum, the exploitation of the prostitution of others or other forms of sexual exploitation, forced labor or services, slavery or practices similar to slavery, servitude or the removal of organs (United Nations, 2000).

**Identity theft:** a crime that involves the illegal access and use of an individual's personal or financial information without permission (Bailes et al, 2013; Finklea, 2014).

**Impact of Crime on Victims Classes (ICVCs):** enhance adult offender acceptance of responsibility for their previous criminal conduct, understand the impact of crime on victims, develop personal safety skills, learn about healthy relationships with others, and contribute to their communities in a way to prevent future victimization (Carson, Chenault, & Matusiak, 2016).

**Incapacitated rape:** occurs when the victim cannot consent because of self-induced consumption of drugs, alcohol, or any other intoxicant (Daigle & Muftic, 2016).

**Incapacitation:** Sentencing goal that disables offenders from committing a crime, mostly through imprisonment.

**Initial Appearance:** The defendant's appearance before a magistrate or a judge in a reasonable period after his or her arrest.

**Institutional corrections:** Housing individuals in secure facilities, usually jails or prisons.

**Intangible costs of victimization:** costs such as pain, suffering, and reduced quality of life and fear of crime, as well as psychological costs to the offender's family and community, are more difficult to measure, but economists make efforts to use varied methods to place a dollar value on those losses (Cohen, Miller, & Rossman, 1994).

**International Crime Victim Survey (ICVS):** The most comprehensive large-scale crime and victimization surveys conducted in 78 countries by 2005.

**Internet fraud:** any fraudulent scheme in which one or more components of the Internet, such as websites, chat rooms, or e-mail are used to defraud victims or to otherwise take advantage of them (Rose, 2005).

**Intimate partner violence:** any "physical, sexual, or psychological harm committed by a current or former spouse, opposite-sex cohabitating partner, same-sex cohabiting partner, date, or boyfriend or girlfriend" (Breiding et al., 2015, p. 11). IPV can take on many forms but is generally categorized into four defining harms: physical, sexual, psychological, and economic abuse (Tong, 1984; Breiding et al., 2015).

**Jails:** Local facilities generally hold individuals who are awaiting trial or awaiting transfer to other facilities after a conviction and misdemeanor offenders serving sentences of one year or less.

**lex talions:** the principle of an-eye-for-an-eye. Here criminals would be dealt punishment equal to that of the harm caused.

**Lifestyle-Exposure Theory:** refers to "lifestyle" as routine daily activities that include vocational (work, school, keeping house, etc.) and leisure activities (shopping and going to bars etc.). A person comes into contact through his or her lifestyle and/or behaviors with potential offenders. Therefore, a person who participates in activities away from the home, particularly at night, and with nonfamily members is more likely to be victimized.

**Low Self-Control Theory:** low self-control is the most important predictor for delinquent and analogous behaviors (Gottfredson & Hirschi, 1990; Jones & Quisenberry, 2004). Why some people turn to criminal behavior and others do not is because offenders have a propensity or tendency to take advantage of opportunities for criminal behavior. This propensity to engage in criminal behavior results from a lack of direct control or guidance by parents or caregivers early in life.

**Mandated reporting:** is the legislative requirement that certain professionals must report cases of suspected child abuse or neglect for investigation to a designated authority within a specified amount of time (USDHHS, 2015).

**Modus operandi (MO):** a term used by law enforcement to develop a description of the way particular criminals operate. Sometimes referred to by its initials, MO.

**Multicultural competence:** gaining knowledge, understanding, supporting, and appropriately responding to victims across different languages and cultures.

**Multidisciplinary Team (MDT):** multidisciplinary teams include, but not be limited to, personnel with a background in (1) law enforcement, (2) child protective services, (3) juvenile counseling and adolescent mental health, and (4) domestic violence (Wasserman, 2005). Under a multidisciplinary team, each discipline provides information relevant to the case, and the ultimate decision is made by one person.

**Multiservice intervention:** includes 24hr hotlines, counseling, support groups, transitional housing programs, safety planning, financial education, employment training and assistance, legal advocacy, and programs specifically designed for children (O'Reilly et al., 2010; Sullivan, 2011).

**National Census of Victim Service Providers (NCVSP):** surveys victim service providers to better understand the field and includes such information as the type of organization and the types of victims served (Office for Victims of Crime, 2013).

**National Crime Victimization Survey (NCVS):** the most comprehensive nationwide household survey providing a detailed picture of crime victims and the consequences of crime, unreported crime, and victimization trends.

**National Incident-Based Reporting System (NIBRS):** national data collection system that gathers each reported crime incident and arrest for 46 specific crimes called Group A offenses as well as 11 lesser offenses from the arrest data (FBI, 2000).

**National Survey of Victim Service Providers (NSVSP):** Follows up on the NCVSP, the NSVSP will seek more specific information about victim service providers (Office for Victims of Crime, 2013).

**Near-repeat victimization:** a victimization that occurs in a place that is close by or near in proximity to a place that was victimized previously.

**Neglect:** failure or refusal of a parent, guardian, or other caregiver to provide for a child's basic needs. The abuse includes harm due to the action or inaction of the caregiver.

**Noncontact sexual abuse:** does not involve any physical contact between the perpetrator and the victim. The noncontact occurs without the victims' consent or when they are unable to consent or refuse and includes sending unwanted pornographic images or videos via text messaging or e-mail or verbal sexual harassment (e.g., making sexual comments) (Center for Disease Control and Prevention, 2017). Some acts of noncontact sexual abuse can occur without the victim's knowledge, where comments or pictures are posted on social networking sites or the Internet (Daigle & Muftic, 2016).

**Normalization of abuse:** when the victim doesn't recognize the violence as unacceptable or rationalizes the abuse as being deserved.

**Normative ethics:** moral duties or the set of considerations as to how one should act.

**NVASC Ethical Standards of Professional Conduct:** the National Victim Assistance Standards Consortium (NVASC) was formed by the Office for Victims of Crime at the U.S. Department of Justice and crafted standards of ethics for those who work in the victim services fields to support them in everyday workplace decision making.

**One-stop centers:** also referred to as family justice centers, allow crime victims to receive various services, including health, welfare, counseling, and legal services in one location.

**Opportunity Model:** takes from the lifestyle-exposure and routine activity theory and expands on them and identifies further factors that may play an integral role in victimization. These factors are exposure, guardianship, proximity of potential perpetrators, attractiveness of potential targets, and properties of specific offences. The inclusion of these factors relocates the prominence of the theory from the characteristics of the perpetrator to the characteristics of the situation (Saponaro, 2013).

**Parens Patriae:** The doctrine that gives the state the authority to act as the parent when a child's parents fail to provide appropriate parental supervision.

**Parole:** the conditional release of a prison inmate ending their term under the supervision of parole officers.

**Partnership:** a collaborative relationship between entities to work toward shared objectives through a mutually agreed division of labor (World Bank, 1998, p. 5).

**Polyvictimization:** a person experiences multiple victimizations of different kinds, such as sexual abuse, physical abuse, bullying, and or exposure to family violence.

**Precipitation:** the extent to which the victims contributed to the criminal event that harmed them, and it can take two forms, victim facilitation and victim provocation.

**Preliminary hearing:** A hearing that determines if sufficient evidence exists to allow charges to be passed against the defendant.

**Primary prevention:** The efforts that focus on preventing or eliminating diseases or injuries before they happen. This can be done with education about a healthy lifestyle.

**Prisons:** Facilities that usually hold felony offenders who have been sentenced to one year or more.

**Probation:** commonly used as an alternative to incarceration where offenders can live under supervision in the community

**Professional ethics:** a specific type of applied ethics focusing on the ethical rules that govern specific professional standards (Pollock, 2010).

**Provocation:** occurs when the victim overtly acts to incite another person to commit an illegal act resulting in his or her victimization

**Rape kit, or sexual assault kit (SAK):** A package of items used for gathering and preserving multiple pieces of evidence from a sexual assault victim.

**Recurring victimization:** occurs when a person or place is victimized more than once by any type of victimization (Daigle, 2013).

**Regulations:** usually come from federal or state governments. Noncompliance of regulations could result in sanctions, which would likely be a fine.

**Repeat victimization:** occurs when the same victimization happens more than once to the same individual, household, place, business, vehicle, or other target (Grove & Farrell, 2011).

**Residential placement:** Placement for youth in residential facilities that might be publicly or privately operated and could be a prison- or a home-like setting.

**Resilience:** a person's ability to maintain a balanced state in the face of challenges. In other words, it is the ability to "bounce back" after being traumatized, where the person is able to process and make sense of the disruption in his or her life, identify his or her resources, and successfully handle the crisis (Bonanno 2004; 2005).

**Resources:** traits, characteristics, or abilities to meet the demands of a stressor event that can be available at the individual, family, or community level.

**Restitution:** The most common form of restitution is financial, which requires the offender to make payments to the victim for crime-related losses. Those would include medical expenses, lost wages, lost or damaged property, and funeral expenses (Herman & Waul, 2004).

**Restoration:** Sentencing goal that focuses on restoring the harm done to victims, family, and friends of victims and the community.

**Restorative justice:** a framework that focuses on repairing the harm done to victims and the community through a process of negotiation, mediation, victim empowerment, and reparation (Zehr, 1990).

**Retribution:** Sentencing goal that considers punishment as justifiable or deserved given the seriousness of the crime that the offender committed.

**Routine Activity Theory:** This theoretical perspective argues not why certain demographics are susceptible to criminal victimization but rather why daily routine activities create the opportunity for criminal victimization (Cohen & Felson, 1979). The propositions of this theory are that for victimization to take place, there must be three elements: (1) a motivated perpetrator/s, (2) suitable targets (victim), and (3) the absence of a capable guardian at a given place and time (Cohen & Felson, 1979, p. 592)

**Safety:** a sense of protection, well-being, and security. It is the feeling people experience when they are not in danger.

**Safety Planning:** involves, amongst other things, discussing and agreeing on a safe place to go when victims leave their partners, opening and/or hiding money in a separate account, getting a second set of keys made for the house or car, having a packed bag with clothes and important documents ready to go when needed, or left with someone the victim trusts, practicing getting out of the house safely, avoiding rooms with no exits and/or weapons (e.g., bathrooms, kitchen), teaching children to not get in the middle of a fight, and memorizing emergency numbers (Campbell, 2001; Parker et al., 2016).

**Secondary prevention:** an intervention that addresses the early detection and treatment of a disease or an injury. An example is a regular checkup to identify and treat disease for those who have risk factors

**Self-care:** is the opposite of self-harm. When victims engage in self-care they are expressing to others that they value their health and are finding ways to move on from the traumatic event. Self-care activities are important for every human being (Herman, 1997).

**Sex trafficking:** when a person is coerced, forced, or deceived into prostitution—or maintained in prostitution through one of these means after initially consenting (U.S. Department of State, 2016).

**Sexual Assault Nurse Examiners (SANE):** trained nurses who conduct a forensic exam and provide comprehensive care to sexual assault victims.

**Sexual Assault Response Team (SART):** serves sexual assault victims by building, expanding, formalizing, and maintaining strong interagency responses to sexual violence. SART models could be a more informal cooperative partnerships to more formalized coordinated and multidisciplinary responses at the local, regional, state, tribal, or territory levels (National Sexual Violence Resource Center, 2011).

**Sexual coercion:** Unlike using physical violence or the threat of physical violence to have sexual intercourse; sexual coercion is instead the act of using psychological manipulation, threat of nonphysical punishment, or pressuring or pestering for sex (Daigle & Muftic, 2016). Sexual coercion generally exists in environments where there is an imbalance in power and control, where offenders exploit behaviors or status that make people vulnerable to victimization through fear, obligation, and guilt and/or the ability to recognize sexually aggressive behavior (Kalra & Bhugra, 2013).

**Social Learning Theory:** individuals learn behavior by observing and imitating other people through the absorption of experiences and reinforcement. In other words, behavior that is either rewarded, or goes unpunished, develops into the observer's library of what is acceptable behavior (Akers, 1998).

**Solitary confinement:** inmates are locked in their small cells alone 23 hours a day and spend one hour in a recreation space, which is only slightly larger than their prison cell. Inmates have little contact outside of guards and prison staff.

**Standards:** a basis for accreditation in the private or the public sector. Noncompliance of standards could result in sanctions, which would likely be a fine.

**Statutory rape:** refers to a relationship between a juvenile and an adult that is illegal under the age of consent status but does not involve the degree of coercion or manipulation sufficient to qualify under criminal statutes as a forcible sex crime (Lee & Jordan, 2014). The minimum age that most states set is between 14 and 18; however, the legal definitions and terminology for statutory rape vary between states.

**Strategic planning:** address high level questions of mission, vision, and goals having the greatest social impact (Backer, 2001; Mckinsey & Company, 2001).

**Stress:** any demand made on a person that causes a reaction either biologically or psychologically.

**Subpoena:** a written order stating the time and place of appearance

**Supermax prison:** the prison with the highest level of security that holds the most dangerous offenders

**Tangible costs of victimization:** costs as a direct consequence of crime, for example, crime-incurred expenses such as property damage and loss and productivity. Productivity includes lost wages, fringe benefits, and housework and loss of schooldays of victims and their families. Also, criminal justice costs such as police investigations and incarceration and costs in preventing future crime victimizations

**Tertiary prevention:** an intervention that addresses the problems that are already present, softens the impact of an ongoing illness or injury that has a lasting effect, and reduces the likelihood of recurrence.

**Theories:** the ideas that provide a framework for investigating the cause-and-effect relationship of events.

**Title IX:** a civil rights law that prohibits discrimination on the basis of sex in any educational program or activity that receives federal funding. This includes most schools, including private institutions and grades K-12 (Marcotte & Palmer, 2016).

**Transitional housing:** programs that may provide assistance for 90 days, or in some cases depending on the organization, up to two years. Victims are usually placed in apartment style facilities or in a communal house at no cost to the family or individual. In some cases when there is no housing space available, vouchers for a motel stay or hotel room may be given to victims and their families.

**Trauma:** the result of severe distress and causes damage. Some stressors may be single incidents of relatively short duration, whereas others may occur over longer periods of time, resulting in prolonged exposure to the threatening stressor (Collins & Collins, 2005).

**Trauma-informed care:** a strengths-based framework that is grounded in an understanding of and responsiveness to the impact of trauma, that emphasizes physical, psychological, and emotional safety for both providers and victims, and that creates opportunities for victims to rebuild a sense of control and empowerment (Hopper et al., 2009).

**Uniform Crime Report (UCR):** national crime data compiled by the FBI that includes crimes reported to local law enforcement departments and the number of arrests made by police agencies

**United Nations Universal Declaration of Human Rights:** The declaration is a document drafted by representatives with different legal and cultural backgrounds from around the world. Its aim is to set a common standard of achievements of all peoples and all nations to protect their fundamental human rights (United Nations, 2004).

**Unwanted sexual contact:** may involve the intentional touching, either directly or through the clothing of any part of a person's body without his or her consent, or of a person who is unable to consent or refuse. Furthermore, unwanted contact sexual can include the perpetrator making a person touch them (Center for Disease Control and Prevention, 2017).

**Values:** elements of desirability, worth, or importance (Pollock, 2010).

**Victim advocates:** trained professionals who offer victims information, support, and help finding resources and assisting victims with paperwork.

**Victim assistance:** a fully-fledged advocacy and service field dedicated to meeting the physical, financial, and psychological needs of victims and their families (OVC, 1998).

**Victim Impact Panels (VIPs):** Three or four speakers who have been seriously injured or whose friends or family members were killed by a drunken driver share their personal stories about how the event affected their lives to a group of offenders in a nonblaming manner.

**Victim impact statements (VIS):** The format of the VIS could be a written statement, a sworn or unsworn oral presentation, or even a prerecorded audio or video statement, and it commonly addresses the harm or trauma, the economic loss or damage to victims as a result of the crime, and a victim's reaction to the proposed sentence or disposition (Schuster & Propen, 2010).

**Victim Notification System (VNS):** a free computer-based system through which federal crime victims can access information on an offender's custody and release status.

**Victim-offender mediation:** a trained mediator coordinates a meeting of a victim and an offender to discuss the offense for which they were involved and facilitate a dialogue. The mediator usually has a separate premediation session with the offender and the victim.

**Victim and Witness Assistance Programs:** Programs that provide information on rights and services to victims and witnesses, and encourage victims to participate in the criminal justice system to the extent they wish.

**Victim and Witness Protection Act of 1982:** the goals of the legislation are (1) to enhance and protect the necessary role of crime victims and witnesses in the criminal justice process; (2) to ensure that the federal government does all that is possible within limits of available resources to assist victims and witnesses of crime without infringing on the constitutional rights of defendants; and (3) to provide a model for legislation for state and local governments. (U.S. Department of Justice, https://www.justice.gov/usao-wdla/programs/victim-witness)

**Victims:** "Persons who individually or collectively have suffered harm, including physical or mental injury, emotional suffering, economic loss or substantial impairment of their fundamental rights, through acts or omissions that are in violation of criminal laws operative within Member States, including those laws proscribing criminal abuse of power" (United Nations General Assembly, 1985).

**Victims' of Crime Act (VOCA):** The act established the Crime Victims Fund, which was made up of federal criminal fines, penalties, forfeitures, and special assessments, for state compensation programs and local victim assistance programs. Subsequent revisions to the act expanded victim eligibility to include victims of domestic violence, drunk driving accidents, nonresident commuters and visitors, and saw the establishment of the Office for Victims of Crime (Hook & Seymour, 2004; Young & Stein, 2004).

**Violence Against Women Act (VAWA) of 1994:** enacted as part of the Violent Crime Control and Law Enforcement Act of 1994, it acknowledges domestic violence and sexual assault as crimes, along with providing federal resources to encourage community-coordinated responses to combating violence against women.

# References

Abbott, S., & Barnett, E. (2015). *The Crossover Youth Practice Model (CYPM) in brief: Behavioral health and crossover youth*. Washington, DC: Center for Juvenile Justice Reform.

Abramson, S. (1991). Use of court-appointed advocates to assist in permanency planning for minority children. *Child Welfare, 70*(4), 477–487.

Acar, K. V. (2016). Sexual exploitation of children in cyberspace. *International Journal of Cyber Criminology, 10*(2), 110–126.

Acierno, R., Hernandez, M. A., Amstadter, A. B., Resnick, H. S., Steve, K., Muzzy, W., & Kilpatrick, D. G. (2010). Prevalence and correlates of emotional, physical, sexual, and financial abuse and potential neglect in the United States: The national elder mistreatment study. *American Journal of Public Health, 100*(2), 292–297.

Acierno, R., Hernandez-Tejada, M., Muzzy, W., & Steve, K. (2009). The National Elder Mistreatment Study. Retrieved from: https://www.ncjrs.gov/pdffiles1/nij/grants/226456.pdf.

Acker, M., & Lawrence, D. (2009). Social work and managed care: Measuring competence, burnout, and role stress of workers providing mental health services in a managed care era. *Journal of Social Work, 9*(3), 269–283.

Adams, W., & Flynn, A. (2017). *Federal prosecution of commercial sexual exploitation of children cases, 2004–2013*. U.S. Department of Justice, Office of Justice Programs, Bureau of Justice Statistics.

Adams, W, Owens, C., & Small, K. (2010). *Effects of federal legislation on the commercial exploitation of children*. Washington DC: U.S. Department of Justice, Office of Justice Programs, Office of Juvenile Justice and Delinquency Prevention. Retrieved from https://www.ncjrs.gov/pdffiles1/ojjdp/228631.pdf.

Addington, L. (2008). *Current issues in victimization research and the NCVS's ability to study them*. Prepared for presentation at the Bureau of Justice Statistics Data Users Workshop, February 12, 2008, Washington, DC. Retrieved from https://www.bjs.gov/content/pub/pdf/Addington.pdf.

Aderden, M., & Ullman, S. (2012). Gender difference or indifference? Detective decision making in sexual assault cases. *Journal of Interpersonal Violence, 27*(1), 3–22.

Adkins, G., Huff, D., & Stageberg, P. (2000). *The Iowa Sex Offender Registry and recidivism*. Iowa Department of Human Rights Division of Criminal and Juvenile Justice Planning and Statistical Analysis Center.

Adler School Institute on Public Safety and Social Justice: Illinois Coalition for Immigrant and Refugee Rights. (2011). *White paper on restorative justice: A primer and exploration of practice across two North American cities*. Chicago: Author.

Administration on Aging. (2017). A profile of older Americans. Retrieved from http://www.aoa.gov/AoARoot/Aging_Statistics/Profile/2011/docs/2011profile.pdf.

Afifi, T. O., & Macmillan, H. L. (2011). Resilience following child maltreatment: A review of protective factors. *The Canadian Journal of Psychiatry, 56*(5), 266–272.

Agarwal, S., Driscoll, J. C., Gabaix, X., & Laibson, D. (2010). *What is the age of reason? Issue in Brief* 10–12. Chestnut Hill, MA: Center for Retirement Research.

Ake, J., & Arnold, G. (2018). A brief history of the antiviolence-against-women movements in the United States. In C. M. Renzetti, J. L. Edleson, & R. K. Bergen (Eds), *Sourcebook on violence against women* (3rd edition), (pp 3–25). Thousand Oaks, CA: Sage.

Akers, R., Greca, A., Sellers, C., & Cochran, J. (1987). Fear of crime and victimization among the elderly in different types of communities. *Criminology, 25*(3), 487–506.

Akers, R. L. (1973). *Deviant behavior: A social learning approach*. Belmont, CA: Wadsworth.

Akers, R. L. (1998). *Social learning and social structure: A general theory of crime and deviance*. Boston, MA: Northeastern University Press.

Akers, R. L, & Sellers, C. S. (2009). *Criminological theories: Introduction, evaluation, and application* (5th ed.). Oxford, UK: Oxford University Press.

Alexander, M. (2012). *The new Jim Crow: Mass incarceration in the age of colorblindness*. New York, NY: The New Press.

Allen, J. G. (2005). *Coping with trauma: Hope through understanding*, (2nd edition). Washington, DC: American Psychiatric Publishing.

Alliance for Safety and Justice (2016). *The first-ever national survey of victims' views on safety and justice*. Retrieved from http://www.allianceforsafetyandjustice.org/wp-content/uploads/documents/Crime%20Survivors%20Speak%20Report.pdf.

Alvarez, M. B., & Alessi, E. J. (2012). Human trafficking is more than sex trafficking and prostitution. *Implications for Social Work*, 27(2), 142–152.

American Association of Children's Residential Centers. (2010, December). *Redefining residential: Trauma-informed care in residential treatment*. Milwaukee, WI: Author.

American Association of University Professors (AAUP). (2012). *Campus sexual assault: Suggested policies and procedures*. Retrieved from https://www.aaup.org/file/Sexual_Assault_Policies.pdf.

American Association of University Professors (AAUP). (2016). *The history, uses, and abuses of Title IX*. Retrieved from https://www.aaup.org/file/TitleIXreport.pdf.

American Psychiatric Association. (2013). *Diagnostic and statistical manual for mental disorders* (5th ed.). Washington, D.C.: Author.

American Psychological Association (APA). (2012). Elder abuse and neglect: In search of solutions. Retrieved from http://www.apa.org/pi/aging/eldabuse.html.

Anderson, D. K., Saunders, D. G., Yoshihama, M., Bybee, D. I., & Sullivan, C. M. (2003). Long-term trends in depression among women separated from abusive partners. *Violence Against Women*, 9(7), 807–838. doi:10.1177/1077801203009007004

Anderson, K. B. (2016). *Mass-market consumer fraud: Who is most susceptible to becoming a victim?* (Working paper No. 332). Washington, DC: Bureau of Economics Federal Trade Commission.

Anderst, J., & Dowd, M. D. (2010). Comparative needs in child abuse education and resources: Perceptions from three medical specialties. *Medical Education Online*, 15.

Andrews, A. B. (1990). Crisis and recovery services for family violence survivors. In A. R. Roberts (Eds.), *Helping crime victims: Research, policy and practice*, (pp. 206–232). Newbury Park, CA: Sage.

Andrews, B., Brewin, C. R., Rose, S., & Kirk, M. (2000). Predicting PTSD symptoms in victims of violent crime: The role of shame, anger, and childhood abuse. *Journal of Abnormal Psychology*, 109, 69–73.

Arabian, A. (2009). *The sexual assault counselor-victim privilege: Jurisdictional delay into an unclaimed sanctuary*. Retrieved from http://law.pepperdine.edu/law-review/content/the-sexual-assault-counselor-victim-privilege.pdf.

Ashworth, A. (2002). Restorative rights and restorative justice. *British Journal of Criminology*, 42, 578–595.

Ayres, D. (1997, Feb.11). JurydecidesSimpsonmust pay$25 million in punitive award. *New York Times*. Retrieved from http://www.nytimes.com/1997/02/11/us/jury-decides-simpson-must-pay-25-million-in-punitive-award.html.

Backer, T. E. (2001). Strengthening nonprofits: Foundation initiatives for nonprofit organizations. In C. J. De Vita & C. Flemming (Eds.), *Building capacity in nonprofit organizations* (pp. 33–84). Washington, DC: The Urban Institute.

Badenes-Ribera, L., Bonilla-Campos, A., Frias-Navarro, D., Pons-Salvador, G., & Monterde-i-Bort, H. (2016). Intimate partner violence in self-identified lesbians. *Trauma, Violence, & Abuse*, 17(3), 284–297.

Bailes, J., Cummins, K., Joyce, E., Rocap, K., Arthur, S., Chandler, P., Kleffer, C., & Lopez, I. (2013). *Taking action: An advocate's guide to assisting victims of financial fraud*. The Financial Industry Regulatory Authority (FINRA) Investor Education Foundation and the National Center for Victims of Crime.

Baker, A. J. L., & Festinger, T. (2011). Emotional abuse and emotional neglect subscales of the CTQ: Associations with each other, other measures of psychological maltreatment, and demographic variables. *Children and Youth Services Review*, 33, 2297–2302.

Baker, C. K., Holditch-Niolon, P., & Oliphant, H. (2009). A descriptive analysis of transitional housing programs for survivors of intimate partner violence in the United States. *Violence Against Women*, 15(4), 460–481.

Balaswamy, S. (2004). Rating of interagency working relationship and associated factors in protective services. *Journal of Elder Abuse & Neglect*, 14(1), 1–20.

Bandes, S. (1999). Reply to Paul Cassell: What we know about victim impact statements. *Utah Law Review*, 545–552.

Banks, C. (2009). *Criminal justice ethics: Theory and practice* (2nd ed.). Thousand Oaks, CA: Sage.

Bard, M., & Sangrey, D. (1986). *The crime victim's book* (2nd ed.). New York, NY: Brunner/Mazel.

Barlow, D. H. (2002). *Anxiety and its disorders*. New York, NY: Guildford Press.

Barnett, O. W., Miller-Perrin, C. L., & Perrin, R. D. (2011). *Family violence across the lifespan* (3rd edition). Thousand Oaks, CA: Sage.

Barnoski, R. (2005). *Sex offender sentencing in Washington State: Has community notification reduced recidivism?* Olympia: Washington State Institute for Public Policy.

Barrile, L. (2014). I forgive you, but you must die: Murder victim family members, the death penalty, and restorative justice. *Victims & Offenders, 10*(3), 239–269.

Bartholomew, K., Regan, K. V., Oram, D., White, M. A. (2008). Correlates of partner abuse in male same-sex relationships. *Violence and Victims, 23*, 344–360.

Basile, K. C., & Black, M. C. (2011). Intimate partner violence against women. In C. M. Renzetti, J. L. Edleson, & R. K. Bergen (Eds.), *Sourcebook on violence against women* (2nd ed., pp. 111–131). Thousand Oaks, CA: Sage.

Baum, K., Catalano, S., & Rand, M. (2009). *National Crime Victimization Survey: Stalking victimization in the United States*. Washington, DC: Bureau of Justice Statistics (Special Report).

Bazemore, G. (1998). The "community" in community justice: Issues, themes, and questions for the new neighborhood sanctioning model. In D. R. Karp (Ed.), *Community justice: An emerging field* (pp. 327–369). Lanham, MD: Rowman & Littlefield.

Bazemore, G., & Maruna, S. (2009). Restorative justice in the reentry context: Building new theory and expanding the evidence base. *Victims & Offenders, 4*(4), 375–384.

Bazemore, G., & Umbreit, M. (2001). *A comparison of four restorative conferencing models*. Juvenile Justice Bulletin. Washington, DC: U.S. Department of Justice, Office of Justice Programs, Office of Juvenile Justice and Delinquency Prevention.

Beaulaurier, R. L., Seff, L. R., Newman, F. L., & Dunlop, B. (2005). Internal barriers to help seeking for middle-aged and older women who experience intimate partner violence. *Journal of Elder Abuse & Neglect, 17*, 53–74.

Beck, A., Berzofsky, M., Caspar, R., & Krebs, C. (2013). *Sexual victimization in prisons and jails reported by inmates, 2011–12*. Washington, DC: Bureau of Justice Statistics.

Becker, J. V., Skinner, L. J., Abel, G. G., Howell, J., & Bruce, K. (1982). The effects of sexual assault on rape and attempted rape victims. *Victimology: An International Journal, 7*, 106–113.

Becker-Dreps, S., Morgan, D., Pena, R., Cortes, L., Marten, C. F., & Valladares, E. (2010). Association between intimate partner violence and irritable bowel syndrome: A population-based study in Nicaragua. *Violence Against Women, 16*, 832–845.

Beirne, P. (1994). Adolphe Quetelet and the origins of positivist criminology. In P. Beirne (Ed.), *The origins and frowth of criminology* (pp. 101–130). Aldershot: Dartmouth.

Belenko, S., & Logan, T. K. (2003). Delivering more effective treatment to adolescents: Improving the juvenile drug court model. *Journal of Substance Abuse Treatment, 25*(3), 189–211.

Beloof, D. E. (1999). The third model of criminal process: The victim impact model. *Utah Law Review*, 289–303.

Beloof, D. E., & Pugach, D. (2014). Comparing modern victims' rights in Israel and America: Israeli victims' rights need remedy. *International Perspectives in Victimology, 8*(1), 11–37.

Bender, K. (2010). Why do some maltreated youth become juvenile offenders?: A call for further investigation and adaptation of youth services. *Children and Youth Services Review, 32*, 466–473.

Benedetti, G. (2012). *Innovations in the field of child abuse and neglect prevention: A review of the literature*. Chicago, IL: Chaplin Hall at the University of Chicago.

Benzmiller, H. (2013). The cyber-samaritans: Exploring criminal liability for the "innocent" bystanders of cyber-bullying. *Northwestern University Law Review, 107*(2), 927–962.

Beran, T., & Li, Q. (2005). Cyber-harassment: A study of a new method for an old behavior. *Journal of Educational Computing Research, 32*(3), 265–277.

Bernat, F. P., Aleman, S., & Gitelson, R. (2003). White and Mexican heritage elders' crime victimization perspectives. *Journal of Ethnicity in Criminal Justice, 1*(3/4), 41–65.

Berns, N.S. (2004). *Framing the victim: Domestic violence, media, and social problems.* New York, NY: Routledge.

Bilchik, S. (1997). *Balanced and restorative justice for juveniles: A framework for juvenile justice in the 21st century.* Ft. Lauderdale, FL: Community Justice Institute, Center for Restorative Justice and Mediation.

Black, M. C., Basile, K. C., Breiding, M. J., Smith, S. G., Walters, M. L., Merrick, M. T., Chen, J., & Stevens, M. R. (2011). *The National Intimate Partner and Sexual Violence Survey: 2010 summary report.* Atlanta, GA: National Center for Injury Prevention and Control, Centers for Disease Control and Prevention.

Black, M. C., & Breiding, M. J. (2008). Adverse health conditions and health risk behaviors associated with intimate partner violence, United States 2005. *Morbidity and Mortality Weekly Report, 57,* 113–117.

Blanton, K. (2012). *The rise of financial fraud: Scams never change but disguises do.* Financial Security Project at Boston College, 12–5. Retrieved from http://crr.bc.edu/wp-content/uploads/2012/03/Scams-RFTF.pdf.

Bloom, B., Owen, B., & Covington, S. (2003). *Gender-responsive strategies: Research, practice, and guiding principles for women offenders.* Washington, DC: National Institute of Corrections.

Boardman, A. E., & Vining, A. R. (2000). Using service-customer matrices in strategic analysis of profits. *Nonprofit Management and Leadership, 10*(4), 397–420.

Bonanno, G. A. (2004). Loss, trauma, and human resilience: Have we underestimated the human capacity to thrive after extremely aversive events? *American Psychologist, 59*(1), 20–28.

Bonanno, G. A. (2005). Resilience in the face of potential trauma. *Current Directions in Psychological Science, 14*(3), 135–138.

Bonnie, R. J., & Wallace, R. B. (2003). *Elder mistreatment, abuse, neglect and exploitation in an aging America.* Washington, DC: National Academies Press.

Booth, T. (2012). "Cooling out" victims of crime: Managing victim participation in the sentencing process in a superior sentencing court. *Australian & New Zealand Journal of Criminology, 45*(2), 214–230.

Boss, P. G. (2002). *Family stress management: A contextual approach* (2nd Edition). Thousand Oaks: CA: Sage.

Bostaph, L. M. G., & Throndyke, B. (2017). Professionalization of the victim assistance discipline. In L. G. B. Bostaph, & D. D. Swerin (Eds.), *Victimology: Crime Victimization and Victim Services* (pp. 409–424). New York, NY: Wolters Kluwer.

Bostock, J., Plumpton, M., & Pratt R. (2009). Domestic violence against women: Understanding social processes and women's experiences. *Journal of Community & Applied Social Psychology, 19,* 95–110.

Boudoukha, A., Altintas, E., Rusinek, S., Fantini-Hauwel, C., & Hautekeete, M. (2013). Inmates-to-staff assaults, PTSD and burnout. *Journal of Interpersonal Violence, 28*(11), 2332–2350.

Boyce, C. A., & Maholmes, V. (2013). Attention to the neglected: Prospects for research on child neglect for the next decade. *Child Maltreatment, 18*(1), 65–68.

Boyd, C. (2010). *Shelter for Asian women focuses on community's culture.* Retrieved from https://www.minnpost.com/community-sketchbook/2010/06/shelter-asian-women-focuses-communitys-culture.

Boyle, D., Ragusa-Salerno, L., Lanterman, J., & Marcus, A. (2013). Overview of "An evaluation of day reporting centers for parolees: Outcomes of a randomized trial." *Criminology & Public Policy, 12*(1), 117.

Bracha, H. S. (2004). Freeze, flight, fight, fright, faint: Adaptationist perspectives on the acute stress response spectrum. *CNS Spectrum, 9*(9), 679–685.

Brandl, B., Dyer, C. B., Heisler, C. J., Otto, M. J., Stiegel, L. A., & Thomas, R. W. (2007). *Elder abuse detection and intervention: A collaborative approach.* New York, NY: Springer.

Brandl, B., Herbert, M., & Rozwadowski, J., & Spangler, D. (2004). Feeling safe, feeling strong: Support groups for older abused women. *Violence Against Women, 9*(12), 1490–1503.

Branson, C., Baetz, C., Horwitz, S., Hoagwood, K., & Kendall-Tackett, K. (2017). Trauma-informed juvenile justice systems: A systematic review of definitions and core components. *Psychological Trauma: Theory, Research, Practice, and Policy, 9*(6), 635–646.

Breiding, M. J., Basile, K. C., Smith, S. G., Black, M. C., & Mahendra, R. R. (2015). *Intimate partner violence surveillance: Uniform definitions and recommended data elements, Version 2.0.* Atlanta, GA: National Center for Injury Prevention and Control, Centers for Disease Control and Prevention.

Breiding, M. J., Chen, J., & Black, M. C., (2014). *Intimate partner violence in the United States.* Atlanta, GA: National Center for Injury Prevention and Control, Centers for Disease Control and Prevention.

Brenner, S. (2007). Cybercrime: Re-thinking crime control strategies. In Y. Jewkes (Ed), *Crime online* (pp. 12–28). New York, NY: Routledge.

Bressi, S., & Vaden, K. (2017). Reconsidering self-care. *Clinical Social Work Journal, 45*(1), 33–38.

Briere, J. N., & Elliott, D. M. (1994). Immediate and long-term impacts of child sexual abuse. *The Future of Children, 4*(2), 54–69.

Briere, J. N., & Elliott, D. M. (1994). Immediate and long-term impacts of child sexual abuse. *The Future of Children, 4*(2), 54–69.

Brisson, D., & Roll, S. (2012). The effect of neighborhood on crime and safety: A review of the evidence. *Journal of Evidence-Based Social Work, 9*(4), 333–350. doi:10.1080/15433714.2010.525407

Broder, T., & Neville, S. (2015). Benefits for immigrant survivors of trafficking, domestic violence, and other serious crimes in California. *National Immigration Law Center.* Retrieved from: https://www.nilc.org/wp-content/uploads/2015/12/TraffickingReport-2015-09.pdf.

Brown, C., O'Brien, K., & Deleon, P. (1998). Understanding stress and burnout in shelter workers. *Professional Psychology: Research and Practice, 29*(4), 383–385.

Brown, T. N. T., & Herman, J. L. (2015). *Intimate partner violence and sexual abuse among LGBT people: A review of existing research.* The Williams Institute. Retrieved from https://williamsinstitute.law.ucla.edu/wp-content/uploads/Intimate-Partner-Violence-and-Sexual-Abuse-among-LGBT-People.pdf.

Browne, A. (2004). Fear and the perception of alternatives: Asking 'why battered women don't leave' is the wrong question. In B Price & N. Sokoloff (Eds.), *The criminal justice system and women,* (3rd edition), (pp. 127–146). New York, NY: McGraw-Hill.

Bruce, G. (2013). Definition of terrorism: Social and political effects. *Journal of Military and Veteran's Health, 21*(2), 26–30.

Brush, L. D. (2011). *Poverty, battered women, and work in U. S. public policy.* New York, NY: Oxford University Press.

Bryant-Davis, T. (2005). *Thriving in the wake of trauma: A multicultural guide.* London, UK: Praeger.

Bryce, J. (2011). Online sexual exploitation of children and young people. In Y. Jewkes & M. Yar (Eds.), *Handbook of Internet crime* (pp. 320–342). London, UK: Routledge.

Buchhandler-Raphael, M. (2011). The failure of consent: Re-conceptualizing rape as sexual abuse of power. *Michigan Journal of Gender and Law, 18*(1), 148–228.

Bunger, C., Chuang, E., & McBeath, B. (2012). Facilitating mental health service use for caregivers: Referral strategies among child welfare caseworkers. *Children and Youth Services Review, 34*(4), 696–703.

Bureau of Justice Statistics. (2012). *Half of violent victimizations of the elderly in Michigan from 2005–2009 involved serious acts of violence.* Retrieved from https://www.bjs.gov/content/pub/press/vcerlem0509pr.cfm.

Bureau of Justice Statistics (BJS). (2015). *Data collection: National Crime Victimization Survey (NCVS).* Washington, DC: Author. Retrieved from https://www.bjs.gov/index.cfm?ty=dcdetail&iid=245.

Bureau of Justice Statistics. (n.d). *Community corrections.* Retrieved from https://www.bjs.gov/index.cfm?ty=tp&tid=15.

Burgess, A. W., & Holmstrom, L. L. (1974). Rape trauma syndrome. *The American Journal of Psychiatry, 131*(9), 981–986.

Burgess, A., Regehr, C., & Roberts, A. (2013). *Victimology: Theories and applications* (2nd Edition). Burlington, MA: Jones & Bartlett Learning.

Burt, M. R. (1980). Cultural myths and supports for rape. *Journal of Personality and Social Psychology, 38*(2), 217–230.

Button, M., & Cross, C. (2017). *Cyber frauds, scams and their victims.* London, UK: Routledge.

Button, M., Lewis, C., & Tapley, J. (2014). Not a victimless crime: The impact of fraud on individual victims and their families. *Security Journal*, 27, 36–54.

Buzawa, E., & Buzawa, C. (2003). *Domestic violence: The criminal justice response*. Thousand Oaks, CA: Sage.

Buzawa, E., Buzawa, C., & Stark, E. (2017). *Responding to domestic violence: The integration of criminal justice and human services* (5th ed.). Thousand Oaks, CA: Sage.

Calhoun, K. S., McCauley, J., & Crawford, M. E. (2006). Sexual assault. In R. D. McAulty, and M. M. Burnett (Eds.). *Sex and sexuality: Sexual deviation and sexual offenses* (pp. 97–130), (Vol. 3). London, UK: Praeger Perspectives.

Camacho, C., & Alarid, L. (2008). The significance of the victim advocate for domestic violence victims in municipal court. *Violence and Victims*, 23(3), 288–300.

Campbell, J. (2001). Safety planning based on lethality assessment for partners of batterers in intervention programs. *Journal of Aggression, Maltreatment & Trauma*, 5, 129–143.

Campbell, J. (2002). Health consequences of intimate partner violence. *The Lancet*, 359(9314), 1331–1336.

Campbell, J., & Soeken, K. (1999). Forced sex and intimate partner violence. *Violence Against Women*, 5(9), 1017–1035.

Campbell, R. (2008). The psychological impact of rape victims' experiences with the legal, medical, and mental health systems. *American Psychologist*, 63, 702–717.

Campbell, R., Bybee, D., Townsend, S. M., Shaw, J., Karim, N., & Markowitz, J. (2014). The impact of sexual assault nurse examiner programs on criminal case outcomes: A multisite replication study. *Violence Against Women*, 20(5), 607–625.

Campbell, R., Feeney, H., Pierce, S. J., Sharma, D. B., & Fehler-Cabral, G. (2016). Tested at last: How DNA evidence in untested rape kits can identify offenders and serial sexual assaults. *Journal of Interpersonal Violence*, 1–23.

Campbell, R., Greeson, M. R., & Fehler-Cabral, G. (2013). With care and compassion: Adolescent sexual assault victims' experiences in sexual assault examiner (SANE) programs. *Journal of Forensic Nursing*, 9, 68–75.

Campbell, R., Patterson, D., & Lichty, L. F. (2005). The effectiveness of sexual assault nurse examiner (SANE) programs: A review of psychological, medical, legal, and community outcomes. *Trauma, Violence, & Abuse*, 6(4), 313–329.

Campbell, R., Townsend, S. M., Long, S. M., Kinnison, K. E., Pulley, E. M., Adames, S. B., & Wasco, S. M. (2006). Responding to sexual assault victims' medical and emotional needs: A national study of the services provided by SANE programs. *Research in Nursing & Health*, 29, 384–398.

Capaldi, D. M., Knoble, N. B., Shortt, J. W., & Kim, H. K. (2012). A systematic review of risk factors for intimate partner violence. *Partner Abuse*, 3(2), 231–280.

Caplan, J. (2010). Parole release decisions: Impact of victim input on a representative sample of inmates. *Journal of Criminal Justice*, 38(3), 291–300.

Cappell, C., & Heiner, R. B. (1990). The intergenerational transmission of family aggression. *Journal of Family Violence*, 5, 135–152.

Carr, W., Baker, A., & Cassidy, J. (2016). Reducing criminal recidivism with an enhanced day reporting center for probationers with mental illness. *Journal of Offender Rehabilitation*, 55(2), 95–112.

Carroll, L. (2013). Problem-focused coping. In M. D. Gellman & J. R. Turner (Eds.), *Encyclopedia of behavioral M=medicine*. (Vol. 1, pp. 1540–1541). New York, NY: Springer.

Carson, J., Chenault, S., & Matusiak, R. (2016). Reintegrating to the prison community. *The Prison Journal*, 96(4), 623–644.

Carver, C. S. (2011). Coping. In R. J. Contrada & A. Baum (Eds.), *The handbook of stress science: Biology, psychology, and health*, (pp. 221–229). New York, NY: Springer.

Casanueva, C., Stambaugh, L., Tueller, S., Dolan, M., & Smith, K. (2012). *NSCAW II Wave 2 Report: Children's services, final report*, (OPRE Report #2012-59). Washington, DC: U.S. Department of Health and Human Services.

Cauffman, E., Feldman, S. S., Waterman, J., & Steiner, H. (1998). Posttraumatic stress disorder among female juvenile offenders. *Journal of the American Academy of Child & Adolescent Psychiatry*, 37(11), 1209–1216.

Cavanagh, C., & Cauffman, E. (2015). The land of the free: Undocumented families in the juvenile justice system. *Law & Human Behavior (American Psychological Association)*, 39(2), 152–161. doi:10.1037/lhb0000097

C'de Baca, J., Lapham, S., Liang, H., & Skipper, B. (2001). Victim impact panels: Do they impact drunk drivers? A follow-up of female and male, first-time and repeat offenders. *Journal of Studies on Alcohol*, 62(5), 615–620.

CdeBaca, L., & Sigman, J. N. (2014). Combating trafficking in persons: A call to action for global health professionals. *Global Health Science and Practice*, 2(3), 261–267.

Cecil, C. A. M., Viding, E., Fearon, P., Glaser, D., & McCrory, A. J. (2017). Disentangling the mental health impact of childhood abuse and neglect. *Child Abuse and Neglect*, 63, 106–119.

Center for Juvenile Justice Reform. (2015). *The Crossover Youth Practice Model (CYPM)*. Retrieved from https://cjjr .georgetown.edu/wp-content/uploads/2015/09/CYPM-Abbreviated-Guide.pdf.

Centers for Disease Control and Prevention. (2017). *Sexual violence: Definitions*. Retrieved from https://www.cdc .gov/violenceprevention/sexualviolence/definitions.html.

Champion, D. R., Harvey, P. J., & Schanz, Y. Y. (2011). Day reporting centers and recidivism: Comparing offender groups in a western Pennsylvania county study. *Journal of Offender Rehabilitation*, 50(7), 433–446.

Chang, E. C., Kahle, E. R., & Hirsch, J. K. (2015). Understanding how domestic abuse is associated with greater depressive symptoms in a community sample of female primary care patients: Does loss of belongingness matter? *Violence Against Women*, 21, 700–711.

Charbone-Lopez, K., Kruttschnitt, C., & Macmillan, R. (2006). Patterns of intimate partner violence and their associations with physical health, psychological distress, and substance use. *Public Health Reports*, 121, 382–392.

Chen, R., & Dong, X. (2017). Risk factors of elder abuse. In X. Dong (Ed.). *Elder Abuse Research, Practice and Policy* (pp. 93–107). New York, NY: Springer.

Cherniss, C. (1980). *Staff burnout: Job stress in the human services*. Beverly Hills, CA: Sage.

Cheung, M., & McNeil Boutté-Queen, N. (2010). Assessing the relative importance of the child sexual abuse interview protocol items to assist child victims in abuse disclosure. *Journal of Family Violence*, 25(1), 11–22.

Child Welfare Information Gateway. (2014). *Differential response to reports of child abuse and neglect*. Washington, DC: U.S. Department of Health and Human Services, Children's Bureau.

Child Welfare Information Gateway. (2015). *Mandatory reporters of child abuse and neglect*. Washington, DC: U.S. Department of Health and Human Services, Children's Bureau.

Child Welfare Information Gateway. (2017). *Foster care statistics 2015*. Washington, DC: U.S. Department of Health and Human Services, Children's Bureau.

Chisholm, C. A., Bullock, L., & Ferguson, J. E. (2017). Intimate partner violence and pregnancy: Epidemiology and impact. *American Journal of Obstetrics and Gynecology*, 217(2), 141–144.

Chisolm, J. F. (2014). Review of the status of cyberbullying and cyberbullying prevention. *Journal of Information Systems Education*, 25(1), 77–87.

Cissner, A. B. (2009). *Evaluating the mentors in violence prevention program preventing gender violence on a college campus*. Washington, DC: U.S. Department of Education.

Clarke, R., & Goldstein, H. (2003). *Reducing theft at construction sites: Lessons from a problem-oriented project*. U.S. Department of Justice, Office of Community Oriented Policing Services. Retrieved from http://www.popcenter .org/library/reading/pdfs/constructiontheft.pdf.

Clawson, H. J., Dutch, N., Solomon, A., & Grace, L. G. (2009). *Human trafficking into and within the United States: A review of the literature*. U.S. Department of Health and Human Services. Retrieved from http://www.wunrn.com/ news/2009/10_09/10_05_09/100509_trafficking.htm.

Clayton, E. W., Krugman, R. D., & Simon, P. (2013). *Confronting commercial sexual exploitation and sex trafficking of minors in the United States* (Eds). Washington, DC: The National Academies Press.

Clements, C., Sabourin, C., & Spiby, L. (2004). Dysphoria and hopelessness following battering: The role of perceived control, coping, and self-esteem. *Journal of Family Violence*, 19, 25–36.

CNN. (2015). *Famous Supermax prisoners*. Retrieved from http://www.cnn.com/2015/05/12/us/gallery/famous-supermax-prisoners/index.html.

Coalition Against Trafficking in Women. (2014). *Annual report*. New York: Author. Retrieved from http://www.catwinternational.org/Content/Documents/Reports/Annual%20Report%202014-3.pdf.

Coates, S., & Gaensbauer, T. I. (2009). Event trauma in early childhood: Symptoms, assessment, intervention. *Child and Adolescent Psychiatric Clinics of North America*, 18(3), 611–626.

Coffey, P., Leitenberg, H., Henning, K., Bennett, R. T., & Jankowski, M. K. (1996). Dating violence: The association between methods of coping and women's psychological adjustment. *Violence and Victims*, 11(3), 227–238.

Cohen, L. E., & Felson, M. (1979). Social change and crime rate trends: A routine activity approach. *American Sociological Review*, 588–608.

Cohen, L. E, Kluegel, J. R, & Land, K. C. (1981). Social inequality and predatory criminal victimization: an exposition and test of a formal theory. *American Sociological Review*, 46, 505–524.

Cohen, M. A., Miller, T. R., & Rossman, S. B. (1994). The costs and consequences of violent behavior in the United States. In J. Roth & A. Reiss (Eds.), *Understanding and preventing violence, Volume 4* (pp. 67–166). Washington, DC: National Academy Press.

Coker, A. L., Cook-Craig, P. G., Williams, C. M., Fisher, B. S., Clear, E. R., Hegge, L. M., & Garcia, L. S. (2011). Does teaching bystanding behaviors increase bystanding and change social norms supporting violence? The University of Kentucky experience. *Violence Against Women*, 16, 777–796.

Cole, H. (2009). Human trafficking: Implications for the role of the advanced practice forensic nurse. *Journal of the American Psychiatric Nurses Association*, 14, 462–470.

Colello, K. J. (2017). The elder justice act: Background and issues for congress. *Congressional Research Service*. Retrieved from http://www.crs.gov.

Collins, B. G., & Collins, T. M. (2005). *Crisis and trauma developmental-ecological intervention*. Boston, MA: Houghton Mifflin/Lahaska Press.

Comijs, H. C., Penninx, B. W., Knipscheer, K. P. M., & van Tilburg, W. (1999). Psychological distress in victims of elder mistreatment: The effects of social support and coping. *Journal of Gerontology: Psychological Sciences, 54*, 240–245.

Commission on the Status of Women City and County of San Francisco. (1991). *San Francisco's response to domestic violence: The Charan Investigation 1991*. San Francisco, CA: Author.

Compassion Capital Fund National Resource Center. (2010). *Identifying and promoting effective practices. Strengthening Nonprofits: A Capacity Builder's Resource Library*. Health and Human Services Contract Number HHSP23320082912YC. Portsmouth, NH: Dare Mighty Things.

Comstock, A., & McDaniel, N. (2004). The casework process. In C. Brittan & D. Hunt (Eds.). *Helping in child protective services: A competency based casework handbook* (2nd ed., pp. 31–49). New York, NY: Oxford University Press.

Conklin, J. (2012). *Criminology* (11th Edition). Englewood Cliffs, NJ: Prentice Hall.

Conner, D. H. (2014). Financial freedom: Women, money, and domestic abuse. *William & Mary Journal of Women & Law, 20*(2), 339–397.

Conrad, D., & Kellar-Guenther, Y. (2006). Compassion fatigue, burnout, and compassion satisfaction among Colorado child protection workers. *Child Abuse & Neglect, 30*(10), 1071–1080.

Cook, A., Blaustein, M., Spinazzola, J., & Kolk, B. (2003). *Complex trauma in children and adolescents*. White Paper from the National Child Traumatic Stress Network Complex Trauma Task Force. Los Angeles, CA/Durham, NC: National Center for Child Traumatic Stress.

Cook, J. M., Dinnen, S., & O'Donnell, C. (2011). Older women survivors of physical and sexual violence: A systematic review of the quantitative literature. *Journal of Women's Health, 20*(7), 1075–1081.

Cooper, A., Delmonico, D. L., & Burg, R. (2002). Cybersex users, abusers, and compulsives: New findings and implications. *Cybersex: The dark side of the force A special issue of the Journal of Sexual Addiction & Compulsivity, 7*, 5–27.

Cooper, A., & Smith, E. L., (2011). *Homicide trends in the United States, 1980–2008 annual rates for 2009 and 2010*. Washington, DC: U.S. Department of Justice, Office of Justice Programs, Bureau of Justice Statistics.

Cordner, G. (2010, January). *Reducing fear of crime strategies for police*. U.S. Department of Justice Office of Community Oriented Policing Services. Retrieved from http://www.popcenter.org/library/reading/pdfs/ReducingFear-Guide.pdf.

Corvo, K., & Carpenter, E. (2000). Effects of parental substance abuse on current levels of domestic violence: A possible elaboration of intergenerational transmission processes. *Journal of Family Violence, 15*, 123–137.

Council on Child and Adolescent Health. (1998). The role of home-visitation programs in improving health outcomes for children and families. *Pediatrics, 101*(3), 486–489.

Courtney, M. (1994). Factors associated with the reunification of foster children with their families. *Social Service Review, 68*, 81–108.

Courtney, M., & Heuring, D. H. (2005). The transition to adulthood for youth "aging out" of the foster care system. In D. W. Osgood, E. M. Foster, C. Flanagan, & G. R. Ruth (Eds.), *On your own without a net* (pp. 27–67). Chicago. IL: University of Chicago Press.

Courtney, M., Piliavin, I., Grogan-Kaylor, A., & Nesmith, A. (2001). Foster youth transitions to adulthood: A longitudinal view of youth leaving care. *Child Welfare, 80*(6), 685–717.

Coyne, I. J., Farley, S., Axtell, C., Sprigg, C. A., Best, L., & Kwok, O. (2017). Understanding the relationship between experiencing workplace cyberbullying, employee mental strain and job satisfaction: A disempowerment approach. *International Journal of Human Resource Management, 28*(7), 945–972.

Craig, M. (2000). *Fear of crime among the elderly: A multimethod study of the small town experience*. New York, NY: Garland.

Crandall C., & Helitzer, D. (2003). *Impact evaluation of a Sexual Assault Nurse Examiner (SANE) program* (Award Number 98-WT-VX-0027). Washington, DC: National Institute of Justice.

Crandall, C., & Helitzer, D. (2003). *Impact evaluation of a sexual assault nurse examiner (SANE) program.* (NIJ Document No. 203276). Washington, DC: National Institute of Justice.

Crime Victims' Institute Sam Houston State University Criminal Justice Center. (2005). *Inviting victim participation in pleas agreements*. Retrieved from http://dev.cjcenter.org/_files/cvi/no22005.pdf.

Cronch, L. E., Viljoen, J. L., & Hansen, D. J. (2006). Forensic interviewing in child sexual abuse cases: Current techniques and future directions. *Aggression and Violent Behavior, 11*(3), 195–207.

Cruickshank, A., & Collins, D. (2012). Culture change in elite sport performance teams: Examining and advancing effectiveness in the new era. *Journal of Applied Sport Psychology, 24*(3), 338–355. doi:10.1080/10413200.2011.650819

Currie, J., & Tekin, E. (2006). *Does child abuse cause crime?* National Bureau of Economic Research (working paper). Retrieved from http://www.nber.org/papers/w12171.

Cutuli, J., George, R., Coulton, C., Schretzman, M., Crampton, D., Charvat, B., . . . Lee, E. (2016). From foster care to juvenile justice: Exploring characteristics of youth in three cities. *Children and Youth Services Review, 67*, 84–94.

Cyberbullying Research Center. (2017). *Advice for adult victims of cyberbullying*. Retrieved from https://cyberbullying.org/advice-for-adult-victims-of-cyberbullying.

Dabby, C. (2017). *A to Z advocacy model: Asians and Pacific Islanders build an inventory of evidence-informed practices.* Oakland, CA: Asian Pacific Institute on Gender-Based Violence.

Dahlberg, L. L., & Krug, E. G. (2002). Violence—A global public health problem. In E. G. Krug, L. L. Dahlberg, J. A. Mercy, A. B. Zwi, & R. Lozano. (Eds.), *World report on violence and health* (pp. 3–21). Geneva, Switzerland: World Health Organization.

Daigle, L. (2013). *Victimology: The essentials*. Thousand Oaks, CA: Sage.

Daigle, L., Fisher, B., & Cullen, F. (2008). The violent and sexual victimization of college women: Is repeat victimization a problem? *Journal of Interpersonal Violence, 23*(9), 1296–1313.

Daigle, L. E., & Muftic, L. R. (2016). *Victimology*. London, UK: Sage.

Danieli, Y., Rodley, N., & Weisaeth, L. (1996). Introduction. In Y. Danieli, N. Rodley, & L. Weisaeth (Eds.), *International responses to traumatic stress* (pp. 1–14). New York, NY: Baywood.

Danis, F. S. (2003). The emerging field of crime victim assistance: Are social workers ready? *Professional Development: The Journal of Continuing Social Work Education, 6*(3), 13–19.

Dank, M., Khan, B., Downey, P. M., Kotonias, C., Mayer, D., Owens, C., Pacifici, L., & Yu, L. (2014). *Estimating the size and structure of the underground commercial sex economy in eight major U.S. cities.* The Urban Institute. Retrieved from https://www.urban.org/sites/default/files/alfresco/publication-pdfs/413047-Estimating-the-Size-and-Structure-of-the-Underground-Commercial-Sex-Economy-in-Eight-Major-US-Cities.PDF.

Daquin, J., Daigle, L., & Listwan, S. (2016). Vicarious victimization in prison. *Criminal Justice and Behavior, 43*(8), 1018–1033.

Davidson, H. (2011). The CAPTA Reauthorization Act of 2010: What advocates should know. *Child Law Practice, 29*(12), 177–185.

Davies, K. (2010). Victim assistance programs, United States. In B. S. Fisher & S. P. Lab (Eds.), *Encyclopedia of victimology and crime prevention* (pp. 968–969). Thousand Oaks, CA: Sage.

Davis, L. (2001). Victimization risk of vehicle hijacking victims: A routine activity approach. *Acta Criminologica, 14*(2), 108–116.

Davis, M. H., Hall, J. A., & Meyer, M. (2003). The first year: Influences on the satisfaction, involvement, and persistence of new community volunteers. *Personality and Social Psychology Bulletin, 29*(2), 248–260.

Davis, R., Lurigio, A., & Skogan, W. (1999). Services for victims: A market research study. *International Review of Victimology, 6*(2), 101–115.

Davis, R. C., & Henderson, N. J. (2003). Willingness to report crimes: The role of ethnic group membership and community efficacy. *Crime & Delinquency, 49*(4), 564–580.

Davis, R. C., Henley, M., & Smith, B. E. (1990). *Victim impact statements: Their effects on court outcomes and victim satisfaction.* New York, NY: New York City Victim Service Agency.

Davis, R. C., & Smith, B. E. (1994). Victim impact statements and victim satisfaction: An unfulfilled promise? *Journal of Criminal Justice, 22*(1), 1–12.

Davis, R. C., & Ullman, S. E. (2013). They key contributions of family, friends and neighbors. In R. C. Davis, A. J. Lurigio, & S. Herman (Eds.), *Victims of crime* (4th ed., pp. 233–250). Thousand Oaks, CA: Sage.

DeGraff, A., & Schaffer, J. (2008). Emotion-focused coping: A primary defense against stress for people living with spinal cord injury. *Journal of Rehabilitation, 74*(1), 19–24.

DeGue, S. (2014). *Preventing sexual violence on college campuses: Lessons from research and practice.* Centers for Disease Control and Prevention. Retrieved from https://www.notalone.gov/schools.

DeGue, S., Holt, M. K., Massetti, G. M., Matjasko, J. L., Tharp, A. T., & Valle, L. A. (2012). Looking ahead toward community-level strategies to prevent sexual violence. *Journal of Women's Health, 21*(1), 1–3.

DeHart, D. D. (2010). Collaboration between victim services and faith organizations: Benefits, challenges, and recommendations. *The Journal of Religion & Spirituality in Social Work, 29*(2), 349–371.

Dehue, F., Bolman, C., & Vollink, T. (2008). Cyber bullying: Youngsters' experiences and parental perception. *Cyber Psychology and Behavior, 11*, 217–223.

Delisi, M., & Hochstetler, A. L. (2002). An exploratory assessment of Tittle's control balance theory: Results from the national youth survey. *The Justice Professional, 15*(3), 261–272.

DePaolis, K., & Williford, A. (2015). The nature and prevalence of cyber victimization among elementary school children. *Child Youth Care Forum, 44*, 377–393.

Department of Defense. (2016). *Victim and witness assistance council.* Retrieved from http://vwac.defense.gov/military.aspx.

DePrince, A. P., Belknap, J., & Gover, A. (2012). *The effectiveness of coordinated outreach in intimate partner violence cases: A randomized, longitudinal design.* The National Institute of Justice and Evaluation on Violence Against Women, (Document No: 238480, Award No: 2007-WG-BX-0002). Retrieved from https://www.ncjrs.gov/pdffiles1/nij/grants/238480.pdf.

Deshpande, N. A., & Nour, N. M. (2013). Sex trafficking of women and girls. *Reviews in Obstetrics & Gynecology*, 6(1), 22–27.

Development Services Group, Inc. (2014). *Commercial sexual exploitation of children/sex trafficking.* Literature review. Washington, DC: Office of Juvenile Justice and Delinquency Prevention. Retrieved from https://www.ojjdp.gov/mpg/litreviews/CSECSexTrafficking.pdf.

Dhami, M., Mantle, G., & Fox, D. (2009). Restorative justice in prisons. *Contemporary Justice Review*, 12(4), 433–448.

Dickerson, S., & Kemeny, M. (2004). Acute stressors and cortisol responses: A theoretical integration and synthesis of laboratory research. *Psychological Bulletin*, 130, 355–391.

Diehl, C., Glaser, T., & Bohner, G. (2014). Face the consequences: Learning about victim's suffering reduces sexual harassment myth acceptance and men's likelihood to sexually harass. *Aggressive Behavior*, 40(6), 489–503.

Dishion, T. J., & Patterson, G. R. (2006). The development and ecology of antisocial behavior in children and adolescents. In D. Cicchetti & D. J. Cohen (Eds.), *Developmental psychopathology: Vol. 3: Risk, disorder, and adaptation* (pp. 503–541). New York, NY: Wiley.

Donegan, R. (2012). Bullying and cyberbullying: History, statistics, law, prevention and analysis. *The Elon Journal of Undergraduate Research in Communications*, 3(1), 33–42.

Dong, X., Simon, M., Mendes de Leon, C., Fulmer, T., Beck, T., & Hebert, L. (2009). Elder self-neglect and abuse and mortality risk in a community-dwelling population. *Journal of the American Medical Association*, 302(5), 517–526.

Dooley, J. J., Pyzalski, J., & Cross, D. (2009). Cyberbullying versus face-to-face bullying: A theoretical and conceptual review. *Journal of Psychology*, 217, 182–188.

DuBow, F., McCabe, E., & Kaplan, G. (1979). *Reactions to crime: A critical review of the literature.* Unpublished report, Center for Urban Affairs, Northwestern University.

Dunn, L. L. (2014). Addressing sexual violence in higher education: Ensuring compliance with the Clery Act, Title IX and VAWA. *Georgetown Journal of Gender & the Law*, 15, 563–584.

Duquette, D. N. (1990). *Advocating for the child in protection proceedings.* Lexington, MA: Lexington Books.

Durfee, A. (2012). Situational ambiguity and gendered patterns of arrest for intimate partner violence. *Violence Against Women*, 18(1), 64–84.

Duron, J., & Cheung, M. (2016). Impact of repeated questioning on interviewers: Learning from a forensic interview training project. *Journal of Child Sexual Abuse*, 25(4), 347–362.

Durose, M. R., Harlow, C. W., Langan, P. A., Motivans, M., Rantala, R. R., & Smith, E. L. (2005). *Family violence statistics: Including statistics on strangers and acquaintances.* Washington, DC: U.S. Department of Justice.

Dussich, J. P. J. (2015). The evolution of international victimology and its current status in the world today. *Revista de Victimologia/Journal of Victimology*, 1(1), 37–81.

Dussich, J. P. J., & Mundy, K. G. (2006). *Raising the Global Standards for Victims: The proposed convention on justice for Victims of Crime and Abuse of Power.* Tokyo, Japan: Seibundo.

Dutton, M. G. (1995). Male abusiveness in intimate relationships. *Clinical Psychology Review*, 15, 567–581.

Duwe, G., & Donnay, W. (2008). The impact of Megan's law on sex offender recidivism: The Minnesota experience. *Criminology*, 46(2), 411–446.

Eckenrode, J., Laird, D., & Zahn-Waxler, C. (1993). School performance and disciplinary problems among abused and neglected children. *Developmental Psychology*, 29(1), 53–62.

Edmunds, C. N., & Underwood, T. L. (2003). Victim advocacy and public policy. In T. L. Underwood and C. Edmunds (Eds.), *Victim assistance: Exploring individual practice, organizational policy, and societal responses* (pp. 225–238). New York, NY: Springer.

Eisenburg, M. E., Lust, K. A., Hannan, P. J., & Porta, C. (2016). Campus sexual violence resources and emotional health of college women who have experienced sexual assault. *Victim and Violence*, 31(2), 274–284.

Ekstrand, L. E. (1996). *Preventing child sexual abuse: Research inconclusive about effectiveness of child education programs.* Washington, DC: General Accounting Office.

Ellemers, N., & Boezeman, E. J. (2010). Empowering the volunteer organization: What volunteer organizations can do to recruit, content and retain volunteers. In S. Stürmer & M. Snyder (Eds.), *The psychology of prosocial behavior: Group processes, intergroup relations, and helping* (pp. 245–268). Oxford, UK: Wiley-Blackwell.

Ellis, R., & Sanchez, R. (2016, September 4). *Jacob Wetterling: Remains of missing Minnesota boy found, authorities say.* Retrieved from http://www.cnn.com/2016/09/03/us/jacob-wetterling-remains-found/index.html.

Ellis, R. B., & Hart, K. J. (2003). Barriers to services. In T. L. Underwood & C. Edmunds (Eds.), *Victim assistance: Exploring individual practice, organizational policy, and societal responses* (pp. 51–65). New York, NY: Springer.

Englebrecht, C., & Chavez, J. (2014). Whose statement is it? An examination of victim impact statements delivered in court. *Victims & Offenders, 9*(4), 386–412.

English, V. (2012). *Medical ethics today: The BMA's handbook of ethics and law.* London, UK: British Medical Association.

Epstein, R., & Edelman, P. (2013). *Blueprint: A multidisciplinary approach to the domestic sex trafficking of girls.* Based on the conference "Critical connections: A multisystems approach to the domestic sex trafficking of girls." Washington, DC: Georgetown Law.

Erez, E. (1990). Victim participation in sentencing: Rhetoric and reality. *Journal of Criminal Justice, 18*(1), 19–31.

Erez, E., & Belknap, J. (1998). In their own words: Battered women's assessment of the criminal processing system's responses. *Violence and Victims, 13*(3), 251–268.

Erez, E., & Laster, C. (1999). Neutralizing victim reform: Legal professionals' perspectives on victims and impact statements. *Crime and Delinquency, 45*(4), 530–553.

Erez, E., & Roberts, J. (2013). Victim participation in criminal justice. In R. C. Davis, L. J. Arthur, & S. Herman (Eds.), *Victims of crime* (4th ed., pp. 251–270). Thousand Oaks, CA: Sage.

Erez, E., & Roeger, L. (1995). Crime impact vs. victim impact: Evaluation of victim impact statements in South Australia. *Criminology Australia, 6*, 3–8.

Erez, E., & Rogers, L. (1999). Victim impact statements and sentencing outcomes and processes: The perspectives of legal professionals. *British Journal of Criminology, 39*(2), 216–239.

Erez, E., & Tontodonato, P. (1992). Victim participation in sentencing and satisfaction with justice. *Justice Quarterly, 9*(3), 393–417.

Ericksen, J., Dudley, C., McIntosh, G., Ritch, L., Shumay, S., & Simpson, M. (2002). Clients experience with a specialized sexual assault service. *Journal of Emergency Nursing, 28*, 86–90.

Erickson, M. F., & Egeland, B. (2002). Child neglect. In J. E. Myers, L. Berlinger, J. Briere, C. T. Hendrix, C. Jenny, & T. A. Reid (Eds.), *The APSAC handbook on child maltreatment* (2nd ed., pp. 3–20). Thousand Oaks, CA: SAGE.

Eriksson, L., & Mazerolle, P. (2015). A cycle of violence? Examining family-of-origin violence, attitudes, and intimate partner violence perpetration. *Journal of Interpersonal Violence, 30*(6), 945–964.

Estes, R, & Weiner, N. A. (2003). *The commercial exploitation of children in the U.S., Canada and Mexico: An executive summary of the U.S. national study.* Retrieved from: http://www.sp2.upenn.edu/restes/CSEC_Files/Exec_Sum_020220.pdf

Estes, R. J., & Weiner, N. A. (2001). *The commercial sexual exploitation of children in the U.S., Canada, and Mexico.* Retrieved from http://news.findlaw.com/hdocs/docs/sextrade/upenncsec90701.pdf.

Estes, R. J., & Weiner, N. A. (2002). *The commercial sexual exploitation of children in the U.S., Canada and Mexico* (Full revised report of the U.S. national study). Retrieved from http://www.sp2.upenn.edu/restes/CSEC_Files/Complete_CSEC_020220.pdf.

Estes, R. J., & Weiner, N. A. (2005). The commercial sexual exploitation of children in the United States. In S. W. Cooper, R. J. Estes, A. P. Giardio, N. D. Kellogg, and V. I. Vieth (Eds.), *Medical, legal & social science aspects of child sexual exploitation* (Vol. 1, pp. 95–128). St. Louis, MO: GW Medical.

Ewick, P., & Silbey, S. (1995). Subversive stories and hegemonic tales: Toward a sociology of narrative. *Law & Society Review, 29*(2), 197–226.

Exum, M., Hartman, J., Friday, P., & Lord, V. (2014). Policing domestic violence in the post-SARP era. *Crime & Delinquency, 60*(7), 999–1032.

Falk, N. L., Baigis, J., Kopac, C. (2012). Elder mistreatment and the elder justice act. *The Online Journal of Issues in Nursing, 17*(3).

Faller, K. C., Cordisco Steele, L., & Nelson-Gardell, D. (2010). Allegations of sexual abuse of a child: What to do when a single forensic interview isn't enough. *Journal of Child Sexual Abuse, 19*(5), 572–589.

Fanflick, P. L. (2007). *Victim responses to sexual assault: Counterintuitive or simply adaptive?* Arlington, VA: The American Prosecutors Research Institute: The Research and Development Division of the National District Attorneys Association.

Fattah, E. (1991). *Understanding criminal victimization: An introduction to theoretical victimology.* Ontario, Canada: Prentice Hall.

Fattah, E. (2000). Victimology today: Recent theoretical and applied developments. *UNAFEI Resource Material Series, 56,* 60–70.

Fattah, E. A. (2000). Victimology: Past, present and future. *Criminologie, 33,* 17–46.

Fattah, E. A. (2010). The evolution of a young, promising discipline: Sixty years of victimology, a retrospective and prospective look. In S. G. Shohom, P. Knepper, & M. Kett (Eds.). *International handbook of victimology* (pp. 43–94). Boca Raton, FL: Taylor & Francis.

FBI. (2016). *Internet crime report.* Internet Crime Complaint Center. Retrieved from https:///pdf.ic3.gov/2016_IC3Report.pdf.

Federal Bureau of Investigation (FBI). (2000). *Uniform crime reporting: National Incident-Based Reporting System.* Washington, DC: Author. Retrieved from https://www2.fbi.gov/ucr/nibrs/manuals/v1all.pdf.

Federal Bureau of Investigation (FBI). (2014a). *Human trafficking in the Uniform Crime Reporting (UCR) program.* Washington, DC: Author. Retrieved from https://ucr.fbi.gov/human-trafficking.

Federal Bureau of Investigation (FBI). (2014b, December 11). *Frequently asked questions about the change in the UCR definition of rape.* Washington, DC: Author. Retrieved from https://ucr.fbi.gov/recent-program-updates/new-rape-definition-frequently-asked-questions.

Federal Bureau of Investigation (FBI). (2015, December). *FBI releases 2014 crime statistics from the National Incident-Based Reporting System.* Washington, DC: Author. Retrieved from https://ucr.fbi.gov/about-us/cjis/ucr/nibrs/2014/resource-pages/summary-of-nibrs-2014_final.pdf.

Federal Bureau of Prisons. (2017). *Statistics.* Retrieved from https://www.bop.gov/about/statistics/population_statistics .jsp.

Ferguson, C., & Turvey, B. E. (2009). Victimology: A brief history with an introduction to forensic victimology. In B. E. Turvey & W. Petherick (Eds.), *Forensic victimology: Examining violent crime victims in investigative and legal contexts* (pp. 1–32). Amsterdam: Elsevier Science.

Ferraro, K. F. (1995). *Fear of crime: Interpreting victimization risk.* Albany: State University of New York Press.

Ferraro, K. F. (1996). Women's fear of victimization: Shadow of sexual assault? *Social Forces, 75,* 667–690.

Ferri, E. (1908). *The positive school of criminology.* Chicago, IL: Charles H. Kerr & Company.

Figley, C. R. (1995). *Compassion fatigue: Coping with secondary traumatic stress disorder in those who treat the traumatized.* New York, NY: Brunner/Mazel.

Finkelhor, D., Cross, T. P., & Cantor, E. N. (2005). *How the justice system responds to juvenile victims: A comprehensive model.* Juvenile Justice Bulletin (NCJ210951), 1–12. Washington, DC: Office of Juvenile Justice & Delinquency Prevention.

Finkelhor, D., Paschall, M. J., & Hashima, P. (2001). Juvenile crime victims in the justice system. In S. O. White (Ed.), *Handbook of youth and justice* (p. 1128). New York, NY: Plenum.

Finklea, K. (2014). *Identity theft: Trends and issues* (Congressional Research Service No. 7-5700).Washington, DC: Congressional Research Service. Retrieved from http://fas.org/sgp/crs/misc/R40599.pdf.

Finklea, K., & Theohary, C. A. (2015). *Cybercrime: Conceptual issues for congress and U.S. Law Enforcement.* (Congressional Research Service, 7-5700). Washington, DC: Congressional Research Service. Retrieved from https://fas.org/sgp/crs/misc/R42547.pdf.

FINRA Investor Education Foundation. (2013). *Financial fraud and fraud susceptibility in the United States research report from a 2012 national survey.* Applied Research & Consulting LLC. Retrieved from https://www.saveand invest.org/sites/default/files/Financial-Fraud-And-Fraud-Susceptibility-In-The-United-States.pdf. ·

Fishe, G. (2000). Plea bargaining's triumph. *Yale Law Journal, 109*, 855.

Fisher, B. S., Cullen, F. T., & Turner, M. G. (2000). *The sexual victimization of college women*. Washington, DC: U. S. Department of Justice.

Fisher, B. S., Daigle, L. E., & Cullen, F. T. (2008). Rape against women: What can research offer to guide the development of prevention programs and risk reduction interventions? *Journal of Contemporary Criminal Justice, 24*(2), 163–177.

Fisher, B. S., Daigle, L. E., & Cullen, F. T. (2010). *Unsafe in the ivory tower: The sexual victimization of college women*. Thousand Oaks, CA: Sage.

Fisher, B. S., Daigle, L. E., Cullen, F. T., & Turner, M. G. (2003). Reporting sexual victimization to the police and others: Results from a national-level study of college women. *Criminal Justice and Behavior, 30*(1), 6–38.

Fisher, B. S., Reyns, B. W., & Sloan, J. J., III. (2016). *Introduction to victimology: Contemporary theory, research and practice*. New York, NY: Oxford University Press.

Fisher-Stewart, G. (2007). *Community policing explained: A guide for local governments*. U.S. Department of Justice. Office of Community Oriented Policing Services.

Fitzpatrick, C. (2014). Breaking barriers to "Breaking the Cycle." *Seattle Journal for Social Justice, 13*(2), 603–648.

Flanagan, J., Sullivan, T., & Connell, C. (2015). Profiles of intimate partner violence victimization, substance misuse, and depression among female caregivers involved with child protective services. *Journal of Family Violence, 30*(8), 999–1005.

Florida State University Institute of Family Violence Studies. (2012). *Domestic violence fatality review information and resources*. Retrieved from http://familyvio.csw.fsu.edu/wp-content/uploads/2013/06/annotated_bib.pdf.

Floyd, G. (1970). Compensation to victims of violent crime. *Tulsa Law Review, 6*(2), 100–145.

Foa, E. B., & Rothbaum, B. O. (2001). *Treating the trauma of rape: Cognitive-behavioral therapy for PTSD*. New York, NY: Guilford Press.

Folkman, S., & Moskowitz, J. T. (2004). Coping: Pitfalls and promise. *Annual Review of Psychology, 55*(1), 745–774.

Follette, M., Polusny, M., & Milberk, K. (1994). Mental health and law enforcement professionals: Trauma history, psychological symptoms, and impact of providing services to child sex abuse survivors. *Journal of Clinical and Counseling Psychology, 25*(3), 275–282.

Follingstad, D. R., Rutledge, L. L., Berg, B. J., Hause, E. S., & Polek, D. S. (1990). The role of emotional abuse in physically abusive relationships. *Journal of Family Violence, 5*(2), 107–120.

Forbes, G. B., Adams-Curtis, L. E., Pakalka, A. H., & White, K. B. (2006). Dating aggression, sexual coercion, and aggression-supporting attitudes among college men as a function of participation in aggressive high school sports. *Violence Against Women, 12*, 441–455.

Ford, J. D., Chapman, J. F., Hawke, J., & Albert, D. (2007). *Trauma among youth in the juvenile justice system: Critical issues and new directions*. Research and Program Brief. Delmar, NY: National Center for Mental Health and Juvenile Justice.

Fors, S. W., & Rojek, D. G. (1999). The effect of victim impact panels on DUI/DWI rearrest rates: A 12-month followup. *Journal of Studies on Alcohol, 60*, 132–153.

Fraser, H. (2005). Women, love, and intimacy "gone wrong": Fire, wind, and ice. *Affilia, 20*(1), 10–20.

Friedman, K., Bischoff, H., Davis, R., & Person A. (1982). *Victims and helpers: Reactions to crime*. Washington, DC: U.S. Department of Justice, National Institute of Justice.

Gaboury, M., Seymour, A., & Heisler, C. (2012). *Elder abuse: Office for victims of crime, training and technical assistance center*. Office for Victims of Crime. Retrieved from http://www.ncdsv.org/images/OVCTTAC_ElderAbuse ResourcePaper_2012.pdf.

Gagnon, K. L., & DePrince, A. P. (2017). Head injury screening and intimate partner violence: A brief report. *Journal of Trauma & Dissociation, 18*(4), 635–644.

Gallagher, B. (2007). Internet-initiated incitement and conspiracy to commit child sexual abuse (CSA): The typology, extent and nature of known cases. *Journal of Sexual Aggression, 13*(2), 101–119.

Gallagher, B., Fraser, C., Christmann, K., & Hodgson, B. (2006). *International and Internet child sexual abuse and exploitation: research report*. Huddersfield, UK: Centre for Applied Childhood Studies; University of Huddersfield.

Gallagher, R. (2013). Compassion fatigue. *Canadian Family Physician, 59*(3), 265–268.

Gannon, M., & Mihorean, K. (2005). Criminal victimization in Canada, 2004. *Juristat*, 25(7). Ottawa: Statistics Canada. Retrieved from http://www.oea.org/dsp/documents/victimization_surveys/canada/Canada%20-%20Victimization%20Report%20with%20Methodology%202004.pdf.

GAO. (2017). *Costs of crime: Experts report challenges estimating costs and suggest improvements to better inform policy decisions*. Washington, DC: U.S. Government Accountability Office.

Garcia-Moreno, C., Henrica, A. F. M., Watts, C., Ellsbery, M., & Heise, L. (2005). *WHO multi-country study on women's health and domestic violence against women: Initial results on prevalence, health outcomes and women's responses*. Geneva: World Health Organization.

Garofalo, J. (1981). The fear of crime: Causes and consequences. *Journal of Criminal Law and Criminology*, 72(2), 839–857.

Gaudin, J. M. (1993). *Child neglect: A guide for intervention*. U.S. Department of Health and Human Services, Administration for Children and Families, Administration on Children, Youth and Families, National Center on Child Abuse and Neglect. Washington DC: Westover Consultants, Inc. Contract no: HHS-105-89-1730.

Gelles, R. (2005). Protecting children is more important than preserving families. In D. Loseke, R. Gelles, & M. Cavanaugh (Eds.), *Current controversies on family violence* (pp. 329–340). Thousand Oaks, CA: Sage.

Gelles, R., & Cornell, C. (1990). *Intimate violence in families* (2nd ed.). Newbury Park, CA: Sage.

George, R. M. (1990). The reunification process in substitute care. *Social Service Review*, 64, 422–457.

Gercke, M. (2012). *Understanding cybercrime: Phenomena, challenges and legal response*. Infrastructure Enabling Environment and E-Application Department, ITU Telecommunication Development Bureau.

Gewirtz, A., & Edleson, J. (2007). Young children's exposure to intimate partner violence: Towards a developmental risk and resilience framework for research and intervention. *Journal of Family Violence*, 22(3), 157–163.

Giannelli, P. C. (1997). Rape trauma syndrome. *Faculty Publications*, 346, 270–279. Retrieved from: http://scholarly commons.law.case.edu/faculty_publications/346.

Gibbons, J., & Katzenbach, N. (2006). *Confronting confinement: A report of the commission on safety and abuse in America's prisons*. New York, NY: Vera Institute of Justice.

Gibbs, D., Hardison Walters, J. L., Lutnick, A., Miller, S., & Kluckman, M. (2014). *Evaluation of services for domestic minor victims of human trafficking*. Research Triangle Park, NC: RTI International.

Gibel, S., Carter, M. M., & Ramirez, R. (2016). *Evidence-based decision making: A guide for victim service providers*. Silver Springs, MD: Center for Effective Public Policy.

Gibson, L., Holt, J., Fondacaro, K., Tang, T., Powell, T., & Turbitt, E. (1999). An examination of antecedent traumas and psychiatric comorbidity among male inmates with PTSD. *Journal of Traumatic Stress*, 12(3), 473–484.

Giffords, E. D., & Dina, R. P. (2004). Strategic planning in nonprofit organizations: Continuous quality performance improvement—A case study. *International Journal of Organizational Theory and Behavior*, 6(4), 66–80.

Gilbert, E. (2017). Victim compensation for acts of terrorism and the limits of the state. *Critical Studies on Terrorism*, 1–20.

Gill, C., Weisburd, D., Telep, C., Vitter, W., & Bennett, Z. (2014). Community-oriented policing to reduce crime, disorder and fear and increase satisfaction and legitimacy among citizens: A systematic review. *Journal of Experimental Criminology*, 10(4), 399–428.

Girgenti, A. (2015). The intersection of victim race and gender. *Race and Justice*, 5(4), 307–329.

Glisson, C., Landsverk, J., Schoenwald, S., Kelleher, K., Hoagwood, K., Mayberg, S., & Green, P. (2008). Assessing the organizational social context (OSC) of mental health services: Implications for research and practice. *Administration and Policy in Mental Health and Mental Health Services Research*, 35(1–2), 98–113.

Godbout, N., Pier-Vaillancourt-Morel, M., Bigras, N., Briere, J., Hebert, M., Runtz, M., & Sabourin, S. (2017). Intimate partner violence in male survivors of child maltreatment: A meta-analysis. *Trauma, Violence, & Abuse*, 1–15.

Goldfarb, S. (2008). *Expert group meeting on good practices in legislation on violence against women*. United Nations Office at Vienna, Austria, 26–28 May. The legal response to violence against women in the United States of America: Recent reforms and continuing challenges. Retrieved from http://www.un.org/womenwatch/daw/egm/vaw_ legislation_2008/expertpapers/EGMGPLVAW%20 paper%20 (Sally%20Goldfarb).pdf.

Goodkind, S., Shook, J., Kim, K., Pohlig, R., & Herring, D. (2013). From child welfare to juvenile justice. *Youth Violence and Juvenile Justice*, *11*(3), 249–272.

Goodman, D. J. (2013). *Enforcing ethics: A scenario-based workbook for police and corrections recruits and officers* (4th ed.). Upper Saddle River, NJ: Pearson.

Goodno, N. H. (2007). Cyberstalking, a new crime: Evaluating the effectiveness of current state and federal laws. *Missouri Law Review*, *72*(1), 125–196.

Goodrich-Liley, D. (2017). Victimization of the elderly. In L. G. Bostaph & D. D. Swerin (Eds.). *Victimology: Crime victimization and victim services* (pp. 305–321). New York, NY: Wolters Kluwer.

Goodrum, S. (2007). Victims' rights, victims' expectations, and law enforcement workers' constraints in cases of murder. *Law & Social Inquiry*, *32*(3), 725–757.

Goolkasian, G. A. (1986). *Confronting domestic violence: A guide for criminal justice agencies*. Washington, DC: U.S. Department of Justice.

Gordon, J., & Baker, T. (2017). Examining correctional officers' fear of victimization by inmates: The influence of fear facilitators and fear inhibitors. *Criminal Justice Policy Review*, *28*(5), 462–487.

Gosselin, D. K. (2014). *Heavy hands: An introduction to the crimes of intimate and family violence*. Boston, MA: Pearson

Gottfredson, M. R. (1981). On the etiology of criminal victimization. *Journal of Criminal Law and Criminology*, *72*, 714–727.

Gottfredson, M. R., & Hirschi, T. (1990). *A general theory of crime*. Stanford, CA: Stanford University Press.

Government Accountability Office (GAO). (2011). Elder justice: Stronger federal leadership could enhance national response to elder abuse. Retrieved from http://www.gao .gov/assets/320/316224.pdf.

Gray, D., Citron, D. K., & Rinehart, L. C. (2013). Fighting cybercrime after *United States v. Jones*. *Journal of Criminal Law and Criminology*, *103*(3), 745–801.

Green, A., Albanese, B., Shapiro, N., Aarons, G., Deleon, P., . . . et al. (2014). The roles of individual and organizational factors in burnout among community-based mental health service providers. *Psychological Services*, *11*(1), 41–49.

Green, F. (2015). *Witnessing executions*. Retrieved from https://pdfs.semanticscholar.org/050a/3fba129bafbba454 dc806cca59e2ca5a35d5.pdf.

Greenbaum, J. (2014). Commercial sexual exploitation and sex trafficking of children in the United States. *Current Problems in Pediatric Adolescence Health Care*, *44*, 245–269.

Greenbaum, J. (2016). Identifying victims of human trafficking in the emergency department. *Clinical Pediatric Emergency Medicine*, *17*(4), 241–248.

Greene, E., Koehring, H., & Quiat, M. (1998). Victim impact evidence in capital cases: Does the victim's character matter? *Journal of Applied Social Psychology*, *28*(2), 145–156.

Greeson, M. (2014). *Sexual assault response team (SART) functioning and effectiveness from the national SART project*. Retrieved from https://www.nsvrc.org/sites/default/ files/publication_researchbrief_sexual-assault-response-team-functioning-effectiveness.pdf.

Greeson, M. R., & Campbell, R. (2013). Sexual Assault Response Teams (SARTs): An empirical review of their effectiveness and challenges to successful implementation. *Trauma, Violence, & Abuse*, *41*, 327–350.

Gregory, D. E., & Janosik, S. M. (2003). The effect of the Clery Act on campus judicial practices. *Journal of College Student Development*, *44*(6), 763–778.

Griffin, T., & Wooldredge, J. (2013). Judges' reactions to Ohio's "Jessica's law." *Crime & Delinquency*, *59*(6), 861–885.

Grobman, G. (1999). *The nonprofit handbook*. Harrisburg, PA: White Hat Communications.

Groenhuijsen, M. (2009). Current status of the Convention on Justice for Victims of Crime and Abuse of Power. In J. P. J. Dussich and K. G. Mundy (Eds.), *Raising the global standards for victims: The proposed convention on justice for victims of crime and abuse of power* (pp. 7–20). Tokyo, Japan: Seibundo.

Groenhuijsen, M. (2013). International protocols on victims' rights and some reflections on significant recent developments in victimology. In R. Peacock (Ed.), *Victimology in South Africa* (2nd Edition), (pp. 313–332). Pretoria: Van Schaik.

Groff, E. R. (2007). Simulation for theory testing and experimentation: An example using routine activity theory and street robbery. *Journal of Quantitative Criminology, 23,* 75–103.

Gross, S., & Matheson, D. (2003). What they say at the end: Capital victims' families and the press. *Cornell Law Review, 88*(2), 486–516.

Gross, S., & Mauro, R. (1989). *Death and discrimination: Racial disparities in capital sentencing.* Boston, MA: Northeastern University Press.

Grossman, S., Lundy, M., George, C., & Crabtree-Nelson, S. (2010). Shelter and service receipt for victims of domestic violence in Illinois. *Journal of Interpersonal Violence, 25*(11), 2077–2093.

Grove, L. E., & Farrell, G. (2011). *Repeat victimization.* Oxford Bibliographies. Retrieved from http://www.oxfordbibliographiesonline.com/view/document/obo-9780195396607/obo-9780195396607-0119.xml?rskey=rK3dlN&result=1&q=repeat+victimization#firstMatch.

Grube, J. A., & Piliavin, J. A. (2000). Role identity, organizational experiences, and volunteer performance. *Personality and Social Psychology Bulletin, 26*(9), 1108–1119.

Guidoni, O. (2003). The ambivalences of restorative justice: Some reflections on an Italian prison project. *Contemporary Justice Review, 6*(1), 55–68.

Gunter, T., Arndt, S., Wenman, G., Allen, J., Loveless, P., Sieleni, B., & Black, D. (2008). Frequency of mental and addictive disorders among 320 men and women entering the Iowa prison system: Use of the MINI-Plus. *Journal of the American Academy of Psychiatry and the Law, 36*(1), 27–34.

Hafer, C. L., & Bégue, L. (2005). Experimental research on just-world theory: Problems, developments, and future challenges. *Psychological Bulletin, 131*(1), 128–167.

Haight, W., Bidwell, L., Choi, W. S., & Cho, M. (2016). An evaluation of the Crossover Youth Practice Model (CYPM): Recidivism outcomes for maltreated youth involved in the juvenile justice system. *Children and Youth Services Review, 65,* 78–85.

Halder, D., & Jaishankar, K. (2011). *Cyber-crime and the victimization of women: Laws, rights, and regulations.* Hershey, PA: IGI Global.

Halder, D., & Jaishankar, K. (2016). Policing initiatives and limitations. In J. Navarro, S. Clevenger, and C. D. Marcum (Eds). *The intersection between intimate partner abuse, technology, and cybercrime: Examining the virtual enemy* (pp. 167–186). Durham, NC: Carolina Academic Press.

Halder, D., & Karuppannan, J. (2009). Cyber socialization and victimization of women. *The Journal on Victimization, Human Rights and Gender, 12*(3), 5–26.

Hannan, M., Martin, K., Caceres, K., & Aledort, N. (2017). Children at risk. In M. Chisolm-Straker & H. Stoklosa (Eds.), *Human trafficking is a public health issue* (pp. 105–121). New York, NY: Springer.

Hanson, R. F., Sawyer, G. K., Begle, A. M., & Hubel, G. S. (2010). The impact of crime victimization on quality of life. *Journal of Traumatic Stress, 23*(2), 189–197.

Harrell, E. (2012). *Violent victimization committed by strangers, 1993–2010* [Special Report]. Washington, DC: U.S. Department of Justice, Office of Justice Programs, Bureau of Justice Statistics.

Harvard University Library. (n.d.). *Jane Addams (1860–1935).* Harvard University Library Open Collections Program. Retrieved from http://ocp.hul.harvard.edu/ww/addams.html.

Haskett, M. E., Nears, K., & Ward, C. S. (2006). Diversity in adjustment of maltreated children: Factors associated with resilient functioning. *Clinical Psychology Review, 26*(6), 796–812.

Hatten, P., & Moore, M. (2010). Police officer perceptions of a victim-services program. *Journal of Applied Social Sciences, 4*(2), 17–24.

Hayes, R. M., Lorenz, K., & Bell, K. A. (2013). Victim blaming others: Rape myth acceptance and the just world belief. *Feminist Criminology, 8*(3), 202–220.

Hayes, S., & Jeffries, S. (2013). Why do they keep going back: Exploring women's discursive experiences of intimate partner abuse. *International Journal of Criminology and Sociology, 2,* 57–71.

Haynie, D. L. (1998). The gender gap in fear of crime, 1973–1994: A methodological approach. *Criminal Justice Review, 23*(1), 29–50.

Hazelwood, R., & Burgess, W. (Eds.). (2008). *Practical aspects of rape investigation: A multidisciplinary approach* (4th ed.). New York, NY: CRC Press.

Hazelwood, S. D., & Koon-Magnin, S. (2013). Cyber stalking and cyber harassment legislation in the United States: A qualitative analysis. *International Journal of Cyber Criminology*, 7(2), 155–168.

Hedayati Marzbali, M., Abdullah, A., Razak, N., & Maghsoodi Tilaki, M. (2012). The relationship between socio-economic characteristics, victimization and CPTED principles: Evidence from the mimic model. *Crime, Law and Social Change*, 58(3), 351 371.

Heise, L., & Garcia-Moreno, C. (2002). Violence by intimate partners. In E. G. Krug, L. L. Dahlberg, J. A. Mercy, A. B. Zwi, & R. Lozano (Eds.), *World report on violence and health* (pp. 87–121). Geneva: World Health Organization.

Heise, L., Moore, K., & Toubia, N. (1995). *Sexual coercion and women's reproductive health: A focus on research*. New York, NY: Population Council.

Hellman, C., & House, D. (2006). Volunteers serving victims of sexual assault. *The Journal of Social Psychology*, 146(1), 117–123.

Henning, K., & Feder, L. (2005). Criminal prosecution of domestic violence offenses: An investigation of factors predictive of court outcomes. *Criminal Justice and Behavior*, 32(6), 612.

Henning, K., & Klesges, L. (2003). Prevalence and characteristics of psychological abuse reported by court-involved battered women. *Journal of Interpersonal Violence*, 18, 857–871.

Henning, K. N. (2009). What's wrong with victims' rights in juvenile court: Retributive versus rehabilitative systems of justice. *California Law Review*, 97(4), 1107–1170.

Herek, G., Gillis, J., & Cogan, J. (1999). Psychological sequelae of hate-crime victimization among lesbian, gay, and bisexual adults. *Journal of Consulting and Clinical Psychology*, 67(6), 945–951.

Heretick, D., & Russell, J. (2013). The impact of juvenile mental health court on recidivism among youth. *Journal of Juvenile Justice*, 3(1), 1–14.

Herman, J. L. (1997). *Trauma and recovery: The aftermath of violence from domestic abuse to political terror*. New York, NY: Basic Books.

Herman, S., & Waul, M. (2004). *Repairing the harm: A new vision for crime victim compensation in America*. Washington, DC: National Center for Victims.

Herrenkohl, T. I., Hong, S., Bart Klika, J., Herrenkohl, R. C., & Jean Russo, M. (2013). Developmental impacts of child abuse and neglect related to adult mental health, substance use, and physical health. *Journal of Family Violence*, 28(2), 191–199.

Herz, D., Lee, P., Lutz, L., Stewart, M., Tuell, J., & Wiig, J. (2012). *Addressing the needs of multi-system youth: Strengthening the connection between child welfare and juvenile justice*. Washington, DC: Center for Juvenile Justice Reform (CJJR), Robert F. Kennedy Children's Action Corps. Retrieved from https://cjjr.georgetown.edu/wp-content/ uploads/2015/03/ MultiSystemYouth_March2012.pdf.

Hill, H. (2014). Rape myths and the use of expert psychological evidence. *Victoria University of Wellington Law Review*, 45(3), 471–485.

Himes, C. L. (2002, June). Elderly Americans. *Population Bulletin*, 56(4), 3–40. A Publication of the Population Reference Bureau.

Hindelang, M. J., Gottfredson, M. R., & Garofalo, J. (1978). *Victims of personal crime: An empirical foundation for a theory of personal victimization*. Cambridge, MA: Ballinger.

Hinduja, S., & Patchin, J. W. (2007). Offline consequences of online victimization: School violence and delinquency. *Journal of School Violence*, 6(3), 89–112.

Hinduja, S., & Patchin, J. W. (2008). Cyberbullying: An exploratory analysis of factors related to offending and victimization. *Deviant Behavior*, 29, 129–131.

Hinduja, S., & Patchin, J. W. (2010). *Cyberbullying by gender*. Cyberbullying Research Center. Retrieved from http://www .cyberbullying.us/2010_charts/cyberbullying_gender_ 2010.jpg.

Hines, A., Lee, M., Osterling, P., & Drabble, A. (2007). Factors predicting family reunification for African American, Latino, Asian and White families in the child welfare system. *Journal of Child and Family Studies*, 16(2), 275–289.

Hockenberry, S., & Puzzanchera, C. (2015). *Juvenile court statistics 2013*. Pittsburgh, PA: National Center for Juvenile Justice.

Hodge, D. R. (2014). Assisting victims of human trafficking: Strategies to facilitate identification, exit from trafficking, and the restoration of wellness. *Social Work*, 59(2), 111–118.

Hoffman, H. (1992). What did Mendelsohn really say? In S. Ben-David and G.F. Kirchhoff (Eds.), *International faces of victimology* (pp. 89–104). Monchengladbach: WSV.

Holcomb, J. E., Williams, M. R., & Demuth, S. (2004). White female victims and death penalty disparity research. *Justice Quarterly*, 21, 877–902.

Holtfreter, K., Reisig, M. D., & Pratt, T. C. (2008). Low self-control, routine activities, and fraud victimization. *Criminology*, 46(1), 189–220.

Homan, R. (1991). *The ethics of social research*. Harlow, UK: Longman.

Hook, M. (2005). *Ethics in victim services*. Baltimore, MD: Sidran Institute Press & McLean, VA: Victims' Assistance Legal Organization.

Hook, M., Murry, M., & Seymour, A. (2005). *National Victim Assistance Academy Videotape Series: Meeting the needs of underserved victims*. Washington, DC: U.S. Department of Justice, Office of Justice Programs.

Hook, M., & Seymour, A. (2004). *A retrospective of the 1982 President's Task Force on Victims of Crime: A component of the office for victims of crime oral history project*. Retrieved from https://www.ncjrs.gov/ovc_archives/ncvrw/2005/pg4d .html.

Hopper, E. K., Bassuk, E. L., & Olivet, J. (2009). Shelter from the storm: Trauma-informed care in homelessness services settings. *The Open Health Services and Policy Journal*, 2, 131–151.

Howard, K. S., & Brooks-Gunn, J. (2009). The role of home-visiting programs in preventing child abuse and neglect. *Pediatrics*, 101(3), 486–489.

Huang, H., Ryan, J., & Herz, D. (2012). The journey of dually-involved youth: The description and prediction of rereporting and recidivism. *Children and Youth Services Review*, 34(1), 254–260.

Hughes, D. M. (2002). The use of new communications and information technologies for sexual exploitation of women and children. *Hastings Women's Law Journal*, 13(1), 127–146.

Identity Theft Resource Center (ITRC). (2017). *Data breaches increase 40 percent in 2016*. Retrieved from http://www.idtheftcenter.org/2016databreaches.html.

Iliffe, G., & Steed, G. (2000). Exploring the counselor's experience of working with perpetrators and survivors of domestic violence. *Journal of Interpersonal Violence*, 15(4), 393–412.

Institute for Law and Justice. (2005). *National evaluation of the Legal Assistance for Victims Program*. Alexandria, VA: Author.

International Labor Organization. (2017). Forced labour, modern slavery and human trafficking. *International Labour Organization*. Retrieved from http://www.ilo.org/global/to/pics/forced-labour/lang--en/index.htm.

Internet Crime Complaint Center (IC3). (2016). *2016 Internet crime report*. Retrieved from https://pdf.ic3 .gov/2016_IC3Report.pdf.

Irazola, S., Williamson, E., Niedzwiecki, E., Debus-Sherrill, S., & Sun, J. (2015). Keeping victims informed: Service providers' and victims' experiences using automated notification systems. *Violence and Victims*, 30(3), 533–544.

Jackson, A. L., Lucas, S. L., & Blackburn, A. G. (2009). Externalization and victim-blaming among a sample of incarcerated females. *Journal of Offender Rehabilitation*, 48(3), 228–248.

Jackson, S. (2017). Adult protective services and victim services: A review of the literature to increase understanding between these two fields. *Aggression and Violent Behavior*, 34, 214–227.

Jacobs, J., Fleisher, M., & Krienert, J. (2009). *The myth of prison rape: Sexual culture in American prisons*. Lanham, MD: Rowman & Littlefield.

Jacobson, S. K., McDuff, M. D., & Monroe, M. C. (2015). *Conversation education and outreach techniques* (2nd edition). Oxford, UK: Oxford University Press.

James, R., & Gilliland, B. (2005). *Crisis intervention strategies* (5th ed.). Belmont, CA: Thomson Brooks/Cole.

Jannoff-Bulman, R. (1992). *Shattered assumptions: Towards a new psychology of trauma*. New York, NY: The Free Press.

Janosik, S. M., & Plummer, E. (2005). The Clery Act, campus safety and the views of assault victim advocates. *College Student Affairs Journal*, 25(1), 116–130.

Javid, A. (2014). Feminism, masculinity and male rape: Bringing male rape 'out of the closet'. *Journal of Gender Studies*, 25(3), 283–293.

Jeltsen, M. (2014). Why didn't you just leave? Six domestic violence survivors explain why it's never that simple. *The Huffington Post*. Retrieved from https://www.huffingtonpost.com/2014/09/12/why-didnt-you-just-leave_n_5805134.html.

Jennings, A. (2004). *Models for developing trauma-informed behavioral health systems and trauma-specific service*. Abt Associates.

Jennings, W. G., Piquero, A. R., & Reingle, J. M. (2012). On the overlap between victimization and offending: A review of the literature. *Aggression and Violent Behavior*, 17(1), 16–26.

Jewkes, R. (2002). Intimate partner violence: Causes and prevention. *The Lancet*, 359(9315), 1423–1429.

Jewkes, R., Sen, P., & Garcia-Moreno, C. (2002). Sexual violence. In E. G. Krug, L. L. Dahlberg, J. A. Mercy, A. B. Zwi, & R. Lozano, *World report on violence and health* (pp. 149–181). Geneva: World Health Organization.

Johnson, I. M. (1992). Economic, situational, and psychological correlates of the decision-making process of battered women. *Families in Society*, 73, 168–176.

Johnson, I. M., & Morgan, E. F. (2008). Victim impact statements—Fairness to defendants? In L. J. Moriarty (Ed.), *Controversies in victimology* (pp. 115–131). London, UK: Routledge Taylor & Francis Group.

Johnson, S., Bernasco, W., Bowers, K., Elffers, H., Ratcliffe, J., . . . et al. (2007). Space-time patterns of risk: A cross national assessment of residential burglary victimization. *Journal of Quantitative Criminology*, 23(3), 201–219.

Joinson, C. (1992). Coping with compassion fatigue. *Nursing*, 22(4), 116–121.

Jones, L,. Mitchell, K., Finkelhor, D. (2012). Trends in youth internet victimization: Findings from three youth internet safety surveys 2000–2010. *Journal of Adolescent Health*, 50, 179–186.

Jones, L. M., Cross, T. P., Walsh, W. A., & Simone, M. (2005). Criminal investigations of child abuse: The research behind "best practices." *Trauma, Violence, & Abuse*, 6(3), 254–268.

Jones, S., & Quisenberry, N. (2004). The general theory of crime: How general is it? *Deviant Behavior*, 25, 401–426.

Jonson-Reid, M., & Barth, R. P. (2000). From maltreatment report to juvenile incarceration: The role of child welfare services. *Child Abuse & Neglect*, 24(4), 505–520.

Juvenile Justice Evaluation Center. (2003). *Evaluability assessment: Examining the readiness of a program for evaluation*. Washington, DC: Author.

Kaeble, D., & Bonczar, T. P. (2016, December 21). *Probation and parole in the United States, 2015*. Washington, DC: Bureau of Justice Statistics.

Kaeble, D., & Cowhig, M. (2018). *Correctional populations in the United States, 2016*. Washington, DC: Bureau of Justice Statistics.

Kagan, M. (2015). Immigrant victims, immigrant accusers. *Scholarly Works*, 902, 915–966.

Kakar, S. (1998). *Domestic abuse: Public policy/criminal justice approaches towards child, spousal and elderly abuse*. San Francisco, CA: Austin & Winfield.

Kalra, G., & Bhugra, D. (2013). Sexual violence against women: Understanding cross-cultural intersections. *Indian Journal of Psychiatry*, 55(3), 244–249.

Kara, S. (2009). *Sex trafficking: Inside the business of modern slavery*. New York, NY: Columbia University Press.

Karjane, H. M., Fisher, B. S., & Cullen, F. T. (2005). *Sexual assault on campus: What colleges and universities are doing about it*. Washington, DC: U.S. Department of Justice Programs, National Institute of Justice.

Karmen, A. (2013). *Crime victims: An introduction to victimology* (8th Edition). New York, NY: Wadsworth.

Kassing, L. R., & Prieto, L. R. (2003). The rape myth and blame-based beliefs of counselors-in-training toward male victims of rape. *Counseling & Development*, 81(4), 455–461.

Katz, J. (2006). *The macho paradox: Why some men hurt women and how all men can help*. Naperville, IL: Sourcebooks, Inc.

Katz, J., Pazienza, R., Olin, R., & Rich, H. (2015). That's what friends are for. *Journal of Interpersonal Violence*, 30(16), 2775–2792.

Kelly, S., & Blythe, B. (2000). Family preservation: A potential not yet realized. *Child Welfare*, 79(1), 29.

Kemp, B., & Mosqueda, L. (2005). Elder financial abuse: An evaluation framework and supporting evidence. *Journal of the American Geriatrics Society*, 53(7), 1123–1127.

Kempe, C., Silverman, F., Steele, B., Droegemueller, W., & Silver, H. (1962). The battered-child syndrome. *Journal of the American Medical Association*, 181(1), 17–24.

Kennedy, M. A., Klein, C., Bristowe, J. T. K., Cooper, B. S., & Yuille, J. C. (2007). Routes of recruitment: Pimps' techniques and other circumstances that lead to street prostitution. *Journal of Aggression, Maltreatment & Trauma* 15(2), 1–19.

Kessler, R., & Wang, P. (2008, April). The descriptive epidemiology of commonly occurring mental disorders in the United States. *Annual Review of Public Health*, 29, 115–129.

Kilpatrick, D. G., & Acierno, R. (2003). Mental health needs of crime victims: Epidemiology and outcomes. *Journal of Traumatic Stress*, 16(2), 119–132.

Kirby, R., Shakespeare-Finch, J., & Palk, G. (2011). Adaptive and maladaptive coping strategies predict posttrauma outcomes in ambulance personnel. *Traumatology*, 17(4), 25–34.

Kirchhoff, G. F. (2005). *What is victimology?* Tokyo, Japan: Seibundo.

Kirchhoff, G. F. (2010). History and a theoretical structure of victimology. In S. G. Shohom, P. Knepper, & M. Kett (Eds.). *International handbook of victimology* (pp. 95–123). Boca Raton, FL: Taylor & Francis.

Klain, E. J., & White, A. R. (2013). Implementing trauma-informed practices in child welfare. *ABA Center on Children and the Law*. Retrieved from http://www.centerfor childwelfare.org/kb/TraumaInformedCare/Implementing TraumaInformedPracticesNov13.pdf.

Klein, A., Tobin, T., Salomon, A., & Dubois, J. (2008). *A statewide profile of abuse of older women and the criminal justice response* (NCJ Publication No. 222459). Washington, DC: U.S. Department of Justice.

Kolko, D. J., & Swenson, C. C. (2002). *Assessing and treating physically abused children and their families*. Thousand Oaks, CA: SAGE.

Kraft, E., & Wang, J. (2010). An exploratory study of the cyberbullying and cyberstalking experiences and factors related to victimization of students at a public liberal arts college. *International Journal of Technoethics*, 1(4), 74–91.

Kramer, H. (2003). *What works: Promising youth justice through restorative alternatives*. Waterbury: Vermont Agency of Human Services, Planning Division.

Krebs, C., Lindquist, C., Berzofsky, M., Shook-Sa, B., Peterson, K., Planty, M., Langton, L., & Stroop, J. (2016). *Campus climate survey validation study final technical report*. Washington, DC: Bureau of Justice Statistics, U.S. Department of Justice.

Krebs, C. P., Lindquist, C. H., Warner, T. D., Fisher, B. S., & Martin, S. L. (2007). *The campus sexual assault (CSA) study*. Washington, DC: National Institute of Justice, U.S. Department of Justice.

Krebs, C. P., Lindquist, C. H., Warner, T. D., Fisher, B. S., & Martin, S. L. (2009). College women's experiences with physically forced, alcohol-or other drug-enabled, and drug-facilitated sexual assault before and since entering college. *Journal of American College Health*, 57(6), 639–647.

Kreuter, M., Lezin, N., & Young, L. (2000). Evaluating community-based collaborative mechanisms: Implications for practitioners. *Health Promotion Practice*, 1(1), 49–63.

Krivo, L., & Peterson, R. (2000). The structural context of homicide: Accounting for rational differences in process. *American Sociological Review*, 65, 547–559.

Kuhn, E. S., & Laird, R. D. (2014). Family support programs and adolescent mental health: review of evidence. *Adolescent Health, Medicine and Therapeutics*, 5, 127–142.

Kury, H., Obergfell-Fuchs, J., & Ferdinand, T. (2001). Aging and the fear of crime: Recent results from East and West Germany. *International Review of Victimology*, 8(1), 75–112.

Lachs, M., & Pillemer, K. (2004). Elder abuse. *The Lancet*, 364(9441), 1263–1272.

Lackie, L., & deMan, A.F. (1997). Correlates of sexual aggression among male university students. *Sex Roles*, 37, 451–457.

La Monica, E. (1981). Construct validity of an empathy instrument. *Research in Nursing and Health*, 4(4), 389–400.

Langton, L. (2011, August). *Use of victim serviced agencies by victims of serious violent crime, 1993–2009* [Special Report]. Washington, DC: U.S. Department of Justice, Office of Justice Programs, Bureau of Justice Statistics.

Langton, L., Berzofsky, M., Krebs, C., & Smiley-McDonald, H. (2012, August). *Victimizations not reported* to the police, 2006–2010 [Special Report]. Washington, DC: U.S. Department of Justice, Office of Justice Programs, Bureau of Justice Statistics.

Langton, L., Planty, M., & Lynch, J. P. (2017). Second major redesign of the National Crime Victimization Survey (NCVS). *Criminology & Public Policy*, 16(4), 1049–1074.

Latane, B., & Nida, S. (1981). Ten years of research on group size and helping. *Psychological Bulletin*, 89(2), 308–24.

Laub, J. (1990). Paterns of criminal victimization in the United States. In A. J. Lurigio, W.G. Skogan & R. C. Davis (Eds.), *Victims of crime: Problems, policies and programs* (pp. 23–49). London, UK: Sage.

Lauritsen, J. L., & White, N. A. (2001). Putting violence in its place: The influence of race ethnicity, gender, and place on the risk for violence. *Criminology and Public Policy*, 1, 37–60.

LaViolette, A. D., & Barnett, O. W. (2014). *It could happen to anyone: Why battered women stay* (3rd ed). Thousand Oaks, CA: SAGE.

Lawyer, S. R., Ruggiero, K. J., Resnick, H. S., Kilpatrick, D. G., & Saunders, B. E. (2006). Mental health correlates of the victim-perpetrator relationship among interpersonally victimized adolescents. *Journal of Interpersonal Violence*, 21(10), 1333–1353. doi:10.1177/0886260506291654

Lazarus, R. S. (1993). Coping theory and research: Past, present, and future. *Psychosomatic Medicine*, 55, 234–247.

Lazarus, R. S., & Folkman, S. (1984). *Stress, appraisal and coping*. New York, NY: Springer.

Lea, S., Fischer, P., & Evans, K. (2009). *The psychology of scams: Provoking and committing errors of judgement. A report for The Office of Fair Trading*. Retrieved from http://www.oft.gov.uk/shared_oft/reports/consumer_protection/oft1070.pdf.

Leary, M. (2014). Fighting fire with fire: Technology in child sex trafficking. *Duke Journal of Gender Law and Policy*, 21, 289–323.

Ledray, L. E. (1999). *Sexual assault nurse examiner (SANE) development & operation guide*. Washington, DC: U.S. Department of Justice, Office of Justice Programs.

Lee, J., & Miller, S. (2013). A self-care framework for social workers: Building a strong foundation for practice. *Families in Society*, 94(2), 96–103.

Lee, R., & Jordan, J. (2014). Sexual assault. In L. R. Jackson-Cherry and B. T. Erford (Eds.). *Crisis assessment intervention, and prevention* (2nd edition), (pp. 193–217). New York, NY: Pearson.

Lee, R., & Slowinski, R. L. (1990). *South Carolina v. Gathers*: Prohibiting the use of victim-related information in capital punishment proceedings. *Catholic University Law Review*, 40(1), 215–249.

Lee, W. A. (2003). Progress report from BITS on fraud prevention effort. *The American Banker*, 1.

Lenhart, A., Purcell, K., Smith, A., & Zickuhr, K. (2010). *Social media and mobile Internet use among teens and adults*. Pew Research Center Publications. Retrieved from http://www.pewinternet.org/2010/02/03/social-media-and-young-adults.

Lenhart, A., Ybarra, M., Zickuhr, K., & Price-Feeney, M. (2016). Online harassment, digital abuse, and cyberstalking in America. *Data & Society Research Institute*. Retrieved from https://www.datasociety.net/pubs/oh/Online_Harassment_ 2016.pdf.

Lens, K., Pemberton, A., Brans, K., Braeken, J., Bogaerts, S., & Lahlah, E. (2015). Delivering a victim impact statement: Emotionally effective or counter-productive? *European Journal of Criminology*, 12(1), 17–34.

Lerner, M. J. (1980). *The belief in a just world: A fundamental delusion*. New York, NY: Plenum Press.

Letschert, R., & Groenhuijsen, M. (2011). Global governance and global crime—Do victims fall in between. In L. Letschert & J. Van Dijk (Eds.), *The New Faces of Victimhood: Globalization, Transnational Crimes and Victims' Rights* (pp. 15–40). New York, NY: Springer.

Leung, P. (1996). Is the court-appointed special advocate program effective? A longitudinal analysis of time involvement and case outcomes. *Child Welfare*, 75(3), 269–284.

Levenson, J. S., D'Amora, D. A., & Hern, A. L. (2007). Megan's law and its impact on community re-entry for sex offenders. *Behavioral Sciences and the Law*, 25, 587–602.

Lewis, C. (1996). The Jacob Wetterling Crimes Against Children and Sexually Violent Offender Registration Act: An unconstitutional deprivation of the right to privacy and substantive due process. *Harvard Civil Rights–Civil Liberties Law Review*, 31(1), 89.

Li, S., Levick, A., Eichman, A., & Chang, J. (2015). Women's perspectives on the context of violence and role of police in their intimate partner violence arrest experiences. *Journal of Interpersonal Violence*, 30(3), 400–419.

Like-Haislip, T., & Miofsky, K. (2011). Race, ethnicity, gender, and violent victimization. *Race and Justice*, 1(3), 254–276.

Lim, N., Greathouse, S. M., & Yeung, D. (2014). *The 2014 technology summit for victim service providers identifying challenges and possible solutions*. Retrieved from https://www.rand.org/content/dam/rand/pubs/conf_proceedings/CF300/CF326/RAND_CF326.pdf.

Limber, S. P., Olweus, D., & Luxenberg, H. (2013). *Bullying in U. S. schools, 2012 Status Report*. Hazelden Foundation.

Linzer, N. (2004). An ethical dilemma in elder abuse. *Journal of Gerontological Social Work*, 43(2–3), 165–173.

Lipsky, S., Caetano, R., Field, C. A., & Larkin, G. L. (2005). Psychosocial and substance-use risk factors for intimate partner violence. *Drug and Alcohol Dependence*, 78(1), 39–47. doi:10.1016/j.drugalcdep.2004.08.028

Listwan, S. J., Colvin, M., Hanley, D., & Flannery, D. (2010). Victimization, social support, and psychological well-being. *Criminal Justice and Behavior*, 37(10), 1140–1159.

Litz, B. T., Gary, M. J., Bryant, R. A., & Adler, A. B. (2002). Early intervention for trauma: Current status and future directions. *Clinical Psychology Science and Practice*, 9(2), 112–134.

Logalbo, A., & Callahan, C. (2001). An evaluation of teen court as a juvenile crime diversion program. *Juvenile and Family Court Journal*, 52(2), 1–11.

Logan, T. K., Walker, R., & Hunt, G. (2009). Understanding human trafficking in the United States. *Trauma, Violence & Abuse*, 10(1), 3–30.

Long, L. (2017). Rape victim advocates experiences with law enforcement in the emergency room. *Feminist Criminology*, 1(1), 1–18.

Lonsway, K., Archambault, J., & Lisak, D. (2009). False reports: Moving beyond the issue to successfully investigate and prosecute nonstranger sexual assault. *The Voice*, 3(1), 1–12.

Lonsway, K. A. (2017). *Effective victim advocacy in the criminal justice system: A training course for victim advocates*.

End Violence Against Women International (EVAWI). Retrieved from http://www.evawintl.org/library/ DocumentLibraryHandler.ashx?id=32.

Lovrich, N. P., Pratt, T. C., Gaffney, M. J., Johnson, C. L., Asplen, C. H., Hurst, L. H., & Schellberg, T. M. (2004). *National forensic DNA study report*. Washington, DC: National Institute of Justice.

Luckett, J. B., & Slaikeu, K. A. (1990). Crisis intervention by police. In K. A. Slaikeu (Ed.), *Crisis intervention: A handbook for practice and research* (2nd ed., pp. 227–242). Boston, MA: Allyn & Bacon.

Luxton, D. D., June, J. D., & Fairall, J. M. (2012). Social media and suicide: A public health perspective. *American Journal of Public Health*, 102(S2), 195–200.

Lynch, J. (2006). Problems and promise of victimization surveys for cross-national research. *Crime and Justice*, 34(1), 229–287.

Lyon, E., Lane, S., & Menard, A. (2008). *Meeting survivors' needs: A multi-state study of domestic violence shelter experiences, final report* (Document number: 225025). U. S. Department of Justice. Retrieved from http://www.ncjrs .gov/pdffiles1/nij/grants/225025.pdf.

Macy, R. J., & Graham, L. M. (2012). Identifying domestic and international sex-trafficked victims during human service provision. *Trauma, Violence, & Abuse*, 13(2), 59–76.

Madeira, J. L. (2010). Why rebottle the genie? Capitalizing on closure in death penalty proceedings. *Indiana Law Journal*, 85, 1477–1525.

Mahajan, B. (2017). Victim offender mediation: A case study and argument for expansion to crimes of violence. *The American Journal of Mediation*, 10. Retrieved from http://www.americanjournalofmediation.com/pg1.cfm.

Maier, S. (2008). "I have heard horrible stories . . . " *Violence Against Women*, 14(7), 786–808.

Maier, S. (2011). The emotional challenges faced by sexual assault nurse examiners: "ER nursing is stressful on a good day without rape victims." *Journal of Forensic Nursing*, 7(4), 161–172.

Măirean, C. (2016). Emotion regulation strategies, secondary traumatic stress, and compassion satisfaction in healthcare providers. *The Journal of Psychology*, 150(8), 961–975.

Makic, M. B. (2015). Taking care of the caregiver: Compassion satisfaction and compassion fatigue. *Journal of PeriAnesthesia Nursing, 30*(6), 546–547.

Malby, S., Jesrani, T., Banuelos, T., Holterhof, A., & Hahn, M. (2015). *UNODC: Study on the effects of new information technologies on the abuse and exploitation of children.* Vienna: UNODC.

Malley-Morrison, K., & Hines, D. A. (2004). *Family violence in a cultural perspective: Defining, understanding, and combating abuse.* Thousand Oaks, CA: SAGE.

Marc, S. (Ed.) (2004). *LGBT: Encyclopedia of lesbian, gay, bisexual, and transgender history in America.* New York, NY: Cengage Learning.

Marcenko, O., Lyons, S., & Courtney, M. (2011). Mothers' experiences, resources and needs: The context for reunification. *Children and Youth Services Review, 33*(3), 431–438.

Marcotte, D. E., & Palmer, J. (2016). *Sexual violence, Title IX and women's college enrollment* (IZA Discussion Paper No. 10345). Retrieved from https://ssrn.com/abstract=2868311.

Mariner, J. (2001). *No escape: Male rape in U.S. prisons.* Retrieved from https://www.hrw.org/legacy/reports/2001/prison/report.html.

Marshall, L. L., & Rose, P. (1990). Premarital violence: The impact of family of origin on violence, stress, and reciprocity. *Violence Victims, 5,* 51–64.

Martin, E. J., & Stern, N. S. (2005). Domestic violence and public and subsidized housing: Addressing the needs of battered tenants through local housing policy. *Clearinghouse Review: Journal of Poverty, Law and Policy,* 551–560.

Martin, J. (2015). "It's just an image?": Practitioners' understanding of child sexual abuse images online and effects on victims. *Child & Youth Services, 35*(2), 96–115.

Martin, P. Y. (2007). Coordinated community services for victims of violence. In L. L. O'Toole, J. R. Schiffman, & M. L. Kiter Edwards (Eds). *Gender violence: Interdisciplinary perspectives* (2nd ed), (pp. 443–450). New York: New York University Press.

Martin, S. L., Ray, N., Sotres-Alvarez, D., Kupper, L. L., Moracco, K. E., Dickens, P. A., . . . Gizlice, Z. (2006). Physical and sexual assault of women with disabilities. *Violence Against Women, 12*(9), 823–837.

Martin, Y. (2005). *Rape work: Victims, gender, and emotions in organization and community context.* London, UK: Routledge.

Maruna, S. (2013). Foreword. In K. S. van Wormer & L. Walker (Eds.), *Restorative justice today: Practical applications* (pp. xv–xiv). Thousand Oaks, CA: Sage.

Maryniak, I. (2000). Something to think about. *Index on Censorship, 29*(2), 76–82.

Maslach, C., & Leiter, M. (1997). *The truth about burnout.* San Francisco, CA: Jossey-Bass.

Maslach, C., Schaufeli, W., & Leiter, M. (2001). Job burnout. *Annual Review of Psychology, 52,* 397–422.

Masten, A. S. (2014). Global perspectives on resilience in children and youth. *Child Development, 85*(1), 6–10.

Masters, R. E., Way, L. B., Gerstenfeld, P. B., Muscat, B. T., Hooper, M., Dussich, J. P. J., Pincu, L., & Skrapec, C. A. (2010). *CJ: Realities and challenges.* New York, NY: McGraw-Hill.

Masters, R., Way, L. B., Gerstenfeld, P. B., Muscat, B. T., Hooper, M., Dussich, J. P. J., & Skrapec, C. A. (2017). *CJ: Realities and challenges* (3rd edition). New York, NY: McGraw Hill Education.

Mastrofski, S. (2006). Community policing: A skeptical view. In D. Weisburd & A. Braga (Eds.), *Police innovation: Contrasting perspectives* (pp. 44–73). New York, NY: Cambridge University Press.

Matthews, B., Yang, C., Lehman, E. B., Mincemover, C., Veridliglione, N., & Levi, B. H. (2017). Educating early childhood care and education providers to improve knowledge and attitudes about reporting child maltreatment: A randomized controlled trial. *PLoS ONE, 12*(5): e0177777. Retrieved from https://doi.org/10.1371/journal.pone.0177777.

Mawby, R. I., & Walklate, S. (1994). *Critical victimology: International Perspectives.* London, UK: Sage.

Max, W., Rice, D. P., Finkelstein, E., Bardwell, R. A., & Leadbetter, S. (2004). The economic toll of intimate partner violence against women in the United States. *Violence and Victims, 19,* 259–272.

McCollister, K. E., French, M. T., & Fang, H. (2010). The cost of crime to society: New crime-specific estimates for policy and program evaluation. *Drug and Alcohol Dependence, 108*(1), 98–109.

McCubbin, H. I., & Patterson, J. M. (1982). Family adaptation to crisis. In H. I. McCubbin, A. E. Cauble, & J. M. Patterson (Eds.), *Family stress, coping, and social support* (pp. 26–47). Springfield, IL: Charles C Thomas.

McCurley, C., & Snyder, H. N. (2004). *Victims of violent juvenile crime*. Juvenile Justice Bulletin. Office of Justice Programs. Washington, DC: Office of Juvenile Justice and Delinquency Prevention.

McDaniel, N., & Lescher, N. (2004). The history of child protective services. In C. Brittan & D. Hunt (Ed.), *Helping in child protective services: A competency based casework handbook* (2nd ed., pp. 31–49). New York, NY: Oxford University Press.

McDermott, J., & Garofalo, J. (2004). When advocacy for domestic violence victims backfires. *Violence Against Women, 10*(11), 1245–1266.

McDevitt, J., Balboni, J., Garcia, L., & Gu, J. (2001). Consequences for victims: A comparison of bias- and non-bias-motivated assaults. *American Behavioral Scientist, 45*(4), 697–713.

McGarrell, E. (2001). *Restorative justice conferences as an early response to young offenders*. Juvenile Justice Bulletin. Washington, DC: Office of Juvenile Justice and Delinquency Prevention.

McGregor, K. (2008). *Surviving and moving on: Self help for survivors of child sexual abuse*. New York, NY: Routledge.

McHolm, F. (2006). Rx for compassion fatigue. *Journal of Christian Nursing, 23*(40), 12–19.

Mckinsey & Company. (2001). *Effective capacity building in nonprofit organizations*. Virginia: Venture Philanthropy Partners. Retrieved from http://www.vppartners.org/sites/default/files/reports/full_rpt.pdf.

McLoughlin, C., Meyricke, R., & Burgess, J. (2009). Bullies in cyberspace: How rural and regional Australian youth perceive the problem of cyber bullying and its impact. ISFIRE, Symposium Proceedings.

McNamee, C., & Murphy, M. (2006). Elder abuse in the United States. *National Institute of Justice Journal*, (255).

McNamee, L., & Peterson, B. (2016). High-stakes volunteer commitment: A qualitative analysis. *Nonprofit and Voluntary Sector Quarterly, 45*(2), 275.

Mega, L. T., Mega, J. L., Mega, B. T., & Moore, B. (2000). Brainwashing and battering fatigue psychological abuse in domestic violence. *North Carolina Medical Journal, 61*(5), 260–265.

Mercer, D. L. (1990). *A national study of victims and non-victims functioning as county level victim advocates for Mothers Against Drunk Driving (MADD)*. Unpublished paper.

Merchant, L., & Whiting, J. (2015). Challenges and retention of domestic violence shelter advocates: A grounded theory. *Journal of Family Violence, 30*(4), 467–478.

Messing, J. T., Becerra, D., Ward-Lasher, A., & Androff, D. K. (2015). Latinas' perceptions of law enforcement: Fear of deportation, crime reporting, and trust in the system. *Affilia: Journal of Women & Social Work, 30*(3), 328–340. doi:10.1177/0886109915576520

Messinger, A. M. (2011). Invisible victims: Same-sex IPV in the National Violence Against Women Survey. *Journal of Interpersonal Violence, 26*(11), 2228–2243. doi:10.1177/0886260510383023

Messman-Moore, T. L., & Bhuptani, P. H. (2017). A review of the long-term impact of child maltreatment on post-traumatic stress disorder and its comorbidities: An emo-tion dysregulation perspective. *Clinical Psychology and Science Practice, 24*(2), 154–169.

Meyer, C., Tangney, J., Stuewig, J., & Moore, K. (2014). Why do some jail inmates not engage in treatment and services? *International Journal of Offender Therapy and Comparative Criminology, 58*(8), 914–930.

Mick, J. (2006). Identifying signs and symptoms of intimate partner violence in an oncology setting. *Clinical Journal of Oncology Nursing, 10*(4), 509–513.

Miers, D. (1992). The responsibilities and the rights of victims of crime. *Modern Law Review, 55*, 482–505.

Miers, D. (2014). State compensation for victims of violent crime. In I. Vanfraechem, A. Pemberton, and F. M. Ndahinda (Eds.), *Justice for victims: Perspectives on rights, transition, and reconciliation*. New York, NY: Routledge.

Mihaljcic, T., & Lowndes, G. (2013). Individual and community attitudes toward financial elder abuse. *Journal of Elder Abuse and Neglect, 25*(2), 183–203.

Miller, T. R., Cohen, M. A., & Wiersema, B. (1996). *Victim costs and consequences: A new look*. National Institute of Justice Research Report. Retrieved from https://www.ncjrs.gov/pdffiles/victcost.pdf.

Miller-Perrin, C. L., & Perrin, R. D. (2012). *Child maltreatment: An introduction.* Thousand Oaks, CA: Sage.

Miller-Perrin, C. L., Perrin, R. D., & Renzetti, C. M. (2018). *Violence and maltreatment in intimate relationships.* Thousand Oaks, CA: Sage.

Minnesota Department of Corrections. (2003). *Level three sex offenders residential placement issues 2003 report to the legislature.* Retrieved from https://ccoso.org/sites/default/files/MNresidencerestrictions.pdf.

Modi, M. N., Palmer, S., & Armstrong, A. (2014). The role of violence against women act in addressing intimate partner violence: A public health issue. *Journal of Women's Health, 23*(3), 253–259.

Moffitt, T. E. (2006). Life-course persistent versus adolescence-limited antisocial behavior. In D. Cicchetti & J. Cohen (Eds.), *Developmental psychopathology: Risk, disorder, and adaptation* (2nd ed., pp. 570–598). New York, NY: Wiley.

Moreno-Walton, L., Ryan, M., Nunez, R., & Alexander, B. (2012). A sexual assault response team (SART): An urban hospital emergency department experience. *Journal of Emergency Medicine, 43*(5), 940.

Morgan, K. D., & Smith, B. (2005). Parole release decisions revisited: An analysis of parole release decisions for violent inmates in a southeastern state. *Journal of Criminal Justice, 33*(3), 277–287.

Morgan, R. E., & Kena, G. (2017). *Criminal victimization, 2016.* U.S. Department of Justice, Office of Justice Programs.

Moriarty, L. (2005). Victim participation at parole hearings: Balancing victim, offender, and public interest. *Criminology & Public Policy, 4*(2), 385–390.

Moriarty, L. J. (2008). Introduction. In L. J. Moriarty (Ed.), *Controversies in victimology* (pp. ix–xii). London, UK: Routledge Taylor & Francis Group.

Morrissette, P. (2004). *The pain of helping: Psychological injury of helping professionals* (Psychosocial Stress Series, 11th ed.). New York, NY: Taylor and Francis Books.

Morsink, J. (1999). *The Universal Declaration of Human Rights: Origins, drafting, and intent.* Philadelphia, PA: University of Pennsylvania Press.

Mosqueda, L., Wiglesworth, A., Moore, Alison A., Nguyen, A., Gironda, M., & Gibbs, L. (2015). Variability in findings from adult protective services investigations of elder abuse in California. *Journal of Evidence-Informed Social Work, 13*(1), 34–44.

Muelleman, R., & Feighny, K. (1999). Effects of an emergency department–based advocacy program for battered women on community resource utilization. *Annals of Emergency Medicine, 33*(1), 62–66.

Mullen, P. E., Martin, J. L., Anderson, J. C., Romans, S. E., & Herbison, G. P. (1996). The long-term impact of the physical, emotional, and sexual abuse of children: A community study. *Child Abuse & Neglect, 20*(1), 7–21.

Murphy, S., Johnson, L., Wu, L., Fan, J., & Lohan, J. (2003). Bereaved parents outcomes 4 to 60 months after their children's deaths by accident, suicide, or homicide: A comparative study demonstrating differences. *Death Studies, 27*(1), 39–61.

Muscat, B. (2010). Child protective services. In B. S. Fisher & S. P. Lab (Eds.), *Encyclopedia of victimology and crime prevention* (pp. 99–100). Thousand Oaks, CA: Sage.

Mustaine, E. E., & Tewksbury, R. (2002). Sexual assault of college women: A feminist interpretation of a routine activities analysis. *Criminal Justice Review, 27*, 89–123.

Myers, B., Roop, A., Kalnen, D., & Kehn, A. (2013). Victim impact statements and crime heinousness: A test of the saturation hypothesis. *Psychology, Crime & Law, 19*(2), 129–143.

Myers, J. E. B. (2008). A short history of child protection in America. *Family Law Quarterly, 42*(3), 449–463.

Nadler, J., & Rose, M. (2003). Victim impact testimony and the psychology of punishment. *Cornell Law Review, 88*, 419–456.

Nagoshi, J. L., Adams, K. A., Terrell, H. K., Hill, E. D., Brzuzy, S., & Nagoshi, C. T. (2008). Gender differences in correlates of homophobia and transphobia. *Sex Roles, 59*(7–8), 521–531.

Najjar, N., Davis, L., Beck-Coon, K., & Doebbeling, C. (2009). Compassion fatigue. *Journal of Health Psychology, 14*(2), 267–277.

Namie, G. (2014). *Workplace bullying survey.* WBI. Retrieved from http://workplacebullying.org/multi/pdf/WBI-2014-US-Survey.pdf.

Namkee, C., & Mayer, J. (2000). Elder abuse, neglect, and exploitation: Risk factors and prevention strategies. *Journal of Gerontological Social Work, 23*(2), 5–25.

Narayan, A. P., Socolar, R. R., & Claire, K. (2006). Pediatric residency training in child abuse and neglect in the United States. *Pediatrics, 117*(6), 2215–2221.

Nathanson, A. M., Shorey, R. C., Tirone, V., & Rhatigan, D. L. (2012). The prevalence of mental health disorders in a community sample of female victims of intimate partner violence. *Partner Abuse, 3*(1), 59. doi:10.1891/1946-6560.3.1.59

National Association of Crime Victim Compensation Boards. (2016). *Victim compensation programs help victims cope with the costs of violent crime.* Retrieved from http://www.nacvcb.org.

National Center for Hate Crime Prevention, Education Development Center. (2000). *Responding to hate crime: A multidisciplinary curriculum for law enforcement and victim assistance professionals.* United States Department of Justice, Office for Victims of Crime.

National Center for Missing & Exploited Children (NCMEC). (2017). *Online safety.* Retrieved from http://www.missingkids.com/education.

National Center for Victims of Crime (NCVC). (2012). *The trauma of victimization.* Retrieved from https://victimsofcrime.org/help-for-crime-victims/get-help-bulletins-for-crime-victims/trauma-of-victimization.

National Center for Victims of Crime (NCVC). (2016). *About sexual assault.* Retrieved from https://victimsofcrime.org/our-programs/dna-resource-center/untested-sexual-assault-kits/about-sexual-assault.

National Center for Victims of Crime. (1997). *Promising practices and strategies for victim services in corrections.* Retrieved from http://victimsofcrime.org/library/publications/archive/promising-practices-and-strategies-for-victim-services-in-corrections#1.

National Center for Victims of Crime. (1999). *Promising practices and strategies for victim services in corrections.* Washington, DC: U.S. Department of Justice, Office of Justice Programs.

National Center for Victims of Crime. (2002a). *Victim input into plea agreements.* Retrieved from https://www.ncjrs.gov/ovc_archives/bulletins/legalseries/bulletin7/ncj189188.pdf.

National Center for Victims of Crime. (2002b). *Victim impact statements.* Retrieved from http://victimsofcrime.org/help-for-crime-victims/get-help-bulletins-for-crime-victims/victim-impact-statements.

National Center for Victims of Crime. (2003). *Crime victim compensation.* Retrieved from http://victimsofcrime.org/help-for-crime-victims/get-help-bulletins-for-crime-victims/crime-victim-compensation.

National Center for Victims of Crime. (2012). *Issues: constitutional amendments.* Retrieved from http://www.victimsofcrime.org/our-programs/public-policy/amendments.

National Center for Victims of Crime. (2013). *Common ground: What crime victims need from the juvenile justice system.* [Executive Summary]. Retrieved from https:// victimsofcrime.org/docs/casey-foundation-roundtable/common-ground-what-victims-expect-from-juvenile-justice.pdf?sfvrsn=0.

National Center for Victims of Crime. (2017). *Mass casualty shootings.* Retrieved from https://ovc.ncjrs.gov/ncvrw2017/images/en _ artwork/Fact _ Sheets/2017NCVRW _ MassShootings_508.pdf.

National Center on Elder Abuse. (1998). *The National Elder Abuse Incidence Study.* Washington, DC: American Public Human Services Association.

National Center on Elder Abuse. (2014). *An introduction to elder abuse for professionals: Overview.* Retrieved from. https://ncea.acl.gov/Resources/docs/Intro-EA-Pro-Overview-2014.pdf.

National Center on Elder Abuse. (2015). *What are the warning signs of elder abuse.* Retrieved from https://ncea.acl.gov/faq.

National Center on Elder Abuse. (2017). *What is elder abuse.* Retrieved from https://ncea.acl.gov/faq.

National Center on Protection Orders and Full Faith & Credit. (2014). *Advocate confidentiality statutes* [Revised 2014]. Retrieved from http://www.bwjp.org/assets/documents/ pdfs/advocate_confidentiality_statutes.pdf.

National Clearing House on Abuse in Later Life (NCALL). (2017). *Defining elder abuse.* National Clearing House on Abuse in Later Life. Retrieved from http://www.ncall.us/defining-abuse-in-later-life-and-elder-abuse.

National Coalition Against Domestic Violence (NCADV). (2017). *National statistics domestic violence.* Retrieved from https://ncadv.org/statistics.

National Coalition of Anti-Violence Programs. (2017). *Lesbian, gay, bisexual, transgender, queer, and HIV-affected hate violence in 2016.* New York, NY: Author.

National Coalition to Prevent Child Sexual Exploitation (NCPCSE). (2012). *National plan to prevent the sexual abuse and exploitation of children*. Retrieved from http://www.preventtogether.org/Resources/Documents/National Plan2012FINAL.pdf.

National Court Appointed Special Advocate Association. (2017). *Evidence of effectiveness*. Retrieved from http://www.casaforchildren.org/site/c.mtJSJ7MPIsE/b.5301295/k.BE9A/Home.htm.

National Crime Victim Law Institute. (2010). *National survey of state victim impact statement laws and whether defendant has right of cross-examination with respect to victim impact evidence*. Retrieved from https://law.lclark.edu/live/files/12746-national-survey-of-state-victim-impact-statement.

National Highway Traffic Safety Administration (NHTSA). (2005). *Strategies for addressing the DUI offender: 10 promising sentencing practices*. Retrieved from http://www.alcoholandcrime.org/images/uploads/pdf_research/10promising_nhtsa_2005.pdf.

National Institute of Justice. (2007). *Commercial sexual exploitation of children: What do we know and what do we do about it?* (Publication NCJ 215733). Washington, DC: U.S. Department of Justice, Office of Justice Programs.

National Institute of Justice. (2007). *Victim impact panels*. Retrieved from https://www.nij.gov/topics/courts/restorative-justice/promising-practices/pages/victim-impact-panels.aspx.

National Network to End Domestic Violence (NNEDV). (2017). *About financial abuse*. Retrieved from http://nnedv.org/resources/ejresources/about-financial-abuse.html?highlight=WyJmaW5hbmNpYWwiLCJhYnVzZSIsImFidXNlJ3MiLCJmaW5hbmNpYWwgYWJ1c2UiXQ==.

National Network to End Domestic Violence. (2011). *11th annual domestic violence counts report*. Washington, DC: Author. Retrieved from http://nnedv.org/downloads/Census/DVCounts2016/Whole%20Census%20Report%20(smaller).pdf.

National Network to End Domestic Violence. (2016). *Violence against women act*. Retrieved from http://nnedv.org/policy/issues/vawa.html.

National Organization for Human Services (NOHS). (2016). *Ethical standards for human service professionals*. Retrieved from http://www.nationalhumanservices.org/ethical-standards-for-hs-professionals.

National PREA Resource Center. (n.d.). *Prison Rape Elimination Act*. Retrieved from https://www.prearesourcecenter.org/about/prison-rape-elimination-act-prea.

National Sexual Violence Resource Center (NCVRC). (2012). *Assisting trafficking victims: A guide for victim advocates*. Retrieved from https://www.nsvrc.org/sites/default/files/publications_nsvrc_guides_human-trafficking-victim-advocates.pdf.

National Sexual Violence Resource Center. (2011). *Sexual assault response team development: A guide for victim service providers*. Enola, PA: Author.

National Sexual Violence Resource Center. (2015). *National sexual violence resource center: Info & stats for journalists. Statistics about sexual violence*. Retrieved from https://www.nsvrc.org/sites/default/files/publications_ nsvrc_factsheet_media-packet_statistics-about-sexual-violence_0.pdf.

National Sheriffs' Association. (2008). *First response to victims of crime: A guidebook for law enforcement officers*. Washington, DC: Office of Justice Programs.

National Victims' Constitutional Amendment Passage (NVCAP). (2016). *Victims' rights amendments adopted in more three states*. Retrieved from http://www.nvcap.org.

Navajo Nation Human Rights Commission. (2016). *The status of Navajo women and gender violence*. Retrieved from http://www.nnhrc.navajo-nsn.gov/docs/NewsRpt Resolution/PublicHearingReports/The%20Status%20of%20Navajo%20Women%20and%20Gender%20Violence%20Report%20-%20Copy.pdf.

Neill, K., Christensen, C., & Williams, D. J. (2017). Sexual violence. In L. G. Bostaph and D. D. Swerin (Eds.). *Victimology: Crime victimization and victim services* (pp. 153–186). New York: Wolters Kluwer.

Nerenberg, L. (2008). *Elder abuse prevention: Emerging trends and promising strategies*. New York, NY: Springer.

Network of Victim Assistance (NOVA). (2016). *Different types of child abuse*. Retrieved from http://www.novabucks.org/otherinformation/childabuse/#physical.

Newlin, C., Steele, L. C., Chamberlin, A., Anderson, J., Kenniston, J., Russell, A., Stewart, H., & Vaughan-Eden, V. (2015). *Child forensic interviewing: Best practices*. Washington, DC: U.S. Department of Justice, Office of Justice Programs, Office of Juvenile Justice and Delinquency Prevention.

Newmark, L. (2006). *Crime victims' needs and VOCA-Funded services: Findings and recommendations from two national studies*. Virginia: The Institute for Law and Justice.

Ngo, F. T., & Paternoster, R. (2011). Cybercrime victimization: An examination of individual and situational level factors. *International Journal of Cyber Criminology*, *5*(1), 773–793.

Nicholson, J., & Higgins, G. E. (2017). Social structure social learning theory: Preventing crime and violence. In B. Teasdale and M. S. Bradley (Eds). *Preventing crime and violence: Advances in prevention sciences* (pp. 11–20). Switzerland: Springer International.

Nickerson, A., Steenkamp, M., Aerka, I. M., Salters-Pednault, K., Carper, T. L., Barnes, B., & Litz, B. T. (2013). Prospective investigation of mental health following sexual assault. *Depression and Anxiety*, *30*(5), 444–450.

Nicksa, S. (2014). Bystander's willingness to report theft, physical assault, and sexual assault. *Journal of Interpersonal Violence*, *29*(2), 217–236.

Nopper, T. (2014). Asian Americans, deviance, crime, and the model minority myth. In S. Bowman (Ed.), *Color behind bars* (pp. 207–243). Santa Barbara, CA: Praeger.

Norman, J. (2010, May 3). Health care law includes long-sought abuse protection for the elderly. *CQ Weekly*, 1066.

Norris, F. H., Kaniasty, K., & Thompson, M. P. (1997). The psychological consequences of crime: Findings from a longitudinal population-based studies. In R. C. Davis, A. J. Lurigo, and W. G. Skogan (Eds.), *Victims of crime* (pp. 146–166). Thousand Oaks, CA: Sage.

Norris, F. H., & Krysztof, K. (1994). Psychological distress following criminal victimization in the general population: Cross-sectional, longitudinal, and prospective analyses. *Journal of Consulting and Clinical Psychology*, *62*(1), 111–123.

North Carolina Bar Association. (1996). *Crime survivors' handbook: What do I do know?* Retrieved from https://www.ncbar.org/media/74954/crimesurvivorshandbook.pdf.

Notar, C. E., Padgett, S., & Roden, J. (2013). Cyberbullying: Resources for intervention and prevention. *Journal of Educational Research*, *1*(3), 133–145.

Nugent-Borakove, M. E., Fanflik, P., Troutman, D., Johnson, N., Burgess, A., & O'Conner, A. L. (2006). *Testing the efficacy of SANE/SART programs: Do they make a difference in sexual assault arrest and prosecution outcomes?* Washington, DC: National Institute of Justice.

O'Leary, K. D. (2015). Psychological abuse: A variable deserving critical attention in domestic violence. In R. Maiuro (Ed.), *Perspectives on verbal and psychological abuse* (pp. 23–42). New York, NY: Springer.

O'Reilly, R., Wilkes, L., Luck, L., & Jackson, D. (2010). The efficacy of family support and family preservation services on reducing child abuse and neglect: What the literature reveals. *Journal of Child Health Care*, *14*(1), 82–94.

Office for Victims of Crime. (1998). *New directions from the field: Victims' right & services for the 21st Century*. Washington, DC: United States Department of Justice.

Office for Victims of Crime (OVC). (2001). *OVC handbook for coping after terrorism: A guide to healing and recovery*. Washington, DC: Department of Justice.

Office for Victims of Crime. (OVC). (2002). *Restitution: Making it work*. Legal Series, Bulletin 5. Retrieved from https://www.ncjrs.gov/ovc_archives/bulletins/legalseries/bulletin5/ncj189193.pdf.

Office for Victims of Crime. (2004). *Responding to victims of terrorism and mass violence crimes: Coordination and collaboration between American Red Cross workers and crime victim service providers*. Washington, DC: U.S. Department of Justice Office of Justice Programs. Retrieved from: https://ojp.gov/ovc/publications/infores/redcross/ ncj209681.pdf.

Office for Victims of Crime. (2012). *Elder abuse/mistreatment*. Retrieved from https://ovc.ncjrs.gov/topic.aspx? topicid=100.

Office for Victims of Crime. (2013). *Vision 21: Transforming victim services, final report*. U.S. Department of Justice Office of Justice Programs. Retrieved from https://ovc.ncjrs.gov/vision21/pdfs/vision21_report.pdf.

Office for Victims of Crime (OVC). (2016). *Crime victims' rights*. Retrieved from http://www.ovc.gov/rights/legislation .html.

Office for Victims of Crime. (2017). 2017 *national crime victims' rights week resource guide: Crime and victimization fact sheets*. Washington, DC: Author.

Office Victims of Crime. (OVC). (n.d.). *Crime victims' rights*. Retrieved from https://www.ovc.gov/rights/ legislation.html.

Office of Justice Programs. (2011). *SART toolkit: Resources for sexual assault response teams*. Washington, DC: Author. Retrieved from https://ovc.ncjrs.gov/sartkit/about/about-sart.html.

Office of Juvenile Justice and Delinquency Prevention (OJJDP). (2017). *OJJDP statistical briefing book*. Retrieved from http://www.ojjdp.gov/ojstatbb/structure_process/qa04101.asp?qaDate=2016. Released on March 27, 2017.

Office on Women's Health. (2015). *Signs of domestic violence or abuse*. Retrieved from https://www.womenshealth.gov/relationships-and-safety/domestic-violence/signs-domestic-violence.

Olinger, J. P. (1991). Elder abuse: The outlook for federal legislation. *Journal of Elder Abuse & Neglect*, 3(1), 45–52.

Olivet, J., Bassuk, E., Elstad, E., Kenney, R., & Jassill, L. (2013). Outreach and engagement in homeless services: A review of the literature. *The Open Health Services and Policy Journal*, 3, 53–70.

Ooms, T. (2006). *A community psychologist's perspective on domestic violence: A conversation with Julia Perilla, PhD*. Building Bridges: Marriage, Fatherhood, and Domestic Violence, 2006 Conference. Retrieved from http://www.vawnet.org/summary.php?doc_id=2864&find_type=web_sum_GC.

Orth, U. (2003). Punishment Goals of Crime Victims. *Law and Human Behavior*, 27(2), 173–186.

Ospina, M., Harstall, C., & Dennett, L. (2010). *Sexual exploitation of children and youth over the Internet*. Canada: The Institute of Health Economics (IHE).

Ostermann, M. (2009). An analysis of New Jersey's day reporting center and halfway back programs: Embracing the rehabilitative ideal through evidence based practices. *Journal of Offender Rehabilitation*, 48(2), 139–153.

Ottoni-Wilhelm, M., & Bekkers, R. (2010). Helping behavior, dispositional empathic concern, and the principle of care. *Social Psychology Quarterly*, 73(1), 11–32.

Overlein, C. (2010). Children exposed to domestic violence: Conclusions from the literature and challenges ahead. *Journal of Social Work*, 10(1), 80–97.

Owen, B., Wells, J., & Pollock, J. (2017). *In search of safety*. Oakland: University of California Press.

Palmer, N. D., & Edmunds, C. N. (2003). Victims of sexual abuse and assault: Adults and children. In T. L. Underwood and C. Edmunds (Eds.), *Victim assistance: Exploring individual practice, organizational policy, and societal responses* (pp. 138–175). New York, NY: Springer.

Palmer, N. D., & Edmunds, C. N. (2003). Violence within family systems. In T. L. Underwood and C. Edmunds (Eds.), *Victim assistance: Exploring individual practice, organizational policy, and societal responses* (pp. 191–211). New York, NY: Springer.

Parker, E. M., Gielen, A. C., Castillo, R., Webster, D. W., & Glass, N. (2016). Intimate partner violence and patterns of safety strategy use among women seeking temporary protective orders: A latent class analysis. *Violence Against Women Journal*, 22(14), 1663–1681.

Parkhill, M. R., Norris, J., Gilmore, A. K., Hessler, D. M., George, W. H., Davis, K. C., & Zawacki, T. (2016). The effects of sexual victimization history, acute alcohol intoxication, and level of consensual sex on responses to sexual assault in a hypothetical scenario. *Violence and Victims*, 31(5), 938 956.

Parson, L., Goodwin, M. M., & Peterson, R. (2000). Violence against women and reproductive health: Toward defining a role for reproductive health care services. *Maternal and Child Health Journal*, 4(2), 135.

Parsonage, W. H., Bernat, F. P., & Helfgott, J. (1992). Victim impact testimony and Pennsylvania's parole decision making process: A pilot study. *Criminal Justice Policy Review*, 6(3), 187–206.

Patchin, W. P., & Hinduja, S. (2016). *Summary of our cyberbullying*. Retrieved from https://cyberbullying.org/summary-of-our-cyberbullying-research.

Paternoster, R., & Deise, J. (2011). A heavy thumb on the scale: The effect of victim impact evidence on capital decision making. *Criminology*, 49(1), 129–161.

Pavelka, S. (2016). Restorative justice in the states: An analysis of statutory legislation and policy. *Justice Policy Journal*, 2(13), 1–23.

Payne, B. K., & Gainey, R. (2005). *Family violence and criminal justice: A life course approach* (2nd ed.). Cincinnati, OH: Anderson.

Peacock, R. (2013). Overview of concepts in victimology. In R. Peacock (Eds.), *Victimology in South Africa* (pp. 3–9). Pretoria: Van Schaik.

Pearlman, L., & Saakvitne, K. (1995). Treating therapists with vicarious traumatisation and secondary traumatic stress disorders. In C. Figley (Ed.), *Compassion fatigue* (pp. 150–177). New York, NY: Brunner/Mazel.

Pence, D., & Wilson, C. (1994). *Team investigation of child sexual abuse*. Thousand Oaks, CA: Sage Publications.

Pennsylvania Coalition Against Rape. (2006). *Meeting the needs of prison rape victims: A technical assistance guide for* sexual assault counselors and advocates. Retrieved from http://www.ccasa.org/wp-content/uploads/2014/01/Prison RapeGuide.pdf.

Pergolizzi, F., Richmond, D., Macario, S., Gan, Z., Richmond, C., & Macario, E. (2009). Bullying in middle schools: Results from a four-school survey. *Journal of School Violence, 8*, 264–279.

Petersen, D. L. (2003). Trauma and the crime victim. In T. L. Underwood and C. Edmunds (Eds.). *Victim assistance: Exploring individual practice, organizational policy, and societal responses* (pp. 95–123). New York, NY: Springer.

Petersen, D. L., & Walker, S. D. (2003). The psychological and physiological impact of stress. In T.L. Underwood & C. Edmunds (Eds.), *Victim assistance: Exploring individual practice, organizational policy, and societal responses* (pp. 66–94). New York, NY: Springer.

Peterson, A. C., Joseph, J., & Feit, M. (2014). *Committee on child maltreatment research, policy, and practice for the next decade: Phase II; Board on Children, Youth, and Families; Committee on Law and Justice; Institute of Medicine; National Research Council, New directions in child abuse and neglect research.* Washington DC: National Academies Press.

Petersen, D. L., & Walker, S. D. (2003). The psychological and physiological impact of stress. In T. L. Underwood & C. Edmunds (Eds.), *Victim assistance: Exploring individual practice, organizational policy, and societal responses* (pp. 66–94). New York, NY: Springer.

Petrellis, T. R. (2007). *The restorative justice living unit at Grande Cache Institution: Exploring the application of restorative justice in a correctional environment.* Ottawa: Correctional Services of Canada.

Pickens, I. (2016). Laying the groundwork: Conceptualizing a trauma-informed system of care in juvenile detention. *Journal of Infant, Child and Adolescent Psychotherapy, 15*(3), 220–230.

Pierce, G. L., & Radelet, M. L. (2011). Death sentencing in East Baton Rouge Parish, 1990–2008. *Louisiana Law Review, 71*, 647–673.

Pietrantonio, A. M., Wright, E., Gibson, K. N., Alldred, E., Jacobson, D., & Niec, A. (2013). Mandatory reporting of child abuse and neglect: Crafting a positive process for health professionals and caregivers. *Child Abuse and Neglect, 37*(2–3), 102–109.

Pillemer, K., Burnes, D., Riffin, C., & Lachs, M. S. (2016). Elder abuse: Global situation, risk factors, and prevention strategies. *The Gerontologist, 56*(2), 194–205.

Piquero, A. R., & Hickman, M. (2003). Extending Tittle's control balance theory. *Criminal Justice and Behavior, 30*(3), 282–301.

Planty, M. G., Langton, L., & Barnett-Ryan, C. (2014, September). *The nation's two crime measures.* Washington, DC: U.S. Department of Justice, Office of Justice Programs, Bureau of Justice Statistics. Retrieved from https://www.bjs.gov/content/pub/pdf/ntcm_2014.pdf.

Poertner, J., & Press, A. (1990). Who best represents the interests of the child in court? *Child Welfare, 69*(6), 537–549.

Polaris Project. (2016). Hotline statistics. Retrieved from https://polarisproject.org/resources/2016-hotline-statistics.

Pollock, J. (2010). *Ethical dilemmas and decisions in criminal justice* (6th ed.). Belmont, CA: Wadsworth.

Popiel, D. A., & Susskind, E. C. (1985). The impact of rape: Social support as a moderator of stress. *American Journal of Community Psychology, 13*, 645–675.

Post, L., Klevens, J., Maxwell, C., Shelley, G., & Ingram, E. (2010). An examination of whether coordinated community responses affect intimate partner violence. *Journal of Interpersonal Violence, 25*(1), 75–93.

Power, C., Koch, T., Kralik, D., & Jackson, D. (2006). Lovestruck: Women, romantic love and intimate partner violence. *Contemporary Nurse, 21*, 174–185.

Pratt, T. C., Holtfreter, K., & Reisig, M. D. (2010). Routine online activity and Internet fraud targeting: Extending the generality of routine activity theory. *Journal of Research in Crime and Delinquency, 47*(3), 267–296.

Presser, L., & Van Voorhis, P. (2002). Values and evaluation: Assessing processes and outcomes of restorative justice programs. *Crime & Delinquency, 48*(1), 162–188.

Prins, S. (2014). Prevalence of mental illnesses in U.S. state prisons: A systematic review. *Psychiatric Services, 65*(7), 862–872.

Prospero, M., & Vohra-Gupta, S. (2008). The use of mental health services among victims of partner violence on college campuses. *Journal of Aggression, Maltreatment, and Trauma, 16*, 376–390.

Puleo, S., & McGlothlin, J. (2014). Overview of crisis intervention. In L. R. Jackson-Cherry and B. T. Erford (Eds.), *Crisis assessment, intervention, and prevention* (2nd edition), (pp. 1–25). New York, NY: Pearson.

Purnell, R., Teng, S., & Warrier, S. (2012). *Cultural competency in California's domestic violence field.* Blue Shield of California Foundation. Retrieved from https://www.blueshieldcafoundation.org/sites/default/files/ publications/downloadable/Cultural%20Competency%20 in%20California's%20Domestic%20Violence%20Field %20_Jan%20 2012_FINAL.pdf.

Putnam, F. (1997). *Dissociation in children and adolescents: A developmental perspective.* New York, NY: Guilford Press.

Puzzanchera, C. (2014). *Juvenile arrests 2012. Juvenile Offenders and Victims: National Report Series.* Washington, DC: U.S. Department of Justice, Office of Justice Programs, Office of Juvenile Justice and Delinquency Prevention.

Puzzanchera, C., Adams, B., & Sickmund, M. (2010). *Juvenile court statistics 2006–2007.* Pittsburgh, PA: National Center for Juvenile Justice.

Puzzanchera, C., & Addie, S. (2014). *Delinquency cases waived to criminal court, 2010.* U.S. Department of Justice. Washington, DC: Office of Justice Programs, Office of Juvenile Justice and Delinquency Prevention.

Quinn, M. J., & Heisler, C. J. (2004). The legal response to elder abuse and neglect. *Journal of Elder Abuse & Neglect, 14*(1), 61–77.

Radelet, M. L., & Pierce, G. L. (2011). Race and death sentencing in North Carolina, 1980–2007. *North Carolina Law Review, 89,* 2119–2160.

Raj, A., & Silverman, J. (2002). Intimate partner violence against South-Asian women in Greater Boston. *Journal of the American Medical Women's Association, 57*(2), 111–114.

Randa, R., & Reyns, B. W. (2014). Cyberbullying victimization and adaptive avoidance behaviors at school. *Victims and Offenders, 9,* 255–275.

Rantala, R. R., & Edwards, T. J. (2000). *Effects of NIBERS on crime statistics.* Washington, DC: Bureau of Justice Statistics, Office of Justice Programs, U.S. Department of Justice.

Rape, Abuse, and Incest National Network (RAINN). (2016). *Scope of the problem: Statistics.* Retrieved from https://www.rainn.org/statistics/scope-problem.

Regehr, C., Hill, J., & Glancy, G. (2000). Individual predictors of traumatic reactions in firefighters. *Journal of Nervous and Mental Disease, 188*(6), 333–339.

Regehr, C., LeBlanc, V. R., Barath, I., Balch, J., & Birze, A. (2013). Predictors of physiological stress and psychological distress in police communicators. *Police Practice and Research, 14*(6), 451–463.

Reingold, D. A., Solomon, J., & Levin, M. (2014). *Elder abuse intervention: The shelter model and the long-term care facility,* Elder Abuse and Its Prevention: Workshop Summary. Washington DC: National Academies Press.

Reisig, M. D., Pratt, T. C., & Holtfreter, K. (2009). Perceived risk of Internet theft victimization: Examining the effects of social vulnerability and financial impulsivity. *Criminal Justice and Behavior, 36*(4), 369–384.

Reisner, R. L., & Nelligan, P. J. (2002). A comparative analysis of victim impact testimony in capital cases in New Jersey and Texas. In R. Muraskin & A. R. Roberts (Eds.), *Visions for change: Crime and justice in the twenty-first century* (pp. 238–264). Upper Saddle River, NJ: Prentice Hall.

Rennison, C., & Dodge, M. (2018). *Introduction to criminal justice: Systems, diversity, and change* (2nd ed.). Thousand Oaks, CA: Sage.

Renzema, M., & Mayo-Wilson, E. (2005). Can electronic monitoring reduce crime for moderate to high-risk offenders? *Journal of Experimental Criminology, 1*(2), 215–237.

Resnick, H. S., & Kilpatrick, D. G. (1994). Crime-related PTSD: Emphasis on adult general population samples. The National Center for Post-Traumatic Stress Disorder: *PTSD Research Quarterly, 5*(3), 1–8.

Reyes, H. (2007). The worst scars are in the mind: Psychological torture. *International Review of the Red Cross, 89*(867), 591–617.

Reyns, B. W., Henson, B., & Fisher, B. S. (2012). Stalking in the twilight zone: Extent of cyberstalking victimization and offending among college students. *Deviant Behavior, 33,* 1–25.

Rheingold, A. A., Zinzow, H., Hawkins, A., Saunders, B. E., & Kilpatrick, D. G. (2012). Prevalence and mental health outcomes of homicide survivors in a representative US sample of adolescents: Data from the 2005 National Survey of Adolescents. *Journal of Child Psychology and Psychiatry, 53*(6), 687–694.

Rich, J., Wakeman, S., & Dickman, S. (2011). Medicine and the epidemic of incarceration in the United States. *The New England Journal of Medicine, 364*(22), 2081–2083.

Rich, K., & Seffrin, P. (2013). Police officers' collaboration with rape victim advocates: Barriers and facilitators. *Violence and Victims, 28*(4), 681–696.

Richards, K., Campenni, C., & Muse-Burke, J. (2010). Self-care and well-being in mental health professionals: The mediating effects of self-awareness and mindfulness. *Journal of Mental Health Counseling, 32*(3), 247–264.

Rivara, F. P., Anderson, M. L., Fishman, P., Bonomi, A. E., Reid, R. J., Carrell, D., & Thompson, R. S. (2006). Healthcare utilization and costs for women with a history of intimate partner violence. *American Journal of Preventive Medicine, 32*(2), 89–96. doi:10.1016/j.amepre.2006.10.001

Roberts, L. D. (2009). Cyber-victimization. In R. Luppicini & R. D. Adell (Eds.), *Handbook of Research on Technoethics* (pp. 575–592). Hershey, PA: IGI Global.

Robinson, L., de Benedictis, T., & Segal, J. (2012). *Elder abuse and neglect: Warning signs, risk factors, prevention, and help*. Retrieved from http://www.helpguide.org/mental/elder_abuse_physical_emotional_sexual_neglect.htm.

Robinson, M. B. (1998). Burglary revictimization. The time period of heightened risk for repeat burglary victimization. *British Journal of Criminology, 38*(1), 78–87.

Rock, P. (2007). Theoretical perspectives on victimization. In S. Walklate (Ed.), *Handbook of victims and victimology* (pp. 37–61). Devon, UK: Willan.

Rodriguez, N. (2007). Restorative justice at work: Examining the impact of restorative justice resolutions on juvenile recidivism. *Crime & Delinquency, 53*(3), 355–379.

Rogovin, C. H., & Velde, R. W. (1969). *Law enforcement assistance administration*. Retrieved from https://www.ncjrs.gov/pdffiles1/nij/2157.pdf.

Rojek, D. G., Coverdill, J. E., & Fors, S. W. (2003). The effect of victim impact panels on DUI rearrest rates: A five-year follow-up. *Criminology, 41*, 1319–1340.

Roman, John K. (2011). How do we measure the severity of crimes? New estimates of the cost of criminal victimization. In John MacDonald (Ed.), *Measuring crime and criminality: Advances in criminological theory*, Volume 17, 37–70. New Brunswick, NJ: Transaction.

Roose, R., Verschelden, G., Vettenburg, N., & Vanthuyne, T. (2012). Working with volunteers in victim support: Mirror or camouflage? *International Social Work, 55*(2), 269–281.

Rose, D. E. (2005). Internet fraud. In L.M. Salinger (Ed.), *Encyclopedia of white-collar & corporate crime* (pp. 439–441). Thousand Oaks, CA: SAGE.

Rosenthal, M., Smidt, E., & Freyd, J. (2016). Still second class: Sexual harassment of graduate students. *Psychology of Women Quarterly*, 1–14.

Rothman, E., Hathaway, J., Stidsen, A., & Vries, H. (2007). How employment helps female victims of intimate partner abuse: A qualitative study. *Journal of Occupational Health Psychology, 12*(2), 136–143.

Roussos, S., & Fawcett, S. (2000). A review of collaborative partnerships as a strategy for improving community health. *Annual Review of Public Health, 21*(11), 369–402.

Ruben, G. J., & Wessley, S. (2013). The psychological and psychiatric effects of terrorism. *Psychiatric Clinics, 36*(3), 339–350.

Rutledge, N. M. (2011). Looking a gift horse in the mouth—The underutilization of crime victim compensation funds by domestic violence victims. *Duke Journal of Gender Law & Policy, 19*, 223–273.

Ryan, J. P., Hong, J. S., Herz, D., & Hernandez, P. M. (2010). Kinship foster care and the risk of juvenile delinquency. *Children and Youth Services Review, 32*(12), 1823–1830.

Ryan, J. P., & Testa, M. F. (2005). Child maltreatment and juvenile delinquency: Investigating the role of placement and placement instability. *Children and Youth Services Review, 27*(3), 227–249.

Saakvitne, K. W., Pearlman, L. A., & Abrahamson, D. J. (1996). *Transforming the pain: A workbook on vicarious traumatization*. New York, NY: W.W. Norton.

Saar, M. S., Epstein, R., Rosenthal, L., & Vafa, Y. (2015). *The sexual abuse to prison pipeline: The girls' story*. Washington, DC: Center for Poverty and Inequality, Georgetown University Law Center.

Sacco, L. N. (2015). The violence against women act: Overview, legislation, and federal funding. *Congressional Research Service*. Retrieved from https://fas.org/sgp/crs/misc/R42499.pdf.

Sahin, M., Aydın, B., & Sarı, S. V. (2011). Cyber bullying, cyber victimization and psychological symptoms: A study in adolescents. Çukurova University Faculty of Education *Journal, 41*(1), 53–59.

Salloum, A., Kondrat, D. C., Johnco, C., & Olson, K. R. (2015). The role of self-care on compassion satisfaction, burnout and secondary trauma among child welfare workers. *Children and Youth Services Review, 49*(C), 54–61.

Saltzman, L. E., Johnson, C. H., Gilbert, B. C., & Goodwin, F. (2003). Physical abuse around the time of pregnancy: An examination of prevalence and risk factors in 16 states. *Maternal and Child Health Journal, 7,* 31–42.

Sampson, R. (2004). *Theft of and from autos in parking facilities in Chula Vista, California: A final report to the U.S. Department of Justice, Office of Community Oriented Policing Services on the field applications of the problem-oriented guides for police projects.* Washington, DC: U.S. Department of Justice.

Sanday, P. R. (2007). *Fraternity gang rape: Sex, brotherhood, and privilege on campus* (2nd Edition). New York: New York University Press.

San Diego Family Justice Center. (2018). Retrieved from https://www.sandiego.gov/sandiegofamilyjusticecenter.

Saponaro, A. (2013). Theoretical approaches and perspectives in victimology. In R. Peacock (Ed.), *Victimology in South Africa* (2nd ed., pp. 11–30). Pretoria: Van Schaik.

Scarce, M. (1997). *Male on male raper: The hidden toll of stigma and shame.* New York, NY: Insight Books.

Schafer, S. (1968). *The victim and his criminal: A study in functional responsibility.* New York, NY: Random House.

Schafer, S. (1977). *Victimology: The victim and his criminal.* Reston, VA: Reston.

Schaufeli, W. B., & Enzmann, D. (1998). *The burnout companion to study and research: A critical analysis.* London, UK: Taylor & Francis.

Schmidt, N. B., Richey, A. R., Zvolensky, M. J., & Maner, J. K. (2008). Exploring human freeze responses to a threat stressor. *Journal of Behavior Therapy and Experimental Psychiatry, 39*(3), 292–304.

Schnebly, S. (2008). The influence of community-oriented policing on crime-reporting behavior. *Justice Quarterly, 25*(2), 223–251.

Schneider, S. K., O'Donnell, L., Stueve, A., & Coulter, R. W. S. (2012). Cyberbullying, school bullying, and psychological distress: A regional census of high school students. *American Journal of Public Health, 102*(1), 171–177.

Schopper, D. (2017). Sexual violence in armed conflict: Responding to the needs of survivors of sexual violence: Do we know what works? *International Review of the Red Cross, 96*(894), 585–600.

Schram, D. D., & Milloy, C. D. (1995). *Community notification: A study of offender characteristics and recidivism.* Olympia: Washington State Institute for Public Policy. Retrieved from http://www.wa.gov/wsipp/crime/cprot.html.

Schreck, C. J. (1999). Criminal victimization and low self-control: An extension and test of a general theory of crime. *Justice Quartly, 16*(3), 633–655.

Schreck, C. J., Wright, R. A., & Miller, J. M. (2002). A study of individual and situational antecedents of violent victimization. *Justice Quarterly, 19,* 159–180.

Schuster, M., & Propen, A. (2010). Degrees of emotion: Judicial responses to victim impact statements. *Law, Culture and the Humanities, 6*(1), 75–104.

Sears, J. F. (2008). *Eleanor Roosevelt and the universal declaration of principles* (p.4). Retrieved from https://fdrlibrary.org/documents/356632/390886/sears.pdf/c300e130-b6e6-4580-8bf1-07b72195b370.

Selye, H. (1956). *The stress of life.* New York, NY: McGraw Hill.

Seymour, A. (2000). Collaboration for victims' rights and services. In A. Seymour, M. Murray, J. Sigmon, M. Hook, C. Edmunds, M. Gaboury, & G. Coleman (Eds.), *2000 National Victim Assistance Academy* (Chap. 19). Retrieved from https://www.ncjrs.gov/ovc_archives/academy/welcome.html.

Shadal, D., Pak, K., & Sauer, J. H. (2014). *Caught in the scammer's net: Risk factors that may lead to becoming an Internet fraud victim: AARP Survey of American adults age 18 and older.* Retrieved from https://www.aarp.org/content/dam/aarp/research/surveys_statistics/econ/2014/Caught-In-The-Scammer%E2%80%99s-Net-Risk-Factors-That-May-Lead-to-Becoming-an-Internet-Fraud-Victim-AARP-Survey%20-of-American-Adults-Age-18-and-Older-AARP-res-econ.pdf.

Shapland, J., & Hall, M. (2007). What do we know about the effects of crime on victims? *International Review of Victimology, 14,* 175–217.

Sharma, R. (2007). *Fundamentals of sociology*. Delhi, India: Nice Printing Press.

Sheedy, C. A. (2016). Clinic and intake forms. In K. L. Eckstrand, J. M. Ehrenfeld, K. L. Eckstrand, & J. M. Ehrenfeld (Eds.), *Lesbian, gay, bisexual, and transgender healthcare: A clinical guide to preventive, primary, and specialist care* (pp. 51–63). Cham, Switzerland: Springer.

Sherman, L., & Berk, R. A. (1984). The specific deterrent effects of arrest for domestic assault. *American Sociological Review, 49*(2), 261–272.

Sherman, L. W., Gartin, P. R., & Buerger, M. E. (1989). Hot spots of predatory crime: Routine activities and the criminology of place. *Criminology, 27*, 27–56.

Shinar, D., & Compton, R. P. (1995). Victim impact panels: Their impact on DWI recidivism. *Alcohol, Drugs and Driving, 11*(1), 73–87. Los Angeles: UCLA Brain Information Service/Brain Research Institute.

Shorey, R., Tirone, V., & Stuart, G. (2014). Coordinated community response components for victims of intimate partner violence: A review of the literature. *Aggression and Violent Behavior, 19*(4), 363–371.

Sickmund, M., & Puzzanchera, C. (2014). *Juvenile offenders and victims: 2014 national report*. Pittsburgh, PA: National Center for Juvenile Justice.

Sickmund, M., Sladky, T. J., Kang, W., & Puzzanchera, C. (2015). *Easy access to the census of juveniles in residential placement*. Retrieved from http://www.ojjdp.gov/ojstatbb/ ezacjrp.

Siegel, L., & Welsh. B, (2012). *Juvenile delinquency: Theory, practice, and law*. Boston, MA: Cengage Learning.

Siegel, L. J., & Welsh, B. C. (2015). *Juvenile delinquency: Theory, practice, and law* (12th ed.). Stamford, CT: Cengage Learning.

Sievers, V., Murphy, S., & Miller, J. J. (2003). Sexual assault evidence collection more accurate when completed by sexual assault nurse examiners: Colorado's experience. *Journal of Emergency Nursing, 29*, 511–514.

Simonin, B., Samali, M., Zohdy, N., & Laidler-Kylander, N. (2016, May 19). Why and how do nonprofits work together? *Philanthropy News Digest*. Retrieved from http://philanthropynewsdigest.org/columns/the-sustainable-nonprofit/why-and-how-do-nonprofits-work-together.

Sims, B., Yost, B., & Abbott, C. (2006). The efficacy of victim services programs. *Criminal Justice Policy Review, 17*(4), 387–406.

Singleton, T. (2013). *The top 5 cybercrimes*. American Institute of CPAs.

Smith, D. W., Kilpatrick, D. G., Falsetti, S. A., & Best, C. (2002). Postterrorism services for victims and surviving family members: Lessons from Pan Am 103. *Cognitive and Behavioral Practice, 9*, 280–286.

Smith, W., & Torstensson, M. (1997). Gender differences in risk perception and neutralizing fear of crime: Toward resolving the paradoxes. *BJ Criminology, 37*(4), 608–634.

Snell, T. (2014). *Capital punishment 2013*. Statistical tables. Washington, DC: Bureau of Justice Statistics. Retrieved from https://www.bjs.gov/content/pub/pdf/cp13st.pdf.

Snell, T. (2017). *Capital punishment 2014–15*. Washington, DC: Bureau of Justice Statistics. Retrieved from https://www.bjs.gov/content/pub/pdf/cp1415sb.pdf.

Sorenson, S. B. (2002). Preventing traumatic stress: Public health approaches. *Journal of Traumatic Stress, 15*(1), 3–7.

Sousa, C., Bart Klika, J., Herrenkohl, T. I., & Packard, W. B. (2016). Family violence. In C. A. Cuevas and C. M. Rennison (Eds.). *The Wiley handbook on the psychology of violence* (pp. 277–370). Oxford, UK: Wiley.

Southworth, C., Finn, J., Dawson, S., Fraser, C., & Tucker, S. (2007). Intimate partner violence, technology, and stalking. *Violence Against Women, 13*(8), 842–856.

Spalek, B. (2006). *Crime victims: Theory, policy, and practice*. New York, NY: Palgrave Macmillan.

Sprang, G. (1997). Victim impact panels: An examination of the effectiveness of this program on lowering recidivism and changing offenders' attitudes about drinking and driving. *Journal of Social Science Research, 22*(3), 73–84.

Starnes, B. J., & Wymer, W. (2000). Demographics, personality traits, roles, motivations, and attrition rates of hospice volunteers. *Journal of Nonprofit and Public Sector Quarterly, 7*(2), 61–76.

Stein, K. (2017). Elder abuse. In X. Dong (Ed.), *Elder abuse prevention interventions* (pp. 433–457). New York, NY: Springer.

Stelle, C. (2010). Adult protective services. In B. S. Fisher & S. P. Lab (Eds.), *Encyclopedia of victimology and crime prevention* (pp. 10–12). Thousand Oaks, CA: Sage.

Stewart, A., Livingston, M., & Dennison, S. (2008). Transitions and turning points: Examining the links between child maltreatment and juvenile offending. *Child Abuse & Neglect, 32*, 51–66.

Stewart, C., Langan, D., & Hannem, S. (2013). Victim experiences and perspectives on police responses to verbal violence in domestic settings. *Feminist Criminology, 8*(4), 269–294.

Storer, H., Lindhorst, T., & Starr, K. (2013). The domestic violence fatality review: Can it mobilize community-level change? *Homicide Studies, 17*(4), 418–435.

Strang, H. (2002). *Repair or revenge: Victims and restorative justice.* Oxford, UK: Clarendon Press.

Straus, M., & Gelles, R. (1988). *Intimate violence.* New York, NY: Simon.

Straus, M. A. (2005). Women's violence toward men is a serious social problem. In D. Loseke, R. Gelles, & M. Cavanaugh (Eds.), *Current controversies on family violence* (pp. 55–77). Thousand Oaks, CA: Sage.

Strom, K., & Hickman, M. (2010). Unanalyzed evidence in law-enforcement agencies. *Criminology & Public Policy, 9*(2), 381–404.

Strom, K. J., & Smith, E. L. (2017). The future of crime data: The case for the National Incident-Based Reporting System (NIBRS) as a primary data source for policy evaluation, *Criminology and Public Policy,16*(4), 1027–1048.

Sullivan, C. M. (2011). Victim services for domestic violence. In M. P. Koss, J. W. White, & A. E. Kazdin (Eds.), *Violence against women and children. Navigating solutions,* Vol. 2 (pp. 183–197). Washington, DC: American Psychological Association.

Sundby, S. E. (2003). The capital jury and empathy: The problem of worthy and unworthy victims. *Cornell Law Review, 88*(2), 343–381.

Sutherland, E. H., Cressey, D. R., & Luckenbill, D. F. (1992). *Principles of criminology* (11th edition). New York, NY: General Hall.

Takahashi, Y. (2017). Jessica's law. In M. Hooper & R. Masters (Eds.), *The criminal justice system (Vol. 2): Law enforcement, Court* (pp. 648–649). Ipswich, MA: Court Salem Press.

Takahashi, Y. (2017). Special needs of elderly victims. In C. Roberson (Ed.), *The Routledge handbook on victims: Issues in criminal justice* (pp. 156–168). New York, NY: Routledge.

Tanner-Smith, E., Lipsey, E., & Wilson, M. (2016). Juvenile drug court effects on recidivism and drug use: A systematic review and meta-analysis. *Journal of Experimental Criminology, 12*(4), 477–513.

Tannura, T. A. (2014). Rape trauma syndrome. *American Journal of Sexuality Education, 9*(2), 247–256.

Tatara, T., Kuzmeskus, L. B., Duckhorn, E., & Bivens, L. (1998). *The national elder abuse incidence study: Final report.* Washington, DC: The National Center on Elder Abuse at The American Public Human Services Association in Collaboration with Westat, Inc.

Taylor, M. (2015). *The 2015–16 budget: Improving state programs for crime victims.* Retrieved from http://www.lao.ca.gov/reports/2015/budget/crime-victims/crime-victims-031815.pdf.

Teasdale, B., Daigle, L., Hawk, S., & Daquin, J. (2016). Violent victimization in the prison context. *International Journal of Offender Therapy and Comparative Criminology, 60*(9), 995–1015.

TeBockhorst, S., O'Halloran, M., & Nyline, B. (2014). Tonic immobility among survivors of sexual assault. *Psychological Trauma: Theory, Research, Practice, and Policy, 7*(2), 171–178.

Teicher, M. H., & Samson, J. A. (2016). Annual research review: Enduring neurobiological effects of childhood abuse and neglect. *Journal of Child Psychology and Psychiatry, 57*(3), 241–266.

Teller, J., Munetz, M., Gil, K., & Ritter, C. (2006). Crisis intervention team training for police officers responding to mental disturbance calls. *Psychiatric Services, 57*(2), 232–237.

Teplin, L. A., McClelland, G. M., Abram, K. M., & Weiner, D. A. (2005). Crime victimization in adults with severe mental illness: Comparison with the National Crime Victimization Survey. *Archives of General Psychiatry, 62*, 911–921.

Tharp, A. T., DeGue, S., Valle, L. A., Brookmeyer, K. A., Massetti, G. M., & Matjasko, J. L. (2013). A systematic qualitative review of risk and protective factors for sexual violence penetration. *Trauma, Violence, & Abuse, 14*(2), 133–167.

Thomas, C., Park, R., Ellingen, M., Ellison, Menanteau, B., & Young, L. (2011). *Developing legislation on violence against women and girls.* United Nation Women. Retrieved from http://www.endvawnow.org/uploads/modules/pdf/1355776748.pdf.

Thornberry, T. P., & Krohn, M. D. (2000). The self-report method for measuring delinquency and crime. In D. Duffee, R. D. Crutchfield, S. Mastrofski, L. Mazerolle, D. McDowall (Eds.), *Criminal justice 2000: Measurement and analysis of crime and justice* (Vol. 4, pp. 33–83). Washington, DC: U.S. Department of Justice, Office of Justice Programs.

Thurman, Q. C. (1995). Community policing: The police as a community resource. In P. Adams & K. Nelson (Eds.), *Reinventing human services: Community- and family-centered practice* (pp. 122–145). New York, NY: Aldine De Gruyter.

Tillyer, R. (2018). Assessing the impact of community-oriented policing on arrest. *Justice Quarterly, 35*(3), 526–555.

Tittle, C. R. (1995). *Control balance: Toward a general theory of deviance.* Boulder, CO: Westview.

Tjaden, P., & Thoennes, N. (2000). *Extent, nature, and consequences of intimate partner violence: Findings from the National Violence Against Women Survey.* Washington, DC: U.S. Department of Justice, Office of Justice Programs, National Institute of Justice.

Todres, J. (2016). Can mandatory reporting laws help child survivors of human trafficking? *Law Review Forward* 69–78; Georgia State University College of Law, Legal Studies Research Paper No. 2016–12. Retrieved from https://ssrn.com/abstract=2767583.

Tong, R. (1984). *Women, sex, and the law.* Totowa, NJ: Rowman & Allanheld.

Townsend, S. M., & Campbell, R. (2018). Services for survivors of sexual violence: Moving from care to comprehensive services. In C. M. Renzetti, J. L. Edleson, & R. Kennedy Bergen (Eds.), *Sourcebook on violence against women* (pp. 353–372). Thousand Oaks, CA: Sage.

Trojanowicz, R. C. (1985). *Job satisfaction: A comparison of foot patrol versus motor patrol officers.* East Lansing: Michigan State University, National Neighborhood Foot Patrol Center.

Truman, J. L., & Morgan, R. E. (2016). *Criminal victimization, 2015.* Washington, DC: Bureau of Justice Statistics.

Truman, J., & Langton, L. (2015, September). *Criminal victimization, 2014.* Washington, DC: U.S. Department of Justice, Office of Justice Programs, Bureau of Justice Statistics. Retrieved https://www.bjs.gov/content/pub/pdf/cv14.pdf.

Tsui, V., Cheung, M., & Leung, P. (2010). Help-seeking among male victims of partner abuse: Men's hard times. *Journal of Community Psychology, 38*(6), 769–780. doi:10.1002/jcop.20394

Tugade, M. M., & Fredrickson, B. (2007). Regulation of positive emotions: Emotion regulation strategies that promote resilience. *Journal of Happiness Studies, 8,* 311–333.

Tullis, P. (Jan. 4, 2013). Can forgiveness play a role in criminal justice? *New York Times.*

Tyhurst, J. S. (1957). Psychological and social aspects of civilian disaster. *Canadian Medical Association Journal, 76*(5), 385–393.

Tyler, K. A., Hoyt, D. R., & Whitbeck, L. B. (1998). Coercive sexual strategies. *Violence and Victims, 13*(1), 47–61.

Ullman, S. E. (1996). Correlates and consequences of adult sexual assault disclosure. *Journal of Interpersonal Violence, 11,* 554–571.

Umbreit, M. S. (1994). *Victim meets offender: The impact of restorative justice and mediation.* Monsey, NY: Criminal Justice Press.

Umbreit, M. S. (2001). *The handbook on victim offender mediation: An essential guide to research and practice.* San Francisco, CA: Jossey-Bass.

Umbreit, M. S., & Coates, R. (1992). The impact of mediating victim-offender conflict: An analysis of programs in three states. *Juvenile and Family Court Journal, 43*(1), 21–28.

UNCG. (2013). *Safety strategies: Safety strategies for survivors of domestic violence and their children.* UNCG Department of Counseling and Educational Development. Retrieved from www.dvsafetyplanning.org.

Underwood, T. L. (2003). Concepts of victim assistance. In T. L. Underwood & C. Edmunds (Eds.), *Victim assistance: Exploring individual practice, organizational policy, and societal responses* (pp. 1–20). New York, NY: Springer.

United Nations. (2000). *The convention on organized crime.* Retrieved from https://www.unodc.org/unodc/en/treaties/CTOC/index.html.

United Nations. (2004). *Basic facts about the United Nations.* New York, NY: News and Media Division United Nations Department of Public Information.

United Nations. (2010). *Manual on victimization surveys.* Geneva. Retrieved from https://www.unodc.org/documents/data-and-analysis/Crime-statistics/Manual_on_Victimization_surveys_2009_web.pdf.

United Nations General Assembly. (1985). *Declaration of Basic Principles of Justice For Victims of Crime and Abuse of Power.* Retrieved from http://www.un.org/documents/ga/res/40/a40r034.

United Nations Office for Drug Control and Crime Prevention (UNODCCP). (1999). *Handbook on justice for victims: On the use and application of the declaration of basic principles of justice for victims of crime and abuse of power.* Retrieved from https://www.unodc.org/pdf/criminal_justice/ UNODC_Handbook_on_Justice_for_victims.pdf.

United Nations Office on Drugs and Crime & United Nations Economic Commission for Europe. (2010). *Manual on victimization survey.* Geneva: Author. Retrieved from https://www.unodc.org/documents/data-and-analysis/Crime-statistics/Manual_on_Victimization_surveys_2009_web.pdf.

United States Census Bureau. (2016). *Computer and Internet access in the United States: 2012.* Retrieved from https://www.census.gov/data/tables/2012/demo/computer-internet/computer-use-2012.html.

United States Census Bureau. (2017). *E-Stats 2015: Measuring the electronic economy economy-wide statistics brief.* Retrieved from https://www.census.gov/content/dam/Census/library/publications/2017/econ/e15-estats.pdf.

United States Congress, House Committee on Energy and Commerce. (2007). *Sexual exploitation of children over the Internet: A staff report prepared for the use of the committee on energy and commerce.* U. S. House of representatives, 109th Congress. Retrieved from https://www.gpo.gov/fdsys/pkg/CPRT-109HPRT31737/pdf/CPRT-109HPRT31737.pdf.

Urban Institute. (1999). *The Violence Against Women Act of 1994: Introduction, background, and legislative intent.* Retrieved from http://www.ncdsv.org/images/UI_EvaluationOfTheSTOPGrants-1996Report_3-1-1996.pdf.

U.S. Department of Education, Office for Civil Rights. (2011). *Dear colleague letter: Sexual violence background, summary, and fast facts,* Retrieved from https://obamawhitehouse.archives.gov/sites/default/files/fact_sheet_sexual_violence.pdf.

U.S. Department of Education, Office for Civil Rights. (2015). *Title IX resource guide.* Retrieved from https://www2.ed.gov/about/offices/list/ocr/docs/dcl-title-ix-coordinators-guide-201504.pdf.

U.S. Department of Education, Office for Civil Rights. (2017). *Title IX letters.* Retrieved from https://www2.ed.gov/about/offices/list/ocr/letters/colleague-title-ix-201709.pdf.

U.S. Department of Health and Human Services. (2005). *Mental health response to mass violence and terrorism: A field guide.* Rockville, MD: Center for Mental Health Services, Substance Abuse and Mental Health Services Administration.

U.S. Department of Health and Human Services (DHHS). (2012). *Services available to victims of human trafficking: A resource guide for social service providers.* Washington, DC: U.S. Department of Health and human Services. Retrieved from www.acf.hhs.gov/trafficking.

U.S. Department of Health and Human Services. (2017). Stopbullying.gov. *USDHHS.* Retrieved from https://www.stopbullying.gov/cyberbullying/what-is-it/index.html.

U.S. Department of Health and Human Services, Administration on Children, Youth and Families. (2004). *Child maltreatment 2002: Reports from the states to the National Child Abuse and Neglect Data System.* Washington, DC: U.S. Government Printing Office.

U.S. Department of Homeland Security Blue Campaign. (2017). *One voice. One mission. End human trafficking.* Retrieved from https://www.dhs.gov/blue-campaign/indicators-human-trafficking.

U.S. Department of Justice. (2012). *Equal access to education: Forty years of Title IX.* Retrieved from https://www.justice.gov/sites/default/files/crt/legacy/2012/06/20/titleixreport.pdf.

U.S. Department of Justice. (2014). *National crime victimization survey.* 2009–2013. Bureau of Justice Statistics.

U.S. Department of Justice. (2014). *Services to crime victims.* Retrieved from https://www.justice.gov/ usao/priority-areas/victims-rights-services/services-crime-victims.

U.S. Department of Justice. (2017). *An update on the defi-nition of rape*. Retrieved from https://www.justice.gov/archives/opa/blog/updated-definition-rape.

U.S. Department of Justice, Federal Bureau of Investigation. (2015). *Sex offenses reported via NIBRS in 2013*. Wash-ington, DC: Author.

U.S. Department of Justice, Federal Bureau of Investigation. (2017). *Hate crime statistics, 2016*. Retrieved from https://ucr.fbi.gov/hate-crime/2016.

U.S. Department of Justice, Office of Justice Programs. (2013). *Vision 21: Transforming victim services: Final report*. Washington, DC: Author.

U.S. Department of Justice, Office of Violence Against Women (2007). *The President's Family Justice Center Initiative Best Practices*. Washington, DC: Author.

U.S. Department of State. (2016). *Trafficking in persons report*. Washington, DC: Author. Retrieved from https://www.state.gov/documents/organization/258876.pdf.

USDHHS. (2004). Gateways to prevention: What everyone can do to prevent child abuse. *Department of Health and Human Services*. Retrieved from https://www.childwelfare.gov/pubPDFs/2004guide.pdf.

USDHHS. (2015). Mandatory reporters of child abuse and neglect. *U.S. Department of Health & Human Services*. Retrieved from https://www.childwelfare.gov/pubPDFs/manda.pdf#page=1&view=Introduction.

USDHHS. (2017). Child maltreatment 2015. *U.S. Department of Health & Human Services: Administration for Children and Families; Administration on Children, Youth and Families; Children's Bureau*. Retrieved from http://www.acf.hhs.gov/programs/cb/research-data-technology/statistics-research/child-maltreatment.

Van Camp, T. (2017). Australia's reintegrative shaming approach. Restorative justice. In M. Hooper & R. Masters, *The criminal justice system (Vol. 2): Law enforcement, court* (pp. 562–563). Ipswich, MA: Salem Press.

van Camp, T. (in press). Recovery stages. In M. Hooper and R. Masters (Eds.), *Salem science. The criminal justice system* (2nd edition). New York, NY: Grey House.

Van Dijk, J. J. M. (1997). Towards a research-based crime reduction policy. *European Journal on Criminal Policy and Research, 5*(3), 13–27.

van Dijk, J., van Kesteren, J., & Smith, P. (2007). *Criminal victimisation in international perspective: Key findings from the 2004–2005 ICVS and EU ICS*. Bibliotheek WODC. Retrieved from http://unicri.it/services/library_ documentation/publications/icvs/publications/ICVS2004_05report.pdf.

van Kesteren, J. N, & van Dijk, J. J. M. (2010). Key victimological findings from the international crime victims survey. In S. G. Shoham, P. Knepper, & M. Kett (Eds.), *International handbook of victimologi* (pp. 151–180). London, UK: CRC Press.

Vang, P., & Bogenschutz, M. (2011). Hmong women, marital factors and mental health status. *Journal of Social Work, 13*(2), 164–183.

Vasquez, A. (2017). *Comprehensive legal services for victims of crime*. Illinois Criminal Justice Information Authority. Retrieved from http://www.icjia.state.il.us/articles/ comprehensive-legal-services-for-victims-of-crime.

Villmoare, E., & Benvenuti, J. (1988). *California victims of crime handbook: A guide to legal rights and benefits for California crime victims*. Sacramento, CA: Victims of Crime Resource Center.

von Hentig, H. (1940). Remarks on the interaction of perpetrator and victim. *Journal of Criminal Law and Criminology, 31*(3), 303–309.

von Hentig, H. (1948). *The criminal and his victim: Studies in the sociobiology of crime*. New Haven, CT: Yale University Press.

von Marees, N., & Petermann, F. (2012). Cyberbullying: An increasing challenge for schools. *School Psychology International, 33*(5), 467–476.

Wagner, B. B. (2010). Why mortgage fraud matters. *Mortgage Fraud Working Group Financial Fraud Enforcement Task Force*. Retrieved from https://www.justice.gov/sites/default/files/usao/legacy/2010/05/27/usab5803.pdf.

Wallace, H. (1998). *Victimology: Legal, psychological, and social perspectives*. Boston, MA: Allyn and Bacon.

Wallace, H. (2007). *Victimology: Legal, psychological, and social perspectives* (2nd ed.). Boston, MA: Pearson A&B.

Walts, K. K. (2011). Human trafficking and exploitation of children and youth in the United States. *A Publication of the Center for the Human Rights of Children*. Chicago, IL: Loyola University.

Wardell, F., Lishman, J., & Whalley, L. (2000). Who volunteers? *The British Journal of Social Work, 30*(2), 227–248.

Warrier, S., Williams-Wilkins, B., Pitt, E., Reece, R., Groves, B., Lieberman, A., & McNamara, A. (2002). "Culturally competent responses" and "Children: Hidden victims." *Violence Against Women, 8*(6), 661–686.

Wasco, M., & Campbell, R. (2002). A multiple case study of rape victim advocates' self-care routines: The influence of organizational context. *American Journal of Community Psychology, 30*(5), 731–760.

Washington Lawyers Committee. (2017). *Abuse of prisoners with mental illness in the Federal Supermax addressed by settlement*. Retrieved from http://www.washlaw.org/news/576-abuse-of-prisoners-with-mental-illness-in-the-federal-supermax-addressed-by-settlement.

Wasserman, E. (2005). Multidisciplinary teams and child protection teams. In *IHS/BIA Child Protection Handbook—2005*. Retrieved from http://www.icctc.org/Difference%20between%20MDT%20and%20CPT.pdf.

Websdale, N. (2001, July). Domestic violence fatality reviews: Implications for law enforcement. *The Police Chief*, 65–74.

Weisel, D. (2005). *Analyzing repeat victimization*. Retrieved from http://www.popcenter.org/tools/repeat_victimization.

Weiss, D. P. (2017). Members of the LGBT community as victims of crime. In Roberson (Ed.), *Routledge handbook on victims' issues in criminal justice* (pp. 127–141). New York, NY: Routledge.

Wellford, C. F. (2017). Improving our conceptualization and measurement of crime. *Criminology & Public Policy, 16*(4). 1021–1026.

Wells, K., & Guo, S. (1999). Reunification and reentry of foster children. *Children and Youth Services Review, 21*, 273–294.

Wentz, E., & Archbold, C. (2012). Police perceptions of sexual assault victims: Exploring the intra-female gender hostility thesis. *Police Quarterly, 15*(1), 25–44.

Wexler, R. (2005). Family preservation is the safest way to protect most children. In D. Loseke, R. Gelles, & M. Cavanaugh (Eds.)., *Current controversies on family violence* (pp. 311–327). Thousand Oaks, CA: Sage.

Whitty, M. T. (2013). The scammers persuasive techniques model: Development of a stage model to explain the online dating romance scam. *British Journal of Criminology, 53*(4), 665–684.

Whitty, M. T. (2015a). Anatomy of the online dating romance scam. *Security Journal, 28*(4), 443–455.

Whitty, M. T. (2015b). Mass-marketing fraud: A growing concern. *IEEE Security & Privacy, 13*, 84–87.

Whitty, M. T., & Buchanan, T. (2012). *The psychology of the online dating romance scam report*. Leicester: University of Leicester. Retrieved from http://www2.le.ac.uk/departments/media/people/monicawhitty/Whitty_romance_scam_report.pdf.

Widom. (2017). Long-term impact of childhood abuse and neglect on crime and violence. *Clinical Psychology Science and Practice, 24*(2), 186–202.

Wilcox, P. (2010). Victimology, theories of. In B. S. Fisher (Ed.) *Encyclopedia of victimology and crime prevention* (Vol. 1, pp. 978–986). Thousand Oaks, CA: Sage.

Willard, N. E. (2007). *Cyberbullying and cyberthreats: Responding to the challenge of online social aggression, threats, and distress*. IL: Research Press.

Williams C., & Arrigo, B. (2012). *Ethics, crime, and criminal justice* (2nd ed.). Saddle River, NJ: Pearson.

Williams, J. C. (1998). Domestic violence and poverty: The narratives of homeless women. *Frontiers: A Journal of Women Studies, 19*(2), 143–165. doi:10.2307/3347163

Willmoare, E., & Benvenuti, J. (1988). *California victims of crime handbook: A guide to legal rights and benefits for California crime victims*. Sacramento, CA: Victims of Crime Resource Center.

Wilson, J., & Websdale, N. (2006). Domestic violence fatality review teams: An interprofessional model to reduce deaths. *Journal of Interprofessional Care, 20*(5), 535–544.

Wilson, L. C., & Miller, K. E. (2015). Meta-analysis of the prevalence of unacknowledged rape. *Trauma, Violence, & Abuse, 17*(2), 149–159.

Winters, G. M., & Jeglic, E. L. (2017). Stages of sexual grooming: Recognizing potentially predatory behaviors of child molesters. *Deviant Behavior, 38*(6), 724–733.

Wistrich, A. J. (2008). Procrastination, deadlines, and statutes of limitation. *William & Mary Law Review, 50*(2), 607–667.

Wolak, J., Finkelhor, D., & Mitchell, K. (2012). *Trends in law enforcement responses to technology-facilitated child sexual exploitation crimes: The third national juvenile online victimization study (NJOV-3).* Durham, NH: Crimes Against Children Research Center.

Wolak, J., Finkelhor, D., Mitchell, K., & Ybarra, M. (2008). Online "Predators" and their victims: Myths, realities and implications for prevention and treatment. *American Psychologist, 63*(2), 111–128.

Wolf, M., Ly, U., Hobart, M., & Kernic, M. (2003). Barriers to seeking police help for intimate partner violence. *Journal of Family Violence 18*, 121–129.

Wolfe, D. A. (2003). Elder abuse in residential long-term care settings: What is known and what information is needed? In R. J. Bonnie & R. B. Wallace (Eds.), *National Research Council (US) Panel to review risk and prevalence of elder abuse and neglect.* Washington, DC: National Academies Press.

Wolfgang, M. E. (1958). *Patterns in criminal homicide.* Philadelphia: University of Pennsylvania Press.

Wolpert, S. (2015). Predictive policing substantially reduces crime in Los Angeles during months-long test: UCLA-led study suggests method could succeed in cities worldwide. *UCLA Newsroom.* Retrieved from http://news-room.ucla.edu/releases/predictive-policing-substantially-reduces-crime-in-los-angeles-during-months-long-test.

Women's Support Project. (2014). *Commercial sexual exploitation.* Retrieved from http://www.womenssupport-project.co.uk/content/commercialsexualexploitation/173, 172.

Wood, A. R., & Janosik, S. M. (2012). The Clery Act: Crime reporting concerns. *URMIA Journal Reprint.* Retrieved from http://www.higheredcompliance.org/resources/Wood-Janosik_CleryCrimeReporting_20120621.pdf.

Wood, J., Foy, D., Layne, C., Pynoos, R., & James, C. (2002). An examination of the relationships between violence exposure, posttraumatic stress symptomatology, and delinquent activity. *Journal of Aggression, Maltreatment & Trauma, 6*(1), 127–147.

Wooldredge, J., & Steiner, B. (2012). Race group differences in prison victimization experiences. *Journal of Criminal Justice, 40*(5), 358–369.

World Bank, Partnerships Group, Strategy and Resource Management. (1998, May 20). *Partnership for development: Proposed actions for the World Bank.* Discussion paper.

World Health Organization (WHO). (n.d.). *Health topics: Epidemiology.* Retrieved from http://www.who.int/topics/epidemiology/en.

World Health Organization. (2012). *Understanding and addressing violence against women: Intimate partner violence.* Retrieved from http://apps.who.int/iris/bitstream/10665/77432/1/WHO_RHR_12.36_eng.pdf.

World Society of Victimology. (2016). *World society of victimology.* Retrieved from http://www.worldsocietyof victimology.org

Yang, B., Zhang, H., Ge, W., Weder, N., Douglas-Palumberi, H., Perepletchikova, F., & Kaufman, J. (2013). Child abuse and epigenetic mechanisms of disease risk. *American Journal of Preventative Medicine, 44*, 101–107.

Yeager, K. R., & Roberts, A. R. (2005). Bringing the past and present to the future of crisis intervention and crisis management. In K. R. Yeager and A. R. Roberts (Eds.), *Crisis intervention handbook: Assessment, treatment, and research* (4th edition), (pp. 3–35). Oxford, UK: Oxford University Press.

Yen, R. (2000). Racial stereotyping of Asians and Asian Americans and its effect on criminal justice: A reflection on the Wayne Lo Case. *Asian American Law Journal, 7*(1), 1–28.

Yin, P. (1980). Fear of crime among the elderly: Some issues and suggestions. *Social Problems, 27*(4), 492–504.

Yllö, K. (2005). Through a feminist lens: Gender, diversity, and violence: Extending the feminist framework. In D. Loseke, R. Gelles, & M. Cavanaugh (Eds.), *Current controversies on family violence* (pp. 19–47). Thousand Oaks, CA: Sage.

Yoshihama, M. (1999). Domestic violence against women of Japanese descent in Los Angeles: Two methods of estimating prevalence. *Violence Against Women, 5*(8), 869–897.

Young, M. (1982). Victimology: A theoretical framework. In Hans Joachim Schneider (Ed.), *The victim in international perspective*. Berlin: Walter de Gruyter.

Young, M. A. (1989). Emerging issues in victim assistance. *Pepperdine Law Review, 17*(1), 129–143.

Young, M. A. (1991). Survivors of crime. In D. Sank and D. I. Caplan (Eds.), *To be a victim* (pp. 27–42). New York, NY: Springer.

Young, M. A. (1993). *Victim assistance: Frontiers and fundamentals*. Washington, DC: Kendall Hunt.

Young, M., & Stein, J. (2004). *The history of the crime victims movement in the United States: A component of the office for victims of crime oral history project*. Retrieved from https://www.ncjrs.gov/ovc_archives/ncvrw/2005/pg4c .html.

Zanin, N., Shane, J., & Clarke, R. (2004). *Reducing drug dealing in private apartment complexes in Newark, New Jersey: A final report to the U.S. Department of Justice, Office of Community Oriented Policing Services on the field applications of the problem-oriented guides for police projects*. Washington, DC: U.S. Department of Justice.

Zaykowski, H. (2014). Mobilizing victim services: The role of reporting to the police. *Journal of Traumatic Stress, 27*(3), 365–369. doi:10.1002/jts.21913

Zaykowski, H., & Campagna, L. (2014). Teaching theories of victimology. *Journal of Criminal Justice Education, 25*(4), 452–467.

Zehr, H. (1990). *Changing lenses: A new focus on crime*. Scottdale, PA: Herald Press.

Zehr, H., & Mika, H. (1998). Fundamental concepts of restorative justice. *Contemporary Justice Review, 1*, 47–55.

Zevitz, R. G., & Frakas, M. A. (2001). *Sex offender community notification: Assessing the impact in Wisconsin*. Washington, DC: Department of Justice.

Zinzow, H., Rheingold, A., Byczkiewicz, M., Saunders, B., & Kilpatrick, D. (2011). Examining posttraumatic stress symptoms in a national sample of homicide survivors: Prevalence and comparison to other violence victims. *Journal of Traumatic Stress, 24*(6), 743–746.

Zinzow, H. M., Thompson, M. P., & Rheingold, A. A. (2013). Homicide survivors. A summary of the research. In R. C. Davis, A. J. Lurigio, & S. Herman (Eds.), *Victims of crime* (4th ed., pp. 133–160). Thousand Oaks, CA: Sage.

Zucker, B. (2014). Jessica's law residency restrictions in California: The current state of the law. *Golden Gate University Law Review, 44*(2), 101.

Zur, O. (1994). Rethinking "don't blame the victim": Psychology of victimhood. *Journal of Couple Therapy, 4*(3/4), 15–36.

Zweig, J., & Burt, M. (2007). Predicting women's perceptions of domestic violence and sexual assault agency helpfulness: What matters to program clients? *Violence Against Women, 13*(11), 1149.

# Index

risk factors for, 266, 268
Understanding and Managing your Stress
    case study on avoiding, 267
Button, M., 228
Bystanders
    definition of, 86
    informal victim support by, 86

California
    California Elder Justice Coalition (CEJC), 278
    California Victim Compensation Program (CalVCP), 111
    California Victims of Crime Compensation Program in, 79
    Central Valley Against Human Trafficking (CVAHT) in,
        180, 181
    compensation paid to victims in, 108, 109 (figure)
    juvenile human trafficking court, 142
    Proposition 83 (version of Jessica's Law), 130
    Welfare and Institutions Code (2005) on restorative
        justice, 153–154
California Elder Justice Coalition (CEJC), 278
California Victims of Crime Compensation Program, 79
Canons of Police Ethics, 255
Capital punishment. *See* Death row inmates
CAPTA Reauthorization Act (2010), 175–176
Caring for Terminal Patients case study, 269
Caron murder, 289
Casanueva, C., 172
Case studies
    Arile Castro's plea bargain, 99
    C.R. Caring for Terminal Patients, 269
    Female Workers Face Rape, Harassment in U.S.
        Agriculture Industry, 291
    Forgiveness Given to Conor McBride, 125
    "Good Touch/Bad Touch," 167–168
    predictive policing (UCLA–LAPD joint study), 49
    Restorative Justice in Practice, 156–157
    Ridgeway Carjacking, 58–59
    "Sexually Harassed at Work," 208–209
    "Sneaking Out," 19
    "Someone Had Taken Over My Life: An Identity Theft
        Victim's Story," 229–230
    "Taken Advantage Of By My Own Child," 182–183
    *Thurman v. City of Torrington,* 88
    Understanding and Managing Your Stress, 267
    Wisconsin Department of Justice rape kits, 90
    "You Can Either Have Your Friends and Your Family,
        Or You Can Have Me," 194–196
Castro's plea bargain case study, 99
Catalano, S., 240
Center for Investigative Reporting, 291
Center for Juvenile Justice Reform (CJJR), 147
Central Valley Against Human Trafficking (CVAHT)
    [California], 180, 181

Child abuse and neglect responses
    education and outreach, 177
    group counseling programs, 174
    home visitation programs, 174
    legal support for victims of child abuse, 174–176
    multiservice interventions, 173–174
Child Abuse Prevention and Treatment Act (CAPTA),
    113, 166, 175–176
Child abuse/maltreatment
    court hearing in case of, 145
    definition of neglect and, 166
    effect on victims, 171–173
    effective responses to, 173–177
    first recognized as social problem (1960s), 6–7
    "Good Touch/Bad Touch" case study, 167–168
    human trafficking, 177–181
    link between juvenile delinquency and, 145–147
    Mary Ellen Wilson case of, 6
    out-of-home placement and reunification outcomes of, 145
    provision of services in case of, 144–145
    psychological effects of, 171, 246–247
    screening and investigation of, 144
    signs and symptoms of, 168–171
    substantiation of, 144
    *See also* Children; Family violence;
        Neglect; Physical abuse
Child labor, 178–179
Child pornography, 245
Child Protective Services (CPS)
    child abuse referrals and assistance by, 165–166
    out-of-home placement and reunification process by, 145
    provision of services by the, 144–145
    victim services offered through, 82–84
Child sexual abuse
    cyber child sexual exploitation, 243–249
    description of, 164
    "Good Touch/Bad Touch" case study on, 167–168
    incest, 37 (table)
    Internet-initiated incitement or conspiracy to commit, 245
    signs of, 170–171
Child victims
    bereaved parents of, 91–93
    court-appointed special advocates (CASA) for, 113
    effective of child abuse on, 171–173
    Parents of Murdered Children (POMC), 8, 92
    victim assistance for abused, 165–166
    Wisconsin Department of Justice rape
        kits case study on, 90
Child welfare (CW) social worker, 147–148
Child welfare system
    association between youth in juvenile court
        and, 145–147
    case flow of children in the, 143 (figure)

court hearing, 145
Crossover Youth Practice Model (CYPM), 147–148
out-of-home placement of children, 145
provision of services, 144–145
reunification of children, 145
screening and investigation, 144
substantiation of child maltreatment, 144
*See also* Juvenile justice system
Children
complex trauma in, 148–151
cyber child sexual exploitation, 243–249
family preservation model approach to assisting, 286–287
human trafficking of youth and, 177–181, 218–219
IPV victims' fear over losing their, 205
out-of-home placement and reunification of, 145
*See also* Child abuse/maltreatment; Families; Youth
The children's movement, 6–7
Christmann, K., 244
Circles (dialogue method), 156
Civil justice system
lower standard of proof than criminal courts, 109
O.J. Simpson sued in the, 109
victims choosing to go through the, 108–109
*See also* Criminal justice system
Civil legal assistance, 112
Civil rights movement (1950s and 1960s), 5
Clery Act (1990), 211, 222, 224–225
Coalition
California Elder Justice Coalition (CEJC), 278
as collaborative approach component, 277–278
definition of, 277
Coalition Against Trafficking in Women (CATW), 277–278
Code of ethics, 255–256
Code of Ethics (NASW), 256
*Code of Hammurabi*, 3
*Code of Ur-Nammu*, 3
Codes of ethics
Code of Ethics (NASW), 256
description and examples of, 255–256
NVASC Ethical Standards of Professional Conduct, 256–258
CODIS (combined DNA Index System), 89
Cognition skills
elder abuse risk due to declining, 185
resilience facilitated by strong, 67
trauma and impairment of child's, 149, 150–151
Collaboration
as collaborative approach component, 276 (table)–277
definition of, 276
improving international victim assistance and, 300–301
Collaborative approach to victims
collaboration, 276 (table)–277
collaborative working relationships in the, 281–283

cooperation, 275, 276 (table)
Coordinated Community Response (CCR)
example of, 287–288
coordination, 275-276 (table)
description and advantages of, 274–275
Domestic Violence Fatality Review Team (DVFRT), 289–290
Female Workers Face Rape, Harassment in U.S. Agriculture Industry case study on, 291
five steps of the process of, 279–281
multidisciplinary teams (MDTs), 278–279
one-stop centers (Family Justice Center) example of, 290–291
service delivery models for using the, 283–287
Sexual Assault nurse Examiner (SANE Nurse) example of, 14, 214, 216, 289
Sexual Assault Response Teams (SARTs) example of, 14, 214–215, 216, 288–289
*See also* Victim assistance programs; Victim services providers
Collaborative service delivery models
domestic violence prevention model, 283–285
family preservation model, 286–287
public health model, 285–286
Collaborative working relationships
challenges to having successful, 282–283
multiple advantages of having, 281–292
College campus sexual violence
campus responses to, 221–225
description and overview of, 219–221
Columbine High School shooting, 61
Communities
community-oriented policing (COP) strategy used in, 77–78
NVASC Ethical Standards of Professional Conduct on coordinating with, 257–258
resources for overcoming trauma, 65
sex-offender laws and notification to, 128–130
Sexual Assault Response Teams (SARTs) of, 14, 214–215, 216
victim-offender programs in the, 126
*See also* Neighborhoods
Community-oriented policing (COP) strategy, 77–78
Community reparation boards, 126
Community work service programs, 126
Community/neighborhood impact statements, 126
Compassion fatigue
Treating Terminally Ill Patients case study on, 269
victim assistance professionals and, 268
Compassion satisfaction, 269
Compensation
definition of, 107
paid to victims in California, 108, 109 (figure)
victim compensation programs, 107–108

Complex trauma. *See* Trauma
Computer-assisted telephone interviewing (CATI), 41
Confidentiality
    juvenile justice system, 137
    of rape victims' communication, 256–257
Connecting Mental Health & Education, Inc., 68
Control balance
    description of, 32
    Extended Control Balance Theory on, 24 (table), 31–32
Cooperation
    collaborative approach component of, 275, 276 (table)
    definition of, 275
Coordinated Community Response (CCR), 287–288
Coordination
    collaborative approach component of, 275-276 (table)
    definition of, 275
Coping
    definition of, 66
    with trauma and stress, 66–67
    *See also* Resources
Correctional systems
    capital punishment and death row inmates, 117–118
    day reporting centers (DRCs) alternative to, 122
    death row inmates and murder victim's family, 118–119
    electronic monitoring (EM) alternative to, 122–123
    Forgiveness Given to Conor McBride case study, 125
    institutional corrections, 115–116
    parole, 120
    prisons, 116–117
    probation, 120
    solitary confinement, 117
    Victim Impact Panel (VIP), 126–128
    victim participation in the parole process, 120–122
    victim services and programs in the, 123–126
    witnessing executions, 119–120
    *See also* Sentencing
Costs of victimization. *See* Victimization costs
Council of Europe, 301
Court-appointed special advocates (CASA), 113
Court process
    arraignment, 100–102
    bail hearing, 98
    booking, 97
    initial appearance, 98
    plea bargaining, 98–99
    preliminary hearing/grand jury, 99–100
    sentencing, 102
    victim and witness assistance programs, 97
    victim involvement in the, 102–113
Coyne, I. J., 239
C.R. Caring for Terminal Patients case study, 269
Credit card skimming, 231
Crime in the United States (FBI), 36

Crime prevention, predictive policing (UCLA–LAPD joint study) on, 49
Crime Victims Bill of Rights, 111
Crime Victims Fund, 10
Criminal justice system
    the court process, 97–113
    initial contact with the police, 78–80
    the investigative process, 77–81, 86–95
    justice system principles of the, 3
    juvenile, 6, 135–143, 148–158
    process and important terms related to, 76
    victim advocates' role in, 13, 80–81, 112–113
    victim services available through the, 13, 82–85
    victims receiving follow-up by type of action (2000–2009), 52 (figure)
    *See also* Civil justice system; Legal services; Victims
Crisis centers
    responding to sexual victimization, 213–214, 216, 217
    Santa Barbara Rape Crisis Center, 216
Crisis intervention
    Crisis Intervention Team (CIT) model used by police, 82
    definition of, 82
Crisis Intervention Team (CIT) model, 82
Cross, C., 228
Crossover youth, 140
Crossover Youth Practice Model (CYPM), 147–148
Culture
    description and significance when interacting with victims, 262–263
    multicultural competency in victim services, 262–264
Cyber-bullying
    definition and overview of, 237–238
    effective responses to victims of, 240–243
    extent of the problem of, 239–240
Cyber-Bullying Research Center, 239
Cyber child sexual exploitation
    defining, 243–244
    effective responses to, 247–249
    extent of, 245–247
    Internet-based child pornography, 245
    Internet-initiated grooming, 244–245
    Internet-initiated incitement or conspiracy to commit child sexual abuse, 245
    victim assistance programs, 248
Cyber-crime
    cyber child sexual exploitation, 243–249
    description and overview of, 227–228
    identity theft, 229–231, 237
    Internet fraud, 228, 230–234
    investment fraud, 231–232
    mass marketing fraud, 233
    mortgage and lending fraud, 232